HUGH JOHNSON

THE INTERNATIONAL BOOK OF

TREES

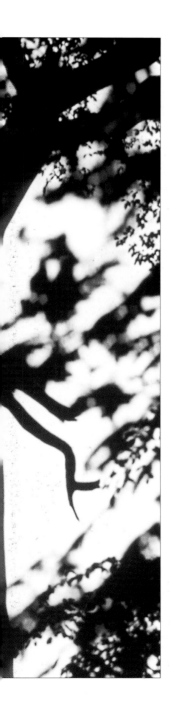

HUGH JOHNSON

THE INTERNATIONAL BOOK OF

TREES

TREES
BOTANY
TREES
PLANTS

CHANCELLOR PRESS

Poplars
by Gwen Raverat

Hugh Johnson's Encyclopedia of Trees was edited and
designed by Mitchell Beazley International Limited,
Artists House, 14-15 Manette Street, London W1V 5LB

Editor   Dian Taylor
Designer   Ruth Levy
Editorial Assistants   Sue McKinstry
   Alison Hancock, Charles Mitchell

First published in Great Britain in 1973 by Mitchell Beazley
(also published as *Hugh Johnson's Encyclopedia of Trees*)

This 1999 edition published by Chancellor Press
an imprint of Bounty Books, a division of the
Octopus Publishing Group Ltd
2-4 Heron Quays, London, E14 4JP.

Reprinted 1978, 1979; revised 1984; revised 1993

ISBN: 0 75370 097 2

Produced by Toppan (HK) Ltd
Printed and bound in Hong Kong

Contents

Forward

to original edition
by Sir George Taylor
D.Sc., F.R.S., Ll.D., F.R.S.E., V.M.H.,
Former Director of the Royal Botanic Gardens, Kew

People are planting more trees, and care more about trees, than ever before. The spread of urban blight and ugliness and the new ecological awareness have prompted many of us to see in trees the best and surest living antidote to the despoliation of our towns, and there is a growing appreciation of the countryside to which we all endeavour to escape.

But how to find out more about trees? During my 15 years as Director of the Royal Botanic Gardens at Kew I realized that there was a significant gap in the popular literature about them. There are scientific books and papers and a plethora of works for the specialist, particularly the aboriculturist and the gardener; very rewarding but in many cases not always easy in their application. And there is the sentimental approach; sympathetic but somewhat unhelpful. Everyman's tree book, which did justice to this complex and enthralling subject, didn't seem to exist.

This is why I feel that Hugh Johnson's timely book is likely to become a familiar and much-consulted work for many, many readers throughout the temperate regions of the world. It is just what is needed: the work of a talented writer well versed in the subject without being fully immersed; one who can see it from an outsider's point of view. I have been impressed by its comprehensiveness, pleased to find it so full of accurate information, and truly delighted to see a subject which has preoccupied much of my life made so fresh and such fun.

Hugh Johnson has travelled widely and delved deeply in quest of trees and tree lore and he writes without prejudice or inhibition, eager to share his vivid enjoyment and remarkable understanding. If you start reading his book with a feeling for trees I don't see how you can finish it without loving them.

George Taylor

Introduction

A traveller should be a botanist, for in all views plants form the chief embellishment –

Charles Darwin

I remember a before-and-after sequence of two photographs in *Time* magazine. Before: main street in some New England town; all harmony; comely cream clapboard dappled with light from the crowns of an avenue of tremendous elms. After: the elms gone; comeliness has become nakedness. What was all proportion and peace is desolate.

Darwin could have been more specific. Not of all landscapes, but of most, he could have said 'trees form the chief embellishment'. Of all plants they are the most prominent and the most permanent, the ones that set the scene and dictate the atmosphere.

This is the aspect of trees that I have written a book about. I have not harped on the value of trees as creators of the air we breathe, or as our most versatile and universal raw material. Nobody is in any doubt today about the necessity of trees to keep our planet in being.

My aim in this book is to bring trees into focus for everybody like myself, who was aware of trees, loved trees, but in a way so vague that it now seems to me quite shameful. It is a personal account. I am not a botanist, nor a forester, nor even (except in my own garden) a gardener, but a writer who has found in trees a new point of contact with creation, a source of wonder and satisfaction which has the inestimable advantage of growing almost everywhere.

What I hope this book does is to make vivid through words and pictures the essential differences between the great groups of trees, to tell their story, and then go on to enjoy the pleasures of their subtly, elaborately, almost endlessly varying designs – the

species and varieties of familiar families from all over the temperate world.

A theme with countless variations is a never-ending source of pleasure. It is true of wine: it is even more true of trees. The theme is simply a plant with a trunk, branches, twigs, leaves. Yet think of a giant elm, and think of a cherry, stooping with soft flowers – and think of a resiny old fir crusted with lichen. Can anything make a more fascinating collection? For once possession is not the point. Trees are wonderfully public property. Wherever you go you are enjoying somebody's trees: and not a penny changes hands.

I have tried not to be pedantic about what is or isn't a tree. There is a classic definition. It calls for a woody plant (capable of) growing 20 feet high and tending to a single stem (though it may have more). What do you do, though, if the thing is single-stemmed as can be, palpably tree-like and permanent, but has never grown over ten feet? Or what do you do if it is 30 feet high but hopelessly and incurably bushy?

My answer has tended to be inclusive rather than exclusive. It is one of the wonders of the subject that the first cousin of a 200-foot mammoth can be a two-foot pigmy. And the relationship adds enormously to the pleasure of growing the pigmy – which is all most people have room for.

Lionel de Rothschild, one of the world's greatest growers of rhododendrons, was once lecturing a city gardening club. 'Gentlemen', he began, 'no garden, however small, should be without its two acres of rough woodland.' For most of the human race those must be two acres of the mind. But what pleasure there is, and how much to be learned about our place in God's universe, in going about them observantly, equipped with even a little knowledge.

I could not possibly have written this book without the extraordinary generosity and enthusiasm of the lifelong professional

plantsmen who have been at my elbow to answer my questions and curb my too sweeping conclusions. Sir George Taylor I must thank first, for giving me the confidence to get started. Alan Mitchell of the Forestry Commission has not spared himself nor his incredible store of information. Ken Beckett, former Technical Editor of the Gardener's Chronicle, Roy Lancaster, the curator of Hillier's arboretum in Hampshire, and Oscar Traczewitz, head forester of the International Paper Company, have answered innumerable questions and put me right countless times. Dame Sylvia Crowe, past President of the Institute of Landscape Architects, was good enough to read my chapters on the use of trees the garden and landscape and make valuable suggestions. The Librarians of the Royal Botanic Gardens at Kew, the Royal Horticultural Society and the Cambridge University Library have been exceptionally helpful. Well over a hundred photographers have been involved. Among them all I must single out one of the world's remarkable amateurs, Dick van Hoey Smith; himself the owner of a famous arboretum, Trompenburg, in Rotterdam. Nearly 150 of the pictures of rarer trees in this book are his.

The International Paper Company and the publishers somehow between them found the money to make this the beautiful book it is. You can imagine how grateful I am to them.

As for the publisher's staff, my colleagues and friends, I can only hope the book itself is some reward to them for the effort, far beyond mere duty, which they unhesitatingly made for it.

Opposite
Hugh Johnson in his garden in Essex.

How a Tree Grows

Below *Part of a ginkgo twig with a short (or spur) shoot, which grows only a millimetre a year, enough to form new buds for leaves and flowers.*

It is winter—the time of drought and dormancy in the plant world. The herbs have taken refuge beneath the soil. Grass and the daisies and violets crouch low, hoping for a covering of snow to protect them from the drying wind. Yet far above the trees sail in the scudding clouds; invulnerable; asleep.

What distinguishes a tree from all other plants is the wooden structure it raises above the ground. By annual additions it builds a tall scaffold on which to hang its leaves, its flowers and its fruit. Each new year's growth is no more than a crop of twigs. Yet those twigs contain in essence the identity of the tree: in time they become branches; eventually perhaps huge limbs. In the winter tower of tracery you can still detect the way the buds formed along the first frail shoots.

Each year's shoot springs from a bud, and ends by forming new buds. The buds are the resting stage common to most trees of the temperate world, where day-length and temperature sharply differentiate the seasons. Each contains in miniature a whole new shoot—either of twig and leaves or of flowers. Even before the shoot of the current year has reached its final size the next year's buds are brewing. By June or July they are complete—even though the embryo growth they hold will not appear until the following March or April. So it was last year's spring that determined the extent of this year's growth.

One bud on each shoot is different from the rest. It is the bud farthest from the tree's roots—the last on the limb: the leader. The nearer this bud is to a vertical position over the centre of the tree the more marked its dominance will be. The force of gravity, you might say, is its authority. It is able to assert its dominance through the agency of hormones. It forms the hormone auxin in its growing tip; gravity distributes it to the buds lying behind. Auxin has the effect of moderating vigour—leaving more of the available sap for the leader to use in in-

creasing its lead, and in forming the biggest of the buds, the one that will be dominant next year.

This is the plan for a tree with the simplest construction—for example a spruce. In a broadleaf tree the same chemistry applies—but soon to a number of leaders as the tree's crown widens out.

Meanwhile what of the other buds, the ones that are being deprived? The shoots they produce are shorter, with a different function. They are the leaf and flower bearers. Their role is to fill out the canopy of the tree to take advantage of all the light, or to carry the flowers and fruit.

Take away the leader, however, and the auxin-making function is inherited by the next shoot down: one that would otherwise have remained in subjection; perhaps a spur with a few leaves. A new leader is born.

The buds are many, but they are not formed at random. They stick to the characteristic pattern of the species, which is the

Left *A section of a trunk showing how even 'suppressed' buds which are held in reserve in case the leader is lost grow outwards each year just enough to keep pace with the annual growth-ring. The lower left bud on the trunk is totally suppressed. The one above it has formed a short shoot like the ginkgo's (above). On the right a mature branch has been lost but a*

suppressed bud from when it was much younger has kept up with the thickening of the trunk round it and will probably break to make a new shoot.

Below *Some of the buds formed two years ago in the angles of the leaves are still suppressed. The horse-shoe scar under the bud, where the leaf stood, still shows rings where its veins were attached.*

A three-year-old twig of horse chestnut shows three annual growth-rings. Its centre is still pith, which disappears with age.

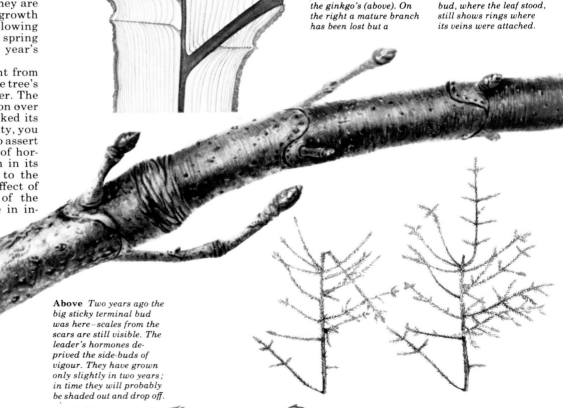

Above *Two years ago the big sticky terminal bud was here—scales from the scars are still visible. The leader's hormones deprived the side-buds of vigour. They have grown only slightly in two years; in time they will probably be shaded out and drop off.*

Right *There are three possible budding and branching patterns: alternate (one bud at a time: left) opposite (two at a time: centre) and whorled (three or more: right).*

Above *Where a leading shoot with its power of dominating and suppressing the lower branches is broken its function is inherited by the stronger side-shoot just behind it. The process is easiest to watch in conifers like the spruce*

above. As soon as a side-branch takes over to grow upright it changes its own budding and branching pattern. Instead of producing only side-shoots in one plane it starts branching all round in whorls.

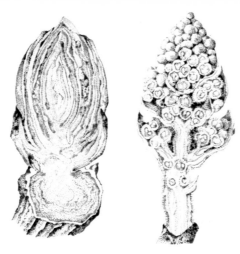

A cross-section of a bud (far left) shows the shoot and all its leaves ready formed. They are complete by mid-summer of the year before they appear. Beside it is the flower bud of the same plant, the common lilac. Here the whole flower-structure with scores of little flowers, also ready formed, is packed within scales that are modified leaves.

Logically you would expect the final tree to consist of all its annual increments: to be able to count all the annual shoots since it was a seedling. Up to a certain age most conifers (which make a single whorl or tier of branches every year) allow you to do this. Some poplars and alders do the same. But with most broadleaf trees the scent quickly gets cold.

One thing that simplifies it is the death-rate among twigs. Most of the older side-shoots are disposed of in this way. In ten years, if a branch produced and kept only two side-shoots a year, the total number would be 19,683. In fact the count on a ten-year-old birch was 238. As the tree moves on beyond them, casting them into shade, they simply drop off.

What complicates it are the external influences forcing or persuading the tree to take up a certain attitude. Of these gravity, light and wind are the most important.

Above In contrast to the horse chestnut where the side-buds are generally suppressed by the terminal bud, the side-buds of the spruce always develop. They elongate very rapidly.

same as the arrangement of its leaves. Each bud forms in the angle which a leaf makes with the twig.

The tree's ultimate aim is to form a head which will give it the maximum exposure to the light. In the forest all the light is overhead: side-branches are shaded out and die: nothing but a narrow crown of up-reared branches can reach the light amid the press of other trees. But in the open field a tree builds up its head in its own characteristic way. There is no mistaking the tall fan of the elm or the oak's zigzag rhythm.

The two-year-old section of the twig (below) lies between two rings of old bud-scars. One of the buds has developed into the one-year-old side-shoot; the other remains suppressed.

Above The sticky bud which contains the coming year's new shoot, enclosed in scales which are themselves a form of leaf and covered with protective resin (more common in conifers than broadleaves). Unless the main shoot is destroyed its side-buds will probably get no farther than the little shoots on the far left.

There are no side-shoots yet on the one-year-old twig, but buds are ready just above where the old leaves fell. One or both of the buds above left will shoot and bear leaves this year. The surface of the twig is marked with breathing pores ('lenticels') to supplement the activity of the leaves.

Last year's growth started at the bud-scars (left). Each succeeding pair of leaves and side-buds is at right angles to the one before.

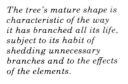

The tree's mature shape is characteristic of the way it has branched all its life, subject to its habit of shedding unnecessary branches and to the effects of the elements.

An oak (above) starts with a distinct main stem, but by the age of 20 it is already hard to say which is the leading shoot. Dominance is shared by all the main branches that can reach the light. The crown soon becomes and

remains rounded to expose the maximum leaf-area. Most oaks grow on from a side bud. Hence their restless zig-zag pattern of branches.

A pine at 12 years (small tree above) is a pyramid of almost-regular whorls of branches: one whorl for each year of its life. As it grows it gradually shades out and kills its own lower branches. Much later in life than the oak it starts to spread:

the leader loses dominance and the upper branches compete, making a broad crown.

A willow is a prolific producer and shedder of twigs all its (comparatively short) life. Every new twig is at an acute angle

to its parent and hence reaches as far into the light and competes strongly with it. It is easy to see the big tree as an extended version of the little one, and both as an extended much-twigged branch.

The Leaves

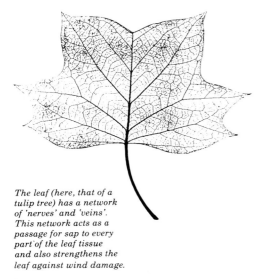

The leaf (here, that of a tulip tree) has a network of 'nerves' and 'veins'. This network acts as a passage for sap to every part of the leaf tissue and also strengthens the leaf against wind damage.

The permanent wooden structure is peculiar to trees. The temporary organs that clothe it—the leaves, the flowers and fruit—are not. Their functions are the same as in every other plant.

The leaf has the task of collecting food. Ninety per cent of the solid matter that makes up the trunk, the branches and the roots themselves is carbohydrates plucked, as it were, out of the sky by the feeding leaves. A leaf becomes self-supporting remarkably quickly. Before it is even half-grown it has started exporting nourishment to the rest of the tree.

Leaves get nourishment out of both the air and the ground. They do the first by photosynthesis: they hold up to the sunlight delicate vessels impregnated with chlorophyll and filled with water. The chlorophyll causes an exchange of hydrogen (from the water) with carbon and oxygen (from the carbon dioxide in the atmosphere). Carbon is the tree's chief food: from it it can make

the sugars and starches it needs.

The leaves are extremely effective evaporating plants; very nearly as efficient as an open water surface like a pond. Their turnover of water is far greater than photosynthesis demands. It is responsible for the whole circulation of sap round the tree. As the leaves lose water to the air they draw it up through the twigs, the branches and the trunk out of the roots, and ultimately out of the soil, below them. With the water, which can be as much as two or three hundred gallons a day in summer, they draw dissolved minerals from the soil. This is the tree's secondary source of solid supplies—and also of course its whole system of getting the supplies to where they are needed.

Leaves have a short life—perhaps six months on the average. The longest any leaf hangs on a tree is seven or eight years (on certain firs). But most leaves, even of 'evergreen' trees, fall and are replaced every year. Evergreen leaves can simply be defined as leaves that are adapted to survive the winter. The adaptation consists of a more miserly evaporation system: a thicker skin, generally a simpler shape (since the longer the margin of any surface in relation to its area the more water vapour will 'flow off' it), and very often a coating of wax, giving the leaves a bluish cast, into the bargain.

The only thing that can be said about leaf shape is that in itself it can't be very important: so many variants arise from tree to tree of the same species, and even from branch to branch and twig to twig. Most broadleaf trees have produced versions with 'cut' leaves—leaves with jagged, deeply embayed margins. Many conifers (see pages 118–9) have congested or otherwise eccentric varieties. They seem to make no difference to the tree's functioning.

Leaf colours can vary within species almost as much. A red pigment overlaying the green of the chlorophyll gives a 'copper' effect. Sometimes a low level of chlorophyll makes the leaves yellow or golden. But lack

of chlorophyll means less photosynthesis and hence less food: yellow trees are slower-growing.

The last act for many leaves is the most colourful. It is their function, before they die, to convert starch into sugar which the tree can store as reserve supplies. But cold nights prevent them passing on to the tree the sugar they have made, so it builds up in the leaf tissue. In many leaves the result is a red pigment. As the chlorophyll is decomposing at the same time, whatever pigment the leaf contains (in such cases red, but usually yellow) is no longer masked by green: its chrysanthemum colours emerge.

Many trees, especially conifers, have different leaf-designs on shoots of different ages. Here a seedling Thuja occidentalis has its seed-leaves at the base of the stem, then 'juvenile', then 'mature' foliage. A few trees (some junipers, for example) keep juvenile foliage all their life.

Leaves tightly packed in the bud begin to expand with the arrival of spring. Once expanded the leaves draw the sap up the trunk of the tree. The force which makes the sap rise to swell the leaves remains a mystery.

Here the swelling of the leaves of a horse chestnut forces the enfolding bud-scales (themselves a modified form of leaf) to hinge back. Once clear of the bud-scales the leaves, already fully formed, unfold (see pages 224–5).

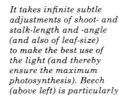

It takes infinite subtle adjustments of shoot- and stalk-length and -angle (and also of leaf-size) to make the best use of the light (and thereby ensure the maximum photosynthesis). Beech (above left) is particularly

effective at making an almost unbroken mosaic of leaves which casts deep shade. Some maple leaves (above right) have to grow stalks as long as themselves to manoeuvre into the light.

Deciduous leaves are either 'simple'—i.e. the blade is in one piece—or 'compound'—i.e. composed of a number of separate leaflets.

The leaf is the tree's feeding and breathing organ. Below right are the deciduous (i.e. one-season only) leaf of an oak and the evergreen leaves or needles of a pine. Evergreen leaves, designed to survive a winter when water is more or less unobtainable, usually have a much smaller area than deciduous leaves. The total leaf area of a typical conifer is one quarter that of a broadleaf tree the same size. A big oak has some 250,000 leaves. The stalk gives them mobility, which helps them survive gales. Points and lobes make rain-water run off quickly. The upper side of the leaf has a waxy cuticle to prevent excessive transpiration. The lower side has minute hairs to keep water from coating the surface. Water prevents the proper function of the breathing pores and encourages fungal infection.

The elm's is an example of a simple leaf with a serrated edge.

Most conifers have needle leaves (though many such as Thuja and cypress have tiny 'scale' leaves).

Maple leaves are described as 'palmate', from the palm of a hand.

Horse chestnut has 'compound' leaves in a 'palmate' pattern.

The commonest compound leaf-form is 'pinnate', from the Latin for feather.

Below left The magnified cross-section of a leaf shows its cell-structure. On the upper surface the cuticle; then a clear layer of epidermis cells; then a layer of 'palisade' cells full of chlorophyll, through which run the veins; then a spongy layer in which a further set of cells containing chlorophyll float in contact with the carbon dioxide imbibed through the breathing pores in the lower epidermis. Each pore is closed by a ring of two guard-cells; this becomes flaccid when sap is in short supply, but stiffens like an inflatable lifebuoy and opens the hole when water is available.

Open breathing pore

Deciduous leaves fall when cells break down in the area known as the 'abscission layer' between leafstalk and twig. Later a layer of cork forms over the wound producing a leaf-scar. Some leaves (e.g. of young beech) fail to form such a layer. They die but cannot break off, so they hang dead on the tree until new leaves push them off in spring.

Cold autumn nights prevent the passage of sugar from the leaves to other parts of the tree. The resulting build-up of sugar leads to brilliant colours.

Evergreen conifer needles (those of a 'five-needled' pine, above) have a harder cuticle and often a thicker layer of wax to slow down their transpiration—essential in winter in northern zones because of the lack of water. Their breathing pores are concentrated in lines, often white with ac-cumulated wax, usually on the underside (or inner side where needles are bunched together).

Hydrogen 6.2%   Carbon 43.5%
Nitrogen 1.5%   Oxygen 44.4%
Potassium 0.9%   Other minerals 3.5%

Above Between 80 and 90 per cent of the bulk of a living tree is water drawn from the ground by the roots. Of the remaining 10 to 20 per cent no less than 91 per cent is derived from the atmosphere by the leaves, which are thus the tree's main feeding organs, collecting all the carbon and oxygen the tree needs. Apart from water, with its all important supply of hydro-gen, the roots provide nitrogen, potassium, calcium, phosphorus sulphur, iron and magnesium.

The Flowers

It is always hard not to fall into the trap of anthropomorphism—in other words of attributing to inanimate objects our own feelings and motives. It is specially hard when you come to talk about sex. Why, we are bound to ask, do plants have to go through the whole risky business of sexual reproduction, entrusting their seed to the elements, or to insects, when it can give them no pleasure and must enormously reduce the chances of successfully reproducing at all?

Most plants, after all, can reproduce themselves by other means: either by sending out suckers from the root, or forming new roots on a side branch in contact with the ground, or just detaching a piece to start a new life on its own. A few depend on such means: their sexual system has broken down and their seeds are never fertile. Yet all plants have some arrangements for mixing their own characteristics with others of their kind. It is a prerequisite of evolution: a genetic lottery where a new combination may make a superior product.

And strange to say (anthropomorphism creeping in again) it is when they feel their life in danger, either through old age or because nutrition is lacking, that they make the most efforts at reproduction and produce the most flowers. Richly-manured orchards bear little fruit. Big flower (and fruit) years follow sunny and dry summers, when nutrients (except carbohydrates from the sun) are in short supply.

Flowers are the plant's sex organs. They exist to exchange genes (and hence characteristics) with neighbours of the same species. Chancy as it obviously is to try to establish physical contact between a speck of dust on one tree and a minute egg on another, this is what they have to achieve.

There are as many forms of flowers as there are plants. Indeed our system of classifying and naming plants is largely based on flower designs. There is such a thing as a 'perfect' flower. In it both sexes are present, which should make things much

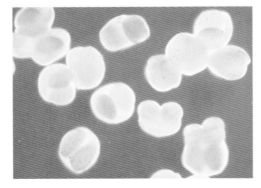

Above *Pollen grains of Korean fir magnified 40 times, showing the two balloon-like compartments that help them float on air.*

Left *Pollen designs. From left to right: holly magnified 800 times, birch and ash both magnified 1,200 times.*

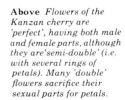

Above *Flowers of the Kanzan cherry are 'perfect', having both male and female parts, although they are 'semi-double' (i.e. with several rings of petals). Many 'double' flowers sacrifice their sexual parts for petals.*

The diagram below shows how the characters of the parents of a hybrid, though blended in the first generation of the cross (e.g. red and white flowers producing a pink offspring) are still retained as possibilities in the hybrid's genetic makeup. The first cross (F1) gets half its chromosomes from each parent. But it can make red- or white-flower pollen and ovules. These have four possibilities for recombination (F2); two of them pink, two like the original parents. The offspring of the second cross (F3) will be white, pink and red. The white and red have reverted to the parental colour; only the pink shows its hybrid parentage.

The two main agencies of pollination (i.e. of conveying pollen from one tree to another) are insects like the bee (top) which are attracted to the flower by nectar created for the purpose, and the wind; in the lower picture pollen is being dispersed by the wind from the male 'flowers' of a Scots pine. The 'flowers' or strobili are usually crowded on shoots near the bottom of the tree.

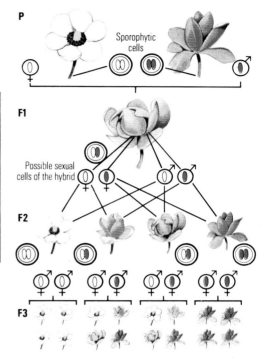

P

Sporophytic cells

F1

Possible sexual cells of the hybrid

F2

F3

easier. However (in the words of C. C. Sprengel, who in 1793 discovered the relationship between flowers and insects) 'Nature wishes crossing to occur'. All sorts of checks and barriers are built in to see that a flower does not fertilize itself. The pollen ripens at a different time from the ovule. Often the pollen is incompatible with its own tree's ovules. Or if by any chance they do couple the self-fertilized flower often falls off the tree before it can become a fruit.

What the flower hopes for (so to speak) is a fine breezy day for the pollen to be carried away in a golden shower to the next tree. And for the tree to windward to oblige with a similar gilding.

Wind pollination tends to be the rule for forest trees. Their flowers, in consequence, are nothing much to look at and have no smell. Trees that need to attract insects to carry their pollen (which are often the trees of the open ground at the forest edge) go in for more elaborate designs. They are the cherries, the magnolias, the willows, and all the chief ornaments of our gardens.

Most forest trees, in fact, have separate flowers for each sex (some for pollen, others for ovules) but have both types of flower on every tree. This is true, too, of all the conifers except the yew and its allies, *Araucaria*, and juniper which have separate all-male and all-female trees. But most ornamental trees have both sexes in each flower.

To speak of conifers in terms of flowers is not strictly correct. Their female organs are called strobili. They tend to be on the upper branches, while their pollen organs are on the lower: a simple precaution against the pollen falling too easily on to the ovules of the same tree.

Flowers enable the forester or the nurseryman to combine characteristics he likes in two different trees by making a hybrid. The trees have to be genetically very close. He can no more cross a willow and an oak than a dog and a cat. But if he sees, say, two beautiful pines, one taller and the other straighter than all the rest, he can ensure the pollination of one by the other. He puts a bag over the branch-end carrying the female strobili before they are mature, and injects into the bag pollen from the other tree. With luck the pine trees from the resulting seeds will be both tall and straight.

In the nursery business crossing has given us many of our most useful garden trees. There remain, I should perhaps add, gardeners who believe no hybrid can have the grace and perfection of a natural species. It is too late to introduce them to C. C. Sprengel.

Catkins are a common form of tree-flower. The alder, shown here, has separate male long catkins and female short ones on the same tree. The latter are strangely analogous in appearance to those of a conifer.

Left *An example of a hybrid camellia in which the sexual parts have been converted into more petals. Cuttings are the only way of propagating sterile forms like this.*

Left *The 'perfect' flower of Magnolia × soulangiana. The primitive race of magnolias all have 'perfect' flowers containing the organs of both sexes.*

The Fruit

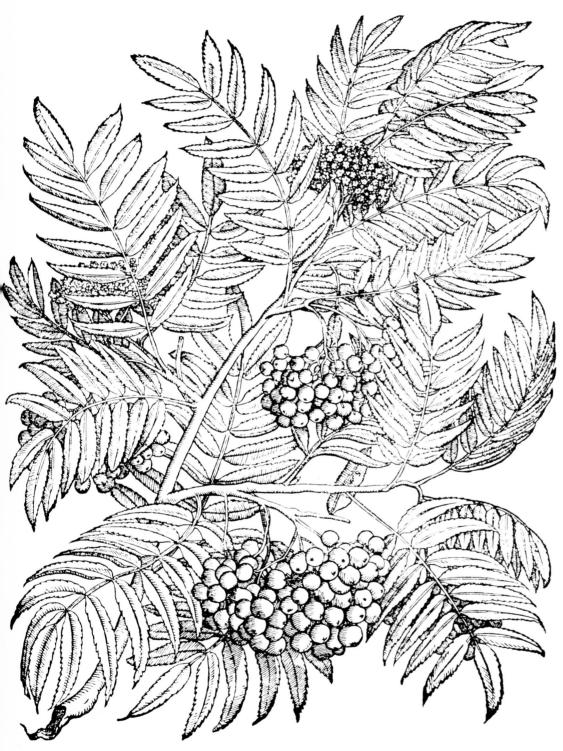

This engraving of the common mountain ash of Europe, or rowan, with its heavy trusses of scarlet berries, was made in Venice in 1565 by Petrus Andreas Mathiolus. His superb illustrations were re-used time and again in early herbals.

The fruit of a broadleaf tree (or any flowering plant) is the female part of the flower – the ovary, with the ovule inside – fertilized and grown to ripeness. The ovule becomes the seed; the ovary the seed's covering. Taking the peach as an example, the ovule is the kernel of the stone, the ovary is its shell. Round it is a fleshy covering which is a development not of the flower itself, but of the stem just below it.

Conifers are technically quite different. Their ovules never have ovaries; the kernel has no shell. They may, however, (as juniper berries do) have a fleshy covering; again derived, like the peach's flesh, from their former stalks.

Fruit always has one simple purpose: to put as much distance as possible between itself and its parent tree. Some of nature's most inventive adaptations come into play to persuade the birds, the beasts and the elements to cooperate.

When a tree clothes its seed in a substantial parcel of sweet flesh, as plums for example do, it is sacrificing a great deal of hard-won starch to make sure of interesting the birds. Come to that the flowers alone, put out to attract insects, use a fair quantity. Someone calculated that the 200,000 flowers on one cherry tree used 25 pounds of starch.

Almost all fruit serves simply to feed animals. Yet so big and so long-lived are the forest-trees that if one in a hundred of the acorns produced escapes being eaten, and one in a hundred of these germinates, and one in a hundred of the seedlings survives to make a mature acorn-bearing oak, the oak population will remain the same.

Most seed ripens in the autumn – conifer seed in the second autumn after its fertilization. It is designed to spend the winter dormant either on the tree or on the ground; then to germinate the following spring. Winter cold is actually necessary to activate it and break its dormancy: a precaution against it germinating as soon as it falls only to be killed by the ensuing cold weather. When the gardener exposes his seed to cold and damp he calls it 'stratifying'. Seeds have been known to stay dormant for 1,000 years.

In the ripe seed there are the beginnings of a little root and a tiny shoot, with one or more seed-leaves which act as storage organs for food and usually as the first operating leaves of the new plant. These are the cotyledons, whose rather obscure influence pervades the whole world of plant classification. Trees with two or more cotyledons produce wood in concentric rings: the classic tree pattern. Trees with only one grow as a cluster of fibrous bundles that gets longer but not fatter. The great 'Monocot' is the palm.

Above *Alders in nature are waterside trees: their seeds (released from fruit very like cones) are equipped with tiny bladders full of air which float them off downstream to a damp place to germinate.*

Below *The 'keys' of the maple family rely on aerodynamics to make them flutter and spin far enough from the parent tree to make propagation possible.*

Below *Thousands of broadleaf species have their seeds distributed by birds who feed on their berries: it is an unusual adaptation for conifers. The thrush (shown here) feeds on yew berries for their fleshy coating; the poisonous seed passes through the digestive system unaffected.*

Above *In hoarding acorns for winter feed, squirrels inevitably lose some in the ground so that they are effectually planted. Jays– particularly greedy and forgetful–are also one of the oak's best friends.*

Above *Poplars and willows produce very light seeds with a little sail of cottony fluff which catches the wind and can carry them for miles. This is probably the most effective of all means of distribution.*

Below *A few species like the witch hazel have contrived a spring mechanism to catapult their seeds into open ground, often as much as 40 feet away from the parent tree.*

Below *Four stages in germination–the progress from seed to seedling. First, usually in the spring after the seed has been sown, the root-tip splits the outer covering of the seed. The tiny seed-leaves (or* cotyledons) *are fully developed at this stage, but remain in the seed husk.*

There is enough fuel stored in the seed to power the rootlet until, guided by gravity, it has turned downwards and buried its tip in the earth. *From that moment it can supplement the seed's supplies and provide energy for the seed-leaves to swell up and emerge.*

The final stage in germination is reached when the stem of the seedling straightens and the seed-leaves fan out and start the process of photosynthesis. Now the tiny bud in their midst will swell to produce the stem and first true leaves of the new tree.

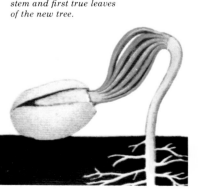

How a Tree Works

The heart of a tree is dead. All its life goes on just under the surface, in a band of cells no thicker than a film that separates the bark from the wood. If you scratch through the bark of any living twig you will find a thin green layer. Immediately within this lies the cambium (from the Latin for 'exchange'). Only the cambium has the power of making new wood. If you destroy a band of it round the trunk the tree dies.

It is the remarkable power of the cambium layer to make three different kinds of new cells at once. Every year it deposits new wood cells on its inner side, thickening the trunk of the tree. So it has to grow itself, to surround the increased bulk. It also has to keep adding 'phloem', or inner bark, to keep up with the expanding circumference.

Within this narrow zone of bark, cambium and the new outer ring of wood, the tree's whole circulation system functions. The sap goes up in the new wood, and comes down in the phloem. So much has been known for centuries through the simple experiment of girdling. If you strip a ring of bark off a tree (leaving the cambium intact) the top continues to get its water supply: what suffers is the roots. The water coming down from the leaves with its store of carbohydrates, the product of photosynthesis, fails

to reach them. They lose their ability to grow and exploit new ground: eventually the whole tree lacks its ration of minerals and nitrogen from the soil, and dies.

It is still a matter for wonder how frail leaves, transpiring as much as 300 feet or even more above the ground, can have the power to pull a column of water up that distance to supply themselves. It used to be thought that the roots pushed it up – which is, of course, equally mysterious. Now it is known that the roots have some pushing power in spring, before there are leaves to pull, but that leaves are perfectly capable of this feat of suction. What makes it possible is the cellular structure of the wood, which takes the fullest advantage of the principle of surface-tension. Water particles are highly mobile, but they are reluctant to part company with each other. It is almost as hard to tear them apart as it is to compress them. So if you pull one end of a long thin stream, the rest has the strength to hang on and follow.

A wood structure with longer cells that made the passage of sap more efficient was one of the evolutionary improvements on the ancient conifers that the newer broadleaves made. There is a simple experiment you can do to compare the two. If you strip a small vertical piece of bark off a tree and

stab the bare wood across the fibres with a penknife, a white mark above and below the cut shows where the air has filled the cells. On a broadleaf tree the mark is much longer than it is on a conifer.

The price for having bigger cells, though, is the danger of air bubbles in the sap-stream breaking the flow. Ice creates the problem. When water freezes (as sap obviously does in trees in a very cold winter) air dissolved in it forms bubbles. In small cells (as in conifers) they simply disappear when the sap thaws. But what happens in bigger ones? The water columns, once ruptured, might never be restored.

What has only recently been discovered is that most of the sap in broadleaves rises in the ring of wood made that very year. The sap need not rely even on the previous year's wood to give it a passage upwards, so efficient is the cambium at making new wood in the spring before the leaves have started drawing the sap up. 'This fabulous efficiency' – I quote Zimmermann and Brown's *Trees: Structure and Function* – 'takes place at the expense of safety.' It was the downfall of the American chestnut and may well be of the elm: the fungi that kill both do so by blocking the current year's wood cells, and with them the main stream of sap.

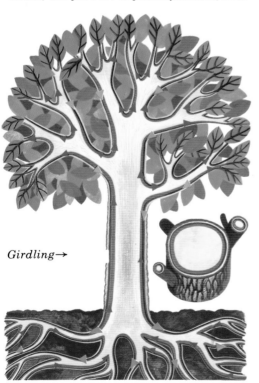

Girdling→

The circulation of sap (that is, water containing food) is shown in the diagram left. The red lines and arrows indicate water (drawn from the ground by the roots) moving upwards in the outermost layers of wood to the leaves. Most of this water is lost to the air by evaporation from the leaves. The blue lines and arrows are the sap on its downward journey in the inner layer of the bark, outside the cambium (see opposite). This pattern of circulation was discovered by removing the bark or 'girdling' and finding that it was the roots that were thus deprived of nourishment, not the tree above.

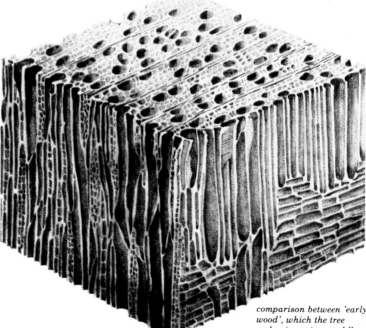

A magnified section of an annual ring of wood shows the long vertical cells in which the sap moves up the trunk, crossed at right angles in places by 'rays' of shorter cells. 'Rays' are used for conveying reserve supplies across the tree

to where they are needed. Where the vertical cells appear to be interrupted they are simply hidden by ray-cells. The only breaks in the tubes are the perforated cell ends, which help to support unbroken a column of water some-times over 300 feet high. A

comparison between 'early wood', which the tree makes in spring, and 'late wood', which it makes in summer, would show that early wood tube-cells are much bigger, having much more water to carry to the developing leaves, shoots and flowers. The difference in cell size gives the characteristic lighter and darker shading of annual rings.

The texture of the bark
is largely decided by the
bark or cork cambium.
In many trees it
grows in shallow over-
lapping arcs; the bark
eventually (left) cracks
at their edges as the
trunk swells. In others
(right, eucalyptus) it
forms a thin peeling sheath
near the surface, which is
constantly renewed.

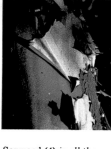

This cross-section of a tree trunk breaks it down into five principal concentric layers: bark, inner bark or phloem, cambium, sapwood and heartwood.

The bark (1) is a protective layer, sometimes (as on birches) a mere skin but on some trees (redwoods, for example) as much as a foot thick. This outer bark is continually being produced by its own specialised cambium. The photographs (above) show how the position of this cambium determines whether the bark peels or cracks.

The inner bark or phloem (2) is a spongy layer providing an easy downward passage for the sap. The sap carries sugar from the leaves to feed new wood cells and supply the roots with energy.

If the cambium layer (3) could be detached (as here) from the bark and wood it would be practically invisible, being only one cell thick. Yet the power of the tree to live and grow is contained in this infinitesimal film. The cambium is continually producing on its inner side wood (xylem) cells and on its outer phloem cells.

Sapwood (4) is all the wood that still functions; it carries sap up the tree, stores nutrients, or transports them from one part of the tree to another. Most sap flows in the new ring of wood made in the current year (see next page for a discussion of annual rings). If this is blocked, as it is by such fungus infections as Dutch elm disease, the tree may die; the older rings cannot keep it alive on their own.

The heartwood (5) is dead. It is a receptacle for the tree's waste matter, which makes it toxic to most organisms that might feed on it (and also darkens it). Yet if air reaches the dead heart of a tree it soon decays and leaves the tree hollow. The only function of heartwood is to give the tree strength and rigidity. It has not been explained how a tree can bend its dead heartwood in order to reach out to the light.

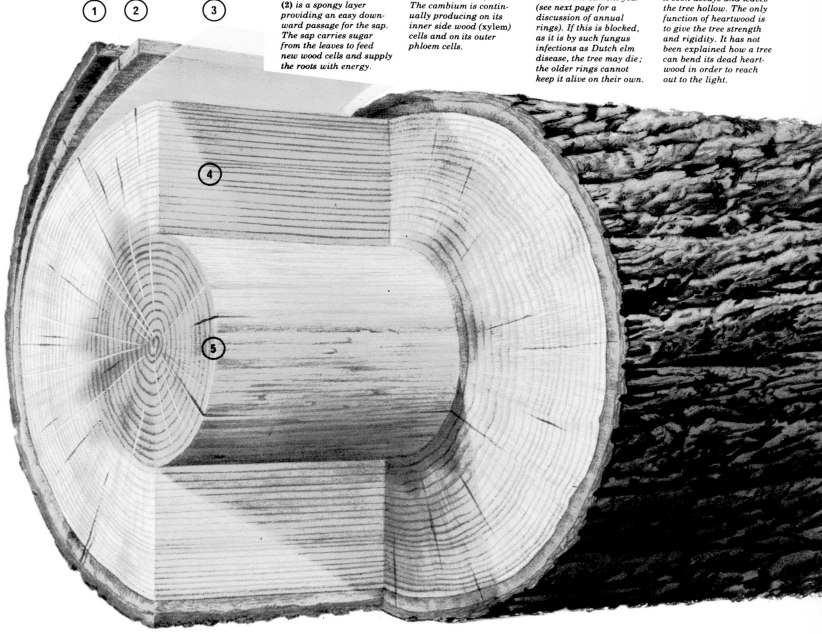

The History in a Tree

As a tree trunk thickens it surrounds the adjacent parts of its own branches. The branch's own annual rings run at an angle to those of the trunk forming a 'knot'. Foresters aim at eliminating knots by the natural self-pruning of lower branches in the darkness of a close forest stand.

Every year the growing tree buries its past in another ring of functioning wood. The oldest part of the tree, the middle, having died, grows harder in death and provides the tree with its backbone. So long as it is sealed off from the air by living tissue on the outside it is virtually incorruptible. Each year's new ring remains just as it was when it was added: a faithful record of one year of the tree's history. Count them, and you know the tree's age.

The size of the new shoot the tree makes each year is decided by the weather of the previous summer when the bud was formed. Not so the annual ring. What affects its width seems to be (subject of course to such outside influences as fertilizers) the weather while it is actually forming. The rainfall of the previous winter is important, since it provides the ground-water of the spring — the sap which will flood up the new ring as it forms. Even more decisive, because more variable, are the sun and rain of the current spring and summer. Growth-rings, therefore, are an immediate record of the weather of the growing season.

But rings are rarely perfect. Trees are not so often round as oval, or fluted, or just plain lop-sided in cross-section.

A forest tree, sheltered on all sides and striving upwards for the light, is likely to be the nearest to a perfect cylinder. The more open-grown and wind-buffeted a tree is the more it will taper, broadening at the base where the leverage of the top applies the greatest strain.

Conifers and broadleaves react in different ways to the strains of wind; conifers putting on extra growth on the leeward side, broadleaves on the windward. The same applies to the strain of gravity on horizontal branches; conifers build up the branch on its underside, broadleaves on its upper. Both result in an oval cross-section, longer in the axis of gravity or prevailing wind.

The annual growth rings of a tree record more than just the fat and lean years when it grew quickly or scarcely at all. The right is a complete record of typical events in the life of a tree.

The tree was felled when 47 years old. A rough guide to the age of most normal trees is to allow one year for each inch of the girth at shoulder-height: e.g. a tree ten feet round is about 120 years old.

1 At five years old the slender tree, growing straight, was knocked sideways by the fall of a neighbour. It reacted by growing twice as strongly on the lower side in an attempt to correct its slant. Five years later it was upright again.

2 When the tree was 14 years old a ground-fire swept through the forest. The bark and cambium on the windward side were destroyed. In subsequent years they grew over the wound by degrees: it took six years to close it completely.

3 Other trees growing around gradually deprived the tree of light and robbed it of moisture. When it was 27 years old 'thinning' of the woods suddenly brought it into the open. There was a great leap in growth-rate, still visible in the rings.

4 Six years of rapid growth followed. Then came a drought; its effects on the tree are visible for six rings. Very serious drought can damage the roots enough to slow down growth even for years after normal rainfall returns.

20

This bristlecone pine in the White Mountains of California may be 3,000 years old. More than half the tree is dead: the live part grows infinitesimally slowly. Dead wood does not rot in the desert atmosphere.

Shipping a gigantic slab of a 3,000-year-old redwood over to England in 1851 was a piece of pure showmanship. Europe has no prehistoric trees: everyone was awed that anything should live so long.

Since the 1950s there has been much more constructive activity in the far west, based on the discovery of pines far older (though far smaller) than the redwoods. It is not their age alone, however, that makes them so exceptionally interesting. It is the strange conditions under which they grow, 10,000 feet up in the White Mountains of California, in a state of chronic drought. Where redwoods grow it rains without fail: every year they add a ring of wood about the same size. But where the bristlecone pine grows there is so little rain that the tree is a super-sensitive rain gauge. Every annual ring is different: and the story they tell goes back (so far) no less than 8,200 years.

There is no tree that old still alive. The oldest living specimen is 4,900. But a special department of the University of Arizona has developed a technique for matching samples of wood from living and dead trees—even from broken-off bits lying on the desert floor—to build up a continuous series of rings.

The rings are microscopically narrow. On one sample there are 1,100 rings in the space of five inches. But the sequence of relative widths never repeats for more than a year or two. Any substantial sample has enough rings either to be unique or to overlap with another. A computer soon finds out which and puts it in its place.

The University expects eventually to push the records back to 10,000 years of weather—back in fact to the centuries when the last ice age was in retreat. The value of the work to weathermen is obvious. But in 1969 another startling issue came to light.

Wood whose age was exactly known was tested by the Carbon-14 method, the accepted means of dating prehistoric sites. But the answer came out wrong. The pines revealed that the basic assumption of C-14 dating, that the carbon in the atmosphere is at a constant level, holds good only for the last 3,500 years. Before that time the errors mount up rapidly: there was a 700-year error within the millennium before 1500 B.C.

As a result the presumed dates of some of the most important early structures have had to be changed. Stonehenge has been back-dated 1,000 years—upsetting the notion that technology was inherited by western Europe from the East. The implications of all this have yet to be gone into fully. But the fact remains that a Californian desert tree is able to bear witness to events long before history began.

Bristlecone pines have been growing for 8,200 years on desert land too dry for any other vegetation. This 'forest' at 10,000 feet, annual rainfall 12 inches, was discovered in 1955.

Above *The University of Arizona prefers whole sections of trees for dating, but can take a 'core' sample of a living tree without harming it. The core is extracted by hand with a fine auger.*

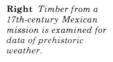

Right *Timber from a 17th-century Mexican mission is examined for data of prehistoric weather.*

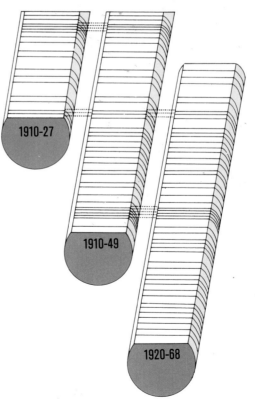

1910-27

1910-49

1920-68

Dendrochronology is historical research through tree-rings. The rain-sensitive bristlecone pine keeps a faithful record of the year's rainfall with thicker or thinner growth-rings. No log sequence is remotely likely to be repeated: a computer, therefore, can match any sample 'core' of wood (like those illustrated here) with others that overlap it in date, pushing the series farther and farther back into prehistory as more samples are analysed. Rings vary in absolute width between specimens, but the relative widths of every year are reliably the same.

Roots and the Soil

There is a discipline about the top-hamper of a tree. It obeys its own specific rules of growth. In contrast the roots are opportunists; they go wherever they find the feeding best. E. H. Wilson told the story of a particularly happy-looking ivy on the walls of Magdalen College, Oxford, which turned out to have got into the cellar and drunk a whole barrel of port.

We know much less about the roots of trees than about their branches, simply because they are out of sight. Very rarely has a tree been excavated *in toto*, like the example on the opposite page.

The roots have three jobs to do. They anchor the tree in the ground; they are the tree's chief source of water; and they have to forage for the elements from the soil that are a small but vital part of every cell.

The first root every tree (and every plant) puts out from its germinating seed is a tap-root. Its course is directed by gravity. All the seed knows is that the ground is downwards. The tap-root is a sort of emergency action to plug into the supplies as quickly as possible. Thereafter most trees soon concentrate on exploiting the top-soil, normally the richest in organic matter. Most feeding roots of most trees are found within six inches of the surface.

Spruces, beeches and poplars are examples of trees which rarely root deep, even when young. Firs, most oaks and many pines on the other hand go on with a tap-root for several years, which makes them much harder trees to transplant. What happens then depends on the soil. The deepest a tree root has been followed into the ground was 21 feet; that was a pine on sand—the most permeable of soils. Far more commonly the tap-root withers away and side-roots take over.

Roots go where it is easy to go. If they can they will follow old worm-tunnels or spaces where previous roots have died and rotted. They have to be wary only of the water-table; the level below which the soil is permanently wet. Their policy here is brinkmanship: they need the water, but they need oxygen too. They like to keep a toe in, but if they are submerged for long the roots of most trees drown. On the whole a fluctuating water-table is not such a safe bet as the rain permeating from above.

As the crown of the tree spreads, the roots extend to keep up with it. They are at their most active under the drip-line, where the rain falling on the crown runs off round the circumference. Trees like Lombardy poplars with upright branches that encourage the rain to run down their trunks have more roots close in where it falls.

Root growth is almost constant, stopping

The shape of a tree's root system depends less on the type of tree than the type of soil. Certain trees predominate on certain soil-types, but where their roots go is a question of tapping the supply of nutrients, water and oxygen with the least physical obstruction in the way. On these two pages four typical forest soil-types are depicted.

On this page are some of the roots of an oak in 'brown earth'; the typical soil of deciduous woodlands in areas of relatively low rainfall, slightly acid but rich in bacteria which quickly break down into humus the surface layer of vegetable litter. Flowers and fungi typical of such woodlands (known as 'dry oakwood') are
1 *Wood meadow-grass*
2 *Bilberry*
3 *Lactarius quietus*
4 *Pignut*
5 *Boletus pulverulentus*
6 *Inkcap*
7 *Stinkhorn*
8 *Woodsorrel*
9 *Foxglove*
The soil is about five feet deep, free-draining, loose-textured and fertile. Most of the tree's feeding roots are in the top 12 inches, the 'topsoil' layer with the most humus. There are no definite 'horizons', or layers of different material. Topsoil fades off into subsoil; 'sinker' roots find matter to exploit right down to the bedrock. The upper subsoil gets its rich rust colour from iron which oxidises readily in well-aerated conditions and is the most visible of all minerals in the soil. In more acid soils the iron oxides dissolve and are 'leached' into lower layers, as opposite. Here they remain evenly distributed on all levels, as do the other essential minerals (phosphorus, potassium, nitrogen, sulphur, calcium and magnesium).

Above Some of the creatures of the brown earth forest floor. The woodlouse, *which loves damp ground, lives on decaying plants and rotting wood. The snail, commonest where the herb* layer is lush, loves nettlebeds. The earthworm, valuable for aerating the soil with his tunnels, pulls fallen leaves underground for food with remarkable strength. The centipede lives under stone or bark: its front legs are poison-claws for killing larvae for food. The grey slug, commonest on beech trunks in wet weather, hides under the bark in dry weather.

A root elongates in the area behind the tip. The function of the cap is to produce a constant supply of new cells to be sloughed off as the tip advances. These discarded cells lubricate the root's passage through the soil.

The function of the root-hairs is to increase the absorbing capacity of the root. Water and mineral salts pass through the cortex into the xylem; the start of the transpiration stream which ends with evaporation from the leaves.

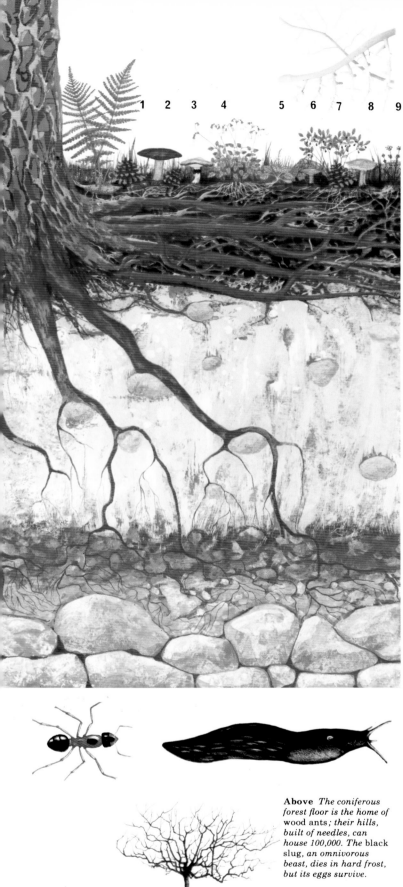

Left *Fungi have the secret of making tree-roots more efficient. Trees in forests usually rely on their characteristic mycorrhizae. They supplant the tree's own root-hairs, feeding on the tree's carbohydrates but in exchange giving the roots increased access to the nutrients in the soil.*

Left *The roots of a pine are growing in a 'podsol', a common soil-type in regions of high rainfall where the net water movement in the soil is downward (because little dry weather draws sub-soil water to the surface by evaporation). The calcium in the surface layers is dissolved and washed ('leached') to lower levels, leaving the topsoil very acid. Bacteria cannot flourish in such acidity, so leaves and other organic matter are broken down into humus very slowly. Earthworms are also absent, so the soil lacks their air-tunnels and has relatively little oxygen. Typical surface plants on such soil are*
1 *Male fern*
2 *Boletus badius*
3 *Boletus luterus*
4 *Twin-flower*
5 *Winter green*
6 *Lactarius deliciosus*
7 *Bilberry*
8 *Boletus granulatus*
9 *Bell heather*
Iron and aluminium in the soil dissolve under acid conditions. With so much water passing downward they too are carried to lower levels, leaving a pale 'horizon' without minerals below the topsoil. Under this, just above the bedrock, is the 'deposition layer' where the leached goodness ends up. The pine as a young tree struck out with a taproot, which found rich nourishment when it reached the deposition layer. Later 'sinker' roots, made by the growing tree looking for anchorage against the wind, also penetrated the leached layer with little branching, but proliferated with rootlets when they reached the buried minerals. Meanwhile most of the feeding roots occupy the same top 12 inches as those of the oak, where they can benefit not only from the humus but also from the help of mycorrhizae (see above).

Left *The total root spread of a tree can be far wider than its crown. This 26-year-old apple tree was unearthed complete by the East Malling Research Station in Kent, the pioneers of 'dwarfing' rootstocks.*

Above *The coniferous forest floor is the home of wood ants; their hills, built of needles, can house 100,000. The black slug, an omnivorous beast, dies in hard frost, but its eggs survive.*

Woodland known as 'damp oakwood' has a 'gley' soil. Gley occurs where drainage is bad, the soil has little oxygen and iron cannot oxidise. Often an impermeable layer of clay keeps the water level high. Airless, water-logged soil below is seen as a dark grey 'horizon'. Oak, ash and hazel grow well but root shallow. Herbs include wild angelica, bramble, woundwort, herb robert, tufted vetch, vernal grass.

Typical chalk-land soil ('rendzina') is a very shallow layer of fertile topsoil with good humus breakdown and efficient drainage. Below is nothing but chalk or limestone. The surface can (through 'leaching') be acidic even a few inches above pure calcium. Beech and ash are typical rendzina trees; most conifers are unhappy. Herbs include dog's mercury, ramsons, fescue, bugle, avens, wood sanicle.

only in freezing weather. It is only new and growing roots that function actively in collecting supplies. In the area where the action is, just behind the root-tip, root, root-hairs and soil are intimately knit together.

Not only are cells from the root-tip constantly being sloughed off to lubricate its passage, but drops of acids (chiefly carbonic) are exuded from the growing cells to dissolve the elements they need. The root's relation with the soil is as much chemical as physical: if the free water in the soil has all gone it can even tap water which is chemically part of the soil.

Many roots have allies: fungal friends or mycorrhizae with which they form a close association and which are characteristic of the tree (as truffles are of certain oaks). The fungi act as go-betweens. The roots supply them with sugars; they supply the roots with minerals from the soil. The reason why alkaline soil is fatal to many trees is that it kills these essential partners.

The acidity or alkalinity of soil is expressed as its 'pH'. The rating is based on the concentration of hydrogen ions in solution: the higher the concentration the more acid the soil. A neutral solution has a hydrogen ion concentration of one in 10 million (i.e. 1:10,000,000, or $\frac{1}{10^7}$, or 10^{-7} (ten to the power of minus seven). The figure seven is the pH. A lower pH number therefore means a higher concentration of acidic ions. A pH of 6 is ten times more acid than a pH of 7.

How Trees are Named

When we talk about a species we mean a group of similar plants, which grow together in nature, breed together, and produce offspring like themselves.

When we talk about a genus we mean a group of such species, consistently different in detail, not normally inter-breeding, but usually linked in a fairly obvious way. The English settlers arriving in New England recognized the oaks as oaks, even though the species they knew back home was not among them. From ancient times these two broad categories of natural objects have been instinctively acknowledged.

But a more searching scrutiny of the natural world has also suggested (to Aristotle in the first place) that there are broader groups and deeper relationships to be found. It is easy to think up ways of classifying anything. You could make lists of trees with yellow flowers, or peeling bark, and have a system of a sort. But it would prove nothing because it would be limited to the characteristic you happened to choose. You could neither deduce nor predict anything from it. Aristotle guessed that there is a natural order of relationships where everything has a place. There was no clue, though, as to where to look for it.

Even Linnaeus, who is known as the father of modern taxonomy (the science of classifying natural objects), was in the dark about the 'natural order'. He classified plants by their sexual characteristics: number of stamens, ovaries and so forth. His instinct was right, yet he admitted his system was artificial and would be superseded when the key came to light.

What natural links he did see he incorporated in a 'fragment of a natural system'. So far as it goes it still holds good. Taxonomists who followed him built on it until by the middle of the last century most of the genera of flowering plants had been assigned to 'families'.

Yet still the key, the link (if any) between genus and genus, between family and family, was unguessed at. It was left to Charles Darwin to supply it: plants are alike because they have common ancestors.

Darwin said: 'All true classification is genealogical . . . community of descent is the hidden bond which naturalists have unconsciously been seeking.'

Since Darwin's day taxonomy and phylogeny (the science of the ancestry of things) have marched side by side–without, it must be admitted, getting very much further. Proof of ancestral links 100 million years ago are not easy to find. Fossil evidence has hardly ever helped: largely because the taxonomically significant bits–flower parts–rarely make legible fossils.

Evolutionary history has been likened to a tree. Only the most recent shoots are visible, but breaks in the canopy show that two or three of the shoots come from one branchlet, or maybe that two or three branchlets come from one branch. The main bulk of the tree, the trunk and limbs which are the early stages of evolution, is invisible. The taxonomist's job is to reconstruct it from what he can see; the plants of today.

He gets most help in discovering links from flower structure. Flowers reflect the chances of mutation, the way the genetic dice fell. They have been less influenced by environment than, say, leaves or buds.

The daisy family, the *Compositae*, is an example of how far apart ecological adaptation can take related plants. It includes trees, shrubs, vines, herbs, even succulents –in every climate, on every soil, using every method of pollination and distribut-

Theophrastus (died 287 B.C.), a pupil of Aristotle, the first man to classify plants as 'woody' or 'herbaceous', though better known for his classification of the 'characters' of men.

Pinaceae *(pine family): narrow leaves in spirals, though sometimes in rows or tufts. Woody cones have two seeds per scale: bracts of flowers often remain visible in cone (as here in* Abies koreana*).*

Magnoliaceae *(magnolia family): bisexual flowers with stamens and petals attached below protruding female organs, which develop into a cone-like mass of seeds with a substantial food-store or endosperm.*

Taxodiaceae *(swamp cypress family; sequoia illustrated): narrow leaves arranged in a spiral. Roundish cones with spiralling leathery or woody scales.*

Cupressaceae *(cypress family): tiny scale-like leaves pressed close to the twigs. Small roundish cones start fleshy and ripen woody. Male 'flowers' are at branch tips.*

Taxaceae *(yew family): typical conifers in leaves and habit, unusual in being either male or female. Single-ovule female 'flowers' develop into open-ended berry-like 'cones'.*

Ginkgoaceae *(ginkgo family): has the oldest genus of tree still living, alone in its family, unaltered for 100 million years. The ginkgo's naked seeds relate it to the conifers; it has catkins for male flowers.*

Cyatheaceae *(tree ferns): reproduction like that of all ferns in two stages: the spores under the leaves have no sex. They drop off and grow into little flat plants (right). These have sexual spores which create another tree fern.*

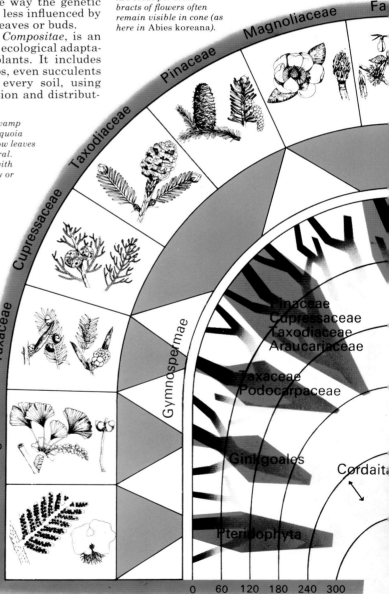

The evolution of trees can only be diagrammatically represented in the most tentative way. The symbolic tree here branches through concentric rings of 60 million years each. The green areas among its branches are suggestions as to the origins of the plant divisions, widest at the period of their greatest importance. The Angiosperm division (for example) came into prominence between 60 and 120 million years ago. Round the margin and described in the captions above are examples of important tree families deriving from the evolutionary groups, with the principal characteristics (largely of their flowers) by which they are classified.

Carl Linné (Linnaeus) (1707–78), the great Swedish naturalist, is considered to be the founder of modern botany. The binomial system for naming plants was established by his work.

Fagaceae *(beech family): male and female flowers on same tree, male flowers tassel-like. Fruit surrounded by a woody cup. Seed has no endosperm.*

Salicaceae *(willow family): sexes on different trees, male and female flowers both catkins. Fruit a capsule of many hairy seeds without endosperm. Leaves alternate and simple.*

Charles de Lécluse (Clusius)(1526–1609) from Flanders made the first real botanical (as opposed to medicine-herb) garden at Leiden in Holland.

Rosaceae *(rose family): bisexual flowers usually with parts in fives. Fruit depends on development of 'receptacle' and number of ovules (Prunus, here, has one). Leaves have tiny leaflets at base.*

ing seeds. Yet a common flower-design, of a group of tiny florets making a composite flower, is the clear link between all the family's members.

On the other hand there is an appeal open to common sense. The maples could, on the strength of their flowers alone, be chopped up into several different genera. Yet maples all have such similar fruit, all have the opposite branching pattern, and most of them have such obviously related leaves that to split them up would be pedantry.

The microscope has given us new aspects of plants to examine. Wood structure and the design of pollen grains are two of the most important. They have frequently confirmed what had already been deduced from the flowers.

The species is the basic category of plant, but it is not the smallest. Within the species there may be several varieties;

often local forms with an ecological reason (extreme exposure, for example) for being the way they are. It is a matter of botanical judgement what constitutes a species and what a variety. As Arthur Cronquist of the New York Botanic Garden says: 'Custom, in such matters, is merely the sum of a series of individual opinions, plus inertia.'

Custom has been given teeth, however, by an international rule of nomenclature that says that the first person to have given an accurate description of a species from a specimen and named it in print (and of course in Latin) was right. To prevent any confusion the 'author's' name–in a shortened form (e.g. L. for Linnaeus)–becomes part of the full name of the plant in botanical works (but not in this). About a quarter of a million flowering plants now have such names. On pages 264–67 is a list of tree-names and their exact meanings.

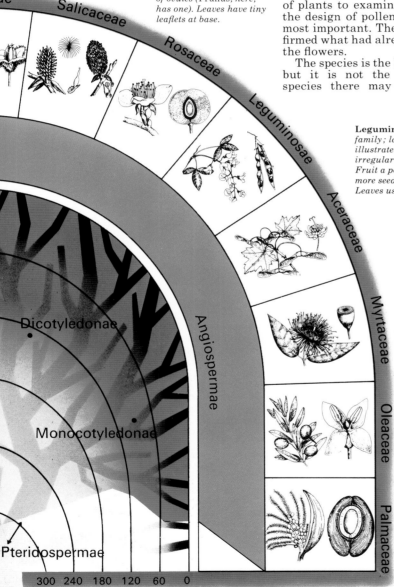

Leguminosae *(pea family; laburnum illustrated): most flowers irregular with five petals. Fruit a pod with two or more seeds, no endosperm. Leaves usually compound.*

Aceraceae *(maple family): opposite leaves and 'keys' for fruit consisting of two winged nutlets joined at their bases. Flowers have five petals, five sepals but eight stamens.*

Myrtaceae *(myrtle family; eucalyptus illustrated): bisexual flowers in clusters; the many stamens often have coloured stems. Fruit a berry, drupe or capsule. Leaves leathery and opposite.*

Oleaceae *(olive family): opposite leaves and bisexual flowers, usually with four petals and two stamens. Fruits vary: olive has drupes; ash, winged nuts.*

Palmaceae *(palms; coconut illustrated); unbranched stems of uniform thickness with terminal spiral of divided frond-like leaves. Flowers small, usually uni-sexual. Three ovules; one matures into seed with massive endosperm.*

Right *The classification of a garden plant starts (at the bottom) with the smallest division: cultivar. It works up in bigger and bigger groupings. Laburnum is a member of* the pea family, the Rosales *order, the* Rosidae *sub-class, Dicotyledon class, Angiosperm Division of the Plant Kingdom.*

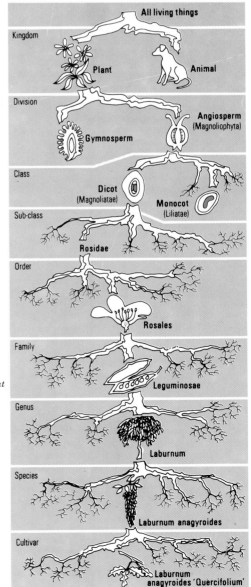

25

Trees and the Weather

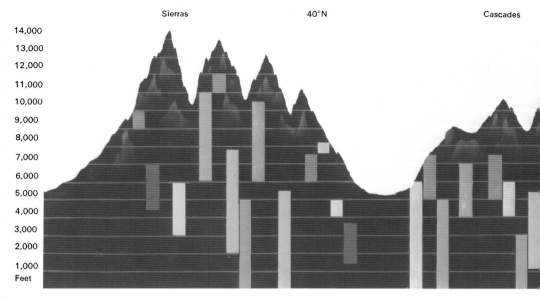

Climate is the crucial factor in deciding what trees grow where. Its broadest movements in geological time have governed the evolution of tree species. Relatively recent climate changes have settled the present natural distribution of these species round the globe.

The ancestors of all our trees were tropical plants. In the tropics the seasons are only vaguely marked by temperature changes: what alters most from one time of year to another is rainfall. Most tropical plants are evergreen, and can grow either constantly or intermittently whenever there is enough moisture, without fear of damage by cold.

Trees that adapted to life in the temperate zones, with marked winters, did so by learning to live with the seasons. A temperate-zone tree in its own habitat is precisely adapted to the exact weather pattern its parents and grandparents have undergone. It is what we call 'hardy', because it has learnt to do the right thing at the right time and not risk exposing its vulnerable stages of growth to weather that can harm them.

It has developed a clock that tells it when, judging by past experience, it is safe to get started in the spring, and when it had better pull in its horns for the winter.

The most graphic illustration of how trees find (literally) their own climatic level is seen along the course of a mountain range that runs from north to south. At the top of this page is a diagram of the western ranges of the United States and Canada. The tapering pattern of each tree's range from south to north tells the story. In the Sierras it finds its ecological niche at considerable altitudes. In the Cascades (and farther north still, in the Coast Range) the same basic climatic conditions, the length of time the snow lies, the number of days above 40°F. in which it can grow and ripen new wood, force it right down to sea-level.

As soon as a tree is moved (or its seed is planted) out of its accustomed zone it is in potential danger. It seems odd that a larch from Siberia (for example) would be anything but delighted to be moved to a softer climate. You would expect it to luxuriate in the longer growing season, while still being totally 'hardy'; whereas what happens in practice is that it is lured out of its safe dormancy by higher temperatures than it expects too early in the spring. It starts growth, only to be cut back by late spring frosts. This happens repeatedly, and it dies.

The converse happens when a southern tree is moved north. It is relatively safe in the spring: it waits for warmer weather. But it keeps growing too late in the summer

Above *Snow can be a vital protection to trees; especially to evergreens in dry mountain sunshine and intense cold. Here firs are completely shrouded in snow in the mountains of Hokkaido, northern Japan.*
Right *More damage is done to trees by untimely spring frost than by winter cold. A typical spring frost merely makes these alder leaves wilt. Less hardy trees can lose their new leaves.*

A prevailing wind can deform trees by preventing them shooting on the windward side. New shoots can grow only in the shelter of old ones; the tree trails over to leeward.

and its new wood is still soft and green when the first autumn frosts strike. Again, lack of hardiness really means being programmed for the wrong climate.

Perhaps more surprising is the difficulty trees experience in moving from the west coast to the east of North America – or from the East to Europe. The difference between a continental climate and an oceanic one can be more upsetting to the rhythm than a simple move from north to south. Western conifers are as unhappy in New England as oaks from Ohio are in Britain or France.

The most extreme example is a cold-climate tree which is moved to the sub-tropics. What can happen here is that its buds may fail to open at all. Built into its schedule is the need for a cold spell (the winter) to break their dormancy. If there is perpetual warmth it is stuck: in all probability it will die.

In forestry the question of provenance (i.e. exactly where the seed comes from) is clearly of the greatest importance. The forester's object is to extend the growth period of his trees as far as he can without putting them in danger of frost damage. He has little room for manoeuvre, but if he can even add a week to the growing season by getting seed from 100 miles farther south without the trees suffering he has added (say) a whole year's growth in 20 years, or five per cent. In practice much better results, even up to 30 per cent, are achieved.

Where winter damage, as opposed to damage by late or early frost, is concerned, trees from different zones are on a more equal footing. Many, if not most, temperate-

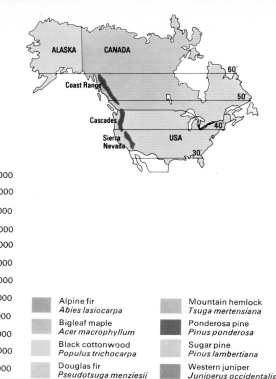

50°N   Coast Range   60°N

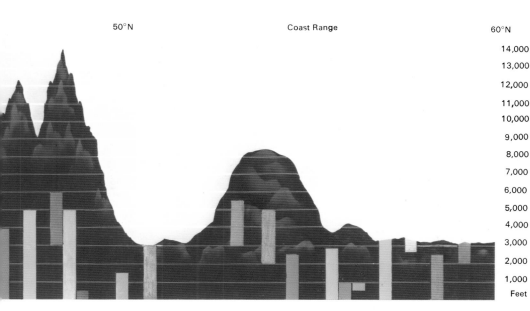

14,000
13,000
12,000
11,000
10,000
9,000
8,000
7,000
6,000
5,000
4,000
3,000
2,000
1,000
Feet

Alpine fir
Abies lasiocarpa

Bigleaf maple
Acer macrophyllum

Black cottonwood
Populus trichocarpa

Douglas fir
Pseudotsuga menziesii

Engelmann spruce
Picea engelmanii

Grand fir
Abies grandis

Mountain hemlock
Tsuga mertensiana

Ponderosa pine
Pinus ponderosa

Sugar pine
Pinus lambertiana

Western juniper
Juniperus occidentalis

Western red cedar
Thuja plicata

Western white pine
Pinus monticola

zone trees can stand being frozen solid while they are dormant (although some are more used to it than others, and none like it to happen suddenly). What more often hurts, and can kill, is winter drought.

While the ground is frozen in winter there is no water available to the roots. But high winds and often low humidity keep on evaporating water from the branches. Even the twigs of leafless trees transpire to some extent in these conditions. So the tree begins to dry out. On evergreens it shows in the browning of the leaves by the end of even a normal winter. A longer period of intense cold with clear skies and a high wind can easily prove fatal.

The Arnold Arboretum at Boston has perhaps (of all scholarly institutions) the most experience of testing temperate trees in hard winters. It argues that if one statistic is to be used to try to map plant hardiness zones it should be minimum temperature. Rainfall is important; soil has its influence; microclimates (see illustrations on right) are vital. But on a broad front it is the lowest regular winter temperatures that decide whether a tree will survive or not.

On pages 30 and 31 the hardiness zone map developed by Dr. Alfred Rehder at the Arnold Arboretum for the whole of North America is matched by a similar map on the same principles done (for the first time) for Europe. On pages 250 and 251 maps show the natural forest vegetation of the same areas, so that it is possible to follow the apparent effects of minimum temperatures on the selection of species to be found in the wild.

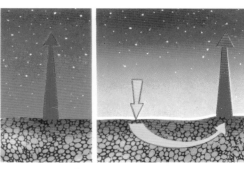

Local frost: cause and effect

Above *Where either clouds or a tree canopy insulate the layer of warm air above ground from the open sky, heat (red) cannot escape; frost is unlikely. On a night without cloud, heat is free to leave the ground, until (above right) soil temperature falls below air temperature. Then soil takes heat (yellow arrow) from air near to the ground, causing 'radiation' frost.*

Below left *Cold air created in a thin layer at ground level will flow downhill and collect like water in hollows and valleys, which thus become 'frost pockets'. The height to which this hollow fills with frost is marked by the dead lower branches of the trees.*
Below right *The house and its garden are protected from frost. Trees uphill prevent it flowing down the hill, the slope below lets it run off. But the valley floor is unprotected: cold air comes in from the left foreground hill.*

The Advance of Spring

The ripple of bursting buds, of woods growing amber with catkins, white with dogwood, tender green with the opening leaf, moves inexorably northward in the spring. Even in the dead of the year there are stirrings of swelling buds, early catkins on willows, eccentric bushes with winter flowers. But it is when the last frosts of spring pass that the full flush transforms the woods. In Florida and Naples this is as early as the first week of March. In New England not until about eight weeks later, about the first of May. At Edinburgh it is the last week of April.

The rising temperature is the prime mover in releasing leaves and flowers from their protecting buds. Spring moves north at a predictable pace in flat and open country. But local factors can cause wide variations on the same latitude. Latitude clearly bears little relation to the relative timing of spring in Europe and eastern North America.

Altitude is important. The temperature drops 1°F. for every 300 feet you climb. The practical effect of this on tree growth depends on other local conditions, but 300 feet extra altitude has been observed to shorten the total growing season in the eastern States by five days, in the Alps by six and in Scotland by twelve.

Cities have the reverse effect. With the warmth and shelter they provide they can greatly advance the spring. London has pear blossom three weeks before a country garden only 50 miles away. Even a sheltering house wall can bring a tree into blossom a week or two ahead of its neighbour standing unprotected in the open.

Daylength is the other deciding factor. However unseasonably warm it may be at the end of winter, or however miserably cold in the spring, trees are governed in the cycle by the photoperiod: the number of hours of darkness.

In the tropics daylength varies no more than do the seasons: day and night are always about equal; trees grow year-round. As far north as Oslo, however, there is a bare seven hours of daylight in January, compared with 17 in June. At the March equinox the north catches up with and overtakes the south in daylight hours. Thereafter its plants can begin to make up for their shorter growing season by using the extra light.

The tables on these pages show the hours of daylight at different latitudes in Europe and America from January to June, together with the actual blooming and leafing dates of nine species of trees. The dates are averages worked out over some 20 years.

The interaction of temperature, daylength and local factors gives some surprising results. For example a magnolia which blooms in London in mid-March waits until mid-May in Fribourg in Switzerland, five degrees of latitude to the south but in the northern foothills of the Alps. The same magnolia flowers in late March in both Seattle and Washington D.C. (8° to the south)—but here it is the continental climate of the east which holds it back. It is interesting to speculate on the relevant influences using

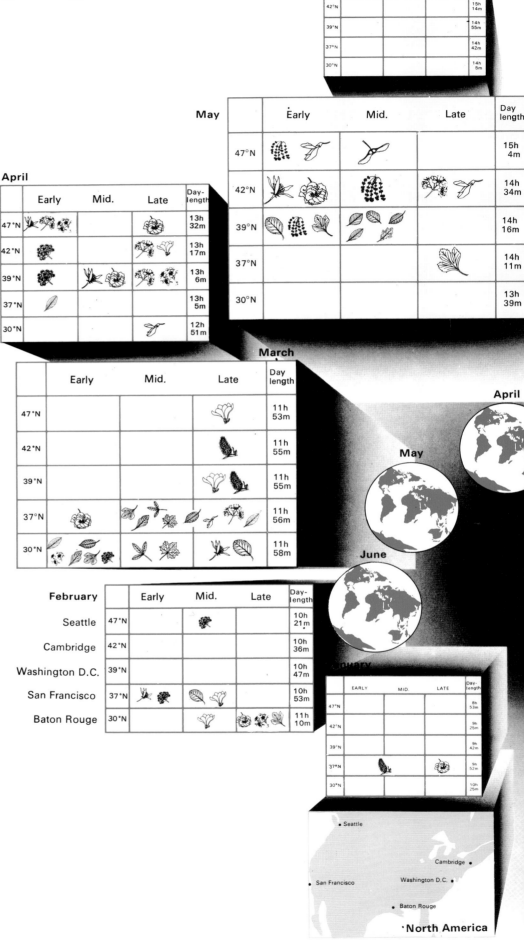

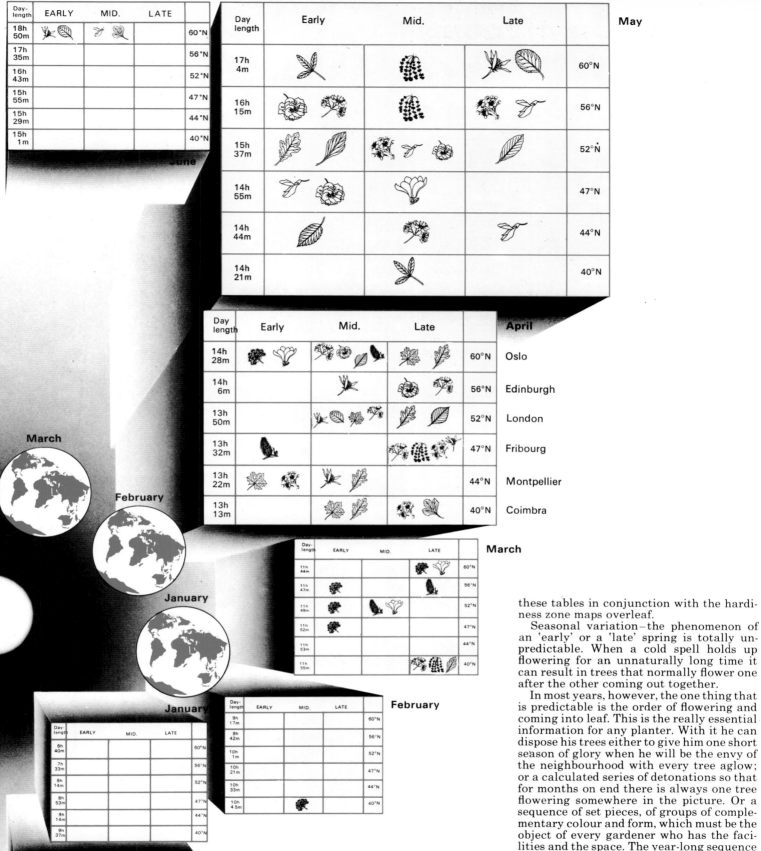

these tables in conjunction with the hardiness zone maps overleaf.

Seasonal variation—the phenomenon of an 'early' or a 'late' spring is totally unpredictable. When a cold spell holds up flowering for an unnaturally long time it can result in trees that normally flower one after the other coming out together.

In most years, however, the one thing that is predictable is the order of flowering and coming into leaf. This is the really essential information for any planter. With it he can dispose his trees either to give him one short season of glory when he will be the envy of the neighbourhood with every tree aglow; or a calculated series of detonations so that for months on end there is always one tree flowering somewhere in the picture. Or a sequence of set pieces, of groups of complementary colour and form, which must be the object of every gardener who has the facilities and the space. The year-long sequence of special features (flowers, foliage and fruit) of 100 species is given on pages 316-17 in the Reference Section.

Common laburnum *Laburnum anagyroides*

Cornelian cherry *Cornus mas*

English oak *Quercus robur*

European pussy willow *Salix caprea*

Hawthorn *Crataegus monogyna*

Japanese or oriental cherry *Prunus serrulata*

Magnolia *Magnolia × soulangiana*

Norway maple *Acer platanoides*

Shadblow *Amelanchier × grandiflora*

Zones of Tree Hardiness in North America and Europe

Whether a tree will live and grow in any region, given suitable soil and adequate moisture, depends on the lowest temperatures it will encounter (see pages 26–27). On this page we reproduce the map of the hardiness zones of North America compiled by the Arnold Arboretum on the basis of average annual minimum temperatures–a map that has long been taken as a guide by the horticultural industry. Opposite is a map of Europe on the same basis.

As an example of how they work the phrase 'zone 9' in the text (and in the notes in the A-Z Index of Tree Species) identifies a tree that will survive in temperature

zone 9–as marked on the maps–or south of it, but only in exceptional circumstances in the next zone northwards, zone 8. Such broad generalizations of course have many exceptions: altitude lowers the temperature locally; big lakes have the opposite effect.

The North American map is dominated by the influence of the great land- (and ice-) mass to the north. You can picture the situation as cold radiating from somewhere in Manitoba. Only the mountain ranges (and to some extent the warm Gulf of Mexico) distort this continental influence. Otherwise minimum temperatures rise in concentric bands to the subtropical fringes

of southern California and Florida.

The rainfall map (top of the page opposite) shows that most of the major centres of population in North America fall in zones of adequate average rainfall for most trees (over 30 inches a year)–though this does not mean that trees will not benefit from deep watering in dry spells. The annual figures do not show, for example, that California's rain comes mainly in winter, making watering very necessary in summer. In most of the United States more rain falls between May and October than between November and April.

The overwhelming influences on Europe

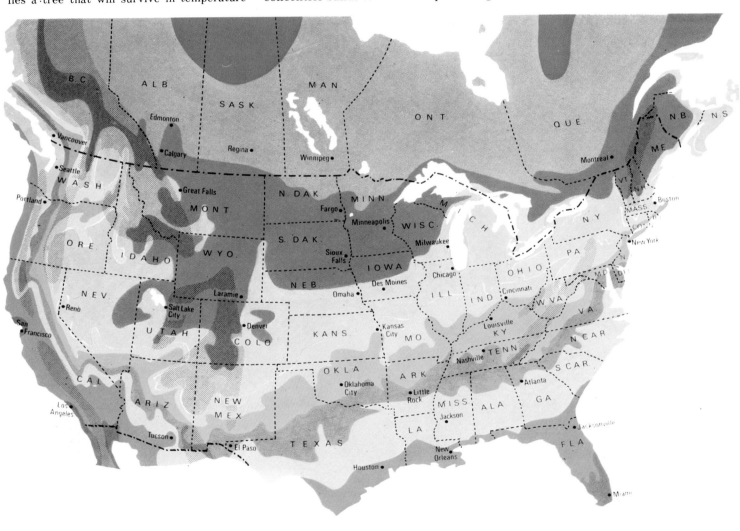

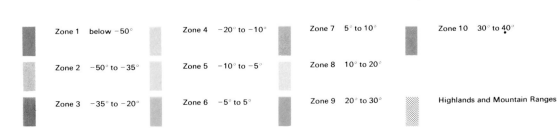

Zone 1	below −50°	Zone 4	−20° to −10°	Zone 7	5° to 10°	Zone 10	30° to 40°
Zone 2	−50° to −35°	Zone 5	−10° to −5°	Zone 8	10° to 20°		
Zone 3	−35° to −20°	Zone 6	−5° to 5°	Zone 9	20° to 30°	Highlands and Mountain Ranges	

are the Atlantic Ocean, the cold land-mass of Asia, and the warm-air-mass over the Sahara. The ocean with its warm Gulf Stream is so effective in keeping winter temperatures up that, mountains apart, the hardiness zones of Britain and most of northern Europe run west-east rather than north-south. Where the Atlantic and Saharan influences coincide in southern Spain, winter temperatures are as high as in Florida, ten degrees of latitude or 700 miles farther south.

Rainfall also follows a mainly west-east pattern, but as in America annual levels are adequate in most populated regions.

Inches		Inches	
Above 60		20 to 30	
40 to 60		10 to 20	
30 to 40		below 10	

Trees and Wildlife

A sand dune is very poor in wildlife. A forest is immensely rich. The more different kinds of trees a forest contains the richer its wildlife will be.

The shores of Lake Michigan provide an opportunity (in the Indiana Dunes National Park, for example) to see the process of enrichment in action. The lake has retreated, leaving ponds interspersed with sand dunes. The plant communities on the dunes are stages between sand and forest.

Those nearest the lake have only a sketchy covering of marram grass, sandreed and *Artemisia*. Eventually, they begin to bind the sand with their roots and enrich it with their litter. Insects diversify enormously. The pond starts to silt up.

At the second stage there is enough soil (sand plus humus from herbs) to support shrubs and pioneer trees: willow, cottonwood, sand cherry and wild plum. Insects increase and attract birds. The margins of the pond contract with flourishing vegetation. Bass give way to catfish. Beavers carry wood into the water.

The pond has become marshy ground by the fourth stage. On the dune there are pines and junipers, even a few young oaks. Water insects reach and pass their climax, to be succeeded by bees, flies, ants, beetles.

Squirrels and ruffed grouse arrive.

Soil builds up in the old pond hollow and changes chemically. Earthworms and snails appear. At first the forest is fairly open with oak and hickory as the big trees above a dense scrub of blackberry, hazel, redbud, cherries, roses and blueberry. The range of insects grows and with it the range of birds. Mammals of all kinds appear.

The final stage of dense beech and maple forest can succeed the oak and hickory. But both types also coexist on dunes of the same age. Owls, woodpeckers and hawks join the birds. Deer are fairly common and black bear put in an appearance.

Below *The illustrations show the progress of the dunes from bare beach to high forest, the chart the successive increase of the different populations.*

The Grass Stage
The pond below has black bass, the dunes grass and termites.

The Scrub Stage
Grasses give way to scrub and pioneer trees. The pond grows a rushy edge and starts to silt up, helped by the work of the beaver. Pollen-gathering and wood-boring insects and mosquitoes attract birds. Amphibian life reaches a peak; at the end of this stage reptiles emerge.

The Pine Stage
The pond is now marsh, fish vanish, aquatic insects reach a climax. Conifers are dominant: jack pine and juniper on the dunes, larch (tamarack) on the marsh-land. New kinds of insects and fruit bring more birds. Mammals begin with the squirrel.

The Oak/Hickory Stage
Oak and hickory dominate a mature community with a rich undergrowth. Plenty of light allows innumerable species of plants. Insect, bird, reptile (snakes) and mammal life continues to diversify with white-tailed deer among the higher mammals.

The Beech/Maple Stage
A denser forest of beech and maple may finally take over. Undergrowth diminishes but all forms of life continue to proliferate. The black bear symbolizes a rich and mature wildlife population.

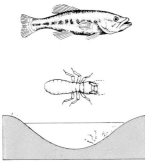

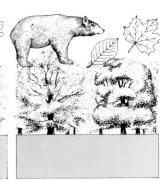

Stage One *Grassy Dunes*	Stage Two *Shrubs*	Stage Three *Pine Forest*	Stage Four *Oak and Hickory Forest*	Stage Five *Beech and Maple Forest*

Plants

Insects

Birds

DUNES

PONDS

Exactly what animals and birds, then, does a forest shelter and feed? Over the page is a portrait of the larger creatures of the Black Forest, one of Europe's ancient and little-changed woodlands, lying at between 1,200 and 5,000 feet in southwest Germany. The scene is a forest clearing in midwinter . . .

The fox will readily live anywhere, even in city suburbs. In the forest, an old badger's earth suits it very well. Its diet is largely small rodents, which it catches by pouncing, but it is not averse to a duck or a hen and even at times berries. Generally a nocturnal creature, with acute senses which make it adept at avoiding man, the fox's strong scent is usually the only indication of its presence.

The wild cat, the commonest feline predator of Europe, is now encountered only in relatively undisturbed areas such as the Black Forest.

Like the fox, it is a nocturnal animal living on small mammals and birds. It usually hides during the day in a well-concealed burrow or a hole in a tree.

The pine marten is a rare member of the weasel family, often called the 'sweet-mart' in contrast to the 'foul-mart' or polecat. It lives in hollow trees, squirrel dreys or abandoned birds'-nests. It hunts by day, often catching squirrels and dormice in the treetops, but will also eat anything from very young roe-deer, hares and small mammals to mountain-ash berries and other kinds of fruit.

The polecat usually spends the day in a burrow and hunts at night, catching anything up to the size of a rabbit – including domestic hens. It climbs poorly, but swims with ease. If frightened or attacked it emits a foul-smelling fluid from its anal glands.

The red deer is the largest European deer (three to four and a half feet at the shoulder; five to six and a half feet long). It is generally found in sexually segregated herds, but during the breeding season forms groups of a stag and a number of hinds. Old stags are generally solitary. Only the males (and they not always) develop antlers. During the rutting season the stags advertise their presence by 'roaring', usually in a special area from which they have cleared all debris.

Red deer often browse on the bottom branches of forest trees.

The wild boar, the only wild pig to be found in Europe, is now rare and survives only in large forests like the Black Forest.

The sow builds a 'nest' (a circular barricade of twigs and earth) within which the young are born and kept until they are old enough to accompany her. At first the young are striped for camouflage, but this is lost in the autumn. Although the boars are solitary, the young and the sows form small family herds. Wild pigs, like their domestic relatives, are fond of rooting in the forest floor and love wallowing in boggy ground.

The red squirrel is a tree-dweller, usually portrayed eating hazel nuts, but greedy for all sorts of nuts, berries, mushrooms, young shoots and eggs.

It stores food in autumn and spends much of its time in winter in a *drey* (a large globular tree-nest built of twigs lined with moss, fine grasses and wool) coming out to feed on warm days (only occasionally in the snow). It is unobtrusive if man is around and can move silently, but is less cautious if it does not realise it is being observed.

The squirrel spends much time on the ground, but always close to a tree up which it will run if disturbed, often uttering sharp staccato cries.

The long-eared owl is a nocturnal predatory bird of coniferous forests, spending most of the day sitting close to the trunk of a tree. It feeds on mammals – to rabbit size – birds and large insects.

At the beginning of the breeding season the male 'displays' by flying through or above the trees clapping his wings. The nest is built in another big bird's abandoned nest or occasionally on the ground.

The goshawk is a large predatory bird adapted for flying through the trees in pursuit of prey, which can be mammals or birds of its own size or smaller. The prey is usually taken to a plucking post in a tree where there is a good all-round view.

The nest is large and substantial, built of twigs and small branches.

The woodcock This large member of the snipe family is well adapted to life in the forest: it has a long, sensitive bill that enables it to probe for worms in the soft forest floor and its colouring blends perfectly with its surroundings.

During the breeding season a 'roding' male can often be seen flying over the trees patrolling his territory and uttering a peculiar croaking call. The nest is a scrape on the ground lined with a few leaves and pieces of grass. The bird's eyes are so placed on the sides of the head that it can see in an almost perfect circle: it is not easily approached. When flushed a sitting bird will often 'tower' (suddenly fly straight up).

The black woodpecker is the largest woodpecker of the Black Forest, about the size of a crow. It is fairly common generally in old deciduous and coniferous forests.

At the beginning of the breeding season the male can be heard 'drumming' (i.e. tapping his bill on a dead branch). The sound carries through the trees for a considerable distance. The nest is a hole in a tree which the bird digs out with its bill. No nest material is used and the eggs are laid on wood chips.

The black woodpecker feeds on the adults and larvae of wood-boring insects, which it extracts by chopping open trees and rotten logs with its massive ivory-coloured bill. During the winter it sometimes burrows beneath the snow to get at red ants' nests at the base of rotten stumps.

The capercailie The chief enemy of this turkey-sized bird of the grouse family is the sportsman: it has few natural predators. The female, like most grouse, is brownish and well camouflaged sitting on her nest on the ground. At the end of April and in early May the males gather at a display-ground and there perform noisily for the benefit of the females.

From autumn to spring the capercailie feeds almost exclusively on the shoots and buds of conifers and can cause great damage in plantations.

The ring ouzel is found in the more open areas of the Black Forest and like many thrushes feeds on the ground, eating ground-living invertebrates. In the autumn it eats berries.

It migrates to the Mediterranean in winter.

The black grouse is found almost everywhere in the Black Forest.

From mid-March to mid-June the male bird is found at a 'lek', a circular display ground which its father and grandfather used before it. The birds gather just after dawn or in the late afternoon to display and to challenge other males, calling with a peculiar dove-like bubbling.

From late April to early May the females (grayhens) visit the 'lek', choose their mate, and then go off to build their nest (a rough scrape in the ground under some cover) and rear their young.

The black grouse feeds mostly on vegetable material with some small invertebrates in the breeding season.

1 Holly *Ilex aquifolium*	**15** Capercailie
2 and **13** Mountain pine	**16** Woodcock
Pinus mugo	**17** Long-eared owl
3, 4, 6 and **12** Norway	**18** Ring ouzel
spruce *Picea abies*	**19** Pine marten
5 Silver birch	**20** Wild boar
Betula pendula	**21** Black grouse
7 Sycamore	**22** Polecat
Acer pseudoplatanus	**23** Red deer
8 Beech *Fagus sylvatica*	**24** Goshawk
9 Hornbeam	**25** Black woodpecker
Carpinus betulus	**26** Fox
10, 11 and **14** Silver fir	**27** Red squirrel
Abies alba	**28** Wild cat

Trees and Wildlife

Forests are the richest areas on earth for wildlife. Here, in a clearing in the Black Forest in mid-winter, are gathered most of Europe's remaining larger animals. They are described on the previous page.

Man and the Forest

Old-fashioned forestry, in the days when it seemed inconceivable that the supply of trees would ever run out, consisted of choosing the biggest and best, chopping them down and sawing them up.

Modern forestry works differently. The great virgin woods of Europe were exhausted centuries ago. In America they would be exhausted by now had conservationists not begun lobbying in the early years of this century for control of what was cut where. Instead of cutting and moving on, the modern forester has to assume that the trees will have to go on coming off the same land for ever.

Modern forestry means planting as many trees as you cut, or more; protecting the stock from disease, animals, people, fire; and cutting it on a rotation basis. It also means sowing only seed that is perfectly suited to the soil and climate, and only the seed of really good fault-free trees. The climate question is discussed on pages 26–27. The basic principles of tree-breeding are shown on pages 14–15.

The process of making the forester's dream, the fast and flawless tree, is a recent one. Since the 18th century landowners have realized that it makes sense to leave one or two of the biggest trees, rather than

unusable runts, to reseed and restock land they have cut over. But juggling with chromosomes is very much a 20th-century idea.

In practice it means running seed orchards, where the fertilizing of trees can be done under supervision and the results controlled. A typical seed orchard would be a few acres of young pine trees, too young to bear seed themselves. On them are grafted the upper, seed-bearing branches of the best of the older trees. To collect such branches the forester takes his gun into the woods. When he sees a tree taller and straighter than all the rest he shoots off branch-tips where the flowers will be.

A 'stand' of larch, halfway to maturity, is being 'thinned'—having the less successful trees cut for pulp to allow the best to develop for timber. The logs are sawn to eight-foot lengths and debarked by

this machine. In some very modern forests a chipping machine reduces the whole tree to pulpable chips on the spot. In this way even the branches can be used and transport is made much easier.

Extraction of timber from the woods is often a problem. On flat ground special tractors can drag or carry it to collection points for trucks on forest roads.

Trees hide tents. Forests can absorb more holiday-makers than any other landscape. The possibilities for pleasure in productive forests have long been exploited in North America: in Europe the idea is relatively new.

In the orchard the flowers are within reach. It is easy to protect them from random pollination and fertilize them only with pollen from another chosen tree. Then in due course it is easy to collect the cones and know just what seed you are sowing.

Along with care of the stock goes care of the land. Most forest is in unfarmable country; often on precipitous terrain. The difficulty here is in getting the wood out without irreparably damaging the soil, which is often held in place only by the trees. Road-building in the mountains is so expensive that helicopters and even balloons have been used to airlift timber.

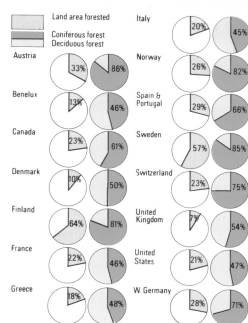

Land area forested
Coniferous forest
Deciduous forest

Austria	33%	86%
Benelux	13%	46%
Canada	23%	61%
Denmark	10%	50%
Finland	64%	81%
France	22%	46%
Greece	18%	48%
Italy	20%	45%
Norway	26%	82%
Spain & Portugal	29%	66%
Sweden	57%	85%
Switzerland	23%	75%
United Kingdom	7%	54%
United States	21%	47%
W. Germany	28%	71%

On land that has been cut over a few of the best trees are sometimes left to sow their (superior) seed. Seed is also sown by aeroplane today, and experiments in dropping seedlings in tiny 'bombs' of soil are being carried out.

One means of combating forest fires is the hilltop fire-tower, set on stilts. In summer the towers are manned for 24 hours a day.

Logging on steep watershed areas brings problems—the soil is easily disturbed; timber may have to be lifted by helicopter and sometimes balloon.

The forester's ideal tree is one with the longest possible straight trunk without branches. Close planting ensures bottom branches will die in the shade and drop off, leaving knot-free timber.

By leaving appropriate indigenous trees in special situations (willow or alder by waterside, for example) the forester can help overcome the perils of monoculture, offering a habitat to a much wider

range of wildlife. An old oak is the most valuable wildlife tree of all: hundreds of different insect species are found on oak—particularly on dead branches.

The Ice Ages

We should glance back a moment at the origins of the forest. When the club-mosses reared up from the swamp and ferns formed the first trees—perhaps some 400 million years ago—they existed in a blanket of carbon dioxide. There was no living creature; there was no breathable air. But there was photosynthesis.

The coal in the ground is the carbon from that unbreathable sky. Tens of millions of years of forest, building trees with carbon and leaving oxygen as the by-product, was the origin of our world. Life on earth was made possible by trees.

We must leap unknowable millennia of evolution to reach the relatively recent past. The period known as the Tertiary, from (perhaps) 38 million to (perhaps) 12 million years ago, was furnished with trees shaped just as we know them. What was different was their numbers. The forest was boundless; it reached from pole to pole. And it was homogeneous; the same species, from a range far wider than we know today, might occur anywhere in that great sea of trees.

In early Tertiary times the climate was distinctly warmer than today: the vegetation of Europe was like that of modern Southeast Asia. By the Pliocene (i.e. late Tertiary) era gradual cooling had killed off the subtropical components of the northern temperate forest or caused them to become mere herbs, leaving a rich mixture of all the families found round the world today at these latitudes. Asia, America and Europe alike had swamp cypress, magnolia, sequoia, sweet gum, ginkgo, incense cedar, umbrella pine, as well as oak, beech and the other common trees we know.

This was the situation about a million years ago when the climate began to change for the worse, and went on changing till the sea froze at the poles, and trees died, and their offspring too, unless they could find a place unoccupied by other trees where the ice had not yet reached.

There was not one ice age, but four: Gunz, Mindel, Riss and Würm (or such are the comic-opera names science has given them). They were leisurely affairs. Between Gunz and Mindel (which was the coldest, and saw the ice reach its maximum dimensions) there was a temperate period of something like 60,000 years, when conditions may have been similar to our time. Come to that, we are quite probably merely enjoying an interglacial period ourselves.

Vast numbers of species perished for ever as the arctic cold came south. Geography was the decisive factor. Where there was a line of retreat, a continuous land-mass, species could fall back in tolerably good order. America and eastern Asia provided these conditions. Where there was a high east-west mountain range, or a sea with no way round, vegetation had its back to the wall. Between them the Alps, the Pyrenees and the Mediterranean cut off the last hope of most of the species of Europe (which up to that time had been as rich in trees as the rest of the world). Only about 36 genera, and very few species of these, survive as European 'natives'; whereas in China there are only six of the whole temperate world's genera missing.

The southern hemisphere, particularly Africa, suffered earlier than the north; a great glacier over South Africa advanced into the Tropics some 250 million years ago; retreat to the north was prevented by an ocean where the Sahara now lies. Tropical Africa today has nothing like the richness of flora of South America or Southeast Asia.

There were special conditions which sometimes allowed survival from the ice. One was extreme drought: in a place where rain (or snow) rarely fell, in the lee of a great mountain range, the ice may never have built up. Some botanists believe that such refuges were numerous, particularly at high altitudes, and account for many of today's local species. On the other hand there were conditions which extinguished a race even where the ice was miles away: there is no harder barrier for a plant to cross than a closed community of other plants, taking up all the available space. This may well have been the case in, say, the south of France, which was never frozen but which failed to provide a refuge for many plants from the north.

The total effect of the ice ages was an enormous acceleration of evolution. Without them the world would still be in the age of reptiles. The effect of refugee plants streaming across the continents was to stimulate genetic crossing, to favour what would previously have been unsuitable mutations. Nor is the process by any means at a standstill today. We can watch the pines for example still in full cry, reconquering the hills.

Fourteen thousand years ago the ice retreated for the last time (so far). The variations in climate since that time have been relatively slight, but enough to favour different trees at different times. What flourished when is known to us primarily by the analysis of the pollen grains found in recent lake sediments in the strata of peat.

In the immediately post-glacial 'subarctic' period, the areas where the ice had been were still raw mineral soil and an unchecked wind allowed only the toughest trees—dwarf birches and willows—to make the first colonizing moves.

Bottom *One million years ago, just before the first ice age, typical European forest vegetation included the present oaks, birch, spruce etc. but also scores of trees we think of as American or Asiatic: magnolias, redwoods, hickories, white pines, incense cedars, umbrella pines, plum yews, ginkgos.*

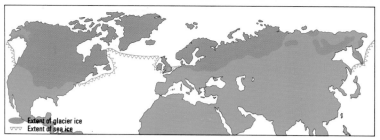

Extent of glacier ice
Extent of sea ice

Left *The last ice age reached its fullest extent of glaciation 20,000 years ago, covering most of North America, all of Scandinavia and north-western Asia, some of northern Europe and all the northern oceans. The ice-sheet built up chiefly where westerly winds brought rain. Siberia, mostly low-lying and* completely sheltered from the west by the Asiatic land-mass, largely escaped glaciation; no solid front of ice descended into China as it did into America and Europe. The whole of China was therefore a refuge for such trees as could stand the cold. In America trees retreated south; in Europe most of them perished.

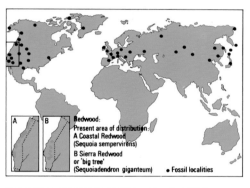

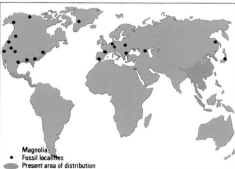

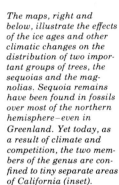

Left *Since the last ice age ended in about 10,000 B.C. the world's climate has not been static. The temperature rose irregularly through the 'Boreal' periods to a maximum in the 'Atlantic' period about 4,000 B.C. Since then, again irregularly, it has cooled. This chart records the effect of these changes on the tree populations of Europe and the United States. The leafier the stem (on the chart) the more the trees in question flourished. 'Pollen counts' in datable strata (usually in peat) provide the evidence. Overall there appears to be a certain symmetry in the pattern, pivoting approximately round the 'Atlantic' period. To this extent it bears out the theory that we are living between two ice ages.*

The maps, right and below, illustrate the effects of the ice ages and other climatic changes on the distribution of two important groups of trees, the sequoias and the magnolias. Sequoia remains have been found in fossils over most of the northern hemisphere – even in Greenland. Yet today, as a result of climate and competition, the two members of the genus are confined to tiny separate areas of California (inset).

Right *Fossil remains of magnolias show that before the ice ages they were well distributed round the northern hemisphere; certainly more so than the present evidence (on the map) proves. But they belonged to one of the families that the ice ages wiped out entirely in Europe. The combination of the Mediterranean and the Alps left them no route southward. All our magnolias today come from Asia and America.*

Redwood:
Present area of distribution:
A Coastal Redwood (Sequoia sempervirens)
B Sierra Redwood or 'big tree' (Sequoiadendron giganteum)
● Fossil localities

Magnolia:
● Fossil localities
Present area of distribution

Since then, starting some 11,000 years ago, there was a build-up through a cool, then a more continental and extreme climate to a climax of relative warmth and wetness – the 'Atlantic' period of between 7,500 and 5,000 years ago, the era when some of the bristlecone pines still alive today were seedlings.

Their lifetime has seen a reversal of the previous trends; another dry, continental and extreme period followed by about 1,500 years of lower temperatures and more rain, the era (in human terms) of the classical civilizations and the Dark Ages. About 1000 (A.D.) another trend becomes discernible – now with plenty of still-living trees to give evidence: the relatively warm and dry period in which we live.

To speak in terms of broad trends is the best anyone can do, reviewing such a span of time. What is worth remembering, however, is that the answer to any particular question need not lie in the great averages of history. Cataclysms and catastrophes are as much a part of evolutionary history as the gradual attrition of the ages. Whether or where a species exists can be decided by one great frost; one plague of locusts; one unaccountable wave of natural competition. The movements of nature can take millennia – or they can happen in a flash.

Left *The theory of continental drift holds that one huge land-mass broke up and has been drifting apart since, taking plants with it. But geologists say the rift (if any) was at least 200 million years ago: too early for modern plant distribution.*

The Old World

Tree distribution since the last ice age has been the slow setting to rights of what the ice disjointed. At first the process was infinitely gradual, through colonization and evolution. But later, since the dawn of civilization when man began moving plants about, redistribution has happened at a faster and faster pace—so that today, in countries which the ice overran and which have since seen a succession of civilizations, the question of what tree is native has little meaning.

Native when? When the ice advanced? Or retreated? Before man set about destroying the forest? In the earliest written account?

We know little of the early years. We know that the peach tree and the mulberry came from the Orient, the walnut from the Caucasus, the fig from Persia.

But what trees the Romans brought, or what plants they moved from one part of their empire to another, are questions we can no longer answer.

Plants of usefulness are cultivated and transported before plants of ornament. If the Romans took the sweet chestnut and the walnut with them to France and Britain it was for their fruit.

But the Romans were rose-lovers as well as gourmands and fanatical ablutionists.

The walnut from Persia was one of the useful trees introduced into cultivation in classical times. Engraving from a 16th-century Swiss herbal.

Diggings at Chichester (their port of Regnum) have uncovered a palace garden made exactly to Pliny's instructions—to the very size and depth and spacing of the flower-beds. It would be surprising if the nurserymen of Rome did not export to officers abroad the plants they loved at home.

The systematic study of plants had been initiated by the Greeks. It was continued by the Romans. Then in the Middle Ages it lapsed into a mixture of carpenter's know-how, herbalist's mumbo-jumbo and poetical symbolism. Chaucer made a catalogue of trees, which is a fair sample:

> The bilder ook, and eek the hardy asshe;
> The piler elm, the coffre unto careyne;
> The boxtree piper; holm to whippes lasshe;
> The sayling firr; the cipres, deth to pleyne;
> The shooter ew, the asp for shaftes pleyne;
> The olive of pees, and eek the drunken vyne,
> The victor palm, the laurer to devyne.

The Renaissance brought the classical systems to light again. Learned apothecaries in the north of Europe found that the plants of ancient Greece failed to tally with the local flora. Modern botany began with their 'herbals'.

The gardens of the Villa Lante, north of Rome, were begun by Vignola in 1566. In such Renaissance gardens trees were treated as architectural elements.

Albertus Magnus (1193–1280), a German Dominican monk, was the greatest exponent of Aristotle's botanical work in the Middle Ages. He taught at Cologne and Paris.

John Gerard (1545–1612) was author of the famous Herball or Generall Historie of Plantes, published in 1597. It is vivid writing, but still largely concerned with medicine.

John Parkinson (1567–1650), early plant collector, and author of Paradisus in sole Paradisus terrestris, or a garden of all sorts of pleasant flowers which our English ayre will permitt to be noursed up . . .

John Tradescant (died 1637?) was gardener to King Charles I, travelled to Russia and Algiers and made a collection of plants at Lambeth. His son John followed in his footsteps, sailing to Virginia.

Europe's earliest botanic garden at Leiden, Holland, was made in 1594 by the

The cedar of Lebanon was introduced to Britain from Turkey in 1638.

This engraving is from an early 17th-century French herbal.

The first herbal in English was William Turner's, published in 1546. Gerard's popular and readable *Herball*, largely plagiarized from the work of the Dutchman Dodoens, appeared in 1597; John Parkinson's *Paradisus in Sole* in 1629. Parkinson was an ardent collector and may himself have introduced new species into cultivation.

At the same time, what had seemed an inexhaustible supply of timber began to look disturbingly thin. By the beginning of the 16th century Royal Statutes were enjoining replanting. The Great Wood of Scotland (the Caledonian Forest) is described as 'utterly destroyed'. Books of husbandry (the first, Fitzherbert's, in 1523) began to give instructions for planting trees.

The first botanical expeditions (in the same period) covered the ancient world, most of it then in the Turkish empire. One might say that consolidation and realization of the trees of the Old World, including the world of the Bible, took up to the middle of the 17th century. About 1600 Europe received the horse chestnut from Asia Minor; by mid-century she had the cedar of Lebanon.

There is a great stock-taking in John Evelyn's *Sylva* of 1662. The monarchy had been restored to an England worse off than ever for timber – particularly for oak, without which there could be no navy. National security literally depended on oak trees – as France realized in the following century. Evelyn was commissioned by the Royal Society to discourse on growing trees. He did it with such gusto (and apparent knowledge) that his discourse was still being printed a century later.

While England was worrying about warships, France was getting on with the serious business of planting avenues. The same year as *Sylva* saw the culmination of the French style of landscaping: Le Nôtre's design for the park of Vaux-le-Vicomte.

Landscape design had advanced hand in hand with baroque building. Concern was entirely with form: plants were treated as far as possible as lifeless absolutes: an avenue and a colonnade came to the same thing; so did a hedge and a wall. Handled by masters, trees did what they were told.

As Kip's engravings of English country houses of the period show, however, there were fewer masters than gardens. A banal formality was the general rule. The first botanic gardens were not much advanced in design from the knot gardens of the Tudors.

This engraving of Vaux-le-Vicomte shows how the vast formal gardens of France were conceived as settings for self-satisfied people in huge numbers. Trees were mere building materials.

great botanist Clusius. His original plan has been reconstructed recently.

John Ray of Essex (1627–1705) originated the division of plants into monocotyledons and dicotyledons. His Historia Plantarum *was published in 1686–1704 and included the first printed account of American trees.*

The Swiss Jean Bauhin c. 1541–1613 established a botanic garden at Lyon, France. His Historia Plantarum Universalis, *not published till 1650, set new standards in accurate and concise plant description.*

André Le Nôtre (1613–1700) was the chief practitioner of the majestic French style of landscaping of the 'Grand Siècle'; he designed the parks of Versailles and Vaux-le-Vicomte. Vanbrugh in England was influenced by him.

John Evelyn (1620–1706), diarist, dilettante and friend of Charles II, published his great Sylva, *a Discourse on Forest Trees in 1662.*

The New World

Henry Compton (1632–1713) was the first great patron of botany in North America, sending botanically-trained missionaries to the Indians.

Peter Collinson, London merchant and Quaker, formed a famous friendship with the American botanist John Bartram.

John Bartram (1699–1777), the first native American botanist, was responsible, through his correspondence with Collinson, for introducing many American trees to Europe.

A strong current had started to run by the time of England's Civil War. King Charles I's gardener went to Russia (whence he may have introduced the larch to England) and Spain and North Africa. His son, the second John Tradescant, sailed for Virginia. With the Tradescants begins the introduction of the trees of the New World.

Whether it was actually the younger Tradescant–who went three times to Virginia–or correspondents of his father, or other returning colonists who brought them, we shall never know. But by 1656 the plant-list of the 'museum' the Tradescants kept in their Lambeth garden included many of the biggest and most striking of the trees of the American east coast: the black locust or false acacia, named *Robinia* after Tradescant's friend Jean Robin, curator of the Paris Jardin dés Plantes; the tulip tree; the swamp cypress; the eastern red cedar.

Evelyn mentions the tulip tree (which he calls the Virginia poplar) and the *Thuja.* He speaks of 'great opportunities . . . we have of every day improving our stores with so many useful trees from the American plantations'.

The man who seized the opportunities was the Bishop of London, Henry Compton, a nobleman and former mercenary. From his palace at Fulham he directed the spiritual affairs of the colonies, sending missionaries among the Indians, and choosing for his men such as could spot an unknown plant and, spotting it, get it safely home.

His palace garden became an important centre for the plants of America. Among the trees introduced there (by his missionary John Bannister) was the first magnolia grown in Europe, the swamp-bay, *Magnolia virginiana*. The black walnut, the box elder, the balsam poplar, the balsam fir, the scarlet oak, the flowering dogwood were others.

The first home-grown American botanist was John Bartram, the son of a Quaker settler at Philadelphia, who farmed the banks of the Schuylkill River. By a happy chance he was put in touch with a London linen-draper named Peter Collinson, another Quaker, who had a passion for plants, particularly for trees, and (not being in a position to send out missionaries) was looking for an American to collect plants and seeds for him. Their correspondence began in 1732 and continued until Collinson died a third of a century later. By then Linnaeus was ready to describe Bartram as 'the greatest living botanist in the world'.

His discoveries numbered some 200 species. He found them by wandering about alone in Indian country, from the Great Lakes down to Georgia. Courage has always been as important as eyesight to people who seek new plants.

The list of Bartram's trees is awe-inspiring. It includes the sugar and silver maples; the American ash, elm and lime; the black, red and white oaks; *Magnolia grandiflora*; the river birch; the long-leaf and the short-leaf pines. Nor was it entirely a one-way traffic. The cedar of Lebanon (in 1746) and the horse chestnut (in 1753) were two of the

Bishop Compton's Fulham Palace on the river Thames had the first garden in Europe to boast such trees as magnolia, flowering dogwood, white pine and scarlet oak.

Right *The 18th century saw the making of England's great 'natural' landscape gardens. Capability Brown's Stowe, shown here, is typical. But the great influx of new trees was virtually ignored.*

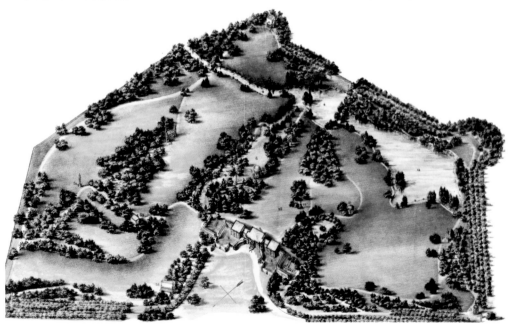

John Stuart, *3rd Earl of Bute (1713–92), was a great amateur botanist,* *first effective Director of Kew and later a deplorable Prime Minister.*

William Aiton, *the first Superintendent of Kew (from 1759 to 1793).* Philip Miller *of Chelsea Physick Garden, father of horticultural journalism.*

André Michaux *introduced such trees as the ginkgo to America at his* *Charleston nursery and wrote the first study of American oaks.*

trees Collinson sent Bartram for his own collection, America's first botanic garden.

What started as a private arrangement became almost a public institution as the results began to be seen. Collinson shared the costs with subscribers: at first the young Lord Petre, whose estate was at Ingatestone in Essex; then the Dukes of Richmond, of Bedford, of Norfolk; then Frederick, Prince of Wales, father of King George III, who with his wife, Princess Augusta, lived at Kew House by the Thames, just west of London.

The story of Kew, the greatest of the world's botanic gardens, begins here. The Prince and Princess provided a nucleus for the mushrooming interest in new plants. They employed the great William Kent (and later Capability Brown) to landscape their grounds. They asked the Earl of Bute, a Scot and (one might almost say therefore) no

mean botanist, to supervise their planting. The Prince died in 1751, but Princess Augusta pressed on. In 1759 she appointed William Aiton the first Curator of the Royal Botanic Garden. He was another Scot, trained at the already famous Chelsea Physick Garden by its celebrated curator, Philip Miller, the author of *The Gardener's Dictionary*. Between them Aiton and his son were at Kew for no less than 82 years.

What perhaps has more to do with trees is the interest some of the great landowners began to take in the new introductions. The Duchess of Beaufort at Badminton, the Duke of Argyll at Hounslow and the Duke of Atholl in Perthshire became passionate tree-planters. Lord Weymouth at Longleat planted so many of the new white pines from New England that they became known by his name. Records begin here for the growth of many trees that are still alive today, with

every biographical detail known.

What was strange and disappointing, however, was the ignorance of all this by the great landscapers. England was at that very moment going through the greatest redecoration she has ever had. The old parks and gardens were being rooted up wholesale, to be replaced by the placid quasi-natural landscape favoured first by Bridgeman and Kent, then by the all-powerful Brown.

As Humphrey Repton, their more sophisticated successor, remarked: 'Their trees are of one general kind, while the variety of nature's productions is endless, and ought to be duly studied'.

The Royal Botanic Garden at Kew, *originally a private royal collection, now the world's greatest botanical institution, is dominated by its pagoda.*

André Michaux's greatest *work was his* Flora of North America *of 1803 from which this painting of leaf and flower of the tulip tree is taken.*

The World Expands

China is the mother of gardens. The Chinese emperors loved and collected plants for almost 5,000 years. Large parts of China have been cultivated for so long that the notion of a wild plant is laughable: everything desirable is cultivated; everything else extinct. Species of the most prized plants–paeonies, chrysanthemums, camellias–have been improved and treasured for century after century.

But China had no intention of letting the barbarians in. After Marco Polo's 13th-century visitation there was a pause of more than 300 years before another contact was allowed, under the pressure of a western world curious and hungry for trade. It was the 18th century before any westerner got even a toehold to look for plants.

The toehold was one of the East India Company's 'factories' on the coast; the westerner was James Cunningham, a surgeon with the company, who visited Amoy in the Formosa strait in 1698 and Chusan, an island south of Shanghai, in 1700. He was forbidden to ramble outside the port, but he procured paintings of Chinese plants and specimens of what the nurseries had to sell.

The French were more subtle–and more successful. They had no trading rights but gained entry to the country by sending missionaries trained in skills the Chinese lacked: glass-blowing; clock-making; engineering. By this means Father Pierre d'Incarville reached Peking in 1742 and stayed for 15 years. He had the commission of France's greatest botanist, Bernard de Jussieu, to collect for the Royal gardens and the Jardin des Plantes in Paris. He also had London correspondents–among them the insatiable Collinson. The fruits of his labours included the tree of heaven, the silk tree (*Albizia julibrissin*), the *Toona*, the *Sophora*, the Chinese *Thuja*, the Chinese juniper and the golden-rain tree (*Koelreuteria paniculata*).

All connections with China, however,

Right Alexander von Humboldt *(1769–1859) visited Mexico and Peru on one of the greatest of all scientific journeys. Botany was only one of his many interests: the Humboldt current bears his name. The first major tree-collection in temperate South America was made by William Lobb in Chile in the 1840s for Veitch's nursery.*

Above left Duhamel du Monceau *(1700–82) was a distinguished French engineer and agriculturist. The* Nouveau Duhamel, *a posthumous edition of his work on trees, was superbly illustrated by Redouté.*

Left Engelbert Kaempfer *(1651–1715), a doctor to the Dutch Company in Japan, took part in diplomatic missions to Tokyo in the spring of 1690 and 1691 and brought the West its first Japanese flowering cherries, and also magnolias. He discovered the ginkgo.*

Right Carl Peter Thunberg *(1743–1828), a pupil of Linnaeus at Uppsala in Sweden, held the same post as Kaempfer 85 years later. He ran a nursery on Deshima, the Dutch island in Nagasaki harbour, and collected maples, oaks, cherries and conifers amongst other plants. He published in 1784 the first* Flora Japonica.

Below Philipp Franz von Siebold *(1791–1866), held the same physician's post as Kaempfer and Thunberg from 1826 to 1830, when he was expelled from Japan for spying. He introduced azaleas, camellias, hydrangeas and other garden plants during this stay, and later* Paulownia *and Japanese crab.*

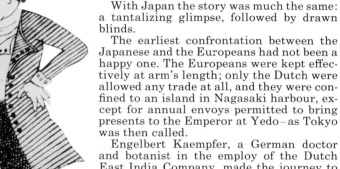

Left *The Orient became a rage in 18th-century Europe. English gardens were decked out in fanciful 'Chinese' style.*

Above left Captain James Cook *proclaimed New South Wales a British possession at Botany Bay in 1770. Sir Joseph Banks was on the expedition.*

Above Bernard de Jussieu *(1699–1777) foreshadowed the 'natural system' of botanical classification, ran the Jardin des Plantes in Paris and started a botanical garden at the Trianon, Versailles, for Louis XV.*

were subject to the imperial whim. D'Incarville had been lucky; after him the doors closed again. But a glimpse had been enough: *chinoiserie* was all the rage in Europe – in furnishing, in decoration; even, for a while, in gardening (witness the pagoda built in 1761 at Kew).

With Japan the story was much the same: a tantalizing glimpse, followed by drawn blinds.

The earliest confrontation between the Japanese and the Europeans had not been a happy one. The Europeans were kept effectively at arm's length; only the Dutch were allowed any trade at all, and they were confined to an island in Nagasaki harbour, except for annual envoys permitted to bring presents to the Emperor at Yedo – as Tokyo was then called.

Engelbert Kaempfer, a German doctor and botanist in the employ of the Dutch East India Company, made the journey to Yedo twice, in 1690 and 1691, and gave the first report of Japanese trees. The ginkgo (a Chinese tree, but imported to Japan, like the art of gardening itself, at a very early period) was his most important discovery; he also sent back to Holland maples and flowering cherries. He was the last European botanist to visit Japan for more than 80 years.

By the time his successor, Carl Thunberg, a pupil of Linnaeus, reached Yedo in 1776 there was a new spirit abroad in Europe. Captain Cook had visited Australia; Francis Masson (the first professional plant-collector) had returned from the Cape; the botanist William Roxburgh had left for Calcutta. The French were heading for Peru.

The new spirit was summed up in the person of Sir Joseph Banks, Lord Bute's successor at Kew and one of the most knowledgeable and enthusiastic (and richest) patrons that exploration has ever had. He himself had sailed with Cook. Now he saw to it that every expedition was equipped with a competent young botanist. And incidentally, that the loot should come to swell the great collection he was making at Kew.

The chart of tree-introductions on pages 318-19 illustrates perfectly the situation at the end of the 18th century. Introductions from the Mediterranean had come in a steady flow for centuries. A colossal flood from eastern North America had steadied to a stream, largely from the work in the southeast of another emissary of Kew, John Fraser. But the rest – the Far East, the American west and the whole of the southern hemisphere – were about to be ransacked for the undreamt-of wealth of trees that was to treble the number known to the western world within the next century.

Giants and Gentility

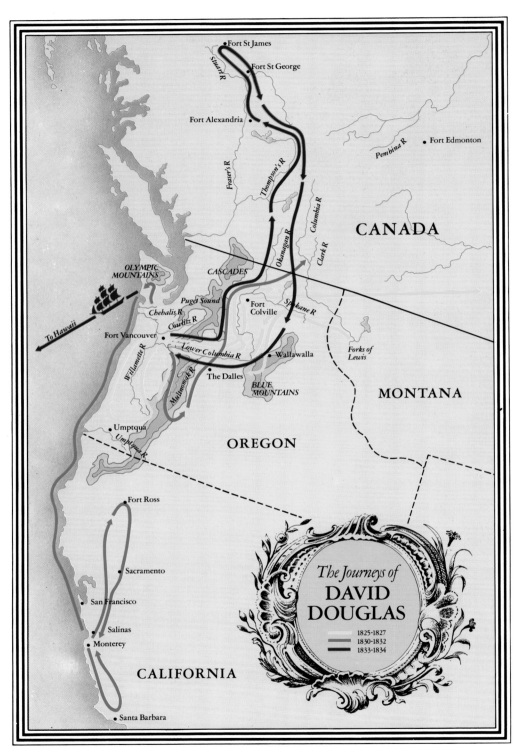

The Journeys of David Douglas

The Journeys of
DAVID
DOUGLAS

1825-1827
1830-1832
1833-1834

The first news that the Pacific coast of America held something quite exceptional for the botanist came from Captain Vancouver's voyage of 1792. His botanist – I almost said his Scotsman – was Archibald Menzies. With justifiable excitement Menzies reported the Douglas fir, the Alaska cedar (or Nootka cypress), the Sitka spruce and the coast redwood: all trees twice as high as anything he had seen before.

John Bartram had dreamed of an expedition to the west many years before. His scheme eventually took place, 37 years after his death, when Thomas Jefferson organized the 40-strong Lewis and Clark expedition. But it lacked Bartram, or even a lesser botanist. The expedition returned from the coast (having spent two and a half years on the way) with a very modest collection of seeds, without apparently having even seen Menzies' great trees.

When in 1824 London got round to sending a collector Sir Joseph Banks was dead, and Kew (temporarily, for political reasons) out of favour and short of funds. It was the Horticultural Society (founded in the year Lewis and Clark set out from St Louis) which commissioned the trip. At the recommendation of the great William Jackson Hooker, then at Glasgow but later to be the most illustrious director Kew has ever had, the man chosen was David Douglas, son of a stonemason from Scone in Perthshire, a self-taught botanist who had impressed Hooker as having unusual qualities.

Courage is common currency among plant-collectors. The stories of their exploits, and not infrequently of their uncomfortable ends, has made many a good book. But by any standards Douglas was special. He was a Highlander with an obsession. He addressed himself to the northwestern wilderness with the energy of a fanatic. The Indians learnt to treat this strange 'grassman' (as they called him) with the utmost respect.

In a Stewart tartan coat, and with tea (of which he drank gallons) as his only comfort, he travelled thousands of miles of trackless country, very often quite alone, carrying on his back (and above his head through icy torrents) a prodigious load of specimens, seeds, cones – even, at one time, two living eagles. To be wet through, to be wounded, to be starving apparently meant nothing to him if he scented a new tree farther on.

His first expedition to the Columbia River (not counting the eight and a half month voyage out, of which no less than six weeks was spent waiting to cross the dangerous sand-bar at the river-mouth) lasted from April 1825 to March 1827, when he left for home overland by the Hudson's Bay Com-

Archibald Menzies (1754–1842), naval surgeon and botanist, sailed on Vancouver's 'Discovery' on its voyage of exploration to the Northwest in the 1790s. He was the first botanist to see the colossal conifers of the Pacific coast. The Latin name of the Douglas fir (Pseudotsuga menziesii) commemorates him.

Thomas Nuttall (1786–1859), from Liverpool, tried several times to cross North America and finally succeeded at the age of 50 after a gruelling journey over the mountains. From 1822 to 1834 he was Curator of the Harvard Botanic Garden.

John Claudius Loudon (1783–1843), journalist and encyclopedist, made the first complete record of hardy trees then known and their implications for horticulture in his astonishing Arboretum et Fruticetum Britannicum, shortened to 1,200 pages in 1842 as Trees and Shrubs of Great Britain. He coined the 'gardenesque' style.

A. J. Downing was the Loudon of North America, publishing his The fruits and fruit trees of America in 1845. He was also the leading American landscape designer of his day, pioneering the creation of urban parks for recreation.

Frederick Law Olmsted was inspired by Sir Joseph Paxton's design of Birkenhead Park, Liverpool, to compete in designing Central Park, New York (1858). Having won the competition he went on to become the father of the U.S. National Parks.

pany's 'express'. His haul from this journey, in trees alone (and there was much else besides) included the Douglas fir, the Sitka spruce, the noble and lovely firs, the bigleaf maple, the ponderosa, the bigcone, the sugar and the western white pines. He wrote to Hooker 'you will begin to think that I manufacture pines at my pleasure'.

He reached the Columbia river on his second expedition in 1830. This time he also went to California and made Monterey his base. All the time he was sending home not packets but chests of seeds. His job was not just to discover but to introduce, which he did so effectively that his finds were able to go immediately into circulation to scores of collections. His trees were becoming well known while he was still camping in the wilderness.

St Petersburg's famous botanical garden was among his clients. He was invited by the Czar to make the appalling journey homewards through Alaska and Siberia. In 1832, full of enthusiasm, he set off from Fort Vancouver. But this expedition came to grief in the wilds of British Columbia. He had to return, canoe-wrecked and dispirited, now blind in one eye.

Douglas met his end in Hawaii 18 months later. He fell into a bull-pit and was killed by a wild bull. He was only thirty-five.

For 20 years after Douglas's death the West was alive with botanists and the world agog to see what they found. Thomas Nuttall arrived by the Hudson Bay route the following year (and found the dogwood of the west, Cornus nuttallii, which Douglas must have been very unlucky to miss). Theodor Hartweg, sponsored by the Horticultural Society, sent home seed of the redwood, the Monterey cypress and the chinkapin. A group of Scots landowners formed themselves into the Oregon Association and sent John Jeffrey (who found the Jeffrey pine and the western hemlock and introduced Douglas's grand fir). Veitch's famous nursery at Exeter sent William Lobb, who had pioneered exploration in Chile. He brought back, among new trees, the giant sequoia, the western red cedar (Thuja plicata), the white fir and the lovely Santa Lucia fir. That was in 1853: the gold-rush was on; there were hotels in the west.

If there is a contemporary of Douglas's to compare with him in prodigious output, though in a different field, it is John Claudius Loudon. Douglas delved; Loudon (you might say) span. Loudon was the author of the seven volumes of the Arboretum et Fruticetum Britannicum, the first attempt to describe, from both the botanist's and the gardener's point of view, the vast range of trees then available; most of them new. He was also the editor of his own magazine and author of (among other thick books) an Encyclopedia of Cottage, Farm and Villa Architecture and The Suburban Gardener and Villa Companion.

The last gives all too clear a picture of the world to which these glorious trees were being introduced. This is Loudon on plant-introduction: 'It is the beautiful work of civilization, of patriotism, and of adventure, first to collect these all into our country, and, next, to distribute them to others.'

Loudon divided all gardens into four classes – from first-rate to fourth-rate. Most modern gardens would make him rush to add an eighth- and ninth-rate. He is full of good practical information and advice. But whereas the 'natural' landscapers and their school had swept all garden fussiness aside, ignored new trees and dealt only in 'prospects', Loudon preached a more dangerous creed: 'When it is once properly understood that no residence in the modern style can have a claim to be considered as laid out in good taste, in which all the trees and shrubs employed are not either foreign ones, or improved varieties of indigenous ones, the grounds of every country seat, from the cottage to the mansion, will become an arboretum.'

The first crossing of North America to the Pacific was made in 1804–06 by Captains Lewis and Clark. For botany it had more symbolic than practical significance.

Loudon's Suburban Gardener and Villa Companion (1838) set the scene to which the discoveries of the dauntless botanists were introduced. Gardening reached a low ebb at the very moment when it received its greatest opportunity.

Explorers in the East

Botanists were running hither and thither like ants as the 19th century opened. The only places where they still met more than physical difficulties were in the Far East. Work there was by maddeningly remote control: East India Company factories on the coast of China were the only point of contact. Plant-hungry collectors (of whom there were more and more) resorted to commissioning the masters of East Indiamen to visit the nurseries of Macao and Canton on their behalf. They got beautiful cultivated flowers, but still no idea of the trees and shrubs of the unknown interior.

The enterprise of a Bavarian eye-doctor, Philipp von Siebold, was richly rewarded when he managed (on the strength of his ability to cure cataract) to steal into Japan and take a first proper survey of her flora. That was in 1823. But the frustrations continued until China was finally bullied into opening her frontiers in 1844, and until Commodore Perry and his warships made it plain to the Japanese (in 1853) that what America was not given willingly she was quite prepared to take.

The story of who went where in that amazing hunting ground, and what they found, is told in the accompanying map and illustrations. There was (and is) a lot to absorb in a single sustained draught–which is more or less the way it happened. We have still hardly taken stock of the superb flora of western China–particularly of the south-western reaches of the Himalayas. One thing which has clearly emerged, though, is the close relations between the species of China and North America. Their similar ice-age history continually crops up in parallel survivals.

The same period saw the exploration of Sikkim and the hugely fertile middle heights of the central Himalayas, initially by Joseph Hooker, son of the director of Kew (who was later to take his turn in that august chair). The great English craze for rhododendrons starts here.

Father Jean Marie Delavay, *the first European botanist in western China (1838–95), discovered scores of good garden plants in Yunnan. A magnolia and silver fir bear his name.* 3C

Jean André Soulié *(1858–1905) discovered the butterfly-bush* buddleja *and several rhododendrons in Szechwan.* 3C

Father Paul Perny *(1818–1907) discovered the holly which bears his name.* 3D

Paul Guillaume Farges *(1844–1912) sent seeds to Vilmorin, including the first Davidia. He discovered many rhododendrons and the splendid silver fir that bears his name.* 2D

▲ **Above Father Armand David** *(1826–1900) was a distinguished French zoologist and botanist. Apart from Davidia, he discovered numerous species called* davidii *and* armandii. *1 and 3C*

SZECHWAN *Province*
Chengku **Centre of botanical interest**
Fortune 1860 **Botanist with main date of visit (where known)**

Thomas Lobb *(1809–63) collected for the London nursery firm of Veitch (who also sent William Lobb to Chile and California). A Cryptomeria bears his name.* 3B

◀ **Left Sir Joseph Hooker** *(1817–1911), later Director of Kew Gardens, returned from the Himalayas in 1850 with magnificent rhododendrons. He introduced the Himalayan birch and reported, amongst other trees, the biggest of all magnolias, Magnolia campbellii.* 3A *and* B

Henry John Elwes *(1846–1922), co-author of a great book on trees (see page 50), visited Sikkim in 1870.* 3B

Victor Jacquemont *(1801–32) reported the deodar cedar. Several plants are named after him.* 2A

Nathaniel Wallich *(1786–1854), a Danish surgeon, 30 years Director of the Calcutta Botanic Garden, introduced* Rhododendron arboreum, Himalayan white pine, *and* Cotoneaster frigidus; *he also discovered many garden plants.* 2A, 3 *and* 4B

Frank Ludlow *and* **George Sherriff** *made the most famous of recent Tibetan expeditions, finding mainly rhododendrons and primulas.* 3B

Engelbert Kaempfer *(see pages 44/5).* 2F

Right Frank Kingdon-Ward *(1885–1958) from Manchester explored and collected for over 40 years between Tibet and Burma. Plants named* wardii *(including a rhododendron, camellia, holly and cherry) are his introductions.* 3B, 4B *and* C. ▶

Right Robert Fortune
(1812–80) was the first collector in China to have relative freedom. He was sent by the Horticultural Society in 1843 and introduced many essential garden plants. His trees included the false larch, the Chinese plum yew, the umbrella pine and the Cryptomeria. *2 and 3D, 3 and 4E, 2F*

James Cunningham, *the first botanist to introduce Chinese plants (in 1698), is commemorated by the Chinese 'fir',* Cunninghamia. *4D, 3E*

Carl Peter Thunberg *(see page 45). 2E*

Pierre d'Incarville *(1706–57), a Jesuit priest, whose introductions, from Peking, included the tree of heaven, pagoda tree and goldenrain tree. 2D*

Philipp von Siebold *(see page 45). 3E, 2F*

Right Carl Maximowicz
(1827–91) of the St. Petersburg Botanic Garden became the greatest living authority on the plants of Manchuria and Japan in the 1860s. He introduced magnolias, Stewartia pseudo-camellia, oaks, firs, pines, maples. The monarch birch, later introduced by Sargent, bears his name. 2D, 1 and 3E, 1 and 2F

Dr. Clarke Abel *(1780–1826) visited Peking in a diplomatic mission, reported the Chinese elm, and introduced the ornamental apricot and the shrub* Abelia. *2 and 4D*

William Kerr *(died 1814) was sent from Kew to China by Sir Joseph Banks and lived there eight years. The Chinese juniper is the most important tree he introduced. 4D*

Grigori Nicolaevich Potanin *(1835–1920) explored 'Tebbuland' (plants from here are called 'tangutica'). The Chinese larch bears his name. 2C and D*

Right Ernest Henry 'Chinese' Wilson
(1876–1930), first for Veitch's nursery, then for the Arnold Arboretum made the greatest individual collection of Chinese trees in four journeys. His trees include the paperbark maple, giant dogwood and Magnolia wilsonii. *3C, 3 and 4D, 2F*

Left John Gould Veitch *of the famous Chelsea nursery family visited Japan in 1860. He collected* Magnolia stellata *and 17 new conifers, including the Japanese larch and Japanese fir from Fuji, and the Yezo, Hondo and tiger-tail spruces. His son J. H. Veitch did much to popularize Japanese flowering cherries. 1 and 2F*

Below George Forrest *(1873–1932) was the greatest of all collectors of rhododendrons, introducing hundreds of species including* R. protistum *var.* giganteum *and* R. sinogrande *to the Edinburgh Botanic Garden. He also specialised in primulas. He introduced a beautiful silver fir and a snakebark maple, both called* forrestii. *4C*

Map of China, Korea and Japan showing plant collectors and their collecting areas:

MONGOLIA · Bunge 1830

MANCHURIA · Maximowicz 1853–60 · Meyer 1905–18

ORDOS · Potanin 1880

Peking · D'Incarville 1740–56 · Abel 1815 · Fortune 1843–62 · Maximowicz 1853–60 · Potanin 1880

SHANTUNG · Tsingtao · Meyer 1905–18

SHENSI · HONAN · HUPEI · Hers 1919–30

Ichang · Henry 1882–1900 · Wilson 1899–1911

Perny 1858–67 · Fengkieh · Ichang · Maries 1877–79 · Wilson 1899–1911

ANHWEI · Fortune 1843–62 · Soochow · Meyer 1903–18 · Shanghai · Fortune 1843–62

CHUSAN · Cunningham 1698–1707 · Fortune 1843–62

Canton · Kerr 1803 · Abel 1815 · Macao · Beale 1792–1842 · Hong Kong · Wright 1854

FORMOSA · Cunningham 1698–1707 · Henry 1882–1900 · Wilson 1899–1911

Amoy · Cunningham 1698–1707 · Fortune 1843–62

SOUTH KOREA · Oldham 1862–63 · Masan · Thunberg 1776

HOKKAIDO · Maries 1877 · Sargent 1892 · J. H. Veitch 1892–93 · Sapporo

Hakodate · Maximowicz 1860–64 · J. G. Veitch 1860

HONSHU · Aomori · Sargent 1892 · J. H. Veitch 1892–93

Sendai · Sargent 1892 · J. H. Veitch 1892–3

Collingwood-Ingram 1927 · Wilson 1914

Tokyo · Kaempfer 1691–92 · Siebold 1827–62 · Fortune 1860 · Sargent 1892 · J. H. Veitch 1892–93 · Wilson 1914

Yokohama · Maximowicz 1860–64 · J. G. Veitch 1860

Fukuoka · Hiroshima · Kaempfer 1691–92

Nagasaki · Siebold 1827–62 · Maximowicz 1860–64 · Oldham 1862–63

KYUSHU · Collingwood-Ingram 1927

JAPAN

Yellow Sea · East China Sea · South China Sea

Scale in miles · 0 · 200 · 400 · 600 · 800

Alexander von Bunge *(1803–90) collected in north China for St. Petersburg; discovered* Pinus bungeana. *1D*

Richard Oldham *(1838–64), the last official collector for Kew, introduced the Japanese snowbell tree. 2 and 3E*

Charles Maries *(1851–1902), sent by Veitch's nursery, pioneered in far-northern Japan, finding 'Maries' fir'. He had a less successful visit to China. 3D, 1F*

Frank Meyer *was sent to China by the U.S. Department of Agriculture in 1905. He drowned in the Yangtze in 1918. He imported millet, rice and* Acer tataricum *spp.* ginnala, *Chinese horse chestnut and* Juniperus squamata *'Meyeri'. 1, 2 and 3E*

Reginald Farrer *(1880–1920) and* **Euan Cox,** *botanical writers, visited Yunnan in 1919 and introduced the coffin-tree juniper,* J. recurva *var.* coxii. *1, 2 and 3C*

Augustine Henry *(1857–1930), an Irish doctor, began to botanize out of boredom at Ichang. His haul from central China included ten new maples, cherries, elms, Chinese honey-locust and coffee-tree,* Tilia henryana *and* T. oliveri. *He joined Elwes in writing* The Trees of Great Britain and Ireland. *4C, 3 and 4D*

Charles Sprague Sargent *(1841–1927) founder of the Arnold Arboretum (see page 50) collected the superb Sargent's cherry and crab in Japan. 1 and 2F*

Collingwood Ingram *has been since 1927 the greatest collector and exponent of Japanese flowering cherries (see page 198). 2 and 3F*

Right Joseph Rock, *born in Vienna, collected for the Arnold Arboretum in 'Tebbuland', which he described as 'a garden of Eden' with an enormous variety of plants. A beautiful mountain ash bears his name. 2 and 4C*

Left Lady Amherst, *wife of the Governor-General of India, seen here tree-viewing from an elephant, is the only woman in this story. She introduced* Clematis montana, *and splendid pheasants— but no temperate trees. 2A*

49

Collectors and Creators

What happened to the fruits of all these expeditions? Who were the collectors and do their collections still survive? Did they take Loudon's advice and ban everything not imported or improved from their grounds? Did a school of gardening emerge that could keep up with such a wealth of wonderful new material?

The answer to the last question is yes–eventually. To the second last it is no–thank goodness. The collections made in the last century do still exist, many of them: but they have reached full maturity; often over-maturity.

Perhaps the most important tree collection to be founded in the last century was the Arnold Arboretum, attached to Harvard University. It occupies part of the Boston park system, which was magnificently landscaped by Frederick Olmsted in the 1860s. It depended, as Kew had done, on a giant to get it going. The giant was Charles Sprague Sargent, a patrician Bostonian whose name crops up everywhere in this or any book on trees. Sargent himself introduced a number of species of flowering cherries and crab apples from Japan. But most important he created the study of native American trees, particularly eastern ones, and their suitability for ordinary gardens. Today, despite Boston's hard climate, the Arboretum is one of the world's greatest collections, particularly strong in flowering trees; crabs and cherries and hawthorns.

After Sargent's death Ernest Wilson, two of whose Chinese journeys had been for the Arboretum, took charge. But he was killed in a car accident in 1930. Among the important books to emerge from the Arnold Arboretum are Sargent's own great 14-volume *Silva of North America*; Alfred Rehder's *Manual of Cultivated Trees and Shrubs*; several very enjoyable and rather lushly-written books by Wilson; and Donald Wyman's *Trees for American Gardens*.

What is now the National Arboretum of France was founded about the same time. The name Vilmorin is another that constantly arises in tree-talk. Maurice de Vilmorin was one of a family that had patronized botanical collection (and run a nursery) since the 18th century. At les Barres, near Montargis in the Loiret, he received seeds from all over the world and made a great collection of trees. When he died in 1918 it was given to the state. But its somewhat remote situation is against it. It is a fascinating (rather than a beautiful) place to visit today. Its only importance is as a school for foresters.

In England the great private achievement of the last century was the Holford family's arboretum at Westonbirt in Gloucester-shire. Two generations of Holfords concentrated for 96 years on their superb collection, which is now virtually the British national arboretum, run by the Forestry Commission. In this century the National Pinetum at Bedgebury in Kent has been added to the country's virtual reference-library of living trees of the temperate world.

Britain has never been in danger of losing the lead as the greatest tree-collecting nation. Perhaps because of the poverty of her natural flora, certainly because of her mild and gently rainy climate, the number of considerable collections of exotic trees is immense. In Scotland it is staggering. Perhaps the same combination of national characteristics and climatic conditions have made the British collect trees and lay down their famous cellars of wine.

The literature of trees kept pace with the collections. The first decade of this century saw the publication of the two greatest reference books on arboriculture. The first, which was privately published for subscribers, was the seven volumes of Elwes and Henry's *Trees of Great Britain and Ireland*. As a piece of scholarship it is unlikely ever to be repeated. Both the authors were immensely travelled (Henry was an early collector in China) and they knew between them where every tree grew and to what size. They had no difficulty in citing specimens in Ecuador or Edinburgh, illustrating many of them with those inimitable full-plate platinum photographs of the period.

The second book was W. J. Bean's *Trees and Shrubs Hardy in the British Isles*, which is still the standard reference work on the subject (and not just in Britain). The revised edition in four volumes is being published by stages at the moment.

That turn-of-the-century period was vitally important in questions of taste as well as scholarship. The gruff, opinionated William Robinson joined forces with the shrewd and sensitive Gertrude Jekyll. Both wrote extraordinarily influential books and both made gardens along quite new lines. Perhaps we should throw into the pot the influence of Josiah Conder, whose book on the landscape gardening of Japan showed the West for the first time what the great oriental tradition of gardening was really like – in photographs.

Robinson's approach is easy to illustrate with a quotation: 'The idea that every choice tree in our pleasure grounds should be set out by itself like an electric lamp-post is deeply impressed on the gardening mind.'

What he and Gertrude Jekyll advocated was a form of gardening exactly opposite to the laborious formalities of the Victorian age. It needed much more knowledge of plants and far greater sensitivity and observation. It looked easy, but in fact was far harder than bedding out in rows. What they wanted was to use the thrilling new exotics in a context of natural (or natural-looking) woodland so that both they and the humdrum natives came to life in a new way.

It is hard to know where to begin or where to end in a list of the great gardens that benefited by their ideas. Certainly English wealth was never more effectively used to create beauty than by men like Leonard Messel at Nymans in Sussex, Lord Aberconway at Bodnant in Wales, or Sir Eric Savill in Windsor Great Park. The influence of these practical examples of constructing the earthly paradise by really knowing the plants of other countries and blending them with one's own has been felt all over the world.

As Repton had said, 'the variety of nature's productions is endless, and ought to be duly studied'.

Charles Sprague Sargent (1841–1927) was America's greatest dendrologist. He was the first Director of the Arnold Arboretum, travelled in the East, employed 'Chinese' Wilson, and perhaps most important set America to studying her rich ornamental tree-resources.

1 *Gertrude Jekyll's* Wood & Garden *of 1898 had an enormous influence on the English (and hence on the world's) attitude to gardens. She saw beauty in natural effects, as here in her illustration of Scots pines broken by a snowstorm.*

2 *William Robinson's* The English Flower Garden *of 1883 was reprinted almost annually for over 25 years, while a whole generation of gardeners imbibed his outspoken rejection of Victorian fussiness and formality.*

3 *Josiah Conder's* Landscape Gardening in Japan *of 1893 showed the western world the gardens of the East for the first time. It was illustrated with excellent photographs and explanatory diagrams.*

4 *The seven volumes of Elwes and Henry's book, privately published in 1906–13, publicly for the first time only in 1969, are one of the greatest compilations of tree-data and descriptions. This epic work celebrates the last golden age of tree-scholarship and arboretum-making.*

5 *W. J. Bean's still-standard reference book,* Trees and Shrubs Hardy in the British Isles, *has swollen from two volumes to four in 60 years as knowledge and experience has been amassed. Bean was curator of Kew Gardens. In 1914 when his book was first published many of the Chinese species mentioned were so recently discovered that they had never flowered in cultivation.*

1

2

3

4

5

The Modern Nursery

Nursery cultivars or varieties of trees which will not 'come true' from seed must be propagated by cuttings; and if cuttings will not root, by grafting on to related but easier 'stocks'. Grafting and preparing cuttings is done in a special 'house' next to the 'mist house'.

A big open barn holds tractors and implements.

The mist house has benches fitted with spray bars which maintain a heavy mist in the air around boxes of cuttings: ideal conditions for the cuttings to root. Temperature in the house is kept at about 70 F.

While explorers have brought thousands of new species into cultivation from the wilds, nurserymen have contributed almost as many to the huge range of trees for gardens through the less dramatic processes of breeding and selection.

An explorer brings home a new species, or a new variety of a known species. A nurseryman crosses one species with another to give us a hybrid with better garden performance–faster growth or more flaunting flowers–than either parent. Also, he watches his seed-beds like a hawk for any interesting deviant that nature may send his way. Many of the most-planted trees today are man-made, or at least man-maintained. Some 'cultivars' (varieties selected for desirable qualities) reproduce themselves faithfully through seed. But a great number can only be kept in being through the arts of propagation that by-pass the sexual system: rooting cuttings or grafting. Otherwise the special qualities of these 'clones' will go back into the genetic melting pot.

The names of many of the famous nurseries of the past are preserved in the names of the plants they bred or selected: Lucombe of Exeter, Späth of Berlin, Vilmorin of Paris, Veitch of Chelsea. These names are as familiar to the gardener as the great names of today: Hillier, Treseder of Truro, Hesse of Bremen, Germany, Gulf Stream of Virginia or Wayside Gardens of Mentor, Ohio.

The bread and butter work of a nursery, however, is simply a production system for a wide range of plants. The modern trend inevitably is to narrow the range to what the public regularly calls for. We have modelled the nursery on this page after one that determinedly does the opposite. It is a very reduced version of the workings of Hillier of Winchester, England. Hillier's *Manual of Trees and Shrubs*, which was formerly their catalogue, is a descriptive list of almost 8,000 species of trees and shrubs that at one time their nursery could supply. No other nursery in the world has attempted such a range: to be, in fact, a commercial botanic garden. Where trees in this book prove hard to find—as alas a number of them will—Hilliers is still a good place to start the hunt.

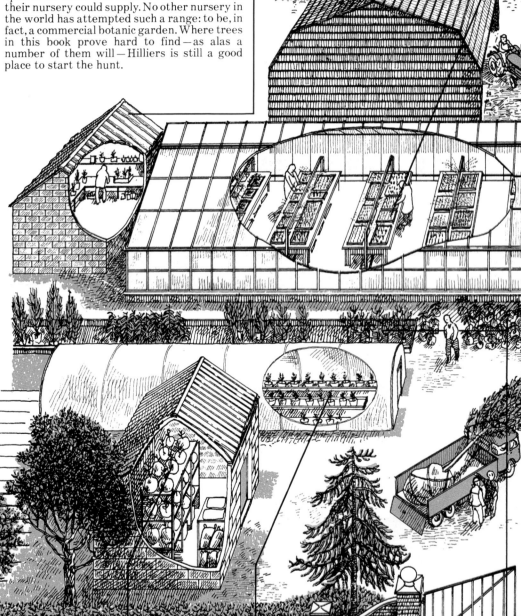

Where seed of popular trees is available in quantity it is sown in a field by a tractor like any crop. An operator on the back controls the flow of seed.

Seed in bulk and cuttings waiting for handling are kept in a cool store at about 38° F. Cuttings can usually be kept in good condition for months. They have survived after being carried across the world with their ends stuck in a potato.

'Tunnel-houses' covered with polythene are a common form of money-saving greenhouse for nurturing young plants just struck from cuttings. Cuttings need to have a weaning period in a humid atmosphere.

Container-grown trees are stored in container beds full of damp sand and peat. These trees, and the bigger ones in pots or cans in front of the mist-house, are ready for sale at any time of the year.

Certain trees such as maples and flowering cherries and crabs are 'lined out' in the open ground until ready for sale. They are 'lifted' by hand and despatched either bare-rooted or 'balled' in burlap or sacking.

A tractor with a spray-bar can spray several lines of seedlings at once with insecticides, or selective weed killer, from nozzles designed to spray over or between the rows.

It is essential to keep the young trees' roots compact and densely fibrous. The technique used is to 'undercut' them with a sharp blade pulled by a tractor. Any tendency for the tree to make an unmovable tap-root is thus thwarted.

Small quantities of seed are sown by hand in beds with irrigation pipes permanently fixed. Behind, low 'tunnel-cloches' have 'mist' pipes for striking cuttings (of, for example, Leyland cypress) in summer.

One area is permanently planted with the stock trees from which cuttings (and sometimes seeds) are taken. Short side shoots are generally needed for propagating most broadleaf species.

Modern potting is done by a machine. Rooted plants are taken from the mist house or lifted from frames and potted up by the hundred in the potting-shed. In the corner is a heap of potting compost.

In this production nursery the sales centre is separate. The vast range of species for sale at different sizes to thousands of customers can necessitate the use of a computer for accounting.

The chemical armoury of a modern nursery is formidable. Insecticides and other chemicals are kept in a locked store and their use strictly regulated. Fertilizers are stored in a separate room.

53

Choosing the Species

Trees are the most telling plants in any landscape. In a garden they are decisive. They control more than its character: its sense of scale; its sense of privacy. If trees are used boldly they can create powerful effects with an almost incredible economy of means.

The various functional uses to which trees are put in gardens and streets and parks are discussed on the following pages. But the first essential is to choose a tree; to know what forms and colours and textures have what other characteristics; to be able to weigh up the various siren-voices (like speed of growth, colour, flowers).

Consider the position of the man with room for one tree outside his house–my dilemma when I lived in London. I wanted it to do everything a tree can. I thought bright gold or silver foliage would be nice, so long as it had brilliant autumn colour. But then of course I wanted it to be evergreen, to get full value from it in winter. I knew there were trees with lovely pink and peeling bark, so I wanted that. And the flowers were to be amazingly double, persistent, and fill the house with scent–and of course lead with hardly a pause to large scarlet fruit which the birds found bitter (but I, of course, found sweet).

(I planted a plane.)

Every tree-lover with a garden goes through the stage of picking the most different trees: the ice-blue spires; the bright-yellow turbans; the leaves like dinner-plates. There is a special bed in my vegetable garden for them while I make up my mind where they will go. The answer very often should be nowhere.

For there is a link, even in the suburbs, between the garden and the land. And the clue is to find it, and exploit it, and push the contrast further and further, yet still keep it in control: never to start by fighting it with the most different tree you can find.

Almost everywhere there is a dominant tree, or trees; even in the suburbs. America's

lovely style of having undifferentiated private areas (the very opposite of Europe's tight fencing and hedging) in a common sward, often with big trees in common, or apparently so, sets the scene perfectly.

Where suburbs have gone over–as so often in England–to Nowhere trees like the dreary purple-leafed plum they need bringing back to the dominance of something real. It will be to everybody's relief when a big forest tree starts asserting itself. It could even (to be in keeping) flower, if it–let us say–were a tulip tree or a big wild cherry.

Let us consider the feeling that a tree is only really there if it is covered with flowers; a common feeling among gardeners, especially with small gardens. First, it is true that the frothy mass of blossom gives the sense of spring in a way nothing else can. But even if you pretend that the two weeks of blossom is really two months–the whole spring– that leaves ten. Not many flowering trees earn their keep in a small space on this basis. Nearest to it are the few cherries that colour well in autumn, or perhaps the crabs that bear fruit long after their leaves have gone.

The same frantic feeling of wanting more than just a tree is expressed in the need for coloured leaves. A single red-leaved, silver-grey or gold-variegated tree, among green ones, can have the effect of enhancing and setting off both itself and its surroundings. By the streetful, on the other hand, red or yellow trees have the very opposite effect, like a whole meal of soup or sweet.

Does the same thing apply to odd-shaped trees? Should we prefer the standard big-head in standard green?

The answer lies in the surroundings. Does your neighbour 20 yards away have a weeping willow? One is enough. If there is none in the street, and you have 50 feet each way to spare, there are few more rewarding trees to grow: among the earliest in spring with their golden young leaves; among the latest to fall, still fresh and green in October.

Is an evergreen really better value? Func-

Forming prospects, shifting hills, planting clumps, damming and diverting streams all have an 18th-century flavour today. Yet today far more landscaping is being done than in the 18th century.

Earth-moving is now much cheaper and easier. And we have a wider knowledge and choice of trees than did Repton (at work here, from his Observations . . . on Landscape Gardening, 1803).

tion aside (if you need it to hide the power-station, there is no argument) the seasons emphatically expressed by a deciduous tree are much more satisfying. It didn't take me long to love the winter sketch of my plane tree against the sky as much as its fat buds bursting, its big leaves forming, its new shoots lengthening and all the rest of its miraculous performance.

Forms, Patterns and Textures

As far as the army is concerned a tree is either a Christmas tree or a bushy-topped tree. But as soon as a civilian starts analysing the range of tree characters it is amazing how many clear categories appear. To take form (in the sense of overall shape) alone: I can think of trees that are tower-like, cloud-like, vase-like, tiered, weeping, multi-trunked (like huge shrubs), columnar, globular, pyramidal (or more strictly speaking conic), mound-like, and just plain irregular and picturesque, like an old Scots pine.

Humphrey Repton (whose late 18th-century writings on landscape design are still the great textbook) points out how–to go no further than army distinctions–the jagged lines of Christmas trees produce a sense of drama (he calls it harshness); whereas the cloud-like outlines of bushy-topped trees give an air of serenity. He went on to urge the association of each with the most unlike architecture: B.T.T.'s with Gothic (which is vertical in emphasis and C.T.'s with Grecian (which is horizontal).

The more open and characterful forms belong in the foreground of the picture. It is easy to see that a silver birch, an olive or a Lebanon cedar (or a tight column like an

1 Vase-like: Zelkova
2 Multi-trunked: Amelanchier
3 Picturesque: Pine
4 Columnar: Cypress
5 Tower-like: English elm
6 Cloud-like: Ash
7 Conic: Spruce
8 Weeping: Willow

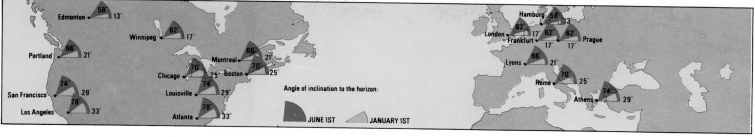

Trees near a house can provide shade just where it is needed, or they can make it gloomy all the year round. The angle of the sun is the decisive factor. In winter it rises to only about a quarter of its summer height. The chart above shows its January and June height at mid-day at different latitudes.

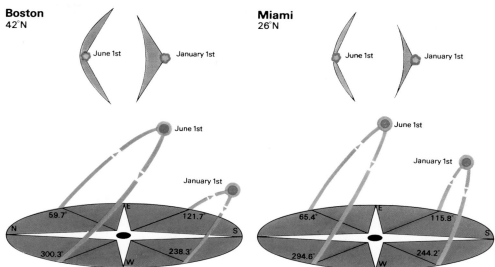

Boston
42°N

June 1st   January 1st

June 1st

January 1st

59.7°   121.7°

300.3°   238.3°

Miami
26°N

June 1st   January 1st

June 1st

January 1st

65.4°   115.8°

294.6°   244.2°

The sun's path through the sky is also very much shorter in winter. The diagrams (right) show the course of the sun in January and June in two places, Boston (or Provence) and Miami. In summer it travels round about two-thirds of the compass, rising in the northeast, climbing high at noon (in Miami almost to the zenith) and setting in the northwest; in winter only about one-third, rising in the south-east, and setting in the southwest. The smaller diagrams show the total daily shadow of a tree in the same places, resulting from the sun's trajectory.
An evergreen tree due west of a house will therefore not shade it at all in mid-winter, but will provide shade on a summer afternoon. Deciduous trees between a house and the low winter sun show their branch-pattern in winter and are perfectly lit in summer.

Italian cypress) provides a good frame for what is beyond, whereas a solid billowing shape like a sycamore or oak, or a broad dark pyramid like a fir, gives the impression of blocking off the view – even if it really hides no more of it.

The strongest effects are undoubtedly obtained by letting one form dominate a scene, using another only to emphasise how very cloudy, moundy, towery or whatever your principal theme is. To have one of everything is bound to produce too diffuse and uncertain an effect; a problem Repton called 'flutter' – he distinguished 'flutter' from 'intricacy'.

I also rather fancy you would arrive at a state of 'flutter' by planting two contrasting forms in equal numbers; say a homogeneous mixture of oak and larch. Both would be more appreciated if there were twice as much of one as of the other. Of course this is not a rule which only applies to trees: equal areas of grass and paving in a garden produce a similarly uneasy effect.

Pattern and texture are only slightly less important than form – though perhaps harder to pin down into categories. The most obvious example of pattern is the bare deciduous tree, where the balance, the boldness or delicacy, the thrust or swoop of its twigs and branches are dominant in the winter scene. But another is the positive modelling of some trees; beech with its graceful layers of foliage; oak with its firm hummocks; or palm with its arching fans. Huge leaves (the tree of heaven's for example) create patterns; small ones (of elm or many of the Japanese maples) are more a matter of texture. The glitter of English

holly or the marvellous mattness of the fern-leaf beech, absorbing all light, are other examples of distinct tree textures.

Here light is the crucial factor. Modelling and texture (and also colour) are obliterated if the light is behind them; bare branch patterns are lost if the light is behind you, the viewer. This is a question that has exercised great minds. Leonardo da Vinci was firm: 'The trees which are between you and the sun are far more beautiful than those which have you between the sun and themselves.' Humphrey Repton held the same opinion, illustrating it with two views of the Thames at Purley. 'All natural objects' (he went so far as to say) 'look best with the sun behind them; all artificial objects with the sun on them.'

But then both were thinking big: of great landscapes where detail was lost in distance and where there was more colour from the shafts of the sun or the lilac haze of distance than from jolly variegated shrubs and

Colorado blue spruces in the foreground.

In garden terms the message is that views to the south (in the northern hemisphere) should always be treated as having the light behind in winter, and from both sides and behind in summer. And views to the north as having the light in front in winter, and from both sides and the front in summer. Bearing in mind of course that the sun in mid-winter is about a quarter as far above the horizon as in mid-summer, which makes an enormous difference to what it reaches.

So the place for deciduous trees is to the south of the house and for evergreens to the north (where they also, happily, give shelter). But for trees of any kind whose colour or texture (or flowers) you particularly enjoy – assuming that the house is your viewpoint – the south is the angle to avoid. This is only to touch on the question of light in the landscape, which can obviously be elaborated for gardening, as it can for painting, ad infinitum.

In a Riviera garden: an unusual example of tree forms to provide shade. In the foreground a tight group of London planes shades the terrace. Beyond a regular planting of mop-head acacias makes a pattern of shade on the lawn.

Planning for Planting

'It is difficult to lay down rules for planting. Time, neglect and accident will often produce unexpected beauties'–Repton again.

The trick is to know a 'beauty' when you see one, and to be able to make the most of it.

Planning and planting are subjects in the round. There is no one right approach to them. One can consider the available material; the objectives; the techniques. Yet there remains a body of lore gleaned from long experience that is worth fitting to the circumstances.

A Dutch landscape designer (a change from Repton, at least) produced an epigram that bears a lot of thinking about: 'The axe is my pencil.' If Repton had thought of it he'd have said it, because three-quarters of the grand new effects he created for his clients, and demonstrated to them in advance with before-and-after 'slides' (as he called them) in his famous Red Books, he contrived simply by selectively cutting down what was there already. This is cold comfort for the owner of a new garden in the middle of an old airfield. But it is surprising how often it does apply once you start to look at a place with open eyes, to sum up what Lancelot Brown referred to as its Capabilities.

There is besides a wicked satisfaction in cutting down trees and clearing bushes which anyone who only plants, and would defend any growing thing with his life, should experience and realize. The most memorable moments to me in taking over a new garden have been when a tree came down, to almost feel the new view rushing in to make its contribution.

Heaven forbid that anyone should think I am advocating indiscriminate clearing, which is generally the misconceived act of developers (who later find, to their chagrin, that they have bulldozed away a good part of the value of their new houses with the trees). The modern world is full of unlovely things crying out to be hidden by trees. Taking stock should be a lengthy business. One must contrive to 'see' the place as it will be with some of the existing trees removed. One must wait four seasons, to find out how leaf-fall changes the total effect. One must go through the site with great care, even if it is only 'scrub': there may be saplings in it which will make a marvellous new start if they are left in place. And finally one must do the job by degrees, and be ready to call a halt if an unexpected effect is achieved. 'Accident will often produce unexpected beauties.'

What one can hope for by clearing is to 'borrow' some of the surroundings for one's own enjoyment. In the 18th century nobody

One of Frank Lloyd Wright's most famous houses, Falling Water (at Bear Run, Pennsylvania) is a brilliant example of the use of existing trees as part of an architectural whole. Where most developers would have cleared the birches Lloyd Wright used their delicacy to interact with his massive slabs. In winter sunshine their lacy handwriting combines with light reflected from the water to make concrete fluid.

thought it particularly wilful if a landlord shifted the village a mile or two to clear a new prospect from his library windows. It is surprising how much one can achieve even while leaving the village exactly where it is.

There was a church spire two blocks away from my old London garden. In winter you could see it looking rather glum and grey through the branches of a sycamore. But I only had to take two branches off the tree to make a leafy frame so that in summer when the light fell on the spire it was as good as in the garden.

'A plain space near the eye gives it a kind of liberty it loves.' This time a quote from Shenstone, an 18th-century English poet whose garden (the famous Leasowes, near Birmingham) was rather more distinguished than his verses.

It sounds rather like another excuse for clearing, or at any rate for not planting. It can't apply, in any case, where the whole

*The human eye takes in a
vertical picture 80° deep.
Only 27° is above the
horizontal line of your
eye–at say five feet
from the ground.
The diagram (right)
shows how a tree need*

*therefore be only 17½ feet
high to give the impres-
sion of complete enclosure
at a distance of 25 feet. At
200 feet you can take in
the whole of a tree
107 feet high.*

garden is 'near the eye' and a plant must either be there or nowhere. It was a basic tenet of the English landscape school, though, that the house should be set in plain lawns and the eye encouraged to go out to the limits of the ground (and beyond). Balustraded terraces round the house came later as part of the general Victorian fussiness. It is lovely to look out from under trees, but not to gaze slap into the side of a big one at short range. William Robinson went (characteristically) too far when he said 'No forest tree should ever be planted near a house'. Close in to the wall is often an excellent place for a tree, if the foundations are sound and you are prepared to take a little trouble directing the young branches. I will always remember a house in Connecticut that had been built round a stand of pines, with an upstairs gallery right among the trees, so you could touch them. It wouldn't have been up Shenstone's street, though.

'Plant close together'–expensive advice from almost every landscape designer (and not just from the nursery trade). Trees like the company of other trees. To 'dot a few starveling saplings on an open lawn' is a recipe for slow-starting, discouraged specimens. Capability Brown always planted in thick clumps–which his clients usually forgot to thin out later as they were meant to. The technique in those days was not to pay a nursery for a few very expensive standard trees (which in any case take years to shake off the dish-mop look and develop much real character) but to plant lots of small ones, mixed in with shrubs. In the open country five or six hollies or hawthorns went in for every one big tree. The trees at that size needed no stakes, which was a real saving (and looked better).

The great argument for planting big trees today is that they are harder for vandals to kill. In public places this overrides everything else. But it is doubtful whether they get away faster in anything except the short

term–up to say five years. In ten to 15 years it is very likely that a tree planted at half the height will have raced ahead.

It is not necessarily a natural look you are after in planting a garden. But Nan Fairbrother (whose book *New Lives, New Landscapes* puts her among the most influential–and enjoyable–of modern writers on the subject) had a few words to say about the Fitted-Carpet Complex. She points out that the normal situation in nature is a tree layer above a shrub layer above a herb layer. Anything that separates these is a garden style. Public authorities are all too prone to plant the trees and then simply mow under them (at great expense) to produce the fitted carpet look, on the mistaken assumption that it is either easier, or tidier, or both. She instances roadsides where the householders have to watch the traffic across a wide strip of grass between tree trunks, whereas the natural regeneration of the area, with a nudge in the right direction and a spot of fertilizer, could have given them a belt of beauty, with a rich mixture of self-sown native trees and shrubs punctuated by the row of trees (if, indeed, a row as such was needed at all).

How much you can use perspective and other tricks to enlarge the apparent size of your garden–or for that matter reduce it–is a question to ponder. Trees here are the crucial factor. They play the essential role of visually linking land and sky. Without them there is a sense of bleakness: man's puny six feet is too open to comparison with the globe, not to mention the firmament. You have only to stand in the middle of the vast and treeless parterres at Versailles or Vaux-le-Vicomte to know the moon-walking feeling.

Happily, however, the human eye, which scans the surroundings for 90 degrees from left to right, peeps out through a comparative slit at the scene above the horizontal. Your eyebrows limit you to seeing 27 degrees of the scenery above eye-level at,

say, five feet from the ground.

A simple diagram at the top of the page demonstrates that in order to make you feel well and truly enclosed a tree at a distance of 100 feet needs to be only 60 feet high; at 50 feet only 30.

Various ways suggest themselves of using this information. Essentially, you have here the clue to the future effect of new tree planting, and of establishing a vertical scale as well as a ground plan to the picture.

A surveyor's pole, ten feet high with the feet marked off in alternate red and white stripes, was Repton's instrument for gauging the interaction of height and distance. He is guilty of the truism 'objects appear great or small by comparison only'. Your Japanese with his 'distancing pine' would of course agree. You plant the big trees at this end of the garden and the small ones at the far end, and (without a ten-foot pole to give the game away) your boundary slinks off into the middle distance.

There is a point about colour that is worth a thought here. Hot colours (yellows and reds) seem nearer to the eye; cool ones (blues and greys) farther from it. Given a reasonable distance for the illusion to get a start you can certainly increase the effect of depth by grouping foliage in this way. It would mean, for example, keeping red-leafed maples near to the house and planting bluish cypresses or a silver lime farther away from it.

It has always been a planter's axiom to use uneven numbers of one kind of tree. Three trees, or five, or seven, but never two, or four, or six–unless in an avenue or as a definite pair flanking a gate. The point that matters is that you should decide whether an effect is supposed to be regular or not–and in either case go the whole hog. Irregularity means trees of different sizes, spaced widely in one place, crowded together in another. Regularity should be exact, or it looks tatty. In the long run, as any ancient avenue will tell you, irregularity wins.

*The art of planting to
look natural was keenly
studied by the 19th-
century landscapers.
These two illustrations
from Humphrey Repton's
Art of Landscape show
(left) how even irregular
planting can easily look
artificial and (right) how,*

*by planting some trees
very close together, by
planting trees and bushes
of different heights at the
same time, even by plant-
ing some trees at an angle
to each other, you can
create the effect of
natural open woodland.*

Trees for Shade, Shelter and Seclusion

The Japanese, with their formalized style of garden design, would never decide (or should I say dare?) just to stick in a tree where they thought it would look nice. They would have to rationalize the situation—in practice by giving the tree a title. That is the Tree of the Sun at Tea-time, or the Gasworks-Hiding-Tree, they would say.

There is a lot to be said for their approach. In a small garden with no space to spare it is almost essential for each tree to have a *raison d'être*. Even in a big one the more controlled and purposeful the planting the greater will be the effect.

Besides, there is no end to the functions of trees once you start to analyse them.

There is shelter (from the weather). Nearly always essential on at least one side of a garden; the side of the prevailing wind. And often essential on the side of the cold winds of early spring as well. Shelter-belts should consist of native trees if possible, to blend in with the landscape. If they are evergreens they give the garden the same feeling of having a protecting shell all the year around. Sylvia Crowe in her *Landscape Design* says such wise words that I would be doing you a disservice not to quote her. She says, in essence, 'Shelter-belts should always be homogeneous: two species are plenty. Get an idea and make a thing of it: a belt *can't* be too tall and thin, for example: if that's the character you're after, make it a single line of Lombardy poplar. Never be indeterminate; to go all out for something is the only way to a rich effect with simple (or any) materials.' That is what she says about shelter-belts, but it is wisdom for any aspect of the garden when you think about it.

There is shade–the avowed purpose of all the street trees in America. In southern Europe (in relatively unpolluted areas) pines and other conifers are widely used to great effect. Deciduous trees are much more popular in the United States, their leaves having a more cooling effect in very hot weather–and indeed casting more shade. A big shade tree very near a house can be almost like air-conditioning. (It can also, however, play havoc with its roots and branches if you are not careful.) In England

Few gardens *in the western world are planned with the functional precision of the Japanese style. Yet purposeful tree-planting defines the structure and scale of all well-designed gardens. The pictures above illustrate aspects of one old garden in eastern England, at Saling Hall, where big old specimens of the regional natives, oak and elms, have been the background to original and intelligent tree-planting for the last 35 years.*

Top *Looking southeast from the front of the house. The only evergreen is a round-headed Platycladus orientalis and a yew hedge defining the front yard. But a simple screen of Lombardy poplars on the west, giving shelter from prevailing winds in summer, provides a strong structural base line and emphasises the perspective of the view, without hiding the low winter sun. The matching crowns of tall English elms on the left also emphasise the distance.*

Above left *In May the sun sets in the northwest, behind just-leafing hybrid black poplars. A white cherry (Prunus avium 'Plena') shows off its flowers against a dark Monterey cypress (providing shelter from northwest winds).*

Above *Trees give shelter, seclusion, shade in summer and a frame to the view both of the house and (top left) from it. A 25-year-old Japanese flowering cherry, 'Shirofugen', is massively horizontal in contrast to the upright Lombardy*

few trees are planted primarily for shade – but we seek the shade of trees in grass to lie under every summer none the less.

There is seclusion – also known as screening. This can involve anything from a whole airport to a bathroom window. In most cases trees are the only possible medium. The point to bear in mind here is that the screen planted near the eyesore has to be far bigger than the one planted near the eye. You can hide a whole house with one bush in the foreground; over against it you will need a whole row of trees.

There is structure: the role of hedges and walls where the scale is fairly modest, but in the landscape the job of trees: to define spaces. The old English landscape of wood, field and meadow, all compartmented by tall lines of elms, or lower barriers of hawthorn, is the perfect example. In a garden in winter the structure tends to fall back on the evergreens; the thing to remember when planting them.

There is the sense of scale – a speciality of the Japanese gardener, who would persuade you that he has half the coastline of Japan in his back-yard. His Distancing Tree is a small pine on a small mound which with half-shut eyes you *might* take for a big pine on a mountain. Trees influence the whole sense of the size of a garden – and more. This aspect is discussed and illustrated on previous pages.

There is the question of framing of views, which we touched on on the previous pages. It is worth noting how photographers instinctively scramble to the nearest tree to frame a picture of a new hotel or generating station. I suspect they often have to take a branch with them to hold in front of the camera.

And finally there is the tree as sculpture; triumphant, central, and intended to be admired for its own sake. In Japanese gardens this is often the tonsured pine leaning negligently over a stone at the water's edge. In western terms it is usually known as 'the lawn tree'. It is worth long pondering whether a magnolia or a cedar or a strawberry tree or a weeping ash deserves this place of honour.

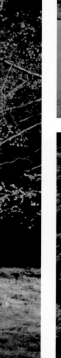

poplars. Beyond it a bird cherry and Prunus 'Kanzan' have reached 30 feet. A low grey willow draws attention to the pond in the foreground. Beyond the roof of the house a 65-foot Scots pine has the effect of a vegetable pediment.

Top right A walled garden to the west of the house is sheltered from the north by a screen of hybrid black poplars 50 feet high (though only 13 years old). Their leaves are copper-pink in spring. The trees within the walls are planted formally: a regular row of clipped upright cypresses along each wall and a row of apple trees pruned into a contrasting flat mushroom shape on the lawn. Being kept low they give shade on the lawn but not on the flower beds. Old pear trees in the centre are used as a framework for clematis, and a purple-leafed plum is trimmed into an upright shape and also smothered in summer with clematis. Two tall clipped Irish yews flank a gateway in the far end wall.

Above A little pool in a hollow, approached by stone steps, has been thickly planted on the north and east sides with lush-foliaged trees to give a sense of privacy. From right to left they are smokebush, Parrotia persica, swamp cypress, Liquidambar and a Caucasian maple whose red summer shoots contrast spectacularly with the blue foliage of Scots pine behind. On the extreme left a feathery grey-green Lawson cypress, 'Pottenii'.

Planting Trees

Moving full-grown trees is no new notion: though modern machinery has made it much less laborious. But even under ideal conditions and at the right season (in autumn or spring) there is a considerable risk of killing the tree.

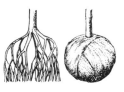

Trees are sold by a nursery with their roots either **bare of soil**, in which case they must be planted, either temporarily ('heeled in') or permanently, straight away; **balled** (i.e. lifted from

the ground with a ball of earth round the roots and wrapped in burlap or sacking; these also need rapid planting); or grown in **pots** or **cans**: these can be moved at any time but preferably not in summer.

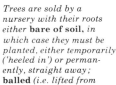

Broadleaf trees can be bought at different ages and sizes, trained in different ways. Left, **bush-form** (i.e. un-trained) is best for multi-stemmed trees, or any tree you want to train yourself.

Feathered (i.e. with all the lower branches intact) is normally the best way to buy specimen trees. They are cheaper and have all their natural character. It is up to you whether you leave the lower branches or not.

Semi-standard and standard are respectively smaller and larger versions of the same thing: a tree with its lower branches removed and the upper branches trained into a balanced head with a more or less definite leader.

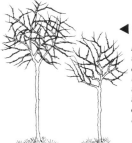

Semi-mature trees are standards grown on in the nursery to 12 feet or more. They tend to be disproportionately expensive and should only be used where the threat of damage to smaller trees is too great.

The first step in planting any tree is to dig a hole big enough to accommodate the roots fully spread out. The soil should be dug out and mixed with a fertilizer (or best of all leafmould) to a depth of at least two feet—depending on the size of

If you are prepared to take enough trouble you can move a tree of almost any size without killing it. The catch is that the trouble increases sharply above a fairly small size, perhaps 15 feet, while the chance of success diminishes. Sir Henry Steuart would not agree with me, and neither would Arbor-Haul Consolidated (if there is such an enterprise). But for us ordinary folk it is one of life's trying little facts.

Old Sir Henry was a 19th-century Scottish landowner who shifted full-grown trees round his park like milk-churns round a dairy. He boasted that he had never lost a tree, and never spent more than 12 shillings (call it two dollars) on moving one. When you consider that for this he employed ten men for two weeks disinterring every scrap of root and reinterring it just down the road (so beautifully that his trees never needed stakes or guy-ropes) you will see why America filled up so quickly with ingenious Scotsmen in the 19th century.

To have any hope of successfully moving a big tree you need either a vast labour-force or a huge machine. However huge the machine, though, it will probably kill the tree unless it has been laboriously prepared beforehand. It means digging a trench first round one side of the tree, then the other (with a year in between) and filling the

trench with leaf-mould. The tree will react by filling the leaf-mould with fibrous feeding roots, making a compact enough root-system to move without losing half of it. Nurseries that grow trees with the intention of selling them extra-large annually undercut the roots with the same object. Unless this is done, and the tree moved at the right season, the chances are it will die.

The easiest trees to shift, and ones that amateurs can move around within their own gardens, are typical garden conifers: cypresses and *Thujas* which have small zones of dense root close to the foot. It is easy for two men in a day to prepare a new hole (the first move) and then unearth and transfer a tree up to say 20 feet, hardly losing any root. With a good stake or guy-ropes and constant watering for at least a year there should be no problem.

But it is best to buy trees small. As a counter-blast to the feeling of impatience which small trees seem to engender in most people I can do no better than to quote the inevitable Humphrey Repton—at his most dogmatic. 'There is no error more common than to suppose that the planter may not live to see his woods unless they consist of (fast-growing) firs and larches .... man outlives the beauty of his trees, where plantations do not consist of oak.'

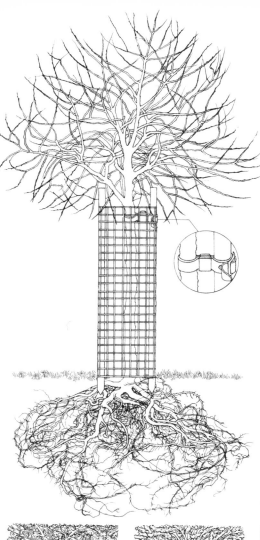

Semi-standard and larger trees must be securely tied to a stake for the first two years after planting (left). The inset picture shows a practical form of tree tie consisting of a plastic belt with a buckle, going through a band which keeps the tree and stake apart.
The tree (left) has a tall wire guard, normally necessary only in public places. Damage from rabbits (or lawn-mowers) can be prevented with a special plastic sleeve which covers the bottom two feet of the trunk. In hot-summer areas the bark of young trees can suffer from scorching after planting out. Paper wrapping material can be bought to shield it.

Above is a method of attaching a conifer to a stake: it can be difficult to get the stake near enough to tie the trunk in the usual way: the branches can be used instead.

It is easy to forget the exact name of a tree, and especially the date that you planted it. A permanent label is not easy to devise. This one is a small rectangle of sheet aluminium, the name and date punched on it with a steel letter-punch.

Lacking the facility Repton must have had of glancing the other way for 20 or 30 years, I have an alternative case to make: that in fact the planter, as soon as he has planted his small tree, begins to get great pleasure from it: greater even perhaps than the pleasure he will have when it is big.

I have kept a letter I had from Alan Mitchell, one of England's greatest dendrologists, when I first started planting. 'Very young trees', he wrote, 'have singular advantages that seem to escape many people . . . There is great aesthetic pleasure in seeing trees at their formative and most vigorous growth . . . when flourishing young foliage is at eye-level and leading shoots four feet long can be seen and measured.' Which is my experience exactly.

Planting a tree seems simple. You dig a hole and stick it in. This, literally, is the way forestry trees in their tens of thousands are planted: there is no time for fancy business. There are touches of finesse, however, that make a great deal of difference to garden trees (which are normally planted considerably bigger). Some of them are outlined on the left.

In places with a deadly winter all planting is best left to early-to-mid spring, when the ground is thoroughly thawed and not too sodden. In more temperate places, deciduous trees are best planted about the time their leaves fall. Their roots can grow surprisingly in mild winter weather, giving them a better chance to put on leaves than if they were planted in the spring. Cold spring winds are also less likely to dehydrate them if they have had a winter in the ground to make roots. Evergreens in the same places can be planted either in early autumn or spring: if in the spring not until the ground is well warmed up and the danger of frosty winds is over. Broadleaved evergreens would rather have some of their leaves cut off than bear the full strain of their transpiration. A jet-age alternative is 'transplanting spray'; a thin plastic coating that reduces transpiration.

Trees in pots or cans are in theory safe to plant at any time. Obviously the best planting season for them is the same as for any other trees. If you plant them in midsummer you must water them much and often. In many nurseries, however, the flourishing-looking tree has been in the can quite a lot too long: its roots are going round and round looking for a way out. For this tree proper planting is going to be quite as much a trauma as for a tree sold bare-rooted. Unless you unscramble the roots (which means shaking the soil off them) they will go on going round and never get a good start in their new home.

A shallow basin over the root area is s simple way of making sure irrigation water reaches the roots.

Where water is precious, roots can be irrigated by perforated pipes driven into the ground.

'Mould-planting': even swamp trees like to be raised a little above very wet ground when planted.

'Basin-planting': in very dry areas trees can be planted in little hollows to encourage water flow.

tree. Break up the bottom of the hole with a fork to ensure good drainage. Anything bigger than a feathered tree (see above left) needs **staking**. Drive a strong wooden stake into the hole at one side deep enough to keep the tree rigid.

Try the tree in the hole. Note that with bare-root trees the **soil-line** on the trunk must be the same as before. If necessary refill the hole until the tree is the right height. Then spread the roots out into their natural position (mainly horizontal).

Start **backfilling** by hand, sifting soil carefully between all the roots and rootlets. Pack them in tight. Mix the backfill soil with compost or leafmould to make it crumbly if necessary.

When the hole is full (all the soil should go back in) **firm the ground** round the trunk by stamping on it. Pull the tree upwards by the trunk: it should not move at all.

Maintenance

A gang was once chopping down a great fir in the Northwest. After a week of axing they thought they heard an echo to their axes. Their foreman mounted his horse and rode round the tree, to find another gang chopping at the other side. Many ingenious devices like the one below were invented to ease the labour of tree-cutting. But only in the last generation has the chain-saw revolutionized it.

I don't know if anyone has sat down cold-bloodedly to calculate how many of the trees planted for ornament survive to do their job. Forestry trees have a good record: 90 per cent success is the average. I suspect that with ornamental trees the failure rate is far higher, despite the fact that so much more trouble is taken, and despite the expensive nursery rearing. It is not only harder to get a four- or five-year-old tree off to a good start, but the risk of damage and the consequences of neglect are more serious. Trees need maintenance. There is a huge difference between a property where the trees are looked after and one where they are supposed to look after themselves.

The first need of trees in the year after planting is water. If the rainfall of the area is less than 30 inches a year, reasonably spaced out through the seasons with a good proportion in the spring, three or four heavy waterings in the first year, and for the next two or three years if possible, will make an enormous difference. Heavy watering means at least 25 gallons to a tree poured on slowly just where the roots are. Irrigation is rarely practised for established trees (i.e., trees that have been planted for more than four or five years) except in areas of notorious drought.

The roots of a newly-planted tree are so near the surface, and so limited in extent, that grass growing over them competes for whatever rations are going. The tree's response is to shade out the grass with its branches – but nursery training removes the low branches that would give the shade. The tree must be helped. Botanical gardens and new commercial orchards always keep a three- to five-foot circle of earth hoed free of grass and weeds round every young tree. In a normal garden this is laborious and not very pretty. The alternative is to mulch the tree with something that will keep down grass and weeds and at the same time help to keep the soil moist. In short grass the perfect material is to hand: the turf you have

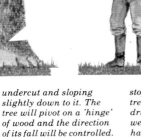

There is an art in safely cutting down a tree and making it fall exactly where planned. The first stage is the 'undercut': a wedge of wood is removed with two cuts, one horizontal and the other *at an angle downwards to meet it. The undercut must point exactly where the tree is intended to fall. The second stage, the felling cut, is made from the opposite side starting at a point just above the* *undercut and sloping slightly down to it. The tree will pivot on a 'hinge' of wood and the direction of its fall will be controlled. Big trees with hard wood can be further controlled if the felling cut is* *stopped short and the tree pushed over by driving in a broad iron wedge with a sledge-hammer.*

cut out to plant the tree, simply turned upside down and stamped down again round the stem. In long grass the answer is a thick pile of cut long grass (and weeds) to cover the ground for two or three feet all round the stem to a depth of four to six inches. Nothing can grow through the pile: it slowly rots down to add a layer of humus to the soil.

There is normally no need to interfere with the branches while the tree is small. It knows what is expected of it. The temptation is there, none the less, to see the twigs of today as the limbs of the day after tomorrow and make sure they form a

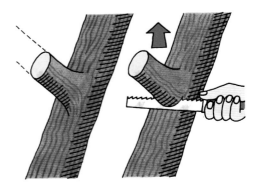

A branch should never be cut off in one piece: the bark will tear. The first step is to cut off the greater part a foot or two from the trunk or main limb. Start even this cut from underneath.

Saw upwards under the remaining branch-stub as close as possible to the tree until the saw starts to 'bind' in the cut.

Take off the stub by cutting downwards to meet the undercut, again as close to the tree as possible so that no stump is left.

Clean off any rough bits of wood or bark with saw, knife or chisel and paint the surface of the wound thickly with fungicide paint. The tree can now rapidly heal the wound with a covering of new bark.

harmonious, balanced pattern. Most of all to see that the trunk or a central leader has the dominance that will give the tree stature.

Some trees grown in the open without competition begin to be complacent, to stop growing upwards and round out their crowns while they are still quite small. It is perfectly sound practice in such a case to shorten the side branches and give the tree a vertical emphasis again. Rather than just cut back any branch and leave a stump in mid-air it is always worth finding a fork with a shorter angled branch you can leave, cutting off the longer arm of the branch flush at that point.

This sort of adjustment to older trees, particularly where it is concerned with repairing damage and fighting disease, is called tree surgery. It is scarcely a job for amateurs. There are real tree-cowboys who can stand (no hands) on a branch 80 feet from the ground while they use a chain-saw. I have got as far as learning to use the ropes and harness to get up there, but I shudder at the thought of actually doing anything (except hang on) at that height.

The tree-surgeon's bible is a book called *The Pruning of Trees, Shrubs and Conifers* by George E. Brown, Assistant Curator at Kew. I cannot attempt here to reproduce its lore and learning. There is, however, one basic lesson to be learned: how a tree heals itself. Bark will grow over a flat clean cut flush with the trunk – but a tree cannot heal a stump. A stump is the royal road for rot, bugs, disease and death.

Never take off a branch in one piece. There is nothing you can do to stop it falling by its own weight before the cut is finished, and taking with it a torn piece of the bark. Remember that the life of the tree lies just inside the bark.

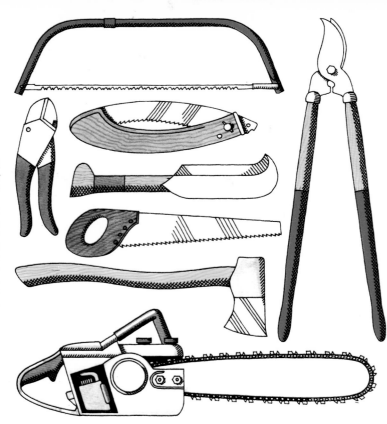

Above *A tree surgeon uses a chain-saw high in an old Scots pine.*

The only reliable method is to cut the branch off a foot or two from the trunk (undercutting to prevent tearing) and then make a separate log of the short stump you have left. Saw from underneath until the blade jams in the cut. Then saw downwards as close to the trunk as you can get to meet the undercut. If there are ragged bits of wood where the two saw-cuts met, saw or chisel them off. Then paint the cut thickly (this is vital) with tree-paint, which is a tarry substance containing a fungicide. If you can't get tree-paint, ordinary household exterior paint is better than nothing. All wounds on trees, and certainly all wounds over one inch in diameter, should be dressed like this. Big wounds, over which it will take the bark several years to grow, should be painted again every year or two.

Unfortunately the gardener quickly learns that many trees which to him are a feast to the eye are quite a different sort of feast to all manner of creatures. A tree stripped of leaves by caterpillars or aphids is a pathetic sight and trunk-borers which work out of sight are no better: they can kill a tree.

Nature is redder in tooth and claw in this regard in North America than in Europe. The extremes of the continental climate, above all the wrecking power of ice-storms, also help to make tree upkeep much more of a problem in the U.S.A. and Canada. On pages 320-1 is a review of some of the commoner pests and diseases that threaten trees, with measures to combat them. The General Index mentions particular susceptibilities to forewarn you of the possible need to keep a spray-gun handy.

The Sitka spruce (right) had a diameter of two inches after 20 years on poor land. In 1960 70 lbs. of phosphate per acre was applied. The tree added half an inch diameter that year. By 1966 the diameter was six inches.

Some of the tools used in pruning and maintaining trees are shown on the left, (not to scale). From left to right and top to bottom they are: a bow-saw, which can be used by one man or two. This is the ideal implement for removing branches. The narrow flexible blade is easy to pull through the wood, but it needs fairly frequent 'setting' (that is, splaying the teeth) and sharpening. Lopping shears have a curved cutting blade pressing on a shallow hook that fits round a small branch. Long handles give great leverage. A good tool for branches up to one inch diameter. Secateurs are for pruning twigs and unwanted new growth. A folding pruning-saw is a useful pocket implement for minor bits of surgery. It can be used with more precision than lopping shears for similar work. A bill-hook should only be used for clearing dead wood or scrub, or 'brashing' (taking small side-branches off felled trees). A carpenter's saw is preferred to a bow-saw by some tree-surgeons, but only for small branches.

The axe is used more for splitting logs than felling trees today. The old forester's axe had a six-pound head on a three-foot ash-wood handle.

The chain-saw with a petrol engine is the standard tree-felling tool today. A chain carrying alternate blades and 'rakers' to clear the saw-dust runs in a track round a steel plate. It is noisy, hot and heavy, but much quicker and easier than the axe.

The Effect of Fertilisers

During their first years, when their roots suffer competition from grasses, trees need food. It is wise to plant them with some fertiliser – and for four or five years to keep a circle at least three feet in radius clear of grass and well mulched.

Each of the three main ingredients of fertilisers, nitrogen, phosphorus and potassium, has a specific effect. Nitrogen promotes strong vegetative growth and enriches leaf colour. Phosphorus is necessary for good root-growth and potassium induces fruiting, and the proper ripening of wood and fruit. Excess nitrogen inhibits fruiting and, by inducing late growth, prevents proper ripening of wood.

At planting, mix a few ounces of super-phosphate with the soil in the hole; as growth starts, add a top dressing of fertiliser with a high nitrogen content. Sandy soils need more fertiliser after heavy rain.

Old trees on closely mown lawns suffer from malnutrition, becoming thin in the crown and prematurely senile. They are best fed by drilling holes over the area and filling them with general fertiliser.

Pruning and other Arts

Hedges are the everyday example of trees bidden by man. We accept the idea of enough beech trees, say, or yews, to make a substantial wood, all being restrained by cutting every year to take the form of a mere wall. Yet other forms of tree-discipline are frowned on as unnatural.

The Japanese think differently. To them a natural pine, whether compact or straggling, is less appealing than a bidden pine engineered into dancing a sort of pine-ballet. The garden is a stage, and the actors are called upon to do more than just stand around in their ordinary clothes passing the time of day.

Are we in the west perhaps too functionally minded? We cordon an apple tree to make it bear more fruit. We pollard a willow to get osiers for fencing and baskets. But if we have any fancy notions about shapes it is usually to carve quite unvegetable things in topiary – be it quasi-architecture, the Sermon on the Mount (in an ancient Warwickshire garden) or even a hunt in full cry, which is frozen in yew on the point of crossing the drive to a French château.

Not that functional forms are without beauty. The methods for maintaining the maximum number of fruiting spurs on an apple or a pear tree give the symmetry and order of the espalier, the fan and the cordon. Where there used to be a demand for regular supplies of long straight poles there are woods of coppiced hazel or chestnut: every six or seven years each tree was cut back to the ground, where it formed a 'stool' and sent up a porcupine of new shoots. They were not very lovely perhaps when they were in production; but old, abandoned coppice is some of the prettiest woodland. In gardens the idea is taken up with trees distinguished for their foliage; regular cutting down giving a bush, usually with bigger leaves than those of the natural tree, forced by roots out of proportion to the top. I have seen eucalyptus, golden poplar, catalpa, box elder all hacked mercilessly to

Bonsai can start with a one-year-old seedling.

Next year the main stem is cut off leaving a branch.

At three years the process is repeated.

At four years the tree starts to look old.

the ground, all bounding back in the same year with eight-foot shoots covered with mammoth leaves.

Pollarding is simply the coppice principle applied six feet above the ground, where grazing beasts can't reach the new shoots. It is the coppice of the meadow, as opposed to the woodland. The word pollard has the same root as poll – meaning head.

Willows are the most commonly pollarded trees, but oak, ash and hornbeam have often been cut for firewood in this way in the past. Sometimes in fact with old spreading trees it is hard to see whether they were once cut off six feet above the ground or not.

Generally you can say that if all the branches start from the same point on the trunk they were.

Pollarding is little used for ornament. The happiest effect I have seen achieved with it has been that of instant fen-land; a group of willows with brilliantly red-barked young shoots standing glowing in the winter sunlight above their reflections in a pond.

Bonsai is the end of the road. The deliberate use of all a tree's forces and (as it were) instincts to make a toy is gardening of a very sophisticated kind. It has special value for a city-dweller, whose chance to observe the forces of nature is limited and

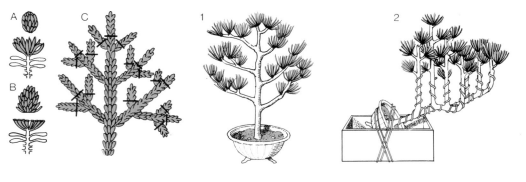

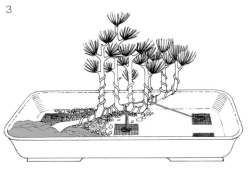 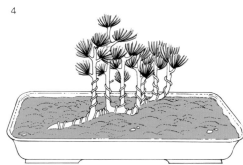

Fruit trees are often pruned and shaped to prevent them growing vertically. They react by producing more fruit. Three shapes are used against walls and along wires. **Right** *the espalier.*

Left *The cordon, more often used on wires, is shown here before and after its annual pruning. Side branches are reduced by three-quarters in winter to induce flower and fruit formation.*

Right *A fan-trained tree, usually grown against a wall. The central leader is cut off after strong side branches have formed the basic fan. No branch is allowed to grow vertically.*

All conifers for bonsai must have their growing tips regularly shortened. **Top left** *Needle-leaf trees must be carefully pinched back (**A**) as cut needles (**B**) will turn brown. Scale-leaf trees (**C**) need a few tips nipping off more or less daily in spring.*

*The process of turning a small pine into a bonsai pine-grove is shown in the drawings above. The tree, its shoots controlled by pinching back (**1**), is lashed into a horizontal position. Stiff wire is wound round its branches*

*to train as many as possible upwards (**2**); the rest are cut off. Wire is also used to bend the trunk. The tree is then transplanted to a wide flat container (**3**) and held down on to the soil with wires passed through the*

*drain-holes. The soil is kept level with the trunk (**4**) and the tree left in a sheltered light place out of the sun where it will form roots from the trunk.*

– adapted from **Bonsai-Saikei** *by Toshio Kawamoto and Joseph Y. Kurihara Nippon-Saikei Co., Tokyo.*

Topiary is gardening with a sense of humour. This garden at Box Hill in the south of England, blends the whimsical and mock-monumental effects which can be achieved by

carving dense-leafed trees and bushes like yew and box. Because it can never be taken completely seriously topiary suits cottage gardens better than formal ones.

distorted to the point of psychological danger. One little tree in a pot can teach you more than a fortnight in a forest about the processes of plant life, if you work with it, as the Japanese do, to bring out its essential character.

Some of the techniques of bonsai are illustrated on the left. Big-tree modelling comes to much the same thing, with the difference that the roots have no restrictions: the size of the tree is only controlled by the amount you stop each year's growth. In practice of course this does restrict the roots, too.

One underlying principle affects all pruning: every time you cut off a growing tip you transfer the energy due to it to the next bud or growing tip back down the line. There is no guesswork in what will happen when you cut off a twig. The last remaining bud will take up the struggle and go whichever way it is pointing. If you want a branch to grow to the right you must choose a bud pointing that way and cut off what lies beyond it, as close to the bud as possible (leaving no 'snag' or stump to die and attract fungi or disease).

Any branch you cut below its lowest bud, simply leaving a stump, will do one of two things, neither of which you want. Either it will die or it will produce epicormic shoots (see page 10) of no beauty or value; just a bunch of straight whiskers.

With this in mind it is not difficult to pick on the branches you want to encourage to grow straight on and those you want to change direction; those you want to shorten or remove and those you want to make dense and bushy.

The trick is to see the tree's natural tendency and help it along. If it tends to form, for instance, flattened whorls of branches with all their leaves facing upwards, remove everything which doesn't conform to the horizontal pattern. The Japanese go further and clip the top of each tier of a pine-tree like a lawn to make it dense and even.

A common form of pollard in fen country; the willow (or osier) cut back every year or two for its pliant new rods for weaving into baskets or fences. The trunks of such pollards usually rot inside and become hollow sleeves, . still supporting a flourishing crown. Varieties with coloured young bark treated in this way in spring are gay shock-heads the next winter.

In a bonsai nursery near Tokyo ready-made bonsai, such as the miniature grove of pines (right, middle-ground) fetch high prices. Enthusiasts, not content with buying off-the-peg, walk in wild mountain areas looking for stunted seedlings to
take home, sometimes even starting to train them in situ. Of all trees, pines and junipers make the most natural-looking miniatures. Flowering trees are popular, but nothing can shrink the blooms. Well-tended bonsai trees can live over 100 years.

The urban pollard, symbol of a tidy-minded municipality. All over continental Europe one sees such trees, usually (as here, at Ghent in Belgium) London planes, cruelly cropped of each year's shoots till they develop great fists at their
extremities. The volume of green produced by such trees and the length of its season are both minimal.

The Conifers

Conifers bear cones. That is their hallmark. Not all cones look like cones. Nobody would suspect a juniper berry, for instance, of being any such thing. But technically a plant whose female flower offers its eggs naked to the world for fertilization, and then develops into a 'fruit', usually of wood, to enclose them while they ripen, is a conifer. And all conifers are trees – or at least woody plants. There are no herbaceous conifers.

The conifers include the world's biggest plants – by far. There is a startling gap between the record heights of broadleaf trees and conifers. In the American championship table there are no broadleaves over 180 feet or so. Then a pause. Then an astonishing list of champions from 250 feet right up to 350 feet – all conifers.

Again, conifers hold all the age records. Millenarians are commonplace. The arguments concern how many thousands of years the oldest of the pines have been growing.

In the natural course of evolution the heyday of the conifers is over. They are one of the oldest plant families. They flourished long before the broadleaves. But they have been on the decline, numerically and territorially, for millions of years.

Yet man has found them a more efficient plant for his purposes, for timber and paper, than the up-to-date broadleaves. Partly it is their willingness to grow under the unlikeliest circumstances; on land too poor or wet or exposed – above all too far north – for farming. Partly it is their simple design with all the emphasis on a thick trunk – the branches being no more than something to hang the foliage on. But mainly it is their speed: the conifers are adapted to use the low sun of the higher latitudes to its utmost; they nearly all keep their leaves and thus have the means to make and store food the year round. Under northern conditions, therefore, they add wood to their bulk at a rate unsurpassed by any broadleaved tree.

There are about 650 species of conifers, in 50 genera in only eight families. They all grow in the temperate zones – most of them moreover in the colder parts; if they grow in the tropics at all it is only on mountains with a temperate climate.

The vast majority – 33 out of the 50 genera – are confined to the northern hemisphere. Nearly all of them are evergreen trees with tough, dark-green needle-like leaves which make dense and deeply shady forests. In the gloom their lower branches rapidly die and drop off; their trunks develop into flawless pillars, often rising to an awesome height.

Yet from the same race, through odd freaks and sports, come small, precisely formal and even miniature trees of exquisite detail and often brilliant colouring – man's other reason for taking the conifers under his protection.

The Ginkgo or Maidenhair Tree

The ginkgo has not changed its design in 150,000,000 years. This fossil leaf found at Scarborough in Yorkshire is part of the evidence that the ginkgo grew world-wide. Eventually it retreated to the mountains of central China.

The ginkgo has neither needles nor cones, yet you might guess its ancestral relationship to the conifers from this picture. Trunk and limbs ascend stiffly; the top is like a spire; the small foliage softens the shape without disguising its basic outline.

One feels a certain respect for a creature which has simply declined to evolve. I believe there are lowly crabs, and also insects, which have been much the same for 100 million years or so. But for a forest tree to survive its relations, its descendants, the conditions which gave it birth: to look unmoved on the drift of continents, the rise of mountain ranges, the coming and going of aeons of reptiles and ages of ice – to survive all this unaltered, for 200 million years, argues a degree of tenacity. Not to mention a sound design.

The ginkgo's unmistakable leaf is as startling as Man Friday's footprint among the tangle of tree-ferns in fossil strata of the Paleozoic era. The tree ranged world-wide in those days. Before the modern conifers evolved, long before the rise of the broadleaves, the ginkgo flourished in America, in Asia, in Australia; and on the Isle of Mull. It went into decline even before the Ice Ages, it seems. And yet it remained viable. There was still somehow a niche for this strangely sophisticated primitive.

By the time man came on the scene the ginkgo had retreated to the mountain forests of Chekiang in easternmost China, and Szechwan in the far west. It may still exist there in a natural state. Nobody seems sure. But its re-emergence is due to the priestly planting of it in temple gardens, first in China, then in Japan. An eighth-century Chinese writer mentions it. A 16th-century one calls it the duck's-foot tree–referring to the shape of its leaves. Its modern name is the Japanese version of the Chinese yin-kuo, meaning 'silver-fruit'. (The fruit was another reason for planting it: the kernels, roasted, were eaten when liquor was flowing freely; the peanuts and cashews of the ancient Chinese.)

The West heard of the ginkgo when Kaempfer wrote of his visit to Japan in 1690. In 1730 the first plant arrived in Europe, in Utrecht, and in 1754 Kew Gardens bought the tree which still grows there from a nurseryman in east London. It was at this stage that it was christened maidenhair tree ('adiantifolia') from the maidenhair fern, the only plant with leaves of similar shape. Thirty years later it was introduced to the United States, to Philadelphia . . . and its new lease of life began.

One of the advantages of living on after your era is that your enemies have all, as they say, gone before. Doubtless there were epidemics of ginkgo disease, and hordes of ginkgo-eating insects–millions of years ago. But today, as oaks wilt and elms wither, the ginkgo can just look inscrutable. Even air-pollution in its deadliest form–on Fifth Avenue for example–leaves its odd duck's-foot leaves fresh and wholesome. It will even grow in shallow concrete tubs at the pavement's edge where buses breathe their unbreathable breath. It is the answer to the Parks Department's prayer.

Neither in Europe nor America, though, is it planted very often simply as the eccentric beauty it is. A young ginkgo's branches rise stiff and straight, rather like an Atlantic cedar's: in summer much softened by the pale green leaves drooping on long stalks; in winter sculptural–if you like it, or stark, if you don't. With age the branches dip at the end and fan out. It may just be fancy, but the ginkgo's distant relationship to the modern conifers seems to be reflected in its stance even in old age.

The tree's best moment is in the late autumn, when the leaves turn from their well-sustained green to clear butter-yellow, without a hint of orange or brown. They fall soon after, but the fleeting effect on a big ginkgo, fuller and more pendulous in figure, is marvellous.

Seventy or 80 feet is normally full size: one at Milan reached 125 feet. Hot summers will certainly have helped it. As to the spread, much depends on the clone: there is a very narrow upright one known as the 'sentry' ginkgo propagated in America for street planting, but the most graceful trees are the broad and droopy kind. One of the advantages of the 'sentry' is that it is a male tree: ginkgo fruit, if any, is malodorous when ripe.

Above *Ginkgo autumn colour is short-lived but lovely; a clear yellow which emphasises the fineness of the foliage. Here at Sheffield Park in Sussex, a garden famous for its autumn display, a ginkgo is flanked by its great grandchildren: cryptomeria (left) and oriental spruce (right).*

Above *The autumn colouring of ginkgo leaves emphasises their peculiar shape; like long-stemmed fans with more or less wavy edges and a notch in the middle. Leaves on young shoots are divided almost in two by the notch.*

The Pines of North America

Pines are to the conifers what oaks are to the broadleaves: the most widespread, most varied and most valuable trees of their order. The biggest family of conifers goes by their name, the *Pinaceae*. It includes the firs, spruces, cedars, larches–almost all the needle trees. But the actual genus *Pinus*, the pines proper, is limited to 100 or so species with certain clear and obvious characteristics, of which the easiest to see and remember is the relatively long evergreen needles in tight bundles, each bundle (of from two to five needles, according to species) wrapped at its base in a papery sheath.

The yearly growth of each shoot of a pine takes the form of a 'candle'. Firs and spruces and the rest add to their branches every year more or less horizontally; pine-candles tend to grow vertically, only settling down to their place as part of the branch later, as they grow heavier.

In contrast to its aspiring new shoots, however, a pine is much less forceful than its cousins in its defiance of gravity. A fir or a spruce is a spire as a young tree, and a spire it remains. Most pines, where they have room to expand, take a course in middle age which brings them nearer to the wide-spreading broadleaves. The result–an eccentric flourish of bold branches, often on a bare stem, usually with beautifully coloured and patterned bark–is one of the most triumphantly picturesque of all trees.

As old trees pines are the standard-bearers of the skyline. But the owner of a young pine has, if anything, even more to enjoy: a vigorous plant at eye level, fantastically rich in its detail, its thick and sappy shoots bristling with bright new needles, embossed with male and female parts of splendidly original and suggestive design.

The natural range of the pines is enormous. They grow from the Arctic Circle to the Equator. If anything they favour rugged conditions: drought and extreme exposure on mountains; on sandy seashores, where the subsoil is permanently frozen; or, like the famous Jeffrey pine, on a rocky dome high above Yosemite, where there seems to be no soil at all. If pines have a headquarters in our era it is in Mexico, whose tropical highlands they seem to relish. With their evolutionary tactics of interbreeding they keep botanists busier there than anywhere else on earth.

Of the hundred-odd known pine species 36 are natives of North America. They divide readily into northeastern, southeastern and western stables. Anyone planting one should certainly consider the trees of his own area first–not forgetting, of course, the imports from Europe, Asia and Mexico.

The great pine of the northeast is the

The needles of the Montezuma pine are pale greyish green, up to a foot long, grouped round bright red-brown buds. Unfortunately this beautiful tree is particularly susceptible to hard frost.

Above *Given the space, light and air the billowing broadleaf shape comes as naturally to most pines as the narrow spire. One of the most beautiful of all is the Mexican Montezuma pine, whose* long (up to 10 in.) bluish-green needles droop gracefully from the branches. This specimen is in the garden of the Villa Melzi on the shore of Lake Como in northern Italy.

Sugar pine (on the right of the picture) in the mountains of California. Long horizontal upper branches and the longest of all cones make it one of the easiest pines to recognize. Sweet resin from the trunk, used by the Indians as food, gave the tree its name. The world's biggest pine tree is a sugar pine growing in Siskiyou National Forest, California.

Ponderosa pine shares the same California mountain country as sugar pine and grows to almost the same size. Beautiful fissured bark ranging in colour from ochre to pink is characteristic of ponderosa. So are the needles in stiff round bunches at the ends of shoots. The tree between the trunks is another ponderosa, showing the typical crown shape.

Right Northern pitch pine is the almost indestructible pine of dry barrens in the northeastern United States. Chalk soil is the only thing it won't stand. It makes a medium-sized tree with long branches and an open crown. The picture shows its habit –unique among pines– of producing tufts of needles from the trunk. The needles are $3\frac{1}{2}$–$4\frac{1}{2}$ in. long and grouped in threes.

white or Weymouth pine (*Pinus strobus*). The old New England forest, which was relentlessly butchered over a period of 300 years, contained vast stands of it, with trees 200 feet high and eight or nine feet across. Its beautiful soft white wood supplied half Europe's needs, as well as building boats and panelling mansions throughout the eastern States. It was introduced to Britain in the 18th century by Viscount Weymouth, who planted it at Longleat. In Britain it has never been a great success: but in France and Germany there are good woods of it. Its thin, pale needles of a delicate blue-green make it a beautiful garden tree; it will keep long branches low-down, where you can see them. But it will make a giant eventually – far too big for the ordinary garden. Neither of the other two northeastern pines shown on page 73, the red pine (*P. resinosa*) and the pitch pine (*P. rigida*), are nearly as big or as beautiful. The red is a sombre tree, dark green with dark red bark, its foliage heavy like that of the Corsican pine; the pitch pine is generally considered a last-resort tree for really rough conditions, where it can cut a rugged, romantic figure. Its peculiarity of sprouting tufts of green leaves from its trunk makes it easy to pick out. In Canada the jack pine (*P. banksiana*) and in the eastern States the scrub pine (*P. virginiana*) are small trees which play similar tough roles.

Southeastern pines are of enormous economic importance, and of great interest and vigour. They cover thousands of square miles of torpid, otherwise unprofitable country. Yet none of them is exactly a beauty.

The strange one is the longleaf pine (*P. palustris*). Long indeed are its needles – as much as 18 inches. But its real quirk is to crouch, a mere grassy mound of potential pine tree, for as much as three or four years before it starts to put on height. In its 'grass stage' it can survive forest fires and at the same time build up a strong root system to boost its later growth.

The southern forester uses four principal pine trees, and does a complicated equation to know which to plant where (the factors are speed, quality and resistance to rust disease). Longleaf is slow-growing but fairly resistant. Shortleaf (*P. echinata*) is even slower, but more resistant. Loblolly (*P. taeda*) is the biggest, best and fastest, at any rate on rich land, but highly susceptible to rust. Slash pine (*P. elliottii*) is the best and fastest on poor soil, but again liable to the disease. Slash has another advantage: a thicker bark, which makes it possible to burn the forest floor to suppress competition while the trees are young. ▶

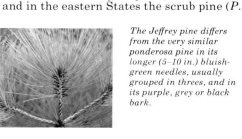

The Jeffrey pine differs from the very similar ponderosa pine in its longer (5–10 in.) bluish-green needles, usually grouped in threes, and in its purple, grey or black bark.

Male flowers cover the entire shoot below the new tuft of needles on a bishop pine, native of the South California coast.

The Pines of North America

Opposite *Pines are adapted to a wide range of climatic conditions.* **Right** *A young shore pine in the snow at Bluff Lake, Oregon.* **Middle right** *Monterey pines luxuriate in the temperate climate of Monterey Bay in California.* **Far right** *Knobcone pines flourish near Bear Basin in California.*

▶ The western pines are in a rather different league. David Douglas, having canoed and portaged for weeks on end to find the sugar pine (*P. lambertiana*), called it 'the most princely of the genus: perhaps even the grandest specimen of vegetation'. Having met the grandfather of all sugar pines in a valley in the Siskiyou mountains of Oregon I can only say Amen. The monster stands 270 feet or so, not as a pole with a shaggy top, as western giant trees tend to be, but mightily branched most of the way up; a forester's nightmare.

Sugar pine branches are straight, and of immense length. Even a 200-foot tree tends to be a well-proportioned T, so each branch near the top must be 70 feet long, weighed down only slightly with its colossal two-foot cones at the tips. Nobody would call it a garden tree, or even a beautiful one. In European collections it has grown to about 100 feet and then perished, being, like all American five-needled pines, liable to the rust disease.

The only other western pine which reaches a comparable size is the ponderosa (*P. ponderosa*), which grows alongside the sugar pine on the same mountain slopes, and reaches its apogee (246 feet) in the same Siskiyou valley. The early settlers' name for the ponderosa was the bull pine, which well expresses the weight and vigour and solidity of this most impressive production. The bark forms into huge rectangular plates of warm pink, etched in grey. The needles are dense and stiff, up to almost a foot in length. In ideal conditions ponderosa has grown 120 feet in 50 years, perfectly straight and only slightly tapering. Of all the big western pines this is the one to choose for a (big) garden in Europe. It transplants well to almost any soil.

Jeffrey pine is similar to ponderosa with more of a liking for high places. Western white pine (*P. monticola*), in the mountains, is not unlike sugar pine–though a far better garden tree, the western equivalent of the New England white pine, with beautiful soft foliage. It has the same rust problem, though. Of the other California mountain pines perhaps the most rewarding to grow is the bigcone (*P. coulteri*)–not a tall tree but a broad one. The reward here–and hence the name–is the cones, as big as a baby's head and armed all over with eagle's claws.

Of the bristlecone pine (*P. aristata*), the oldest living creature on earth, I have written on pages 20–21. Anyone who wants to try this patriarch in his own garden will find it very slow. For the first few centuries the curious little dew-drops of resin on the leaves are probably the best part. The knobcone (*P. attenuata*) is another small and slow species. Its curving cones, as solid as hand-grenades, stick close to the trunk and never fall or open until a forest fire comes their way.

The shore pine (*P. contorta*) seems to be the most adaptable. It grows from the seacoast right up to 11,000 feet (where the variety is called lodgepole). Not only is it adaptable and hardy, but it has beautiful dense foliage, usually from head to foot, and striking red buds which make it look as though it is flowering. Happily it is turning out to be a first-class forestry tree in Britain, suppressing even Scottish heather with its rapid early growth. After the Sitka spruce it is the most-planted species–and should be more so in gardens with acid soil.

The remainder of the western pines belong on the coast, in milder conditions, with the on-shore gale as their chief foe. The most important is the Monterey pine (*P. radiata*), perhaps the lushest and most lordly of the whole tribe. Nature had restricted this incredibly vigorous, but rather tender, plant to a few square miles round Monterey in southern California. Man has changed all that: it is now the chief forestry pine of the southern hemisphere. Results in New Zealand are sensational. In its fifth year one tree there put on 20 feet. Where it is happy the

 Bigcone	Loblolly	 White (or Weymouth)	Red
Bristlecone	Lodgepole	Sugar	Slash
Pitch	Monterey	Shortleaf	Jelecote
Ponderosa	Longleaf	Western white	Mexican white
Torrey	Jeffrey	Knobcone	Montezuma

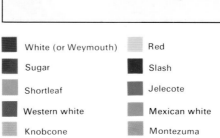

Monterey pine grows vast branches and keeps them densely clad in bright bottle-green needles. Even in southern England it grows four feet a year, not even making a resting bud in winter but charging right on, only pausing in cold weather.

The bishop pine (*P. muricata*) is along the same lines, but slightly duller in colour, often somewhat slower and hardier – an excellent front-line defence against sea winds.

In the same seaside context the Torrey pine (*P. torreyana*) has a limited southern range. It is a short, open, spreading tree with its bundles of five needles as heavy as darts: the leaves of plants below are punctured by them as they fall.

In New Mexico the piñon pine (*P. cembroides*) is grown for its seeds rather than for its looks. They are the pine-nuts which were an important food for the Indians. Mexico also produces three species which should be much better known. Perhaps the best-looking pine of all is the Montezuma (*P. montezumae*). It spreads pale grey needles in wide whorls round deep, resinous, orange buds almost like some titanic Michaelmas daisy. An old tree is a vast low dome of these stiff, brush-like shoots. Such specimens are rare – and there are less dramatic varieties under the same name from other parts of Mexico.

The jelecote or spreading-leaf pine (*P. patula*) could hardly be more different. The most feminine tree of all the pines, it has pale, drooping needles, as thin as threads, hanging from the tips of gently curving limbs. For all its delicate appearance it grows like the devil in a warm climate.

The third Mexican pine which occurs here and there in collections abroad is the Mexican white pine (*P. ayacahuite*). To the non-expert its smooth grey bark and fine needles make it a recognizable relation of the white pines of the eastern and western States – and come to that of the Himalayas.

The maps on the left show the natural range of North America's most important pines. The illustrations (below) show the needles, the cones and the manner of growth of sixteen of them. The trees shown are in their prime, shaped as they would be if growing in open ground. In forests they would be narrower with longer trunks clear of branches; with greater age they will grow wider in the crown and more branchy without putting on much more height.

Bigcone pine: P. coulteri; *small mountain tree; clawed cones weigh up to 5 lbs. Needles at 90° to shoot.*

Bishop pine: P. muricata; *small tree for poor or swampy soil. Needles stiff; cone has sharp prickles.*

Eastern white pine: P. strobus; *biggest most beautiful conifer of northeast. Has grown to 220 ft.*

Jelecote pine: P. patula; *small graceful Mexican tree. Footlong bright-green needles droop.*

Loblolly pine: P. taeda; *biggest (to 150 ft.) and fastest southern pine on good land. Weak wood.*

Lodgepole pine: P. contorta latifolia; *small vigorous mountain tree, hardy to 11,000 ft.*

Longleaf pine: P. palustris; *important and pretty southern forestry pine; 18-in. needles.*

Monterey pine: P. radiata; *beautiful, fast and dense tree; dark grassy-green needles.*

Pitch pine: P. rigida; *small and spreading; needs light; good by sea; stiff needles stick out.*

Ponderosa pine: P. ponderosa; *most important western timber pine with huge range. To 240 ft.*

Red pine: P. resinosa; *fast, dense, well-shaped; good on sandy soil.*

Shore pine: P. contorta; *vigorous coastal form of lodgepole. Big red buds.*

Slash pine: P. elliottii; *best and fastest southern pine for poor land.*

Sugar pine: P. lambertiana; *the world's biggest pine; to 270 ft.*

Western white pine: P. monticola; *to 180 ft. in Idaho; soft blue-green.*

Whitebark pine: P. albicaulis; *small mountain tree of northwest.*

The Pines of Asia

Looking at a photograph of Japan it is sometimes hard to know whether the scene is wild coastline or suburban garden. The lanterns and the carefully-placed stones soon give the game away, but the main visual element which links the two, and carries at least a momentary conviction, is the pine trees. Wind-contorted, shank-shrunk dotards of pine trees are the soul of the Japanese landscape. A gardener's business is to bend a sapling to his whim, to give it premature grey hairs by constant bullying, by weighing down branches, by pinching out shoots, by a salon-full of cosmetic tricks.

The principal victim of all this flattering attention – and the one on the willow-pattern china – is the Japanese white pine (*P. parviflora*). Its natural form already suggests the more highly-coloured coiffured version. It is short, wide-crowned, often with several stems; it holds its twigs and needles in flat plates, facing upwards. The needles are short, dark, grey-blue, with a slight twist and a paler inner surface which gives them a certain vivacity.

Japanese trees came west with a rush in the 1860s. The Japanese white, red and black pines all appeared here within ten years. The red pine (*P. densiflora*), however, is so similar to the Scots pine that there is little need for it, except to a collector. This is the skyline pine of the Japanese garden: the ragged, red-barked head on the quasi-distant hill. Its semi-dwarf variety, 'Umbraculifera', is the most interesting for the western gardener. It makes a broad dome, no more than seven feet high but with age perhaps twice as much across; a tent full of snaking branches. There is also a variety called

The shadow of a Japanese white pine snakes across rock and raked gravel in a formal Japanese garden. The white pine is the small and often contorted tree in the famous willow pattern.

The Japanese umbrella pine, so called because its needles look like the spokes of an umbrella, is quite different from the umbrella or stone pine of Italy. It forms a tall, bright green bush; very hardy on lime-free soil.

A Japanese white pine in a romantic landscape garden. The tree has been trimmed and trained to stoop elegantly over the water, supported on a single crutch. Each year's new shoots need shortening to maintain the balance and the perfect tier-structure of the tree.

Below The Japanese red pine is the eastern equivalent of the Scots pine; a tall-growing, broad-headed tree with red bark. The picture shows one trained in a naturalistic style, contrasting with the mannered effect in the tree on the left. Again a prop is used for a long low bough over the water.

Right Nature outdoes art in this umbrella version of the Japanese red pine growing at the French National Arboretum at les Barres. This tree is seven feet high with a spread of nearly 15 feet. It has taken 40 years to reach this size, probably its maximum.

dragon's-eye with variegated foliage.

There would be no difficulty in growing either of these species in any temperate garden—or in a tub, or even on a plate, as bonsai. The red is very much faster than the white to start with; apparently it has reached 100 feet in California, but 50 feet is the most it has done in Britain. On the other hand the white, like most five-needled pines, transplants well when it is bigger.

The Japanese black pine (*P. thunbergii*) can be bracketed with the European black pines—particularly the Corsican. It has proved itself the best of all windbreak trees for the seashore in New England. Poor sandy soil does not worry it: it slowly forms a head of long unpredictable branches, bearing tufts of dark foliage—another opportunity (which the Japanese do not miss) for crimping and curling and theatrical effects.

The repeating pattern of black, red and white pines, whether it has a sound botanical basis or not, certainly helps one to classify, to recognize and remember certain types. There are two more Asiatic trees with typical 'white pine' characteristics—silky light green foliage, with the young bark smooth and grey. The Himalayan white pine is fairly well known under various names (*excelsa*, *griffithii*, the Bhutan and the Nepalese pine, as well as the up-to-date name, *wallichiana*). In *Trees for American Gardens* Donald Wyman names Seattle and Philadelphia as two places where it does particularly well, whereas Boston is too cold for it. The best trees in the British Isles (over 100 feet) are in Devon and Ireland, the mildest areas. It is one of the few five-needled pines to resist the rust disease. It grows quickly to start

Mature and immature cones of the Japanese red pine. The green female flowers are ripening to become real cones. The botanical name P. densiflora refers to the dense clusters of male flowers which result in such tight-packed cones.

with, then settles down at 50 feet or so as a broad, open tree of beautiful colour and gleaming texture.

The Chinese white pine (*P. armandii*) is much rarer. I have seen splendid young trees with long, grey-green needles growing at the French National Arboretum at les Barres, south of Paris. But by all accounts the eventual tree is less attractive than the Himalayan one.

The connoisseur's Chinese pine is the lacebark (*P. bungeana*), a tree which often

The dwarf Siberian pine is a bushy Asiatic version of the Alpine cembran pine. Its stiff and twisted needles are grey-blue; its male flowers brilliant red.

makes several stems—and the more the better, since the bark is the main attraction. Areas of white, buff, grey, rust-red, purple and green are revealed where the bark comes off. The bole is smooth and bulky, in fact not at all unlike a London plane in feeling. There are trees you can plant for immediate satisfaction, but the lacebark pine is not one of them: it is essentially a tree to bequeath (or inherit).

Apart from these two rare species, Chinese pines are oddly absent from the West. Korea makes an excellent contribution with a pine rather like the Swiss cembran, only, to my mind, much more decorative. The Korean pine (*P. koraiensis*) has the same way of keeping its upholstery from top to bottom, but it is a fine shade of deep grass-green, with what seems an abnormal amount of needles. The National Arboretum in Washington D.C. has a remarkable 20-foot specimen on which all the needles change direction by about 45 degrees a quarter of the way along. It is a well-proportioned tree, and this extra bushiness makes it quite vibrant with colour and life.

One more valuable tree from the Far East must find a place here—though it is only the most distant relation of the pines. The *Sciadopitys* is usually called the umbrella pine, because its long, succulent, bright green needles radiate from the branches like the spokes of a half-open umbrella. It grows slowly in a perfect full-dress cone-shape: a formal but very satisfying feature on a lawn or among low shrubs. There are 100-foot umbrella pines in Japan (and a 75-foot one in Kent) but 30 feet is a more probable maximum in most gardens.

A lacebark pine, one of the most ornamental of all pines, growing near Sochi in the USSR. In the wild the lacebark tends to have an almost white bark. In cultivation the bark is grey-green, flaking to show a patchwork of colours.

75

The Pines of Europe

Nobody would deny pride of place to the Scots pine (*P. sylvestris*) among the pines of Europe–even perhaps among the pines of the world. I find its beauty unrivalled. The richness of its colouring, its wild poise set it apart. No matter how grey the winter's day, the papery bark, flaking in butterfly wings of salmon and green, glows with the warmth of a fire in the sky. And if the bark is richly red, the leaves are no less richly blue. To handle a heavy, resinous spray and see the unripe cones, little jade carvings in the deep sea lights and shadows of the needles, is an intoxication.

In its natural range, from Siberia to the Highlands to the Mediterranean, the Scots pine is unique. It was the sole north European pine to survive the Ice Ages. In the Alps the cembran came through in some mountain refuge. Only along the shores of the Mediterranean and the Atlantic did half a dozen other species survive.

Of the great Caledonian forest where the Scots pine grew only a few remnants have come down to us, among them one of the most beautiful and romantic woodlands in the world: even its name, the Black Wood of Rannoch, has primeval vibrations. It lies at the head of a glen, on the high moorland round Loch Rannoch, in the centre of Scotland. Among the vast pines, not tall but broad and somehow darker than their descendants, widely spaced in the heather and bilberry, grow great fountainous gold birches, at the same time taller and more weeping than any you have seen. A little alder grows by the burn which slides on long granite slabs to the loch. A rowan stoops under a hundredweight of scarlet berries.

Until recent times, hard as it is to believe, these few pines of Rannoch Wood were the only pines in Britain. Early man had massacred the rest. An untravelled contemporary of Shakespeare's would never have seen the tree the English have come to know, with cheerful ignorance, as 'the fir'.

North Germany, the Baltic and Scandinavia grow the same pine. At higher latitudes and altitudes it narrows its crown, becoming almost a spire. But the Alps have their own pines: the slow, solid, columnar cembran or Arolla of Switzerland (*P. cembra*) and farther east the Austrian black pine (*P. nigra* var. *nigra*), closely related to the black pine of Corsica and the south of Italy (*P. nigra maritima*). Of all European pines the Austrian is probably the toughest: it will transplant well even at ten feet tall; it will grow in clay (which most pines would shun); it doesn't mind lime in the soil. It has special value in growing on ground which has been

Above *The Bosnian pine grows in naked rock in the mountains of northern Italy and Yugoslavia. It thrives in drought and chalky soil; dense, dark but full of character. Its cones are blue.*

Left *The female flowers of Scots pine are dark red, in bunches of two to five on the end of vigorous new shoots: they take two years to ripen seed, in the meantime turning dark green. New needles are bright green but turn steel blue in a season.*

Left *Male flowers of Scots pine cover weaker shoots in May, while their needles are still emerging. Varieties of Scots pine include a very blue one, 'Argentea', and a small form, 'Aurea', which turns brilliant light gold in late winter.*

Tall, spreading Scots pines on the shores of Buttermere, Westmorland. Forms vary through its wide range; snowy Scandinavia has some very narrow trees. This is not a slow pine; two or three feet a year is normal growth for 20 or 30 years.

The stone (or umbrella) pine of Italy is one of the classic Mediterranean landscape trees. It has been widely planted for centuries. Here at Ravello near Naples it grows over the Church of the

Annunciation. Its shape is remarkably constant, in formal gardens and in the wild. A famous tree at Kew with four stems has an enormous table-like top. The large seeds of the stone pine are edible.

Below The mountain pine (P. mugo) is very hardy and tolerant of poor, limy soil, forming a dense, sagging bush or a low tree of many grey, curving stems with dark green mopheads.

Below right The Corsican pine is southern Europe's biggest. In southern Italy it has grown to 180 feet; a long-branched tree with dense, black foliage. An excellent windbreak.

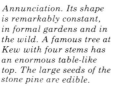

churned up by contractors, where the topsoil has been buried or pilfered. You see it in such unpromising places as Kennedy airport and the filling-stations on Italian autostradas, where its big bushy crown makes a quick sight-screen and windbreak. It is a rough and rather dark and dull tree, but I have one to break the northeast wind behind the house, and I wouldn't be without its long strong branches for all the flowering cherries in Japan. The Crimean variety of the same tree, *P. n. caramanica*, is even more heavily branched and more handsome.

Both the common black pines of Europe are trees of use rather than beauty. The Corsican version, which is also the Calabrian, is a useful forestry tree for poor sandy ground, quicker than the Austrian, narrower and less branchy. At home in Calabria it has grown as tall as 180 feet, and in Corsica to 150. The Italian navy used it for masts—but the French thought that too much resin made it 'as hard and translucid as horn'. The size for a Scots pine mast (which was the best), in the terms of the 18th-century mast-brokers of Riga on the Baltic, was over 18 inches diameter and about 80 feet long. Smaller trees were sold as spars or termed 'Norway masts'—since Norway had no big trees to sell.

Unquestionably the most distinctive of

European—perhaps of all—pines is the stone (or umbrella) pine of Italy (*P. pinea*). It was a godsend to the Roman and Renaissance gardeners, who were in the habit of confusing vegetation and architecture: it provided them with the perfect foil for the black pillars of their cypresses—a dense black canopy on a nice tidy pole. The pine tree's tendency to flatten out on top is epitomized in the stone pine: its twigs seem to multiply in the crown to leave no chink for light—while all the lower branches disappear without a trace. It is a reasonably hardy tree and could be grown in more northern gardens than it is. Indeed it should be, for there are few big trees which interfere less with what goes on underneath.

In the kind of country where the stone pine grows there is often another less shapely pine with grey-green needles and a crooked leaning trunk; the Aleppo pine (*P. halapensis*). Typical Aleppo pine country (the hills between Marseilles and St. Tropez are an example) is perilously inflammable. Old trees are rare.

In some ways the most useful pine, though not a glamorous tree, has been the pinaster (*P. pinaster*). The pinaster's place is the seashore. It was the means by which the biggest man-made forest on earth was developed on shifting sand in southwest France during the last century. In 1789 M. Bremontier started to plant 12,500 acres of sand-dunes, open to the Bay of Biscay, with pinaster and broom seed together. He laid brushwood over the top, and waited. The result was to fix what was thought unfixable. Three million acres were added to cultivation in the wake of his experiment. Today the pines of the Landes are still tapped for turpentine and used for coalmines and railways—but it is the third and fourth generations of them, and in the meanwhile their roots and needles have made the land so fertile that farms are taking it over.

One scrub pine of the Alps (*P. mugo*), not really a tree but a bush, is well-known to rock-gardeners in various forms. But there are two other European hill pines which are little known, and which are even tougher and less choosy about soil than the cembran. The Bosnian pine (*P. heldreichii*) is one we should see more of, especially in small gardens. It grows slightly quicker than the cembran, is certainly more attractive in youth, and has bright blue young cones into the bargain. The other, also from Yugoslavia, is the Macedonian pine (*P. peuce*). It makes a broad, dark, well-furnished spire under almost any conditions. At the Conifer Conference in 1972 it was described as 'undoubtedly the most useful five-needled pine for landscape planting'.

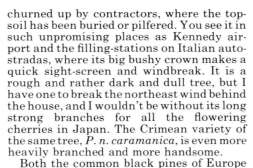

Above Pines can adapt to impossible conditions. Macedonian pine is here invading the upper slopes of Mount Olympus in Greece. The strata of the bare rock are plainly visible—yet the trees can find enough soil to grow.

The cembran pine is the typical tree of the Alps; a column with dense leaves from base to tip. Its female flowers are red among the yellow-green foliage. Being slow-growing and shapely this pine could be used more in formal garden layouts.

The Silver Firs of North America

To most of us the silver or true firs are probably the least familiar of the common members of the pine family. The word fir is loosely bandied about. It has been applied to every pointed tree; almost every evergreen. But the true firs are a conservative genus. They rarely dominate the scene; each species keeps to a relatively narrow range: many, indeed, are well on the way to extinction. Superficially they look very like spruces and moreover all firs tend to dress rather alike.

Yet as a sensuous experience the fir tree is hard to beat. There is, first of all, its smell. Firs have been called balsams in North America for a long time. They seem to exude the scented gum from every pore. Their barks carry fat blisters of sweet resin; their shoots are full of it; their leaves, crushed, coat your hands with the delicious glue. Every species has its own peculiar scent: of lemon, or turpentine, or tangerine.

The form of the tree expresses vigour under stern control. Within the strictest spire shape of any tree, the liveliest branching pattern darts into space. The view up the side of a fir tree is of thousands of little aircraft zooming out from the centre: shoots and side-shoots create a design of crystalline energy and rigour against the sky.

A juicy rigidity is equally well expressed in the needles: plump, leathery and firm, apparently adhering to the stout shoots with little round sucker pads. Dried branches of most firs keep their needles firmly on: spruce sprays disintegrate. There is rigidity in the way the branches thrust out horizontally in regular whorls, rarely drooping as spruce branches do. The cones stand up on the branch-ends, and, when they break up and scatter their seeds, leave their centre spikes standing there; spruce cones hang down, and fall off, leaving nothing on the tree. There is a simple test to tell whether a tree is a fir or a spruce. Pull a living needle off a twig. If it leaves a neat round mark, a slight dent, it is a fir. If a little piece of bark comes too, leaving a torn scar, it is a spruce. When spruce needles fall naturally, though, the minute pegs which form their bases stay on the twig, making it rough to the touch. Fir branches are pegless, and consequently smooth.

The cones of firs are the most attractive cones of all, but since they mostly grow high up on tall trees they are hard to collect. Some species have green or brown ones; most are dark and dusty purple, and so solid-looking that their habit of collapsing in your hands is quite disconcerting.

Botanists have named about 50 species of the firs. In a tribe as homogeneous as this there arise disagreements over what is a

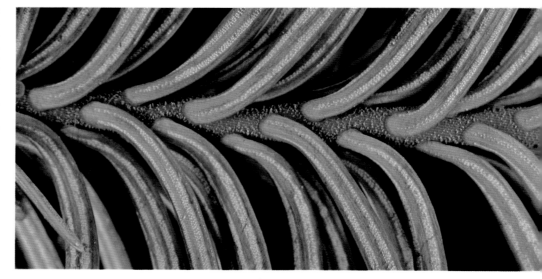

Fir needles are attached to the shoot by round sucker-like bases. This magnified (× 6) shot of the underside of a noble fir shoot shows the roundish needles, marked with white pores.

species and what a variety. Populations sometimes flow into each other with enough intermediate specimens to keep everyone guessing. All are limited to the cooler hills and mountain-ranges of the northern hemisphere. On the whole they are relatively self-indulgent trees, liking deep moist soil and not attempting the cold dry hills of the far north.

North America has nine of the firs; two in the east and seven in the west. The eastern species, the balsam fir of Canada and the Lake States (*Abies balsamea*), and Fraser's fir (*A. fraseri*), of the Great Smoky Mountains, are on an altogether smaller scale than the western ones, hence more often grown in gardens. The balsam certainly puts up with the worst climate of any of them, growing slowly to a maximum height of about 60 feet. It keeps a good shape, a dark spire complete with lower branches, even when crowding has killed the foliage. The scented needles are used to give the 'pine-woods' smell to soap and such–and in Quebec the resin from the trunk is collected as glue. 'Canada balsam' is the finest cement for glass in optical instruments. The wood, strange to say, is the one part which has no smell of resin.

It was, inevitably, David Douglas who discovered the biggest of all the firs, the grand fir (*A. grandis*). This tree of prodigious vigour thrives where the rainfall is highest–Vancouver Island has grand firs

Left *The female flowers standing upright on the branches of the alpine fir are dull crimson. All the silver or true firs have upright cones, contrasted with the spruces, whose cones hang down.*

Above *Alpine fir grows high in the mountains of the Olympic Peninsula of Washington. It is sculpted by the snow; where the snow lies round the base thousands of short shoots make a broad skirt.*

Left *New growth on the flat, comb-like shoots of the grand fir. On lower branches, as here, the long needles grow in even rows on either side. Higher up the tree they curl upwards.*
Below left *Grand fir, the biggest of its genus, reaches 300 feet on the coastal plain of the Pacific northwest.*

Below *Red fir growing in the Sierra Nevada of California. Most firs have stronger, more horizontal or upswept branches than spruces. The blackish trunk of the trees on the left is typical of red fir. The tree on the right is a Balfour pine.*

Cones of noble fir cluster round the top of the tree. Since fir cones fall to pieces on the tree, leaving only their centre spike standing, they are rarely seen complete. These are typical in being barrel-like with overlapping scales and extruding bracts.

nearly 300 feet high. But even more startling is its speed. Atlantic rain apparently suits it as well as Pacific, or better: trees in Scotland have grown 160 feet in 50 years. Even in drier areas it is a quick grower.

There is a childish simplicity about its design. The leaves are straight, parallel-sided, of shiny mid-green, neither dark nor light. They are set each side of the twig in flat rows, as straightforward as the teeth of a comb. Their undersides have two pale blue lines – but these you rarely see; the branches hang flat and low.

Where it stands above its fellows, exposed to the wind, the grand fir often loses its top. But an accident like this is only an excuse for another display of strength; three or four new tops will grow as tall as the first, creating a massive square head.

The red silver fir (*A. amabilis*) occupies ground only slightly higher; it too likes to have its roots in deep soil, to have a long growing season and an equable climate.

But its name is for beauty rather than size or speed. Its Latin name translates literally as lovely fir. Thick lustrous leaves set off its pale and smooth grey trunk blotched with white stains of resin. Though a foothill tree, it bears the pointed crown which is usually the mark of the snow-covered heights.

The red fir (*A. magnifica*) and the noble fir (*A. procera*) keep the middle altitudes of the Cascades and the Sierras from Canada to southern California. Noble fir has the north of the territory and red the south. In the middle is the Shasta fir of Mount Shasta, a variety of the red.

There is no striking difference between these trees. The noble fir has the biggest cones of any, and bears them most freely. Its needles are shorter, more crowded, with grooved upper-sides (which red firs never have). But their general appearance is the same: of immense vigour somehow restrained within a narrow space, as if there were a glass funnel inverted over the tree.

In western gardens both do equally well; in exceptional eastern gardens fairly well; in European gardens the noble fir, on the whole, rather better. In nature it is the bigger tree – to nearly 250 feet.

One of the mountain firs, oddly enough, is the most cultivated in gardens. The Colorado white fir (*A. concolor*) seems to be the most adaptable to conditions in the east and in Europe. Its natural range is enormous; it grows all the way from New Mexico to Oregon, where its variety Low's silver fir (*A. c. lowiana*) merges with grand fir. The tendency of its long needles towards blue-green has produced garden cultivars in shades of piercing silver-blue: 'Candicans' and 'Violacea' are two of the best known. The alpine fir (*A. lasiocarpa*) has a similar, rather more northerly, range, yet its garden performance has not been good. Its sub-species, the cork fir (*A. l. arizonica*), from the southernmost part of its range, is healthier, and also prettier, with silvery-blue needles.

The Santa Lucia fir (*A. bracteata*) is the odd one out. It is a rare tree, not often cultivated and found naturally only in canyons in the Santa Lucia mountains, behind Monterey and Big Sur overlooking the Pacific. To me it is the most beautiful and memorable of all firs.

Where the others have plump needles with blunt ends, crowding and curling along the shoots, Santa Lucia's needles are long, slim, straight and hard, brilliant green with two white lines underneath ending in a sharp point. They fan out below the shoot; on top they surge forward to the tip where, in place of a fat, round, resinous bud, there is an elegant parcel of folded parchment.

The cone is equally eccentric: a fat little brown barrel decorated with what look like long green feelers.

Best of all, though, is the Santa Lucia's shape: a sharp, broad-based spire, terraced with branches which dip in the middle under the weight of drooping branchlets, and turn up at the end like a spaniel's tail.

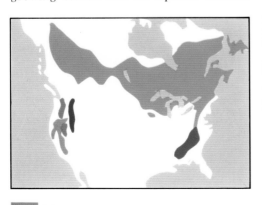

- Balsam
- Fraser
- Red
- Shasta
- Noble

- Alpine
- Grand
- Santa Lucia
- Cork

- Red silver
- Colorado white
- Low's silver

The Silver Firs of Europe and Asia

Decorative, strong-growing species of fir abound in Asia, but not all of them have been properly tried out in the western world. Since most of them are too big for widespread garden use, and forestry prefers local kinds, they remain in a quite unwarranted obscurity. Even among Europe's three native firs only one, the common silver fir, has been planted widely. The Spanish and Greek firs are acknowledged handsome and hardy; yet we are only just beginning to put them to use.

The silver fir of Europe (*A. alba*) was for many millennia the second tallest European tree. In Britain it was the tallest until its reign was brought to an end (at 180 feet) by a Douglas fir in 1955. From its natural home in the mountains in a band stretching from the Pyrenees through Burgundy and the Vosges as far as Poland it was introduced as a forestry tree throughout Europe. It reached Britain in 1603 and grew so big that it was forgiven its susceptibility to spring frosts. Until the northwest American coni-

fers came on the scene more than 200 years later it had no competition for speed of growth and eventual height. Even then it was a relentless aphid which decided the question in favour of the newer exotics. None of the first trees survive, but there are some 17th-century specimens still left in Scotland. They tend, perhaps because of frost damage, to make big-branched trees rather than spires: huge, open-headed, grey-barked, dark-foliaged constructions of no special elegance or beauty. They are at their best when, as younger trees, their bark is as silvery as a beech's.

Two firs which are very much alike, perhaps survivors of the same race long decimated by the Ice Ages, have taken up their residence at the extreme corners of southern Europe, *A. cephalonica* in Greece and *A. pinsapo* in the mountains behind the Costa del Sol in southern Spain. This Mediterranean strain gives blue-grey trees with stiff, hard leaves emerging hedgehog-like from

all round the shoot; uncomfortable to handle. *A. numidica* is another, from Algeria—a rather denser and less prickly tree. Where the Spanish and Greek firs are particularly worth planting is in chalky, well-drained districts where other firs have reservations about growing. They are not fast, but they have character from the start.

Caucasian trees in general have a fine reputation. The Caucasus mountains lie on the same latitude as northern California (and Tasmania, another rich plant-kingdom, in the southern hemisphere). With the Black Sea on one side and the Caspian on the other, with Russia to the north and Persia to the south, they are one of the great meeting places of weather-systems; and also of genetic contributions. Mount Ararat lies just to the south. One might easily fancy the garden of Eden was in these hills—in which case the Caucasian fir (*A. nordmanniana*) would have been one of its more distinguished decorations.

A young plant of the Caucasian fir is the most delectable of evergreens. You look down on dense tiers of long, shiny, deep green needles. Underneath they have two icy stripes marking the pores. The tree is always one of the happiest, best-fed looking of the firs, right into its gianthood when its long branches, still dense and shining, cascade in rich tiers to the ground.

The supply of beautiful firs from farther east, from the Himalayas, China, Korea and Japan is almost overwhelming. Probably the best known of them at the moment is the Korean fir (*A. koreana*) which is obliging enough to cone prolifically at eye-level. The ripe cones remind me of those decadent displays of Fabergé imitating confectionery in ivory and rubies, or scrambled eggs in amber and gold; they are plump, and piercing purple, with brown contour-lines and spangles of translucent resin—and like presents in dreams they crumble when you pick them up.

Two Japanese firs, the Nikko (*A. homo-*

Above *Nikko firs on Hokkaido, the northern island of Japan. The Nikko makes a very large, hardy tree with a pale and faintly pink bark, turning an attractive purplish grey-brown with age.*

Above *Forrest's fir from southwest China is one of the handsomest. Its bright green leaves grow stiffly all round the shoot and its flowers and cones are blue. The buds are just bursting and the male flowers are prominent in this photograph.*

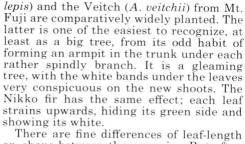

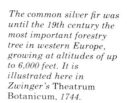

lepis) and the Veitch (*A. veitchii*) from Mt. Fuji are comparatively widely planted. The latter is one of the easiest to recognize, at least as a big tree, from its odd habit of forming an armpit in the trunk under each rather spindly branch. It is a gleaming tree, with the white bands under the leaves very conspicuous on the new shoots. The Nikko fir has the same effect; each leaf strains upwards, hiding its green side and showing its white.

There are fine differences of leaf-length or -shape between these species. But often the most noticeable feature is the colour of the new shoot within the covering of leaves. The Veitch fir has brown shoots, the Nikko fir white; a third Japanese species, Maries' fir (*A. mariesii*), has almost red shoots and its winter buds are coated with resin.

A short list of the best Chinese firs would certainly include George Forrest's variety of the fir named after the Abbé Delavay, who virtually initiated botanizing in west-central China. *A. delavayi* var. *forrestii* (reclassified *A. forrestii*) sums up for me the juicy feeling of well-being which makes the firs such satisfying trees. My notes here get as far away from objectivity as they do at the end of a good wine-tasting: 'thick squirrel-brown shoots: needles crowding all round, brilliant white beneath; buds are red globes, shiny and succulent with resin; very bunchy and rich-looking'.

Another on the list would be *A. fargesii*, which was brought back by E. H. Wilson from the same area. Another would be the Manchurian version of the Nikko, *A. holophylla*, which Alan Mitchell at the 1972 Conifer Conference singled out as a good doer.

One couldn't close the list without at least one of the Himalayan firs. *A. spectabilis* (a tree very like the *A. delavayi* I have described) grows on the highest Himalayan slopes and *A. pindrow* on lower ground. *A. pindrow* (the west Himalayan fir) has distinct long thin needles dividing at the end into two tiny spikes.

The Douglas Fir

A tree with the forester's idea of perfect form: a Douglas fir, nearly 200 feet high and five feet thick at the base, tapering gradually with no branches at all for the first 100 feet.

The bark of an old Douglas fir is deeply creviced and richly brown. This tree in the Mount Rainier National Park in Washington is in typical Douglas country. This tree would be about 400 years old.

The soft green foliage of Douglas fir with an unripe cone showing the unique trident-shaped bracts between the scales. For forestry purposes the exact provenance of the seed is vitally important. It decides the length of the tree's growing season.

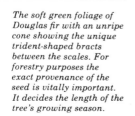

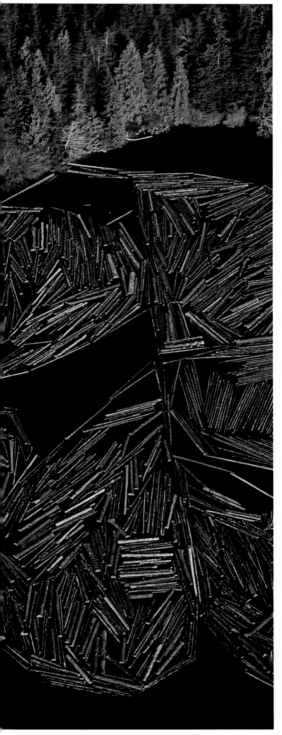

Rafts of Douglas fir logs in an inlet in the coast of British Columbia. Trees lining the shore are Sitka spruce, more resistant than Douglas to salt and flooding.

With the greatest respect to the giant sequoias, the Douglas fir (*Pseudotsuga menziesii*) can be fairly called the world's biggest *beautiful* tree. There is no suggestion of the amazing survival from another era about the Douglas; it is in the prime of life, with a natural range all the way from Canada to Mexico – as well as close relations in China and Japan.

The Douglas is alone in its botanical compartment. It is not a silver fir. Its cones hang down, and remain in one piece. It is not a spruce either. Its leaves have tiny stalks and suckers like the fir's. It deserves better from botanists, however, than the Latin name they gave it. For *Pseudotsuga* means 'false hemlock'. The 'pseudo', with its implication of moral turpitude, I (on its behalf) most categorically refute. It was never a hemlock, and it never pretended to be.

Happily the rest of the Douglas's nomenclature celebrates the two deserving explorers who found it and introduced it to cultivation. Menzies, sailing with Vancouver's expedition in 1791, was the first. David Douglas, the tireless envoy of the London Horticultural Society, sent home the seeds in 1827. Some trees planted in 1828 still stand in Britain today.

The forest that Douglas found is also still unplundered in a few spots in the northwest. Mount Rainier National Park is one. Penetrating even 100 yards into a stand of old growth Douglas fir makes it hard to believe that this is the country Douglas crossed and recrossed, sometimes with Indian guides, often on his own. Every few yards a fallen log the size of a truck stops your progress. Great rotting snags tower above the brilliant emerald of the mounting young trees; Douglas and red silver fir, western red cedar, red alder. Rivers, of course, were the only way of covering long distances. But to portage through these woods . . . !

The seeds from which those first cultivated Douglases grew crossed the continent in this way. The cones were entrusted to the Hudson's Bay Company's 'express' – an annual expedition of a score of *voyageurs* who paddled and clambered 2,000 miles from Hudson Bay to the mouth of the Columbia River to collect pelts.

The Douglas is a relatively easy tree to recognize. The clearest indicators are the buds at the ends of the twigs, which are reddish-brown and pointed, very much like rather fat beech buds. If the tree has cones, they are unlike any others: egg-shaped, hanging, with three little paler points, an upside-down trident, extruding from beneath each dark-brown scale. The bark of a big Douglas is unmistakable: immensely craggy and rutted with dark corky cracks.

The hang of the whole tree is distinctive too: the foliage is dense and dark and soft, weighing down the side-shoots in swags below the branches; eventually weighing down the longest branches until they dip to the ground.

In the hills of the northwest occasional trees are so pendulous that they could, at a distance, be Brewer's spruce. Like all the western trees, though, they become stiffer, narrower and paler as they go south and higher into the mountains. The Rocky Mountain form of Douglas fir has the sub-specific name 'Glauca' – though it is by no means bright blue – and is hardy where the big vigorous green tree is not (in northern New England for instance). 'Glauca' is also happier on chalk or lime. Ordinary Douglas will grow in a limy soil but, at least in my garden, turns yellow-green. When I first saw it I thought it was a golden cultivar.

Given reasonably good soil the Douglas is one of the best timber trees on earth. It makes wood like good quality pine at a prodigious rate. A tree planted 80 years ago is now, at 175 feet, one of the tallest trees in Britain. It stands by a woodland pool on the Duke of Atholl's estate in Dunkeld in Scotland. But Scotland has a long way to go. The tallest sequoia is 20 feet taller than this tree and its reflection added together.

A Douglas fir cone which has released its seed. Male flowers crowd the branch ends except for the tips where the female flowers cluster round the buds. Male and female flowers ripen at different times so that the tree will not pollinate itself.

David Douglas, the greatest of all botanical explorers, who introduced the Douglas fir to cultivation from the wilds of the Pacific northwest.

His numerous other finds include the sugar pine, whose huge cones reminded Douglas of sugar loafs in a grocer's shop.

The Spruces of North America

The spruces remind one more than any other conifer that they evolved in the age of reptiles. Those thin unwavering shoots groping at the sky are like tentacles. Few spruces, indeed, are very graceful. They seem to lack the plump poise of the firs, their nearest relatives. They are uncomfortable trees; their needles hard and spiny, their twigs rough, the bark thin and scaly. With age they become gaunt and gappy, their branches skeletons of corroded old twigs. The beauty of their new shoots is out of reach as they grow old. You have to be a forester to appreciate the sturdy pole which holds the tattered top against the sky.

There are about 40 species of spruce, as there are of silver fir. The spruces, on the other hand, are more varied than the firs in their habit, their colour and manner of growth. They contain in their number a handful of trees more strikingly ornamental than any other conifers–so ornamental, in fact, that it is hard to know whether to think of them as *haute couture* or Carnaby Street.

The spruces far outnumber the firs. From the mountains of the south, where the two share the same tastes and habits, the spruces fan out northwards into much colder, wetter country. The tree-map of the great land-masses of the north, Siberia, Canada and Alaska, shows the astonishing hardiness of the race.

Three spruces, the red (*Picea rubens*), the black (*P. mariana*) and the white (*P. glauca*), grow in the far north. Their range extends south to the Great Lakes–the red as far as the mountain tops of the Great Smokies. Their importance lies in their wood, which makes some of the best paper pulp. As

Above *The shoot of a Sitka spruce, magnified five times, shows the woody pegs at the base of the flattened needles and the plaited effect* *of the ribbed shoot itself. The leaves are dark green above; this shot from below shows the breathing pores, white with a waxy coating.*

Left *Ripe cones of Sitka spruce. Each scale has opened and released a seed. The cones of all spruces hang from the upper branches of a tree and fall in one piece shortly after they have dropped their seeds.*

Above *Sitka spruce from the coastline of British Columbia has become one of Europe's most important forestry trees. This young plantation is in Bavaria. Snow provides useful protection from drying winds.*

ornamental trees they are only planted where nothing else will grow. But the spruces have the peculiarity, much more than the firs, of producing odd branch 'sports' of dwarf form or unusual colour—and the northern spruces are no exception. *P. glauca albertiana* 'Conica', a bright green bushy form of the white spruce which was found in the Rockies in Alberta, is one of the best-known garden conifers—though bearing little resemblance to its parents. *P. mariana* 'Doumetii' is a similar production of the black spruce.

The biggest member of the spruce family (*P. sitchensis*) comes from the land of giants—the northwest. It takes its name from Sitka, the old Russian capital of Alaska on Baranof Island off the southeast Alaskan coast. Along the fog-bound straits and inlets there, where whales and log-rafts loom up intermittently out of the gloom, the spruces grow trunk to trunk to the water's edge. Melancholy ramrods of trees almost 300 feet high are found, their moss-grown bases splaying out as though to get a purchase in the saturated soil.

Farther south, on the Oregon coast, the Sitka is the first tree to front the sea-wind on crags and promontories above a beach buried deep in jetsam lumber. The grey water-worn snags below, the grey wind-torn branches above, epitomize the staying-power of the spruce. The same qualities have made it one of the most-planted forest trees in northern Europe in this century. One of Douglas's originals still stands in Ireland, 160 feet high. During its life-time some 2,000,000 acres of swampy exposed ground have been made productive by its kin.

It is barely 100 miles from the coast where Sitka grows to the heights of the Siskiyou mountains. But the spruce of the Siskiyous belongs to a different world. Brewer's spruce, or the weeping spruce (*P. breweriana*), is certainly the most beautiful tree of its race—possibly the most beautiful of all conifers. Its mountain home, above the valley where the world's biggest pine trees grow, is a garden of rare and graceful plants: the Lawson cypress is wild here, growing with pendulous western hemlock and Douglas fir, tufted incense cedar, tangerine-scented white fir, brilliant-leafed dogwood and bigleaf maple, and neat, dark-green bulwarks of Sadler oak. The weeping spruce, though, would stand out in any company. Its arching branches carrying long shawls of green-black lace hold arcs of sunlight or snow, receding tiers in different angles of profile; an exquisitely satisfying design.

But whereas Lawson cypress, equally limited in nature, has been prolifically fast and easy in cultivation, Brewer's spruce needs wooing. It is slow to start, demands moisture (in the air as well as in the ground) and takes several years before its weeping habit really shows. Branch cuttings weep sooner, but need staking to develop a leading shoot. In the eastern States it rarely does well: in Europe, on the other hand, there are superb examples. One in the British National Arboretum at Westonbirt has grown to 40 feet in 35 years. It is a tree to try, and to keep trying.

There could not be a greater contrast than the blue spruce of Colorado (*P. pungens*). High altitude and bright light give the species its stiff habit of growth, the grey-blue cast in its leaves. But the cultivars a rejoicing nursery trade has found are surely bluer and stiffer than God ever intended. They include the most piercingly ice-blue of all plants. Various forms of the cultivar 'Glauca', notably 'Koster' and 'Moerheim', have a totally artificial air: they rise in stiffly perfect terraces of ice to a stiffly perfect pinnacle. They are perhaps the hardest of all plants to place successfully in a garden; and it is worth remembering that they are best in youth; gaps and dead twigs show up all too clearly on a pale ground.

The answer is to compromise, and plant the much less common, softer and more graceful Engelmann spruce (*P. engelmannii*). The 'Glauca' version of this is also very pale blue. But in place of the stiff icy terraces it has long furry tails for shoots; the needles run along the shoots towards the tip. The species is an important timber tree of the Rockies, with a more northerly range than the Colorado blue spruce.

Above and left *The handsomest of the spruces; Brewer's weeping spruce from the Siskiyou mountains in western Oregon. It is still rare in gardens, taking years to establish its weeping habit. Mature trees are highly prized.*

New growth on black spruce from the northeastern States. All spruces look best in the spring when the soft young shoots in paler colours light up the tree. The crushed foliage of the black spruce is strongly scented of balsam.

A stand of Engelmann spruce, a native of the western States, ranging from Alberta to New Mexico. In the wild Engelmann can reach 150 feet; in cultivation it tends to make a much smaller tree with a narrow, pointed crown.

The Spruces of Europe and Asia

Half of all the species of spruce are natives of China. We have two or three good ones from Japan and the Himalayas. As usual, Europe's contribution in numbers is minimal—only two species. On the other hand they are probably the two most important of all the spruces to the gardener.

The Norway spruce (*P. abies*) is Europe's tallest native tree: 200 feet is within its reach. It was the first of the pointed trees to re-enter Britain, whence the Ice Ages had expelled it. As long ago as 1500 it was planted and admired. As the source of much of Britain's light lumber (deal, as we call it) which was bought in the Baltic, it also

Left and above *Serbian spruce is shapely, quick-growing and adaptable; one of the best garden conifers. It grows with the same narrow spire-shape in the wild (above) in Yugoslavia.*

Above *The Himalayan weeping spruce growing in the foothills of the Himalayas in Kashmir. In cultivation it is often more distinctly weeping than these wild trees. It has reached 124 feet in Scotland.*

brought the word spruce into the English language: it derives from Pruce, the old English name for the Kingdom of Prussia. Today in most of northern Europe it is, at any time of year, 'the Christmas tree'.

From the forestry point of view it has one advantage over the faster-growing Sitka: it is frost-hardy from the start. There are cold areas where sapling Sitka suffers. For the gardener its importance lies in its profusion of off-beat cultivars. It comes in drooping, upright, golden, dwarf, bush, prostrate, tabular, globular, congested and exploded forms. A few of them are shown on pages 118–19. They could afford the subject of a whole collection in themselves.

More beautiful and useful in its normal form, however, is the Serbian spruce (*P. omorika*) from the mountains of eastern Yugoslavia. There are no difficulties with limy soil, or indeed soil of any kind, with this adaptable tree. Moreover, it can manage in city air. It grows tall (but not too tall), stays slim (but is satisfyingly solid at the bottom), forms a strong but graceful pattern with its short arching branches. It flatters buildings by introducing a harmony and rhythm which they often lack. Most important of all, it grows fast; two or three feet a year to about 50 feet. In fact it is hard to think of anything else you could stand on a ten-foot square base which would do the environment so much good.

The oriental spruce (*P. orientalis*) is not quite as exotic as it sounds: it comes from nearest Asia; from the Caucasus mountains—the home of a number of our best garden trees. One can't be dramatic about the oriental spruce: its strength is simply in its neatness. It has short needles which sit tidily on its twigs; a model of grooming. For all that, it makes a big tree, and a handsome one. It also has a cultivar, 'Aurea', which greets the spring with startling creamy-white (instead of green) new shoots. A bit gimmicky, but effective none the less.

None of the far-eastern spruces can be reckoned essential garden material, like the above. Encomiums have been lavished on one or two, particularly the Sargent spruce (*P. brachytyla*), from western China. The dragon spruce, which has been called China's version of the Norway spruce, is one of the best known, valuable for its densely needled, dark and stolid appearance. Its Latin name, *asperata*, celebrates the way it identifies itself to anyone who is rash enough to stroke its branches: a file is less asperate.

The dragon's bark is its bite, but beware of the tiger-tail's needles. The Japanese tiger tail, *P. torano*, with creamy-buff shoots and chestnut red buds, has the sturdiest leaves of

all spruces. Stout, stiff and extremely sharp, its shoots bristle with arms like those of medieval Japanese knights.

Of the other Chinese spruces one very pretty one is well known for its flowers—indeed it is probably the only conifer which is planted primarily for that reason. The Likiang spruce (*P. likiangensis*), from Yunnan in southwest China, becomes spectacularly uxorious in the spring, loading its branches with crimson male and bright red female flowers, the females (the cones-to-be) standing up boldly at the tips of the branches until pregnancy weighs them into the correct spruce position, dangling down. It is

Above *The dull green of the Norway spruce is enlivened in May with the bright yellow-green of the new shoots. They decorate the tree for about two months before darkening.*

Top *Cones of the Norway spruce hang from the tips of the upper branches. They have leathery scales and are twice the size of the cones of the Sitka spruce, the other widely-planted forestry species.*

fair to add that this performance only starts
when the tree is 25 or 30 years old.

Of all the Asiatic spruces possibly the
best known is the Himalayan weeping
spruce (*P. smithiana*). Were it not for the
existence of Brewer's this would be a re-
spectable entry as *the* weeping spruce. As it
is, this much bigger (to 118 feet in the south
of England), broader, less densely furnished
tree, tending indeed to become decidedly
skeletal with age, must take second place.
It may be the answer in places like New
England, where Brewer's is unhappy. But,
as a young tree, it has trouble with late
spring frosts.

Norway spruce is
Europe's tallest native
tree, reaching about 200
feet. Here it is growing in
the Italian Tyrol, in the
Alpine foothills.

The Hemlocks

One or other of the hemlocks (*Tsuga*) is a familiar sight from Alabama to Nova Scotia, and from San Francisco to Alaska; between them the four local species cover most of eastern America and most of the west coast. In Europe, on the contrary, it is a surprise to most people that there is such a tree at all. (If hemlock means anything to them it is the waterside weed which Socrates is supposed to have taken as poison.) The hemlock is one of the few important races of conifer which occur in America and Asia but have no representative in Europe; it has scarcely been planted outside its native habitat – very much to Europe's loss.

In appearance the hemlocks (all except one) come somewhere between a spruce and a yew. They are botanically close to the spruces; the yew likeness lies in their flat, blunt-ended, relatively broad needles. The hallmark of the hemlock, however, lies in its manner of growth. Of all the needle trees it is perhaps the most graceful in texture and

Above *The western hemlock, biggest and best of its race, grows with Douglas fir in the Pacific northwest. Open-grown it makes a broad pyramid with a characteristic drooping leading shoot.*

Left *Hemlock foliage is soft and fine, with the needles arranged in two ranks on the shoots. Shelter and moisture are essential for its lush growth.*

The mountain hemlock; an old tree, its top gone, at Snow Lake, 4,000 feet up in the Cascade Mountains of Washington.

Eastern hemlock is often a several-stemmed, spreading tree. Its weeping form is small and slow-growing; one of the best conifers of this shape. The ordinary variety makes dense and hardy hedges, much used in New England.

detail. Without drooping or dangling it suggests elegant repose.

You need to look no further than its leading shoot to see the hemlock's philosophy. It nods in a sleepy curve. Instead of neat ranks, or jostling crowds, its needles look faintly dishevelled. The side ones are longer than the top ones, and no two exactly agree on the direction to go. But they are a lovely soft green on top, marked white underneath, and dense enough to create an almost furry appearance.

The important differences between the hemlocks are questions of habit and habitat rather than twigs and leaves. They all answer the description above except the mountain hemlock of the Pacific northwest (*T. mertensiana*), whose needles surround each shoot, pointing onwards and outwards. Soft hemlock-green, in this case, is also overlaid with the bloomy grey cast typical of the mountain-tree – a subtle and telling colour in the garden.

The familiar pattern repeats itself: the eastern hemlock is the hardy one, usually shorter in stature. The western one (*T. heterophylla*) is the giant, the spoilt child of moist ferny litter, tall shelter and perpetual mist. Where it succeeds (and the moisture and shelter are both important) it can be breathtakingly graceful. Its long branches form loose layers, softer and more sloping than those of a cedar but almost as broad and architectural. It keeps a tall, narrow crown with a nodding shoot even as a tree 140 feet high. What clinches it for me is the foliage – a sort of subdued brilliant green . . . This is the one for the two-acre lawn.

The eastern hemlock (*T. canadensis*) very often grows up with several leading shoots, to make a spreading shape more like a typical broadleaf parkland tree. Its foliage has an odd feature in a line of little blunt needles lying upside down, with their white undersides showing along the top of the shoot. Eastern American gardeners have

found it so adaptable that they think of it more as raw material for shaping (particularly into a hedge) than as a tree with ideas of its own. Among its own ideas (it has almost as many as the Norway spruce) are gold, upright and dwarf versions, and an extremely effective weeping one – perhaps the best low evergreen weeper for the lawn. The maximum height of this form (*T. canadensis* 'Pendula') is nine or ten feet, but its spread might be 20 or 30.

The Carolina hemlock (*T. caroliniana*) is to all intents a local form of the eastern one. If there is any advantage in either of the two Japanese hemlocks (*T. diversifolia* and *T. sieboldii*) it is only a still-denser supply of needles. The sole discouragement from growing any of this graceful group is their distaste for limy soil, which is strong in the western, the Japanese and the Carolina, and less so in the mountain hemlock. The obliging eastern one hardly seems to be bothered by lime at all.

At Crater Lake in Oregon. mountain hemlocks at higher altitudes have the short branches and narrow profile of trees accustomed to long months of snow. Their leaves have a grey-blue sheen like most high-altitude conifers, but their nodding tops proclaim them hemlock.

Male flowers of western hemlock shedding pollen. The short leaves are blunt, with little notches in the tips. Underneath they are marked with two broad white lines where waxy resin accumulates round the breathing pores.

Unripe cones forming from the female flowers of western hemlock. They ripen dark brown but remain only an inch long. Hemlock seeds germinate freely even in the shade of big trees.

The True Cedars

The cedar of Lebanon at Wilton House in Wiltshire is typical of the cedar's long association with noble country-house architecture. This tree, 85 feet high and 28 feet in girth, was probably planted in the 18th century. Many of them lose their high dome and become flat-topped.

The layman uses the name cedar for any tree with dark, spice-scented timber. Thus America has the incense, the western red, the eastern red, the Alaskan yellow and the Port Orford cedar; Japan the plume cedar and the Hiba cedar. The botanist uses much stricter rules and recognizes only four, none of them from America (or the Far East) and none of them remotely like the American 'cedars'. For once I would say (as a committed layman) that the botanist is right.

There is nothing like the true cedars in the whole coniferous kingdom. Not even the pines produce a tree of such majestic architecture. Partly no doubt because of their biblical background–they are the trees most mentioned in the Bible, and always as an image for fruitfulness and strength–Europeans regard them with something approaching awe. Countless cedars in English churchyards and on the lawns of country houses are celebrated in village lore as having come back with the Crusaders. Villagers' geography, in this case, is better than their history. Few of the giant trees which cut such a timeless figure are more than 150 years old. On the other hand crusading country is just where they do come from.

Three of the four species of cedar come from the shores of the Mediterranean; the fourth comes from the western Himalayas. The cedar of Lebanon (*Cedrus libani*) is the most celebrated and by far the oldest in cultivation. The remaining grove of ancient trees on the slopes of Mount Lebanon (at 6,200 feet–4,000 feet below the summit) has been a place of pilgrimage for centuries; from all accounts the cedars have remained exactly the same since travellers began writing about them. There are roughly 400 of them, the biggest 48 feet in girth and calculated (by guesswork) to be about 2,500 years old. The biggest natural woods of Lebanon cedar surviving are in the Taurus mountains in southeastern Turkey.

A grove of the great cedars from which King Solomon is said to have built his temple still stands on the slopes of Mount Lebanon, 4,000 feet below the 10,000 foot summit. In biblical times the cedar stood as a symbol for everything fertile and abundant. Its wood was highly prized for its strength, colour and scent.

The young female cones of the cedar of Lebanon are surrounded by clusters of protecting needles. The white, waxy lines of pores on the dark yellow-green needles are clearly seen in this picture.

The blue Atlas cedar is the most popular cedar and one of the most popular of all conifers today; the picture shows a garden version of the tree from the Atlas mountains of Morocco. The first tree to be introduced to Britain, planted by Lord Somers in Herefordshire on the Welsh border in 1845, is still healthy.

The great Sir Joseph Hooker, incidentally, poured cold water on the idea that Solomon's temple was built of these trees. In his view builders' merchants of Solomon's day were no better botanists than they are nowadays: the wood they called cedar was probably a sort of juniper.

Despite such recollections of antiquity it is still remarkable that the first cedar of Lebanon to be planted in Britain, the forerunner of a great revolution in English gardens, is alive today. It is in the rectory garden at Childrey in the Thames valley, planted there by Dr. Pocock, the rector, in 1646, soon after his retirement as the Embassy chaplain in Constantinople. Today its trunk is 25 feet in girth, whereas the next oldest tree of known date, at Biel near Edinburgh, measured 23 feet in 1967.

John Evelyn did his best to popularize the cedar of Lebanon in the 1670s, but it was not until the earliest trees started to bear cones that they could be planted on a massive scale. In the mid-18th century they became a craze. The Duke of Richmond planted 1,000 at Goodwood in 1761. The trees on the lawn at Wilton House, illustrated on the left, belong to this era. They were the only exotic trees which Capability Brown used in his landscapes, and they continued to be planted in great numbers until the 1830s, when the new giants from Douglas's travels began to take their place.

The cedars, in fact, are not nearly so slow-growing as their stateliness might suggest; they can reach 50 feet in 30 years in good conditions, and grow stout and impressive in an equivalently short time. The tallest in Britain, at Petworth in Sussex, is 132 feet. Not until they are getting on in years, though, do they strike their splendid attitudes, forming black plateaux low over the lawn, at rooftop height, and again, high above pediment and belfry, spreading a black table in the sky.

The Atlas cedar (*C. l.* spp. *atlantica*) does not plant them. One sees their desperate pale-blue gestures over every little garden wall in some parts of France–particularly the southwest. It is hard to think of any tree less suitable for a small space: colossal spread is its very essence. And heaven knows how you would fell it in a back-yard.

The Deodar (*C. deodara*) is better as a small tree. With longer needles in a quieter colour, a lovely soft silver-green, it nods and droops in delicate attitudes. It tends to maintain its basic conical shape into maturity, rather than rearing all its upper branches together to a high plateau. In its native Himalayas it makes what must be some of the world's loveliest forests.

The fourth true cedar comes from Cyprus. Compared with the others it is unspectacular–and consequently a rarity in cultivation. It grows slowly to about half the size of a Lebanon cedar, and is notable only for its much shorter leaves–whence its Latin name, *C. libani* spp. *brevifolia*.

The weeping form of the blue Atlantic cedar is the most spectacular of all weeping conifers–and also one of the rarest; a difficult tree to grow.

Above right The Deodar is very beautiful as a young tree; the softest in shape and colour of the cedars. This adult tree is at Nymans, Sussex.

have quite the same classical education as the cedar of Lebanon. Its arrival, from the Atlas mountains of Morocco, was not until 1839. A forest of it was planted in 1862 on Mont Ventoux in Provence–a magnificent sight today. It is a bold man, however, who claims to be able to tell the difference between the Lebanon and the Atlas. The only certain way is with a magnifying glass: the Atlas' needles have a minute translucent spine at the tip.

The ordinary green Atlas cedar is not planted nearly so much as the variety 'Glauca', the blue one which is said to be the most popular of all ornamental conifers today. I have not actually seen one in a window box, but it is remarkable where people do

The growing stem of many germinating conifers lifts the seed above the ground. Here the seed-leaves of a cedar are pulling themselves free of the husk and are expanding to begin photosynthesis.

Right *Mature cones of the blue Atlas cedar are plump and pink-brown, sitting up like over-fed skittles on the boughs of brush-like blue foliage.*

Above *A very different version of an adult Deodar cedar growing at Child Okeford in Dorset. This tree has grown tall and open–more like the Deodar in its native Himalayas.*

The Larches

The larches make their mark in autumn when they turn from the anonymity of forest green to warm gold. Here in the Pacific northwest the western larch, the tallest and narrowest of the larches, grows with the alpine silver fir.

Of all the conifers which are widely planted as forest trees the larches make the prettiest woods. It must be because they celebrate the seasons that we find them so friendly and amenable. The advantages of evergreenery are obvious enough – yet we love the larches for being different: for flushing feathery green in April; for glowing gold in November; even for spending the winter as a tangle of bare black rigging, when their colleagues are demonstrating the superiority of their leathery leaves.

Their leaf-dropping lets in the light so that a rich undergrowth of shrub and herb and creature can flourish, and contributes year by year to the fertility of the forest. Yet it by no means detracts from their vigour, as you might think it would do. The larch is one of the fastest-growing of all trees; certainly the fastest to make strong and heavy wood with almost oak-like qualities.

Close to, the larch's summer rig is remarkably like the cedar's. They are clearly the closest kin, with their leaves in little rosettes like those of no other tree. The larch bears no resemblance at all to the two other deciduous conifers, the swamp cypress and the dawn redwood; the confusion comes in telling larch from larch.

North America has three larches, two of them excellent trees. Both Russia and China have two species – of which one forms the world's northernmost forest, on the latitude of the northernmost point of Alaska. The Himalayas, Japan and Europe have one species each. Possibly more important than any of the species, however, is a hybrid, the fruit of a union romantically formed at a ducal seat in the highlands of Scotland.

The family of the Dukes of Atholl has had trees in the blood for generations. It was James, the 2nd Duke, who first saw the possibilities of the larch for reafforesting his naked Perthshire hillsides. The European larch (*Larix decidua*) had been brought to England from the Alps, its native home, in 1620; Evelyn had described it; but it had remained a rarity. In 1738 the Duke planted his first larches beside Dunkeld cathedral on the banks of the Tay, in sight of some of the best salmon water in the world. One of these famous 'mother' larches, as they are always called, can still be seen. It is a matronly figure, as broad as it is high (which is 105 feet) with massive curving limbs; more like an oak than a larch. The seeds from this tree and its companions were planted on a steep slope nearby called Kennel Bank. One of them now stands 131 feet high; its trunk, scarcely tapering at all, soars 90 feet without a single branch, then on to a distant, delicate head of pale, weeping branches.

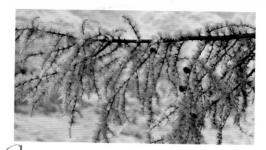

Right *In spring bare larch branches sprout rosettes of pale green needles. This branch of the European larch is typical in its masses of hanging short shoots. Needles on new lengthening shoots are single and not in rosettes.*

Right *The female flower and cone of the larch are truly flower-like and often called a 'larch rose'. On the Japanese larch shown here cones are sometimes strung like beads with the shoot going through their centres (just visible above).*

The 4th Duke was so smitten with the larch that he planted 17,000,000 of them. His example was followed all over Britain, so that by the mid-19th century larch was the most important plantation tree. At that stage an aphid started to prey on it, with disastrous results.

In 1861 the nurseryman Veitch introduced the Japanese larch (*L. kaempferi*) to cultivation. The 7th Duke of Atholl, as larch-minded as his forebears, was quick to plant it, alongside Kennel Bank. By 1904 the first hybrids had come into the world.

As so often happens, the hybrids were better than either parent. The Dunkeld larch proved faster, more resistant to insects and disease, and just as beautiful. Today all three are planted in America and Europe, but the hybrid tends to be first choice.

The two American larches are similar in all respects except size. The tamarack, or eastern larch (*L. laricina*), ranges from Alaska to Illinois. It is a characteristic tree of swampy ground, and rarely grows taller than 75 feet–much less where the ground never dries out. It is ideal for gardens in really cold areas; its little rose-like cones are very decorative. The western larch (*L. occidentalis*) is a native of Montana and Idaho, where it can reach 175 feet–scarcely a garden tree.

The Himalayan larch (*L. griffithiana*) makes a graceful garden tree in milder regions. But the one which deserves to be far better known is a Chinese tree which carries the stigma 'pseudo'–the false larch. The structure of the false larch (*Pseudolarix amabilis*) is no different from that of the larch proper–except that it grows very wide and not so high (or fast). What is different is its texture. The perfect little open rosettes of needles are the softest, silkiest green; there's a porcelain quality about the depth and texture of its autumn apricot-gold. It would need a broad space in a garden–perhaps 30 feet across eventually. But it would be my first choice.

Above *The 18th century saw a craze for larch planting, particularly in Scotland. One of the early trees still stands at Dawyck by the Tweed in the Lowlands. Old larches reach out immense horizontal branches.*
Left *Immature cones on the false larch are the same brilliant fresh green as the needles. Gnarled and often lichen-covered wood increases the contrast with the delicate new growth.*

James, the 2nd Duke of Atholl, who was the first man to plant the larch on a wide scale for forestry.

Left *Male flowers and tender young rosettes of leaves form on tiny, woody, peg-like shoots. This is the false larch from China, a small tree but perhaps the most beautiful in colour and texture of all the larches.*

Above *Larch is a native of the Alps. It grows with silver fir at lower altitudes and with Norway spruce to 7,500 feet. Twigs of the European larch are buff-coloured (making the bare trees in this picture stand out against the dark spruce).*

The True Cypresses

Trees of the pine family have enough in common with the broadleaves for their parts to be easily recognizable. A twig is a twig, a bud is a bud, a leaf, though exiguously narrow, is a leaf. The trees of the cypress family are so different that they seem to have no way of growing, as we usually understand it, at all. You can't see the twigs for the leaves–or, in a sense, the leaves for the twigs. And buds there are none.

'Them ferns' is what an Essex country-man calls the 50-foot Lawson cypresses in my garden. Tree-ferns, if it didn't already mean something palm-like and entirely different, would be a good term for them. They seem as different from other trees as bracken is from a rose-bush. So much so that when in maturity they show their trunks, as stout and straight as any fir's, they look quite incongruous.

All the difference, in fact, lies in the foliage. The little leaves are so closely applied to the twigs they spring from that on most of the more recent shoots leaf green is all you can see: no wood shows through. Without twigs or buds or any of the usual points of reference the foliage is oddly homogeneous. Instead of forming the next year's shoot in miniature during the summer, and protecting it during the winter resting period in a covering of scales, the cypresses merely pause in their tracks during cold weather–and set off again in the spring. A cypress spray in time becomes a cypress branch simply by intermittent expansion.

There is no difficulty, then, in recognizing a member of the family. Certain parts of it, particularly the junipers, distinguish them-selves by unambiguous signs–in their case, by having what seem to be berries instead of cones. With the two genera of cypress proper and false cypress, however, we catch a glimpse of the botanical backroom, where all is by no means so cut-and-dried. The *Thujas*, too, are a group of easily confusable trees, not only among themselves, but with the false cypresses.

And as though this weren't enough, along comes the woodsman and calls three-quarters of the cypress family, indiscriminately, 'cedar'.

On the whole this family is less important to the forester and more important to the gardener. The wood is excellent–durable, light and often sweet-scented. Hence the name 'cedar': a luxury rather than a staple. The Japanese pay thousands of dollars for a big Port Orford cedar (alias Lawson cypress) from Oregon, which they apparently use for lining coffins. There are no great forests of it.

Nurseries, on the other hand, are full of funny cultivars. There is hardly a gawky shape or a gaudy colour which doesn't find an admirer somewhere, particularly among the dwarf trees and little bushes with which the family abounds. On the other hand some of the finest species, fast, hardy and beautiful trees, get overlooked.

Cypresses proper, the nub of the whole family, are trees whose twigs, closely covered in tiny scale-like leaves, branch again not only sideways in one plane, as it were east and west, but north, south, and points between as well. This, together with their much bigger cones, distinguishes them from the false cypresses which (like the thujas) keep their sprays flat. If you hold a false cypress spray horizontal, you will find no twiglets heading upwards or down-wards–only on the level.

The classic cypress (*Cupressus semper-virens*), *the* cypress of literature, is the dense dark column of the Italian garden, of the Greek olive grove–of all the sunwashed landscapes of the Mediterranean where its point of exclamation, alone or in combina-tion with umbrella pines, contributes the essential architecture of the scene. There is no better columnar tree where it is hardy–and we are probably too ready to assume, because of its southern connotations, that it won't be hardy in our gardens. It grows well in the Edinburgh Botanic Garden; the Arnold Arboretum puts it in hardiness zone 7, which brings it as far north as mid-Tennessee and, on the coast, Atlantic City. If it is planted out very young in a reasonably sheltered place it is certainly worth a trial even farther north–although only southern nurseries are likely to stock it. It may have been because the cypress didn't take to the ▶

Above *The Mediterranean cypress, illustrated (far left) in Turner's herbal of 1546 was the only cypress known before 1600. Its habit of growth (above) was then unique among known trees: it has no* *buds, but grows on steadily so that the little leafy spur of one year is the forked twig of the next. The leaves are tiny scales so closely applied to the twig that until they fall years later no wood can be seen.*

The Mediterranean cypress has a unique formality which sets off architecture to perfection. These fine specimens, keeping perfect shape even in old age, stand by the 15th-century convent of Pantanassa at Mistra, northern Greece.

The tiny male flowers on a spray of the smooth Arizona cypress. These flowers will develop within several months into the cones shown on the right. Cypress twigs branch radially, making an open conic shape like tiny Christmas trees.

Male flowers (yellow tips) and unripe cones on a smooth Arizona cypress. As they ripen the cones turn dark grey. They hang on the tree for several seasons, gleaming among the dense, dusky foliage like decorations.

Growing wild among the olive groves of Kato Figalia in Greece, the cypress masses into stately ranks which give the landscape the feeling of a garden. Classical landscape gardening leant heavily on the cypress for this effect. Farther north, where the cypress will not grow, Lombardy poplars are used for the same purpose.

The True Cypresses

▶ Po valley in northern Italy that the Lombards took up their perpendicular poplar as a substitute. There is no real substitute, though, for the peculiar glossy blackness of this tree with its gleaming cones in constellations, towering 50, even 100 feet above the nymphs and gravel of an Italian garden.

The next best tree for texture, though not for form, is the Monterey cypress (*C. macrocarpa*) from California. In hardiness it may have a marginal advantage where winters are wet as well as cold–though zone 7 is given as its limit, as well. Tree-talk returns again and again to Monterey. The same wind-battered bit of Pacific coast which gave us the fastest-growing pine, and the best-looking silver fir (and more besides) has the only two natural groves of *C. macrocarpa*, at Point Lobos and Cypress Point.

The extraordinary junk-yard tangle of the trees which have grown up in the teeth of a gale is no indication of how a Monterey cypress will behave in a garden. What is fairly constant is that it will have several, perhaps many, stems. Whether these all go upwards, or spread to an oak-like head, may be a question of breeding, and is certainly a question of light, for which the tree is conspicuously greedy. Shaded branches die without more ado. The biggest and best of the species I have seen are in the Melbourne Botanic Garden in Australia: they are immensely broad domes. Often, on the other hand, one sees narrow, plume-like specimens, or ones with three or four of these plumes, all playing the leader. In San Francisco there are some which look at a distance like cedars of Lebanon.

The two-year-old you buy in a pot is curiously misleading if you expect the mature tree to look like that only bigger. It is a much paler green than the adult, which is very dark indeed. Transplanting of older trees is not a good idea–nor is it necessary, as cypresses grow at least three feet a year.

The Monterey cypress has spawned various golden forms. 'Lutea', 'Donard Gold' and 'Goldcrest' are all well-known. Of these 'Goldcrest' is probably the best shape and 'Donard Gold' the best colour. It has also produced a weeping form (very rare) and two or three pigmy ones–even one which lies flat on its front.

Odd pockets of cypresses with just enough differences to count as species proliferate in California. Often there is only one stand, reached by a botanist-beaten path. *C. abramsiana* is one such. It lives on the southwest slope of Ben Lomond, about seven miles east of Bonnie Doon School in the Santa Cruz mountains. It is interesting as an indication of the good things still to come–if the one specimen in England, at

The foliage of the Arizona cypress shows the heavy wax coating, which protects it from drying out in the parched desert conditions. Some of the best blue garden conifers come from arid areas of the Rockies or the southwestern States.

The Monterey cypress is limited in nature to the gale-swept promontory of Point Lobos in southern California. The winds make stunted

but still thriving trees with characteristic antler-'like branch formations. The same tree introduced into gardens is one of the most popular of all conifers.

Hillier's nursery in Hampshire, is a guide:
it grew 50 feet and five feet round in the first
15 years. The Gowen cypress, which is
similar, is already in circulation.

More to the point for gardeners north of
zone 7 is *C. bakeri*, from 5,000 feet up in the
very north of California, which the Arnold
Arboretum at Boston has found totally
hardy, and as fast as any tree there.

The dark green of all these is an excellent
background colour for flowering trees and
shrubs. By going inland into Arizona one
finds, as in the other conifers, the lighter
colours, the grey-greens and grey-blues, of
drought-resisting species. The smooth Arizona cypress (*C. arizonica* var. *glabra*) is
one of the best; an extraordinary tree. The
twigs look no more leafy than lengths of
sash-cord, covered (like sash-cord) with a
fine coating of wax. The cultivar 'Pyramidalis' is pale grey with a hint of blue. So cold
a colour that you could almost use an
enclosure of them, with perhaps an icy
eucalyptus, for shooting snow-scenes in
mid-summer.

The Mexican cypress, which owes its
Latin name, *lusitanica*, to its early popularity in Portugal (Lusitania) is the south-
of-the-border version. The name cedar of
Goa—whoever thinks of these names?—
makes it the only true cypress to be called
a cedar.

Of the numerous true cypresses of Asia
only one has really found favour in western
gardens: the Kashmir cypress (*C. himalaica*
var. *darjeelingensis*), not only silvery-blue
but softly weeping. This is really tender,
though: at Kew (zone 8) it lives in the
temperate house under glass. I can find no

mention of it growing in America, but there
are clearly places where it could.

There is also room to wonder why nobody
grows the alerce (*Tetraclinis articulata*),
the North African relative of the true
cypress. The ancient Romans apparently
rated its scented, bird's-eye-figured wood
highly, and called it citrus (a change from
cedar, but still further from the truth). A
little grows in Spain . . Why not in Italy,
if the Romans prized it so highly?

And few people grow the two cypresses of
the southern hemisphere–though the Chilean *Fitzroya* is distinctly decorative, and
the Australian *Callitris* very handy if you
have a parched plain to furnish.

Fitzroya makes a big tree in its native
Andes, and has reached 58 feet in Scotland.
It is like a broad cypress whose hanging
branchlets seem to be made of green plastic
chain . . . except that it is really very pretty.
Its possible role in modern gardens has yet
to be explored.

*The Monterey cypress
grown in gardens to its
full stature can make an
enormous dark dome,
rather like a very bushy*

*cedar of Lebanon.
It is at risk from
exceptional frosts even in
such temperate climates
as the south of England.*

The False Cypresses

From the four common species of this minor branch of the cypress family (minor in nature, that is) so many decorative cultivars have arisen that false cypress might be called the flowering cherry of the conifer world.

In gardens in many parts of the world (the south of England and the north of France are two) false cypresses are such a cliché that it is hard to see them with fresh eyes, or to use them effectively. Yet good specimens are graceful and satisfying plants.

The commonest in gardens, by far, is the Lawson cypress (*Chamaecyparis lawsoniana*). Lawson was a famous Edinburgh nurseryman, and fitting it is that such a nurseryman's staple should bear a nurseryman's name. If I occasionally address my trees as Port Orford cedars it is only to reinforce their dignity a little. For, though botanically way off mark, this is their forest name in the narrow tract of the northwest that is their home.

Port Orfords are common, but never dominant, in the forest which starts on the foggy coastline of Oregon and works back into the Siskiyou mountains, up to that extraordinary Eden populated by the Brewer's spruce. As far inland as the sea's influence is felt in mist and moisture-laden winds, the Port Orford is dotted, singly or in small groups. It stands out as a paler, more finely-detailed tree than the spruce, the Douglas and the western hemlock. On higher and drier spots its place is abruptly taken by the brighter, more tufted, incense cedar. Its love of moisture is a point gardeners should bear in mind. New England and most of California are too dry for it to flourish; it will grow there, as it will all over Europe, but it can be a drab thing where it is unhappy.

What more than anything has singled out the Lawson (to come back to its nursery persona) for intensive cultivation is its tendency to pop up in the seed-bed in eccentric–sometimes quite unrecognizable –forms. No conifer has so many faces. Den Ouden and Boom, authors of one of the standard reference books on conifers, list 200 cultivars of tree or big bush size and some 50 dwarfs.

The main variations are in colour, habit of growth and in leaf shape and arrangement. Some of the best are particularly soft and graceful by virtue of having permanently juvenile foliage–fronds which never reach the size, firmness and flatness of the adult tree. This state of affairs was misunderstood when it was first noticed. It is not peculiar to false cypresses, but occurs in *Thujas* and junipers and even *Cryptomerias* which are not members of the cypress family at all. All were thought to belong to a separate genus, which was labelled 'retinospora'; Victorian gardening books are full of retinosporas. As a genus it was a chimera: on the other hand it is a perfectly valid concept, and all these trees do share an attractive quality.

Two other fairly frequent aberrations of foliage are a sort of congestion, in which twice the usual ration of twigs and leaf-scales crowd into the same space; and the opposite, where they are freakishly spaced out along hanging sprays as thin as strings. The name 'filiformis' (string-shaped) is given

Top *The first of scores of garden versions of the Lawson cypress was 'Erecta Viridis', a tall (to 90 feet) column of emerald-green foliage. Wind and snow tend to break its erect branches unless they are tied up.*

'Fletcheri' is another of the popular-garden Lawson cypresses. It has a bluer tone and more feathery foliage than 'Erecta Viridis' and grows much more slowly; the biggest specimen is 40 feet tall.

The cones of the Lawson
cypress are full-grown but
still green and unripe
here. A few of last year's
cones, brown and with
their scales opened, still
hang above them on the
drooping spray.

The red male and
black female flowers of
the Lawson cypress
become conspicuous all
over the tree in early
spring before any new
growth starts.

to this type of foliage.

There are other differences in branching
which it is harder to classify; ones which
hold their sprays upright but side-on to the
audience, or loose and nodding, or one
with odd, twisted branch tips.

The first and still the greatest of the
cultivars actually arose from seeds shipped
from California to Britain in 1855, so it
has been almost as long in cultivation as
the species itself. It is sometimes called
'Erecta Viridis', sometimes just 'Erecta',
but the first name describes it exactly:
bright green upright—to 90 feet sometimes.
Up to a certain age, and barring accidents,
it is the best of all sentinel trees, as formal
as a footman and as groomed. When most
green cultivars turn grey in winter, it
seems greener than ever. But accidents do
happen to older trees: their fine fronds are
pulled away from the column by wind or
snow and never recover.

The best of the gold-leaved Lawsons are
'Lutea' and 'Lanei'; of the blue (for bright-
ness) 'Spek', 'Pembury Blue' and the ultimately huge 'Triomf van Boskoop'; for
combination of blueness and narrow upright
form 'Columnaris'. For a broad upright
habit like an Irish yew, 'Fletcheri' and
'Ellwoodii'. You can find Lawsons to fit
any scheme or decorative plan. . . . One
can't help thinking of them as garden
wallpaper.

It is easy to confuse the ordinary Lawson
cypress with other false cypresses or with
thuja, which is often found in the same
gardens. The best way to recognize it is to
look at the underside of the foliage. A faint
but distinct pattern of little white crosses
marks the lines of pores.

The Nootka (false) cypress (C. nootkatensis) has never caught on to the same
extent. Its real claim to fame in modern
gardens is in being one of the parents of the
Leyland cypress (see page 101). In nature
the Nootkas are the northern neighbours of
the Lawsons. Under the name Alaska cedar, ▶

False Cypresses and Leyland Cypress

▶or yellow cedar, they are common among Sitka spruce along the coast from Alaska to Vancouver, and farther south (on Mount Rainier for example) at an altitude much higher than the Port Orford cedar. The Nootka of their name is an inlet in the ocean side of Vancouver Island, where the botanist Archibald Menzies first caught sight of them.

The usual garden form of Nootka is different from the Lawson chiefly in the hang of its foliage. The sprays are heavy, and coarse to the touch. They droop as though the tree were desperate for water; and their rather dingy yellow-green suggests it may be too late. The form 'Pendula' is relatively rare in cultivation but superior in every way. Where Nootka just mopes, 'Pendula' is heartbroken. Each long branch bears a cascade of weeping fronds. If Forest Lawn were to revert to the 19th century notion of a graveyard which really looks like a graveyard this would be the tree they would plant by every skull-studded sepulchre.

Two species of false cypress grow on the east coast of the United States. The white cypress, *C. thyoides*, has by far the biggest range of any; being happy in wet ground from Maine to Mississippi. (Florida has its own species: *C. henryae*). It came into cultivation 150 years before the western and oriental species, but today they have more or less eclipsed it. Its best-known forms in modern gardens are the dwarfs, 'Andelyensis' and 'Ericoides'.

The Japanese Sawara cypress (*C. pisifera*) has identity problems like the Lawson. Indeed, if the species itself rather than one of its cultivars were grown few people would recognize it. In two areas of aberration it is conspicuously successful; the string-leafed and the juvenile (or retinospora). It goes so far in the latter that two different degrees of juvenility have separate terms: if it is merely childish it is 'plumosa'; if it is positively infantile it is 'squarrosa'–vernacularly, 'moss'. Seventy feet is not an impossible height for a 'squarrosa' with the finest and fluffiest foliage. One often sees hacked-about specimens ruining the rockeries where they were planted as pigmies years ago. Some of the best true dwarf forms are shown on pages 118–9. A compromise, and probably the best cultivar of all, is a 'squarrosa'-type called 'Boulevard' which grows slowly to 15 feet, and eventually a little more. Its leaves, if you can call them that, are like a silvery froth all over the plant.

The 'filiformis' ones, which come in green and gold but not blue, are even less vigorous than the retinosporas. None the less you finally get a huge gold (or green) bun–as much as 30 feet high and 20 feet through.

The other Japanese false cypress, Hinoki, or *C. obtusa*, is more consistent and in many ways a better tree, keeping dense and healthy-looking when many a Sawara has tired of life.

The hallmark of the Hinoki is the blunt-ended spray of deep shiny green, which gives the whole tree a compact, well-nourished look. Both the species and its golden version 'Crippsii' are first-class garden trees.

The most popular cultivar, and probably the best, is 'Nana Gracilis'; a big bush comparable with *C. pisifera* 'Boulevard' both in size and in its remarkable finish. It consists of a dense random heap of small vivid-green scallops; an unmistakable plant in the millions of gardens which give it pride of place.

Compactness goes berserk in some of the other cultivars; the foliage becomes a congested jumble which would look like a nasty spot of virus trouble if they weren't such sturdy, bright-coloured plants. 'Filicoides', 'Lycopodioides' and 'Tetragona Aurea' seem to make whole trees out of witches' brooms. The last is a good gold colour, but the others, to my mind, have no great virtues to balance their essential freakishness.

Top left *"Ellwoodii' is a bluish cultivar of the Lawson cypress which grows slowly to over 20 feet, keeping a dense, tight and narrow columnar shape as a young tree and broadening with age.*

Above *'Lanei' is one of the best of many golden cultivars of the Lawson cypress. Its soft golden branch-ends contrast prettily with the green of the older leaves. It will eventually reach 30 feet.*

Top right *'Lutea' is a bright, crisp-looking gold cultivar of the Lawson cypress; narrow, with a maximum height of 50 feet or so. All golden forms are brightest in early summer.*

Above *'Nana Gracilis' is the outstanding small cultivar of the Japanese Hinoki cypress: it makes a large bush (to about 10 feet). Its jumbled shell-like growths are brilliant dark green all year.*

'Filifera Aurea' is the best of the string-foliaged golden versions of the Japanese Sawara cypress. It makes a broad bright dome of unique texture.

Up to 1925 the two groups of trees we now call the cypresses and the false cypresses were considered one. So when in 1888 the pollen from a Monterey cypress lit on the female flowers of a Nootka false cypress in the grounds of a Welsh country house the affair was perfectly legal. Hindsight (in the shape of a taxonomic dictate of 1925) has since declared the two parents members of separate genera and their offspring, therefore, a mule.

The mule is the Leyland cypress (× *Cupressocyparis leylandii*). It is still relatively little known in America, but in the last 35 years or so it has been recognized in Britain as one of the most useful trees in the whole list: a paragon combining hardiness, shapeliness, density of foliage and excellent colour. And it grows like the devil.

In normal British gardening conditions the Leyland is the fastest-growing conifer bar none. Cuttings, which root easily, are ready for planting out in one year. Thereafter growth only pauses in really cold weather. The first year out the plant will double in size; three years from a cutting it should be at least six feet tall. It will make a 30 foot specimen in ten years or so, and it has reached 100 feet in 55 years.

There are faster trees for milder climates.

Eucalyptus can go like a train. Even in the north spruces have made six feet in a season. But Leyland is not only tough: it has the good manners of a garden plant: it makes the ideal rapid hedge or tall screen, without gaps or bare patches; it gives a perfect even grey-green background for coloured trees or flowers. Even at 100 feet it keeps its smooth shape like a great green flame with a slightly leaning tip.

Some trial plants in California have taken on a different habit, becoming much broader, more bushy and less elegant. A trio of them in the Golden Gate Park in San Francisco are rather tubby things. Probably it is a tree for cool-temperate areas with decided seasonal changes (which, of course, San Francisco lacks).

The Leyland of the name was C. J. Leyland of Haggerston Hall, Northumberland. It was he who first spotted the hybrid at his brother-in-law's home, Leighton Hall, in Montgomeryshire on the Welsh border. In fact the cross happened both ways: in 1888 it was the Nootka which was the mother, but in 1911 (by the strangest coincidence on the same estate) the Nootka pollinated the Monterey cypress. Leyland's first find is now referred to as 'Haggerston Grey'. It is the common Leyland of commerce. The second cross bears the name of 'Leighton Green'; being harder to propagate it is not so often seen.

To every nurseryman's delight the Leyland has obliged with 'golden' (or at least yellow-green) sports. In 1970 'Castlewellan' appeared, followed five years later by the—slightly brighter—'Robinson'. Both seem to share all the admirable qualities of the green forms.

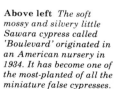

Above left *The soft mossy and silvery little Sawara cypress called 'Boulevard' originated in an American nursery in 1934. It has become one of the most-planted of all the miniature false cypresses.*

Above right *The Hinoki cypress cultivar 'Crippsii' is one of the most interesting-shaped golden plants. It grows slowly to 20 feet or more and keeps a bright colour even without much sun.*

Left *The white cypress* (Chamaecyparis thyoides) *has produced fewer ornamental cultivars than most, but 'Ericoides', bright green in summer and purplish in winter, is a superb small plant.*

The Leyland cypress, a hybrid between the Monterey and Nootka cypresses, has all the qualities of the ideal background tree for gardens (or hedge): fast growth, good colour, dense and even foliage. It is hardy and reliable.

The Thujas or Arborvitae

It is comforting to know that the great Bentham and Hooker, authors of *Genera Plantarum*, one of the definitive systems of arranging plants, lumped *Thuja* and false cypress together. One doesn't feel quite such an idiot. The same flattened fronds, the same well-furnished conical form make the species infinitely more like each other than their own varieties. In the garden *Thuja plicata*, the western red cedar (or giant arborvitae, for it has nearly as many names as branches) and the Lawson cypress are almost interchangeable.

If the trees have cones it is easy to tell which are the thujas: the scales of their tiny, rosehip-shaped cones all hinge at one end. False cypress cones open round a central point: the scales point up and down as well as sideways, forming a sort of skeletal sphere. Perhaps the other most telling point of recognition which applies to all the thujas except one, is their powerfully pungent smell; something between balsam and turpentine. The leaves fairly exude it; you become aware of it just by standing nearby.

The two American species of thuja are by far the best-known. The familiar pattern repeats itself: a small, immensely hardy, not particularly attractive tree shows the flag in the east while out west its great brawny country cousin luxuriates in perfect conditions, developing to a size and beauty which makes it almost a match for the Douglas fir.

The eastern tree, *Thuja occidentalis* ('white cedar')–the roll call of 'cedars' is still not exhausted–was the first American tree to be grown in Europe. There is a record of one in Paris in 1553, almost 200 years before the trees of North America began to make their great impression on the world's gardens.

Its importance today, however, is based on its quirks and foibles in the seed-bed rather than its intrinsic value. It is second only to the Lawson cypress in the number of offbeat seedlings it produces. Professor C. S. Sargent of the Arnold Arboretum,

Boston, once said that if anyone sowed a quantity of seed he 'would be sure to find forms among the seedlings as novel and interesting as any now in cultivation'. The competition, as represented in nurseries today, includes mainly dwarf and several juvenile-leaved varieties, but one of the classic golden conifers, 'Rheingold', is a bush form of *T. occidentalis*.

Thujas on the whole are strong on gold cultivars, shifting from bright gold to dull, bronzy old-gold at the onset of winter. The billowing flanks of a 12-foot 'Rheingold' (12 feet is about its maximum) can be one of the best things in a bleak winter landscape. The winter shift of colour is much less effective on a green tree. Hardy though it is, the white cedar tends to go drably brown as the pigmentation changes in very cold weather. A number of cultivars have been selected for constant colour, among them 'Wintergreen', 'Lutea', an excellent full-size golden form, and 'Spiralis', which is slim, compact and dark green with distinct formal possibilities.

In all except very northerly or badly-drained gardens the western red cedar is a much better tree; greener and more glossy, leafier and of course larger. Old lawn specimens are sometimes creatures of extraordinary character. Their lowest limbs rest on the ground and take root, to spring up and surround the tree with a grove of green buttresses, a tabernacle cavernous and perfumed within, floored and ceilinged in bracken-brown and raftered with branches.

In Washington and Oregon they grow to 200 feet with vastly buttressed bases as much as 35 feet through. One sees old red cedar butts grounded along the shores of Puget Sound, great wooden whales which decay, apparently, can never touch. The Indians hollowed out 50-foot canoes from them and carved them into totem poles. As 'cedar' in commerce today they provide outdoors all-weather wood for shingle roofs, greenhouses and football posts.

The gardener can hardly avoid using such

Western red cedar, the giant of the thuja family, growing in an experimental forest in Britain. In the Pacific northwest it grows to 200 feet and produces the fragrant 'cedar' of the building trade.

Above *A group of young western red cedars (Thuja plicata); ultimately, they will take on a majestic height and form.*
Left *Details of the branchlet system of western red cedar (Thuja plicata) with cones that have released their seeds.*

Above Thuja occidentalis 'Aureospica' has *yellow young shoots, gradually maturing to bronzy gold.*
Right *Cones of western red cedar. Soon they will turn pale brown and gape open, so that the seeds can be dispersed by the wind.*

Left *The Japanese arbor-vitae* (Thuja standishii) *is rare in cultivation outside Japan. In many ways it is a smaller version of* Thuja plicata. *Its blunted leaves are blue-white underneath. They have a rich lemony scent.*

an adaptable tree. It is happier than almost any conifer on chalk soil and in drought conditions—strange when you consider its moist, luxuriant origins. It will start life slowly but surely in quite heavy shade. Given better conditions it can grow three feet a year. It makes an excellent hedge.

'Zebrina', one of the forms of *T. plicata*, is the biggest of any golden conifer. It has reached 70 feet: a remarkable sight in its summer colouring. In winter it settles down to a mixture of gold and green which is still, in such bulk, extremely eye-catching.

Golden varieties are also the main attractions of the Chinese thuja, *T. orientalis*. The green tree is small, often a multi-stemmed, round-headed, substantial bush. One in my garden has been reduced to two of its original five stems, leaving a neat dome on bare poles which is extremely effective. Its sprays, fine and small-scale for a thuja, have a certain springy way of turning on their sides which gives it a tousled look. It is not glamorous, but its green is bright and one grows fond of such things.

This is the only thuja without a pungent smell, and the only one with little down-turning hooks on the scales of its cones: an easy tree to identify. 'Conspicua' and 'Ele-gantissima' are two of its best-known golden forms of small tree size. 'Aurea Nana' is a particularly good golden dwarf.

The Japanese thuja, *T. standishii*, is a rarer tree than the related *Thujopsis*, another native of Japan. Many conifers flirt with green plastic artificiality. Thujopsis goes the whole way. Its scale-leaves, firmly (and very prettily) marked with silvery-white below, are a conifer in kit-form from a cereal box: the precise, shiny, yellow-green of a stamped-out plastic conifer.

Though with a possible height of 60 feet or so it could not be classed as a dwarf conifer, it grows slowly in its early years so that you could happily plant it in a small garden. Young plants may grow only an inch or two a year for as long as ten years.

Left *Eastern white cedar or arborvitae* (Thuja occidentalis) *is usually of columnar form, with rather drab foliage, especially in winter. In cultivation it is usually represented by dwarf and coloured foliage forms, such as the bright green 'Wintergreen' and 'Lutea', a narrow pyramid of golden foliage.*

Right *Under ideal conditions the zebra-striped western red cedar* (Thuja plicata *'Zebrina') can be a most striking and ornamental specimen tree. The twigs are banded green and gold, or more heavily suffused with gold as in this specimen (*T.p. *'Zebrina Extra Gold') at Bedgebury, Kent.*

Above Thujopsis dola-brata, *showing the striking white pattern on the undersides of the plastic-like leaves. The green cone above is not yet mature; the previous season's brown one has opened and shed its seeds.*

Right *The Chinese thuja has claws on its round cones which make it easy to identify. As the cones ripen the waxy white bloom fades to brown and the scales gape open.*

Above *The Chinese thuja is a many-stemmed bright green tree, seldom more than 30 feet. Its golden cultivars are more popular than the species itself. This is 'Elegantis-sima', growing in the Trompenburg arboretum in Rotterdam, Holland.*

The Incense Cedars

Far left *The incense cedar from the forests of northwestern America has become the best of all narrow-column trees in cultivation. It stays narrow for many years, eventually broadening to a huge tower (left).*

Above *Its inch-long cones start off fleshy. When ripe they are woody and open like a book.*

If the incense cedar grew only in its native woods in the Pacific northwest it would rate little more attention than a cousin of the better-known *Thujas* with the peculiarity of holding its branchlets on edge instead of flopping horizontally. It is a common tree in the lower mountains of Oregon and California. The 'incense' of the name is a sweet resinous scent in the leaves and wood–no more so than in many other conifers. But there is more to it than this. It is one of only two conifers with almost identical relations south of the equator–so close that one might almost say its range runs from Oregon to New Zealand. And in

cultivation it has given northern parts what is easily their grandest columnar tree, a formal upright more magnificent in size and much richer in colour and texture than the Mediterranean's cypress.

As far as the northern hemisphere is concerned the incense cedar, *Calocedrus decurrens* (catalogued as often as not under the name *Libocedrus decurrens*), is the sole representative of its genus. Colonel Fremont of the U.S. Corps of Topographical Engineers (an officer whose career embraced everything from botany to mutiny, and who eventually found himself the owner of one of California's richest gold lodes) discovered

the tree in 1848, flourishing in the drier and sunnier spots of the mountains of Oregon and California.

The tree he found is very distinct in colour and texture. Its firm, bright green tufts, vertically set, are a cheerful part of the character of the sunny slopes.. It is never one of the tallest trees; rather it makes its presence felt by keeping more branches than most of the forest trees; often being clothed for most of its length in foliage, giving the woods a dense, well-furnished look. Only in old age does it tend to grow gaunt.

It doesn't, on the other hand, have the habit which makes the garden version so outstanding. In nature the incense cedar is a bushy, irregular tower of foliage, broadest about its middle reaches. Whereas the same tree grown in gardens in Europe and the eastern States soars up with completely parallel sides, the most regular and densest column to the greatest height of any tree. The best have reached 120 feet in 100 years or so, the only unevenness being a faint billowing of the rich greenery–the *embonpoint* of a courtier.

A variegated version also exists, but it is a poor thing, merely sprinkled with yellow branch-tips as though something were lacking from its diet.

The male 'flowers' of the incense cedar are like tiny cones whose scales open to release the pollen. In the wild the tree has none of the statuesque quality it has mysteriously assumed in gardens.

The Junipers

The Utah juniper (J. osteosperma) makes massively gnarled small trees in arid western canyons. Like most junipers it has thin bark which peels in narrow vertical strips.

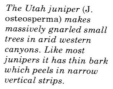

Reading accounts of desirable conifers I sometimes begin to despair that they all want the same (to me unattainable) conditions: acid soil and lots of moisture. What hope of these arid and alkaline acres ever having anything worthwhile to show? And then I remember the yews–and the junipers.

The juniper in particular desires and does almost the exact opposite of the general run of conifers; even of the rest of the cypress family. Where they grow relatively fast she grows at a snail's pace. Where they love shelter she loves the south slope of the hill–unmitigated sunlight. Where they need damp luxurious leaf-mould she likes to get her wiry roots into mineral soil. Where they have both male and female flowers on one tree she (again like the yew) has either one or the other. They have woody cones; she has fleshy berries.

Her slow growth rules her out for the forester, except for such small-scale and specialized uses as providing the scented wood for pencils. The same quality makes the juniper a basic stand-by in planning gardens–particularly small gardens. But the great majority of garden forms of juniper fall far short of tree stature: there is probably more grown as ground-cover than in any other role.

The common juniper (*Juniperus communis*) is the only tree species which occurs naturally in Europe, Asia and America. It is usually dismissed as scrub; its only claim to fame is that its berries provide the flavour for gin. To give it a fair hearing, however, I must quote Gertrude Jekyll, whose sensitive eye made her one of the greatest gardeners of this century. She feels differently. 'Its tenderly mysterious beauty of colouring . . . as delicately subtle in its own way as that of cloud or mist, or haze in warm, wet woodland. It has very little of positive green; a suspicion of warm colour in the shadowy hollows and a blue-grey bloom of the tenderest quality

imaginable on the outer masses of foliage.' She goes on in the same vein, admiring the way the plant recovers from snow damage, the silver lichen on its stems, 'the infinitely various position of the spiny little leaves'. One is driven by such words at least to take a second look.

In fact no nursery will supply the common juniper today except in one or other of its cultivar forms. Three of these are pale grey-green columnar plants of considerable merit: the tallest 'Suecica', as much as 40 feet ultimately; the commonest the Irish juniper, 'Hibernica', perhaps 15 or 20 feet; and the baby, which has no business here but is such a gem I can't leave it out, 'Compressa'; about 18 inches of drum-tight fuzz; one of the best of all miniature trees for a sink garden or rockery.

All common juniper incidentally comes into the category of retinospora–having nothing but juvenile foliage. Some other junipers tend to be very variable, having some branches adult (with scale-leaves, quite cypress-like) and others, or just individual sprays, with fine sharp-pointed leaves: the juvenile form.

The two junipers which between them give more garden varieties than all the rest are *J. virginiana*, better known as eastern red cedar, and the Chinese juniper, *J. chinensis*. Both have this characteristic of variable foliage. The eastern red cedar is widespread in the wild throughout the eastern United States. Occasionally it makes a 100-foot tree of a battered conical outline; but only in the south of its range, south of (say) Pennsylvania. There are said to be 40 cultivars of eastern red cedar in all; nurseries looking for shapeliness concentrate on the narrower, smaller, northern ones. 'Glauca' is a good blue-grey upright one; 'Canaertii' is a selection made in a Belgian nursery: dark green and firmly conical, with the added attraction of regular masses of blue-bloomed berries.

There is not a great deal of difference between the eastern and the Rocky Mountain junipers, or between the Rocky Mountain (*J. scopulorum*) and several other local western forms. According to Sunset Magazine, which caters exclusively and exhaustively for western gardeners, the juniper is the 'most widely-used woody plant in gardens in the west'. I can make no attempt to sort out the Utah from the one-seed or the Californian; the varieties of the worldwide ones are enough to be getting on with. The Rocky Mountain contributes half a dozen good garden varieties, mainly columnar. 'Columnaris' in fact comes from North Dakota. In the wild, to give you some idea of its unhasty progress, it has

Top *The cherrystone juniper (J. monosperma) is a common bush in the Arizona deserts. Under better conditions it can grow to 60 feet. Its name comes from its single stony seed.*

The pale green berry-like male 'flowers' of the common juniper are borne in the angles of the whorls of spiky leaves. Here they are mature and have released their pollen.

Left *The common juniper has little pointed 'juvenile' needles and berry-like cones. In form it varies from prostrate mats to spire-like trees: usually it is bush-size.*

The Junipers

▶been measured at 14 feet in 40 years, 18 feet in 80 years, and 30 feet in no less than 300 years. The western juniper, *J. occidentalis*, is something different, by the way; a rough, big-limbed, unshapely tree from dry sites in eastern Oregon and western Idaho.

Most original of the American junipers is the one known as the 'alligator', *J. deppeana pachyphlaea*. All other junipers have thin bark which peels off, if at all, in brown vertical ribbons. The alligator's cracks up into square patches like the carapace, if that's the word, of the terror of the Everglades. Its leaves are light blue, fine and spiny as befits a tree from the near-desert of Texas and New Mexico.

The Chinese juniper (*J. chinensis*), like the common juniper, is the raw material of dozens of cultivars. It is not often seen in the form nature intended. There is no striking difference between it and the eastern red cedar (*J. virginiana*) unless it be the considerably larger berries of the Chinese plant (when it has berries at all). Both carry foliage of two types, fine-prickly, and cypress-like with scale-leaves. Some of the selected forms break this rule, however; the size of the berries, if any, is probably the most consistent trait to watch for. One cultivar, 'Femina', has been selected on the strength of its profusion of pretty berries.

Of the other selections the golden one, 'Aurea', is probably the most popular, as one of the most reliably bright gold conifers for a small garden. It may reach 40 feet, but it will take 60 or 70 years. 'Keteleerii' is a tidy, solid, dark-toned tree, a broad cone in shape – again very slow. 'Kaizuka' (also known as the Hollywood juniper) is a harum-scarum sort of bush, launching long limbs of bright green in unexpected directions: a good one for a mid-lawn position where it can freely yawn and stretch as wide as 15 feet. In straightforward columns most shades from bright green through grey to blue are available under one name or another. Nursery names often depart from

the strictly botanical; the great thing is to see the tree and like it.

One occasionally sees a very different oriental juniper, a tree with great character which could be used much more: the temple juniper, *J. rigida*. Not column- or cone-shaped, the temple juniper puts out pine-like branches to make a small but venerable-looking open head. Spiky dark foliage droops densely from the branches with an effect like Spanish moss on an old swamp cypress. Thirty feet would be a big one.

In 1930 another drooping juniper was discovered in the Burmese foothills of the Himalayas. *J. recurva* var. *coxii* (after Euan Cox, its finder), has almost the effect of a weeping willow at a distance. The long camouflage-green sprays, so dense and soft to the touch that you can squeeze them like sponges, hang from arching branches. It is more of a forest tree than most junipers; shade, especially near a woodland pool, suits it well.

To stick strictly to the trees of the family I should ignore the much better-known Himalayan juniper, *J. squamata*, whose form 'Meyeri', a prickly, icy-blue bush with drooping shoots, is familiar in so many gardens. I should also fail to mention the ubiquitous *J.* × *Media* 'Pfitzeriana', child of a union between the Chinese juniper and the shrub *J. sabina*, the Savin of southern Europe. 'Pfitzeriana' (and also *J.* 'Hetzii') are vigorous V-shaped bushes capable of covering a remarkable amount of ground. Being capable of growing in pure chalk, dry as a bone and in deep shade, they are the workhorses of the family, inevitably seen in problem corners.

In southern gardens one sometimes sees the Greek juniper, *J. chinensis* 'Pyramidalis'; a tight grey column. From the best accounts the Syrian juniper, *J. drupacea*, is much hardier and more tolerant, as well as being (I quote Alan Mitchell, in his *Conifers in the British Isles*) 'a fresh light green colour unique among junipers'.

Top *A remarkably shapely specimen of the pencil juniper (J. virginiana 'Pseudocupressus') in the Schlossgarten at Baden Baden in Germany. Its many cultivars include bushy and weeping forms.*

Above *The 'Swedish' juniper is an upright form of the common juniper which grows wild in Scandinavia and north Germany (here on Lüneberg Heath near Hamburg).*

Above *The spreading prickly juniper (Juniperus oxycedrus) with 'juvenile' leaves is common all round the Mediterranean. It varies in size from a low shrub to a 30-foot tree.*

Right *The drooping juniper of the Himalayas (Juniperus recurva) is here (in its native land) trimmed and shorn by the weather to a more compact and stiffer shape than it assumes in gardens.*

The Phoenician juniper growing on the Acropolis in Athens. It can live for 1,000 years, and has spread from the East throughout the Mediterranean and to the Canary Islands.

The Phoenician juniper of the Mediterranean has typical mature foliage (compare the prickly juniper opposite). Its berry-cones lose their bloom as they ripen and turn reddish-brown.

The Yews

I am not sure that one could rightly describe the yew as beautiful. My feelings, at least, are not so much of admiration as of respect. The yew is old and wise. It is the colour of ancient widows' shawls; as unkempt and wispy as their hair. Yet senile as it seems, its berries are bright red and there are lusty new shoots from the old trunk. From some secret place in its dark boughs it shakes bright yellow dust to catch the springtime sun.

Folk must always have felt like this about the yew. They have so lavished legend upon it that there is not a 200-year-old churchyard yew which isn't in Domesday Book. My favourite fable is built round the old tree (what is left of it) at Fortingall in the Scottish Highlands. It appears that Pontius Pilate's father was an Imperial official in that area and the stripling Pontius (or so they say) romped beneath those very branches. He scratched P.P. in the bark of the tree and he even added a date: 15 B.C.

Sober report has it that this particular yew is 1,500 years old and thus one of the oldest living inhabitants of Europe. There are no annual rings to count, though. For yews, unlike redwoods, have no thick rind to protect them. Their heart-wood, immensely durable as it is, eventually decays and they become hollow. The Fortingall tree has no centre left at all: it is a palisade of living fragments. Two hundred years ago it measured 52 feet round, but it would be hard to know which bits to measure today.

The association of yews and churchyards is so widespread that everyone has his own explanation of it. I find it easy to believe that people have always respected this ageless evergreen. In England, moreover, it was the only conifer (save the bushy juniper) throughout the middle ages. Along with holly and ivy (both equally associated with Christianity) it was the only green thing in the brown winter world. A practical consideration is that the yew's leaves are poisonous and the churchyard is one of the few places fenced against stock.

For garden purposes it is not the species of yew that matters, but the form. Some authorities, indeed, say there is only one species, and that it alters slightly in leaf size and colour from place to place. *Taxus baccata*, the European species, is in any case the yew of yews. If there is any argument for growing either *T. canadensis* (the northeast American native one), *T. brevifolia* (the Pacific coast version), or *T. cuspidata* (the Japanese yew) it is only a question of local conditions. North of New York, for example, the Japanese yew is recommended; *T. baccata* suffers in winter. But the biggest and best-looking yews are all European–and it is the European yew that has spawned the most celebrated garden forms.

It is one of the oddest coincidences in gardening that the two most distinguished cultivars of the yew arose within a couple of years of each other at the end of the 18th century. In 1777 a Mr. Dovaston at West-felton in Shropshire in the English west midlands spotted a weeping yew among the seedlings offered by a pedlar. And in 1778 or '79 a farmer called Willis saw two female versions of what is now the famous Irish yew (*T. baccata* 'Fastigiata') growing in the wild near Florencecourt in County Fermanagh. They were moved to the Earl of Enniskillen's garden nearby and from them, by cuttings, are descended the millions of upright yews all over the world.

One sees far fewer Westfelton yews–largely, no doubt, because they take up so much space. What the ordinary yew tree lacks in poise and harmony this graceful one provides. It makes a broad symmetrical

The unusually tall yews in the churchyard at Kergrist in Brittany are estimated to be 1000 years old. The usual shape of yews is more squat and spreading, with branches to the ground.

Two stages in the development of a yew 'berry' or single-seeded fleshy cone. The lower ones show the acorn-like cup which later swells up with sticky red pulp. Both the leaves of the yew and the seeds are poisonous.

Left *Male yew 'flowers' or pollen-producing cones are usually borne in abundance on the undersides of the twigs. In February and March they scatter yellow clouds of pollen on the wind.*

Below *Rugged, windswept yews on a hillside in Borrowdale, Cumberland. Common yew grows equally well in the shade of a forest or completely exposed on a bare hill.*

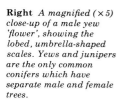

Right *A magnified (×5) close-up of a male yew 'flower', showing the lobed, umbrella-shaped scales. Yews and junipers are the only common conifers which have separate male and female trees.*

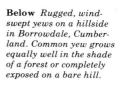

Irish yews, thick columns in nature, clipped into a goblet shape in a churchyard in Tiverton, Devon. All yews thrive with regular clipping and make the best of all hedges.

tree like a huge pavilion, rising to a conical centre. The branches all round have weeping swags of near-black branchlets and often a good crop of red berries in autumn.

Yews are unusual among conifers in being either male or female. The male tree has much bigger flower buds on the new shoots. It is important to distinguish a tree's sex if you either want the berries or don't want the prodigious clouds of pollen that gild the countryside around a virile yew.

Both the weeping and upright yews, at the Great Gardener's command, have done the sporting thing and produced golden cultivars. The golden upright (*T. baccata* 'Fastigiata Aurea') is much the brighter and more effective. Both the golden and green Westfeltons sometimes fail to develop central leaders and flourish as spreading bushes with much less to recommend them.

Yew is incomparably the best hedging plant. It is so dense and even-textured that one can easily think of it as architecture. Many of the greatest gardens have their structure defined in clipped yew: it makes a perfect background for colours in shrubs or borders. It answers the shears perfectly, yet somehow always contributes its own weight to the effect: there is no such thing as a straight line in yew, yet you can hardly perceive just where it sags and softens the design. If the hedge is grown from seedlings there is a constant play of different colours where one plant merges into the next: no two are ever exactly the same green. When the new growth starts in spring a warm coppery bloom spreads in broad jigsaw pieces over the hedge.

If yew hedges are planted much less today than hedges of *Thuja* or Lawson cypress it is partly a question of price but more, I suspect, a question of impatience: yew has the name for growing at a snail's pace. We should learn from the Hon. Vicary Gibbs, who in 1897 planted some seedlings which he fed liberally with nitrate of soda. Eight years later, in 1905, he had trees 12 feet high and 16 inches in girth. Better to wait four years for a six-foot yew hedge which needs clipping only once a year than two for a thuja which bristles with new growth after every rain.

If Gibbs had waited another three years before planting he could have tried the hybrid between the European and Japanese yews, raised in 1900 in Massachusetts. *Taxus × media*, as it is called, was reported at the Royal Horticultural Society's Conifer Conference in 1972 as being 'slightly coarser in texture than English yew, much quicker growing; easily rooted from cuttings'. The last part is important: it could bring down the price of yew hedges.

The Plum Yews and Podocarps

I have yielded here to the temptation to lump together the two families of the yew's relations. They have so much in common that a taxonomist in mild mood might have done the same. They come from California and the Far East. Their leaves are much longer, more spaced-out and lighter green than the yew's. Their fruits are nuts enclosed in flesh like a small plum, not open at one end as the yew's fruit is. They both grow into small, irregular, rather open trees whose main charm is in the strong pattern of their leafing.

The Chinese plum yew, *Cephalotaxus fortunei*, is probably the most-planted of the group. Its long, soft, light green leaves are ranked along the sides of its shoots so that each branch presents a flat upper surface like a young grand fir branch, but bolder in detail. The Japanese plum yew (*C. harringtonia drupacea*) is similar, a bush rather than a tree perhaps, with the leaves tilting up to give a V-shape to the shoot. An excellent form of this imitates the Irish yew almost to the life, with the same way of leafing radially all round the upwards-pointing branches; the only obvious difference being that the leaves are bigger. The fruits of both (it is hard to think of them as cones) are light green ripening to purple, juicy and inviting-looking. Squeezed hard they exude delicious-smelling milky resin. They are plants that grow well in the shade and tolerate chalky soil, and would certainly make a worthwhile contribution to many gardens.

The California nutmeg (*Torreya californica*, named after the same botanist as the rare Torrey pine) makes a bigger tree–the biggest in Britain is 75 feet, to the cephalotaxus's 35 feet. In texture it is much spikier, its needles hard and coming to positive points. The fruit is similar, perhaps a shade bigger. A Japanese species of torreya (*T. nucifera*) has smaller, relatively broader leaves. Neither is a tree that would justify itself in a small garden where other conifers would malinger.

Above *The Huon pine of Tasmania* (Lagarostrobus franklinii) *is a most distinguished weeping conifer, very like the true cypresses in leaf and twig.*

Below *The big-leaved podocarp* (Podocarpus macrophyllus) *is one of the exotic Asiatic conifers we have hardly started to appreciate as a garden tree. Its leaves are as big as six inches by half an inch.*

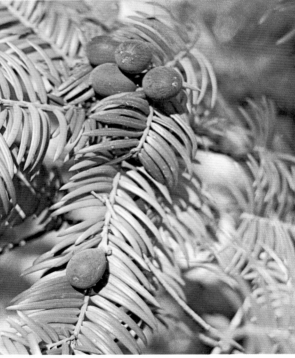

Top *This small specimen of the California nutmeg* (Torreya californica) *is typical of its form in gardens. In its native mountain woods it reaches as much as 90 feet and a nine-foot girth.*

Above *The Chinese plum yew* (Cephalotaxus fortuni) *is the best-looking tree of its genus. Its single-seeded fleshy 'cones' look like plums– but are totally inedible.*

Above *The California nutmeg takes its name from the shape and appearance of its fruits – here in their unripe green state. The ripe fruit is streaked with bands of purple. The fleshy part is thin and resinous.*

The podocarps are largely a submerged clan as far as European and American gardeners are concerned. They are (with the *Araucarias*) the principal conifers of the southern hemisphere. In South Africa, for example, yellow-wood (*Podocarpus latifolius*) is the chief source of timber. Podocarps, in fact, are almost the only native South African conifers. In Australia 'brown pine' and 'black pine' are both podocarps. In New Zealand *P. dacrydioides*, the biggest of the family, up to 200 feet, is called 'white pine'. But only one exceptional species of podocarp, a native of Japan, belongs in the northern hemisphere and the few excellent hardy species from New Zealand and Chile have hardly been used at all.

The fruit of the podocarp (technically a cone) is a purple or red berry in which a nut is embedded. Podocarp leaves vary from yew-length to willow-length; all narrow but the longest ones too tapering at the ends to be described as needles. Perhaps their best quality is their rich yellow-green glossiness, a subtropical quality that draws you to the tree, particularly in winter. *P. salignus*, the willow-leaf podocarp from Chile, and *P. macrophyllus*, the Japanese member of the family, both have this effect. Where they are hardy (zones 7 and 8 respectively) they will eventually grow into fair-sized trees. The biggest willow-leaf one in Britain at present is 64 feet; in the southern States 60 feet is not exceptional for *P. macrophyllus*.

One of the short-leaved podocarps, the Chilean *P. andinus*, is remarkably like the yew for such a distant relation. To make matters worse it has been christened the plum-fruited yew, to the chagrin (one imagines) of the plum yew.

Another yew-like podocarp from Chile was made memorable by being called after the husband of Queen Victoria; *Saxegothaea conspicua* (Prince Albert's family name was Saxe-Coburg-Gotha). 'Prince Albert's yew' is certainly worth planting. It looks like a rather slender weeping willow with black foliage–or at least it does in Edinburgh, where it is perfectly hardy.

The podocarps have their cypress-types as well as their yew-types and willow-types. The *Dacrydium* branch of the family has scale-leaves that suggest cypress (or perhaps juniper). The New Zealand Rimu (*D. cupressinum*) is another small, soft-foliaged, weeping tree, happy in the moderate warmth of San Francisco. The Tasmanian Huon pine (*D. franklinii*) has shown itself a shade hardier. If you can imagine a cypress weeping willow you are somewhere near it. Such a tree, if only one could find it (few nurseries yet have them), would be a superb acquisition for a garden in zone 8.

Above *A mature Huon pine weeps gracefully. Young trees make some of the most elegant of pot-plants for conservatories in zones that (like most of Britain) are too cold to grow them out of doors.*

Below *The distinctive branched clusters of male 'flowers' of plum-fruited yew* (Podocarpus andinus). *Here they are shedding pollen. Male and female flowers usually occur on separate trees.*

The plum-fruited yew, Podocarpus andinus *(from Chile), is surprisingly like a yew in every way except in its fruit, which look like small plums. They change from blue- to yellow-green and eventually turn black.*

Above *The New Zealand Kahikatea or 'white pine',* Podocarpus dacrydioides, *grows in swampy ground in both North and South Islands. Captain Cook measured a specimen with a clean bole to 90 feet. In Britain it is tender,* making a slender, pretty tree only in the mildest garden.

Swamp Cypresses and Dawn Redwoods

Conifer naming is much more confident with the nuts and bolts of varieties and cultivars than with the bafflingly broad horizons of families that have been in existence 100 million years or more. One might say that the big divisions into families and orders are provisional. The Swamp Cypress, Dawn Redwoods, Sequioas, and their allies were, until recently, grouped in a family of their own, *Taxodiaceae*. Since this was based on a combination of characters that they have with those that they lack, modern botanists have found this an unsatisfactory alliance. Recent research has shown that most of the group are better placed in the *Cupressaceae*.

One thing the swamp cypress (*Taxodium*) and its class-mates have in common is great age. Another is colossal size. To this group belong the redwood and the giant sequoia, the Japanese 'cedar' and Chinese 'fir' (the biggest timber-trees of their respective countries) and the biggest conifer of the eastern United States, the swamp or, as it is known in America, bald cypress.

It may seem odd to recommend a conifer for being deciduous, but the swamp cypress, like the larch, makes a virtue of its seeming disability by being the freshest-looking of all the needle trees while it is green, and turning colour superbly in autumn. It complements the larch beautifully, in fact; they should be planted together. For when the larch turns from dark green to autumnal gold, the swamp cypress shifts from pale green by deepening stages to a ripe ginger brown. The two colours together in my garden, interspersed with the steel blue of Scots pine, are one of autumn's most compelling compositions.

Why is the swamp cypress not planted more? Partly, no doubt, on account of its size. Yet of all tall trees in a small garden it can make the most effect while casting the least shade. Partly, I suspect, because everyone assumes it needs a swamp. Curiously, it seems indifferent. For a tree whose home-ground (if that's the word) is the brackish water of swamps in the sub-tropics, it does remarkably well in dry ground in the sub-arctic winters of New England. It needs a good warm summer – it fails on the mild west coast of Scotland – but it freezes without flinching, as the 80-foot tree at the Arnold Arboretum in Boston shows.

The only attraction you will probably lose by planting it in ordinary garden soil is the eventual growth of its unique 'knees' from the roots. Science is puzzled by these spongy knobs, which arise over the points where its deep sinker-roots descend into the mud. Sometimes they form a whole village of odd mounds like ant-hills, coming out of the water or out of the waterside ground.

It seemed reasonable to think that they supplied air to the roots, which would otherwise be in danger of drowning. Yet they seem to have no means of doing this. Like earlobes or little toes they are just there.

The swamp cypress includes two other

Left *Female flowers of the swamp cypress are like tiny open green cones at the tip of the old shoot before the new leaves have emerged. The eventual cone (far left, unripe) is a little ball only one inch across.*

The trunks of swamp cypress in Cypress Gardens, Charleston, S. Carolina, show the fluted, flaring base of a tree adapted to wet, unstable ground. The 'knees' (right of big trunk) may be a way of supplying the roots with oxygen.

Left *Swamp cypress has no objection to a hard winter. By a Swiss lake it forms the same knotty and knobbly roots as by a Florida swamp. The first examples planted in Europe in the 17th century are still healthy trees.*

The dawn redwood was only discovered in 1941 in China. Already it has produced cones in cultivation in several places. These were photographed in the Donaupark, Vienna. They closely resemble the cones of the swamp cypress.

trees in its rather special genus. The pond cypress (*T. ascendens*) is a local form, restricted to the southeastern part of its huge range, which runs from Delaware to the swamps of eastern Texas. Although it is not so hardy, the pond cypress is in some ways an even better tree for the garden: smaller and upright, with its leaves set spirally all round the branches instead of in two ranks.

The other taxodium is evergreen at home in Mexico, only losing its leaves where it is planted near the limit of its hardiness. One specimen, the Montezuma cypress (*T. mucronatum*), can safely be called the world's fattest tree: it is 115 feet in girth. Postcards from Tule, Oaxaca, show nothing but El Gigante: there is no room for anything else.

Asia's nearest approach to a taxodium was a tree of great rarity, reported as living a swamp cypress-like life near Canton in the south of China. Whether there is any *Glyptostrobus* left in the wilds nobody seems sure. There is one in the University of Washington arboretum at Seattle and three tiny ones grow in the south of England, distinguishing themselves by turning a lovely warm pink-brown in autumn.

Then in 1941 a Japanese scholar found the fossil remains of a similar tree in Tokyo. He called his find *Metasequoia glyptostroboides* –an indication, perhaps, of his state of scholarly indecision, rather than of his barbaric ear.

What seems almost incredible is that in the same year, 1941, thousands of miles away, half-way up the Yangtze river in eastern Szechwan near Chungking, a botanist stumbled on three trees of this same unknown genus. It was 1944 before specimens were collected and 1946 before a thorough search of the region was made by the National University. By September that year the Arnold Arboretum, for which Wilson had done most of his collecting in that very area, had joined the search. There were plenty of these trees; they were known to the people as water-larch and fed to the cattle. In 1948 seeds germinated in Boston and Britain and within a year the tree was being planted all over the world.

Like the ginkgo, this survival from among the fossils seems to have left its enemies behind. It grows much faster than the swamp cypress, at least to start with; there are

dawn redwoods (the name that was coined for it) 60 feet high in collections already. So far it has grown as a regular, pointed tree with very light, indeed rather twiggy branches. It remains to be seen whether it will broaden out with age, as swamp cypresses do, to the splendid, branchy, irregular head it possesses in its native habitat. It already shows signs of developing a flaring, fluted bole and of having a special fondness for water: both typical swamp cypress traits.

The ready way to distinguish between the two is by the arrangement of the leaves. Though both have green branchlets in two ranks along the main shoots (which fall in autumn with the leaves) those on the metasequoia are opposite each other, while the swamp cypress's are placed alternately. The same is true of the tiny soft-green needles themselves. Perhaps easier to see is the metasequoia's unique habit of having the next year's buds underneath the branchlets.

Dawn redwood (above and below) holds its light green colour until late in the season. Then it colours well; sometimes creamy-gold, often pinkish; always ending with shades of amber. The

dawn redwood's only drawback as a garden tree is its tendency to put out leaves before the last frost. Yet it repairs damage quickly with more long feathery sprays of its fragile little needles.

Above *Ancient specimens of the swamp cypress completely lose the tidy pyramidal look they had in youth. Old trees in the Everglades of Florida have huge limbs which semaphore with hanging curtains of Spanish moss.*

Right *In the 45 years it has been cultivated the dawn redwood has maintained a neat and narrow profile of perfect symmetry. Time will tell whether it will go on to imitate the gestures of the swamp cypress above.*

Trunks of bigger specimens of dawn redwood are often a maze of deep flutings which writhe down the trunk for two or three feet and then stop. Many of them are rich ginger-red with the bark coming away in strips.

Giant Sequoias and Coast Redwoods

Subject to an unconcluded debate about whether early Australians were just bragging when they reported eucalyptus trees 470 feet high, the redwood is the tallest tree we know and its cousin, the 'big tree' or giant sequoia, is the biggest.

Just how big they are in relation to more everyday trees comes across well in the comparison made by the American dendrologist Rutherford Platt. The lowest branch of the biggest of the 'big trees', in his report, is 150 feet from the ground; but this branch is six feet in diameter and 150 feet long – a branch alone bigger than the biggest elm tree in the world, held horizontally more than an elm tree's height above the ground.

It took even 19th-century Californians in all their vigour and rapacity quite a time to think of a way of cutting down such formidable creatures. There is a note of hysterical triumph in the account of five men working for three weeks boring holes round the trunk of a tree 100 feet in circumference to fell it. It never occurred to them to leave it where it stood.

In times past, before the Ice Ages, redwoods grew in many parts of the globe. Fossil remains of them have turned up in Cornwall, in the southwest corner of England, among other places. But like so many trees they have retreated to the one place on earth that offers them ideal conditions, and as so often that place is California.

There is a recipe for instant confusion in the fact that there are two trees in this story, not one. To make matters worse the tree known to botanists as *Sequoia sempervirens* is called the redwood (or coast redwood) while the tree known to laymen as giant sequoia or 'big tree' is botanically separate in the genus *Sequoiadendron*. It is the only species: *Sequoiadendron giganteum*.

Superficially the two are similar enough. Their foliage in fact is quite different; but what distinguishes them far more is their tastes and habits. The coast redwood reaches its preposterous heights in dense stands in the coastal fog belt of northern California; the 'big tree' builds its bulk in open groves with white fir and ponderosa pine and incense cedar in the relatively dry and extreme climate of the western Sierra, where most of the precipitation comes as snow.

A redwood forest is like no other. The best stands are on rich alluvial flats sheltered by the coast range but still within 30 miles of the sea. Bull Creek Flat in the Rockefeller Forest near Highway 101 is one of the best remaining, with about 10,000 acres of superb trees. The biggest surprise on seeing them for the first time is not so much the height of the trees, for it is almost impossible to stand

One of the biggest of the 'big trees': 'General Grant' is 267 feet high, 80 in girth, and weighs over 2,000 tons. 'Big trees' grow in groves with other species – in contrast to the coast redwood which forms dense stands on its own.

The 'big tree' of the Californian Sierras has succeeded splendidly in cultivation in Europe. Here at the Younger Botanic Gardens at Benmore in western Scotland 70-year-old trees make a perfect avenue between 130–150 feet high.

Right *The foliage of the 'big tree' is scale-like (compare with the redwood's, opposite). The cones here are full-size but still green: they turn dark brown on ripening and release scores of tiny angular seeds.*

The terrific growth-rate millions of years ago still shows in the thickness of the annual rings of a fossilized 'big tree' in the Yellowstone National Park.

back and survey one; it is the way they stand shoulder to shoulder, sometimes leaving scarcely room for a man to squeeze through between two trunks each 20 feet thick.

The whole grove seems to grow from one giant skein of roots. Nothing else except a few ferns can grow in that half light. It is a solemn and simple environment: the soft brown floor of litter; the surrounding trees more like walls than pillars, the dusky brown of their bark lit occasionally with a needle of light from far above. The style of the architecture is distinctly Gothic: the bark splits in deep grooves which end in a narrow Early English arch every ten or 15 feet.

The 'big trees' in the Sierra are more impressive to visit as a spectacle. There is all the fairground stuff of being able to drive through holes in them. You can stand back and see the whole monstrous vegetable: its untapering shaft going up like a road to the tangle of heavy branches that make its head – perhaps 100 feet of lively sprouting above 200 feet of simple, unadorned log. The tallest, a towering 320 feet, is only 47 feet short of the tallest redwood. A tree 100 feet in circumference at the base is 3,500 years old and some of the largest are at least 4,000 years old; there is no question of 'second-growth' trees ever supplanting these, except for logging purposes.

In nature since the trees never grow together there is no opportunity to compare them. In cultivation their foliage – if you can reach it – is the simple way of telling them apart. The 'big tree' is essentially scaly: somewhere between a cypress and a monkey puzzle in size of scale but inclined to the monkey puzzle's reptilian look. The redwood has two kinds of foliage: a little on new shoots like the 'big tree' but most of it more like a yew with regular rows of flat, taper-ended needles. The needles grow steadily shorter towards the end of the shoot, so that each individual shoot is roughly boat-shaped. The texture of both trees is stiff and coarse.

In cultivation the 'big tree' has proved much the hardier and more adaptable. Its arrival in Europe in 1853 caused a sensation. The craze for the cedar of Lebanon was almost over: the 'big tree' took its place. It was christened 'Wellingtonia' in honour of the Iron Duke. There was not a landowner in Britain who failed to plant one. And British conditions suited it perfectly: the trees survived and flourished so that today there is one on every estate; the tallest (in 1970) is in Devonshire and stands 165 feet high.

In the United States there was some attempt to counter-christen the tree 'Washingtonia' – a name already pre-empted by a palm. It is hardy as far north as Rhode

Island on the east coast. But it has never been regarded quite as rapturously as it was in Europe, perhaps for lack of the private parkland in which its opulent symmetry is so telling.

Open-ground cultivation gives the drooping lowest limbs of the 'big tree' the opportunity to layer themselves round the base. Some of the most magnificent specimens have formed vast pyramids in this fashion. The siblings moulded into the general mass are all the more beautiful because the younger growth is noticeably more grey, or silvery-green, than the dark spire above.

It is the nature of the coast redwood to dwell in groves. Single trees tend to resent the exposure to frost and wind. The best specimens outside California, where it is widely used, are in southwest Britain where it has reached 135 feet. But in central France, for example, where the wellingtonia grows well, it is not happy.

I feel obliged to mention what to me is the ugliest tree in the world – the weeping wellingtonia. This freak from a French nursery has branches that grow straight downwards, as near the trunk as they can get. As it gains height it begins to topple from the tip, sometimes curving almost into a loop. To grow one seems to me rather like exhibiting Siamese twins.

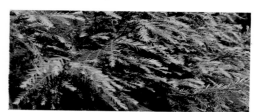

Left *Coast redwood sprouts vigorously from the base of the stump. Cut-down trees put up dense clumps of shoots. The foliage consists mainly of needle-leaves; a few shoots are scaly like those of the 'big tree'.*

Above *Spongy red bark gave the coast redwood its name. It is remarkably fire-resistant; a factor which has helped redwoods survive for up to 2,000 years.*

The coast redwood thrives in the coastal zone of northern California. The remaining acres of old-growth redwood are guarded by the Save-the-Redwood-League, one of the earliest conservation groups in the United States.

The Pacific 'Cedars' and 'Pines'

'A tree of the pine tribe, and perhaps the most miserable-looking ever introduced; something like an *Araucaria*, it is usually full of dead twigs.' Thus William Robinson in *The English Flower Garden*, writing of the glorious, vigorous, shapely (but not terribly hardy) *Cunninghamia*.

Robinson did not approve of the vogue that had set up monkey puzzle trees (or Chile pines, *A. araucana*) as thick as television aerials in the suburbs of late-Victorian England. The highly-flavoured taste of the time would combine these reptilian relics with bogus-rustic arbours and geometrical beds of scarlet salvias. But at least the monkey puzzle flourished. The cunninghamia sinned twice by turning brown.

James Cunningham was the first western plant-hunter ever to reach China. On that voyage in 1700 he discovered and described two magnificent trees, unlike anything then known. The one that bears his name is China's principal timber-producing tree,

coming second only to bamboo; his other find was the *Cryptomeria*, which plays the same role in Japan.

Genealogically these two trees link the sequoias with the weird araucarias of the southern hemisphere. The cryptomeria is very like the giant sequoia in foliage; the cunninghamia, as Robinson says, is like the monkey puzzle. Yet botanically the two belong to the same family.

They are both uncommon if not actually rare trees in gardens today. Only a juvenile-foliaged or retinospora form of the cryptomeria is well-known – as *Cryptomeria japonica* 'Elegans'. It justifies its popularity in every way: its soft plumey foliage changes with the seasons from a pale opal in summer to a bold brick-purple in the coldest months. It is no dwarf: 60 or 70 feet is within its reach. If it does grow so high, though, it has a tendency to topple over or even to bend double under its own weight, and layer its long curving branches in the ground.

Left *Immature male cones of the monkey puzzle. It is unusual to see such a perfect whorl of five cones together, ones and twos being the norm. When mature, each cone will be the size of a small coconut.*

Above *A vista in one of the great monkey puzzle forests of Chile on the slopes of Volcan Llaima. Here the trees extend up to the snow line and thrive in soil that seems to be no more than ash and clinker.*

Top *The reptilian-scaly branchlets of the monkey puzzle (or Chile pine). Each leaf is hard and tough as leather, tipped with a sharp point. At the top of the tree partly mature rounded cones can be seen.*

Typical arching branchlets of Cunninghamia lanceolata, *the Chinese fir. The handsome glossy dark green foliage is only seen at its best in sheltered humid areas; frosts and icy winds will sear or kill it.*

There is a strong argument for bringing back the cryptomeria proper, a tree like a more elegant and lightweight wellingtonia with softer foliage and a less rocket-like silhouette. And also, in milder areas, for re-installing the cunninghamia.

My ideas about these bold reptile-trees (there is no other way of describing their bright green scaliness) were abruptly altered when I saw them being tried out in what are known as 'forest-plots' on the west coast of Scotland.

Where one monkey puzzle (or cunninghamia) looks quite embarrassingly stiff and self-conscious–at least as a young tree–a whole clump of them takes on quite a different air. Seven or eight araucarias, six feet apart and 20 feet high, would make the most magnificent garden sculpture: fairly ferocious-looking, I'll admit.

The other araucarias, the Norfolk Island pine (*A. columnaris*), the candelabra tree (*A. angustifolia*) and the bunya bunya pine (*A. bidwillii*) are too tender, alas, for northern Europe or most of the United States. Alas because they are really much better-looking trees than the monkey puzzle. The Norfolk Island pine is the beauty of the family. It grows for many years with the hypnotic symmetry of a paper cut-out, each perfect whorl of branches holding aloft four perfectly-matched green combs of leaves.

The Pacific Ocean is completely encircled by this family: the redwoods in the northeast, the Chile pines in the southeast, cryptomerias in Japan and the araucarias in Queensland and Norfolk Island. The most southwesterly of all is a genus peculiar to Tasmania, an island with many excellent and original plants. The King William pine (*Athrotaxis selaginoides*) and the smaller *A. cupressoides* and *A. × laxifolia* are nearest to the cryptomerias in appearance; hardy and good-looking, but still very much collectors' pieces. In a tub (as they are often grown) they look quite artificial.

Part of the vast cryptomeria forests of Japan, where it is the most important timber tree and is cultivated with great skill. Cryptomeria needs a high rainfall to grow fast and well. Like the monkey puzzle it had a vogue in Victorian gardens.

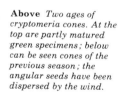

Above *Two ages of cryptomeria cones. At the top are partly matured green specimens; below can be seen cones of the previous season; the angular seeds have been dispersed by the wind.*

Below *The scuffling of human feet and the erosive force of rain have combined in laying bare this pattern of cryptomeria roots near a Japanese temple at Kyoto.*

The Dwarf Conifers

When the nurseryman says sport he doesn't mean violent exercise: nor does he mean jest. He means the tendency of plants and parts of plants to have a mind of their own; to deviate from the norm. The nurseryman's business is to follow up the most promising deviants to see how they develop. It happens in the seed-bed: out of 200 cypress trees one or two may be blue or yellow instead of green, or thin and narrow instead of pyramidal or bushy. It also happens occasionally on one branch of an otherwise blameless tree. There is suddenly a confusion of twisting, twining little shoots. The nurseryman pounces. If he can propagate from this oddity, either by getting a cutting of it to take root, or by grafting it on to other roots, he has a new design of tree of his own. In the past he has celebrated the fact in appalling pseudo-Latin: today he must use a vernacular name.

Sports of conifers which grow very little, or at least slowly, are particularly valuable. They are permanent, often pretty and they take up practically no space. In town gardens which have no room for real trees they offer, pollution permitting, the chance to enjoy the lovely variety of the conifer world in miniature.

There is no clear dividing line between conifers and dwarf conifers. Natural smallness may or may not be permanent; but it can always be made so. By a simple borrowing from the technique of bonsai – just lifting and replanting every few years – it is possible to keep any small conifer (or even any big one) from getting the bit in its teeth and growing away.

On this page are some of the outstanding miniatures. The broadleaf world has no equivalent – only relatively few stunted arctic forms. A certain amount of tact is needed in using dwarf conifers effectively; their scale works best if they are kept to themselves, in a bed or on a rock garden of their own, perhaps with low heather to cover the ground between them.

The most effective way of using dwarf conifers is in a self-contained land-scape. This is the famous Pigmy Pinetum at Devizes, Wiltshire, made by H. J. Welch, author of Dwarf Conifers; the standard work on the subject. The plants in the picture are:

1 Juniperus chinensis 'San Jose'; a blue dwarf ground-cover form.

2 *A golden version of* Chamaecyparis lawsoniana 'Ellwoodii': *'Ellwood's Gold'. It is slower than the green form; a dense little column of gold.*

3 *'Boulevard' is an American improvement on what was called the 'moss retinospora' (Chamaecyparis pisifera 'Squarrosa'). It is a beautiful colour, and can reach 15 feet or more.*

4 *Even the coast redwood has a dwarf form:* Sequoia sempervirens 'Prostrata'. *Full-size shoots that appear need cutting off.*

5 *A dwarf form of one of the best false cypresses;* Chamaecyparis lawsoniana 'Wisselii Nana' *has clustered radially arranged shoots of dark bluish-green. Strong-growing shoots need pruning to keep it small.*

6 Chamaecyparis pisifera *'Plumosa Aurea' is a rich-gold mossy bush which can live among dwarfs for several years.*

7 *A dwarf form of the well-known cultivar* Chamaecyparis lawsoniana 'Ellwoodii', *one of the best of the soft blue columns.*

8 *A white-variegated round bush form of the Chinese juniper (J. chinensis 'Variegata'): eventually much more than dwarf size, becoming pyramidal with densely packed branches.*

A tidy little gold ball: Thuja plicata 'Rogersii'; *a far cry from its giant parent the western red cedar. It will take 30 years to grow to about three feet each way.*

Right *The Waukegan juniper (Juniperus horizontalis 'Douglasii') is one of the best of the blue-grey ground-cover junipers humping up into low billows. In winter it takes on a purple tone.*

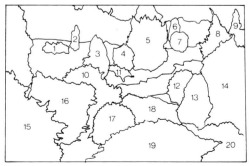

Right *A wild form of the Balsam fir from New Hampshire:* Abies balsamea 'Hudsonia'. *It makes a flat spreading shrub with short, broad leaves of a good green. Slow enough to be treated as a dwarf.*

Chamaecyparis law-
soniana 'Nidiformis'—the
name means 'nest-shaped'
—slowly makes a broad
arching mound of
graceful grey-green
sprays. Only in the short
term is it a true dwarf.

12 The Hinoki cypress
(Chamaecyparis obtusa
'Nana') is shapely,
brilliant green, and one of
the slowest-growing
dwarfs.

13 One of the smallest
and brightest Lawson cy-
presses; C. lawsoniana
'Minima Aurea' is a
golden cone in spring,
growing only a foot in
ten years.

14 'Fletcheri' is a Lawson
cypress cultivar, too tall
for dwarf status. But it is
neat, soft and bluish—and
one can always trim it.

15 Cryptomeria japonica
'Pygmaea' or 'Nana'—a
low flat-topped bush
version of the Japanese
cedar with tiny leaves.

16 The only non-conifer
in the picture: Hebe
lycopodioides from New
Zealand: a conifer-mimic
until its white flowers
appear in summer.

17 The best small golden
thuja (T. occidentalis
'Rheingold'). Grows
slowly to become a bronze-
gold bush with superb
winter colour.

18 Another ground-
hugging juniper (J. pro-
cumbens 'Nana') makes a
blue-green mat.

19 An excellent small
juniper: J. communis
'Hornibrookii' moulds its
miniature green silver-
backed foliage to the
shape of the ground.

20 The prostrate Christmas tree (Picea abies
'Procumbens') starts flat
on the ground, then heaps
up close-pressed tiers of
foliage to make a wide-
spreading, flat-topped
bush. It is one of the most
vigorous prostrate forms
of P. abies.

Above A new, as yet
unnamed form of
Cryptomeria japonica.
Such sports are con-
tinually arising in
nurseries. Worthwhile
ones are given names and
propagated.

Above The bizarre
cockscomb growths of
Cryptomeria japonica
'Cristata' make it perhaps
the most obviously
freakish of conifer
cultivars. It grows slowly
but can reach 30 feet.

9 The golden Chinese
thuja that appears on
page 102 (P. orientalis
'Elegantissima') is slow
enough to live among
dwarfs for several years.
In winter the leaves turn
bright reddish-brown.

10 A miniature version of
the Asiatic 'Schrenk's
spruce'–Picea schrenk-
iana 'Globosa'; a broad
low cone of short but
typical spruce branches.
This form is now rare in
cultivation.

11 Another Hinoki
cypress, C. obtusa
'Mariesii', makes a tiny
but untidy cone shape.
The variegated foliage is
creamy-white in summer,
yellowish-green during
the winter.

Left A young form of
eastern hemlock, Tsuga
canadensis 'Pendula';
eventually it will become
a dome-shaped bush with
pendulous branchlets. It
was first introduced into
cultivation in the 1870s.

Above The dwarf
Alberta spruce (Picea
glauca albertiana
'Conica') grows very
slowly to six feet: a neat,
bright green, well-
furnished cone. It was
found wild in the Rockies
in 1904.

119

The Palms

The palms, the potent symbol of the tropics, occupy a by-way of evolution. In the remotest past they parted company with the family which contains the water-lilies and the magnolias. In strict botanical terms, being properly called flowering plants, which the conifers are not, they come closer to the broadleaves. But unlike any broadleaf tree they come into the class of plants with one seed-leaf, the monocotyledons. The implications of this abstruse detail are far-reaching. From it springs the totally different design and construction of the palm trees.

Palms don't and can't have any real branches. They have no annual rings of growth: they grow taller without growing thicker. All their leaves are produced from the top of the stem, and their flowers and fruits from among their leaves. The workings of a palm tree are shown in the illustration on the right.

There are certain crucial disadvantages in their design. The biggest is that they depend utterly on the cabbage-like bud at the top of the stem . . . . which happens to be a very tasty morsel, much sought by the evolving beasts of every age up to and including man. Its defence has therefore been an important part of their evolutionary story. Witness the fact that mainland palms tend to be more or less furnished with spikes to make them uncomfortable to climb, whereas on remote and mammal-less islands in the Indian Ocean they have no spikes at all.

A hundred and twenty million years ago most of the globe suffered the same tropical climate. Then came the cooling that ended with the Ice Ages. The palms retreated before the cold in just the same way as the rest of the trees, but very few were left in the temperate zone and not many in the sub-tropics; they needed the tropical extreme. Most of the 3500 species of palm need heat and moisture as a way of life.

To palms, therefore, even the subtropical climate of southern California or Florida is chilly. A world-wide group of a very few species venture into the world of frost. Only one, a Chinese species, is at home in a truly northern climate. Overleaf some of the best-known on the borderlines of hardiness are illustrated.

The study of palms is relatively new. The first and still the most considerable work on them was done by the Dutch in the East Indies in about 1800. The classic palm drawings of that period have not been surpassed. For the plain fact is that you have to be a blend of botanist and steeplejack to get very far. Not surprisingly, most botanists stick to trees with branches. ▶

A date palm heavily laden with its bunches of fruit. The date palm is a native of North Africa, but today planted in places with a similar climate all over the world. Suckers can be seen arising from the base of the trunk.

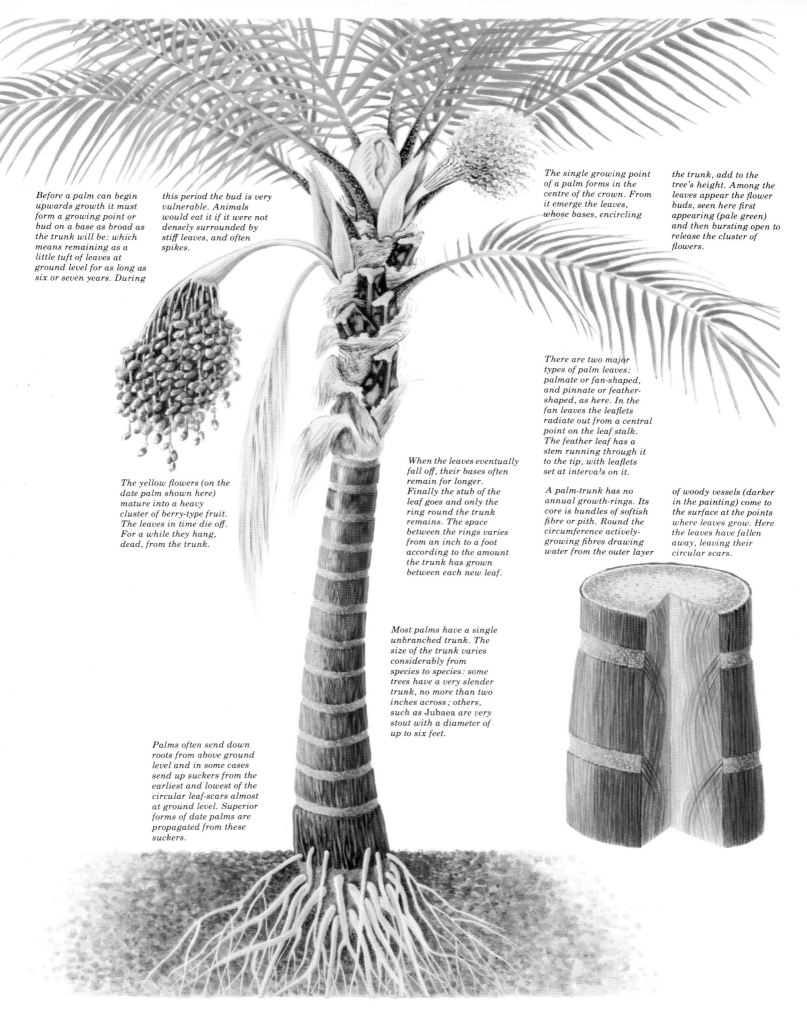

Before a palm can begin upwards growth it must form a growing point or bud on a base as broad as the trunk will be: which means remaining as a little tuft of leaves at ground level for as long as six or seven years. During this period the bud is very vulnerable. Animals would eat it if it were not densely surrounded by stiff leaves, and often spikes.

The single growing point of a palm forms in the centre of the crown. From it emerge the leaves, whose bases, encircling the trunk, add to the tree's height. Among the leaves appear the flower buds, seen here first appearing (pale green) and then bursting open to release the cluster of flowers.

The yellow flowers (on the date palm shown here) mature into a heavy cluster of berry-type fruit. The leaves in time die off. For a while they hang, dead, from the trunk.

There are two major types of palm leaves: palmate or fan-shaped, and pinnate or feather-shaped, as here. In the fan leaves the leaflets radiate out from a central point on the leaf stalk. The feather leaf has a stem running through it to the tip, with leaflets set at intervals on it.

When the leaves eventually fall off, their bases often remain for longer. Finally the stub of the leaf goes and only the ring round the trunk remains. The space between the rings varies from an inch to a foot according to the amount the trunk has grown between each new leaf.

A palm-trunk has no annual growth-rings. Its core is bundles of softish fibre or pith. Round the circumference actively-growing fibres drawing water from the outer layer of woody vessels (darker in the painting) come to the surface at the points where leaves grow. Here the leaves have fallen away, leaving their circular scars.

Most palms have a single unbranched trunk. The size of the trunk varies considerably from species to species: some trees have a very slender trunk, no more than two inches across; others, such as Jubaea are very stout with a diameter of up to six feet.

Palms often send down roots from above ground level and in some cases send up suckers from the earliest and lowest of the circular leaf-scars almost at ground level. Superior forms of date palms are propagated from these suckers.

121

The Palm Family/*Palmae*

The Palms

Middle *The date palm is an important food plant in North Africa, its original home, and in many parts of the world with a similar climate. Here in Tunisia the ripe dates are being stripped by hand from their heavy clusters.*

Above *The royal palm makes one of the best street trees for the tropics with its pale trunk, bulging interestingly at the base and again in the middle.*

Top left *The crown of the coconut palm with its feather-leaves up to 20 feet long. Up the trunk of this tree growing in the West Indies climbs* Scindapsus aureus.

Above *The Canary Island date palm is a squatter, broader tree with a much thicker trunk than the date palm of Egypt. The flowers can be seen appearing from among the leaves.*

▶ Only one palm has come to terms completely with snow and ice: *Trachycarpus fortunei*, the Chusan or windmill palm of the Far East.

It is no beauty. Each year it grows two or three fan-leaves, three or four feet across, and sheds their yellowed forebears. The old leaf-bases remain, covering the trunk with brown furry fibre. As a young tree, a cluster of green fans on a short stalk, it has definite merit, but in age, a 15- or 30-foot column of tatty fur with a tuft of leaves on top, it is a sad creature. Still, a palm is a palm, and the raffish Riviera air it can lend an innocent rose garden is not to be underestimated.

The Riviera, indeed the whole Mediterranean, has its own native palm, a similar fan-leaved affair. *Chamaerops* is not quite so hardy and rarely grows so high. It often forms a bush with a cluster of short trunks, each carrying a bunch of completely rigid fans. At most it will grow, single-stemmed, to 20 feet, and look like a better-groomed Chusan palm.

Most of the palms on the border-line of the temperate zone belong to the group with fan-leaves: in the tropics the feather-leaf is much more common.

There are two other fan-leaf palms, not as hardy as the first two but certainly acquainted with freezing temperatures–the

FAN PALMS
The hardiest palms have fan leaves (right). They will survive in temperate zones but only one, the Chusan palm, is fully frost-proof.
1 *The Chusan palm (Trachycarpus fortunei) can survive temperatures of 10° F. or even lower. It grows slowly with an untidy fibrous trunk.*
2 *The Mediterranean fan-*

palm, seen growing far right in the south of France, is more often a many-stemmed bush or even a hedge.

CABBAGE PALMS
A group of palms with fan-leaves formed round a distinct mid-rib (right) include several moderately hardy species for Mediterranean-climate regions (zone 8).
3 *The cabbage palm (Sabal palmetto) grows to 90 feet with immense fans on stiff spines curving out and down. Its dried leaves furnish the crosses for Palm Sunday services.*
4 Livistona *is a genus from Australia and China. The slow-growing Chinese form has gracefully drooping tips to the lobes of its fans.*

5 Washingtonia, *a sturdy-looking tree surviving temperatures down to 22°F. The Mexican W. robusta is one of the fastest-growing palms, but not as hardy.*
Far right *A young* Livistona australis.

MODIFIED-FAN PALMS
A third form of palm-leaf continues the progression from fan to feather (right); leaflets are curled almost into tubes where they attach to the leaf-spine. Trees with this form of leaf are more tender than fan palms.
6 *The date palm of commerce is planted worldwide in regions with a climate similar to Egypt's. A temperature of 20° F. will defoliate a date palm, but the trunk may survive even lower temperatures.*
7 *The Canary Island date palm is the most impressive of its genus. The less hardy Senegal date palm (Phoenix reclinata) forms graceful clumps of thin stems.*
Far right *The date palm in the Algerian Sahara.*

FEATHER PALMS
The feather-leaved palms (right) are mostly tropical trees with little or no resistance to frost. Their leaves may be as long as 20 feet. The hardiest tree is the Chilean wine palm.
8 *The king palm grows to 70 feet with a smooth green trunk and a broad shapely head.*
9 *The queen palm grows*

rapidly and keeps ramrod-straight to 40 feet with an open crown of long pendulous leaves.
10 *The coconut palm with its curving trunk grows only in frost-free regions, such as, far right, Tahiti.*
11 *The royal palm is at the borderline of its hardiness in southern Florida. Its pale trunks line avenues in many tropical cities.*

Palm-like as it looks, the tree fern (here a species of Dicksonia in Tasmania) is no relation; but a normal fern with its rhizome or root vertical instead of horizontal in the ground. The illustration is from A Narrative of a Visit to the Australian Colonies, *published in 1843.*

Caribbean cabbage palm (*Sabal palmetto*) and the Australian (and Asian) *Livistona*. In both, the leaf-stalk extends through the fan, giving it a distinct mid-rib. That of the cabbage palm – the common palm of South Carolina and Georgia and many beaches of Florida – curves the whole six-foot leaf outwards and downwards. *Livistona australis* is in some ways the most graceful of the fan-leaved palms: the points of the fan's score of fingers are as long as whips and dangle from the crown.

California's only native palm, the petticoat or California fan (*Washingtonia filifera*) is also fan-leaved and moderately frost-proof. The petticoat's peculiarity is to keep its dead leaves indefinitely. They hang round the trunk, eventually making the whole tree look like an Alpine haystack.

The move from fan to feather advances a stage with the date palms. In the date genus (*Phoenix*) leaflets of leaves that are obviously feathers meet the stalk in a pleat with its curling edges facing upwards, a characteristic which apparently relates it to the fan-leaf. Date palms have magnificent crowns – as many as 200 leaves each 20 feet long. They are hardy enough for southern California and central Florida; the Canary Island date (*Phoenix canariensis*), which has an immensely thick stem, being hardier than *Phoenix dactylifera*, the Egyptian date palm. Left to their own devices certain cultivars of the date palm often produce so many suckers from the base that their trunks are lost in fountains of greenery.

There are two more magnificent feather palms hardy enough for southern California and central Florida: the king palm of Australia (*Archonthophoenix alexandrae*) and the queen palm (*Syagurus romanzoffianum*) of Brazil. The king has a worthy crown of short, substantial leaves, rising from a glossy green crown-shaft at the top of a 70-foot trunk. The queen is less than half the height, with a distinctive top.

The royal palm and the coconut palm make no pretence of hardiness. The royal palm (*Roystonea regia*) comes from Cuba, the coconut (*Cocos nucifera*) from almost everywhere in the tropics. Both make enormously stately trees: the royal palm perfectly straight, pale-trunked with a gentle swelling at the base and again half-way up; the coconut tall but never straight, characteristically inclined towards the surf over a dazzling white beach.

The hardiest of the feather-palms seems to be the Chilean wine palm, *Jubaea chilensis* (or *J. spectabilis*). It does very well in California and of all palms has perhaps the most impressive trunk. It can be as much as six feet in diameter.

Above *The Joshua tree,* Yucca brevifolia. *Yuccas, like palms, have only one seed-leaf; they are native to Mexico and the southern United States. The Joshua tree is the most tree-like of the genus. It grows to over 30 feet.*

The Broadleaves

The broadleaf trees belong to the earth's dominant group of plants: the flower-bearers, in the strict sense of the word. Unlike the conifers the families of the broadleaves include plants that are not trees at all. They stem back to tropical climates (where by far the greater number of species still live). In the course of adapting to temperate conditions—above all to freezing winters—they have had varying degrees of success. Only a minority of species has come through as trees. All our herbaceous plants had tree-ancestors in the ancient tropical forests and many of them have tree-cousins still to be found in the forests of today.

Broadleaves originated as an evolutionary improvement on the conifers. What they managed better, above all, was the circulation of sap. The structure of their wood adapted to allow a much freer and stronger flow: this in turn allowed them leaves which could evaporate more water, photosynthesize quicker and thus get more value out of the summer sun.

Having made leaves that were more efficient for the conditions in which they grew, they were in trouble when (in the course of geological time) colder weather came. Some modified their leaves, giving them a tougher structure and a thicker skin: made them, in fact, more like the leaves of their conifer ancestors. These are our broadleaf evergreens.

Some simply became herbaceous, going underground in winter. These no longer exist as trees.

Most adopted a third plan: they went

deciduous. By dropping their leaves they could make the best of the sunny season with big, delicate and efficient leaves, capable of the maximum photosynthesis; but suffer no damage in winter (when they would not be missing much sun anyway).

As far as flowers were concerned the big step forward by the broadleaves was pollination by insects rather than by the wind. It seems to have started with beetles eating the flowers of members of the magnolia family. The great advantage of insect pollination is that it does not need a great crowd of trees of the same species to have a fair chance of success. There is less drain on a tree's protein supply because less pollen is needed. (The nectar that attracts bees is made not from protein but from more easily obtainable sugars.)

The other development, crucial to the science of taxonomy, but without much advantage for the broadleaves, was the introduction of an ovary to contain the seeds. The term Angiosperm, which covers all the flowering plants, refers to this and distinguishes them from the naked-seeded conifers (Gymnosperms).

'In a large group an imperfect organization is better than no organization at all.' So writes Arthur Cronquist, the Senior Curator of the New York Botanic Garden in his *The Evolution and Classification of Flowering Plants*. I am glad I can quote him, because the organization of the broadleaves is a mine-field for the amateur – or, come to that, for the professional. My debt to Dr. Cronquist goes much further, though: the order in which the families appear in the following pages is entirely his. It is based on the relative primitiveness or sophistication of the families, as demonstrated (chiefly) by their flowers. Thus the magnolias, which are accepted as belonging to the most primitive order of all the flowering plants, come first. The rest follow in increasing order of sophistication and modernity.

The common oak, Quercus robur, *in the forest of Fontainebleau, France.*

The Tulip Tree and the Magnolias

Every magnolia is the apple of someone's eye. To be conspicuous but to manage an air of frailty is a good recipe.

There are 80 species of magnolia and two of tulip trees (*Liriodendron*) in the magnolia family. Nearly all have flowers larger than any other tree and leaves bigger than most. They range from the tallest of American broadleaves to cafe-umbrella size. None comes from Europe; some big ones are natives of the southeastern United States; almost all the pretty little garden ones come from China and Japan. Frailty is deceptive: these last tend to be the hardiest.

The tulip tree is the grandfather of the family. It sounds rather less glamorous under the name foresters know it by: yellow poplar. As the tulip tree it sounds like a Walt Disney production. Imagine: 190 feet high; all covered with tulips. The only trouble is that the two selling points cancel each other out. It's true about the tulips, but you often need binoculars to see them.

You can hardly grow a more adaptable, less demanding tree, or one that grows faster. In the wild it grows in the Great Smokies and along the Ohio River, but its range reaches from the Great Lakes to the Gulf of Mexico. It should be planted small: like all magnolias it has vulnerable fleshy roots and one of them is a deep taproot. Ideally it likes deep loose soil and a wet spring. A seedling with all its prayers answered has grown 50 feet in 11 years. But tulip trees soldier on in polluted air, mutilated by amateur tree surgeons, in disease (they catch few) and drought (provided there is a moist sub-soil).

They offer an individuality that makes one think of the ginkgo. There is no other leaf quite this shape. It sets off like a maple leaf, with pointed lobes at the sides, but where the third and biggest lobe should come to a point it is cut off short. Again ginkgo-like, it keeps up an even, fresh, medium green from spring to autumn, then changes to a clear light yellow. I can never understand the prejudice that autumn colour is not colour unless it is red. A hundred feet of fresh farm butter is a stirring sight.

As for the tulips, which open in May or June, it's a pity they are not often within reach: they are sumptuous flowers, beloved by bees, with pale green petals opening to show a soft orange lining and a noble array of parts.

The tree has a remarkably similar Chinese counterpart; less different indeed than one or two odd cultivars which have cropped up. There is also an upright one, a variegated one and one without the side lobes so that the leaves are virtually rectangular.

Magnolias proper can reach almost the same colossal heights, but many stay obligingly near eye-level. It is probably in terms of size that they can be most usefully catalogued; that, and the crucial question of when they flower.

There are really three major types of magnolias. One is the evergreen, of which *Magnolia grandiflora*, the bull bay of the Deep South, is the prime example. The second is the deciduous magnolia that flowers in summer, so that its leaves set off (or hide, as the case may be) the flowers, which are tulip-shaped, opening to saucers. The third is the kind that flowers before the leaves. Most of them are small trees, some are shrubs, and all are from the Far East. There is a superannuated subgenus name for these: *Gwillimias*. It has no more modern validity than *retinospora*, but I like the Welsh feeling about it – and why not make a distinction of plants that are, to you and me, distinct?

Gwillimias in turn can be divided first into tulip-flowered and star-flowered kinds and then into the few big trees (all tulip-flowered) and the rest, which are small-to-medium.

The bull bay (what a dreadfully hearty name for such a voluptuous plant) must be counted the all-round champion of the

Top *The highly original leaves of the tulip tree seem to have the middle lobe cut off. The beautiful orange flowers often occur too high up to be clearly seen.*

The tulip tree is one of the tallest natives of eastern North America: specimens nearly 200 feet high have been known. Its foliage turns pale yellow in autumn.

Magnolia grandiflora, *the bull bay of the southeastern States, is the best evergreen member of the family, even tolerating city air (as here, in London). In northern parts it is often grown against walls.*

Left *Even without its flowers* Magnolia grandi-flora *would be worth growing for its big glistening leaves, coated underneath with brown felt. A spent fruit can be seen at the end of this shoot.*

Left *A magnificent close-up of the fruit of* Magnolia grandiflora, *splitting to disclose one of its bean-like seeds. They germinate the following spring, but the plant takes ten years or more to flower.*

The leaf, flower and fruit of the yellow cucumber tree of Georgia, Magnolia acuminata *var.* subcordata, *are shown here in the painting by the 18th-century botanist André Michaux.*

magnolias. In the forests of the south it grows to well over 100 feet and regularly delivers a heavy, creamy, scented flower on every shoot, making sackfuls of seed. Its leaves are beautiful: best when they unfold with a layer of velvet rust underneath, but always glistening and trim. Furthermore, they dry well and keep for ever: year after year we have, as Christmas decorations at home, some little artificial orange trees made of them.

Towards the north of its range (Philadelphia is about the limit on the east coast; it is hardy in most of Europe and all of Britain) the custom is to grow it up a high south- or west-facing wall, which it totally buries in its magnificent evergreenery. It prefers no lime (but is tolerant of it) and lots of nourishment. Once it gets going it flowers steadily (though not all over except in the south) from June or July to October. Some clones start flowering at a much earlier age (four or five years) and have bigger flowers than others. An 18th-century English selection called 'Exmouth' (or 'Exoniensis') is one of the best on both counts. Another good one, with whopping flowers, is called 'Goliath'.

The first magnolia to reach cultivation was the swamp bay (*M. virginiana*). It lacks the magnificence of the bull bay, either in

leaf—it is only a committed evergreen in the south—or in flower. Its compensations are a delicious fragrance in flowers which persist (at Kew) even into December and almost luminous blue-white undersides to the leaves—but many other magnolias share this.

The bigleaf magnolia (*M. macrophylla*) from the southeastern States has its detractors, but I find it superb. This one is definitely not an evergreen, but then its leaves are really startlingly big—getting on for banana size. Its flowers, moreover, are in proportion. They come in summer, beaming through the two-foot, luminous-green ▶

In climates like that of its native south (here in northern Italy) the bull bay (Magnolia grandi-flora) makes a magnificent evergreen tree, growing as high as 90 feet and flowering profusely.

Top *The scented creamy flower of* Magnolia grandiflora. *Some forms of bull bay, notably 'Goliath', have flowers up to ten inches across, produced in great numbers from mid-summer on.*

Above *The evergreen sweet or swamp bay was the first of the family to be grown in Europe, as early as the 17th century. It lacks the vigour, hardiness and gloss of the bull bay.*

Top *The Chinese evergreen rival to the bull bay,* Magnolia delavayi, *has much bigger leaves with milky-green undersides. It is just as hardy, but has never achieved the same popularity. It flowers in late summer.*

Above *The bigleaf magnolia, with the biggest leaves of all, up to two feet long, is another native of the southern States, but deciduous. Its huge flowers (up to 12 inches across) are sweetly scented.*

The Magnolias

Left *A cross-section of the heart of a magnolia flower, showing the curling female parts, or pistils, each one leading to an ovule. At the base are tight-packed stamens, not yet grown to mature size.*

Below *The lemony flowers of* Magnolia obovata.

▶ leaves. In autumn, if the tree is well sheltered from the wind (this is essential) and the leaves hang on in good condition, they can turn anything from malted milk to espresso. Not classic fall colour exactly, but even more arresting.

I have strayed from the evergreens. The other one is *M. delavayi* from western China. This is the compromise between the bull bay and the bigleaf: it is evergreen, and its leaves are quite big enough to satisfy most people. Its flowers come and go very quickly: the leaves would be the reason to plant it, but again, only if you have a wind-proof corner. It is as hardy as *M. grandiflora*.

The bigleaf is, in fact, a member of class two; deciduous, summer-flowering magnolias. The champion for flowers in this department is the Japanese 'whiteleaf' magnolia (*M. obovata*). Its flowers are long-petalled, white and sweet-scented and the leaves really do set them off: they are long enough to be slightly floppy: their undersides are milky white; and if you are lucky enough to be standing under the tree on a sunny day you will see how they have the translucency of tropical sea-water; a pale green glow suffuses everything beneath.

The cucumber tree of the eastern States (*M. acuminata*) is probably the tallest magnolia in the flower-with-the-leaves department, but it would be misleading to class it as an ornamental flowering tree; the flowers can scarcely be seen in the towering mass of big shiny leaves. In every way the yellow cucumber tree (*M. cordata*), which has been considered a variety, is more of a garden proposition. It is half the size or less, but has masses of yellow flowers, among leaves half the size. The same cucumbery pods appear on both.

Wilson's (*M. wilsonii*), the Chinese (*M. sinensis*) and the Oyama (*M. sieboldii*) are a group of three oriental species without significant differences as far as the gardener is concerned: all flower from May or June onwards, sometimes intermittently for two

or three months. All have flowers which hang their heads so that you have to be underneath to see the red stamens in the white shades and all tend to be big bushes rather than real trees. There is a famous hybrid of *M. sinensis* named *highdownensis* which proved, at Sir Frederick Stern's famous chalk garden at Highdown near Worthing on the south coast of England, to be perfectly happy to grow on that uncompromising rock.

The gwillimias, now. These are the really spectacular ones, covering their bare branches with waxy flowers before a leaf appears, and often while there is still a good chance (in Britain at least) of a frost to wreck the show. *M. campbellii* is the giant tulip tree of the Himalayas. I think I can imagine one 150 feet high and holding aloft no leaves but thousands of big, pink, waxy flowers, but it does set the mind to boggling. It is pretty good at 60 feet, the highest it grows in England. There are several forms with flowers from white to pink/purple, but many demand patience: *M. campbellii* has no flowers at all for 25 years or so. There is one particularly hardy variety, *M. c. mollicomata*, which gets under way rather quicker at about 15 years.

A quick start is obviously a major consideration with a tree which is grown for its flowers. The excellent *M. kobus* has been largely superseded because it takes 15 years or more to start flowering. The ones which start soonest are *M. stellata*, the low bush with white star flowers you see almost everywhere, its more vigorous and splendid hybrid *M. × loebneri*, and the most popular and free-flowering of the tulip-flowered kind, *M. × soulangiana*.

The trick with the very-early flowering kinds like *M. stellata* is to grow them in a comparatively cold spot where their buds will not be wooed open by the spring sunshine too soon. *M. × stellata* and *M. × loebneri* are hardy enough to flourish in a north exposure. *M. × loebneri* grows twice

Top Perhaps the most splendid form of the most popular garden hybrid magnolia: the huge flowers of Magnolia × soulangiana 'Lennei'. *It was discovered in a garden in northern Italy in 1850.*

The magnolia that bears 'Chinese' Wilson's name, Magnolia wilsonii, *was discovered by him in China in 1908. Its pure-white flowers come after the leaves in summer. It makes a wide shrub rather than a tree.*

The cucumber tree of the eastern States has flowers in quiet tones of green-yellow and metallic blue-purple. It forms a tall tree with splendid big leaves. The 'cucumbers' are its fruit.

In the Himalayas the aristocrat of all magnolias, Magnolia campbellii, grows to 150 feet and covers its branches with huge pink flowers. But it is not as hardy as the smaller garden species from the orient and one may have to wait 25 years for flowers.

The Yulan or lily-tree of Japan and China (Magnolia denudata) has sweet-scented snow-white flowers before the leaves appear. Eventually it makes a tree up to 30 feet high, billowing with big branches.

as fast, however, and has bigger flowers, either pink or white to taste.

There are at least a dozen clones of the hybrid *M. × soulangiana*, varying from white through the grades of flush and blush which are typical of the race to a fairly livid purple. They are not trees at all, but spreading shrubs which consume a fair amount of space. Having flowered, they fill the space with not very fascinating foliage. To my mind it is a big garden which can spare the space for them. The Japanese willowleaf magnolia (*M. salicifolia*) is the narrowest-growing gwillimia, and an ardent flower-bearer; perhaps the best for a small garden.

Of the species other than *M. campbellii* which are relatively leisurely about flowering, the Chinese Yulan (*M. denudata*) is the classic. Its flowers have broad, pure white petals of the substance and thickness of an ivory paper knife. The leaves are milky-white beneath.

There is a hybrid between this and the Himalayan giant *M. campbellii* (under the name *M. × veitchii*) which has grown to 85 feet in Cornwall and apparently covers itself with hundreds of pink flowers. Neither of these last two would be at all happy in an alkaline soil.

The catalogue could go on and on, but these are by and large the best, and certainly the best-known, of the big family. There is one more, which doesn't exactly fall into the gwillimia class because, although it starts flowering early, it goes right on into mid-summer. This is the bush-size lily magnolia (*M. liliiflora*), whose variety 'Nigra' is almost new-wine purple on the outside of the petals. I would say crocus rather than lily for the shape of the flowers, though.

The positioning of magnolias is worth some thought. Wind and rain can soon destroy their fragile flowers. Shelter is the vital factor; light woodland shade provides the ideal conditions.

Above *The star-shaped flowers of the Japanese* Magnolia stellata, *the shrub on the left of the big centre picture. It grows slowly, rarely to more than ten feet, often wider than its height.*

Below *The darkest form of the lily-flowered magnolia is known as 'Nigra'. It is a smaller plant than the normal species but flowers even more freely, going on all summer in a good year.*

Above centre *Two of the most popular garden magnolias; the big pink* Magnolia × soulangiana *and the smaller white M.* stellata: *both are reliable and profuse flower-bearers before the leaves in spring.*

Of the many forms of the hybrid Magnolia × soulangiana *'Rustica Rubra' is one of the darkest pink. The 'lily-flowered' magnolia in the picture to the right is the parent that gives the colour.*

The shrub-sized lily-flowered magnolia of China (Magnolia liliiflora) starts flowering before the leaves and goes on far into the summer. It is one of the parents of M. × soulangiana.

The Bays and Laurels

Below left *Sweet bay or laurel was the emblem of victory to the ancient Romans, and poets were crowned with laurel wreaths. For more than 2,000 years it has been used for decoration, medicine and cooking.*

It is as well, first, to denounce the common laurel as the usurper of an honoured name. *The* honoured name, you might say, since the true laurel, to us the bay tree, sweet bay or bay laurel, is the Latin *Laurus nobilis*, whence poets laureate, winning your laurels, passing your baccalaureate and all the rest. Wreaths for distinguished brows were made, in fact, of the leaves we put in courts-bouillon and milk pud. The noble tree of the ancients is the one they clip like a poodle outside the Hôtel de Paris in Monte Carlo and casinos and hairdressers the world over. Whereas the common laurel (page 203) is an evergreen cherry.

Laurels are fairly close to the magnolias. They have in common striking, rather big leaves, usually simple ovals (and where not, as in the tulip tree and *Sassafras*, quite odd and original shapes). They share an aromatic principle: their chemistry is not identical, yet your nose tells you there is something in common between magnolia, bay, camphor and sassafras smells. What they lack, of course, is the fancy flowers. They are essentially foliage trees.

The bay tree comes into the same class as the yew and the box as material for vegetable sculpture. It is a slow grower; naturally a dense cone to no more than 40 feet. But it can easily be trimmed to a pyramid, or more laboriously pruned up to make a ball on a stick. It survives in a tub, or anywhere where the drainage is good. Very hard frost can hurt it, but it is by no means tender.

There is an unusual narrow- and rather wavy-leaved variety of bay (*L. nobilis* 'Angustifolia') which is apparently hardier. Like the golden bay (*L. n.* 'Aurea'), it is not common in cultivation.

Bay is a Mediterranean tree. It has two far-flung relations that are similar in general effect, but curiously different in their (very powerful) smells. The smell of camphor is familiar enough. Camphor comes from the camphor laurel (*Cinnamomum cam-*

phora) of southeast Asia. But there is no short way of describing the smell of *Umbellularia californica*, the California laurel – or, as Oregonians have it, Oregon myrtle. It is the sort of smell that somehow spells danger to me. I would no more put it in my soup than I would petrol – though Californians (and no doubt Oregonians too) play chicken with it in the kitchen, scorning the pungent bay as a spice for weaklings. The crushed leaf has a reputation for giving headaches. I'm prepared to take it on trust.

A smell is not a tree, however. The umbellularia is a very fine evergreen. The biggest one, near Santa Barbara, California,

Above *Looking up into the crown of an ancient bay tree in Italy. Although it is hardy, the bay never grows to this sort of age and size except in a warm climate. But it stands clipping into formal shapes.*

Left *Bay is not grown for its flowers; they are small and cream-coloured. But they can appear in dense masses, to be followed by little black cherry-like berries. The French 'baie' – whence the name – means berry.*

Sassafras is an eastern American relation of the bay. Its deciduous leaves vary from ovals to three-lobed (like maples') or two-lobed (like a mitten), rich green above with a blue-white patina below. Sassafras will grow to about 60 feet.

The camphor tree is
another of the aromatic
relations of the bay. It is
seen here growing wild on
the island of Shikoku in
southern Japan. In
California it makes a
good tree but it is too
tender for Britain.

The California laurel or
Oregon myrtle is the most
pungent member of the
bay family. It makes
dense dark trees in
northern California and
southern Oregon. In
Europe it is hardy,
but rare.

thick black branches. This is for southern parts only.

The deciduous sassafras, the only other hardy member of a family which (like so many) has its real headquarters in the tropics, is by far the most beautiful (and the best-smelling) of the collection. The bark and the roots used to be used to make a fragrant and refreshing pink tea, known colloquially as 'saloop'. Sassafras is rare in Europe, but in its native eastern States it is common enough—and it has a vast natural range, all the way from Florida to Maine and west to Texas.

Sassafras leaves can't even agree among themselves: some are plain, some lobed rather like maple leaves, some lobed on one side and looking like mittens. They stay a really edible, succulent green as late as September; then they turn orange and scarlet.

This excellent tree doesn't take up too much room: its branches are noticeably short for its height. Only its very positive likes and dislikes tell against it. It needs well-drained sandy loam; alkaline soil kills it. It doesn't like being moved except in infancy, and it clearly prefers summers that are summers and winters that are winters; Europe's wishy-washy arrangement gets it confused. The difference shows in the size. The biggest known in Europe is six feet round—although it was introduced nearly 350 years ago. The biggest in America, in Kentucky, is 17 feet round and 100 feet high.

The pawpaw (*Asimina triloba*) is a not-so-distant cousin of the laurels. It had a great name among the early settlers in America as a food in the wilds. John Bartram sent it over to England in 1736. Yet today it is far from common. To collectors of the curious its pleasures are its big, drooping, oval, deciduous leaves; its small, browny-violet flowers and its short brown pods which are edible—but not, I'm told, a gastronomic experience.

is 80 feet high and 100 feet wide. It is a tree that will grow in deep shade before its turn comes to cast it. The big ones have rather wandering trunks of wood, so hard that folk who up and move house (in the land where moving house means moving house) just put umbellularia rollers underneath and shove. It is not so hardy as bay but even in England grows to a bigger tree. Certainly it has a much more interesting shape.

In California the camphor laurel is beginning to be fancied as a street tree. It is slow (like all the family) and rather greedy for a small garden, but it supports a wide canopy of lovely shiny big leaves on

In its native States sassafras colours crimson and orange in autumn: in Europe more usually yellow. It is always a shapely, rather narrow tree with small branches. Like all the bay family it is aromatic.

The greenish-yellow flowers of sassafras, magnified, show the family resemblance to the flowers of sweet bay, opposite. They too are followed by berries with a single seed like a cherry-stone.

Right The paw-paw of the southeastern States is no relation of the tropical fruit of the same name. It is a small tree with maroon-purple flowers. The leaves grow much bigger and sway in the wind. The pod-like fruit is edible.

Witch Hazels, Sweetgums and Parrotias

The witch hazel family stands at the head of a broad class of plants that show symptoms of having developed very early in the evolutionary scheme of things. The class includes a good chunk of the biggest hardwoods of the temperate world: the oaks, elms, beeches, chestnuts, planes, walnuts and hickories. Their relationship is proved only by unobvious technical points: the structure of their wood and pollen in particular. But there are other indications: most of them have catkins for flowers and rely on wind-pollination – possibly because in their day (so to speak) few pollinating insects had evolved. With wind-pollination goes a tendency to flower early in the spring before the forest's leaf-cover gets in the way. There are obvious catkin-trees like the willows and poplars outside this group; but not many.

The witch hazel's own family of close relations gives us some of the best autumn colour outside of the maples in the sweetgum (*Liquidambar*) and the Persian ironwood (*Parrotia*). The witch hazel itself is one of the best winter-flowering shrubs – though scarcely a tree. And two other closely allied families give us a useful range of Australian evergreens, the *Pittosporums*, and one of the most delicate and beautiful of all big trees for the garden, the Japanese katsura or *Cercidiphyllum*. Nobody seems to have come up with a vernacular name for this. It might sell well as the Valentine tree; its leaves are perfect little hearts which turn all kinds of sweetheart colours at the end of the year.

None of these trees survived the Ice Ages in Europe. The witch hazel, which gives the sweet-scented soothing lotion for bruises, was the first one known to botany; the eastern American *Hamamelis virginiana*. Hazel because of its soft oval leaves like the nut tree's; witch, presumably, from witch.

The most tree-like of the witch hazels is the Japanese *H. japonica* 'Arborea'. The best for winterflowering in gardens is the Chinese species, *H. mollis*. They all have beauti-

Top *The sweeping layers of its branch-pattern combine with its little heart-shaped leaves to make* Cercidiphyllum japonicum *(in Japanese 'katsura') one of the most graceful of all medium-sized trees. It needs deep soil and moisture.*

Disanthus cercidifolius *has leaves exactly like the cercidiphyllum's (top) but with brighter autumn colour. A rare member of the witch hazel family, it makes at best a small tree. It needs lime-free woodland soil, moisture and shade.*

Witch hazel (Hamamelis virginiana) is a native of the eastern States, bearing yellow spidery flowers in winter. Its chief use in gardens is as root-stock on which the more reliable Chinese witch hazel (Hamamelis mollis) is grafted.

ful pale yellow leaves in autumn and all tend to grow with a broad horizontal emphasis, covering a fair bit of ground.

The relationship of the sweetgum to the witch hazel is far from obvious. It looks much more like a maple, with leaves lobed in just the same way. It is another tree that ended up everywhere but in Europe. The eastern American version (*Liquidambar styraciflua*) is by far the best known; but the Turkish *L. orientalis* and the Chinese *L. formosana* are very pretty; especially the Chinese, which produces lavender-coloured young leaves in spring.

Sweetgum is not all sentiment in the United States. Any tree that grows to 125 feet and 20 feet round is forestry material. I have seen it grown as the moist bottomland hardwood in Georgia, with its masters expecting quite some performance from it.

It is a fairly slow grower in Europe (10 feet in 12 years), and furthermore is a tree that must be planted small; it has fleshy roots that sucker furiously if they are disturbed. The biggest in England (at Syon House near London) is none the less 93 feet high and a beautiful sight, turning from the same sort of rich shiny green as the sassafras to an autumn motley of scarlet and crimson. There are two simple ways of recognizing the sweetgum. All maples have their leaves and shoots in pairs opposite one another on the twig; the sweetgum's are arranged alternately. And the bark, even of the twigs, has deep ridges of corky material like that of a number of elms.

Its liking for damp ground (though not bogs or floodland) suggests the bank of a pond as the ideal place to plant it. The reflection can be sensational.

Shiny succulence of leaf doesn't always count as a botanical characteristic, but if you see the sweetgum and the parrotia side by side (a good idea, by the way) you can sense a relationship. The parrotia is known to gardeners as a low tree that grows more sideways than up—as does the witch hazel, in

fact. I have the word of Roy Lancaster, the curator of Hillier's nursery/arboretum near Winchester, that in Persia he has seen it straight as an arrow and 60 feet high, but the biggest I have seen in captivity is the Arnold Arboretum's tree; a broad fan with a good dozen stems to maybe 35 feet.

Parrotia, drooping as it does, tends to show you here and there a cascade of rich deep green leaves from above. Other branches will take off like flapping wings of a big bird, making the tree a free-form performance you need to stand back from. Its little blood-red flowers, rather like the elm's, make a lovely early spring incident. In England its autumn colour is patchy, some leaves going orange or red while others stay green, or parti-coloured. The snag is that the ones on the end of the long branches drop off before the inner ones have turned, so you seldom have the whole tree furnished and coloured at the same time.

What with the colours and the flapping I

was prepared to believe that it was the parrot which lent the tree its name. Now I read that it was named in honour of a Herr Parrot, the second man to the top of Mount Ararat (Noah being the first) in 1829.

Among all this lush foliage the cercidiphyllum strikes a blow for quiet good taste. An old tree makes distinct terraces with its swooping, almost-horizontal branches. On them each small, long-stalked leaf stands out precisely; a neat heart in pale green. One of its lovely habits is to produce single leaves from the old wood of its inner recesses, so that when they turn almost pure white as they often do in autumn you catch a glimpse of white hearts against dark bark. Overall it can turn anything from deep pink to ivory; the paler colours stressing all the more the marked separateness of each leaf. Eighty feet is the tallest it has yet grown in England, but it shows promise in America of reaching 100 feet. Virtually pest-free, this is one of the first-choice garden trees.

Above *The sweet gum or* Liquidambar *has leaves like a maple's. Its ridged and corky bark and alternate pattern of branch and leaf are the easiest ways to distinguish it.*

Below *The deep green glossy leaves of parrotia in summer. Before the leaves the parrotia opens petalless crimson flowers like the elm's. They are followed by hard oval capsules.*

Above *Persian parrotia (or ironwood) colours brilliant red and yellow in autumn. It tends to a broad horizontal shape. Mature trees have flaking bark making patterns like that of the London plane.*

Right *Seed capsules of* Pittosporum tobira *on the point of ripeness. They develop from yellow flowers with an orange-blossom scent. Several species are popular in California, where they grow well by the sea.*

Left *The pittosporums are evergreen Australian relations of the witch hazel family, making small trees in a subtropical climate. Here the seed capsules of* Pittosporum tobira *are splitting open to show the red seeds.*

Above *A young sweetgum starting to change colour in autumn. The leaves hold a good bright green until late in the season, then take on tones of scarlet and orange. It is the biggest tree of the family, growing to over 100 feet.*

The Planes

An avenue of young London planes in Belgium. They have been regularly pruned to produce a mop-head effect. Planes take well to such treatment, but it totally destroys their winter beauty of branch-tracery.

The London plane growing by the Thames in a painting by John Varley (1811). Since the / *18th century this hybrid between the oriental and American planes has been London's principal tree.*

It was calculated in 1920 that more than 60 per cent of the trees in London were London planes, most of them planted in the previous 25 years. If that isn't daredevil monoculture I don't know what is. The figure is not very different today, for the fact remains that the plane is, in the words of the Chairman of the tree planting committee, the 'most biddable tree' there is.

The London plane is generally believed to be a cross between the two sorts of plane that occur in the wild. There is an eastern plane (*Platanus orientalis*), native to Turkey and Greece; and the western plane (*P. occidentalis*) which Americans call either buttonwood or sycamore. The first record of the London plane was in England in 1663 – which of course has not prevented the botan-

ists calling it *P. × hispanica*, the Spanish cross. It certainly shows the sort of vigour associated with hybrids. Given a good bit of clay it grows two or three feet a year from the start.

Familiar as the plane is, it is hard to fault it for style. Its great attraction is a trunk as tall as an English elm's, not getting lost in a maze of branches but weaving purposefully to the top, dappled with big patches where the dark outer bark has flaked away and left the inner layer; green ripening to buff. Its winter silhouette is one of the most graceful of all; a tracery in which the weeping twigs form countless little Gothic arches, diversified with dangling black balls, three or four to a string.

The power of this form to save city architecture from itself has been realized for 200 years. It has never been more needed than today. There remain authorities, notably round the Mediterranean but also in the suburbs of most cities, who hack the branches off planes as a symbol of municipal power over nature. This is what is meant by the plane being biddable: it just shoots again undaunted. But streets where it is allowed to fulfil itself, as it is in countless Provençal villages, are among the most stately, be the houses mere hovels.

The three most important planes (there are of course others, of which the Californian, *P. racemosa*, is the most notable) are easily distinguished by their leaves. They all have what are, basically, maple leaves, but the eastern plane's are deep-lobed, the buttonwood's very shallow-lobed and the London plane's something between them. What is odd is that they could hardly

be farther from the maple in the evolutionary sense.

Of the three, the London plane is the most widespread today. It will grow in an astonishing variety of climate and latitude, ranging from North Africa to New Zealand. The French Ministry of Forests has suggested planting it in place of the ubiquitous poplar for its quick-growing timber. But to a tragic extent the range of forestry trees is controlled by what the market is accustomed to.

Where the buttonwood is grown for timber in the southeastern States you can see that the poplar analogy is no exaggeration. A trunk 45 feet high and nine inches thick in ten years is not bad going. Unfortunately this beautiful tree, in many ways even better-looking than the London plane and certainly more handsome than the rather dumpy eastern one, demands the continental climate of the eastern States. Spring frost makes it hard to grow in Britain.

Above *The leaf, fruiting ball (left) and flower clusters of the American plane, known as buttonwood or sycamore. Compare this leaf with that of the oriental plane in the picture to the right. The lobes are very much shallower.*

Right *Late spring foliage of the London plane with young, partly-developed fruiting clusters. The London plane has two to four fruit balls on a stem; the oriental plane four to six and the American buttonwood one or two.*

Above *The deeply-lobed maple-like leaves of the oriental plane, one parent of the London plane, take on warm russet tints in autumn. It is a shorter, less graceful tree which remains rare in cultivation in the West.*

The smooth flaked and marbled bark of the London plane is derived from its American parent, the buttonwood. It gives even enormous trees (the tallest, at Bryanston, Dorset, is 145 feet) the appearance of youth and vitality.

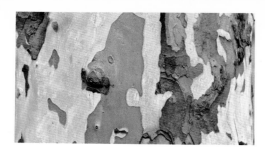

A much-loved London vista and the world centre of nannydom: the 200-year-old planes in Kensington Gardens with the sun setting over the rooftops of Kensington Palace and the spire of St. Mary Abbot's church in the background.

The flaking bark of the American buttonwood. The irregular plates of outer bark are continually falling away, especially in summer, to reveal the creamy inner layer, which changes to a mosaic of green and fawn.

The Elms

A dismal cloud hangs over the elms. Nobody could write without emotion of this most majestic family of trees being under the threat of extinction. In many townships as far apart as New England and East Anglia elms *were* the landscape. Whether the local species is the American elm, immensely high-arched and spreading; the English elm, tall-trunked and balancing a broad fan far above the fields; the wych elm, wide-crowned and weeping, or any of a dozen others it set the scale for life in its countryside. In our flat country it did service for the non-existent hills.

Dutch elm disease is a fungus carried by a beetle. It grows in the new ring of wood, just inside the bark, on which the tree relies almost totally for its flow of sap. When it blocks the sap vessels, the branch dies – and very soon the tree. Two-hundred-year-old trees can be killed in one season. Because the disease battens on wood that is being created that year little can be done to protect the tree. The only hope is to kill the beetles with a DDT-type spray and to inject the sap-stream with fungicide. But this is an expensive operation which might have to be repeated year after year. To whole populations of millions (70 per cent of the hedgerow trees in the English Midlands and eastern counties were elms) it is impossible.

We can only hope that as the disease passes some of the abundant hedgerow sprouts will prove immune and provide our descendants with these irreplaceable trees.

There are about 45 species of elm: nobody is quite sure how many. Donald Wyman in *Trees for American Gardens* says there are 200 or so named clones. There are certainly five species that count, and perhaps another six hybrids and cultivars. Which you consider *the* elm depends entirely on where you were brought up.

I was brought up in the heart of elm-land, in the southeast of England, where three species and several elusive crosses and crosses of crosses clumped or filed all over the landscape. Our chief glory was the English elm (*Ulmus procera*) which, because it sets no fertile seed but reproduces entirely by new saplings springing up from the roots of old trees, maintains its blood free from taint. In a sense all English elms are parts of one gigantic tree, and look like it; the pattern of branching in a line of them is hypnotically repetitive. They all have short horizontal or slightly drooping branches on the lower part of the trunk, then very often a distinct waist half way up, then an almost-symmetrical, half-open fan of long branches forming the top third of the tree. William Gilpin, who wrote late in the 18th century about the aesthetics of trees, pronounced magisterially: 'No tree is better adapted to receive grand masses of light.' The grand masses are not exactly of light, but of the dark green, small-leafed foliage whose cloud-formations seem to hold it. Constable, a native of this landscape, was constantly trying to paint it: and yet his oaks are better than his elms.

The leaves stay green on the English elm longer than on the others; even into November. Their autumn colour is a fine light gold, which coincides with autumnal mist to create effects I can't begin to describe. It is a savage irony that that lovely colour comes early now, and means death.

Elm is the traditional wood for coffins. There is a trenchant old jingle which makes the link between this and the tree's famous tendency to drop a big branch, without warning, on a still summer's day.

> Elem hateth man
> And waiteth.

It is customary in books about trees to repeat this warning and advise against planting elms anywhere where people might walk under them. Well and good; but where does that leave us? There is a much higher death toll from getting run over by lawn-mowers than from standing under elm trees. How often do you hear of anyone being slain in this honourable fashion? ▶

The smooth-leaved elm, Ulmus carpinifolia, *growing on fen-land near Cambridge.*

The Elms of Europe and America

The typical elm-tracery of a superb pair of Hunting-don elms with the tower of St. John's College, Cambridge behind. This is one of the fastest-growing elms, a cross between the wych and the smooth-leaved.

The English elm is essentially the hedge-row, often the parkland tree; not so frequent now in towns. It has been as successful in North America as in Europe. 'Chinese' Wilson in his *Aristocrats of the Trees* remarked that not only did it flourish in New England, but it showed no sign of doing its branch-dropping act.

I have the honour of living in Saling, the village with the biggest smooth-leaved elm (*U. carpinifolia*)—as far as anyone knows—in the world. It isn't what it was (in 1841 it was 114 feet high) but it is 22½ feet round and that, for an elm, is big. In the last 130-odd years it has grown five feet in girth. It must

have been planted between 1600 and 1650, which happens to be just when my house was built. It is all too easy to get damp-eyed about the historic associations of trees, but it is a quality they possess that one can't pass over in silence.

At a casual glance a smooth-leaved elm and a wych elm (*U. glabra*) can look very much the same. They usually fork fairly low and broaden out (like the American elm) into an immense explosion, from the extremities of which the twigs come tumbling in intricate cascades. They are at their most beautiful in winter, when their tracery is on display; not even the grand masses of light

Elm flowers (here on a wych elm) have no petals, but appear as a red bunch of stamens on the bare twigs in very early spring. They can be borne densely enough to colour the whole tree red.

Sunlight emphasises the vein pattern in the big rough-textured leaves of the wych elm. All elm leaves, as here, have one side of the blade extending farther along the leaf-stalk than the other.

Left The fruit of the elm often covers the branches so densely (especially on the wych elm, seen here) that the tree appears to be in premature leaf. It turns brown and falls as the young leaves appear.

Below The weeping wych elm forms a broad crown of branches which climb slowly in shallow arcs, sometimes to a considerable height. Its flat top has earned it the alternative name of the tabletop elm—an ideal tree for a large garden or park.

can compare with what is surely nature's very best pen-and-ink work.

If you can reach a leaf you have your answer to the identity of the tree: the smooth-leaved elm's leaf is smooth (on top) and shiny; the wych elm's is bigger and raspingly rough. The English elm's has the same sandpapery feeling. The trade-mark of all elm leaves is a lop-sided base.

The flowers of the elm are often dismissed as being invisible from the ground, and so not worth bothering with. It has no showy catkins, but early in the spring it carries so many tiny red flowers, which are really just bunches of stamens appearing from a bud, that the whole leafless tree, caught by the sunlight, glows misty crimson. Still before the leaves appear come the winged fruit; little discs more or less the shape of a fried egg, which colour the tree green. They ripen brown and fall as the leaves expand. The fertile ones germinate as quickly as they ripen: the whole performance from flower to new elm is a matter of eight weeks or so.

On a tree like the American elm, which often hangs its branchlets so low that you can examine the twigs, you can see from late summer on which buds are going to produce leaves and which flowers. On the whole the leaf buds congregate near the branch tips, where they will get most light. The flower buds, a little higher up the hanging spray, are twice the size. If you open one with your fingernail you will see that it is all ready to go; packed with pinky-crimson fluff.

One of the many crosses between the smooth-leaved and wych elms, or rather a whole group of such crosses, constitutes most of the elm population of continental Europe, under such names as the Belgian and Dutch elms (*U.* × *hollandica* 'Belgica' and ditto 'Major'). Wandering down to Italy they become the support for many a promiscuous vine; a role they have filled since Virgil's day. Several selected clones have shown themselves more able to resist Dutch elm disease than others. Two offspring of

U. × *hollandica*, 'Christine Buisman' and 'Bea Schwarz', were at one time much fancied as saviouresses – but neither has proved fully immune.

A similar cross, a tree which fountains up to a spectacular height and spread, has long been known and admired in England as the Huntingdon elm (*U.* × *vegeta*). One Huntingdon elm clone called 'Commelin' is also reckoned fairly disease-resistant. Of the local French types that have been selected (as opposed to the unstudied multitudes of the fields) the most widely-adopted is the Jersey elm (*U.* × *sarniensis*) whose narrow head of long ascending limbs makes it possible for (wide) streets and gardens where others would be in a straitjacket.

The really weeping forms of elm you sometimes see on broad lawns (weeping, that is, not just in branchlet and twig, but in the whole branch from the top) are varieties of the wych elm: the lower and rounder 'Camperdownii'; the taller and more angular 'Pendula'.

There has not been such planting of the lesser-known American elms, either in the United States or in Europe. The slippery elm (*U. rubra*) with its big velvety leaves (slipperiness, being in the inner bark, is not an obvious character) and the narrow, short-branched rock elm of the Great Lakes have been overshadowed by the far-ranging American elm (*U. americana*) itself.

There are no native elms west of the Rockies. The lack has been supplied partly from the eastern States and Europe, but also from Asia. The Chinese elm (*U. parvifolia*) – though not remotely elmy to the untutored eye – is a highly desirable garden tree: all rather miniature; its leaves decidedly so; dark green, shiny, almost evergreen, colouring red before its late leaf-fall. In cold places the similar (but less attractive) Siberian elm (*U. pumila*) does service for it. An Asian hybrid under the name 'Sapporo Autumn Gold' holds out hopes of becoming a big disease-free elm.

Left The narrow pyramidal crown of the Jersey (or Wheatley) elm makes it one of the best elms for streets and avenues. The perfect avenue seen here in early spring is at Cranborne Manor, Dorset. The Cornish (or Goodyer) elm is another species of similar shape.

Far right above Disease has drastically reduced the population of American elms, whose wide-spreading crowns used to be landmarks all over the eastern States. A survivor, photographed here, formerly stood in New England.

Above The rugged bark, stained green with algae, and (right) the characteristic shape of the English elm, growing by the Serpentine lake in Hyde Park, London. English elms all conform closely to this narrow-waisted shape.

Zelkovas and Hackberries

The elms are a homogeneous lot; more so even than the oaks. None is evergreen; none has wildly eccentric leaves. Their relations also toe the line. The excellent *Zelkova* (if ever a tree deserved a good common name) is thoroughly elmy, though only a cousin. And the nettle-tree or hackberry (*Celtis*) has much of the same family look about it.

Very few trees have had such a good press as the zelkova. With no flowers or fruit to speak of and with leaves like those of the elm (only singly toothed; elm leaves have paired teeth) it manages it on composure alone. It is a graceful, well-proportioned, short-trunked, many-stemmed, broad-domed, soberly coloured ordinary tree.

Both the zelkovas (the medium-rare ones; there are more, but they are really rare) answer this description. I turned up William Robinson's *The English Flower Garden* to find myself echoed with another forest of commas: 'The longer points, sharper teeth, more numerous nerves and leathery texture, together with the fact that they hang longer, may enable anyone to tell the leaf of the Japan Zelkova (*Z. serrata*) from that of the better-known Caucasian tree (*Z. carpinifolia*).'

I would add to the list of distinctions the thin bark of the 'Japan Zelkova', which in flaking off reveals enticing little patches of quite startling orange. With the wide spread of the long branches from a mere five feet above the ground there is plenty of bark to contemplate.

It is the fruit that distinguishes the hackberries from the elms. Though it is scarcely a reason to grow them, it consists of red, yellow or blackish berries compared with the elm's dry, flattened, winged fruit. Otherwise in proportions and general aspect they are small (rarely much higher than 50 feet) spreading, bush-topped and rather bright green elms, with much to be said for them as street or small garden trees.

One point in their favour is that they root deep. You can grow shrubs under them – if the shrubs can take dense shade, which is what they deliver. Their deep roots, once they have found their depth, are virtually drought-proof.

The best part about the common hackberry (*C. occidentalis*) of eastern North America (which will grow more or less anywhere) is its highly original bark. Corkiness is in the family (several elms have corky twigs) but the hackberry handles it differently. By middle age the tree has deep flanges of cork, widely spaced, running more or less north-south but wandering about on its surface. As a tree for public places the common hackberry is apparently discredited for its habit of forming witches' brooms from which

A superb specimen of the Caucasian zelkova growing in Devon. The short buttressed trunk and extraordinary system of crowded upright branches are unique to this tree. It was discovered in 1760, yet remains almost unknown.

the congested twigs fall off and make a mess.
This shouldn't put anyone off planting a
good and unusual tree in his garden. In its
place the authorities plant either the Mississippi hackberry (*C. laevigata*), with mainly
untoothed leaves, the Chinese hackberry
(*C. sinensis*) with shiny, bright green leaves,
or the southern European hackberry (*C.
australis*). 'Australis' in this usage simply
means southern. The most unexpected fact
about this tree is that its small, dark purple
berry is the Lotos of Tennyson's mild-eyed,
melancholy Lotos-eaters, no less. I'm afraid
the spectacular pollination the poet describes–'Round and round the spicy downs
the yellow Lotos-dust is blown'–would be
quite beyond it. Did I say the berries were
no reason to grow them? I'm not so sure.

The *Eucommia* is a lone Chinese species
that offers proof to the sceptical of the close-
ness of the elms and the fig family (see next
page). The figs include among their tropical
members the rubber plant. The eucommia
looks like a small elm, but has rubber in its
veins. If you tear one of its leaves in half the
barely-visible strands hold the two halves together. It is the only hardy tree that does
contain rubber; not enough to make it a
commercial proposition, but in an attractive and easily-grown tree perhaps enough
of a reason to plant it.

*The same species as the
tree opposite: the
Caucasian zelkova in
summer (and comparative
youth). At this age it is
very like the American
elm in shape. Cities hit by
elm disease are planting
it in the elm's place.*

*The leaves of the Cau-
casian zelkova are less
toothed than those of the
oriental species above.
They turn yellow or
bronze in autumn. The
fruits are hard little nuts,
unlike the elm's flat
wafers and the hack-
berry's berries.*

American Nettle Tree

*The American hackberry
is much more like a small
elm in general appearance
than its leaves and
certainly its berries would
suggest. It is fast-growing
and well-shaped; mature
trees have a corky,
thickly-ridged bark.*

The Figs and Mulberries

Below *A mulberry tree planted by the poet Milton in the garden of Christ's College, Cambridge, was a place of pilgrimage in the 19th century. Centenarian mulberries often need props and wear a look of immense antiquity.*

What can you grow that gives a garden such a sense of established well-being as a fig tree or a mulberry? I've no doubt it is just witless harking back to a three-quarters-mythical past: the fig-tree mentioned so often in the Bible and popping out from under every fallen marble frieze in the ruins of the classical world, and the mulberry appearing from China in the Dark Ages—maybe long before–and with it the Secret of Silk.

Historical stuff apart, it would never have occurred to me that they belonged together, particularly as the one fig species hardy enough to grow in the temperate zone happens to be the only one with distinctly un-mulberryish, deeply-lobed leaves.

All the mulberry family have in common the white sap that contains latex. In the fruit department things are more complicated: mulberries, paper mulberries (*Broussonetia*) and osage oranges (*Maclura*) having essentially raspberry-like fruit, all globules and pips where the old flower-cluster was; the fig having a design of its own in which the flowers bloom (if that's the word) on the inside walls of a little fleshy funnel, which then swells around the pips to become the fig.

The hardy species (*Ficus carica*) can scarcely in fairness be described as a tree at the northern extremes of its range. It is more of a sprawling shrub, whose thin grey branches need support from a wall to reach any height. With a bit of care, however, it can be persuaded to ripen fruit in the south of England and in the United States as far north as New York. The trick to get it to fruit well is to give its roots the minimum space to ramble; feed them well in a tub. Certain cultivars can set fruit without pollination. Of all the late-summer garden pleasures there is nothing to beat a forage through the heavy, dusty-smelling leaves of the tree to find ripe figs. Their own leaves make a plate for them beside a bowl of cream cheese among the wine glasses. I cut them, not because biting them open isn't a pleasure, but to see the purple-violet-indigo of their livery opening to the silver of the knife.

Mulberries are gastronomically neglected. They are somehow not quite right as fruit, combining the extremes of squashiness and pippiness–yet the flavour, searchingly sour and hauntingly sweet, is very special.

The mulberry is an easy, though rather slow, tree to grow. You can plant cuttings even five feet long in autumn with every hope of starting something. The great question is where. It is ultimately a wide, sprawling, low-profile tree with fruit which,

Above left *A young mulberry on the west lawn at Polesden Lacey house, near London. Mulberry trees were much planted in England in the 17th century in the hope of starting a silk industry.*

Lower left *Light and shade in a mulberry tree in summer. The raspberry-like fruit ripen from light to dark red; few people today appreciate their sweet-acid flavour.*

Above right *The silk-moth has been cultivated in the orient for so long that it can no longer fly. Here an adult female moth sits with her eggs beside her silken cocoon.*

Lower right *An almost fully-fed silkworm (the caterpillar of the silk-moth) feeds on a black mulberry leaf. Silk is spun from the very fine thread with which the worm makes its cocoon.*

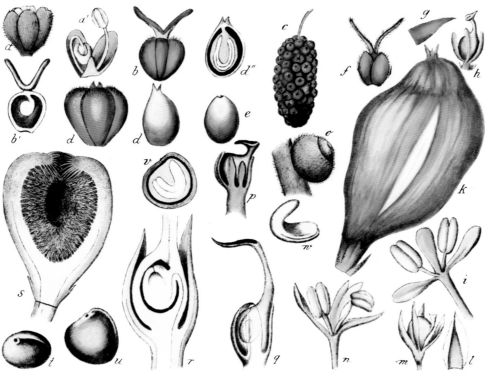

unless you eat it, falls abundantly to stain everything under it a fine shade of crimson. That is the black mulberry; the eating one. If you want to keep silkworms you will want the white mulberry, which grows a bit quicker. But the black makes a better garden set-piece: few small trees grow so gnarled and ancestral-looking.

The paper mulberry helps to link mulberry and fig; in terms of leaves, not fruit. Some of its leaves are more or less heart-shaped like the mulberry's; most are lobed and figgy. The fruit, not edible but pretty, is like a round red mulberry.

Some of the earliest Chinese paper was made from the bark of the paper mulberry by soaking it, smoothing it and finishing it with rice paste. In Japan it is still an important source of super-quality paper. As a tree it has some of the qualities of the common elder; it grows rank and tousled with soft and pithy wood almost anywhere.

One thoroughly off-beat American tree, the osage orange, limited in nature to parts of Kansas, Virginia, Georgia and Texas, can be dimly perceived to be a relation through the formation of its remarkable fruit. It does indeed look like an orange, but its bumpier surface suggests the same composite structure. Each fruit is in fact composed of many smaller ones tightly welded together.

Above *The parts of the flower and fruit of the black mulberry (letters a to g) and the common fig (letters h to v). A cluster of female flowers (f) of the mulberry develops into a cluster (c) of fruitlets (d)* which is a mulberry. The fig-flowers (h) are clustered inside a swelling at the end of the stalk (in cross-section in s and complete in k). The male flowers are at the top; the female further in.

Below *The common fig is a native of the Near East, at home in a Mediterranean climate but hardy surprisingly far north. In Britain it needs shelter and a good summer to ripen its soft sweet fruit.*

Right *The fig turns a bloomy purple and wrinkles when it is ripe. Fresh figs go beautifully with raw Italian ham or with cream cheese at the beginning or end of a meal.*

Left *The osage orange has little globular heads of flowers like the mulberry. They fuse together as they develop to form orange-sized yellow (inedible) fruit.*

The Walnuts

What makes a man proud and happy about having a walnut on his lawn? There can scarcely be a tree that puts on less of a show. It is one of the last bare trees of spring and the first of winter. Its leaves fall a sullen brown. Its catkins are by no means ornamental, coming with the leaves; nor is its fruit. It is stocky, heavy of detail and thick of limb and twig.

Can trees communicate extra-sensorily? A walnut can. It speaks of fatness and fertility even while it stands looking like a puritan about to close the theatres. What it offers is of the highest quality: the best timber and the best of all nuts.

Of the eight or nine species of walnut which inhabit Asia and America two are widely planted—the American (or black) and the English (or Persian). Hickories—those quintessentially American trees—are distantly allied. There is an Asiatic branch, too, the wingnuts, with very similar character and perhaps more beauty than either.

What all the family have in common are catkins; compound (often slightly fragrant) leaves with anything from five to 25 leaflets along a stalk up to two feet long; bold buds above pronounced scars from the old leaves; and nuts. Their twigs are distinctly knobbly and substantial, full of slight changes of

Walnut wood has some of the most beautiful colour and 'figure', or patterns of graining, of any tree. This portable writing cabinet was made in England in the early 18th century.

Below *The black walnut of the eastern States is the most vigorous of the walnuts, whether it is planted in America or Europe. Its deeply furrowed bark is a darker grey than the near-silver of the English (or Persian) walnut; hence its name.*

Bottom left *The leaf, flowers and nut of the English walnut. The catkin is the male flower; two little female ones are just above the nut. The nut is oval and thin-shelled; the leaf has an odd number of oval leaflets.*

Bottom right *The American walnut has a longer leaf than the English with an even number of tapering leaflets, and a round nut with a thick furrowed shell which is hard to crack.*

Below *The English walnut is a smaller, slower-growing tree than the American, with pale bark and thick twigs. One of the last trees to put on leaves in spring, it is the walnut most grown for its fruit all over the world.*

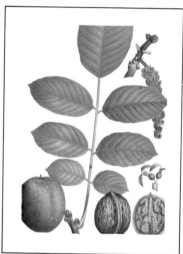

planted in a more desultory way, in hedgerows and gardens. Grenoble in southeastern France has the great name for walnuts as fruit; the Dordogne in the southwest for walnuts as wood. In the Dordogne a walnut tree can be an important family asset. Demand ran away with supply many wars back. Walnuts are indispensable trees for gunstocks: for weight, elasticity and smoothness of touch there is apparently no comparable wood. Today the famous gunsmiths of London make special journeys to the Dordogne to find the best; the rest, one imagines, goes to make 17th-century furniture for the antique shops of Paris.

Circassian ('Persian') walnut from the Caucasus has always had the name for the most beautiful figure of all. It is like a troubled, swirling pool of browns, from parchment to near-black, on the brink of a weir that draws the ripples towards it.

The common English walnut (*J. regia*) grows slowly. It never makes such a big tree as the American (*J. nigra*), either in height or spread. The only attraction it has which the American lacks is a gleaming pale-grey bark: the black walnut's is blackish-brown. America's biggest black walnut is 111 feet high and 125 feet across from branch-tip to branch-tip, with a trunk 21 feet round. It grows almost as well as this in Europe, compared with our native's best performance of 80 feet or so.

The English walnut in fact is first choice for nuts. The American is the choice for ornament or timber, unless your family is prepared to wait twice as long for the ultimate quality; a chancy philosophy.

The American walnut has one nasty habit you should watch: it is capable of poisoning neighbouring trees and shrubs, particularly fruit trees (including its own offspring) with a substance called juglone in its roots. Apple trees near walnuts are often known to die mysteriously. It is a sinister development in the battle for survival; happily a secret the walnut can't impart to other trees.

direction that give them character compared with, say, the ash, which has similar leaves.

With so much in common it is often a job to tell them apart. The way to know a walnut from a hickory (in the absence of a nut) is to slice a twig longways: if the pith is solid it is hickory; if divided with air-pockets, a walnut or a wingnut. If it's a wingnut you're in an arboretum.

The walnut has a history of cultivation as long as the fig's. Its Latin name was concocted for it by the Romans when it came to them (via Greece) from Persia. *Juglans* was derived from *Jovis glans*—Jupiter's acorn.

Our name for it means simply 'foreign nut', from the same old German word Welsh as again meaning simply 'foreign'.

As a fruit tree the walnut has had a good deal of attention paid to it: there are a score or more of named clones, chosen for bigger fruit or more of it or thinner shells. The most famous, perhaps, is *J. regia* 'Franquette', a vigorous wide-spreading French tree with long, oval nuts, not specially big but full of meat, and the meat full of flavour.

The biggest orchards of the English walnut are in central California (125,000 acres) In Europe orchards are rare and it is

One of the best of the lesser-known walnuts is the Texan Juglans rupestris, *a small tree with dense masses of very narrow leaflets that give it a feathery look. It is hardier than its southern origin suggests.*

Hickories and Wingnuts

If the walnuts inherited the dignity in their family, it was the hickories and the wingnuts which inherited the looks.

The hickories are hardly known in Europe; not even for their superlative wood whose smoke goes up like incense from the barbecue-pits of America. Yet the vast forests of the eastern States, with their vitality and variety undreamed of in the Old World, have hardly a more characteristic ingredient.

It is not hard to characterize the hickories as a race. They are like taller and more graceful walnuts; more finely textured; in brighter colours. Their catkins, instead of being a single tassel, fork to become three-pronged. Their wood is the finest of all for the traditional offices of ash–for tool handles and firewood.

The most distinguished of them is the pecan (*Carya illinoensis*). It is also, alas, the least hardy: a native of the Mississippi basin, in Europe not happy north of central France, but ripening fruit in Bordeaux. If the walnut (nut, not tree) has a superior it is this.

Given the soil it likes (deep and moist) the pecan is the fastest of its race and makes the biggest tree–taking spread into account as well as height. A pecan in Tennessee, 106 feet high, is 136 feet in total width. The leaves are composed of many leaflets, the

The hickories are the beauties of the walnut family, with long sweet-scented and rich-textured compound leaves. The shagbark hickory has the fewest and biggest leaflets. All hickories colour well in shades of warm yellow in autumn.

The trunk of a tall shagbark hickory is covered with stiff curling and crackling bark–possibly a defence against nut-hunting animals. The shagbark covers a vast territory, and grows as well in Europe as in North America.

longest of all the hickories', and every leaflet is gracefully curved. Bulk and grace combine to make a most impressive tree.

The pecan has only one problem. All the hickories have it and so to some extent do the walnuts: they hate being moved. Nurseries don't like them, and often don't stock them, for this reason. At best they sulk; usually they die. The only thing to do is to plant them out tiny–or bury some nuts.

The easiest hickory to identify is the shagbark (*C. ovata*). If ever there was a case where the botanist who christened the tree in Latin should have seen it first it is this. But he was Philip Miller, 3,500 miles away at the Chelsea Physic Garden, and all he had was a few leaves and a few (oval) nuts. Had he seen the amazing trunk of the tree he would have ransacked mythology for some old witch in moth-eaten rags to express its appalling look of wear and tear.

It is when the shagbark comes to fruiting age, at 30 or 40 years, that its trim trunk starts to tatter. It may well be an evolutionary adaptation which has proved successful in keeping squirrels away from the nuts. Certainly the sharp-edged strips of bark, still rigid although apparently ready to fall, must present them with a problem.

The shagbark has fewest leaflets per leaf; only five; the end one bigger than the rest.

The bitternut is one of the tallest and most vigorous of the hickories: easy to identify in winter by its bright yellow buds. Hickories must be planted out small: they never grow well after transplanting at larger sizes.

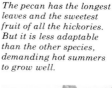

It is an upright, tower-headed tree, its spread only half its height or less. The tallest, 132 feet high and 64 feet across, is in Texas.

The bitternut (*C. cordiformis*) has a pale yellow bud, curving and without covering scales, which is unlike any of the others. This is the most widespread of the family and the commonest, reaching as far north as Minnesota and Maine, where it turns from its gay green to a lovely straw yellow in autumn. It is also unfortunately the one with totally inedible fruit.

The mockernut (*C. tomentosa*)–its fruit, almost empty, is the mockery–has the alternative name of bigbud, which tells its story precisely. The velvety grey end bud is twice as thick as the twig behind it. This is the commonest southern hickory; not a big tree compared with the others, but excellent for timber and liked, also, for having sweet-smelling leaves.

One more, the pignut, is important and relatively distinctive for the smoothness of bud and twig, and glossiness of the undersides of its leaves, which give it its Latin name of *C. glabra* (literally, smooth hickory). It has the same range as the shagbark.

The Caucasian wingnut (*Pterocarya fraxinifolia*) comes into that class of trees, like the worthy *Zelkova*, which are strong, trouble-free, easy to grow, decorative and in every way to be recommended, but which are hardly ever planted, simply because they are strangers. Ideally it likes a climate more continental than the British; the eastern U.S.A. up to say New York would be ideal for it. It also likes moist ground. Given these it quickly forms a huge dome on a short trunk with the liveliness of millions of leaflets on long stalks. By July its winged nuts are developing from the catkins in long yellowy-green streamers all over the tree. The hybrid *Pterocarya × rehderiana* from the Arnold Arboretum is even more prolific in catkins: a tree to stop and gaze at, and at a time of year when flowering trees are few.

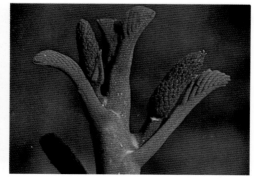

The wingnuts are another group of trees that deserve to be better known. They grow fast to oak-like shapes with long elaborate leaves and catkins, followed by chains of nuts. These are the nuts of the Chinese wingnut (Pterocarya stenoptera).

The dangling nut-chains of the ash-leaved wingnut from the Caucasus, a bigger tree than the Chinese, but with a liking for damp soil and a hot summer.

Top *The wingnuts are at their most ornamental in summer when their pale nut-chains hang all over their spreading crowns. A cross between the Chinese and Caucasian, Pterocarya × rehderiana is the most vigorous and splendid of all of them.*

Above *An expanding shoot-tip of the Caucasian wingnut, covered in a layer of brown wool. The embryo leaves are still tightly folded like fans and the flower spikes before expanding are like little brown catkins.*

The Beeches

A painting of a famous old beech tree at Windsor by the English artist Paul Sandby, 1832. Beeches are not as long-lived as oaks: they rarely survive to become as bulky and gnarled as this tree.

The beech family in its broad sense, embracing beeches, oaks and sweet chestnuts, is the royal family of the broadleaves by any reckoning. It has the oak for king and the beech for queen.

Oaks spread over more of the temperate world than any other broadleaf tree. There are some 450 species, evergreen and deciduous. There are shrubs among them, but most of them are big trees.

There are fewer beeches and less beech forest. None the less, the beech grows in the three northern continents and appears again in a modified but recognizable form in the southern hemisphere. It is the only broadleaf tree to be established in force on both sides of the equator.

The chestnut, closely kin to the oak, is the third major member of the family. What marks all three of them as close relations is their fruit. Acorns, chestnuts and the 'mast' of beeches are all formed in the same way: by the woody base of the female flower growing to form a husk round the seed.

If there is a royal seat it is surely Normandy. It is there that the beech grows to perfection, in woods of amazing purity and grandeur. At Lyons-la-Forêt, near Rouen, illustrated on these pages, beeches that seeded themselves during the French Revolution now soar clear and smooth-boled to 100 feet, into a green canopy 30 feet deep shutting out the sky. One cannot avoid the feeling that the inspiration for the great Norman cathedrals came from the ancestors of this solemn forest.

The beech is a much-shorn tree, excellently adapted for making hedges. Appropriately enough, the monarch of all hedges is of beech. It stands at Meikleour, about ten miles north of Perth in the Highlands of Scotland, a green wall 580 yards long and no less than 95 feet high. It is kept trimmed up to 60 feet – but beyond that ingenuity (and courage, I shouldn't wonder) is exhausted. ▶

The fruit of the beech family clearly links its members. Their nuts are all more or less enclosed in a woody sheath which grows up from the base of the female flower. The 'mast' of the beech (top left) has two nuts completely enclosed until they are ripe and the husk splits open as here. The acorn of the oak has one, sitting in an open cup. The chestnut has one, two or three nuts wrapped entirely in a prickly shell.

The autumn colour of beeches varies from yellow to russet to deep foxy red. They are a small and homogeneous race of trees, easily recognizable even in their ornamental and exotic forms.

Century-old beeches in one of the great beech-woods of Normandy, at Lyons-la-Forêt near Rouen. The beech makes dark woods, casting deep shade with its layers of leaves. All the lower branches die off to leave tall trunks of silver-grey.

The Beeches

Above *The erosive action of rain has laid bare this labyrinthine pattern of beech roots. Surface-rooting is one of the factors that make beech a very competitive tree, able to starve out other species.*

Below *The darkest of the copper or purple beeches is named 'Riversii' after the 18th-century English nursery firm of Thomas Rivers. Many shades of purple exist but all grow darker in late summer.*

▶ Odd that the beech has not seen fit to diversify in the same way as the oak. The eight or nine species are almost interchange-able, save for a bigger, smaller, longer or rounder leaf. The beech is clearly the logical end of its own evolutionary road, just as it is the final winner in a struggle for dominance in the forest.

An old beechwood has the longest echo of any woodland: a sound so eerie and disturb-ing that I remember it vividly from when I was a boy of four living on the chalk hills of Buckinghamshire. (The 'Buck' of Bucking-ham in fact means beech.) The beech thrives on lean chalk where other trees flag. In due course it takes it over completely; scarcely a bramble, barely a toadstool grow in the moss below the massed beech boles of the Chiltern hills. Their layered canopy lets only threads of sunlight through. Hence the long-answer-ing echo; the echo of an empty room.

The beech's domineering methods, of fill-ing the surface of the ground with fine roots, and covering it with heavy shade, certainly don't show in its face. Of all the big trees it is one of the daintiest; one of the most grace-ful in angles and movements, one of the lightest and most feminine in colour, one of the smoothest in texture.

Rather than accumulate calloused old corky stuff to form a protective layer of bark, the beech's cambium stays almost on the surface; its trunk remains smooth and silvery and fresh-looking. By the same token it needs the shade it is so good at making with its layer upon layer of leaves, all hori-zontally aligned. A beech grown in the open keeps branches right down to the ground to protect its trunk from sunlight. To see the sun playing on its pale curves and hollows—paler in the American beech, like the bloom on old aluminium—is one of the winter pleasures. You could argue that the beech is best in early winter. Its leaves turn some-times to the colour of golden burnt butter, sometimes to the clear coppery red of a fox's brush, before they fall. But one in ten of those on young trees hangs on to the lower branches up to eight or nine feet from the ground. Between the red drifts on the ground and the red spume in the air (and dare I men-tion the azure firmament behind?), the silver shaft is dazzling. Summer with its geraniums has no monopoly of nature's colours.

The American beech (*F. grandifolia*) is re-luctant to grow in Europe. The European (or common) beech (*F. sylvatica*) has no such qualms about America: which is just as well, since it is the one with all the interesting cultivars. Beech's commonest manifestation in gardens is in hedges, for which it is per-fectly suited. But next after hedges comes, undoubtedly, the purple or the copper beech

—understandably popular as by far the big-gest red thing there is to grow.

Red beeches have turned up many times in the wilds—usually, for some reason, in the middle of Europe: in Switzerland, Bavaria or eastern France. At their earliest appear-ances they were inevitably rumoured to be the mark of nature's disapproval of some un-natural crime—the blood refusing to lie down. Redness is a fairly stable character-istic of these trees; often their seedlings are red too. A number of shades of red are registered in different varietal names. 'Cuprea' has been used for the lightest, sup-posedly copper-coloured; 'Rivers Purple' for the darkest, a full-blooded purple. But nur-series don't often offer a choice—and since beeches all go through the whole range of colours, from new leaves of rosy-red silk to a browny-purple final stage in autumn, it is hard to know which colour is the one to put a name to.

The fern-leafed beech (*F. sylvatica lacin-iata*) is a more subtle and, truthfully, far more beautiful tree. Its leaves are deeply cut into narrow points that somehow give the whole tree a much finer and less shiny tex-ture: a matt effect which soaks up the light. It is difficult to see why this tree is quite as effective as it is; and yet if any tree in old

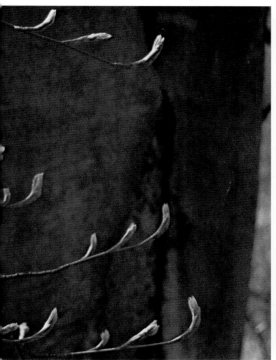

parkland has people streaming up for a closer look it is always this one.

I am probably alone in thinking the weeping beech a monstrosity. But it comes near the bottom of my list of weeping trees; the ash and the elm both weep far more convincingly. The beech's are surely crocodile tears, or indeed – as Hillier's *Manual* perceptively suggests – elephant's. I quote: 'the enormous branches hang close to and perpendicular with the main stem like an elephant's trunk'. Nothing like as bad as a weeping sequoia, which looks like a boa-constrictor trying to take off. But still far from graceful.

Possibly the most useful of all the variants is still a fairly new tree; clearly with a lot of planting ahead of it. It was Mr. Naesmith of Dawyck who found it. Dawyck is an estate in the Tweed valley in lowland Scotland which has been in the hands of tree lovers since Elizabethan times. Mr. Naesmith was the incumbent in 1860 when up sprang a beech with the stance of a Lombardy poplar, the perfect compromise for people who want a beech tree but haven't got room. The Dawyck beech (*F. sylvatica* 'Dawyck') is formal when young, but big ones are huge leafy ovals. As a street tree, where shade was not the main need, it would be hard to beat.

Above *The Botanical Garden at Leiden in Holland has one of the biggest and most splendid weeping beeches in the world.*

Left *The upright, or Dawyck, beech was discovered in a Scottish garden in the last century. It makes a superb tower of pale shining green.*

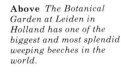

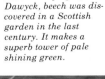

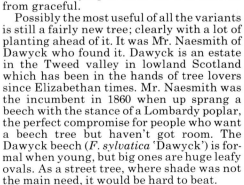

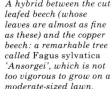

A hybrid between the cut-leafed beech (whose leaves are almost as fine as these) and the copper beech: a remarkable tree called Fagus sylvatica *'Ansorgei', which is not too vigorous to grow on a moderate-sized lawn.*

Above *The demented growth of the 'Tortuosa' beech. These rare trees occur in a line through Denmark, Champagne, and Le Cosquer in Brittany (above). A radioactive meteor centuries ago may have caused the malformation.*

151

The Southern Beeches

The world has been pretty thoroughly ransacked for trees. It is unlikely that even in China any significant genus remains undiscovered. There is, however, one highly significant and decorative one which is still virtually unexploited and unknown: the southern beeches. Here is a race of trees of remarkable singularity, style and speed. But where do you see them? Few nurseries have ever heard of them.

The southern beeches are *Nothofagus*; the beeches, *Fagus*, of the southern hemisphere. The botanical differences between the two are relatively minor. They are very different trees, though, to look at. Some of them are deciduous, some are evergreen, but the hallmark of most is a tiny leaf–at biggest, perhaps half the size of a beech leaf: at smallest, smaller than a box tree's.

What is the advantage of a tiny leaf? To the gardener it is a question of texture. Evenness and flatness may not sound very exciting, but they are the qualities that draw the crowds to the fern-leaved beech (see the previous page).

Close to, it is a question of the pleasure taken in anything miniature and precise. In the Antarctic beech (*N. antarctica*), for example, the leaves are disposed in two neat rows along the slender twigs, each leaf a crinkled, nervy, shell-like *objet*.

There are southern beeches in both Australasia and South America; a fact which confirms that the southern land-masses have separated relatively recently. The hardiest and best-tried are the Chilean species. Novelty can't be the reason for their remaining in an esoteric niche; two of them were introduced to botany in the 1820s.

Of the deciduous Chilean species the Antarctic beech is perhaps the most characteristic and the least rare. It has a tendency in Britain to make a wide bush rather than a tree; one I have seems to be modelling itself after a corkscrew.

The evergreen southern beech Nothofagus cunninghamii *from Tasmania is typical of the genus in its tiny leaves. The red of the new shoots recalls the autumn colour of its deciduous relations.*

'Black beech', Nothofagus solandri, *growing in the foothills of the Southern Alps of New Zealand. It forms enormous pure forests ascending to the snowline.*

The Antarctic beech from
Chile, Nothofagus
antarctica, *sometimes
fails to make a straight
trunk at all, but spreads
into a huge shrub-like
form of twisting branches.*

The deciduous leaves of
the Chilean Antarctic
beech are almost as small
as those of the black
beech. Clusters of yellow
flowers hang from the
branches in spring.

As a piece of autumn colour the Antarctic beech is also quite remarkable; it changes colour leaf by leaf, and into several different shades. The effect is a mosaic of green, red, orange and brown, all over the tree. Its rather obvious and fish-bony branching pattern adds point to the performance.

Two other Chilean deciduous beeches *N. procera* and *N. obliqua*, have bigger leaves. *Procera's* leaves are paler with more marked veins, not unlike a hornbeam's. Its buds stand out from the twigs at an angle like the beech's. *Obliqua*, darker green with shinier and more toothed leaves, looks more like a chestnut. Both are enormously fast-growing and colour well in autumn.

The only evergreen species I have had a chance to get to know is the Chilean *N. dombeyi*. The fishbone branching pattern in this is almost as pronounced as in some young elms. In leaf it is like the Antarctic beech, only darker, the leaves set alternately and rather close together on red twigs, flecked, as the branches of some cherries are, with white horizontal streaks. On the grey trunk these white streaks persist, scaled up.

Another Chilean evergreen, *N. betuloides*, the New Zealand black beech, *N. solandri*, and its form *cliffortioides* are very similar. The Chilean ones are reckoned hardier in Britain, but in a climate like California's they would all grow, one would think, like beans. Their only dislikes are wind and lime in the soil.

Most of the southern beeches are easy to propagate by cuttings. Surely a few more nurserymen must be tempted?

Above and below *The prominently veined leaves of another of the Chilean deciduous southern beeches, Nothofagus procera, are some of the biggest of the genus—up to four inches long. They are remarkably like those of the hornbeam. In autumn (above) they take on various warm shades of pink and brown. The fruit of procera (below, unripe) is very like that of the familiar beeches.*

A typical upright fan-shaped spray of the ever-green black beech of New Zealand. It makes a slender tall tree whose tiny leaves give it great elegance. The form N. solanderi cliffortioides is a close relation with even smaller leaves.

153

The Oaks

'"Robur, the Oak". I have sometimes considered it very seriously, what would move Pliny to make a whole chapter of one only line.' So John Evelyn begins the first chapter of his *Sylva*.

Pliny, and Evelyn, were right. The oak carries such a cargo of symbolism that embroidery is counter-productive.

Robur, the Oak.

'I wonder if you ever thought of the single mark of supremacy which distinguishes this tree? The others shirk the work of resisting gravity; the oak defies it. It chooses the horizontal direction for its limbs, so that their whole weight may tell; and then stretches them fifty or sixty feet . . . to slant upward another degree would mark infirmity of purpose; to bend downwards, weakness of organization.'

This is Oliver Wendell Holmes, *The Autocrat of the Breakfast Table*, chapter Ten. I beg you to find the book and read on to where he goes to look for New England's biggest elm.

In Britain it seems as though a sort of race memory still exists of the time when the whole country was oakwood. Even in Henry VIII's time, 450 years ago, one-third of the whole island was still covered by oak trees. Still, today, if good land is left fallow, oak will very likely find its way there and cover it before ten years are out.

There are 600 species of oak in the world. There is one that started the legend. Oak grows in every form: as tree, as bush, as scrub; deciduous or evergreen: in Europe, Asia and America. But the oak of imagery is the English oak: broad and slow, angular and ponderous-branched; *Quercus robur*.

I should hasten to say that there are two species of oak in England and northern Europe, *Q. robur* and *Q. petraea*; that they are quite distinct (though they often hybridize) and that I have no evidence (or not much) for offering one as the original of the oak-image and not the other.

Typically, the English, common, or pedunculate oak (*Q. robur* has all these names) is the broad tree, not specially tall, that the *Autocrat* was talking about. Typically the durmast or sessile oak (*Q. petraea*) is a taller, more upward-reaching tree.

True, it depends above all on where they are growing. In an open field both will be broad and spreading; in close forest both need to aspire towards the overhead light. You have to remember, therefore, that the pedunculate oak has its acorns on peduncles or stalks; the durmast has them sitting on the twig. The leaves are the other way round: the short-stalked leaves of the pedunculate form stiff rosettes at the ends of the twigs, making the canopy broken, with patches of sky showing through. The stalked leaves of the durmast oak give an even coverage; a shaftless, uniform shade.

The great oak forests of central France where Europe's tallest oaks grow, above all the Forêt de Tronçais, planted by Colbert for the French navy in the 18th century, are durmast woods. In the west of England durmast is in the majority. In an eastern, or midland, or southern English park on the other hand, the huge, broken-headed hulks, reputed (often rightly) to have been there 500 years or more, and all their gnarled and leafy offspring are common oak. As far as the navy was concerned, there were never enough of these trees. Their awkward, angular way of growing gave the shipwright the hugely powerful brackets and angle-pieces that held a 74-gun ship together as she blundered through the troughs on her way into the line.

Queen Elizabeth's Treasurer, Lord Burghley, was the first man to plant oaks. He sowed acorns and holly berries together, shrewdly giving his saplings evergreen cover that would never smother them. It was held that bigger acorns make better trees, so they were sieved and only the biggest were planted.

Intensive cultivation produced its crop of ornamental cultivars. An excellent upright version of the common oak, Lombardy-poplar style (*Q. robur* 'Fastigiata'), is perhaps the best. The rest are rare, but there exist a cut-leafed version (*Q. robur* 'Filicifolia'); a purple version (*Q. robur* 'Atropurpurea'); a golden version (*Q. r.* 'Concordia'); and a rather anaemic variegated version (*Q. r.* 'Argenteovariegata').

By the mid-18th century most of the oaks of Europe and the Mediterranean region were well known and enthusiastically cultivated. A number of hybrids of permanent value arose in the nurseries, where oaks quite foreign to each other were planted side by side.

Turner's oak, the Fulham oak and the Kew oak are all examples that have been famous in their time. The most famous and the most used today was a chance seedling in the Exeter nursery of Lucombe & Pince in 1762. The parents were the vigorous Turkey oak (*Q. cerris*) and the evergreen cork oak (*Q. suber*). The Lucombe oak (*Q. × hispanica* 'Lucombeana') has the most useful attributes of both its parents short of providing cork. It is a most distinguished and huge-growing almost-evergreen, with beautiful glowing-green leaves with a golden cast.

Oaks continue to plant themselves, but not many are planted today. Mainly, one supposes, because they are notoriously slow. It is worth examining, therefore, just how fast or slow they are.

On a piece of land which was completely cleared 15 years ago I have oaks 25 feet high, from acorns presumably sown by jays the year the land was cleared. True, if they were poplars they could be 60 feet by now, but is 25 feet in 15 years (or say conservatively 15 feet in 10 years) so slow? It's certainly a satisfying rate of progress to watch.

One should not underestimate young oaks as ornament. The Lammas shoots which make all oaks glow with new life in mid-summer show up most on a young tree. Last year one particular tree was so covered with new pink and golden leaves that no flowering cherry could have been more spectacular; and it took them six weeks to fade through pale green to dark. The same tree, in a sheltered place, has kept its brown leaves on all winter like a young beech. In that tree's future there is really something to look forward to.

155

The Oaks of Europe and Asia

The tendency to keep their leaves late in the season, dead or alive, is clearly an oak family trait. The oaks as a whole give the impression that evergreenery is never very far away. Many of the oaks of the south, whether in Europe or America, are outright evergreens. Others (especially the big-leafed species) hang on to their leaves for as long as they can. In northern Europe this is often until January. In the south it is until the new crop of leaves takes over in spring.

The holm oak is by far the most familiar of the Mediterranean species and far and away the biggest and best broadleaved evergreen we can grow as far north as Britain. (In the U.S.A., as far north as Washington D.C.) It seems to break all the rules, exposing a mass of leaf to the cruel winter winds. Yet it takes a severe winter to defoliate it, even partially – and even then the tree is often unharmed.

The name 'holm' (and also the Latin name, *Q. ilex*) means holly. It may have been the shock of seeing another green broadleaf in winter which caused the comparison, because, though its young leaves are spiny, the adult leaves have nothing like the shine nor the spines of the holly. Holm oak leaves vary from plain ovals to distinctly toothed shapes, from thumb-nail size to three inches or so, and from quite pale green in shade to a dark gloss in the sun. The tree's best moment, like the yew's, is when the young growth of the spring shows against the near-black background of the old. A white moss of hairs covers the fresh leaves; as they open they glow amber and tawny. The broad dome of a big tree, dressed with drooping branches to the ground, and creaming over with these quiet colours, is spring's most solemn celebration.

Being such good shade-bearers makes close-grown holm oaks quite remarkable. They grow tall and slim like any forest tree, but without losing their lower leaves and branches. I have seen full-dressed trees 60 feet high and not ten across in a forest clearing; perhaps the most elegant of all evergreens. There is no better tree for the architectural backbone of a garden or park.

The other evergreen oak of the Mediterranean is the cork oak, *Q. suber*. It is not quite so hardy as the holm oak, neither is it such a big and good-looking tree. Its interest lies in its bark, which is usually displayed (as the elephant-skin bark of the holm oak is not) by its open and haphazard way of growing. Old cork oaks usually lean at perilous angles which go with the exaggerated cragginess of the trunk to make a convincing picture of age. Cork as a commercial proposition is still pretty well confined to Portugal and Spain. South of the Tagus in Portugal the country is orchard-like for mile

Left *The sessile or durmast oak, native of most of Europe and western Britain, is often a taller and less spreading tree than the common English oak. France's finest oak-forests are of this species.*

Below left *The Turkey oak is the fastest-growing and most adaptable European species. Its acorn is distinctive for its densely mossy cup. The rough leaves vary in shape from oval to oblong.*

Above *The cork oak of Spain and Portugal is still the world's principal source of cork. The thick, rugged bark is stripped off every ten or 15 years.*

Below *The male catkins of durmast oak are yellow and easily visible. The female flowers sit, like the acorns, stalkless in the angles of the leaves. The durmast's leaves are generally bigger than those of the closely allied (and similar) English oak.*

after mile among the spreading, stunted cork-trees. Recently, though, there have been plantations in California and the southern States.

In many ways the ideal plant for a public place is one that is slightly larger than life. Not a ferocious-looking exotic that makes the native greenery look dowdy, but a close relation with a touch of extra ginger. Just enough to wake people up with the surprise of, let us say, an oak with such big leaves.

This alone would be reason enough to bring back the neglected big-leaf oaks of southern Europe, even if they were not in

their own right singularly splendid, vigorous and adaptable trees.

There are three outstanding oaks which once were famous: the Hungarian (*Q. frainetto*), the Algerian (*Q. canariensis*) and the Caucasian (*Q. macranthera*). They all have leaves about six inches long – not as long as some of the American oaks', but long enough to give a distinctively tulgy look.

The Caucasian and Algerian oaks are easily confusable; the Hungarian has much deeper lobes – even two inches deep – in its splendid leaves. All are eventually trees of the biggest size.

Another distinctive pair of oaks from the

The oaks of the orient are still rare in western gardens. Quercus glauca is a beautiful small evergreen species from China with blue-white undersides to the leathery little leaves.

Several southern European oaks have bold and shiny leaves twice the size of the common English oak. The Caucasian Quercus macranthera is one of these noble and eye-catching trees, perfectly hardy in northern Europe.

The English oak has produced several ornamental cultivars, among them the slow-growing but attractive 'Atropurpurea'; the leaves and shoots are suffused with a rich purple, turning greyish-purple on mature trees.

Leaves of the holm (or holly-leaved) oak are glossy but without the glitter of holly. They fall in early summer and resist rotting, which can make them a problem in gardens. The acorns take 18 months to ripen.

Near East have narrow leaves, not lobed (i.e. with the wavy coastline of most oak leaves) but with a regular row of little points, or teeth; ten or 15 a side. The general effect is very much like a chestnut leaf. One of them, in fact, is called the chestnut-leafed oak (*Q. castaneifolia*); the other the Lebanon oak (*Q. libani*). Like chestnuts' their leaves are dark green and shiny; like oaks', they hang on until the new year.

The only one of this southern group which could be called at all common is the Turkey oak, *Q. cerris*. It has the reputation of being the fastest-growing and could perhaps make in time the tallest tree. At one time the navy

had great hopes of it, but its wood proved a disappointment. Its leaves are all points and angles, not oversize but eye-catching. Most important, perhaps, it grows well on unpromising dry and chalky soil.

The oaks of the Far East in cultivation are not (yet, at any rate) such big trees. The outstanding ones are the sawtooth oak (*Q. acutissima*) from Japan, a very similar tree to the chestnut-leafed oak, and the daimyo oak (*Q. dentata*) which has the biggest leaves of any, sometimes over a foot long. *Q. acuta* and *Q. glauca*, both small evergreen trees, and *Q. variabilis*, the Chinese cork oak, occasionally turn up in collections.

Above *The evergreen holm oak of the Mediterranean makes massive hedges and thrives under clipping almost as well as yew. It will grow on all types of well-drained soil. This garden is at the American University in Rome.*

In the middle ages oak was important as a source of pig-food. Forests were assessed by the number of swine which could live on their acorns. The swineherd was still a familiar figure in 16th-century Germany when this engraving was made.

The Oaks of North America

The American Oaks

The oaks of North America present a daunting picture at first. Yet there are certain key features which help one to classify and recognize the individual species. The chart on the right shows the leaves and acorns of 25 of the most important ones. The trees are divided according to their black/white affinities, the shape of their leaf (lobed or unlobed), whether they are deciduous or evergreen, and their native habitat — whether they belong east or west of the Rockies.

Left *The black oak of the eastern States (*Quercus velutina), *one of the tallest of all oaks; a tower of dark glossy green, turning red in autumn, up to 140 feet in good moist soil.*

Above *The white oak, most characteristically oak-like of all the American species with its mighty dome. The leaves turn from autumn purples and reds to golden brown.*

Left *The red oak (*Quercus rubra) *is more amenable to transplanting than either the white or the black and grows faster than any other American oak. It has golden new shoots and red autumn colour.*

Above *The California white or valley oak is the biggest oak of the west, the tree that makes parts of the Central valley look like a park. The best specimen today is 120 feet high, 103 feet in spread and 28 feet in girth.*

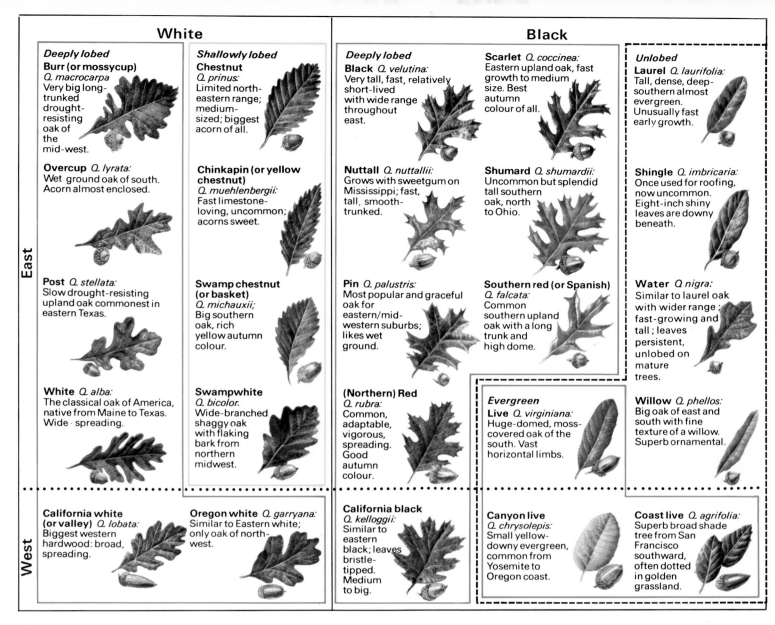

White		Black		
Deeply lobed	**Shallowly lobed**	**Deeply lobed**		**Unlobed**

East

White — Deeply lobed

Burr (or mossycup) Q. macrocarpa: Very big long-trunked drought-resisting oak of the mid-west.

Overcup Q. lyrata: Wet ground oak of south. Acorn almost enclosed.

Post Q. stellata: Slow drought-resisting upland oak commonest in eastern Texas.

White Q. alba: The classical oak of America, native from Maine to Texas. Wide-spreading.

White — Shallowly lobed

Chestnut Q. prinus: Limited north-eastern range; medium-sized; biggest acorn of all.

Chinkapin (or yellow chestnut) Q. muehlenbergii: Fast limestone-loving, uncommon; acorns sweet.

Swamp chestnut (or basket) Q. michauxii; Big southern oak, rich yellow autumn colour.

Swampwhite Q. bicolor. Wide-branched shaggy oak with flaking bark from northern midwest.

Black — Deeply lobed

Black Q. velutina: Very tall, fast, relatively short-lived with wide range throughout east.

Nuttall Q. nuttallii: Grows with sweetgum on Mississippi; fast, tall, smooth-trunked.

Pin Q. palustris: Most popular and graceful oak for eastern/mid-western suburbs; likes wet ground.

(Northern) Red Q. rubra: Common, adaptable, vigorous, spreading. Good autumn colour.

Scarlet Q. coccinea: Eastern upland oak, fast growth to medium size. Best autumn colour of all.

Shumard Q. shumardii: Uncommon but splendid tall southern oak, north to Ohio.

Southern red (or Spanish) Q. falcata: Common southern upland oak with a long trunk and high dome.

Black — Unlobed

Laurel Q. laurifolia: Tall, dense, deep-southern almost evergreen. Unusually fast early growth.

Shingle Q. imbricaria: Once used for roofing, now uncommon. Eight-inch shiny leaves are downy beneath.

Water Q. nigra: Similar to laurel oak with wider range; fast-growing and tall; leaves persistent, unlobed on mature trees.

Evergreen Live Q. virginiana: Huge-domed, moss-covered oak of the south. Vast horizontal limbs.

Willow Q. phellos: Big oak of east and south with fine texture of a willow. Superb ornamental.

West

California white (or valley) Q. lobata: Biggest western hardwood: broad, spreading.

Oregon white Q. garryana: Similar to Eastern white; only oak of north-west.

California black Q. kelloggii: Similar to eastern black; leaves bristle-tipped. Medium to big.

Canyon live Q. chrysolepis: Small yellow-downy evergreen, common from Yosemite to Oregon coast.

Coast live Q. agrifolia: Superb broad shade tree from San Francisco southward, often dotted in golden grassland.

At times the great American forest seems like an oakwood with intruders—so many splendid species are there. Eighty grow in North America and 60 of them are full-fledged trees.

There can be few people who have mastered the whole catalogue, though when you start breaking it down into the more obvious distinctions—region, deciduous or evergreen, whether the leaves are lobed or not and the colour of the bark—the process of identification works pretty quickly. The truth is, however, that in most parts of America there is an obvious oak to plant—the one that grows there already.

The most noticeable distinction is between the live oaks (as the evergreen species are called) and the deciduous ones. The live oaks in fact are few: one in the east and half a dozen in the west.

The real botanical distinction is between white and black oaks (which include the red oaks and all the live oaks). There is no single great give-away here, but enough clear differences to make it quite easy.

In the northeast *the* white oak, *Quercus alba*, has its domain. In what way is it typical of its group? Its name, it seems, comes from the colour of its trunk, which is grey and scaly, contrasting with the blackish and furrowed trunks of the black oaks. The deep lobes of its leaves are rounded at the ends, without points or bristles. Its acorns are reasonably sweet to eat, their cups are shiny inside. And they stay on the tree for only one season; they fall in autumn and germinate straight away—often to be killed by frost before they have got established.

The red oak (*Q. rubra*) is the protagonist of the blacks. Its bark is blackish-brown and corrugated. The leaves have less indented bays, but their lobes are sharp-pointed and their points have little bristles. Acorns last two years on the tree; when they fall they wait until spring before germinating. Their meat is bitter and their cups are downy inside instead of shiny.

By and large the rules of identification apply. Often one of the typical features is missing. There are no bristled lobes, for example, on the (black) willow oaks. In the last resort the botanist's criterion has been the wood structure, which divides the two groups perfectly in accordance with the other evidence. White oak timber is, on the whole, much the better. It is an odd side-light that the white oaks are miserable in Europe and hardly grow at all, while the black have done excellently.

The big variations in leaf shape that occur within each group help the identification process considerably. The chart above shows the principal trees—far more black than white, and far more in the east than in the west. The map overleaf shows the total range of the two groups and the site of the biggest known tree of each species—an indication of where it feels most at home. ▶

The Oaks of North America

▶ Differences in acorns and leaves seem to suggest that there is considerable variation between the species of oaks–but how much, in fact, do they differ in life style?

In outright hardiness they vary surprisingly little; some of the southern oaks will grow even in New York, though they lose the leaves they might have kept, at home, through most of the winter. They all have their favourite haunts: moist river bottoms, gravelly gullies or rocky open hills. In overall size they can certainly vary: from the cliff-like 125 feet of occasional black oaks to the mere 50 feet of, say, the blue oaks of California, not to mention some of the scrub oaks that never make a tree. On the other hand, most oaks with space to spread settle for a medium height: 70 feet or so.

There are three characteristics in particular that single out certain oaks as trees of real beauty: their habit of branching, their texture and their autumn colour.

The classic oak branch pattern–bold, wide and angular on a stocky trunk–is best expressed by the white oak. The Oregon white and the burr oaks are similar. The others in their group approach it, though they are rarely so perfect in form. Overcup oak, for instance, often has a crooked trunk.

Among the second group of white oaks, those with chestnut-style leaves, the trees are often taller in relation to their spread, with shorter or upward-trending branches. They are less typical of the oaks both in figure and in leaf.

The red and the black oaks tend to be narrower than the white; the total effect more tower than dome. The shumard and the Spanish (or southern red) oaks are typically taller and narrower trees; the scarlet oak more branchy and open. The fastest-growing oaks all belong to this group.

Of these the tree most often planted in America for its profile is the pin oak, which has, instead of stout wandering branches, an abundance of thin and straight ones. The upper branches climb to make a rather narrow crown; the lower ones droop, often as low as the ground, hiding the trunk. For an oak it is a lightweight tree; the more so because of the fine texture of its deeply-divided leaves.

The live oak of the south is the most characteristic of all in its shape: it grows twice as wide as it is high. The champion is 138 feet across by a mere 71 feet high.

All oak leaves are lively: the oak is never dull in texture. The burr oak, which has the biggest leaves (sometimes a foot long) has an extraordinarily emphatic pattern. Yet perhaps the finest-textured make the most beautiful trees: fine either in having deep-cut leaves like the pin oak, or in having them slim and small like the willow oak. Small leaves on a big tree do not have the busy effect you might expect: they make a perfect patina for the terrific sculpture of crown and bough.

What matters more to the parks department than the exact shape of tree or leaf is the way the tree transplants. Tap-rooting oaks are notoriously reluctant to move: the white, scarlet and black oaks are all examples. Among the easiest to transplant, and hence the most popular, are the red, water, pin and willow oaks. The last three, alas, need acid soil.

Above *The canyon live oak, a common evergreen species in California, is the oldest American oak. It is a medium-sized spreading tree with smooth pale bark and gold-fuzzy acorn cups.*

Below *The Oregon white oak takes over from the valley oak in north California. It has similar twisted branches but makes a smaller deep-rooting tree. The leaves are deeply lobed.*

Deciduous Black Oaks
1. Black
   125' h. 85' s. Warrensville Heights, Ohio.
2. Blackjack
   47' 4" h. 76' s. nr. Wakita, Oklahoma.
3. California black
   124' h. 115' s. Siskiyou National Forest, Oregon.
4. California blue
   55' h. 87' s. Nevada County, California.
5. Laurel
   102' h. 116' s. Waycross, Georgia.
6. Nuttall
   130' h. 80' s. Rolling Fork, Mississippi.
7. Pin
   93' h. 85' s. nr. Carrollton, Missouri.
   134' h. 99' s. nr. Smithland, Kentucky.
8. Red
   118' h. 128' s. Berrien County, Michigan.
   88' h. 88' s. Ashtabula County, Ohio.
9. Scarlet
   65' h. 80' s. Massapequa, New York.
10. Shingle
    80' h. 80' s. Wayne County, Ohio.
11. Shumard
    130' h. 111' s. Brooksville, Mississippi.
12. Southern red
    128' h. 149' s. Harwood, Maryland.

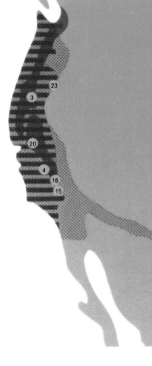

The blue oak of inland California has a bluish cast to its leaves, often the mark of a tree which can withstand drought conditions. In the foothills of the Sierras it grows with little moisture, wide-spreading, rarely over 50 feet.

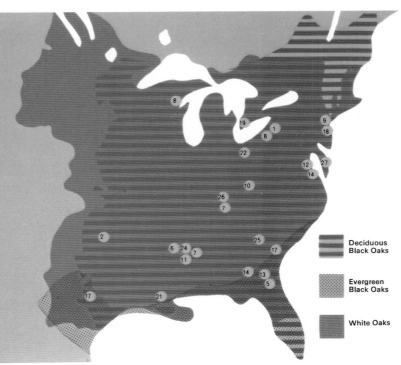

Deciduous Black Oaks

Evergreen Black Oaks

White Oaks

White Oaks

18. Basket
*75′ h. 100′ s.
Northport, New York.*

19. Burr
*128′ h. 104′ s.
Algonac, Michigan.*

20. California white
*120′ h. 103′ s.
nr. Gridley,
California.*

21. Chestnut
*130′ h. 86′ s.
nr. Urania,
Louisiana.*

22. Chinkapin
*72′ h. 62′ s.
Ross County, Ohio.*

23. Oregon white
*98′ h. 72′ s.
Douglas County,
Oregon.*

24. Overcup
*120′ h. 83′ s.
Rolling Fork,
Mississippi.*

25. Post
*86′ h. 42′ s.
nr. Hartwell,
Georgia.*

26. Swamp white
*104′ h. 119′ s.
nr. Tompkinsville,
Monroe County.*

27. White
*102′ h. 158′ s.
State Park,
Wye Mills,
Maryland.*

13. Water
*106′ h. 105′ s.
nr. Waycross, Georgia.*

14. Willow
*125′ h. 106′ s.
Queenstown, Maryland.
112′ h. 125′ s.
nr. Hillman, Georgia.*

Evergreen Black Oaks

15. Canyon live
*72′ h. 80′ s.
Cleveland National
Forest, California.*

16. Coast live
*108′ h. 129′ s.
Chiles Valley, Cal.*

17. Live
*44′ h. 89′ s.
Goose Island State
Park, Texas.
71′ h. 138′ s.
Beaufort County,
South Carolina.*

Top *The live oak of the Deep South; one of the widest-domed of all trees, nearly always decked with shawls of grey Spanish moss which give it an indescribable grace. It will grow on most soils.*

Above *The willow oak (named for its narrow, unlobed, willow-like leaves) has the finest texture of all and makes one of the most magnificent, yet graceful and lightly-built, trees.*

Most brilliant of all oaks in autumn, the scarlet oak has a natural range of nearly a third of the United States and grows excellently in Europe. Its long, relatively slender branches and open crown cast a light shade.

The pin oak is easy to recognize by the hang of its thin branches; the lower ones always sweeping to the ground and the upper ones forming a tidy dome. Deep-cut leaves give it a fine texture in keeping with its almost feminine shape.

The water oak of the southeast will grow considerably north of its natural range and in relatively dry ground. Like many southern oaks it keeps its leaves for half the winter or more, according to the climate.

The Chestnuts

It is hardly a step from some of the chestnut-leaved American oaks to the chestnut itself. Botany has made stepping stones rather than a linking path between the two, preferring to give the golden chinkapin and the tanbark oak, two American species which come firmly between oak and chestnut, and *Castanopsis*, a Japanese one, the status of separate genera. But from the acorn, part in its cup and part out, to the chestnut, all inside, each stage of wrapping is represented.

When you get to the chestnut tree there is no mistaking it. Vivid leafiness proclaims it. Big tongue-shaped leaves, every vein making a valley and every valley ending in a holly-like point. Very commonly the leaves are all the evidence you have of what it is. In Europe because of a still-flourishing industry in chestnut poles, for which the wood is coppiced; cut to the ground every seven or eight years. But in North America because disease has in the last 60 years killed every big chestnut. If anyone is complacent about the elms, let him look at the fate of the chestnuts. At the beginning of this century they were one of the chief components of the eastern forest, bigger than almost any oak, spreading from Alabama to Maine. In 1906 a bark fungus very like the elm disease was introduced accidentally from the Far East. By 1940 the chestnut was expunged from the list of American forest trees. Only because of its immense power of sprouting from the base (which makes it ideal for coppice) does it survive at all, as leafy fountains from where huge old trees formerly stood.

Uncoppiced and unblighted, standing on a lawn, the chestnut is a dense, substantial-looking tree, forming a billowing pyramid of light-catching leaves. In July it is variegated by its long yellow-green catkins. In them lies its only disadvantage: a sickly smell that haunts high summer.

The Spanish or sweet chestnut (*Castanea sativa*) of Europe gets its name from an

Above *Sweet (or Spanish) chestnut in mid-summer, covered with its creamy spikes of flowers. In its native Mediterranean it is the longest-lived of all deciduous trees.*

Below *The catkin-like flower spikes and glossy toothed leaves of the sweet chestnut. The flowers give off a sickly smell but the leaves make it one of the handsomest trees for parkland.*

Below *The fruit of the sweet chestnut: the only beech-family fruit commonly eaten by the human race today. The sweet brown nuts are enclosed in a prickly green case until they are* ripe: one, two or three *nuts to each shell. Varieties with extra heavy crops of good nuts have been selected: 'Marron de Lyon' is the most famous. There are forms with yellow or white leaf margins.*

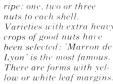

Left *The deep and regular fissures in the bark of the chestnut have the habit of swirling round the trunk in a spiral; often the quickest way to identify a chestnut tree in winter.*

Right *The giant chinkapin is an evergreen relation of the chestnut from northern California and Oregon. It has valuable wood, good fruit and beautiful foliage. It could be planted much more outside its natural range.*

A record-size specimen of the giant chinkapin growing near Saverdun in the foothills of the Pyrenees. The whole tree takes on a fluffy bronze look in mid-summer with its thousands of flowers. Where it will not make a full-size tree (i.e. too far north) the chinkapin is worth growing as a shrub.

ancient city in what is now Turkey: the city of Kastanaia, whence the Latin name; *châtaignier*, the French; and chestnut. The horse chestnut, of another family entirely, has merely borrowed it because its nuts are similar, at least in size and shape.

Where the chestnut demonstrably feels most at home is half-way up a full-sized Mediterranean volcano. The most colossal hulk of a tree ever recorded still flourished in the last century on the eastern slopes of Mt. Etna. It was 204 feet round, counting all the fragments, and supported a small industry of nut-gatherers, who in their simple Sicilian way eventually killed the goose by cutting off its branches to stoke the fire to cook the nuts. At 2,500 or 3,000 years of age (having been an old tree when Plato lived in nearby Syracuse) it finally succumbed to souvenir-hunters.

The Spanish and American chestnuts are as close cousins as any two trees on opposite sides of the Atlantic. Which means, alas, that the Spanish chestnut is susceptible to the blight and can't be planted in America.

To take its place American nurseries have introduced the Japanese and Chinese chestnuts (*C. crenata* and *C. mollissima*). Of the two, the Chinese has the sweeter nuts and makes the bigger and better tree – but still only half the size of the native species.

There are beautiful variegated versions of the Spanish chestnut, with leaf-margins ivory-white or yellow. But these of course are blight-prone in America too.

Happily the stepping-stones are immune. Both are evergreens from the northwest States, Oregon and North California. The more chestnut-like of them in fruit is the golden chinkapin (*Chrysolepis chrysophylla*, formerly *Castanopsis chrysophylla*).

For one of the most original and charming of relatively hardy broadleafed evergreens, this tree remains curiously uncommon outside its natural range. Its leaves vary from willow-slim to broad as bay, dark green above and beneath permanently upholstered

in brown-gold down. Its nuts are very like chestnuts, and can be eaten.

Once golden chinkapins – the name is the Indian for chestnut – grew on a truly western scale, 150 feet high among the redwoods and Douglas firs in the coastal hills. But their wood was too good to last in a region where hardwood is the exception.

The tanbark oak (*Lithocarpus densiflorus*) has less to attract the gardener. It is like a chestnut in leaf and identical to an oak in fruit. Its very tannic bark makes it important for the leather industry, but in gardens it has proved wilful and demanding, without offering very much in return.

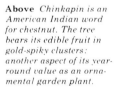

Left *The evergreen foliage of the giant chinkapin (sometimes known as the golden chestnut) is elegantly tapered, dark green above and densely covered below with gleaming gold-amber felt.*

Above *The American sweet chestnut, which, until 60 years ago, rivalled the tulip tree as the tallest deciduous tree of the eastern forests. In the '20s and '30s, it was wiped out by a bark fungus very like the Dutch elm disease.*

Above *Chinkapin is an American Indian word for chestnut. The tree bears its edible fruit in gold-spiky clusters: another aspect of its year-round value as an ornamental garden plant.*

Below *At the beginning of the century a quarter of the hardwoods of the Great Smokies were chestnuts. Today almost the only relic of them is the shingle roofing of the old settlers' cabins.*

The Birches

The evolutionary group that started with the witch hazels and included the elms, the beeches and the oaks ends with the birch family: the birches, the alders, the hornbeams and the hazels.

Both the birches and the alders, the closest cousins, are lightweight trees of the forest's edge, adapted to poor land and extremes of either drought or damp. The birches are the hardiest of all the broadleaves; the only trees native to Iceland and Greenland.

There are some 60 species of birch. It circles the globe in the higher northern latitudes without varying very much in stature (save in tundra where it dwindles to scrub) or in stance; remaining always a light-branched, thin-twigged and graceful tree. Birch species are notoriously difficult to identify. In collections they lose no time in hybridizing–which only makes matters worse. They vary (but not very much) in leaf shape, colour and texture; more in leaf size–up to the six-inch heart-shaped leaves of the monarch birch of Japan, *Betula maximowicziana*. Where they vary most is in the birch's most original feature: the colour of its bark.

The common silver birch of Europe has chalk-white bark; the American canoe (or paper) birch whiter still; the yellow birch yellow; the gray birch white streaked with black; the cherry birch cherry-like brown; the river birch dark shaggy brown; Forrest's birch a purply brown; the Himalayan birch buff or cream; the Chinese paper birch a range from pink to oxblood satin.

In all these (except the river birch) the coloured layer is a stage in the bark's development from a reddish brown to an eventual craggy black. During this stage the outermost layer peels off in the thinnest of ribbons. It has incredible endurance. Pieces of birch bark hundreds of years old have been found intact in peat bogs. In Siberia (at Dworotrkoi, to be exact) it has even been found in its original state attached to wood that has fossilized. To dwellers in the north it is indispensable. Indians make canoes of it; Lapps cloaks and leggings; Norwegians roofs, covering a layer of bark with a foot of earth. When all is sodden in the forest birch bark will burn. To Russian leather (which is tanned with it) it gives its peculiar musty scent.　▶

Left *A dense natural stand of the canoe or paper birch of North America, one of the tallest and most vigorous of the birches, whose waterproof bark formed the hulls of Indian canoes. The biggest tree (in Maine) is nearly 100 feet.*

The outermost layer of bark of a birch is in a constant state of replacement. Few other trees have peeling bark. Above is the bark of the paper or canoe birch; it provides writing material, weatherproof covering or instant kindling for a fire.

Right *The Russian rock birch (Betula ermanii) is another of the northern Asiatic species that have proved a success in northern gardens. A tall tree with pinky-white peeling bark on the trunk and orange-brown branches.*

Left *Northern Asia is the home of dozens of species and varieties of birch. Betula costata (it has no English name) is one of the most decorative. It has pinky-cream bark, narrow oval leaves and glorious autumn colour.*

Below *The North American river or black birch has crackly dark brown bark very different from the usual silky sheath. It is the best species for wet ground. Its diamond-shaped leaves turn clear yellow in autumn.*

The silver birch of Europe is not quite the glowing warm white of the paper birch, nor does it grow so big. But its crown has an unrivalled fountaining elegance. It often seeds itself abundantly and forms dense stands on burned-over woodland.

The bark of the yellow birch (Betula alleghaniensis): yellow more in its magnificent autumn leaves than in its peeling bark, which is amber or golden brown. This is the tallest of the American birches, reaching over 100 feet in the Allegheny mountains.

Right *The gray (or poplar-leaved) birch is often a short-lived, many-stemmed tree colonizing derelict land. Its grey-white trunk is marked with black lines where young branches have been.*

165

The Birch Family/*Betulaceae*

The Birches

Young paper birches grouped on a New England lawn. Birches are most effective in gardens when they are planted in small groups. A dark background helps to emphasise their white trunks. Where there is no space for a spreading tree the lower branches can safely be trimmed.

▶ Bark apart, the birch's beauty lies in its poise; the way it puts dense swarms of lacy twigs in the air with the flimsiest engineering. Perhaps its best time is in spring, when its natural droop is emphasized by the weight of catkins. Beside an oak, or a pine, its natural companions, it looks unmistakably feminine. Coleridge called it 'The Lady of the Woods'. There is no avoiding the inevitable image.

But then there is autumn. Birch leaves turn the purest, most sovereign gold of any tree's. It begs to be planted against a background of dark conifers, where the slender pallor of the trunk, fountaining up to fall in shining leaf tresses can really be seen. Plant birch to the north of your house: not only is it a tree that wants the light shining on, rather than through it, but the moss which tends to grow on the trunk and hide its colour concentrates on the north side of the tree.

Birches are trees to plant in clumps rather than singly, for the maximum effect from their bark. Or you can cut a sapling back right to the base: it will sprout up again as a cluster of stems – but they will take a few years to turn white. The American gray birch (which is perfectly white with interesting dark marks at intervals on the trunk) forms clumps naturally.

There is no need to look for exotic species. The common birch of damp ground in Europe, *B. pubescens*, is not so beautiful as the more drooping silver birch (*B. pendula*) of sandy heaths – above all in Scotland. The common birch has downy twigs; the silver birch rough and warty ones – you can tell them apart even as young trees while their bark is still brown. There are extragraceful versions of the silver birch: the Swedish birch 'Dalecarlica' with deeply lobed leaves, the cultivar 'Tristis', narrowly soaring and weeping, and Young's weeping birch with a low domed head are all striking

Above *The long heart-shaped leaves of the Russian rock birch. The monarch birch of Japan (Betula maximowicziana) has the biggest leaves of the genus: up to seven inches long by five across.*

Below *The leaves of the silver birch with its catkins, conspicuous on the tree all year. One particularly pretty cultivar of this tree, 'Dalecarlica', has its leaves deeply divided and almost ferny.*

and excellent trees. Young's is peculiar for having branches as bare as curtain-rods with all the foliage hanging below them. But can one honestly say they are more beautiful than the species itself? Or than the straightforward canoe birch? Or the Japanese silver birch, *B. platyphylla japonica?*

The coloured-bark species compare with the snake-bark and paper-bark maples as trees with a special value in winter: trees to plant near the house, or at any rate near a path where you will see them at close quarters. Their satin glow seems to reach its warmest on a cruel snowy day.

The paper birch, shown here growing by a lake in New Canaan, Connecticut, is the most widespread of all the American birches, ranging in its natural habitat from Labrador to Nebraska. In the north the bark is used for roofing.

Above *The southern white Chinese birch (Betula albosinensis septentrionalis) is a supreme collector's tree; its bark of pale coppery silk with a greyish bloom makes it perhaps the most beautiful of all birches.*

Middle *The birch of the western Himalayas, Betula utilis var. jacquemontii, in its native Kashmir. Himalayan birch is variable; its bark may be white, cream or brown. Our knowledge of the birches of Asia is far from complete.*

The Alders

Below *Early in the year the alder puts on its most telling performance with its catkins and fruit on its bare branches. When low wintry light strikes the tree it seems to glow with ripeness.*

Above *Alder is the stream-side tree. Its common forms (here the common European alder, growing by a Yorkshire 'beck') tend to be neglected, although pretty at all times of year.*

Alders must be the easiest trees to overlook, or simply to accept as part of the scenery. I lived for 30 years before I became aware of them. Perhaps that's why they give me so much quiet pleasure now.

Alders have their moment in late winter. They are the dark-brown silhouettes at the water's edge, often in single file along a streambank, which gradually become more and more cluttered with dangling bits and pieces as the winter wears on. By spring their silhouette is noticeably denser; the transparency of a winter tree is gone. In its place is an abstract of clustered catkins and cones. Cones on a broadleaf? The alder is the only one that has them.

Having spotted the alders in winter I watched them into full leaf and discovered that their silhouette is still their hallmark. By coincidence they tend to be neat and narrow, as short and lightly-branched as conifers and with their branches almost as regularly arranged. Their leaf-shapes vary in detail from species to species, but all are round or fat-oval in general outline and all tend to be held horizontally. From below, therefore, an alder floats black discs across the sky.

Alders are humble trees. Their place is boggy bottoms in the wild. Since clogs went out of fashion (if fashion is the word) nobody

has wanted their timber, even though half of Venice is built on alder piles. Only in the Pacific northwest, where hardwoods are the exception, is it used for furniture. In gardens the alders tend to be equally ignored.

There is little call, it's true, to plant the common alder of Europe or the American speckled (or grey) alder from the east or red alder from the west – unless to vary the endless willows and poplars that tend to be stuck in wherever ground is boggy.

But the genus has a dressy member in the Italian alder; and a tree, moreover, that seems completely impartial about site and soil. As to soil, indeed, it actually improves

The bunches of male catkins of the red alder of the Pacific northwest are often up to six inches long. Red alder grows densely in swampy land near the sea in Oregon and provides good timber for furniture.

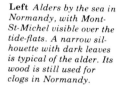

what it finds, having (like the pea family) the trick of introducing nitrogen with its roots.

I first saw the Italian alder (*A. cordata*) growing by the terrace of a mansion that had been burnt down and its ruins demolished. The garden was rank and dispiriting: the ponds choked, the once-trim columns of yew toppling and coming apart. What were those gleaming dark green trees still formal and polished as butlers in the chaos? They made a great impression on me, which has been reinforced wherever I have seen them in a garden (which is not often, I admit).

To be specific: a tall (to 90 feet) and narrow tree, though with branches more horizontal than upright. Substantial (up to four inches) heart-shaped leaves like a birch's, but darker green and glossy. Remarkable little cones: black eggs standing up on the branch-tips in trios.

Natural variation of the common alder of Europe (*A. glutinosa*; so named for the stickiness of its buds and twigs) and the grey alder (*A. incana*, or in America the very similar *A. rugosa*) – grey of leaf – has produced a few garden forms of these unpretentious trees. The most successful are the cut-leafed versions (*A. glutinosa* – or *incana* – 'Laciniata' and *A. glutinosa* 'Imperialis') and the golden ones (A.*g.* or *i.* 'Aurea').

Garden forms of the alder include several golden varieties. This is the golden form of the common alder of Europe (Alnus glutinosa 'Aurea'). There are also alders with ferny, deeply-cut leaves: a leaf-form which gives a lovely texture to the tree.

169

The Hornbeams and Hazels

The alder is not the only sleeper in its family. It's a long time since there was exactly a craze for hornbeam.

Hornbeam's fate is to be passed over as beech, with the feeling that the beech is a bit short of beechiness – the silver trunk and silky leaf we prize it for.

Certainly there is only one superlative that applies to hornbeam. It is the hardest. Iron-wood is another name for it. Before iron became cheap and plentiful the load-taking parts of machines – cogs, axles, spokes – were made of hornbeam. So was the sweet and simple furniture of the dairy: the yoke, the scrubbed white milkpails and the churn. But its engineering role past, what part has it to play today?

The distinctive quality of hornbeam is its texture. An old parkland hornbeam is simply a good broad-headed tree of something less than terrific height, colouring well (the American hornbeam, *Carpinus caroliniana*, splendidly) in autumn. At close quarters, though, the subtle corrugation of its surface gives it special interest. Where the bole of the beech is smooth and round the hornbeam looks as though muscles were straining within, making irregular flutes and ridges. And where the beech's leaves are slips of well-ironed silk, the hornbeam's are corrugated with ribs between the veins.

Where this texture can best be seen and appreciated is in a hedge. Not even the beech takes to the shears so well as the hornbeam. It makes a sturdy windbreak on almost any soil, like the beech keeping many of its dead leaves through the winter. One couldn't call their shade of brown a festive colour, but it has warmth.

Biddable as it is, the hornbeam will do more interesting things than a simple four-square wall. Its most effective use is at Hidcote, the Gloucestershire garden where hedges attain almost the status of art. Hornbeam here makes a hedge-on-stilts, pleached, as the old word is, into a perfect box-shape carried on wide-spaced immaculate stems four feet off the ground. The European *C. betulus* is best for hedge-work.

In hedging hornbeam you lose, of course, its natural shape. You also lose its fruit. The ordinary hornbeams of Europe and North America have little clusters of hanging winged nuts which catch the eye in autumn. But the Japanese ones (*C. cordata* and *japonica*) seem to be covered in bunches of drying hops when the leaves fall.

Hornbeams have a close relation which carries the hop theme far enough to be called the hop-hornbeam. The hop-hornbeams (*Ostrya* species) flourish in America, Europe and Asia, all looking remarkably alike and like hornbeams, save for their

Top *The fruit of the common hornbeam consists of short chains of three-winged nuts. It can hang high in the tree after the leaves fall, a help in distinguishing hornbeam from the similar but unrelated beech.*

Above *Hornbeam is one of the best broadleaf trees for hedging. This famous 'pleached' alley of common hornbeam is at Hidcote Manor in Gloucestershire. It keeps its perfect box shape with only one annual clipping.*

Right The Japanese hornbeam Carpinus cordata
has more substantial
tassels of green fruit, and
bigger, broader leaves
than the European or
American hornbeams. It
makes a small spreading
tree, worth growing for its
hop-like display of fruit
in autumn.

shaggy bark, which recalls the shagbark
hickory. Their long catkins add spring to
their season of display; like the hornbeams
they colour richly yellow in autumn.

The most familiar catkins of all are those
of the homely hazels and filberts, species of
Corylus, which with one exception are
bushes rather than trees. In their lowly
ranks there are some very attractive individuals. There is no more velvety leaf, for
example, than the Californian hazel's (*C.
californica*). And the purple hazel (*C.
maxima purpurea*) is one of the best purple-
leafed shrubs. But the one tree the hazels
can boast is a splendid one. It was brought
to Europe from Turkey at about the same
time as the horse chestnut. Vienna on the
fringe of the old Turkish empire has always
specialized in it. The Turkish hazel (*C.
colurna*) is just a greatly magnified (to 75
feet) version of the familiar one; a shapely,
many-branched tree, bearing trios of nuts
enveloped in whiskery husks.

Left Catkins of the
common hazel come in
late winter, undeterred by
frost. In February they
turn soft yellow. There are
pendulous and also
corkscrew-like forms of the
common hazel.

Above 'Fastigiata', a
form of the common
hornbeam, makes an
attractive medium-sized
tree. Although it starts off
narrow, with age it
becomes vase-shaped with
a short trunk, as here.

The common European
hazel is typical of the
genus with its roundish,
hairy leaf and nut (here
immature, still green) in a
frill of leaf-like material.
The shape of the frill is
the principal way of
distinguishing the
different species.

Right Hop-hornbeam is a
smaller tree than the
hornbeam, pretty both in
spring with long catkins
and in autumn when its
yellow leaves show off its
brown fruit. The fruit has
each little nut in a tiny
bladder.

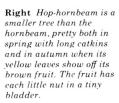

171

The Trees of the Tea Family

The tea family is a link in the ancestral chain between the great group headed by the primitive magnolias and a yet more diverse group that includes the heath family, the limes and – strange to say – the willows. Between the magnolias and their kin, and tea and its kin, come the peonies, a genus without trees, at least in our era. The grounds for such deductions are technical in the highest degree, starting with, of all things, the firing order of the stamens. Thus evolutionary links are obscured by infinity of variation and length of time.

The least spectacular member of the tea family is the tea-tree itself (*Camellia sinen-* *sis*). Its little nodding white flowers hardly prepare you for the glory of its sisters the camellias of the garden, nor the curiously-named trio of *Franklinia*, *Gordonia* and *Stewartia* which represents the family in North America. In Europe, ice-ravaged as ever, there are none.

Nurseries have developed a huge range of camellias from the original species. The process began centuries ago in China. *C. japonica*, the common species, is totally submerged in a sea of hybrids and cultivars. Two other species, however, are still important, both in their own right and for the magnificent hybrids they have generated. *Cam-* *ellia reticulata* from Yunnan in China is one; *C. sasanqua*, from Japan, the other.

All camellias are capable of making small trees (or very big bushes) in time, given the summer heat of Virginia and southwards (in Europe, of Bordeaux or the Italian Lakes), and given the right peaty soil and the right degree of woodland shelter. *C. reticulata* (which flowers in early spring) and *C. sasanqua* (which flowers from late autumn onwards) are or can be the most tree-like of them. Their flowers come in such a range from white to scarlet and from single to double and convoluted that they can match almost any human emotion. But even in

Above *The modest white flowers of the tea-bush seem to have little in common with their cousins the camellias. The tea-plant is kept small by the repeated drastic pruning of the* *harvest. High-quality tea was introduced from China (above, in Hang-chow province) to India in the last century by the British botanist Robert Fortune.*

Left *These splendid trees of* Camellia japonica *in the garden of the Duchess of Campo Bello in Portugal were planted in 1560, some 150 years before the 'official' introduction of one of Asia's greatest flowering plants to Europe. This species of camellia has produced hundreds of large-flowered varieties.*

Right *The deciduous stewartia is perhaps the most valuable tree of the tea-family for temperate gardens where it can grow to 50 feet or more. Here the leaves of the Japanese* Stewartia pseudocamellia *show their characteristic vein-pattern as they begin to turn rich shades of red and purple in autumn.*

Above *The Korean stewartia is a slightly smaller tree than the Japanese, but with bigger flowers. It too has rich autumn colour, and an attractive flaking bark.*

Right *The single camellia-like flower of the Japanese* Stewartia pseudocamellia.

Left *A typical Japanese hybrid of the common camellia, 'Haku-rakuten'. It makes a small but vigorous upright tree.*

regions where growth is slow and flowers are often spoilt by frost it is worth thinking of camellias for their foliage.

The stewartias are by comparison committed trees. (The 'Stewart' in question was John Stuart, the Earl of Bute who was unofficially the first Director of Kew Gardens.) Stewartias are native to both North America and the Far East, but the ones grown to such effect in gardens are Japanese (*S. pseudocamellia*) and Korean (*S. koreana*). Both are small-to-medium trees, often low-forking and branchy, with white flowers like single camellias coming in summer, often for eight weeks on end; and leaves that

turn episcopal shades of crimson and purple before they fall. Their intricately-flaking bark is my reminder of the connection with tea: its colours are the shades of gentle brown in strong tea just clouded with milk.

Franklinia and gordonia are both prizes of the great John Bartram, who collected them for his (and America's first) botanic garden in Philadelphia in the 1760s. He found them down in Georgia, where the gordonia is still to be found as the loblolly bay, but whence the franklinia has totally disappeared.

All the franklinias grown now must be descendants of Bartram's plants. The tree is

not unlike a stewartia, but smaller; less hardy but less fussy about soil – the only members of the family in fact which are happy to grow on lime. They flower rather later, with creamy flowers, and they too colour richly in autumn.

The Franklin, I should add, was Benjamin. Gordon was a London nurseryman, James Gordon of Mile End, supplier of many plants to the infant Kew. His loblolly bay is perhaps the least distinguished of a very fine bunch. It is grown in the southern States for its evergreen foliage like the bull bay magnolia's, but its flowers are out of their class in such company.

Left *The camellia has been coaxed by breeders into every size, shape and colour since the Chinese emperors began to collect it over 1,000 years ago. The process still goes on. 'Yours truly' is a modern hybrid, in this case a slow-growing bushy form.*

Limes, Lindens or Basswoods

Left *The famous lindens of Berlin: a walk in the Tiergarten as October frosts turn the leaves.*
Above *The common European lime or linden has the soft, translucent, heart-shaped leaves typical of the genus, midway in size between its two parents; the small-leafed and big-leafed limes.*
Right *The scented flowers are borne on stalks coming from a long leaf-like bract.*

How many of the great country-houses of Europe do you approach along drives of rearing twiggy monsters: England's limes; France's tilleuls; Germany's lindens; the basswoods of America? It must have been in the 17th century that they first came into fashion as the show-trees of the great. One can see why they were thought the very thing for avenues. They take the form of a tower; a huge rectilinear tree, not spreading wide but with the upper branches going up and the lower ones down. Of all the biggest class of trees they are the most softly leafy, with fine-textured, heart-shaped leaves as big as the palm of a (lady's) hand. And in mid-summer they sweeten the air most mellifluously with the scent of their flowers.

Yet despite its benefits the lime is one of the few trees whose vices outweigh its virtues.

The common lime (*Tilia × vulgaris*) is a hybrid; a cross between Europe's big-leafed and small-leafed limes (*T. platyphyllos* and *T. cordata*). It has all the vigour associated with hybrids; it has reached 150 feet in England, making it the tallest broadleaf in the country. Its problem is its suckers, which spring up all round the base and grow furiously in ungainly competition with the crown. The same exuberance produces great whiskery nobs on the trunk: pruning only makes matters worse. Miles Hadfield, the English tree historian, blames the wide circulation of the common lime on the Dutch nursery trade, which found it one of the easiest, most profitable trees to grow.

But both its parents are widespread natives of Europe, and both are much better trees. The big-leaf lime is often the bigger in stature as well as leaf; otherwise the differences between them are unimportant. Today these are the ones that are commonly planted; particularly the red-twigged form of the bigleaf (*T. p.* 'Rubra')–which makes an excellent hedge, distinctly warm-looking in winter–and a narrow cultivar of the

Left *Limewood is the softest wood for sculpture. The work of the English sculptor Grinling Gibbons, never surpassed for exquisite intricacy, was all done in limewood. This piece (from 1691) is at Trinity College, Oxford.*

Hoheria glabrata, one of the New Zealand ribbon-woods which are related to the limes. As sweet-scented small trees or large shrubs, often stooping under bushels of soft white flowers, they deserve to be better known in the northern hemisphere.

Below *Young specimens of the silver lime, Tilia tomentosa, in the valley of the Loire in western France.*

Right *One of the rare but very pretty and silvery Chinese species of linden or lime, Tilia henryana, has finely-toothed leaves. T. oliveri is similar. These flower-buds of T. henryana were photographed in July on a 30-foot tree at the French National arboretum at les Barres.*

Below *The underside of a spray of the silver linden or lime, Tilia tomentosa. This tree and its weeping counterpart, T. 'Petiolaris', are the best-known of a number with silver-backed leaves which glint in the breeze. The flowers (here fully mature) can have unfortunate effects on bees.*

Above *The big-leafed lime of Europe (Tilia platyphyllos) is a much better park tree than its offspring, the common lime, which tends to send up ungainly suckers. The tower-shape of this specimen is typical of the bigger Tilia species.*

Middle above *The leaves of the big-leafed lime are sometimes six inches long, but those of the American basswood, Tilia americana, can be twice the size or more. Here the flowers of the broadleaved species have ripened into round fruits.*

Above *Limes can grow to a tremendous age. This big-leafed lime at Upstedt, near Hanover, Germany, was planted about A.D. 850 and is mentioned in a document of 1100. Its diameter five feet from the ground is 25 feet.*

small-leaf, the 'Swedish Upright'.

The search for a fault-free lime continues, however. All the foregoing have another problem. They are the regular diet of aphids which cover their leaves all summer with honey-dew. Honey-dew is not the pleasure it sounds; it blackens the leaves and drops stickily on to everything below.

Sad to say the American basswood (*T. americana*) is just as much a victim. It should be a spectacular tree; it has by far the biggest leaves of the family – up to a foot long. But by the end of the summer they can be a sorry sight; blackened and sucked dry, curling and turning brown.

The most aphid-proof of the limes has turned out to be another hybrid, known as the Crimean lime (*T.* × 'Euchlora'). So far this has good reports; if not for its overall shape, at least for its glossy leaves. The only catch here is the mystery of its flowers, which draw the bees in swarms only to knock them out with a narcotic dose that often proves fatal. Feebly buzzing bees cover the ground below the tree.

The same problem is the only possible reason for not planting the two most beautiful trees of the genus, the silver lime and the weeping silver lime (*T. tomentosa* and *T. petiolaris*). Both these trees have the backs of their leaves richly silvered with fine hairs so that when the wind ruffles them they glisten and wink. The weeping version has leaf-stalks twice as long, which makes its leaves stir more readily and gives more glimpses of silver. As weeping trees go it is not, however, the full cascade that say the willow can be.

Does this leave us any lime totally free of faults? There is one lime, or so I'm told, which clears up all the points. Wilson brought it from China in 1900 and called it *T. oliveri*. Alan Mitchell says: 'It has an open upright crown of grey smooth branches bearing very flat, large leaves ... Each leaf is pale green above, silver beneath and elegantly toothed.'

The Willows

The willow family has evolved along a distinct path of its own as a client of the four winds. Although the construction of its flowers puts it in the line of descent from the tea family, it stands on its own in being specially adapted to give the wind its seeds to sow. There are only two members of the family; the willows and the poplars. Both have male and female catkins on different trees and offer nectar to the bees for fertilizing them. Poplars get their other name of cottonwoods from the seed's flying apparatus: all willows and poplars use the same bit of fluff to carry the seed away.

The seed has to be very light, which means it can carry no endosperm, the food supply most seeds include in one form or other. Seed without endosperm has a very short life; germinating conditions must be right straight away. Which may be why willows and poplars tend to grow in moist ground.

Vigour is another family quality, but in this the poplar is more consistent than the willow. For one of the odd things about this original tree is that, fast as it can grow, most of its 250-odd species are shrubs.

America, Europe and Asia share most of the tree species of willow – all except the most famous of all, the weeping willow, which grows wild only in the west of China.

Stories abound of the introduction of *Salix babylonica*, the original weeping willow. Before it was established that it came from China it was thought to have been the tree by the waters of Babylon where the Jews in captivity sat down and wept. Its entry into western gardens came early in the 18th century, from the Middle East, or, according to another story, as a withy used to tie a parcel sent from Spain to Lady Suffolk in London. W. J. Bean recounts how the poet Pope, 'noticing one of the twigs was alive, begged it, and planted it at Twickenham, where it grew into the celebrated weeping willow of his villa garden'.

White willow is one of the fastest-growing of all big trees: a silver cloud with a leaning spine, usually growing straight but rarely perpendicular. Countless fine twigs and white-silky leaves give its reflection in dark water a subtle beauty.

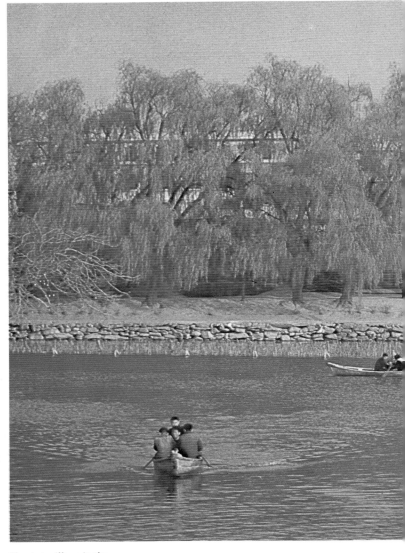

Weeping willows in the grounds of the summer palace, Peking. The weeping willow picked up the name of babylonica on its travels from China to Europe. Most weeping willows in gardens today are hybrids between this and the white willow.

Although the Chilean Maytenus *is no relation of the willow (or any other tree in this book) this is the only place for it. It looks remarkably like a small evergreen weeping willow: a rare but highly desirable tree for any garden.*

The English landscape movement had mixed feelings about this noticeable tree. William Gilpin held that it was 'not adapted to sublime subjects. We wish it not to screen the broken buttresses . . . of an abbey . . . These offices it resigns to the oak, whose dignity can support them. The weeping willow seeks an humbler scene; some romantic bridge. which it half conceals. . . .'

Most books agree that what really popularized the tree was Napoleon's fondness for one on Saint Helena. So fond was he that he asked to be buried under it, whereupon the poor thing was torn twig from limb by tourists. Most Victorian weeping willows claimed to be cuttings from that tree.

The blood of *Salix babylonica* runs in every weeping willow's veins, but the species itself is rare today. Finding that it was quite tender, nurserymen (or possibly in the first place nature) produced crosses of it with hardy native willows. The commonest of these in Europe is *S. × sepulcralis* var. *chrysocoma*, which is *S. babylonica* crossed with the weeping form of the white willow (*S. alba* 'Tristis'). In America other crosses are popular; notably the Thurlow and the Wisconsin weeping willows (*S. × pendulina* vars. *elegantissima* and *S. × p.* var. *blanda*) which are crosses between *S. babylonica* and the crack willow (*S. fragilis*).

The Thurlow has reddish shoots, the Wisconsin a bluish sheen in both shoots and leaves. They weep less than *S. × sepulcralis* var. *chrysocoma*. *S. × sepulcralis* (which is a cross between *S. babylonica* and *S. alba*) is the most vigorously and grandly ascending of weeping willows. The magnificent trees round the lake at Kew are this hybrid.

Today it is accepted that a weeping willow is almost indispensable to any biggish body of ornamental water. Water is not necessary for the tree, but the reflected light apparently encourages it to extend its twigs in that direction. ▶

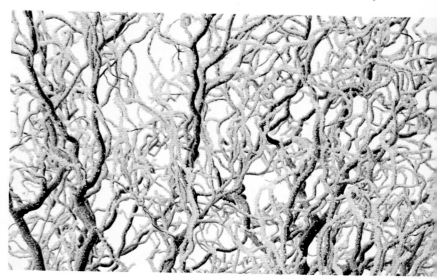

Right *Male catkins of the grey sallow (*Salix cinerea*). This, the similar goat willow (S. caprea), and S. discolor of North America are all known as pussy willows. The male catkins appear before the leaves.*

Top *Hoar-frost accentuates the writhing pattern of the twigs and branches of the twisted willow of Peking,* Salix matsudana 'Tortuosa'. *It makes a fast-growing small tree; its leaves are are among the first to come and the last to go.*

Above *Willows are either male or female plants. In the foreground a female grey sallow has bright silver-green catkins. Behind and slightly to the right is a male tree with yellow catkins (see also close-up in the picture below left).*

The Willows

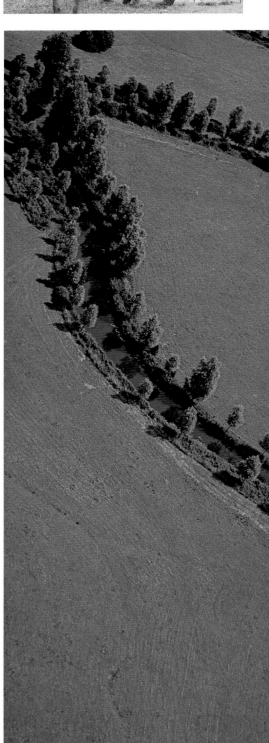

▶ Gilpin went on to call the weeping willow 'the only one of its tribe which is beautiful'. Evidently he was never invited to Woburn Abbey. There the 7th Duke of Bedford made a complete Salicetum: a collection of every known species. For a time the Salicetum was like the Pinetum, the collection of conifers, a desirable – if not essential – part of the grounds of a great house. The importance of osier beds as a way of using undrainable land provided an economic excuse. But the point was that willows are pretty.

Catkins in the early spring are the first obvious attraction. The prettiest catkin-bearers tend to be the shrubby kinds of willows, or sallows – which also fortunately have their catkins within reach. It is the male plants that have the bigger and brighter catkins. There are red-catkinned ones, like *S. gracilistyla*, but it is hard to beat the common European pussy willow (*S. caprea*), with its fat pearly-furred catkins ripening to saffron yellow.

Coloured bark is the other willow speciality. Many of the shrubs, and several of the trees, have brilliantly-painted new shoots. They come in scarlet, yellow, green, orange, white, purple and brown. The colour is brightest on new stems in their first winter. The trick, therefore, is to cut them back hard in the spring, to give them all summer to grow. If you cut them to ground level it is coppicing; to shoulder-level pollarding. Uncut, if the thing becomes a tree, it is scarcely less bright waving in the sky. I can see an ordinary golden white willow (*S. alba* var. *vitellina*) from my desk. Winter morning sun makes it easily the brightest spot in the landscape. The best red is another variety of the white willow (*S. alba* 'Britzensis'); the best purple (overlaid with a soft white bloom), *S. daphnoides*.

The typical willow leaf is racing-boat-shaped: long, narrow and pointed at both ends. Many are bloomy-silvery, the common

The power of the willow to brighten a dull wintry landscape: these red-stemmed white willows were twigs on a tree two years ago. Any willow twig stuck deep in the ground in autumn will start growing as a new tree the next spring.

White willows by the Stour, in eastern England typical white willow and bat-willow country. The smallest trees here are three years old, the biggest 12. Conditions are ideal: plenty of water and full sunlight.

Left *The scarlet willow, Salix alba 'Britzensis' is a blaze of colour in a winter landscape with its brilliant display of scarlet-orange branches. Like S. alba var. vitellina, 'Britzensis' needs to be pruned severely to encourage the growth of its mophead of branches.*

The golden twigs of Salix alba var. vitellina. Every spring the pollards are cut back to the short trunk to encourage the tree to produce a profusion of golden branches for the winter.

Left *The peach-leafed willow (Salix amygdaloides) is found by wild water-courses from Quebec to Oregon (photographed here in Wyoming). The similar almond-leafed willow* (S. triandra) *plays the same role from Europe to the orient. It has long been cultivated for basket-making. Although it is a workaday tree its glossy leaves with pale under-sides make it very pretty.*

white willow (*S. alba*) perhaps most of all. There are surprising variations, though, in this too. The bay willow (*S. pentandra*) has glossy dark-green ovals which look–and even smell–like a bay tree's; *S. magnifica* from China has leaves as big as a magnolia's.

One inspired variation is the twisted leaf. A variety of the original weeping willow (*S. babylonica* 'Annularis') has leaves like little ringlets. In the corkscrew willow (*S. matsudana* 'Tortuosa') the vibrations go right through the whole tree: every inch of twig as well as leaf wiggles. It sounds bizarre: in fact it is elegant. I know of only one willow which has gone too far: *S.* × *erythroflexuosa* tries to do everything at once: to twist, to weep and to look cheerful in orange-yellow bark. The result is a neurotic-looking bush.

The white willow, the crack willow (*S. fragilis*, so-called because its twigs snap off if you pull them) and the super-vigorous variety the bat willow (*S. a.* var. caerulea) are the common tree-willows grown not for their beauty–beautiful as they are–but for their wood. The willow combines first-class timber with rocket-like growth. Whether for cricket bats, the bottoms of quarry carts that have to endure the shock and scrape of stone, or in the terms of the naval timber manual which called it 'the best wood without exception for the formation of small, fast-sailing war vessels', willow is strong.

As for speed, a normal rotation period for bat willow, from planting to felling, is 15 years. By then, on a good site, the tree is 70 feet high and five feet round.

Willow-growing is made absurdly easy by the readiness of the twigs to take root. The sets used for willows are ten feet long; simply a young branch driven into the ground for half its length. 'Sets' are planted in February; by May they are in leaf and growing as new trees. You can even stand a young willow on its head. The branches can become roots and vice versa.

This wonderful instant tree must have its drawbacks. It has several, from its liability to the fatal disease of canker to its attractiveness to aphids; also, curiously for such strong wood, its liability to split in a bad storm. But to me they are outweighed by the advantages: its ability to grow so big and beautiful so quickly.

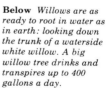

Above *One of the most exquisite of all big shrubs, without even a flower to its name: the Chinese Salix moupinensis, with broad oval leaves from sealing-wax red buds.*

Above *The woolly willow (Salix lanata) is one of the prettiest of the shrub-size willows. Its name is derived from its woolly catkins and its young branchlets which are covered with grey wool.*

Below *Willows are as ready to root in water as in earth: looking down the trunk of a waterside white willow. A big willow tree drinks and transpires up to 400 gallons a day.*

Poplars, Cottonwoods and Aspens

The willow family includes, in the weeping willow and the Lombardy poplar, the two most famous and distinctive of all ornamental trees: a text-book pair of forms planted together for contrast in almost every park in the world.

The weeping willow is a true species: its seed comes up weeping. The Lombardy poplar is a cultivar, in the sense that its seed may or may not grow bolt upright. It is propagated by cuttings, which luckily are as easy to persuade to take root as the 'sets' of willows.

But neither tree is typical of its race. They are exceptional not only in shape but in being considered ornamental at all. Poplars on the whole are thought of, like willows, as wood factories. Like willows they grow alarmingly fast. A cottonwood (*Populus deltoides*) planted on Mississippi bottomland grew 98 feet in 11 years.

Like willows, poplars hybridize among their kind with abandon. As racing trees they have also been subject to a great deal of stud activity. Hence, as J. L. Reed irresistibly puts it in *The Forests of France*, 'their social history is like one of those exhausting novels which describe the adventures and alliances of several generations of an international family established in different capitals'.

The four branches of the family are the black, white, trembling and balsam poplars. The black are the biggest branch, containing all the poplars which aren't white under the leaves, don't smell of balsam in bud (or if the twigs are bruised), and don't tremble (as the aspens do).

The white poplars are natives of Europe, long since established in North America. The basic white poplar (*P. alba*) is an eye-catching tree, even where (which is often on poor land) it grows no higher than 20 or 30 feet. Its leaves toss at the merest breeze to show their silver-white undersides. The standard poplar leaf-shape is more or less like a heart; the white poplar's are lobed like a maple's. In America, furthermore, they often turn red in autumn. In Europe, like other poplars', they turn yellow.

There is an upright version of the white poplar ('Pyramidalis' or 'Bolleana') which is like a rather beamy Lombardy with the distinct advantage of the winking white leaves, and a charming smaller form of the tree known as Richard's poplar, with leaves buttercup yellow on top and white below; unassuming and easy to grow but potentially a knock-out against a background of heavy shade.

The balsam poplars are some of the earliest trees of all to come into leaf. Their big pointed buds on curiously ribbed twigs are sticky with balsam in late winter. In the south of England the strong sweet smell is one of the clearest heralds of spring.

Of the American balsams the confusingly-named black cottonwood (*P. trichocarpa*) (which is neither black nor strictly speaking a cottonwood) is, if the record figure of 225 feet is right, the tallest American broadleaf.

Balsam poplar leaves are markedly shiny and rich green; the long necklaces of yellowish catkins usually arrive just ahead of them. It sounds attractive, yet I would never recommend anyone to plant either the monster black cottonwood or the more modest-sized balsam (or tacamahac) poplar (*P. balsamifera*), or the balm of Gilead (*P. × jackii* 'Gileadensis'). They have no real grace of growth; their winter silhouette is always really that of a huge branch stuck in the ground. The Chinese poplar (*P. simonii*) may be an exception to this—I have seen a row in Seattle which had much softer and less rigid skeletons with hanging twigs.

For the balsam smell alone one can well plant any of them and treat it as coppice: cut half the shoots right to the ground every year. The result is extra-big leaves on wands which are ideal to scent the house. Indeed there is a variety of the balm of Gilead poplar called *P × jackii* 'Aurora' which has creamy, pink-tinged leaves, balsam and all. ▶

Poplars and willows, members of the same family, completely dominate the landscape in many low-lying parts of Europe, as here in the Seine valley. At all seasons they are light and airy trees in pale colours.

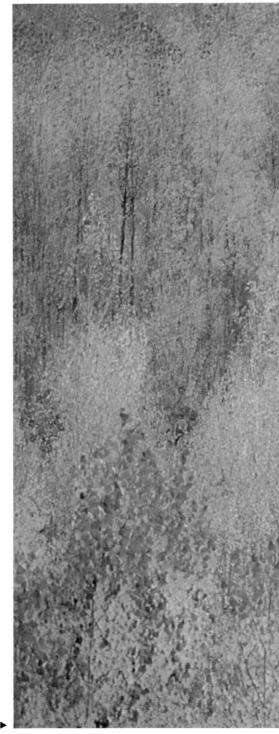

Right *The grey poplar, an old natural cross between the white and trembling ('aspen') poplars, has the typical vigour of a hybrid and combines the long stalk of the aspen with the white-felted leaf of the white poplar.*

*Renoir, Monet, Pissarro...
poplars in autumn seem to
sum up the vision of the
French impressionists.
This is 'Robusta', a
hybrid black poplar which
is now planted in millions
in northern Europe.*

Poplars, Cottonwoods and Aspens

Top *Several upright forms of the black poplar, of which the Lombardy is the best-known, have occurred in nature. This Lombardy-like tree was photographed by the 1972 Everest expedition in the Himalayas.*

Above *The female catkin of the Japanese* Populus maximowiczii *starting to ripen into fruit. Each green capsule will split in mid-summer and release a cotton-wrapped seed: hence the American name cottonwood.*

The cypress-like pattern of the branching of Lombardy poplars is seen here in a stormy light against a hillside in the Lot valley in southwest France. Male trees tend to be very narrow like those on the right, female ones to grow a little more beamy.

Top *Poplars, like willows, are either male or female. The female catkins of the aspen are typical: short woolly tassels before the leaves. The weeping aspen, a male variety, has pretty purplish-grey catkins in February.*

▶ The cottonwood of the western creekbeds is the most familiar black poplar in the wilds. A film director is bound to aim his cameras at it or through it when it is the only tree in the landscape. Its range runs from the Atlantic to the Rockies; in the east it is less conspicuous until it snows cotton in July.

The union of the cottonwood with the black poplar of Europe (*P. nigra*) has brought about most of the rapid commercial poplars that – in France especially – have made their own style of valley landscape. The ordinary black poplar is not distinguished; its varieties 'Italica', the Lombardy poplar, and 'Plantierensis' (which often steps in to take the Lombardy poplar's place) are the important ones. Their value as landscape trees is always before one's eyes: either the single huge tower, sometimes 100 feet high or more, dominating some Alpine valley; or the elegant file through fenland, leading to a lonely farm; or the grand approach to an urban institution. There is no tree which creates an architectural incident so quickly and surely.

The black poplars have made hybrids of varied merits, all fast and some beautiful in a light-leaved, summer-meadow way. 'Robusta', for example, leafs late but coppery – an autumnal colour in May. Its narrow, light-branched crown (which it shares with 'Eugenei') can look like a feather on the skyline. 'Regenerata' and 'Marilandica' are denser and broader; 'Serotina' can make a huge cloud-like head. In the Melbourne Botanic Garden there is a golden poplar (*P. × canadensis* 'Aurea') a good 120 feet high and built like a sunlit thunder-cloud.

Since all poplars have leaf-stalks and many of them long ones, the wind always sets them aflutter. The difference with the aspens, the trembling poplars, is that they feel breezes when the whole world is becalmed. You can lie under an aspen on a stiflingly still day and listen to its incessant whisper. The trick is in the leaf-stalk, a narrow ribbon set at right-angles to the hanging leaf-blade.

The American quaking aspen (*P. tremuloides*) is the tree with the widest distribution on the whole North American continent. It grows from Labrador to Mexico and to the Bering Strait, leaving out only the south-east and part of the midwest. Its life is short and vigorous: it demands light and offers bigger and more permanent trees a light shade for their early years; then they overtake it and it dies. In the east of its range it grows with its sister, the bigtooth aspen (*P. grandidentata*), which has bigger, toothed leaves.

Its favourite place to seed and start a new colony is where fire has been. According to J. C. Loudon, the European aspen (*P. tremula*) took over the ruins of Moscow in 1813, the year after Napoleon had reduced most of the city to ashes.

It is similar to the American aspen, lacking only its pale smooth bark. Both are (or were when Europe had such things) the beaver's favourite tree. Despite its astringency he loves the inner bark. Both species have small weeping forms, particularly pretty with their grey catkins in early spring and again in autumn, when aspens turn a shining yellow.

Aspen crossed with white poplar has produced grey poplar (*P. × canescens*), a common and on the whole stately tree beside French roads. It has a bad habit (which it gets from both its parents) of throwing up suckers. It is a good catkin tree before the leaves come, and the leaves can be almost as silvery as the white poplar's in a breeze. Poplar wood is not generally sought for special qualities, except perhaps its readiness to split into narrow shavings, good for matches and lightweight fruit baskets. Basically it is grown today for pulp. Grey poplar, however, has smooth, non-splintering, non-warping and lightweight wood which has many uses, from silk-rollers to barn doors.

POPLARS

White	Balsam	Black	Trembling

- **alba** (white)
- **maximowiczii** (Japanese balsam) — **trichocarpa** (black cottonwood) — **simonii** (simon) — **balsamifera** (balsam) — **deltoides** (cottonwood)
- **nigra** (black) — **lasiocarpa** (Chinese Black)
- **tremuloides** (American Aspen) — **tremula** (aspen)

'Pyramidalis' — 'Richardii'

x jackii, 'Gileadensis' (Balm of Gilead), 'Aurora'

Hybrid Black Poplars (x canadensis) — 'Italica' (Lombardy) — 'Planteriensis'

x generosa

'Robusta' — 'Serotina' — 'Marylandica' — 'Regenerata' — 'Eugenei'

× = hybrid

x canescens (grey)

The interbreeding of the four different groups of the poplars has given us some of our most useful and fastest trees. The diagram above shows the family story so far as it is known: many of the crosses are intentional, but others happened in nature.

Poplar catkins have a beauty of their own. A male aspen catkin (here magnified twice) shows its purple stamens and their outer covering of white hairs.

The Chinese species Populus lasiocarpa has the largest and lushest leaves of any poplar: shiny green hearts up to a foot long. It was introduced from China in 1900 by E. H. Wilson.

Heather and Strawberry Trees

The heath (or heather) family is the backbone of the gardening style which has distinguished the great gardens of this century. It is the family of the rhododendron and the azalea: the mounds, drifts and terraces of evergreen foliage that unobtrusively back up every garden picture, to burst into life in spring with improbable quantities, sizes and shapes of flowers in every colour, save true blue. So universal are rhododendrons in the great woodland gardens, especially in Britain and the United States, that gardeners who don't have those flourishing mounds of evergreenery to give their gardens substance and backbone often feel at a psychological disadvantage. There are ways round that, but the fact remains: the classic woodland scene is a fantasy largely borrowed from the rainy lower slopes of the Himalayas (and to some extent the mountains of western North America) where conifers and heaths flourish together in ecological harmony on a soil composed of centuries of fallen leaves. A soil without the smallest trace of lime.

The heaths are part of a race derived from the tea family, which through the ages has developed cooperation with soil organisms called mycorrhizae. For some heaths this has gone so far that they are totally dependent: without their fungus friends they can't make their own food at all. The mycorrhizae attached to most of the familiar heaths need acid soil: therefore rhododendrons do too.

The most tree-like of the family are also those that are least particular in this regard. They are the tiny-flowered arbutuses from California, the Mediterranean and Killarney. Southwest Ireland is one of the warmest points in the British Isles and thus a logical outpost for a Mediterranean plant, but in fact the strawberry tree (*Arbutus unedo*) is hardy in much colder places; almost anywhere in Britain and to zone 7 at least in North America.

The flowering of the strawberry tree is a charming piece of understatement: the clustering of hundreds of tiny near-white pitchers among handsome bay-like leaves. It happens in the autumn when flowering trees are few. But the best thing about it is that the fruits from last year's flowers ripen red at the same time. They are more like cherries with roughened, pimply skins than strawberries. The overall effect is of a

The great sweep of the heath (or heather) family is summed up by the flowers above, those of the only true heather (Erica) to grow to tree size – and the flowers opposite, those of a modern rhododendron

hybrid. Despite the huge difference in size the family resemblance is clear. The strawberry tree (below) has flowers very like the heather, although it makes a substantial tree.

Above *A red-flowered form of the strawberry tree, Arbutus unedo 'Rubra'. The normal form has white flowers (as on the left), perhaps just blushing pink. The strawberry tree is evergreen with handsome bay-like foliage.*

Right *Clethra arborea of Madeira is known as the lily-of-the-valley tree. Again, the heather relationship is clear from the flowers; the rhododendron kinship is suggested by the leaves. Clethra needs an oceanic climate.*

quietly prolific plant in glowing good health; a happy thing to have around.

The California version, the madrone (*A. menziesii*) flowers more conspicuously, at the branch-tips, in spring. It is altogether much more of a tree; to 80 or 90 feet. The strawberry tree's maximum is 30 or 40 feet.

The madrone's real beauty lies in its combination of rich green foliage and beautiful smooth red bark on a graceful curving and forking trunk and limbs. A big tree in evening light can show up on a hillside two or three miles away. In flower, in fruit (which is red, yellow or orange) or in mid-winter, when its evergreen foliage is all the more telling, it is one of the finest trees hardy enough for northern Europe. There is a 55-foot specimen in the glorious collection at Hergest Croft on the Welsh border.

The strawberry tree, and also its Greek cousin *A. andrachne* and the splendid hybrid between the two, *A.* × *andrachnoides*, are content to grow with a modest amount of lime in the soil; the madrone would much rather not.

Arbutus flowers betray the relationship of the genus to the heathers; the same little pendant pitchers cluster among the conifer-like foliage of the biggest of the heathers, *Erica arborea* (a big bush, seldom a real tree), and the broad leaves of the madrone.

They appear again in long streamers on the sorrel tree, *Oxydendrum arboreum*, of the eastern United States. Sorrel tree is a deciduous member of the family, the only one of its kind and a plant of very decided character. It wears a sort of oriental grace, its shoots falling away rather like the multiple eaves of a pagoda to form a tall pyramid – as high as 70 feet in the wilds. It flowers very usefully in late summer, is hardy to Cape Cod, and colours fiery red in autumn. Given good rhododendron country, every garden needs one.

And again the tree *Clethra* (*C. arborea*) from Madeira has the same flower design. Most members of the clethra family grow only to large shrub size but *arborea* can make a very attractive multi-stemmed tree, up to 25 feet. In late summer the tree is a cascade of fragrant, white, bell-like flowers on delicate spiky stalks. Sadly it is a very tender tree and will thrive only in the mildest of climates. Ideally it likes a rich, acid soil.

Left *The Pacific madrone is the western American version of the strawberry tree: a magnificent evergreen with a red trunk and red fruit, both contrasting splendidly with the dense green foliage.*

Above *Fruit of a strawberry tree, turning from yellow to red. Flowers can be seen (left of centre).*
Right Arbutus × and-rachnoides *combines the hardiness, vigour and warm red bark of its parents the strawberry tree and* A. andrachne.

The Rhododendrons

Left *A pink form of the tree rhododendron,* Rhododendron arboreum *var.* roseum, *has its trumpet-like flowers marked with red spots inside. There are also white varieties, one of which, 'Sir Charles Lemon', has red-brown felt under the leaves.*

The first known tree rhododendron, Rhododendron arboreum, *has been a vital part of the genetic heritage of hundreds of hybrids. Here it is growing near Senchal lake in Darjeeling in the eastern Himalayas.*

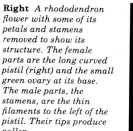

For a non-fanatic to write of rhododendrons at all is foolhardy, but to try to distinguish those that should be called trees, at least without long experience in the Himalayas, is almost suicidal. There never was a rhododendron with the sort of long straight trunk that would tempt a forester, that is certain. Yet who would call a plant 90 feet high, however curving and many-stemmed, a shrub?

Until 1820 the European and American rhododendrons were the only ones known. Of these the rosebay rhododendron, *R. maximum*, from the eastern States, was the biggest—though scarcely a tree.

In 1820 the first seeds of *R. arboreum* arrived in England from the Himalayas, packed by the prudent Nathaniel Wallich in brown sugar. With them arrived the glorious red blood that transformed the relatively tame and dowdy colours of the rhododendrons then known. For though *R. arboreum* was tender at first, and needed a conservatory in Britain, it soon hybridized and started hardy strains. Waterers, the famous nurserymen of Surrey, were the pioneers in adapting this tender giant to cultivation. Most modern rhododendron varieties, even small ones, have the blood of *R. arboreum* in their veins.

Sir Joseph Hooker's expedition to the Himalayas from 1847 to 1850 set the seal on the rhododendron as the supreme flowering evergreen. He introduced 43 species, including the tree-size *R. falconeri*.

Magnificent as they are in flower, a yet greater virtue of the bigger species is their leaves: great glossy tongues of darkest green, often backed with thick brown felt.

Left *These rhododendron hybrids at Squerryes Court, Westerham, Kent, are over 80 years old. Careful training of a single trunk can, as here, create a small tree even of bush-size species.*

The 'bearded' rhododendron (Rhododendron barbatum) might have been better named the unshaven: its twigs and leaf-stalks are covered with bristles up to half an inch long.

Western China has given us one of the hardiest of the tree-rhododendrons with huge evergreen leaves: Rhododendron calophytum.

The Himalayas have more great rhododendron species than California has kinds of pine. Rhododendron thomsonii was another of Hooker's discoveries: a very distinct tree with rounded leaves and deep red waxy bells of flowers.

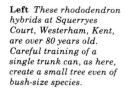

Persimmons, Silverbells and Snowbells

The mainly tropical race that takes its name from the ebony tree of India and Ceylon is another remote descendant of the tea family on lines roughly parallel to the heaths. The ebony (*Diospyros ebenum*) has jet-black heartwood of great value. Its temperate-zone relations are better known for their fruit, the persimmon.

The persimmon is one of many trees which the chances of history have left in China and eastern North America and nowhere else. The Chinese tree (*Diospyros kaki*) gives the edible persimmon; a succulent yellow fruit the size and shape of an apple. The American tree (*D. virginiana*), which is much more impressive, has fruit that is edible only late in the season, after a frost (when it is soft and sweet, but still without flavour). As ornamental trees, however, both have merit. The smaller Chinese tree has long leaves of a glossy green that can turn orange, yellow or purple in autumn. The American is tall and narrow to 60 or 70 feet and its bark is one

Left *The common persimmon of the eastern States makes a straight and stately tree with a distinctive dark bark in a four-square pattern and fine yellow autumn colour. Its fruit is edible.*

Above *The Chinese persimmon is a smaller (up to 40 feet) but more ornamental tree. Though its flowers are green and well-camouflaged, its leaves are broad, glossy and attractive.*

The fruit of the Chinese or kaki persimmon ripens orange as the leaves turn to a noble shade of purple. These are the sweet persimmons or date-plums of the fruit-basket, grown in Japan, the southern States and in the south of France.

of the most arresting of any tree's: clear and regular fissures mark it both ways, dividing it into rectangular blocks of sooty grey. In Washington's National Arboretum it grows well in swampy ground by a stream, among dark-barked river birches. There were no leaves left when I saw it, but I picked the squashy yellow fruit which hung on the dipping boughs.

Persimmons claim no beauty of flower. But three neighbours of theirs on the evolutionary tree (neighbours rather than close relations) are among the trees with the prettiest flowers: the American snowdrop or silverbell tree; the Japanese snowbell; and the American-named Chinese fragrant epaulette tree.

There are two silverbells (called snowdrop trees in Britain): the shrubby Carolina version (*Halesia tetraptera*) and the much more noticeable mountain one (*H. monticola*) from the Great Smokies, which grows to 90 feet and wears big bunches of its bell-flowers on its bare shoots like cherry-blossom in the spring. The flowers are succeeded by fruits—also bell-like but with four little wings—which can hang a whole year.

The Japanese snowbell tree (*Styrax japonicum*) seems more decorative in intention, for when it flowers in June it contrives to put the flowers just where you can best see them, in long rows along the long, low branches. It is a tree with a strong horizontal inclination, often twice as wide as it is high.

The leaves perch in pairs like butterflies along the tops of the branches while the dainty little white flowers hang beneath.

Styrax obassia has fragrant flowers on erect spikes as an added advantage, but its bigger leaves are less neatly disposed.

As for the fragrant epaulette tree, *Pterostyrax hispida*, the lavish way it covers itself with creamy cascades of sweetly-smelling flowers could make it a mid-summer successor to the laburnum. It is the least particular of its group in the matter of soil—the others all shun lime.

Roses, Shadblows, Mespilus and Cotoneaster

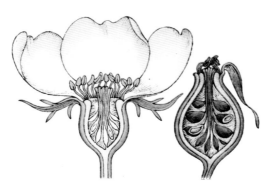

The fruit of the rose family varies more than its flowers. These three cross-sections show the flowers and fruit of the rose (above), the apple (below) and the plum (foot of page).

In each case the ovaries of the flowers are contained in a receptacle which is an extension of the flowerstalk. It is this receptacle that swells to become the flesh of the fruit.

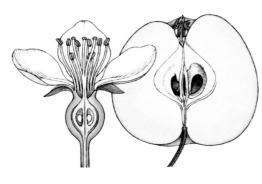

In the rose-hip (top) the receptacle swells very little. It swells much more round the five seeds in one ovary of the apple (above) and the single seed in the ovary of the plum (below).

The thin bony membrane round the apple-seeds is the ovary wall: the ovary wall of the plum hardens to become the shell of the plum-stone.

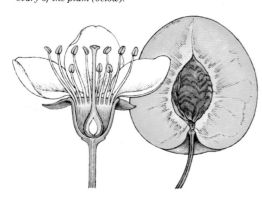

The scope of the rose family is staggering. In the widest botanical sense the broad group of plants or Sub-class that bears the rose's name, the *Rosidae*, contains a third of all the species of flowering plants with two cotyledons. In the narrower Order, the *Rosales*, one-third of this one-third, one-ninth of the vast number belong: about 20,000 species. Of these some 2,000 species belong to the rose family proper; the *Rosaceae*.

Most of our fruit trees and ornamental blossom trees belong to this one family. The cherries, crab-apples, hawthorns, blackthorns, pears, apples, mountain-ashes, whitebeams, quinces, fire-thorns, shadblows, laurels, cotoneasters, medlars, almonds, peaches, apricots and plums are all members. The next 18 pages are full of them, and this is only a selection of the best.

Hardiness is a feature of the family: there are few tropical members. There is no nonsense about acid soil either; to this family alkalinity is a positive virtue. In flower structure the family is distinctive; both sexes are present in the same flower and most flowers have five petals (though the number is often increased in the 'double' flowers that are bred for show).

How near together or far apart in ancestry the various members of the family may be has not been fully determined. There have been some surprising instances of cross-breeding between two very dissimilar trees: *Amelanchier* (the shadblow or snowy mespilus) and *Sorbus* (the mountain ash) for example. On the other hand *Malus* (the crab-apple) will not even graft on to *Sorbus* or *Pyrus* (the pear), let alone hybridize with them. There can never be a cross between an apple and a pear.

There are no tree-roses, or rose-trees. The only way a rose can reach tree height is by climbing, using strong hooked thorns on long shoots as crampons. Some roses can go 40 feet or even higher. Species such as *Rosa filipes* 'Kiftsgate' or the Himalayan musk rose (*R. brunonii*) will scramble out into the sunlight at the top of an old fruit tree and send down astonishing cascades of a hundred sweet-scented flowers in a spray. If there is an old tree in your garden you consider dull you could do much worse than give it such an adornment as a Christmas present.

But even a 40-foot rose is only a shrub with long shoots, as liable to lie on the ground as to ascend into the air.

The tree known in America as shadbush or shadblow or serviceberry, in England as juneberry or snowy mespilus, is one of the most delicately beautiful of the rose's relations, and perhaps the one that gives a

Above *The Himalayan musk rose* (Rosa brunonii) *is among those with the vigour to climb to the top of a tall fruit tree and give it a second flowering season. The white flowers are richly scented.*

Below *The Allegheny serviceberry.* Amelanchier laevis, *produces myriads of delicate white flowers with pink young leaves in May. A hardy small tree, it grows best on soil with no lime.*

The shadblow, tallest of the Amelanchiers, *reaches 50 or 60 feet in the eastern States. Its silvery leaves which accompany the white flowers in May turn scarlet and orange in autumn.*

Left 'Snowy mespilus' is a bushy form of Amelanchier which grows wild in southern Europe, as here in Provence.

Below All Amelanchiers can be treated as garden shrubs; they readily sucker and form a thicket of stems. Their typical autumn colour is a sustained glow, effective even in grey weather.

small garden best value. *Amelanchier* (here is a case where an international name is obviously a relief) is a tree–or sometimes a bush–to watch carefully, even when it is not putting on its main performances.

The genus on the whole is lightly built and all its parts are cast in a fine mould: thin, pale grey limbs and pointed buds, emerging leaves of pale pink and coppery bronze, silver-haired (only a few cherries have the same combination) and accompanying the masses of star-shaped white flowers which froth it over lightly (though in warm weather, admittedly, for only a few days). By June there are bunches of berries like blackcurrants in shining green foliage. And in autumn, for a relatively long spell, the leaves turn the softest red, orange and brown; a glow rather than a flame.

North America has three or four amelanchiers, but there is often some confusion about which is which. When you say shad-blow you mean the bush which blows–or blooms–when the shad are running in the rivers in April . . . or so the story goes. *Amelanchier canadensis* is the name most often used for the tallest, a tree often as much as 50 feet high. But if you follow the latest edition of W. J. Bean, which is much the wisest course, you must call this *A. arborea*. The Allegheny serviceberry is generally smaller, but has the prettiest unfolding leaves and sweet-tasting berries–as the birds know. And there is a hybrid between these two with pink-tinted flowers. Again this is often called *A. canadensis*, although its real name is *A. × grandiflora*. The true *A. canadensis* grows as an upright shrub in wet ground: a wildling.

Strictly speaking (to complete the picture) snowy mespilus is none of these but the European *A. ovalis*, a medium-sized to large shrub, which is snowy in its downy new leaves as well as its flowers.

Here among the rose tribe the shrub-barrier is crossed and recrossed so many times that a distinction must be arbitrary. Most of the species of *Cotoneaster* are shrubs without qualification. Indeed, some have a marked fondness for lying flat on the ground. But up rears the excellent *Cotoneaster × watereri*; a more than half-hearted attempt at an evergreen tree. In my garden it loses most of its dark green leaves by Christmas but keeps its incredible crop of red berries: almost a solid dome of scarlet 15 feet high and the same across. True it has 20 stems, but each one carries a tree's baton in its knapsack. For some reason the pheasants are in no hurry to gobble this crop; in mid-March there is still a good third of it beaming in the sun. Perhaps this restaurant knows more about serving than seasoning.

Shadblow fruit ripening from yellow through red to an eventual purple-black. When fully ripe it is edible though too small to be worth more than an inquisitive nibble.

None of the rose family bears fruit more abundantly, reliably and brilliantly than the almost-evergreen near-tree Cotoneaster × watereri *and its improved forms. The scarlet bunches hang on long into the new year.*

The Hawthorns

'Whenever I smell a May tree I think of going to bed by daylight.' This is William Morris, remembering his childhood on the edge of Epping Forest. Marcel Proust, thinking of Normandy, said the same thing (in a hundred times more words). Hawthorn blossom *is* the smell of early summer in the country.

To the layman there is scarcely a simpler or more consistent genus of tree than the hawthorn. It is a dense, compact, always a wild-looking tree, never a big one. It flowers in a sheet of haunting-scented blossom in May. Its blossom can be pink, is occasionally red, but (says the sentimentalist) ought to be white. It is fiercely armed with thorns, and covered with dark red berries as the year wears on.

In northern Europe it is the hedgerow tree; or rather it is the hedgerow. Its name means hedge-thorn, and long before barbed wire it made it very clear where my property ended and yours began. It was 'laid'

Above and below *The common hawthorn, otherwise known as 'May' or 'Quick', is northern Europe's commonest hedging material; below, in meadows in Burgundy. It is hard to beat for beauty of flower, for scent or for profusion of flower and fruit. Above, its little white flowers are peppered with darker stamens; they come after the deeply-lobed, polished leaves in late spring.*

by being cut half-through with a bill-hook and bent horizontally, to make a barrier that neither man nor beast could pass. Or often where no such fence was needed it grew to make an orchard-shape tree. The meadows (unpurged with selective weedkillers) shone with buttercups just at the season when the hawthorns gave them their dazzling frame.

But if it seems almost elemental to the layman, to the botanist it is a genus to dream of. A thousand species have at one time or another been identified in North America alone. How deceitful that apple-like blossom; those simple, shiny, dark green, tooth-edged leaves . . . that we should have been happy to think of them all as hawthorns, and never suspect. . .

The major differences that need concern a planter lie in the colour of the flower, the colour of the fruit, and the length of time the fruit hangs on the tree. Many species have red or orange leaves in autumn, too.

The best for flower colours, or at least

Left *The common hawthorn has a single seed in each berry or 'haw'. The other famous European species, Crataegus laevigata, has two or three seeds. It also has more different varieties with more ornamental flowers.*

the most varied, is the English hawthorn, *Crataegus laevigata*—not the common May or quick of the hedges, *C. monogyna*, but a tree differing in having two or three seeds to the berry instead of one. There are single- and double-flowered versions of the English thorn in white, pink and red. The best-known cultivar is the famous 'Paul's Scarlet'. Double-flowered cultivars on the other hand bear little fruit; nor does the English hawthorn colour well in autumn.

The common or hedgerow hawthorn has grown to almost 50 feet—and the oldest known is ten feet in girth. It usually has white flowers, but has them in such profu-

sion that they hide the whole tree. The date of its flowering has a strange fascination for people. It was a point of pride that it should flower by May Day, the first of the month, in time for the traditional celebrations of spring (and of course socialism). The poor tree has had a hard time keeping to schedule since 1751, when the calendar was altered by 12 days.

It is a variety of this thorn (*C.m.* 'Biflora') that has earned itself a legend by habitually bearing a precocious crop of flowers at Christmas. The legend goes that Joseph of Arimathea, who visited England to preach Christianity after the Crucifixion, was getting nowhere with a sceptical Somerset audience on Christmas morning when God made his staff (which he had stuck in the ground) burst into leaf and flower.

Some of the American thorns have much bigger fruit than the English (the downy hawthorn, *C. mollis*, is an example) but more have as their advantage orange or red

leaves in autumn. The Washington thorn (*C. phaenopyrum*) turns scarlet; the wide-spreading cockspur thorn (*C. crus-galli*) orange or red; the glossy-leaved thorn (*C. × nitida*) the same. The hybrid *C. × lavallei* has both shiny leaves which last until the end of the year and red fruit which hangs on till spring. The combination is almost like holly in November.

There are also two Chinese hawthorns of character, *C. pinnatifida major* with big leaves, big bright fruit and good autumn colour, and *C. laciniata*, whose leaves are deeply lobed and grey with down and whose fruit is orange.

Above *The brightest and most 'double'-flowered hawthorn is the cultivar 'Paul's Scarlet', which makes a low spreading small tree. No fruit is produced by these sterile flowers.*

Below *The only variegated hawthorn is a variety of the common 'May'. One advantage of the hawthorns is that they are among the first deciduous trees to be green in spring.*

Above *The leaves and blossom of the late-flowering hybrid Crataegus × grignonensis. The flowers are followed by big red fruits; the leaves stay green until well into the winter.*

Below *Long-fingered grey leaves and orange berries make the far-eastern Crataegus orientalis one of the most original and decorative of the hawthorns. It is very tough and hardy.*

Above *The dark and glossy hawthorn Crataegus × lavallei is a cross between the American cockspur thorn and a Mexican species. Its fruit hangs on throughout the winter.*

Below *The American cockspur thorn has the longest (up to three inches) thorns of its prickly genus. Its glossy unlobed leaves colour well in autumn. Its flowers are profuse and its fruit long-lasting.*

Right *The 'Bronvaux medlar' (+ Crataegomespilus dardarii) is a strange cross between hawthorn and medlar (see pages 194–5), originally formed by grafting one tree on the other. It is more like a miniature medlar than a hawthorn.*

Quinces, Medlars and Crab-Apples

Fish is about the only thing we eat on a large scale today which is not specially bred for our consumption – perhaps the reason why we think of it as a luxury. The relationship of our wheat to the original grass, our heifers to the original wild cattle is pretty remote. As for the unselected, unimproved food which is all around us, we leave it for the birds.

In the rose family you can see every stage of selection and improvement – for every purpose. Selection has produced cabbage roses from sweet hedgerow briars, our big juicy apples from sour crabs. In the case of orchard apples it has concentrated on the fruit; in the case of crab-apples it has sought to perfect the flowers.

There remain other trees within the rose family, however, where the fruit has never come up to the standard of interest or flavour (or glamour) that is needed to make it a commercial proposition. It is eccentric to eat medlars or to grow quinces today; they are neither flesh nor fowl; that is, neither standard rations nor spectacular bearers of blossom. They come into the same category as mulberries – and make as alluring a tree to have on the lawn.

The medlar, both in flower and leaf, quickly becomes a centre of interest. It grows short and often crooked with a broad spread of generous leaves, hairy underneath (and in autumn a lovely russet colour). In May – already leafy – it carries quantities of soft round-petalled pinkish-white flowers. Watching these become medlars you can see exactly how, as in roses, the seed receptacle behind the flower's facade of petals swells into ripeness – without even closing at the end in the medlar's case, but leaving ajar the end where the petals were. The medlar is like a big brown rose-hip, perhaps two inches across. In the terms of a healthy Shakespearean exchange of insults, however, 'You'll be rotten ere you'll be half ripe'. The medlar is not ready for eating until it has been 'bletted' by the frost: gone 'sleepy', as they say of pears, with incipient rottenness. And then, truth to tell, it is no gastronomic experience.

The quince on the other hand is a tree to grow for the fruit. You can buy all the apples and pears you need, but the quince is the truffle of the orchard; the mysterious savour that makes an apple pie come alive as no apple – except possibly an old-fashioned russet – can. In Portugal quince jelly in granular pinky-amber slabs is a common confection; the quince ripens better there. Britain is a shade too cool for it. The haunting lemony fragrance hangs about the tree, however, and fills the kitchen.

There is not very much to choose between

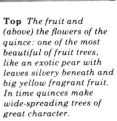

Top *The fruit and (above) the flowers of the quince: one of the most beautiful of fruit trees, like an exotic pear with leaves silvery beneath and big yellow fragrant fruit. In time quinces make wide-spreading trees of great character.*

Top *The fruit and (above) the flowers of the medlar: like the quince, a fruit tree which calls to mind the well-stocked larders of old country-houses. The medlar has long softly hairy leaves and fruit like big rose-hips.*

quince and medlar as trees: their habits are similar. The quince has leaves richly white-felted below; flowers a little showier perhaps; fruit—a shining pale yellow pear—much prettier. The slightly more tender Portuguese quince is the best for flowers and has softly downy fruit; but any quince is a source of pleasure.

In the Middle Ages the crab-apple was important in the kitchen as the source (or a source) of verjus, a powerfully acid liquid that seems to have played the role of vinegar in salad recipes and recipes for preserving. In those days before bottles, when so much wine went bad in the barrel, it is a wonder they needed any other vinegar. But in Elizabethan cookery books there is still a great call for it. In addition, of course, crab-apples make refreshing jelly.

It was not until the end of the 18th century when the Siberian crab was introduced into cultivation that exciting hybrids began to appear with far more telling flowers than the modest white blossom of the old hedgerow tree.

Native American and later Chinese species joined in the criss-cross of breeding so profitably that the pedigree of a modern hybrid would have more 'begats' than the Book of Genesis.

Today crab-apples come second only to

flowering cherries for excellence and popularity among flowering trees. Indeed before planting a flowering cherry it is very well worth examining the claims of the crabs. They have certain marked advantages that usually get overlooked.

In tough conditions of either soil or climate the crabs on the whole are more adaptable and hardy than the cherries. And under any conditions they are normally longer-lived. Like the cherries they rarely have good autumn colour but in compensation they often have very pretty fruit. What's more in many cultivars the fruit stays on the tree long after the leaves have gone—even

into the following February or March. A crab with this peculiarity soon becomes a centre of curiosity and astonishment. I know of one (a 'Golden Hornet') that has nearly caused nasty accidents. It stands, dripping with yellow apples, near a sharp bend in the road. On a brilliant winter day you can't help looking at it as you go by....

Crabs often bear as many flowers as cherries, but few have the weight of petals; the flowers have never quite developed into the same sort of extravaganzas. Some think that with fewer petticoats they have more charm. ▶

Early spring in the département of Calvados. Cider-apple trees share the fields of Normandy with cattle. The cider from the sour apples is distilled to make Calvados apple-brandy; the cattle give superlative cream and cheese.

The Crab-Apples

Left and below left *The Japanese flowering crab has the simplest little single white flowers. It gains its extraordinarily beautiful effect from the backs of the petals, which are cherry-red before they open. Its flowering is delayed until the leaves have expanded, so white, red and bright green are intermingled on the arch-ing tree. This was one of the first flowering trees to be introduced from Japan in 1862.*

Above *'Charlottae' is a superior form of one of America's native crab apples, Malus coronaria. Its big but delicate and subtly-scented flowers come in late spring or early summer.*

Right *A complicated parentage of Chinese and Japanese crabs has pro-duced hybrids with a red tint in both flowers and leaves. One of the most popular cultivars, with deep red flowers, is Malus 'Lemoinei'.*

Above *The hybrid Malus × purpurea is one of the most conspicuous crabs with its profusion of reddish-pink flowers and its dark purple-green leaves. The fruits are like large cherries and hang on dark red stalks.*

Above and left *The Siberian crab is the hardiest of its race; a small tree which regularly smothers its branches in fragrant white flowers. Its fruit is as small as a berry, usually yellow as here but sometimes red.*

▶Several of the species of crab-apples that have contributed most to the breed in the stud book are still very much in circulation in their own right.

Perhaps the best of them is the Japanese crab (*Malus floribunda*), which is one of the first to flower; a thrilling sight in April when its flowers open from bright red (the backs of the petals) to white (the front). The new leaves are still shining grass green and very small; the flowers waiting to open look like scarlet berries among the white stars of those that already have. All this happens at eye level: it is only a short tree and the branches tend to arch and hang. Most important, it does its stuff every year; a number of otherwise excellent crabs take alternate years off.

There is another Japanese species, Sargent's crab (*M. sargentii*) which is as beautiful in flower (white flowers with gold centres) and in its bright red fruit, but which is only a big bush eight or nine feet high and wide.

The selected, bigger-flowered forms of two native American species, themselves closely related, compete in the flowering-cherry league with big soft double pink flowers. Bechtel's crab (*M. ioensis* 'Plena') is a form of the prairie crab–no relation of the prairie oyster–which sacrifices fruit for extra petals. The less temperamental tree of the two, *M. coronaria* 'Charlottae', has the great advantage of noticeably larger and toothed leaves, which colour well in autumn.

Of the many superb Chinese species–China has the richest natural supply–the cutleaf crab (*M. toringoides*) is the most un-usual on account of its leaves, which are not only deeply cut with lobes but colour well in autumn to set off the big red and yellow apples. *M. halliana* 'Parkmanii' has double pink flowers on red stalks; *M. spectabilis* 'Riversii' (or Rivers' crab) is fairly early with its profuse red-bud-pink flower combination; the Hupeh or tea crab which E. H. Wilson found (*M. hupehensis*) is a strange thing with branches which, when they flower late in the season, are like long tentacles of pink and white.

Different parts of Siberia have given us different improvements on the Siberian crab, *M. baccata*. *M.b. mandshurica* is the Manchurian candidate, a big early-flowering tree with fragrant white flowers. In the tree horrifically named *M. pumila* 'Niedzwetzkyana' southwest Siberia or Kazakhstan has made an important contribution of red blood: it has a red pigment that shows in its new shoots, its clusters of purply-red flowers and its plum-coloured fruit. Some of the reddest of the hybrids have this 'blood' in their veins.

'Lemoinei' is a typical example with rich red flowers. The more recent 'Profusion' is another and 'Red Tip' a third. 'Echtermeyer' is a tree with the same colour scheme but a weeping habit. I confess to a quiet loathing of a dark red tone in almost anything except wine–but don't listen to me.

There is obvious confusion lying in wait in the two excellent hybrids called 'Red Jade' and 'Red Sentinel', both of which sound like fellow-travellers but in fact have white flowers. 'Red Jade' is a small weeping tree, 'Red Sentinel' a bigger one. The great value of both lies in the bunches of red

crabs bigger than cherries that hang on and on through the winter.

Of the trees with yellow fruit the 'Golden Hornet' I have mentioned is certainly one of the best and 'Dorothea' (a product of the Arnold Arboretum) is said to be very good. Dorothea's flowers are pink and double.

Even this trugful by no means exhausts the catalogue. 'John Downie' is possibly the best known cultivar of the old English wild crab, *M. sylvestris*. For a crab it makes a big tree which is generous with substantial red and yellow fruit: several crabs make good jelly material but John Downie's fruit is actually good to eat off the tree.

The Siberian crab has a Manchurian variety (Malus baccata mandshurica) which is the first of all the crabs to blossom, though later than some of the early flowering cherries.

Left *The 'cherry' crab (Malus × robusta), a hybrid of the Siberian crab, is another form with particularly striking fruit.*

Above *'Golden Hornet' is a crab apple worth growing for its fruit alone. It is a neat domed tree with unremarkable white flowers but a regular crop of brilliant yellow fruit which stays long after the leaves have fallen.*

The Flowering Cherries of Japan

The flowering cherry is not so much a tree as an event: a milestone in the year which even the most ungardening citizen recognizes. It is (as the Japanese have long known) a suitable object for a cult. Would thousands flock out from the city to see the crabs, the laburnums – even the magnolias – in flower? They do to see the cherries.

The cherry alone manages to look both virginal and voluptuous. It is easy (and fashionable) to turn up your nose at it; to consider it tainted by the suburbs which have become its second home. Yet nature offers no experience of profusion and delight so strong. To stand among the low branches in the fragility of millions of pale petals is in the range of natural experiences that are totally distinct and all-embracing; like standing under a waterfall, or flying through racing scraps of cloud.

It is also, to westerners, a modern experience. Japanese cherry-worship is a thousand years old, but the garden cherries perfected in Japan were not seen in the West (or had not grown to full size) until this century. Most of the work that has led to their popularization was done by one man who is still alive: Captain Collingwood Ingram.

The Japanese have firm notions about which cherries should be planted where. The elaborately double-flowered forms they keep for important sites, where they plant them singly. For the massed effects of hundreds of trees they use single-flowered species and they stick to one kind. The most famous cherry-viewing district near Kyoto is planted entirely with the hill cherry (*Prunus serrulata* var. *spontanea*). It flowers late enough (the second half of April) for the weather to be perfect when its broad crowns turn white against black pines and the pattern of dark and light is reflected in the Kamo River.

The biggest (to 90 feet) and longest-lived (to 1,000 years at least) of these half-wild single cherries is the spring cherry (*P. subhirtella*). But its little pale pink flowers are not up to the standard of cultivated varieties. The important forms of the spring cherry are the weeping *P.s.* 'Pendula' (which was the first Japanese cherry to reach the western world in the middle of the last century); the double-flowered *P.s.* 'Fukubana'; and the winter-flowering *P.s.* 'Autumnalis'. One can forgive the flowers their weak colour and puny size when they are the only ones in the garden. In a mild winter in the south of England the performance is continuous from late October on; most of the flowers clustering tightly round little wispy shoots from the trunk – ideal for cutting and taking indoors. In a harder climate 'Autumnalis' often flowers in November and again in the early spring.

The most popular cherry in Tokyo today is a relatively modern hybrid, the Yoshino (*P.* × *yedoensis*), which flowers early and fills the suburbs with the scent of almonds. Its advantage for a shifting population is that it grows and flowers quicker than the others. The flowers come in tens of thousands, white stained with pink, on branches that droop at the ends as though under their weight. Nurseries often offer selected droopy forms.

Noblest of the common species is the tall great mountain cherry. Picture it on the middle slopes of Mt. Fujiyama. It is known to the West by the name of Professor Sargent of the Arnold Arboretum. Sargent's cherry (*P. sargentii*) candies over with bright pink flowers before the leaves, but the leaves catch up and mingle their ruby-brown with the pink. On a tree 40 or 50 feet high the effect is pretty powerful.

Cherries as a whole are not great autumn-colour trees. Sargent's cherry is an exception, particularly conspicuous for turning orange and red in September while most trees are still green. Its long oval leaves turn their points down and hang rather sadly as summer ends, but when they catch fire the display is all the better for seeing their whole length.

The Japanese use the term *sato zakura*, which means village cherries, for their cultivated productions. There are 40 or 50 of them in cultivation in Europe and America. When they first arrived they were given Latin names relating them all to the species *P. serrulata*, but the tendency today is to use their Japanese names alone without trying to trace the intricacies of their parentage.

The most popular of them all, by far, is the variety called 'Kanzan' (or often, but wrongly, 'Kwanzan'). Its vigour, its freedom with its many-petalled flowers, and above all their piercing pink colour combine to make a fatal appeal. Pink is tricky. There are agreeable clear pinks, salmon pinks, tawny pinks and rosy pinks, but as soon as pink is stained with blue it starts to shriek. Kanzan is calmed by a white background, but its stridency in combination with red brick walls has alone been enough to give the cherries a bad name.

As a little tree in the nursery Kanzan looks well-adapted for a narrow space. Its branches climb steeply in a narrow V-shape. At ten or 15 years, however, the narrowness is a thing of the past: 25 feet or more is a normal spread.

Several other cherries have the same vase-shape, at least in youth. 'Ukon' is a very pretty one with white flowers just touched with enough lime-green to give a sulphury effect. 'Hokusai' is another, eventually spreading wide, with hundredweights of pale pink flowers slowly being overtaken by pinky-brown emerging leaves.

The only flowering cherry that really fits permanently into a narrow space is 'Amanogawa', which is built like a stripling Lombardy poplar; a shape which (soldier-like as it is) makes a laughable combination with petticoat-pink flowers. 'Amanogawa' is a mistake in the open lawn. At the back of a bed or among shrubs where its shape is not overstressed it could be a very useful tree, though.

Flowering cherries have been an important theme in Japanese art and literature since the 12th century. This 17th-century painted screen shows cherry and plum blossom.

Tokyo's favourite flowering cherry is the 'Yoshino' (Prunus × yedoensis). Its faintly pink flowers come early and scent the April air with almonds. Though it grows eagerly to start with it never makes a big tree.

Flowers of the 'hill' cherry, simple and white with bronzy-green young leaves, are the archetype of Japanese cherry-worship. This is the tree planted in groves near Kyoto, the object of pilgrimages in early May.

The weeping form of the 'spring' cherry is so graceful a little tree that even without its early white (or very pale pink) flowers it would be planted, like the weeping birch, for its elegance.

What the flowering cherries really want to do, or look as though they want to do, is to reach long branches low across the lawn. The trees that do this offer you a whole universe of coloured petals to swim in at head height–even to wade in at waist height.

'Shirofugen' is a May-flowering, long-lasting one, pink in bud and maturing white, which does this. 'Shirotae' is an earlier, scented, pure-white one, which makes wonderful use of the bright green of its new leaves to show off its hanging clusters of flowers. The leaves remain a feature of 'Shirotae': their edges are fringed with deep teeth and they have long points. 'Shimidsu' is a third, with pink buds opening late to wide white flowers on stalks six inches long.

The best of all spreading cherries, and all white cherries, however, is 'Tai Haku'–a tree with a fascinating history. In 1923 the owner of a garden in Sussex showed Captain Collingwood Ingram a tree without a name. It had the biggest flowers he had ever seen on a cherry; simple five-petalled flowers, shining white with gold stamens, displayed among huge copper-red young leaves. He promptly took grafts and put it into circulation, knowing nothing of its name or where it originally came from.

On his next visit to Japan Ingram was shown an 18th-century book of flower-paintings. In one of the paintings he recognized his new white cherry. But, he was told, it had been lost to cultivation since the painting was made. There was no 'Tai Haku' in Japan; the Japanese certainly didn't believe it could exist in England.

How it came to that Sussex garden remains a mystery. All the 'great white' cherries in cultivation today, however, are its offspring. Ingram himself recommends planting it by still water where its roots can drink deep and its beauty be reflected.

Top left *Sargent's cherry opens its tens of thousands of single clear pink flowers early in the season, making one of the great landmarks of spring. In autumn, again very early, its leaves turn the fieriest colour of any of the cherries.*

Bottom left *'Amano-gawa' is the only upright cherry: a little column of ascending branches like a baby Lombardy poplar. Its pale pink slightly scented flowers come late in the season. In autumn it turns pinkish amber.*

Top right *The piercing pink and frilly flowers of 'Kanzan' have made it the most popular of the Japanese cherries in the western world. It is a vigorous, wide-stretching tree, growing quickly to over 20 feet.*

Bottom right *The great white cherry has the biggest blooms of any, in the purest white. At the same time the young leaves have a coppery glow. A big 'Tai Haku' near water is the finest sight the Japanese cherries can offer.*

199

The Flowering Cherries

The *Prunus* branch of the rose family has such a strangely various bunch of components that it used to be divided into a number of different genera. The cherries then were *Cerasus*; the almonds and peaches *Amygdalus*; the plums, *Prunus*; the apricots, *Armeniaca*; the bird cherries *Padus* and the laurels, or cherry laurels, *Laurocerasus*. The botanical argument, though, is that they all have a single female organ in a five-petalled flower, and consequently a single-stoned fruit.

Japan has no monopoly of the flowering cherries. In fact Captain Collingwood Ingram, enumerating the species, counts 13 for Japan (not counting, of course, the countless varieties), 23 for China, six for North America and five for Europe. Europe's best have long been known and used both for ornament and for their fruit. For both purposes the leading species is the gean, mazzard or simply wild cherry which flourished over the whole European continent, in Britain and as far east as the Caucasus. Its small cherries are sweet or relatively sweet in the wild; in cultivated varieties of course they are delicious. Seduced by the Japanese varieties, however, we have forgotten how beautiful the gean can be. Its double-flowered variety (*Prunus avium* 'Plena') not only rivals the *sato zakura* in its billowing white flowers but is hardier. The biggest gean, moreover, is of forest tree size, almost 15 feet in girth, and specimens 80 or 90 feet high are not unknown. This is the tree whose wood makes so much splendid French furniture and whose fruit makes the potent Kirsch of Switzerland, the Black Forest and the Vosges.

Above *The wild cherry of Europe, the mazzard or gean, is a tall woodland tree greatly prized for its timber and very beautiful in early spring. Its double-flowered form is among the best white cherries for the garden.*

Left *Leaves of the wild cherry in early autumn. Few cherries are noted for autumn colour, but many turn gentle amber shades and hang their leaves like this. The wild cherry often goes on from this stage to deep red.*

The sweet-fleshed eating cherries are cultivars of the European wild cherry. Morello cherries (here growing in Switzerland) are derived from the sour cherry (Prunus cerasus). The Swiss use their fruit for jam.

Left and below *Bird cherries make their little white flowers conspicuous among their early-appearing leaves by carrying them in spikes like the butterfly-bush buddleia. The American choke and rum cherries do the same. The showiest of them is Waterer's bird cherry (Prunus padus 'Watereri'), shown here.*

Of still older use as a garden ornament is the sour cherry *P. cerasus*, the parent of the dark Morellos from which the Swiss make their marvellous jam. The white double-flowered version of this (*P.c.* 'Rhexii') has been known to gardeners since Elizabethan times at least.

The bird cherry (*P. padus*), which grows all the way from Britain to Japan, is different in having its flowers in spikes; much smaller individually, but almost as effective in being crowded together. Of this too there are selected versions: *P.p.* 'Watereri' with extra-long flower-spikes, 'Colorata' with pink ones and *commutata*, an oriental form which produces leaves exceptionally early.

North America's native cherries have produced no spectacular ornamental trees; the best of them, *P. serotina*–the black or rum cherry–is the equivalent of the bird cherry. It is very common in the woods of the east, but neither its short spikes of white flowers nor its little red cherries attract much attention. The choke cherry (*P. virginiana*) is another 'bird' type with flowers in spikes. The wild red cherry, *P. pensylvanica*, has clustered flowers and fruit like the gean.

E. H. Wilson brought back a number of cherries from China. The most important in cultivation have been *P. hirtipes* which he found in Hupeh, whose variety 'Semi-Plena' is singularly weather-proof; *P. serrula* from western China, whose flowers are not up to much but whose bark is in the birch class, glistening squirrel-brown; and *P. campanulata*, which he picked up in Formosa as a contribution to the gardens of the south. It is one of the reddest-flowered of cherries, but for a warm climate only.

It was not Wilson but an earlier traveller who brought *P. maackii* back from Manchuria to the Arnold Arboretum. It remains rare, but makes a stout tree with bark of a glorious polished golden-brown. There is one like a barrel of honey at Wakehurst Place, Kew's country garden in Sussex.

Nurseries meanwhile have been busy with hybrids and selections; far too many to catalogue. One of the very best was produced by Hillier's and called *P. × hillieri* 'Spire'. Their description of it as 'possibly the best small street tree raised this century . . . flowers soft pink; leaves with rich autumnal tints' is fair comment.

Given a good start in life the cherry is such an easy tree to grow in most soils (it prefers a little lime and good drainage) that its performance is more or less assured. There is one thing it doesn't like, and that is to be hacked about; it tends to go on producing gum from a bad cut until it dies. Its motto is 'Don't Prunus'.

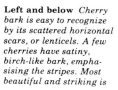

Left and below *Cherry bark is easy to recognize by its scattered horizontal scars, or lenticels. A few cherries have satiny, birch-like bark, emphasising the stripes. Most beautiful and striking is* the Chinese Prunus serrula (left). The Manchurian cherry (below) with flaking honey-coloured bark is less common but a much hardier tree. Neither has spectacular flowers.

Left *The wild red or pin cherry is common in woods in parts of the eastern States. It has white flowers before the bright green, finely-toothed leaves – and shiny little red cherries in great abundance.*

Left *The fruit of the bird cherry is small, black and bitter: far from being the favourite of the birds, which often leave it on the tree all the winter.*

Peaches, Plums and Cherry Laurels

The frivolity of the flowering cherry has been contagious. Peach, almond, apricot and plum have all caught it and produced more or less fruitless varieties with a short season of stunning display.

It comes most easily to the almond, *Prunus dulcis*. Even in countries where the almond is grown seriously for the kernels of its fruit, orchards are a tourist attraction. In Sicily, for instance, they are frothing pink in a countryside not given to such femininities – and as early as February. The fruit is not up to much in northern parts, but the trees are hardy and flower just as well. *P.d.* 'Roseoplena' is the almond's nearest approach to a cherry: pink, many-petalled, and one of the first trees in blossom. Well-protected with evergreens it can be the best thing in a drear March garden.

An almond is a peach with a lean fruit: or a peach is an almond with a fat one. In any case there is little difference besides the sweet flesh. They are close enough kin to breed together. The most ornamental upshot so far was conceived in Australia at the turn of the century and given the name *P.* × *amygdalo-persica* 'Pollardii'. Pollard was the nurseryman; *amygdalus* was in those days the specific name of the almonds (*dulcis* is today) and *persica* of the peaches. The fruits of this hybrid are like hard green peaches; the main attraction is its big pink flowers – bigger and pinker than either of its parents'. Again, a first-class tree for early blossom.

The peaches flower just after the almonds. A well-planned group of trees could use a flowering peach to link the blossom-time of the almond to that of the first cherries so that from early March (or sooner in the south) through to June there would always be a tree in flower. Of the peaches selected and sold for their flowers the most telling are perhaps the double-flowered red or rose-pink cultivars. The best-known is *P. persica* 'Klara Mayer'. Peaches, however, are not the rugged self-supporting individuals that cherries and even almonds are. They have a range of problems, from a curling and crumpling ailment of their handsome long leaves to relatively early decline and death. Growing peaches (or even better their smooth-skinned sisters nectarines) against a wall for fruit is another matter.

The fruit-tree apricot from China (*P.*

armeniaca) is nothing much to look at, though it is hardy and early in bloom. For its fruit, of course, it is eminently worth growing anywhere warm enough to ripen it. The Japanese apricot (*P. mume*) is the one for flowers. It is a shade less hardy than the almond. Double white, double pink and pendulous forms of both are to be had. Their 'floral ardour', as Collingwood Ingram warmly puts it, depends on the sunshine of the summer before.

Most of the domestic plum-trees are thought to be forms of an ancient hybrid between the sloe or blackthorn (*P. spinosa*) and the myrobalan or cherry plum *P. cerasifera*, which originally came from eastern Europe and western Asia. Neither is a very impressive tree in its own right; the blackthorn more often a suckering bush. The blackthorn's flowering, tiny though the white flowers are, is such a feature of hedgerows at the end of March that the spell of cold weather which often occurs in northern

Europe at that time is known as the blackthorn winter.

I was surprised to discover that there is a fancy purple-leaved variety even of the humble blackthorn. The purple version of the cherry plum is all too well known: the grossly over-planted purple-leaved cliché of suburban streets. The culprit for this tree was M. Pissard, the French gardener of the Shah of Persia 100 years ago – whence its name of *P. cerasifera* 'Pissardii'. There are other, slightly different cultivars, but all of them are trees of dreary hue.

It is quite hard to make the mental jump from the deciduous trees of *Prunus* to the big shiny-leaved evergreen shrubs which have borrowed from the bay tree the name of laurels. What could have less in common with a flowering cherry? Yet *Prunus* species they are.

The cherry laurel is the common one that flourishes in the dankest shade. It has a dozen variants; different leaf-shapes,

The almond and the peach are closely related. The ripe fruit of the almond (left) is like a green peach without the thick layer of juicy flesh. Though the almond is remarkably hardy it takes a Mediterranean climate to ripen fruit regularly.

The Japanese apricot, Prunus mume, introduced to the West in 1844, is a pretty little tree with almond-scented pink flowers. It has produced several splendid varieties, including the form shown here: 'Alphandii'.

The wild apricot of China has naturalised itself in parts of Europe. Here it blooms in March above Lake Lugano in Switzerland.

Right *The beautifully-bloomed but intensely sour sloe is the fruit of the blackthorn (Prunus spinosa). Blackthorn in the hedges is a sheet of tiny white flowers just before the more voluptuous pear-blossom appears.*

Below *A cross between the peach and the almond, Prunus × amygdalo-persica, was first made in cultivation in 1623. One of its most ornamental forms is 'Pollardii' which has big, deep pink flowers.*

Bottom *The Chinese Photinia serrulata looks more like a cherry-laurel than its nearer relation the hawthorn. Its great value to gardeners is its almost year-round succession of new shoots bearing bright red young leaves.*

The purple-leaved plum has a short-lived display of almost daisy-like pink flowers, appearing with the coppery-red young leaves. During the summer the leaves grow darker and darker, becoming almost black by autumn.

The evergreen cherry laurel successfully disguises its close relationship to the cherries until its fruit ripens red. Victorian shrubberies have given this magnificently-leaved little tree (or big shrub) a bad name it scarcely deserves.

colours and habits, the most striking of all a tall one with bold curling leaves, *P. laurocerasus* 'Camelliifolia'. The Portugal laurel (*P. lusitanica*) is a very smart round-topped tree up to 30 or 40 feet, glossy and a good bright green all the year round. Game birds enjoy the little cherries. Forms with broader leaves (*azorica*); narrower leaves ('Angustifolia'); and variegated leaves ('Variegata') can be found. The capabilities of these trees as the evergreen foundations of gardens on poor and chalky soil have scarcely been explored.

Better still is the Chinese *Photinia serrulata* – as yet an almost unknown member of the rose family but a hardy, uncomplaining and thoroughly original tree/shrub. This photinia is constantly producing new shoots of brilliant orange-red leaves, which slowly fade to gleaming green. The effect is of a tree never-endingly in flower. I have not seen a photinia as big as the biggest reported – 50 feet – but it must be quite a sight.

203

Pear Trees, Whitebeams and Mountain Ashes

Pears, whitebeams, mountain ashes–they seem strange bedfellows. Two, in fact, the superficially unlike whitebeams and mountain ashes, belong in the same genus–that of *Sorbus*. The pear is *Pyrus*, on its own.

What are the real differences between apples and pears? Flavour is obviously the most important. The pear tends to have a fleshy stalk, not joining the fruit in a dip but on a bump. Its flesh is granular in texture; gritty when unripe and once ripe, soon rotten.

Pears are wild in Europe and Asia; not in the New World. The common pear from which all the orchard varieties are derived occurs frequently in the south of Europe, and is not uncommon in the north. It is one of the longest-lived of fruit trees and eventually reaches a remarkable size: there are records of pear trees 16 feet in girth, and 60 feet is not an exceptional height.

Old common pears are densely twiggy; black and emphatic in winter–which makes their regular early spring covering of delicate white blossom all the more effective. Few (if any) are planted on purpose; where they happen to come up they are none the less very much enjoyed. Their wood is the 'fruit-wood' of French provincial furniture; the light brown that glows in old armoires and dressers.

There are two Chinese wild pears that have a following in the United States these days as ornamental trees. One is the work of the Plant Introduction Station at Glenn Dale, Maryland. From their stock of *Pyrus calleryana* they chose a seedling (known as *P.c.* 'Bradford') which has all the makings of a good medium-sized shade tree; a dense pyramid with plenty of flower and red autumn colour. The other is the Ussurian pear (*P. ussuriensis*) which has a more northerly range. Neither gives edible fruit.

The only pears one would normally consider planting for their beauty in the garden are those with white or silvery young leaves–*P. nivalis* from the Mediterranean and above all the willow-leaved pear (*P. salicifolia*) from the Caucasus. For the particular combination of summer-long silveriness and a weeping habit this has no competitors. If anyone is looking for an instant feature, a theme to form the basis for a new garden, or a corner of an old one, they could hardly do better than this. It has a tendency to overbranch and make a tousled head; this is its only fault (and it can be cured by pruning). I have made a silver plantation using it beside a weeping silver lime in a thicket of silver sea-buckthorn. Some common juniper (also in part silver) is dotted about. Have I overdone it? Very likely.

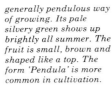

Above and below *Of all garden trees not bred or selected for beauty of blossom, the pear gives the best display. Old pear trees are like clouds of white and gentle green in early spring. Above is a* typical old domestic pear, a cultivar, probably nameless, of Pyrus communis, by a farmhouse in Normandy. Below is pear blossom, white touched with pink, bunched and stiff on the spray.

Above and below *The most decorative of pear trees is the weeping willow-leaf pear: a small tree with narrow silvery leaves, simple creamy-white flowers and a dense, rather congested but* generally pendulous way of growing. Its pale silvery green shows up brightly all summer. The fruit is small, brown and shaped like a top. The form 'Pendula' is more common in cultivation.

Above *Summer leaves and newly-formed fruit of the common pear.*

Right *The autumn colour of pear leaves. They emerge slightly white-furry in spring, but become glossier as the season advances. Pear trees will live to a great age, becoming the stateliest members of their family.*

It is almost a relief, after the frenzied flowering of so many of the rose family, to come to a group of trees which arrange their nuptials more discreetly. Neither whitebeam nor mountain ash, the two broad classes of *Sorbus*, is worth planting for the sake of its flowers. They are white or cream, and although there are plenty of them in broad heads they come with the leaves which not only tend to hide them but are in themselves more eye-catching. The leaves are the strong point of both sections of sorbus, different though they are. And after the leaves, in many cases, the heavy bunches of little coloured berries.

The whitebeams have single, simple leaves; usually just toothed but sometimes lobed, very often white-felt-backed. The white side of the leaf gives the tree its name. The mountain ashes have compound leaves; anything from three to 30-odd leaflets on a stalk. In the days of more naïve botany this was enough to prove them ashes. None of the trees in either class grows to enormous size. Seventy-five feet would be a record.

The mountain ashes outnumber the whitebeams but remain pretty consistent wherever they grow. There are four distinct whitebeam strains; a splendid one of several species with huge leaves in the Himalayas; the locally variable whitebeam (again several species, but very similar ones) of northern Europe; a couple of trees with leaves deeply enough lobed to remind one of the maple, also in Europe; and a superb Japanese tree with hornbeam-like leaves which is the best of all for flowers and fruit. America has no native whitebeams.

It is the way in which the leaves appear that first draws your attention to the whitebeam in the spring. They emerge from the bud rather as the petals do in the tulip, forming a chalice-shape with their points up and displaying their undersides. At this stage the underside (in most cases indeed the whole leaf) is covered with a silvery silk that reflects the light like metal. In the wild the tree is characteristic of chalk and limestone hills; it winks from copses of pale beech or the bronzy black of yew.

By July the brilliance of the leaves has gone. In many years insects get to work on them and leave mere fretwork. But if all is well they have a second stint in October in shades of russet and amber, setting off heavy bunches of red berries.

This is the wild one of Europe, *Sorbus aria*. Cultivation has polished up its performance without greatly changing it in the cultivars *S.a.* 'Lutescens' and 'Majestica' (which has bigger leaves and berries). It has also produced a pale yellow form (*S.a.* 'Chrysophylla') and a weeping one (*S.a.* 'Pendula') which are both very pretty trees.

The Himalayan whitebeams are recognizably the same tree, but with much bigger leaves, rich glossy green on top, chalk-white beneath, and as much as ten inches long. *S. cuspidata* has broad-oval or long, tapered leaves; *S.c.* 'Mitchelli' almost round ones; both are supremely lush and well-nourished looking trees, whose livery of dark green and white lasts well all summer. Their berries are crab-apple size, but not brightly coloured. The place to plant either would be in a wood where their big leaves are given some protection from the wind. They stand out magnificently among the busy patterns of oak or beech.

There are three whitebeams with lobed leaves. The Swedish whitebeam (*S. intermedia*) is just that–intermediate; the second is a native of most of Europe including England with the curious name of the wild service tree; and the third is *S. hybrida*. Learned discussion has produced two alternative theories for the meaning of 'service'. One gives it the same Latin root as *cerveza*, the Spanish word for beer, on the grounds that a drink was once brewed from its berries. The other, more earthily, reckons it is no more than a corruption of sorbus. In any case people with wild service trees tend to be rather pleased with themselves; not because the tree is spectacular (though its leaves like a handsome maple–without a felty side–and its speckled brown berries make an intriguing combination) but because it is wild and native. There are butterflies which get people in the same way. ▶

Left and below *The Swedish whitebeam* (Sorbus intermedia; *left, in autumn) and* S. hybrida *(below) appear to be links between the oval-leafed whitebeams and the closely related but* very different mountain ashes with their divided ash-like leaves. The Swedish tree has slightly lobed leaves; the 'hybrid' deeper lobes, becoming actual divisions towards the base of the leaf.

Its silvery-hairy leaves make the whitebeam (Sorbus aria) *conspicuous. The flowers (like those in the picture on the left) are pretty, but less noteworthy than its young leaves. It is a common wild tree on chalk or limestone soil in Europe.*

Pear Trees, Whitebeams and Mountain Ashes

▶ The wild service tree has hybridized with the ordinary whitebeam to produce the service tree of Fontainebleau (*Sorbus latifolia*) which has both lobes and felt lining. The other hybrids of the family link the whitebeams with the mountain ashes. The upshot in these cases, *S. hybrida* from Scandinavia (now considered a true species) and *S. × thuringiaca*, originally from Thuringia in what is now East Germany, is just what you would expect; compromise leaves with a whitebeam-type oval at the end and a clutch of mountain ash-type leaflets. From the whitebeam they keep white bottom-sides.

An upright version of the Thuringian white-mountain-ash-beam (*S. × t.* 'Fastigiata') earns praise on all sides as a street tree which doesn't take up too much room.

The Arnold Arboretum is also full of praise for the Japanese/Korean sorbus, which is hard to place in either section of the family. This is the one with leaves very like a hornbeam, having the same corrugation where the veins go. Botany has described its leaves as alder-like (its name is *S. alnifolia*) which seems a bit far-fetched. In any case it is the gayest of the race in flower and the most conspicuous in fruit, keeping its red berries long after the leaves have turned red and fallen.

It follows from its leaf-design that the mountain ash is a less substantial, more feathery-looking tree than the whitebeam. It grows to about the same size and has the same flowers and fruit, but otherwise it is remarkably different.

One basic model of mountain ash with only stylistic variations in colour of leaf, size of leaf and colour of berry runs right round the world. Its most famous representative is the rowan; a tree, like the Scots pine, identified inextricably with Scotland (though it is native to most of Europe). I have seen landscapes there in which full dress tartans would have simply disappeared

Whitebeam fruit ripens in glowing colours while the leaves turn shades of buff and yellow. The fruit is rose-hip size and very popular with the birds. Whitebeams never grow much taller than 50 feet.

Above *The Japanese whitebeam* Sorbus alnifolia *is one of the best for autumn colours. It is highly prized by the Arnold Arboretum for its clusters of tiny bright-red fruit that hang on the tree long after the leaves have gone.*

Above *The whitebeams of the Himalayas (here* Sorbus cuspidata) *have huge and handsome leaves, dark shiny green above and furry-white beneath. Their fruit is like a tiny pear.*

Below *The leaves and ripe fruit of the wild service tree, an unusual whitebeam with maple-like leaves, growing to 60 or 70 feet. It is a native of Europe, Asia Minor and North Africa.*

Below *The mountain ash or rowan of Europe is a small tree of the wilds but a willing recruit for gardens, with remarkable quantities of gaudy fruit. Here it is growing with larch in the French alps.*

Above *(both pictures) Among the Chinese mountain ashes E. H. Wilson found this rich-toned widespreading tree: Sorbus sargentiana. Its winter buds are*

crimson and sticky, its young shoots (left) also crimson, its summer colour dark green, its fruit bright and generous and its autumn leaves dark red nudging crimson.

Below *The American mountain ash and the European are very similar. If anything the American has larger leaves and less fruit. It has been known in cultivation since 1782.*

into the background as a perfect disguise. The heather gives a purple ground on which the larches and the birches display their yellow gold. The rowan is gold of a richer tone, set with preposterous carbuncles of scarlet fruit.

It is hard to improve on the common rowan. Various nursery productions offer alternatives; of yellow fruit, for example, in *S. aucuparia* 'Xanthocarpa'; of finely divided, ferny leaves in *S.a.* 'Aspleniifolia'; of a narrow upright head in *S.a.* 'Sheerwater Seedling'; even of edible fruit in *S.a.* 'Edulis'.

North America's native *S. americana* is a similar tree, usually smaller and with smaller fruit. *S. scopulina* is a western version with bigger leaves and fruit – on, if anything, a smaller tree.

The most valuable of the dozen or so Asiatic mountain ashes are those with different coloured fruit and leaves. *S. hupehensis* and *S. cashmiriana*, for example, with grey-green leaves and white or faintly pink fruit; either of them a lovely misty sight in the gloaming. Or *S. sargentiana* which is dark green, with very long leaves with red stalks, red autumn colour and scarlet fruit which hangs on into the winter.

S. discolor (otherwise known as *S.* 'Embley') is very much recommended as a street tree because its branches slant sharply upwards out of the way. It has both big red fruit and red leaves at the same time. Several of them in fact have the same trick of branching: *S. pohuashanensis* from the north of China and very hardy; *S. harrowiana* from the south and rather tender; *S. insignis* from Assam with pink fruit which lasts right through the winter.

Among the best for autumn colour, regularly turning orange, red, purple and everything between, is a gracefully spreading little tree from China called *S. vilmorinii*. A Scottish gardener has told me that birds which lose no time in stripping the other species of their fruit leave this one (whose fruit is white blushed pink) entirely alone.

Left *One of the very best mountain ashes, both for its neat shape with erect branches and for the powerful autumn colour of its leaves and fruit together: Sorbus discolor, alias S. 'Embley'.*

Above *There are mountain ashes with fruit of almost every colour. The Chinese Sorbus prattii is a delicately-formed little tree with ivory-white fruit in small hanging clusters.*

Above *The yellow-fruited mountain ash is one of the forms of the common European rowan. Another form 'Edulis' has fruit which ripens sweet and is quite pleasant to eat.*

China's huge stock of mountain ashes includes the exquisite Sorbus vilmorinii, with grey-green leaves as fine as ferns, thinly arranged on an elegant arching little tree. Its fruit (right) varies between deep pink and blushing white.

207

Locusts and False Acacias

Peas and pea-trees of various kinds grow everywhere on earth. The tropics are their natural base; in the temperate zones they appear more often as herbaceous plants than trees. Peas, beans, lupins are all examples. Even the big trees of the family, however, share the pea-likeness to a remarkable extent. The *Robinia* (which goes by the name of the black locust, false acacia or acacia according to where you happen to be) is the first one that springs to mind. Big tree though it is, it has essentially pea-like flowers, pods for fruit, and much the same sort of finely-divided foliage as all its kin.

Most of the family are cultivated for their flowers. Of the bigger trees grown for their stature, timber and shade four are natives of eastern North America. Europe has been poorly endowed in this department.

The term locust, which has stuck with several members of the family, started as the Latin word for lobster. From lobsters it got transferred to the swarming grasshopper-like insect of the Middle East which, with wild honey, was said to be the diet of John the Baptist in the wilderness. Learned discussion produced the verdict that what he was eating was really the fruit of the carob tree, which thereupon took the name of locust. Thence, via the Bible-reading colonists, the name was attached to the American trees with the same sort of pod: *Robinia* became black locust and *Gleditsia* honey-locust.

The black locust was one of the first American trees to be sent back to Europe. By about 1600 Jean Robin, Henry IV's herbalist, was growing it in Paris. It derives its generic name of *Robinia* from him and its specific name of *pseudoacacia* from its obvious similarity to the subtropical acacias of Africa. There are no European acacias. The acacia can hardly have been a well-known plant in the 17th century. Yet for some reason its name stuck and to this day in England acacia means robinia. (Real

Above *One of the most graceful and decorative of all small garden trees:* Robinia pseudoacacia *'Frisia', a cultivar of the false acacia produced 40 years ago in Holland. Its rich yellow colour from* spring to autumn shows off feathery and graceful leaves which are typical of the pea family.

Above *A cross between the false acacia (or black locust) and the lesser-known clammy locust of the southeastern States has produced two delicate little pink-flowering garden trees: (here)* Robinia × ambigua *'Bella-rosea' and 'Decaisneseana'.*

Left *The false acacia or black locust looks, for a native of the eastern States, remarkably like oriental species. Its branch-pattern is usually decidedly picturesque, both in zig-zag main limbs and in mazy fine twigs.*

Above *The flowers of the false acacia are scented, but scarcely conspicuous enough to enhance the foliage.*

acacia from Australia we call mimosa.)

Whatever the natural range of the black locust may have been, somewhere in the Alleghenies, today it grows wild in large parts of North America and most of Europe. Greedy though it is, with shallow and competitive roots, it is usually welcome. It grows very fast and makes wood which rivals oak for strength and permanence. In the wine-districts of France a copse of 'robinier' is a valuable asset; vine-stakes from it will not need replacing for 50 years.

Moved by its performance and its manifest usefulness, the English journalist William Cobbett came home from America in 1823 to sing its praises. In his enthusiasm Cobbett had started a nursery on Long Island and raised thousands of seedlings for the English market. He sold them, and they grew; but unfortunately crooked-trunked and useless.

Crooked or straight, though, from the ornamental point of view the black locust is an exciting tree. Its signature in the winter sky is unmistakable: branches like forked lightning zig-zagging out from a pale grey trunk with deep-shadowed furrows. It seems to have no over-wintering buds on the twigs; where each bud should be the ridge is crowned with two short sharp thorns.

Like the walnut, it is a black shape for more than half the year. The leaves are late to come and early to fall. They come out tender and yellow-green, deepening to a bluer shade when the white flowers appear. Then for a fortnight there is a faint sweetness in the air and the gaunt framework is transformed into as delicate a salad as anything in the garden.

But the black locust takes up a lot of space for what it does, and casts practically no shade. Nursery work has made a better version of it for street-planting; the cultivar R.p. 'Inermis' which has no thorns – and alas few flowers – but which forms a dense round head of the most mouth-watering green. In town squares in southern Europe it is an ideal shade-tree, leafing only when the sun grows hot and always keeping a neat shape.

For the garden proper there is a smaller golden version, R.p. 'Frisia', which is one of the most desirable of all golden trees. Its annual programme is from pale gold through golden green to golden copper.

The other locust, the honey locust (Gleditsia triacanthos), has also been called acacia in its time. There is no mistaking this tree in nature; it grows thorns in vicious clusters, even on the lower part of the trunk. It will grow to twice the size of the black locust: to 130 as against 70-odd feet. The biggest honey-locust, in Michigan, is 115

feet high and 124 in spread.

The search for an elm-substitute has lit on this tree as being tall, shapely, singularly beautiful in its fine, almost ferny, foliage and not subject to too many pests. Sad to say, though, it has had to be emasculated; disarmed of its thorns and made barren of its long shining brown pods, to satisfy the parks departments. The thornless locust comes by many names from different nurseries: 'Moraine' is perhaps the best known cultivar.

Better still for gardens is the smaller Japanese species of the same tree (G. japonica) which has leaflets so small (about half an inch long) and in so many millions as to look exactly like a big billowing fern.

Honey locust and its near relation the Kentucky coffee tree (Gymnocladus dioica) are unusual in the pea family for having regularly petalled, not pea-like, flowers. Since in both cases they are green they are of no ornamental importance. If the coffee tree is planted it is for its leaves, the biggest and boldest in the family; up to three feet long, easily 18 inches wide. Bare of leaf the coffee tree remains a landmark. For a while the long leaf-stalks hang on. When they fall the tree seems bereft of all its twigs; what is left is so sparse and each shoot so thick.

The American yellow-wood (Cladrastis lutea) is the last of the locust-relations from the same astonishingly species-rich forest of the east. It would pass for a specially showy black locust selected for longer streamers of bigger white flowers. The way to identify it is to look for its buds. They lurk all summer inside the hollow stalks of the leaves.

Its oriental counterparts, the Maackias from Manchuria (Maackia amurensis) and China (M. chinensis) are rare but highly-prized little trees: the Manchurian for its upright blue-white flower heads in summer, the Chinese for ravishing young shoots in spring, emerging dark and bluish with a covering of silver-silk down. ▶

Left The biggest tree among the peas is the magnificent honey locust of eastern North America, which grows to the proportions of the spreading American elm, yet still with fresh and delicate leaflets. Here its pea-like pods are ripening.

Above *'Sunburst' is a recent cultivar of the honey locust with bright yellow young leaves. Its shoots lack the sharp thorns of the ordinary honey-locust, making it a better street tree.*

Below *Older specimens of the honey locust develop dangerous branching thorns on the main trunk. Most barbarously armed of all is the Caspian locust from northern Persia, seen here.*

Left The American yellow-wood is like a smaller false acacia with longer streamers of white flowers in June, falling like wisteria from its rounded crown. Here the tiny pods which succeed the flowers are half-ripe. In time they turn brown.

The Chinese yellow-wood flowers in mid-summer, a month after the American (see top of page) and with upright flower-clusters tinged with pink and cream. Yellow-woods are a useful size: up to 40 or 50 feet at most.

Laburnum, Redbuds and the Silk Tree

▶ Europe's biggest pea-tree is the original locust, the carob (*Ceratonia siliqua*) of the Mediterranean. Apart from the occasional experimental bite into the fleshy brown pod (which is mildly chocolaty; not bad at all) nobody pays the carob much attention. Because it is evergreen its eight-inch pods often escape notice. It merges into the background: short, gnarled, ageless-looking.

But experimental bites into pods are not something to encourage. The little laburnum tree is poisonous in every part. Were it not so beautiful, so regular in profuse flower and so ready to grow anywhere it might well have been banned as a public danger. As things are it is almost as universal in small gardens in Europe (where it is native) as the flowering cherry, with the same drawback: that its big moment is only two weeks of the late spring.

There is common laburnum (*Laburnum anagyroides*), Scotch laburnum (*L. alpinum*; hardier, with shinier leaves and longer spikes – a better tree) and a hybrid between the two (sold either as *L. × watereri* 'Vossii') which seems to flower even more lavishly than either. Any of them used in calculated masses for knock-out effect or scattered among light woodland like natural accidents can be the most telling of all hardy yellow-flowering trees – unless you count broom, another pea-cousin.

Most brooms are shrubs. But it has needed only a slight help from a wall to windward to egg on a Mount Etna broom (*Genista aetnensis*) to 20 feet in my garden. On the way up Mount Etna you pass through a belt of this broom growing in black lava soil: a more startling monochrome landscape it is hard to imagine.

The best of the hardy Asiatic pea-trees, the pagoda tree (*Sophora japonica*), is more in the vein of the American locusts. Among the curiosities of Kew Gardens there is a specimen that reclines its trunk as though

Below *The poisonous pods of the common laburnum, which hang on the tree for months on end. The thickened upper edge of the pod helps to distinguish the common laburnum from the Scotch.*

Above *The laburnum tunnel in the gardens at Bodnant, North Wales, is perhaps the world's most spectacular use of this almost universal tree. It is made of the hybrid* L. × watereri *'Vossii'*

Left *The silk tree from Persia is a remarkably hardy member of a largely tropical family. It makes a low wide-spreading tree covered with pink flowers in mid-summer.*

Above *The hardiest of the true acacias is silver wattle, here growing wild in southern Australia. It needs a Mediterranean climate to reach tree-size, surviving hard frosts only with artificial aid.*

Left *Scotch laburnum is a slightly showier tree than the common laburnum. Here its young flower racemes are developing with the yellow flowers still folded.*

Right *The pea family likeness can be traced in the evergreen leaves of the Mediterranean carob tree. In the top right corner of the picture young pods are ripening. When they are brown they are edible and sweet.*

The young translucent seed-pods of the Judas tree clearly relate it to the peas. They grow to about five inches and ripen purple. The Judas tree and the related redbud flower from old wood, producing flower-buds even from the main trunk near the ground.

on an invisible chaise-longue. It was planted in 1762 – one of the first two or three Chinese trees to reach Europe direct through the offices of M. d'Incarville. In the same year the garden's ten-storey pagoda was finished. Did the sapling gaze up at the 163-foot tower and realize it would never make it?

The pagoda tree remained relatively unknown in the New World, perhaps because the black locust (which was there already) is so similar. Yet a month after the black locust has dropped its leaves the pagoda tree will still be fresh and green. Its chief justification, fine foliage apart, is that it flowers notably late, in August. Its flowers are creamy-white. The variety *S.j.* 'Pendula', a graceful small tree with long weeping branches, would succeed much better than a weeping willow in very dry soil.

The New Zealand kowhai (*S. tetraptera*) is an evergreen relation that needs the mild winters of the south to get beyond the shrub-stage. Its flowers are bigger and bright yellow, coming in May among ferny young grey-green leaves.

Yellow is one characteristic pea flower colour. The other is purply-pink. The red-bud (*Cercis*) genus, represented in Europe by the Judas tree, is probably the most familiar instance of the second kind – aside from sweet peas. The North American redbud (*C. canadensis*) flowers with the dogwood in the woods of the east from Pennsylvania southward, the only native tree with this flowering-cherry colour.

Europe's best display must be the grove of 50-foot Judas trees in the Retiro gardens in Madrid. I remember seeing them being watered one sunny morning by a jet with a great plume like a fire-hose. The big trees, arched with rosy blossom, were entirely covered with drops of water; the sun caught a crystal in each of the million tiny flowers. The tree's peculiarity is to flower not only on young twigs but even from the most calloused old bark of the main trunk.

China has a similar redbud, and also another whose flowers hang in short streamers (*C. racemosa*). They are all worth having for their glossy green heart-shaped leaves, quite apart from their flowers.

The legend that this was the tree from which Judas Iscariot hanged himself marches on. The French name for the tree, however, explains all. They call it *l'arbre de Judée* – the tree from Judaea.

All these trees adhere to the pea's own asymmetrical flower design. It is the mimosa group that rocks the boat. Their ring-leaders are the acacias – the true acacias of the tropics. In the sub-tropics they have concentrated in the southern hemisphere. After the eucalyptus they are Australia's

commonest trees. Mimosa-type flowers are radially designed and symmetrical.

The silk tree (*Albizia julibrissin*) is the one hardy tree of this group that belongs in the northern hemisphere. It was first found in Persia (julibrissin is its Persian name) but its range runs all the way to China. Like the true acacias it has doubly-divided leaves of the finest texture. Unlike most of them it is deciduous and its fluffy heads of flowers are a rather washy pink. In southern gardens it is often called mimosa. A better form (*A.j.* 'Rosea') has been introduced from Korea for the north; both hardier (zone 5) and stronger in flower-

colour, though not happy in Britain. The top of the low, wide-reaching tree is never without a few pink plumes from July to September.

Of the 500 species of Australian acacia, or wattle, only half a dozen are usually attempted in gardens outside the sub-tropics. Only one has ever made a substantial tree in England: the one the Piccadilly flower-sellers call mimosa; the silver wattle (*Acacia dealbata*).

For Californians and Floridians and gardeners on the Mediterranean the wattles to try (apart from the silver) are the coota-mundra, the black and the Sydney.

Above left *The flowers of the New Zealand kowhai or Sophora tetraptera. Their tubular form is unlike that of other pea flowers. Kowhai is evergreen in mild areas, and flowers in late spring.*

Top right and above *A young shoot of the Judas tree grows with a zig-zag gait. The rounded heart-shape of the leaf can clearly be seen. The purply-pink flowers are tiny, but densely massed.*

Above *The first pagoda tree (Sophora japonica) in Britain was planted at Kew in 1762. It is still alive and well, but for some strange reason has adopted a reclining position. Mature trees are covered with white flowers in late summer.*

Right *The eastern redbud blooms in early spring with the dogwood in the eastern States, especially from Pennsylvania to Virginia. A white-flowered form is also available from nurseries.*

The Eucalypts or Gum Trees

Left, below and right
The flower-bud of a eucalyptus (here, the blue gum) is like a little urn (left) with a lid. The flower has no petals, but as the stamens expand they push the lid off (below, the lid coming off and—on the right—the expanding stamens exposed). Right, the flower opens.

Australia is more closely associated with *Eucalyptus* than any other country with any other tree. Three-quarters of all the forest trees of Australia are eucalypts–from the snowy passes of Tasmania to where palms and tree ferns take over in the tropical jungle of northern Queensland. Their ecological range is thus enormous.

The eucalypts are members of the myrtle family, which was probably in ancient times a branch of the rose family. Most of the myrtles (including the eucalyptus) have simple, untoothed, unlobed, straightforward leaves appearing opposite each other in pairs. Very often the leaves have tiny translucent dots which are visible against the light. The eucalyptus is unique in having a flower bud with a lid which comes off when the sexual mechanism inside is ready to receive insects (for whom it supplies abundant nectar). It also has unusually well-marked stages in the two-year growth of its evergreen leaves. Juvenile or new leaves are one shape–often round; mature leaves are totally different, usually long and narrow like larger-than-life willow leaves. More often than not they are grey with wax, at least while they are young. They all have a fragrant oil inside. And finally the bark of many eucalypts is as deciduous as most trees' leaves, resulting in patterns of flaking or tattered strips which are half the tree's character.

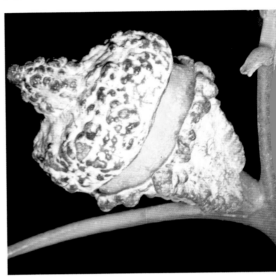

Typical eucalyptus country, in South Australia for instance, is strangely like the ghost of a great English park. If you half-shut your eyes those soft contours with grazing sheep, those huge hummocky broadleaf trees, here in a clump, there standing alone in massive maturity, suggest a Petworth or a Longleat drained of all colour, condemned to everlasting summer, to bone-grey and bone-brown.

In the arid parts towards the desert, where grass gives way to bare earth and stone, the scrubby types of eucalyptus known as

The gum trees have a vast range of habitats, from the tropics to such cool mountain sites as Crater Lake, Tasmania (above), where Eucalyptus coccifera *submits to wintry storms. In garden conditions this tree has brilliantly blue-waxy leaves.*

The ghost gum is so-called for its smooth almost luminous white bark. In very hot climates (here in Dampier, western Australia) gum trees get by with very little foliage to minimize transpiration losses. Their roots also plunge deep for water.

Right *Red resinous gum pours from a wound: hence 'gum tree'. Eucalypts also have a very marked oily fragrance in most of their parts. The oil has many uses, from disinfectant to boot polish, and it also makes a soothing embrocation.*

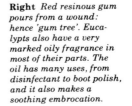

Right *A very marked difference between young and adult foliage is a common gum-tree characteristic. Many like the cider gum and the spinning gum illustrated here have completely disc-like leaves on young shoots giving way to the waxy adult leaves which are more or less willow-shaped.*

Left *Adult foliage of the blue gum, with immature little flower buds. The leaves of young blue gums have an almost silvery hue.*

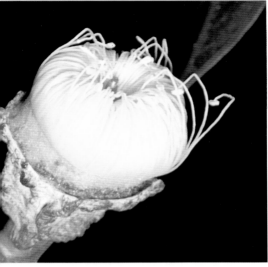

mallee take over as dense brush. And in the towns and villages the red-flowering ones (principally *E. ficifolia*) line the streets like flowering cherries.

There are 600 or so species. Some are very local; others, like the river red gum (*E. camaldulensis*), are native to every State, growing wherever their niche – in this case the riverbank – can be found. There are huge variations in hardiness within a species. In the very common snow gum, for example, it is essential to know whether the seed comes from Tasmania or New South Wales, and from what altitude, before it is possible to say if it will survive in northern Europe or the eastern States.

On the whole eucalypts must be regarded as subtropical trees. In England the commonest, by far, is the Tasmanian cider gum, *E. gunnii*. High altitude strains of *E. pauciflora* ssp. *niphophila*, from 7,000 feet on Mt. Kosciusko in New South Wales in particular, have also come through seasons of icy winds

unharmed. The University of Washington aboretum at Seattle finds this the hardiest, and also grows the startlingly silver-grey Tasmanian snow gum, *E. coccifera*. They are pleasant enough trees, yet somehow they always look spindly and top-heavy; their grey-green foliage always looks as though it has been slept in; they look uneasy among the busy burgeoning and quick corruption of northern summers. Perhaps the most effective use of eucalyptus in a northern climate is to coppice it. This way the foliage is perpetually juvenile: the effect is of a cool little shrub.

In the south it is another matter. California saw the first invasion of the United States by eucalyptus in the 1880s. The blue gum was widely planted with the fanciful notion that it would absorb the 'noxious gases' which were then supposed to be the cause of malaria. The blue gum did so well it gave the whole gum-tribe a bad name. It seeded itself everywhere and filled good ▶

Eucalyptus growing against the mysterious red wall of Ayers Rock, a vast monolith in the flat central desert of Australia. Rainfall in this area is limited to 30 days a year and rarely exceeds ten inches.

Right *Gum tree bark comes in almost every colour, but always has the character of skin, often peeling or flaking away in thin layers to make beautiful patterns, as here on the blue gum. Sometimes the peeling layers hang on the trunk.*

Above *Snow gums in the snow. Eucalyptus pauciflora ssp. niphophila, the snow gum, is one of the hardiest species; a small slow-growing tree worth having in a garden for its beautiful bark (picture on left).*

Eucalypts, Silk Oak, Fire-Bush and Oleasters

Right *Woodward's gum (Eucalyptus woodwardii) is a tender species with its wax-red flower-buds opening to golden flowers.*

Below *The western Australian* Eucalyptus miniata *has bright orange flowers.*

Below right *The red-flowered* Eucalyptus leucoxylon 'Rosea' *is widely grown in Mediterranean climates for its almost cherry-blossom effect.*

Left *The tallest known broad-leaf (327 feet) is a* Eucalyptus regnans, *the species seen here (in the foreground) growing in the Styx valley of Tasmania. The smaller trees are* Eucalyptus obliqua. *Neither species has been extensively tried in the northern hemisphere.*

Left Luma apiculata *makes a beautiful evergreen in regions without hard frost; it is photographed here in Cornwall.*

Right *The cider gum (Eucalyptus gunnii) is rather less spectacular than the trees above, but very hardy and fast growing. It is the one relatively common eucalyptus in British gardens.*

Below *The only real tree of the true myrtles, the Chilean* Luma apiculata, *shows its kinship with the eucalypts in its peeling trunk.*

ground with its greedy shallow roots. None the less it looked splendid, and still does, its blue-rinsed tresses and chaotically shaggy forking trunk mingling magnificently with the native oaks and pines.

If Californians curse the blue gum it is only fair to say that Ethiopians bless it. Its introduction at the end of the last century probably saved their capital city. The native timber had all been cut and the seedlings grazed: Addis Ababa was without fuel. No native tree would grow at anything like the speed of this exotic.

Speed trials with eucalyptus species are going on now in the southern States. The Chinese, with their well-known fertilizing techniques, claim figures so astonishing that every forester is intrigued. But everyone is wary of eucalyptus statistics–from the original claim of a 470-foot tree onwards. What is certain is that the tallest species in Australia, *E. regnans*, is easily the tallest non-conifer in the world. There may be trees 350 feet high in western Australia.

Of the gum-trees I know (which is admittedly a minute fraction of the field) the one that stands out for beauty–alas a tender one, but worth growing even in a greenhouse–is the lemon-scented gum, *E. citriodora*. It possesses a trunk as slim and white as a goalpost, but a goalpost with hips.

Right *The little light-limbed and often almost weeping* Eucalyptus caesia, *hardy down to about 25 F., has some of the prettiest flowers of the genus, in loose clusters in early spring, often recurring later.*

Is it a coincidence that most of Australia's trees come in a rush at this stage of evolutionary history? Between the *Eucalyptus*, the *Acacias* which came just before them, and the *Grevilleas* and *Hakeas* which turn up now in their order of *Proteales*, we have accounted for a high proportion of all Australian trees.

The silk oak *(Grevillea robusta)* is more familiar in the northern hemisphere as a pot-plant or summer bedding plant than as the big tree (to 120 feet) it makes in Australia and California.

The name 'oak' as applied to trees so very unlike oaks as the *Grevilleas*, or the 'she-oak' *Casuarina* (an apparently leafless Australian with bamboo-like twigs), derives from the properties of their timber, which has oak-like broad medullary rays. In California the silk oak grows fast, looks lush and thrives in desperately dry areas. The pincushion tree *(Hakea laurina)* is the other member of the family Californians grow, for its pink and gold pincushion flowers.

Gardens as far north as southern and western Britain can grow the Chilean fire-bush (*Embothrium coccineum*). If there is a more spectacular tree than this in flower I have never seen it. In May and for several weeks the fire-bush covers its whole 20 or 30 feet with tubular scarlet flowers. The variety *E.c. lanceolatum* 'Norquinco Valley' is hardier and even more floriferous.

There is nothing so showy in the allied *Elaeagnus* or *Oleaster* family. The family likeness lies in a subtle silvery-scaliness. In the main they are a collection of the most useful and cheerful of evergreen shrubs, with silver-backed leaves. The one small tree among them (*Elaeagnus angustifolia*, sometimes known as the Russian olive) has the silver-scales both sides of its narrow, willowy leaves. The general effect is like a small olive-tree; even to the olive-like fruit, the many trunks and the domed top. This and its cousin the sea-buckthorn (*Hippophae rhamnoides*), which needs a bit of pruning to make a tree-shape, are two of the best small silver-leaved trees; they deserve a place in the sun with a dark background. When the sea-buckthorn is covered with its orange berries all along its twigs among the leaves (you need both male and female plants to get fruit) the effect is of fire-light on silver hair – a truly autumnal theme.

The oleaster or Russian olive (Elaeagnus angustifolia) *is one of the best small silver-leaved trees, suggesting an olive tree both in colour and in its many-stemmed spreading shape.*

Europe's sea buckthorn has even narrower leaves than the oleaster (left) and often makes a thicket rather than a tree. Female plants bear orange berries (in autumn) only when a male plant is nearby.

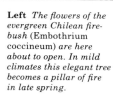

Left *The flowers of the evergreen Chilean fire-bush* (Embothrium coccineum) *are here about to open. In mild climates this elegant tree becomes a pillar of fire in late spring.*

Above *The ferny leaves of the silk oak* (Grevillea robusta) *are silver underneath and golden green above. In cold climates in the north it is used as a summer bedding plant for its foliage alone.*

Australia has a number of trees that mimic conifers with their drought-resisting needle-like leaves. 'Sweet' hakea (Hakea suaveolens) *is a useful small tree in hot dry places.* H. laurina *is more showy with red and gold flowers.*

Right *Rosemary-leaved grevillea is hardier than the silk oak, but reaches only six feet in cultivation. It looks like rosemary with red flowers all summer.*

The Dogwoods

The name dogwood covers more different kinds of shrub and tree than one name rightly should. It covers creeper ankle-high; shrubs waist-high; little trees window-high and big trees of the high forest. There are almost as many designs of flowers as there are sizes. The leaf, always an oval with veins curving to meet the centre axis at both ends, is the only clearly visible link between them all.

Although the dogwood trees have two very different flower designs they are all so whole-hearted about it that the effect comes to much the same thing: a spread of warm white, of branches obliterated under tablecloths of massed flowers which have no equal–not even among the cherries. The common flowering dogwood of eastern north America, the Pacific dogwood and the Japanese dogwood are the proponents of one system of flowering. The giant dogwood of China leads the other school.

What seem to be petals on the flowers of the first are really no such thing: they are the modified leaves known as bracts, which usually play a humble supporting role protecting the unopened flower. Inside that ring of four (sometimes six) white pseudo-petals the real petals are tiny: miniature parts of a cluster of miniature flowers. The second school simply has bigger clusters of bigger flowers, and no fancy bracts.

It is the way the dogwood grows almost as much as its floral ardour that makes it such a spectacle in spring. Its tendency is to throw out long branches sideways. Every flower tells because it is held face upwards on these branches.

From the point of view of habit and flower there is little to choose between the flowering dogwood (*Cornus florida*) of North America and the (normally rather smaller) Japanese dogwood (*C. kousa*)–except their flowering times, which are staggered . . . making it worthwhile planting both.

Unfortunately the American dogwood demands a continental climate; Britain is too temperate for it, and so is the northern Pacific coast. We therefore miss the pink varieties which only occur in this species. The Japanese model does triumphantly in England, however, and in France both succeed as well as they do in New York or Pennsylvania. The Chinese variety of the Japanese (*C. kousa chinensis*) is said to be even better, more vigorous and ardent in flower, than the species.

Having seen dogwood in flower in Connecticut I was prepared to settle for that. It would have been absurd to ask for more. More is what they get on the west coast, though. The most memorable of many stirring forest sights is the Pacific dogwood in mid-October high in the hills of Oregon, not only lighting the depths of the Douglas fir and hemlock with flurries of golden and scarlet leaves, brighter even than the big-leaf maple on the same hill, but lighting its own brilliant branches with a second crop

The autumn leaf colour of the American dogwood in its native land is as great a display as its spring blooming. Unfortunately in Britain we can rely on it for neither.

The true flowers of the dogwood are the unremarkable little cluster, here about to open, in the centre of each set of four big petal-like bracts. These are the 'flowers' of Cornus florida 'Rubra'.

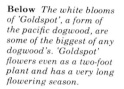

Above *Strange straw-berry-like fruits follow the yellow flowers of* Cornus capitata. *In very mild winters this dogwood is evergreen, although some leaves will turn purplish and fall.*

Below *The white blooms of 'Goldspot', a form of the pacific dogwood, are some of the biggest of any dogwood's. 'Goldspot' flowers even as a two-foot plant and has a very long flowering season.*

of its huge white clematis-like flowers.

Alas this, the biggest of the dogwoods, able to grow to 100 feet in its own woods, is less happy abroad. In the east it suffers from the cold. In Europe it is good, but short-lived and never a big tree.

The biggest tree of the dogwoods we can grow in either Europe or the eastern States is the giant dogwood of China, *C. contro-versa*. This is the one without big white bracts, but with broader clusters of little flowers which at a distance have almost the same effect.

The horizontal branching pattern is most marked in this tree. There are specimens, perhaps slightly aided and abetted by the gardener, which have made perfect wedding-cake tiers year after year on which the flowers lie like a covering of snow. Its freer form is perhaps even more dramatic. The branches go like the swirl of a dancer's skirt or the tipping horizons of distant alps. By 50 feet with most trees a degree of round-headed anonymity is creeping in. Not with the giant dogwood: it builds another majes-tic plateau for its 50th birthday.

Gardens where such an empire-builder would soon take over have the alternative of an exceedingly pretty variegated-leaved version of the same tree, *C. controversa* 'Variegata'. Like most trees with a short share of chlorophyll it grows slowly, but with the same deliberate pattern of whorled branches. The leaf margins are white, so whether the tree flowers much or not makes little difference: you have your wedding-cake all the summer.

The dogwood family is by no means exhausted with these. There is the cornelian cherry (*C. mas*) of Europe, which flowers yellow before the leaves in February, and like all dogwoods gives a good account of itself with autumn colour. For southern gardens there is an evergreen, *C. capitata* from western China, which has pale yellow bract-flowers.

Left *The oriental equivalent of America's flowering dogwood has pointed bract-petals and fades from white to white-and-pink. Flowering is conveniently a month later, making it worth planting both species.*

The 'Cornelian cherry' is so-called for its edible red fruit. It is Europe's big-gest native dogwood; a large shrub or small congested tree that flowers on its bare twigs in mid-winter or earliest spring.

Dove Trees and Black Gums

The dove tree grows to about 60 feet and as much across: a light-limbed and airy tree. The 'doves' (or 'handkerchiefs') grow along the whole length of its long branches in late spring, mingling with its bright green to make a most refreshing sight.

The dove tree looks rather like a linden (or lime) with over-size dogwood flowers. The two 'petals' of each flower have a leaf-like construction and one is four times as long as the other.

So many of the trees of North America have turned up again as survivors of the Ice Ages in China that there is considerable excitement when a family is found that holds out in only one of these refuges.

Leaving aside the ginkgo, no individual tree has caused quite so much wonderment as the *Davidia*, which, in 60 years, has become known as the dove tree, the ghost tree and the handkerchief tree.

Father David, the French missionary who first reported the panda, was also the first to report – in 1869 – a beautiful new tree in the mountains of western China. He told of huge white flowers, hanging like handkerchiefs (or fluttering like doves, according to the weather) from the branches.

Not until 1897 did another missionary, Father Farges, collect seed from the tree and send it home to France, to the great tree-collector Maurice de Vilmorin. Of the 37 seeds he sent only one germinated, but M. de Vilmorin planted it out in his arboretum at les Barres, and it did splendidly. It flowered in 1906 and the West saw its first dove (or handkerchief).

But Veitch's nursery, the most enterprising in Britain at the time, knew nothing of this Gallic transaction. They had just engaged the young Ernest Wilson and the first job they gave him was to collect the davidia. He set off in 1899. His only information about the tree came from Dr. Augustine Henry, the famous amateur botanist who

The fruit of the Davidia *is a green ball, purple-bloomed at first, containing a single hard, ridged, inedible nut. E. H. Wilson brought enough of these back from central China to recoup the costs of his expedition to find the tree.*

Tupelo or black gum is one of the events of the eastern American autumn. It is a swamp-loving tree, oak-like in construction, with lustrous leaves which blaze as bright as any maple when the cold nights come. Its flower is totally inconspicuous; its fruit a small blue oval. Neither (any more than the leaves) suggests its relationship to the dove tree. In Europe its autumn colour is less certain.

had lived in China for nearly 20 years. First Wilson had to reach Henry, who was in Yunnan in the southwest. Then, with Henry's instructions, he had to travel the 900 miles to Ichang in central China where the tree was. Henry drew Wilson a map – to show a solitary tree in an area the size of England.

Wilson was boat-wrecked in rapids. He was travelling through country that was notoriously unsafe; it was the time of the Boxer Revolt; and his Chinese guide was an opium addict.

He found the tree, though. Its stump was standing by a house that had just been built from its wood. 'I did not sleep that night,' he wrote in his diary.

Eventually, by combing the neighbourhood, he found a grove of davidias and collected their seed. When he sent it off to London he was sure it was the first ever to leave China.

He was bitterly disappointed when he came home to find that de Vilmorin already had the tree in his collection. But on closer examination it turned out that there were two different varieties. Farges's was named *Davidia involucrata* var. *vilmoriniana*, Wilson's *Davidia involucrata*.

The two varieties are almost identical, the only difference lying in the colour of the buds and the under-surface of the leaves. But oddly there is a big enough ecological difference for Farges's to be fully hardy in Boston, at the Arnold Arboretum, while Wilson's is not. The arboretum's original (about 1910) specimen of *D. involucrata* is still alive, but every winter cuts down the year's shoots to the ground. It is an interesting case of the borderline between a tree and a herbaceous plant, although few trees would stand such attrition for more than a few years.

The botanists' first impression of the davidia was that it belonged to the dogwoods. For just as in the dogwoods, the apparent petals of the huge white flowers turned out to be bracts. Where the dogwood has four equal ones, however, the davidia has two – and one is four times as long as the other. The leaves, moreover, are heart-shaped; more like those of the linden tree. It was not a dogwood, but it was a close relation. So it was given its own family of *Davidiaceae* (now *Nyssaceae*).

Nothing but a botanist's word would have convinced me that the nearest relation of the davidia, nearer even than the dogwoods, was the tupelo or black-gum, *Nyssa sylvatica*. Tupelo is an eastern American tree; common, though scattered, on moist ground throughout the whole of the eastern States. It has relations in China . . . other tupelos. But it has neither bracts nor heart-shaped leaves; the evidence for its connection with davidia lies in the intricacies of the little flowers and fruit. When tupelo is planted as an ornamental tree it is for its generally glossy and wholesome appearance – a strong and shiny green – and for its whole sunset of autumn colours. It goes with *Liquidambar* as one of the trees for a damp site on the sunny side of a pond. All summer long it deepens the water with its dark reflection; then suddenly in autumn it lights the surface with the reds and yellows of a flaming evening sky.

The Hollies

English holly has produced dozens of different varieties, making a fascinating collection of subtly different leaf-shapes and colours. **Right** *and overleaf are some of the outstanding cultivars and species – most of them growing slowly into big bushes or small trees.*

It must have struck you by now that the evolutionary order of things is a pretty funny one. To leap from poplars to strawberry trees; from laburnums to eucalypts to dogwoods to hollies seems like no kind of order at all. This, however, as far as we know, was how, over tens of millions of years, new trees developed. We can only be thankful that the randomness of evolutionary mutation and selection did produce such a mixed bunch; and wonder humbly how each one of them in its own way manages to be so intricately and originally beautiful.

There is no objective reckoning by which one tree is more beautiful than another. But one can have favourites. One of mine is the holly. And I find I am in good company: this is what John Evelyn had to say (about his holly hedge): 'Is there under heaven a more glorious and refreshing object of the kind than an impregnable hedge about four hundred feet in length, nine feet high, and five in diameter, which I can show in my now ruined gardens at Say's Court (thanks to the Czar of Muscovy) at any time of year, glittering with its armed and varnished leaves?'

Poor Evelyn. His fractured syntax makes it plain that he was distracted by having the Czar in the house. Peter (later the Great) was his tenant. He had come to England to learn about shipbuilding, and needed a house near the naval dockyard at Deptford. Who but a Czar, having discovered that his landlord was a passionate gardener, would have set about wrecking the garden?

The story goes that the Czar amused himself by having his staff wheel him through the holly hedge in a wheelbarrow. But apart from the difficulty (not to mention discomfort) of being any part of an assault on five feet by nine feet by 400 feet of holly, Evelyn's own words seem to contradict it. He goes on '. . . It mocks the rudest assaults of the weather, beasts, or hedge-breakers.' Whichever of the three he considered the Czar, it sounds as though the hedge survived.

Evelyn was, of course, talking about English holly, *Ilex aquifolium*. There are 400 species of holly, even deciduous ones (the American 'Possumhaw' for example). But it is a tree that has been in cultivation for ornament so long that the cultivars and hybrids outnumber the species. Most of the best of these are either variants on the English holly, or forms of a cross between the English holly and the native holly of the Azores.

Strangely, for a native, English holly is not 100 per cent hardy in England. Only a once-in-a-century winter will actually kill a holly tree, but really sharp weather can strip it of leaves. In consequence, its range

in the eastern States is limited to zone 6– from Connecticut southwards. Northwards the American holly (*I. opaca*) is hardy, and can be good for berries. But it lacks one of the English holly's principal virtues; what Evelyn calls its 'varnished leaves'. At its best it makes a distinctively matt, greyish or yellowish-green small tree (the biggest, 53 feet high, is in Texas) on which a good crop of red berries (or in the cultivar 'Xanthocarpa' yellow berries) shows up well.

The typical English holly, left to nature but given some woodland shelter, is slightly bigger (the tallest is 74 feet, the thickest 11 feet round) and almost as pointed as a Christ-

mas tree. But such trees tend to be thin and transparent. The best-looking ones are in hedgerows where the wind has a pruning effect: shorter shoots keep the foliage dense and stress the contrast of glitter and darkness that is half the pleasure. For this reason holly is best in summer, when the new shoots emerge so soft and shiny that they look (and even feel) wet. The new leaves glow with pink, brown and purple tones as well as green.

Most holly trees are either male or female, which means they need a mate if they are to bear berries. Many of the variegated cultivars, unfortunately, are male, and will never ▶

'The holly bears a blossom As white as the lily flower.'– The famous old carol gives the holly the crown of 'all trees in the greenwood'.

Top *Common English holly (Ilex aquifolium) with berries, borne only on female plants. They often last all winter.*

Upper middle *A narrow-leaved variety: I. aquifolium 'Angustifolia'.*

Lower middle *Hedgehog holly, I.a. 'Ferox', has fierce spines on all surfaces of its leaves.*

Bottom *I.a. 'Elegantissima' has wavy leaves with a white edge and faintly marbled centres.*

Top *Holly flowers in early summer, inconspicuously but with a sweet scent.*

Upper middle *I.a. 'Hastata' is a strange variety, with leaves long-spined at the base but with rounded tips.*

Lower middle *The silver hedgehog holly (I.a. 'Ferox Argentea') is both bright and bristly.*

Bottom *'Silver Queen' is a male (berryless) holly with yellow leaf-margins surrounding green and grey-mottled centres.*

Top *One cultivar (I.a. 'Bacciflava') has yellow berries, often in strikingly large quantities.*

Upper middle *I.a. 'Crispa' has thick leaves curling in bizarre contortions.*

Lower middle *Perry's silver weeping holly is a beautiful little dome of a tree. Masses of berries line its drooping branches.*

Bottom *I.a. 'Argenteo-marginata' is one of the several cultivars with silver-edged leaves.*

Holly and Box

▶ have berries. One would hope and expect that their names would give some indication of their sexes–especially as the most famous of them are called either Kings or Queens. But the Joker must have stepped in. 'Golden King' is a female; 'Golden Queen' a male. There is no 'Silver King' but 'Silver Queen' is also a male. These are all variegated with a band of either silver or gold round the margin of the leaf and green in the middle.

The two 'Milkboys', 'Golden' and 'Silver' (both male, reassuringly), have the alternative form of variegation; green round the edge and a beautiful mixture of apparent brush-strokes of dark green, light green and gold (or silver) in the centre. It is these plants with centre-variegated leaves that have a built-in tendency to revert to plain green. If you see any plain green shoots on them you simply cut them off. Sometimes, on the other hand, shoots with no green at all, leaves exactly the colour of that Swiss white chocolate appear.

On the left is a selection of the leaves of some of the best and most distinct hollies. Leaf-shape varies as much as colour. There is hedgehog holly (*I.a.* 'Ferox'–the fierce), both green and green-and-white, which has spines on all the surfaces of its strange hunch-backed leaves. There is 'Crispa', a rare cultivar on which everything–leaf, twig, branch and trunk–curls and contorts: a slow-growing, but ultimately unmatchable, specimen for a courtyard or a lawn. There is weeping silver-variegated holly (*I.a.* 'Argenteomarginata Pendula')–bright as a button and not in the least doleful. There is yellow-berried English holly ('Bacciflava'); there are purple-stemmed, unarmed, narrow-leaved and broad-leaved English hollies. And there are combinations of most of these characteristics. It is hard to think of any tree more worthwhile collecting, or more rarely collected.

Moreover, the crossing of English holly and *I. perado* from the Azores has produced another whole range known as the Highclere hybrids (*I.* × *altaclerensis*). On the whole these tend to be more vigorous than English holly, and less prickly. One of the most magnificent varieties is the camellia-leaved holly (*I.* × *altaclerensis* 'Camelliifolia') which has very few prickles, and those only on the lower branches. 'Golden King' is in fact supposed to come from this stable. 'J. C. van Tol' is famous for his (her) profuse berry-bearing. 'Silver Sentinel' is one of the tallest growing variegated hollies, and female. 'Purple Shaft' has tremendous deep purple shoots. 'Lawsoniana' has gold centres like the 'Milkboy'. . . . There are 20 or so: another whole collection.

Top *Hollies with gold or white margins (here, 'Golden Queen') often produce shoots with no green in the leaves at all.*
Upper middle *'Camelliifolia' is one of the best Highclere hybrids: very vigorous with numerous berries.*

Lower middle *'Lawsoniana' is another of the Highclere hybrids with golden variegation in beautiful brush-strokes and few prickles.*
Bottom *American holly, Ilex opaca, is similar to English. It has good berries but matt leaves.*

Top *'Golden Milkboy' is one of the best centre-variegated hollies, a variety of the English holly. It has no berries.*
Upper middle *'Golden King' is perhaps the most popular Highclere hybrid: a female with broad yellow leaf-margins.*

Lower middle *Ilex pernyi from China is one of the most elegant species with tiny leaves, often making a tall thin bush.*
Bottom *The surprising Ilex pedunculosa is a Japanese holly whose berries are carried on very long individual stalks.*

Below *Formal box. Box is the traditional material for low hedges round flower-beds in formal gardens, as here at Hampton Court Palace near London.*

Bottom *Natural box. Left to themselves, box trees are often many-stemmed and straggling. Their hard, even-grained wood is perfect for wood-engraving blocks.*

Among the species, which come from almost everywhere in the northern hemisphere, my own favourite is Father Perny's holly (*I. pernyi*) which was found by yet another of the French missionaries in western China. It has the smallest leaves of any; each one a crisp green diamond. It makes a sparkling little tree.

At the other extreme the Japanese broad-leaf holly (*I. latifolia*) you would take for a cherry laurel, with its long, wide, serrated but unprickly leaves. The Dahoon holly (*I. cassine*) of the southeastern States is also unarmed, but tender. There is a prettier and much hardier one from Japan which carries its berries on stalks as long as the leaves (*I. pedunculosa*).

There is only one word of warning needed about hollies: they do not like being moved after two or three years. It is very risky indeed to move them without a big ball of soil containing as much as possible of the roots. And even then it is better to move them in very late summer or mid-spring, when the roots can make some headway before the full demand of transpiration starts to dry out the plant. If a holly does seem to be under this sort of stress, take off some, or even all, of the leaves. It can recover from being denuded, but not from drying out. Do not assume, by the way, that a holly is its own protection against grazing animals; rabbits will eat an unprotected little plant down to the ground.

Defenceless box on the other hand they leave alone. Its smell, which is so attractive to us, the smell of old walled gardens in summer, they apparently shun. Box is more of a social than a botanical connection of holly, but it has some of the same virtues and is too modest a tree to have any vices. It seems equally happy cropped down to a six-inch hedglet grilling by a pathway in the sun or reaching up in permanent gloom as the undergrowth of thick woods. Wherever it is its neat, almost round, yellow-green leaves give it a satisfying texture.

Horse Chestnuts and Buckeyes

Far left, below left and below *The fruit, the flowers and the tree in flower. Horse chestnut, the biggest of our ornamental flowering trees, is a native of northern Greece. It is decoration pure and simple, with no economic value.*

There are no identification problems with the horse chestnut. It peddles a whole catalogue of its own patented paraphernalia. Item: one sticky bud – take indoors for an instant spring. Item: one huge fingered leaf, with no competitors for boldness of design. Item: one tall candle of flowers, as original as orchids. Item: one prickly green container, holding the most succulently shiny of inedible fruit – the conker.

Despite its manifest entertainment value, the horse chestnut gets a bad press. It is proclaimed 'dirty': which means it drops things. Its foliage is described as 'coarse': which means its leaves are big. And those responsible for public trees get themselves into terrible knots over the favourite sport of every nine-year-old: chucking sticks up at the conkers.

The horse chestnut was brought into western cultivation from Turkey in Elizabethan times. It soon proved to be not only the biggest of all flowering (or rather ornamentally flowering) trees, but to be completely hardy, to grow fast and to grow in any soil. Also to grow old. The oldest dated trees in Britain were planted in 1664 and one of them (in Surrey) is still 125 feet high.

Yet it remains essentially an ornamental tree, the sign of human habitation, of a park or a village. There are no woods of it:

its timber is hardly worth having. We plant it because we love its paraphernalia, but also its billowing, drooping outlines, its bright shade of green in early summer and its early autumn colouring of a warm yellow. It is one of the first trees to hang out its limp green flags in the spring.

America has its own set of close relations of the horse chestnut: the buckeyes. There is the red buckeye (*Aesculus pavia*) of the south; the sweet buckeye with yellow flowers (*A. flava*) from the Appalachians; the Ohio buckeye (*A. glabra*) with creamy flowers and the California buckeye (*A. californica*) with pink or white flowers. The

first three of these are medium-sized trees. The last, and also *A. parviflora* from the south, are elegant lounging shrubs.

The inevitable cross between the imported horse chestnut and the native buckeye (in this case the red one) has given us the red-flowered horse chestnut, *A.* × *carnea*. It is fashionable to regard this as the ideal horse chestnut for parks; its red (or rather dark pink) flowers and its small stature being regarded as advantages. But truth to tell it is a bit of a runt, and distinctly dowdy, beside the majesty of a full-scale horse chestnut flashing white flowers from ground level up to its cloud-like crown. If you must have

The sticky bud of the horse chestnut swells and begins to open in early spring: among the first trees to come into leaf.

The bud-scales fold back as the growing tip emerges. Six compound leaves and a spike of flowers are all packed into this little parcel.

The inner bud-scales hinge back as the white-furry shoot pushes the swelling leaves clear. An analysis of a horse chestnut shoot appears on pages 10 11.

The fledgling contents of the bud sort themselves out. The year's whole growth is made in this one flush: the thick shoot has all summer to ripen into wood.

The bold design of horse chestnut leaves is magnificent in autumn yellow. The tree colours more reliably in Europe than in America, however, and the leaves fall early.

Below *The red-flowered horse chestnut is a hybrid with the American red buckeye. It is a slower-growing, rounder, ultimately smaller tree than the true horse chestnut (below left). Its buds are not sticky.*

Right *One distant horse chestnut relation, Koelreuteria paniculata (the 'golden-rain tree') comes from China. Its flowers are similar, but hang down. Its bladder-fruit is very different. A wide small tree with beautiful feathery leaves and good autumn colour.*

Above *Japanese horse chestnut flanked by cedar and golden yew at Westonbirt, Gloucestershire. It has splendid three-foot-wide leaves and yellowish-white flowers with red spots.*

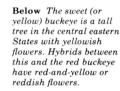

Below *The sweet (or yellow) buckeye is a tall tree in the central eastern States with yellowish flowers. Hybrids between this and the red buckeye have red-and-yellow or reddish flowers.*

Above *A hybrid between the white and red-flowering horse chestnuts, A. × carnea 'Plantierensis' has pale pink flowers but no fruit–often considered an advantage.*

Below *The red horse chestnut is unusual among hybrids in having fertile fruit which produces trees identical to the parents. It has one variety, 'Briotii', selected for deeper pink flowers.*

a smarter version the Swiss cultivar 'Baumanii' with double flowers (and no conkers) is a better choice.

Some of the common horse chestnut's oriental relations offer it serious competition. The Japanese horse chestnut (*A. turbinata*) has leaves as much as three feet wide. And the Indian horse chestnut (*A. indica*) brings into the family an indefinable grace and polish. The leaves are a little shinier, with perhaps a little more emphasis on the centre leaflet of the seven. It is different enough to catch your eye as an extra-handsome specimen, rather than a different and exotic species.

Left *Young leaves of the red buckeye of the southern States have a reddish tinge. Although it is one parent of the red-flowering horse chestnut it is an uncommon tree in cultivation.*

Above *The flowers of the Indian horse chestnut, perhaps the most graceful and distinguished member of its family. It flowers in mid-summer; another reason to plant this admirable tree.*

Above *The southern buckeye, Aesculus parviflora, has the most delicate flowers of the family in late summer. Strictly speaking this buckeye is a shrub: it spreads wide with no central trunk.*

The Maples of North America

The oaks, the hollies, the mountain ashes and the southern beeches get through to the semi-finals. But in the finals there is no competition. The maples are the trees with the most beautiful and varied foliage of all the broadleaves.

The maples' own rules are fairly lax. Among the 150 species there are shrub-sized maples and very big trees. Though there is a tendency to a hand-shaped leaf, interpretation runs through everything from a simple oval to a filigree of 15 fingers. Bark is almost as varied. Nearly all are deciduous. Though autumn colour is very much part of the game, there are maples whose leaves turn crisp and dismal brown, rattling to the ground with the first good frost. Very few maples make a show of flowering. Where their family loyalty is strongest is their fruit: they all have 'keys', consisting of two little nuts with one wing each, linked together by their bases; and in their almost universal rule of branching: two twigs at a time, opposite each other on the shoot.

Maples group curiously well by geography. America provides big and handsome ones, given to brilliant autumn colouring. Eastern Asia contributes small and intricate ones, carefully shaped and often beautifully coloured all summer. Europe has the strong silent ones; the bull of the family, the sycamore, for instance; or the workhorse, the field maple.

Europe has never seen anything like New England's maples in October. There is no describing, nor photographing satisfactorily, the trumpet-pitch of red their leaves achieve. And strangely you never seem to see two trees with the same tone side by side: the whole gamut of the highest-frequency colours is in use.

Sugar maple (*Acer saccharum*) and red maple (*A. rubrum*) grow together through most of the eastern States (though sugar maple not in the south). Both colour supremely well in the northern part of their range, where they get the right combination ▶

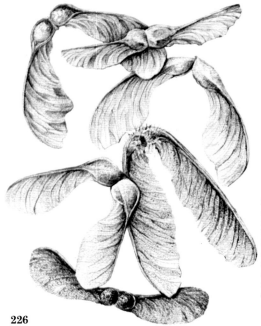

Keys are as much the hallmark of maples as acorns are of oaks. Every species has a different shape. Here, from top to bottom, are the keys of the sycamore, field maple, silver maple, bigleaf maple, sugar maple and Japanese maple.

Sugar trapped in the
dying leaves of maples
turns them an infinity of
fiery colours. New
England, where cold
autumn nights alternate
with sunny days, has the
most pyrotechnical palette
of anywhere on earth.

The Maples of North America

▶of sunny days and freezing nights. Over part of their northern range, they are joined by the black maple (*A. saccharum* ssp. *nigrum*). None, unfortunately, gives quite such a performance in Europe.

It is easy to confuse the sugar and red maples. They are in the same size range; medium to big, but never giants. They are dense trees, close-branched and rather upright; oval shapes in silhouette. Extremely upright forms of both (*A. rubrum* 'Columnare'; *A. saccharum* 'Temple's Upright') have been propagated. The clues are the red buds, flowers and leaf-stalks of the red maple. Its leaves have more acute angles; the sugar maple's leaf-lobes are separated by curves. The red maple grows faster, flowers earlier and often turns red earlier in autumn. Given moisture it will stand city conditions; sugar maple is essentially a countryman.

Silver maple (*A. saccharinum*) is the third one with a similar range. In summer it is a more obviously decorative tree. Its leaves are a cheerful light green backed with a soft silver lustre; their lobes are longer, parted with deep indentations almost like the red oak's. Unfortunately there is a history of accidents with the silver maple. Evidently it was over-commended for its beauty and speed (it is very fast) at the turn of the century in areas where conditions are too tough for it. It got a name for splitting in storms. Yet of all the big American maples this is the happiest in Europe. It makes a beautiful light-shaded wide-crowned tree remarkably quickly and turns a happy pale yellow towards the end of October. There are also cultivars with yellow-green leaves and deeply cut, almost shredded leaves (*A. saccharinum* 'Lutescens' and 'Laciniatum').

One has come to expect the west coast to produce something bigger. In maples it is the leaves. The tall-tree maple of the west coast is the bigleaf or Oregon maple (*A. macrophyllum*), which has whoppers. In the Pacific forest, where broadleaved trees (even narrow-leaved ones) are far outnumbered by conifers, the foot-wide foliage of the bigleaf stands out everywhere. In autumn when it is yellow or orange a single leaf shuffling to the floor among the dark fronds of Douglas fir is an incident worth watching. Bigleaf maple, like many western trees, thrives in Europe but not in the eastern States.

The native maple of the middle-west, so common there that it is often regarded as a weed, is the box elder (*A. negundo*). 'Elder' is easy to understand; it grows to about the same size in the same disorganized bushy way. 'Box' is more difficult. Box elder departs from the expected maple leaf-shape, simply by treating three (or sometimes five) lobes as three (or five) separate short-

Above *The sugar maple has rounded angles between the leaf-lobes, and its trunk is furrowed with distinct vertical lines, almost like boarding. It is one of America's best trees for autumn colour.*

Below *The red maple grows alongside the sugar maple and colours almost as brilliantly in autumn. Red maple leaves have sharp angles between the leaf-lobes.*

stalked leaves. It is the only American maple with this character; in the East there are several more.

There is scarcely an easier or more undemanding tree to be had. It can, and often does, grow in the dustiest and driest places. On the other hand it is dull in form, dull in colour and makes no special effort in autumn. It is one of the rare species in which the variegated form is superior to the normal one in almost every way. *A. negundo* 'Elegans' has yellow edges to its leaves and 'Variegatum' has white. Both are extremely conspicuous trees.

The west coast has its shrubby maple too;

Red maple makes a medium-sized tree, fast-growing and a tidy shape for street-planting. Autumn colour can be yellow (above left) or any shade of red: it rarely colours well on chalky soil. This picture was taken in Vermont.

Below *The flowers and half-grown leaves of the bigleaf maple of Oregon. Full-grown leaves of this tree can be a foot or more across, and the tree 100 feet high with luminous yellow-gold autumn colour.*

Below *Flowers of the red maple have just formed into tiny keys. It flowers early: the leaves are still in bud. Buds, stems and flowers of red maple are red. Young branches have bark (as here) as silvery as beech.*

Below *The box elder has its male and female flowers on separate trees. Here the male flowers appear with the opening leaves, which are in three pieces—each lobe on a separate stalk. Box elder is a common wild tree from New York to the Rockies.*

Below *The vine maple is seen here in the Cascade mountains of Washington in its usual company: giant firs. It is an insubstantial tree, sometimes literally a vine, but its leaves are eye-catching.*

Right *'Moosewood' (Acer pensylvanicum) is the striped-bark maple of America: a slender, light-shading tree with leaves tending to oval. The young stems are jade green and white.*

the vine maple (*A. circinatum*), so-called because in the tangle of the forest it often fails to make a real trunk, but wanders vine-like on the ground and up other trees. It is possible to make a tree of it, but more interesting to let it sprawl. It is one of the most worthwhile small maples for a garden; excellent in autumn and very pretty in spring with its purple and white flowers.

America has one striped-bark maple; a ravishing tree which the settlers christened, with inimitable earthiness, moosewood (*A. pensylvanicum*). A few Asiatic maples have the same characteristic: the constantly smooth, fresh green bark of a tree with its living cambium almost on the surface, vertically striped with bold chalk-marks.

Moosewood is a tall thin tree, as though in a hurry to get out of the moose's reach. Its rather sparse and spindly branches are a beautiful clear green like the trunk, or in one cultivar (*A.p.* 'Erythrocladum') a pretty pale pink, which turns red in winter.

Moosewood leaves are like ovals with wings; a totally different and memorable design. It can be too sparse a tree to plant in the middle of a lawn; one would tend to see right through it. Its place in nature is in light woodland, where its pale snake-bark blends with the fleeting shadows.

The Maples of the East

Right *Late-summer leaves and keys of the aconite-leaved Japanese maple (Acer japonicum 'Aconitifolium'), another low tree of richly distinctive texture which colours crimson in autumn.*

The maples, with the flowering cherries and the pines, are the cornerstone of Japanese gardening. They are the second annual event: April brings white and soft pink to the gardens and the woods; October the flame colours of ripening maple leaves. Composing tone poems with maples, however, is a less exact art than it is with cherries. For you never know exactly what colour a maple will turn. And cherries are constant year after year; maples louder or fainter according to the season.

None of the maples of the East is a big tree. Fifty feet is about as high as any of them go. But they have an incomparably rich range of variations on their elegant theme. Central China is the great reservoir of species. Many of the Japanese trees were imported from China in the distant past.

As far as the West is concerned *the* Japanese maple is the little shrub-size but tree-shaped plant with a domed head and fine-cut, often dark red, foliage. This particular tree, the most popular of all garden maples, is *A. palmatum*. 'Atropurpureum' is the dark red variety. Nurseries have concentrated on two variables; leaf colour and leaf shape. There are bright green, pale gold and bronzy green, as well as various mottlings and marginations, besides the red form. There is a second group, all known as

A. palmatum 'Dissectum', with their leaves cut right down to the stalk in a series of almost needle-like lobes. These are the weakest-growing kinds, never reaching tree height. They also come in red, bronze, purple and green. And there is a third group of relatively vigorous small trees with bigger leaf-lobes; normally seven of them, each with a serrated edge. Three of the best of these are *A. palmatum* 'Senkaki', which has red twigs and colours a thrilling clear yellow in autumn; *A. palmatum* 'Linearilobum', whose green or red leaves are shredded as deeply as the 'Dissectum' maple's; and 'Heptalobum Osakazuki', which simply turns furnace-red for a fortnight in October. The original 'Osakazuki' tree, imported from Japan in 1886, is at the British national arboretum at Westonbirt; 30 feet high with half a dozen stems. Although it is well-shaded by a huge red oak it lights its dark corner like a lantern. A glade at Westonbirt is given to seedlings of *A. palmatum* (which, being seedlings, have no more exact name). The range of shapes, sizes and colours is extraordinary.

The maples which botany knows as Japanese (i.e. the *A. japonicum* group) are not very different. The species tends to have more leaf-lobes (from seven to 11) and to grow a bit bigger, but the detail of a downy

leaf-stalk is the only crucial distinguishing mark. The three named cultivars of *A. japonicum* are all outstandingly beautiful small trees. 'Vitifolium' (vine-leaved) for its broad, fan-shaped leaves; 'Aconitifolium' for its deep-cut leaves and 'Aureum' for its pale warm-yellow leaves. The first two colour magnificently in autumn; 'Aureum' tends to be scorched by the sun and turn brown. With a little guidance all these trees will make wonderfully harmonious shapes, putting on a terrace of leaves here, a terrace there like the hand-movements of a Japanese dance.

Japan has one totally different maple, with simple oval leaves. Only the keys and the opposite branching give away the hornbeam maple (*A. carpinifolium*). It has the same corrugations between the leaf-veins as the hornbeam.

Some excellent species share the characteristic of the box elder: having the lobes of their leaves completely separate and on stalks. One of the rarest and most beautiful of all small trees, the paper-bark maple, *A. griseum*, has little three-leaf leaves, greyish underneath as the name suggests. The bark of this tree is much more like a birch than a maple; it peels away in tatters of rich red-brown. Even the bark of quite thin twigs starts crackling and coming away. As it does

For a combination of elegant shape with brilliant colour there is no small tree to compare with the Japanese maple (Acer palmatum). A score of its cultivars have different leaf shapes and colour. Here A. palmatum *'Osakazuki' blazes in autumn.*

Right *The Japanese maples with very finely-divided leaves (here, Acer palmatum 'Dissectum Atropurpureum') never grow higher than low mounds which perfectly display the beauty of their almost ferny texture.*

Below *The paperbark maple adds to the delicacy and autumn brilliance of its foliage the beauty of birch-like peeling bark in the warmest tones of red-brown. It is among the bigger oriental maples, growing as high as 45 feet, though slowly.*

Below *One of Japan's snake-bark maples, Acer rufinerve, has three-lobed leaves very similar to those of the American moosewood. Its variegated form 'Albolimbatum' is a superb tree.*

Above *The vine-leaved Japanese maple (Acer japonicum 'Vitifolium') has bolder and broader leaves than the others: magnificent as they turn by degrees to their final autumnal scarlet.*

Left *The nikko maple has leaves divided into three separate pieces like the American box-elder. In autumn colour it is far superior, turning shades of brilliant red or purple.*

Above *Japan's horn-beam maple departs entirely from the typical maple leaf design. The leaves are similar in shape and size to the hornbeam's and turn the same autumn colour.*

Hers's Chinese maple (Acer hersii), left, and the very similar A. davidii have some of the best striped bark. The leaves of David's turn yellow in autumn. Hers's turn bright red.

raced shape. It colours rich yellow in autumn. *Hersii* and another species, *A. grosseri*, have botanists in a tangle about whether they are two or one. Hers was a Belgian railway engineer, who improved his leisure, while hunting up timber for his tracks, by some very distinguished botanizing. For the gardener's purposes, rather than the botanist's, it is fair to consider his, David's and *A. grosseri* as one group; immensely decorative and valuable trees.

None of these trees is by any means common. The purple horned maple (*A. diabolicum purpurascens*), the biggest of the red-leaved maples of Japan, is more often planted – both for its leaves and its profuse pink flowers. The trident maple (*A. buergeranum*), with leaves that suggest the name, is popular in California. And the Amur maple (*A. ginnala*), from the north of China, whose leaves are similarly three-pronged but with teeth and a long central lobe, is grown a good deal in the north.

There remains one maple (*A. giraldii*) that tries to combine all the attractions; a paper-bark trunk with snake-bark shoots; big sycamore-like leaves with long pink leaf-stalks; beautiful autumn colour with a rich crop of keys. It only fails in its shape: it tends to long-branched stiffness. Needless to say it is the rarest of them all.

so it catches the light, so that the interior of the tree is always full of reddish lights and shadows. The leaves turn scarlet, and so do its thousands of tiny keys lining the branches. Unfortunately very little of this harvest is fertile: hence the tree's rarity.

The nikko maple (*A. nikoense*) is not common anywhere, even in Japan. Among the three-leaf species it is easily distinguished by having densely furry stems. The whole of a young tree bristles like a moss-rose. It grows into an upright fountain shape and colours brilliantly.

Another group of a good half-dozen has snake-bark more or less like the American moosewood. *A. davidii* and *hersii*, both from central China, are probably the best-known. *A. davidii* is a conspicuously coloured tree all year, with green-and-white bark, shiny green leaves which are heart-shaped and toothed rather than lobed, and bright red leaf-stalks. One of Westonbirt's examples is a wide-spreading tree of a beautiful ter-

Above *One form of the Japanese horned maple (the keys are 'horned') has purple foliage and purply-pink flowers, more conspicuous than those of most maples.*

Top *Acer davidii 'George Forrest' makes an open, spreading small tree with tiers of rich yellow foliage in autumn. It was introduced by Forrest from Yunnan in 1921 and is now the commonest form of David's maple in cultivation.*

The Maples of Europe

Below *'Brilliantissimum' is a most unexpected variety of the ordinary sycamore maple: a small tree whose leaves unfold in tender pink and gold (lower right picture), then turn pale yellow (upper picture), then bronze and finally green.*

Europe hasn't many maples. What she has on the other hand are exceptionally useful. Two of her maples are now basic planting material far beyond her frontiers. The sycamore and the Norway maple are among the fastest, hardiest and least demanding of all big trees. And both of them are prolific in coloured versions for ornament. One would not claim exquisite grace of design for any of them, but they are easy, colourful and on the whole tough and vigorous.

The sycamore-maple (*A. pseudoplatanus*) is the giant of the maple family. Also the beanstalk: it reaches full height in 60 years. It makes a great girthy tree, longer in branch than in trunk, with pale rough bark breaking into plates like rhinoceros armour. Its green winter buds break to produce so many dangling yellow-green flowers that a tree of mine that flowers with a neighbouring laburnum almost rivals it in beauty. The big leaves of the sycamore darken during the summer to yew-green, often overlaid with black by 'tar-spot' fungus. They have no autumn glory; but in compensation they soon fall after a frost.

You can tell a sycamore in spring without raising your eyes from the ground. It sows its seed with such abandon that the ground below is a lawn of its little strap-shaped seed-leaves uncurling. The town-dweller as a result often sees sycamore in the most unlikely and undesirable places. He comes to regard it as a tree weed.

Scotland (where it is known as the 'plane') is where the sycamore grows in its greatest beauty. On the windswept moors of the border country wind-shaped sycamores are drawn like hoods around the cowering farms. In the 'policies' (as they call the parks) of mansion and castle the 'plane' is the dark green cumulo-nimbus that defines where pleasure-grounds end and country begins. Above all the sycamore is the front-line defence against the salt-laden sea-wind. It may crouch, but at least it grows, and provides that minimum shelter in which other plants can start to grow.

Dark as the sycamore is, a purple pigment comes naturally to it and suits it very well. The purple sycamore *A.p.* 'Purpureum' or 'Spaethii' is a subtle tree; green at first glance, but with crimson flashes where the wind lifts a leaf. On top the leaves are green; underneath they are dark purply-red.

The golden sycamore *A.p.* 'Worleei' also works well, particularly in the spring. It is not such a big tree as the green or purple. But the doll of the family, without a doubt, is the almost-miniature *A.p.* 'Brilliantissimum', a little mop-head with leaves of a lovely faint pink at first, turning pale greeny-gold, then a bronzy colour with

Above and right *The European sycamore is one of the biggest of the maple family; fast-growing, immensely hardy and prolific with its seedlings. It makes a broad tree in the open, casting a heavy shade with its big dark green leaves.*

veins etched in green. Maples as a race are shy of the hottest sun. 'Brilliantissimum' should be kept in a light shade.

The Norway maple (*A. platanoides*) is looked on as a more refined tree and often used for street planting. It has many of the sycamore's qualities of speed and indifference to conditions, but less of a liking for the sea. Its leaves are of thinner fabric and a paler colour, and they turn splendid gold, rather briefly, in autumn. A Norway maple should be encouraged to branch as low as possible; its yellow-green flowers are early and relatively conspicuous. They repay a closer look.

Hardly any broadleaf tree, at least big tree, has given us such an imaginative catalogue of forms. There are mop-head, upright, cut-leaf, variegated and red forms, and one with strange angular leaves known as the eagle's-claw maple. The red pigment is not altogether satisfactory in this tree. Either there is too much or not enough. Some forms ('Goldsworth Purple' and 'Faassen's Black' are examples) start wine-red but turn a depressing dull purple-brown by summer. Some on the other hand – and these are much preferable – run out of red and end the season an original kind of bronzed green. 'Schwedleri' and 'Reitenbachii' are of this school. None of the fancy ones is as

good as the straightforward species.

America appreciates Europe's little hedge (or field) maple (*A. campestre*) more than Europe does. On the continent it is used to form hedges, but in Britain its growth is mainly wild. When I see it growing on the chalk downs in Kent I almost wish it came from Japan so that someone would make a fuss of it. Its yellow-gold is not exactly rapturous in autumn, but it makes a neat little tree with its very small leaves, and answers the shears as well as a beech. No doubt with a good choreographer it could adopt poses as graceful as any. Its golden form, *A.c.* 'Postelense', is exceptionally pale and fine.

Towards the Mediterranean its place is taken by the Montpellier maple (*A. monspessulanum*) which has three lobes to its leaves, a little like clover, instead of five.

The Italian maple *A. opalus* and the Turkish *A. cappadocicum* are both uncommon outside their own countries, but both well worth considering, the Italian maple for its yellow flowers, as early as March, and the Cappadocian for its dome of pale yellow in autumn. The variety of *A. cappadocicum* called 'Rubrum' has startling blood-red new shoots in summer. They are all trees of moderate stature; the convenient size for street-planting that urban authorities are always on the lookout for.

Above left and left The Norway maple is one of the fastest-growing and most adaptable trees, beautiful in flower (left) and in autumn colour (above left). It has produced a dozen coloured varieties, including some very dark purple ones.

Cashews and Sumachs

The nuts and leaves of the pistachio tree, by the French artist Redouté. He painted details of over 400 trees for Le Nouveau Duhamel *in 1801–19.*

The sinister principle of poison links the members of the cashew family. They all have to some degree the faculty of giving you a nasty rash. Poison ivy is the extreme example. But even the unroasted husks of cashew nuts can be irritant. Even mangoes (another tropical relation) can give people who eat them raw an extremely sore mouth.

The cashew is a Caribbean tree, a native of Haiti. The hardier nut-bearer of its race is the pistachio (*Pistacia vera*) of the eastern Mediterranean. Anyone who has sat in a cafe in Athens knows that the pistachio is a very profitable item of commerce in that part of Greece; old men and little boys are waiting in the wings to sell you a tiny bag for a huge price. There is another pistachio tree in the same area that produced the chewing gum (mastic; hence masticate for chew) which was issued to the inmates of harems to give them white teeth and sweet breath. Californians and Italians could have a shot at growing either of these useful trees. There is a *very* hardy pistachio (*P. chinensis*), but it has no comestibles to offer. It is grown for its upright shape, moderate size and first-rate autumn scarlet. It will perform in the same way at Palm Springs and Kew Gardens.

The graceful pepper tree from South America (*Schinus molle*) is also limited in Europe to parts with a Mediterranean climate and in America to zone 9. The pepper part of it is its little red berries. But what makes it so popular is the combination of thick gnarled trunk and branches with

The pepper tree of Peru is a feathery evergreen for a warm climate. Its autumn cascades of fruit like red peas make it popular in southern Europe.

The smoke tree envelopes itself in a haze of minute buff-coloured flowers, seen here becoming fruits. Their stems show up clearly against the foliage of the purple-leaved form. All smoke trees colour red in autumn.

Below *The cashew family produces a range of intriguing textures, including swansdown and velvet. The swansdown is the young flowering plumes of the smoke tree, seen at a later stage, below left.*

Stag's-horn sumach is so called for the texture of its shoots – exactly like a stag's horns 'in velvet' in the spring. It makes a low flat-topped tree, much given to suckering and forming a thicket.

The varnish tree (here with its flower spikes half-developed) is the oriental species of Rhus *(or sumach) whose sap makes lacquer: the brilliant paint-like coating of oriental furniture. Like many members of its family (including poison ivy) it contains a severe irritant.*

Right *A detail of a lacquered English chest from the reign of William and Mary (1689–1702). The fashion for lacquered furniture was at its height in the late 17th and early 18th centuries.*

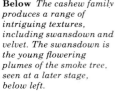
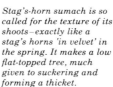

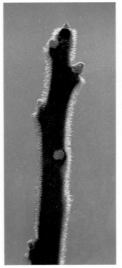

The most elegant garden form of the stag's-horn sumach (Rhus typhina 'Laciniata') has fretted leaflets on its big compound leaves, here in their autumn colour. The sumachs grow in most soils.

droopy, almost weeping branchlets. It reaches its ultimate height and equal spread of 35 or 40 feet in only 20 years. People are apt to install pepper trees in brand-new gardens, only to find that they have commandeered the whole place.

The two members of the cashew family important in northern gardens are *Rhus* and *Cotinus*. Rhus is best represented in the species known as staghorn sumach, from its antler-like growth with supple bends and very few twigs – and also for its antler-like texture; when stag's horns are 'in velvet' in the spring they have the same mossy covering. The species (*Rhus typhina*) is a native of the eastern States; a hardy and tenacious plant despite its exotic, subtropical appearance. Plant it in a border where its roots get pronged when you are forking around and it suckers freely. But it is a little tree well worth having for its scarlet lollipop fruit and its fiery autumn leaves.

Chinese rhus (*Toxicodendron vernicifluum*) is the source of lacquer for furniture. E. H. Wilson gives the recipes for the various colours in his account of his journeys. The natural colour of the dried sap (which can also give you a rash) is black. Oil from *Aleurites fordii* (tung, or Chinese wood-oil tree) is added to make it brown; mercuric sulphide to make it red. Apparently only in a hot climate does the sap give the right results.

Cotinus is the smoke tree. The European *C. coggyria*, common in gardens with its purple leaves and fawn fuzz of flowers, can hardly claim tree status. America's *C. obovatus* is more upright, and by all accounts one of the best-colouring plants even in the fire-box of an eastern autumn.

The Citrus Trees

Rue is a little herb with a strong smell. Few of the 1,600 plants that sail under its flag as *Rutaceae* are trees, but the few include the highly decorative and useful genus *Citrus*; also the eastern American hop-tree or wafer-ash and the Amur (which means, roughly speaking, Manchurian) cork tree.

Their flower structure puts them in the same evolutionary category as the maples. What singles them out as associates of rue is having in their leaves translucent glands filled with aromatic oils. Fastidious Frenchmen of the 18th century 'stopped their noses' with rue.

The orange tree, prettiest of the citrus family and the most able to stand relatively low temperatures, came into cultivation in Arab lands from the Far East at least 1,000 years ago. In 17th-century Europe the orangery, a room with big windows and a stove for over-wintering orange trees, became a craze. The huge white tubs containing the trees were manoeuvred into it in the early autumn and out into the garden again in the spring. The trees barely existed through the winter and would have died without their summer out of doors.

It was an essential part of the upkeep of the ornamental oranges in those days to hose them down regularly–even daily–to keep pests and disease at bay. Oranges are singularly prone to both.

A winter temperature in the upper forties is enough for an orange to thrive and set fruit. Spring is the season of blossom, so sweet-smelling that in orchard areas it can become too much of a good thing. The fruit takes a long time to come to maturity. The following winter is the normal harvest

Top *The charm of orange trees lies in their glossy evergreen foliage against which white flowers and bright orange fruit stand out like decorations – often both at the same time, since fruit takes a year or more to ripen.*

Above *Lemon trees are less hardy than oranges, but no less ornamental. Here at Marlia in Italy the lemon garden has trees in pots. They are put out in the spring and taken indoors for the winter.*

Right *The 'orangery' is a 17th-century invention: a building with tall windows for sheltering oranges through the winter. Here, at Fontainebleau, the orange trees are in their summer order in front of the orangery.*

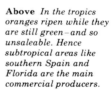

Right *The soft blackish bark of the Amur cork tree from northern China at the Trompenburg arboretum, Rotterdam. The trunk often forks low and massive furrowed branches take over, making a most impressive wide-spreading shade tree.*

Left *The very hardy cork tree has big bright green leaves like the tree of heaven's and small black plum-like fruit. Only the aromatic essence in glands in the leaves suggests its relationship with the rue family.*

period in subtropical conditions, but in cooler parts oranges are not ripe till the following summer–hence the charming combination of fruit and flowers on the same tree together.

The citrus list is formidable. Apart from the sweet oranges there are Seville oranges (bitter; the best for marmalade) tangerines with their reach-me-down skin, lemons (the least hardy trees), limes (which gave their name to all the 'limeys' who sailed on British ships and drank lime-juice to ward off scurvy), grapefruit and its forebear the shaddock, citron with its thick skin, used for flavouring cakes. The list of hybrids is as long. There is the ugli (a cross between grapefruit and tangerine), the citrange, the limequat, the tangor, the orangequat and even the citrangequat. The -quats involve the blood of China's shrubby, sour-fruited kumquat (*Fortunella margarita*), which is a hardier plant.

The Japanese bitter orange (*Poncirus trifoliata*) is hardy even in Britain and up to Boston. It can scarcely be called a tree, but it has plenty of flowers and little oranges that make adequate marmalade.

The same chemistry gives the little hop-tree (*Ptelea trifoliata*) one of North America's best-smelling flowering seasons, and in a smaller degree pervades the Amur cork tree (*Phellodendron amurense*) and the Korean *Tetradium daniellii*. It is occasionally planted as a hardy small tree with midsummer scented flowers. The Amur cork tree is planted more for its corky bark, which looks impressively bulky on its thick, wide-reaching branches. Both these Asiatic trees have long compound ash-like leaves.

Above *In the tropics oranges ripen while they are still green–and so unsaleable. Hence subtropical areas like southern Spain and Florida are the main commercial producers.*

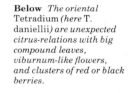

Below *The oriental* Tetradium *(here T. daniellii) are unexpected citrus-relations with big compound leaves, viburnum-like flowers, and clusters of red or black berries.*

Above *Lemon trees need less summer heat than oranges to ripen their fruit–but they also need warmer winters. They should be able to survive where temperatures never fall below about 44° F.*

237

The Ashes of North America and Europe

Right *The weeping ash is a spectacular lawn tree, particularly in winter when its stiffly hanging rod-like branchlets are visible. Weeping branches can be grafted on to a normal ash at any height: even 100 feet up.*

Not even the oak carries quite such significance out of the murk of legendary time as the ash. In which cold land of myth-making was it such a conspicuous tree? Somewhere on the Baltic shores where the Vikings' ancestors spent the dark evenings scaring themselves with sagas and dreaming up dragons, primeval ash-woods must have held them in awe. To them the ash was Yggdrasil, 'the greatest and best of all trees. Its branches spread over the whole world, and even reach above heaven.' At the top (so they said) sat an eagle; at the bottom a dragon. In between a squirrel scrambled up and down like Henry Kissinger relaying endless threats and counter-threats.

Was it size alone that promoted the ash to this position? Certainly it is one of the tallest of Europe's broadleaves. It has reached 150 feet in modern times. Linnaeus' name for it, *Fraxinus excelsior*, stresses its height.

It is not exceptional in leaf: best perhaps when its grey-green leaflets stream in the wind. It is more conspicuous in winter: notably austere, grey-barked and sparse-branched. Dryden wrote 'nature seems to ordain the rocky cliff for the wild ash's reign'.

Botanically the ashes belong to the olive family, which also includes (among common garden plants) privet, lilac and jasmine. The family traits are by no means obvious (unless you count opposite branching, which is common to most of them, but to thousands of other plants too). The fruits of ash and olive could hardly be less alike.

Most of the world's 60 or so ash species conform to the general style of *F. excelsior*. They have compound leaves; the leaflets arranged in opposite pairs (except for the

The manna ash is always a tree to watch, from the tulip-like unfolding of its grey-green buds into leaves and copious flowers to the gentle autumn colouring of its dense and shady foliage.

The common ash seeds itself widely and comes up fast, making a tall, wide-spreading, grey-barked tower of the finest quality timber. This typical tree is in the south of England, at Hambledon near Portsmouth.

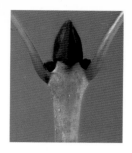

Below *The flowers of the common ash colour the bare branches well before the leaves (which come late to this tree).*

Below right *'Keys' of the ash are rather like half a maple key. They hang in dense bunches, often right through the winter, and germinate almost as prolifically as those of the sycamore.*

Right *The ash carries leaves and buds in opposite pairs, making a branch pattern that often makes a young tree in winter easy to recognize. The common European ash has matt black winter buds unlike any other tree's.*

odd one at the end) on a green stalk seldom more than a foot long. They have simple, single-winged keys for fruit. They are vigorous, dense-rooted and demanding of the soil: easy to transplant but bad to grow near shrubs: liable to commandeer all the rations.

All North America's common ashes follow this general pattern. The white ash (*F. americana*) is the tallest, best for timber and most commonly planted. The basic hardiness of the race comes out in the fact that it grows as well in Europe as in America; not true of American oaks, beeches or elms. White ash is white and downy beneath the leaves; in autumn purple in the north; yellow farther south.

Red ash and green ash (*F. pensylvanica* and *F.p. subintegerrima*) are varieties of one species; the green one (green beneath the leaflets) the commoner of the two, with the biggest natural range of any of them. These, and several other American ashes, have a great advantage as street trees: they are fast-

growing at first, but slow down and form round crowns at about 60 feet.

The same size range includes black ash (*F. nigra*; a far-northern swamp tree), blue ash (*F. quadrangulata*) from the southeast and velvet ash from the southwest. Blue ash has twigs with a square cross-section, and bark which makes blue dye. Velvet ash (*F. velutina*) has a downy layer on both twigs and leaves, together with a dense fashion of leafing that makes it a good shade tree.

Only the Oregon ash of the northwest (*F. latifolia*; a Douglas discovery, named by him for its broad leaflets) grows to the same sort of height as the white ash.

There are European ashes that give relief from this generally business-like approach. There are narrow-leaved kinds (the cultivars and varieties of *F. angustifolia*); an odd one with only one leaf at a time (*F. excelsior* 'Diversifolia') instead of nine or 11; one with dandelion-yellow bark (*F.e.* 'Jaspidea') which is remarkably conspicuous in winter;

and above all the weeping one: to me the best of all weeping broad-leaf trees. Weeping ash (*F. excelsior* 'Pendula') manages to be both stiff and graceful together. It is made by grafting weeping branches on a stem already grown to the required height; this has been done, successfully, to a tree 90 feet high. It is a particularly fine sight in winter when its hanging ramrods of branches are like wooden rain.

But the biggest departure from what we expect of ashes comes in the group that flaunts its flowers. Of these the manna ash of southern Europe (*F. ornus*) is by far the best known. The flowers are showy, creamy-white, in May. But they are only half the story. The whole tree is so voluptuous in glossy leafage that others look quite abashed beside it. It stands out in staid parkland like the velvet-framed bosoms of Nell Gwynn and her contemporaries on ancestral dining-room walls.

A storm-cloud picks out the pale bark of the green ash – America's most widespread species. America's tallest ash is a hybrid between this and the white ash – a 'pumpkin' ash 130 feet high in Missouri.

The yellow ash (Fraxinus excelsior 'Jaspidea') is a fine form of the common ash which colours gold in autumn (the common ash stays green till leaf-fall) and has distinctly yellow bark – very striking in the winter sun.

Olives and Fringe-Trees

If your fairy godmother would let you grow just one tree from outside your climate-zone what would it be? For me the answer is not the coconut palm nor even the lovely weeping blue cypress of Kashmir. I would choose the olive.

Olive-trees have Homeric style. I cannot see flowering cherries in the Elysian fields. I can see grey olive-orchards, black cypresses and pines. Grace and gravity the olive has, living as long as yew, growing as gnarled, yet still leafing with a silver spray.

The olive tree is given to branching low, and its branches to wandering. Down into them through leaves like the white willow's pours Mediterranean light. The range of the olive in Europe has always been taken as the limits of the Mediterranean world. Wherever olives are planted they bring their mood. No Doric columns, no transplanted temple ever brought the classical world into America as powerfully as an olive grove.

Olives love the sun and dread humidity. They like the soil deep but dry. Florida is not such good olive country as California, and of California the south and the central valley is best. They are slow trees to grow. But they have one great advantage: by diligent digging and packing of its roots, you can move even an ancient olive.

The best imitation olive tree I have seen in a northern garden was its cousin *Phillyrea latifolia*, a favourite Victorian evergreen. Phillyrea can be remarkably olivey in shape: only very dark green.

To turn from olive to its cousin privet sounds at first like a descent from the sublime to the ridiculous. And is privet a tree? Common privet isn't: just one of the necessary evils of gardening. But its Chinese counterpart with glossy leaves (*Ligustrum lucidum*) is one of the best hardy (to zone 7) evergreen trees.

Vogue would no doubt call this the wet-look privet. Its leaves are long, camellia-size, dark green and glossy. In summer it carries upstanding batons of white flowers

Olive wood is hard but smooth-grained and ideal for carving into implements. Monks in the monasteries of Mount Athos have made a small industry of olive-wood spoons and bowls.

Far left and left *Unripe green olives and the swollen, wrinkled, oily black ripe fruit. Olives for oil are left on the trees to ripen: eating olives are picked both half-ripe and ripe.*

Above *The ancient marriage of oil and wine; olive trees and vines grow together on the terraced hillsides of the island of Samos in the Aegean, punctuated with black spires of cypress.*

The glossy privet of China is in a class apart from common hedge-privet. It makes a beautiful and hardy small evergreen tree with pointed shiny leaves and masses of white flowers in autumn.

Left *Olive-trees can live for 1,500 years or more. They share with yews the distinction of being Europe's oldest trees. In age they become grotesquely gnarled, in wonderful contrast with their light silvery foliage.*

Below *The olive-harvest in the Mediterranean takes place in the winter. The ripe olives are beaten from the trees with long poles and gathered from the ground. In this close-planted grove in Dalmatia the trees are growing unusually straight and tall.*

with the rather sickly privet smell. Thirty feet (fairly fast) is about as high as it grows, but 30 feet of such intense dark green gloss can be quite a showpiece – especially with such a heavy load of flowers.

One of the stranger tales E. H. Wilson told of backwoods China is the story of the wax-insect. It seems almost as though the insect sensed that the privet and the ash are of one family. In one valley in the west (at Chien-ch'ang to be exact) the wax-insects breed on the leaves of the Chinese ash, *Fraxinus chinensis*. In May they are collected in boxes and carried by coolies, travelling only at night (it being too hot for the insects during the day) for 200 miles to their feeding ground – the leaves of the privet-trees of Kiating. Such extraordinary pains are rewarded by three months of unrelenting wax-laying, when the insects weigh down the privet with hundredweights of the finest wax – used for candles, for coating paper and polishing jade. Whether the Cultural Revolution left the wax-coolies in business we may one day find out. But how did the business start?

With a bit of imagination one can see the fringe-tree (*Chionanthus*) as the missing link in the olive-ash family; close enough to the ash to be grafted on its roots, flowering rather like the flowering ashes and with fruit not unlike the olive.

But a fringe-tree in flower, more fringe than tree, needs no botanical footnotes. Like the ashes it comes late into leaf, but almost at once, in June, puts on a covering of white flowers: five spidery-thin petals joined at the base (whence 'fringe'). It is one of the most stunning small trees (or big shrubs) that a northern garden – on any soil – can grow.

Olives for oil are first crushed with a stone roller (left) then pressed like grapes in a huge vice (right). The ancient process is shown here in a 16th-century Flemish engraving.

There are two species of fringe-tree: Chinese and North American. The American (above left) has drooping flowers in enormous quantities (but not as a young bush). Its leaves appear very late in

the spring. The Chinese fringe-tree (above right) carries its dainty and fragrant flowers in erect clusters – by the million. Both species do best in a continental climate.

The Tree of Heaven and the Cedrelas

It is possible for a tree to be too easy and prolific–to devalue itself by appearing whether it is invited or not. The tree of heaven, *Ailanthus altissima*, makes this mistake. But before dismissing it as an urban weed we should look closer. Its leaves, often dismissed as 'coarse', are among the most impressively tropical-looking of any hardy tree's: plumes, sometimes a yard long, of as many as 30 substantial pointed-oval leaflets. Yet with these splendid leaves it contrives to remain open and light-shaded; often forked and wide-spreading; rarely more than 60 feet high.

Trees of heaven are (usually) either male or female. There are disadvantages to both; the male flowers smell nasty, but then the female has offspring. The female, however, is definitely the tree to buy if you have a choice: its fruit, bunches of propeller-like keys ripening bright red, is as good as a flowering season.

There is said to be no limit to the range of soils and other substances (ash, gravel, garbage) in which the tree of heaven will seed itself and thrive. On the other hand moving bigger trees is not so certain. I have been disappointed by standard trees set in good soil with loving care.

The way many people take advantage of such noble leaves without having to accommodate a whole tree is to cut the whole thing back every year as coppice. The effect in a border is of some ferocious fern, in which you will observe a curious habit: the leaf-stalks, usually in such compound leaves as deciduous as their leaflets, seem undecided as to whether they are leaf-stalks or permanent twigs. Often they let their leaflets fall some time before they let go themselves.

All the tree of heaven's close connections are tropical: the West Indies is the home of several *Quassias* that are relations. The West Indies is also the headquarters of the mahogany family, of which one branch, the Spanish cedar (*Cedrela odorata*) and its Chinese counterpart (*Toona sinensis*) is remarkably like the tree of heaven.

The Spanish cedar gets its inappropriate name from its scented wood; the wood of cigar-boxes. The Chinese Cedrela or toon has little-known gastronomic potentialities. Its young shoots and leaves, which are delicate shades of pink and cream, are said to be delectably oniony: to the Chinese a vegetable. I can't help wondering how long the ones in the streets of Paris would remain so leafy if this were generally known.

The Chinese toon has other advantages over the tree of heaven: its yellow autumn colour and its bigger (and unscented) flowers. On the other hand it is a smaller tree and not quite so hardy.

Only in the south of Britain, and then only as a shrub, can we grow *Melia azedarach*, its near-eastern subtropical relation. Melia is fast-growing and shady; pretty in leaf but prettier after leaf-fall, when the yellow berries stay glistening in its crown.

Above and left *The bead tree or chinaberry; an ideal fast shade-maker in a hot climate, needing little moisture. The small, pale-lilac flowers, left, are fragrant. Above, the tree in early winter, a tangle* *of yellow berries. The berries remain on the tree long after the leaves have fallen. The hard, bony seeds inside them were strung together to form rosaries, hence the name 'bead tree'.*

Right *Three-foot ash-like leaves are perhaps the strongest point of the tree of heaven. They can lend an exotic subtropical air to any group of trees. Cut right down to the ground regularly and* *heavily manured an* Ailanthus *base will throw up monster leaves which can be an exciting ingredient in a shrub or herb border. The variety 'Pendulifolia' has even larger, drooping leaves.*

Left *The Chinese* Idesia polycarpa *(the only tree of its genus) has been described as 'like a small-leaved catalpa', with a splendid autumn display of red berries in heavy clusters.* (Flacourtiaceae)

Top and above *The ash-like fruit of the tree of heaven (on female trees only) is normally faintly coloured like the example at the top. The variety* *'Erythrocarpa' (above) has darker green leaves and bright red fruit which makes a good show from late summer into autumn.*

Above *The tree of heaven gets its name from its height. Tall trees like this, however, are the exception. America's biggest, on Long Island, is 60 feet high and 80 wide.*

Above *Toona (the 'Chinese cedar', or 'toon') has lagged behind the tree of heaven in popularity, although it makes an admirable street tree in Paris (as here) and has the bonus of onion-flavoured leaves.*

Right Ehretia *is another small Chinese genus of trees which remain rare, though they are easy and rewarding to grow. E. dicksonii develops rapidly into a short broad tree with ten-inch leaves and June flowers.* (Boraginaceae)

Empress Trees and Indian Beans

Left *The catalpa (or Indian bean) of the southern States is a remarkably hardy garden tree, suffering only from strong winds which bruise its big soft leaves.*

Below *Catalpa leaves are heart-shaped, softly furry, and as much as ten inches long by eight wide–in young trees even larger. The purple tint of new leaves makes the new shoots conspicuous.*

Big pale crushable leaves give a tree the look of being in tropical kit. In Florida or Cap Ferrat you wouldn't give the *Catalpa* a second glance: which makes it all the more effective in Philadelphia or Frinton.

The catalpa and the *Paulownia* (or empress tree) are two trees northern gardens can grow as a reminder of the jacaranda and other tropical excesses. They are so similar in most ways that one is surprised to find them in different botanical families–respectively the *Bignoniaceae* and the *Scrophulariaceae.* What they have in common are flowers like foxgloves, weak and pithy young wood, and their oversize leaves. The

most obvious difference is that catalpa's flower-clusters hang while the paulownia's stand erect. And that catalpa flowers are white spotted with purple, while paulownia's are purple all over.

Catalpa's other name of Indian bean tree only reinforces the tropical impression. But Indiana bean tree would be nearer the mark. It is a mid-western native; another of the trees that turn up only in North America and China; nothing to do with India–only with Indian beans; its pencil-like pods.

There are two American catalpas: the southern *Catalpa bignonioides*, more common in gardens, and the northern *C.*

speciosa, a far bigger tree, making (surprisingly, considering its pithy shoots) timber that will lie on the wet ground for a century and not rot.

The southern catalpa is also the commonest in Europe. It tends to spread, even to sprawl, from a short trunk, or from none. Its heart-shaped leaves start hairy in the spring, growing shiny above as they reach their full nine or ten inches, at flowering time in mid-summer. Young trees produce only leaves, but old ones sometimes perform prodigiously with clusters of their extremely elaborate flowers.

The place for a catalpa is on a lawn that

Left *The empress tree or royal* Paulownia *is well-named: a conspicuous but impractical tree with huge leaves, weak and pithy wood, and flowers which appear in bud in autumn and often succumb to frost. Its fruit follows the flowers on tall spikes.*

Jacaranda is a flamboyant Brazilian cousin of Catalpa *and* Paulownia*: a gaudy tree in flower even by tropical standards. Its ferny-fine leaves are almost evergreen and its habit horizontal, making it a first-class shade tree for tropical and subtropical cities.*

Kalopanax septemlobus are armed with stout, sharp prickles.
Below *The glossy green leaves of* Kalopanax *are similar in shape to those of the sweetgum or a maple. The tree carries white flowers in flat heads in autumn.*

Left *The scented foxglove-shaped flowers of* Paulownia tomentosa *are a pale shade of heliotrope which easily merges with a bright sky. They need to be offset by a dark background.*

Below *The golden Indian bean tree,* Catalpa bignonioides *'Aurea', is one of the most striking of all yellow-leafed trees. The leaves are big and velvety in texture.*

has both space, sun and shelter from wind. Such rare spots are not lightly allotted, though. A tree must be more than merely conspicuous to compete. There are hybrid catalpas (American crossed with Chinese species) that offer further distractions: double-size leaves in the case of *C.× erubescens* 'J. C. Teas'; purplish ones in the case of *C.×e.* 'Purpurea'. Best of all is the golden cultivar of the southern catalpa, *C.b.* 'Aurea'; the nearest thing to a permanently sunlit hill.

The empress tree (*Paulownia tomentosa*) can be disappointing for flowers in northern gardens. It has the rather illogical habit of forming substantial flower-buds in autumn, which winter-cold often kills. Some gardeners for this reason forget about them altogether and coppice the plant, taking advantage of its natural vigour to force huge furry leaves out of it. It seems that the more recently introduced *P. fargesii* from China may do better with flowers – and also make a bigger tree.

No botanical considerations, only the arresting strangeness of the tree, brings the rare *Kalopanax septemlobus* in here. With the related thorny shrubby *Aralias* (Hercules' club and the Japanese angelica tree) it is botanically nearer the dogwood, with the same little massed florets and seeds arranged in a ball. *K. septemlobus* (sometimes called the castor aralia) is most like a succulent sycamore or a sweetgum in leaf: a striking pile of glossy greenery. But it is its winter frame that is really distinctive: its few, thick and forky twigs make memorable sky-writing. There could be no better tree to sharpen up bland avenues of plate-glass offices.

Aralia is more often shrub than tree. The most worthwhile of the genus are the variegated forms of the Japanese angelica tree (*A. elata* 'Variegata'). The leaves are huge and many-leafleted. In mottled green and creamy-white they look both ferociously tropical and innocently pretty.

The Elders

Evolutionarily new-fangled as they are, elders are still ancient in human history. The Latin *Sambucus* takes us back, via Greece, to very ancient things . . . among them the sackbut that accompanied the Psalms. Elder still makes whistles, as every schoolboy knows, and wine, as every grandmother did.

The elders and viburnums are close kin, as their flat flower-clusters show. The viburnums are unusual in sometimes having two kinds of flowers in one cluster: some working (i.e. sexual) and some purely to attract insects. The related hydrangeas do the same. Most insect-fertilized flowers, as W.J.Bean puts it, 'do their own advertising'. Yet here in this relatively recent design a division of labour is introduced.

In playing to the gallery like this they have played into the nurseryman's hands. The snowball tree (*Viburnum opulus* 'Sterile') is a form of the 'guelder rose' in which the sterile parts have been kept and the sexual rejected: the flower is all the showier.

The elder of elders is the truly tree-like blueberry elder (*Sambucus caerulea*) of the Pacific northwest. It grows in the wild to 50 feet and staggers under its late-summer load of bloomy fruit.

Common elder (*S. nigra*) will be a bush (and very likely a weed, too) if you let it. But such a vigorous and uncomplaining–and immensely hardy–plant can easily be harnessed into service. It will grow in dense shade, on a minimum of soil–and deliver barrow-loads of berries. Its worst point is its smell–not of the flowers (though this is a matter of opinion) but of its pithy new wood. Flies apparently agree: carters used to make chaplets of elder to keep the flies from their sweating horses' heads.

Several viburnums reach tree stature–though not strictly speaking the wayfaring tree, the only one with a tree name. Wayfaring tree (*V. lantana*) is a European hedgerow bush with white-wool-backed leaves which have much the same effect as the whitebeam. It was William Turner the Elizabethan herbalist who likened it to a wayfarer come from a dusty road.

The eastern American blackhaw (*V. prunifolium*) and the sheepberry or nannyberry (*V. lentago*) are the principal viburnums of North America which make small trees. Both are worth growing for their autumn colour, apart from their edible fruit and masses of white (or off-white) flowers.

John Evelyn must have the last word: the pleasure he took in matching trees and words comes so clearly over 300 intervening years. He is speaking of inflammation. 'An extract of elder is efficacious to eradicate this epidemical inconvenience.'

Left *A typically vigorous common elder (here in North Wales). The elder is considered too coarse and vigorous (and free-seeding) for gardens. American blueberry elder is the most ornamental tree-sized species.*
Below Left *The wayfaring tree is conspicuous in spring with its dusty-white shoots and in autumn for its jewel-like fruit which turns from red to black.*

Above *The common elder is weighed down with sweet-scented flowers in early summer. The broad flat heads make heavy clusters of sweet black berries.*
Below *The berries of the 'guelder rose' (Viburnum opulus) turn and remain ruby-red, hanging on far into the winter. It is a tree or tall spreading bush for wet or boggy ground. The lobed, maple-like leaves colour richly in autumn.*

Reference Section and Index

R

Contents

Urban, Pastoral, Classical, Romantic . . .

*Four very different entirely man-made tree-settings,
all photographed in spring, illustrate
the power of trees to create an atmosphere.
The species in the pictures are detailed
in the diagrams opposite.*

The urban *On the East
River in downtown
Manhattan flourishing
trees in private gardens
make a bizarre contrast to
the city skyline. Most
surprising are the firs
(above the footbridge).
Polluted air can kill
conifers more quickly
than most trees, yet these
seem healthy.*

The classical *Stourhead
in Wiltshire, one of the
great English 18th-
century landscape
gardens has been en-
riched (some say over-
enriched) with 19th-
century tree-planting.*

The pastoral *The
simplest native ingredients
give the most powerful
effect of Elysean peace at
Olantigh in Kent.*

The urban
Right

1 Honey locust *Gleditsia triacanthos*

2 Tree of Heaven *Ailanthus altissima*

3 Maidenhair tree *Ginkgo biloba*

4 Colorado white fir *Abies concolor*

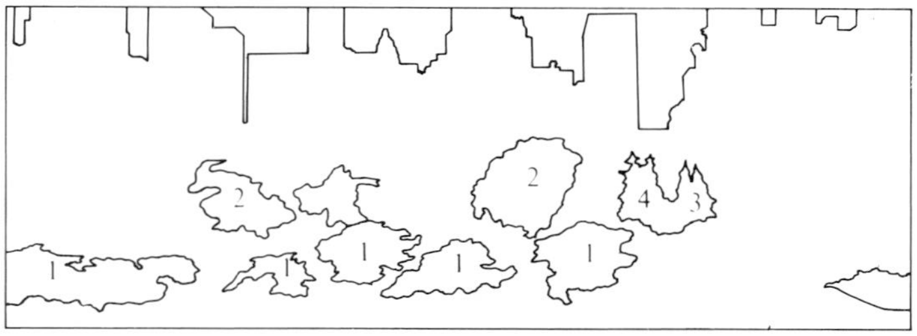

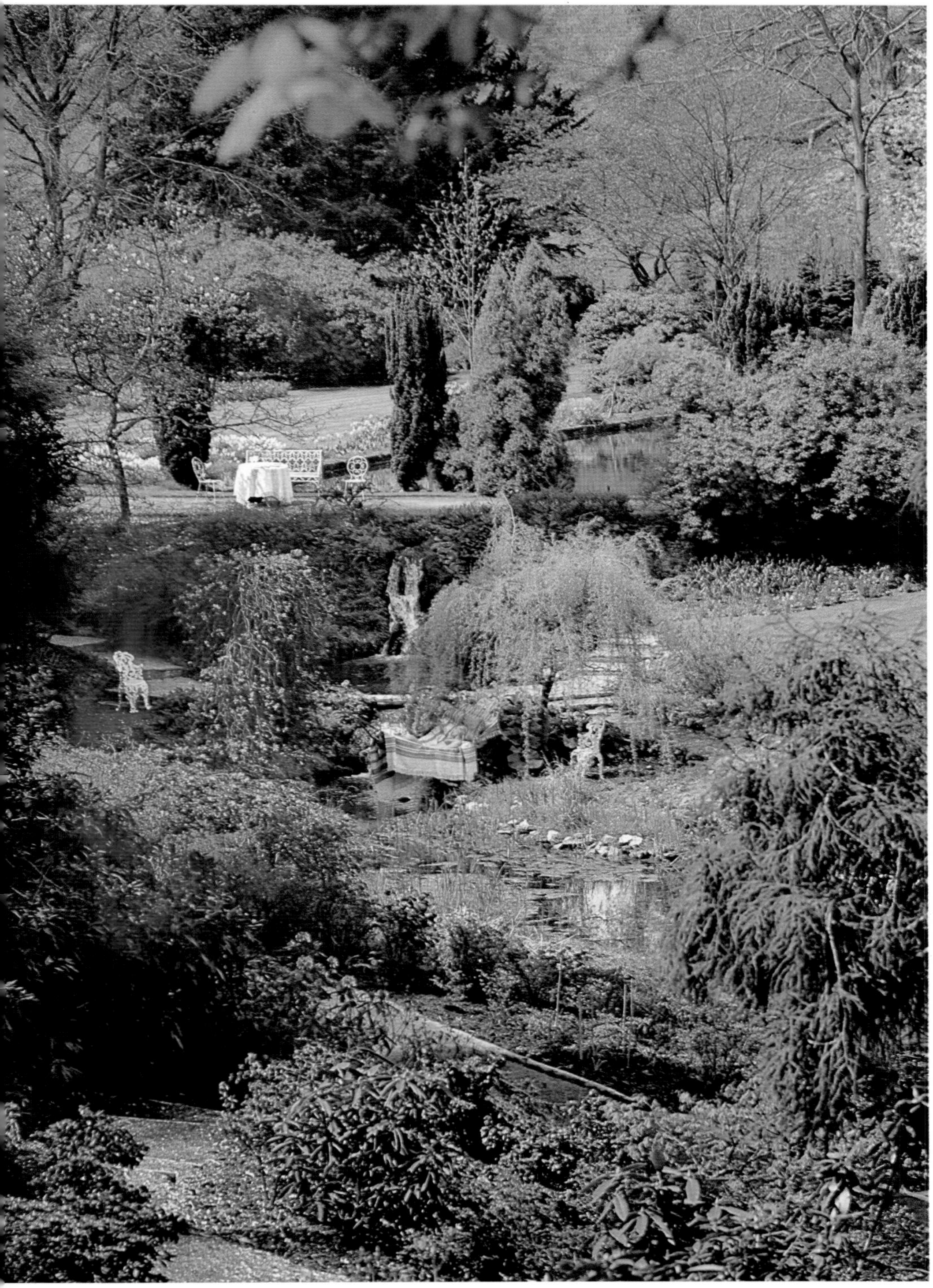

The romantic *A very private paradise-garden in the South of England uses exotic trees and the sense of enclosure to create a fantasy world entirely removed from the surrounding country.*

Right

7 Tree of Heaven *Ailanthus altissima*

8 Weeping silver pear *Pyrus salicifolia* 'Pendula'

9 Weeping willow *Salix × sepulcralis*

10 Rhododendron

11 Coast redwood *Sequoia sempervirens*

The classical
Below

1 and 9 Caucasian fir *Abies nordmanniana*

2 Monkey puzzle *Araucaria araucana*

3 and 5 Weeping ash *Fraxinus excelsior* 'Pendula'

4 Cedar of Lebanon *Cedrus libani*

6 Copper beech *Fagus sylvatica* 'Purpurea'

7 *Chamaecyparis pisifera* 'Filifera aurea'

8 Tigertail spruce *Picea torano*

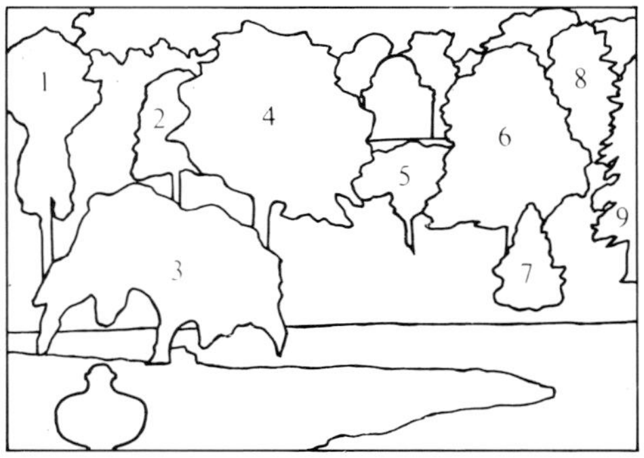

The pastoral
Below

1 Silver birch *Betula pendula*

2 Weeping silver pear *Pyrus salicifolia* 'Pendula'

3 English yew *Taxus baccata*

4 Silver white willow *Salix alba* 'Sericea'

5 *Gunnera manicata* not a tree

6 Weeping willow *Salix × sepulcralis*

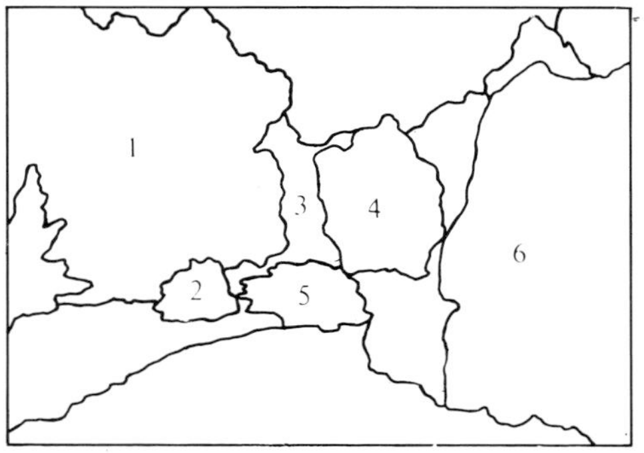

The romantic
Below

1 European beech *Fagus sylvatica*

2 *Magnolia × soulangiana*

3 Irish yew *Taxus baccata* 'Fastigiata'.

4 *Magnolia obovata*

5 *Thuja occidentalis* 'Elegantissima'

6 Paper-bark maple *Acer griseum*

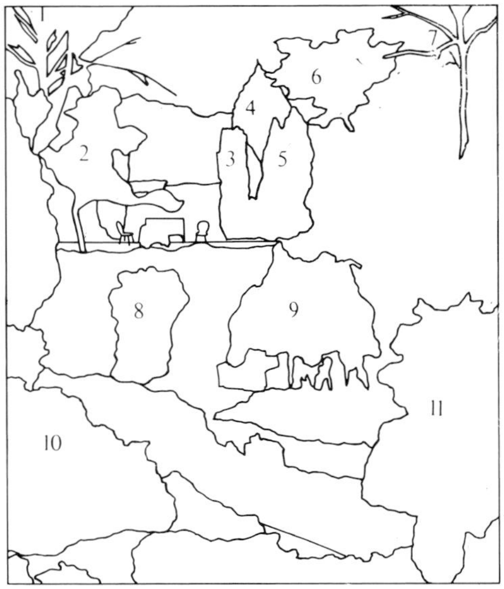

Natural Forest Vegetation

The climate (both prehistoric and modern), the soil, the mountains, the rainfall, the length of nights and angle of the sun are factors that shape natural forest vegetation. On these pages are maps of its outlines in North America and Europe.

The European pattern is relatively simple. Starting in the north, after tundra (where trees, if any, are stunted dwarfs) comes the vast northern coniferous forest of pine and spruce, sprinkled with birch and, further east, fir, larch and spruce.

South of a line on about the latitude of northern Scotland deciduous trees come into the picture in greater numbers. The northern limit of the oak is roughly along this line. All northern Europe comes into the mixed coniferous/deciduous belt with oak, beech, fir, pine etc. as the principal trees, except where mountains make islands of coniferous forest or where heath (Scotland, North Germany) or grassland (Hungary, S.W. Russia) occupies very poor soil.

The Mediterranean zone is approximately marked by the northern limit of the olive. Its forest is largely evergreen (pine, oak, cork oak, carob) alternating with areas of aromatic shrubs and herbs (myrtle, thyme) dotted with olive, juniper and cypress.

North America is much more complex. The forest zones of the east, compared with the hardiness zones on page 30, show the same strong continental influence, modified by river-valleys and mountains. In the west the ocean and the mountains are dominant, largely through their effect on rainfall (see page 31).

The overriding factor in Europe is less one of temperature zones (the vegetation bears little relation to the hardiness zones on page 31) than of daylength. Northern Scotland is on the same latitude as southern Alaska. At these latitudes conifers with their relatively small but permanent leaf-area begin to have marked advantages.

USA Vegetation Zones

1. Pine, fir, spruce, larch, poplar.

2. Pine, spruce, tamarack, balsam fir, poplar, birch.

3. Oak, hickory.

4. Oak, chestnut, yellow poplar.

5. Oak, pine.

6. Beech, maple, birch, hemlock.

7. Beech, chestnut, maple, oak.

8. Hemlock, pine, fir, spruce.

9. Longleaf and loblolly pines.

10. Atlantic pine barrens.

11. Cypress, magnolia, white cedar.

12. Spruce, hemlock.

13. Douglas fir, hemlock.

14. Douglas fir, oak, redwood, cypress.

15. Yellow pine, Douglas fir.

16. Lodgepole, yellow and sugar pine.

17. Piñon, pine and juniper.

18. Californian chaparral.

19. Temperate and semi-desert mesquite grasslands.

20. Yucca, sage brush, cactus, agave.

21. Dwarf willow, birch and alder.

Europe: Vegetation Zones

1. Pine, spruce, Siberian larch, fir, birch.

2. Fir, pine, spruce, sometimes with oak, beech, chestnut.

3. Mixed forest and meadow: oak, beech, fir.

4. Holm oak, cork oak, stone pine, carob.

5. Evergreen maquis and meadow: myrtle, olive, aromatic shrubs.

6. Grassland.

7. Steppe.

8. Heath, moor, sandy coastal wastes.

9. Alpine.

251

A Twelve-Month Succession of Ornamental Flowers, Fruit and Foliage

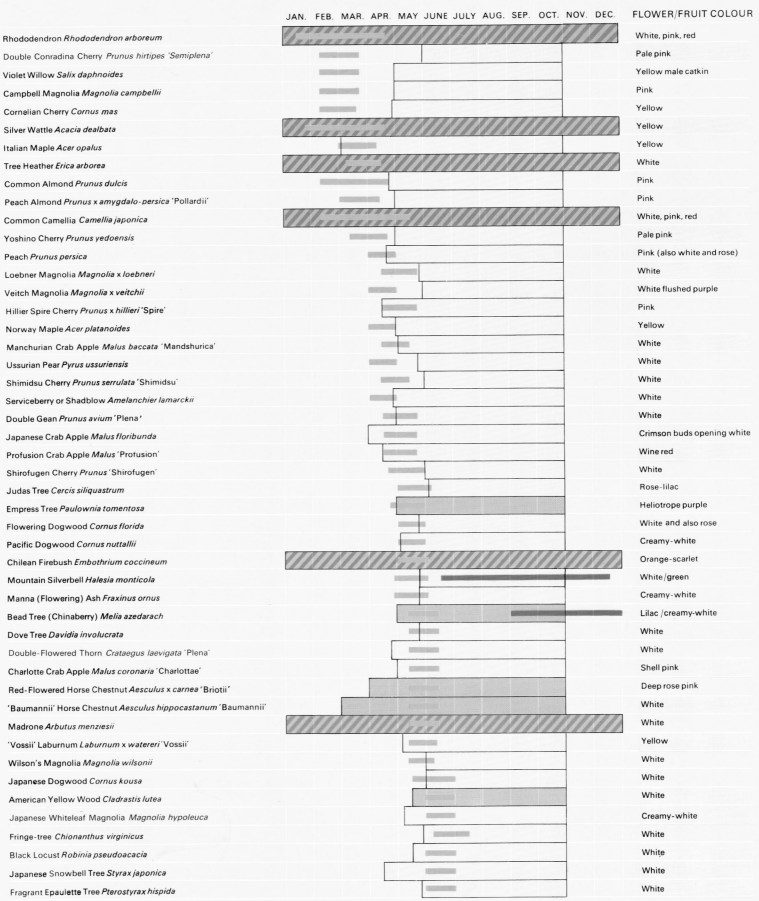

	JAN. FEB. MAR. APR. MAY JUNE JULY AUG. SEP. OCT. NOV. DEC.	FLOWER/FRUIT COLOUR
Rhododendron *Rhododendron arboreum*		White, pink, red
Double Conradina Cherry *Prunus hirtipes 'Semiplena'*		Pale pink
Violet Willow *Salix daphnoides*		Yellow male catkin
Campbell Magnolia *Magnolia campbellii*		Pink
Cornelian Cherry *Cornus mas*		Yellow
Silver Wattle *Acacia dealbata*		Yellow
Italian Maple *Acer opalus*		Yellow
Tree Heather *Erica arborea*		White
Common Almond *Prunus dulcis*		Pink
Peach Almond *Prunus x amygdalo-persica 'Pollardii'*		Pink
Common Camellia *Camellia japonica*		White, pink, red
Yoshino Cherry *Prunus yedoensis*		Pale pink
Peach *Prunus persica*		Pink (also white and rose)
Loebner Magnolia *Magnolia x loebneri*		White
Veitch Magnolia *Magnolia x veitchii*		White flushed purple
Hillier Spire Cherry *Prunus x hillieri 'Spire'*		Pink
Norway Maple *Acer platanoides*		Yellow
Manchurian Crab Apple *Malus baccata 'Mandshurica'*		White
Ussurian Pear *Pyrus ussuriensis*		White
Shimidsu Cherry *Prunus serrulata 'Shimidsu'*		White
Serviceberry or Shadblow *Amelanchier lamarckii*		White
Double Gean *Prunus avium 'Plena'*		White
Japanese Crab Apple *Malus floribunda*		Crimson buds opening white
Profusion Crab Apple *Malus 'Profusion'*		Wine red
Shirofugen Cherry *Prunus 'Shirofugen'*		White
Judas Tree *Cercis siliquastrum*		Rose-lilac
Empress Tree *Paulownia tomentosa*		Heliotrope purple
Flowering Dogwood *Cornus florida*		White and also rose
Pacific Dogwood *Cornus nuttallii*		Creamy-white
Chilean Firebush *Embothrium coccineum*		Orange-scarlet
Mountain Silverbell *Halesia monticola*		White/green
Manna (Flowering) Ash *Fraxinus ornus*		Creamy-white
Bead Tree (Chinaberry) *Melia azedarach*		Lilac /creamy-white
Dove Tree *Davidia involucrata*		White
Double-Flowered Thorn *Crataegus laevigata 'Plena'*		White
Charlotte Crab Apple *Malus coronaria 'Charlottae'*		Shell pink
Red-Flowered Horse Chestnut *Aesculus x carnea 'Briotii'*		Deep rose pink
'Baumannii' Horse Chestnut *Aesculus hippocastanum 'Baumannii'*		White
Madrone *Arbutus menziesii*		White
'Vossii' Laburnum *Laburnum x watereri 'Vossii'*		Yellow
Wilson's Magnolia *Magnolia wilsonii*		White
Japanese Dogwood *Cornus kousa*		White
American Yellow Wood *Cladrastis lutea*		White
Japanese Whiteleaf Magnolia *Magnolia hypoleuca*		Creamy-white
Fringe-tree *Chionanthus virginicus*		White
Black Locust *Robinia pseudoacacia*		White
Japanese Snowbell Tree *Styrax japonica*		White
Fragrant Epaulette Tree *Pterostyrax hispida*		White

There is no difficulty in having beauty and interest in garden trees in the spring. This chart suggests trees to carry on the interest, with either flowers, ornamental fruit or eye-catching leaves, all the year round

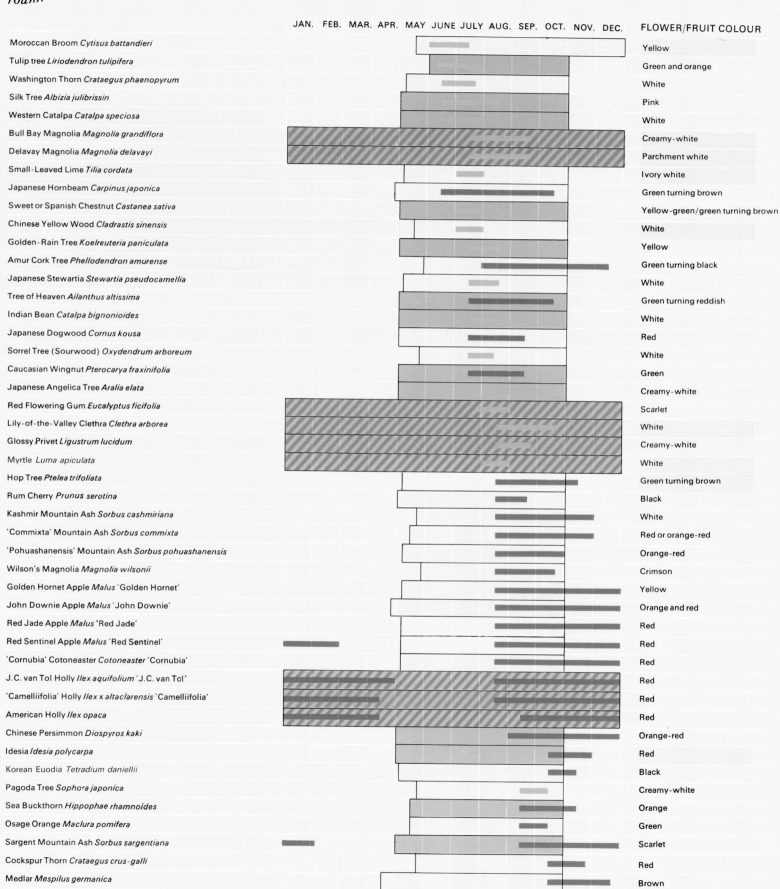

Legend:
- Foliage
- Striking foliage
- Evergreen foliage
- Flowering time
- Fruiting time
- Scented flowers

	JAN. FEB. MAR. APR. MAY JUNE JULY AUG. SEP. OCT. NOV. DEC.	FLOWER/FRUIT COLOUR
Moroccan Broom *Cytisus battandieri*		Yellow
Tulip tree *Liriodendron tulipifera*		Green and orange
Washington Thorn *Crataegus phaenopyrum*		White
Silk Tree *Albizia julibrissin*		Pink
Western Catalpa *Catalpa speciosa*		White
Bull Bay Magnolia *Magnolia grandiflora*		Creamy-white
Delavay Magnolia *Magnolia delavayi*		Parchment white
Small-Leaved Lime *Tilia cordata*		Ivory white
Japanese Hornbeam *Carpinus japonica*		Green turning brown
Sweet or Spanish Chestnut *Castanea sativa*		Yellow-green/green turning brown
Chinese Yellow Wood *Cladrastis sinensis*		White
Golden-Rain Tree *Koelreuteria paniculata*		Yellow
Amur Cork Tree *Phellodendron amurense*		Green turning black
Japanese Stewartia *Stewartia pseudocamellia*		White
Tree of Heaven *Ailanthus altissima*		Green turning reddish
Indian Bean *Catalpa bignonioides*		White
Japanese Dogwood *Cornus kousa*		Red
Sorrel Tree (Sourwood) *Oxydendrum arboreum*		White
Caucasian Wingnut *Pterocarya fraxinifolia*		Green
Japanese Angelica Tree *Aralia elata*		Creamy-white
Red Flowering Gum *Eucalyptus ficifolia*		Scarlet
Lily-of-the-Valley Clethra *Clethra arborea*		White
Glossy Privet *Ligustrum lucidum*		Creamy-white
Myrtle *Luma apiculata*		White
Hop Tree *Ptelea trifoliata*		Green turning brown
Rum Cherry *Prunus serotina*		Black
Kashmir Mountain Ash *Sorbus cashmiriana*		White
'Commixta' Mountain Ash *Sorbus commixta*		Red or orange-red
'Pohuashanensis' Mountain Ash *Sorbus pohuashanensis*		Orange-red
Wilson's Magnolia *Magnolia wilsonii*		Crimson
Golden Hornet Apple *Malus* 'Golden Hornet'		Yellow
John Downie Apple *Malus* 'John Downie'		Orange and red
Red Jade Apple *Malus* 'Red Jade'		Red
Red Sentinel Apple *Malus* 'Red Sentinel'		Red
'Cornubia' Cotoneaster *Cotoneaster* 'Cornubia'		Red
J.C. van Tol Holly *Ilex aquifolium* 'J.C. van Tol'		Red
'Camelliifolia' Holly *Ilex x altaclarensis* 'Camelliifolia'		Red
American Holly *Ilex opaca*		Red
Chinese Persimmon *Diospyros kaki*		Orange-red
Idesia *Idesia polycarpa*		Red
Korean Euodia *Tetradium daniellii*		Black
Pagoda Tree *Sophora japonica*		Creamy-white
Sea Buckthorn *Hippophae rhamnoides*		Orange
Osage Orange *Maclura pomifera*		Green
Sargent Mountain Ash *Sorbus sargentiana*		Scarlet
Cockspur Thorn *Crataegus crus-galli*		Red
Medlar *Mespilus germanica*		Brown
Autumn Cherry *Prunus subhirtella* 'Autumnalis'		Pale pink

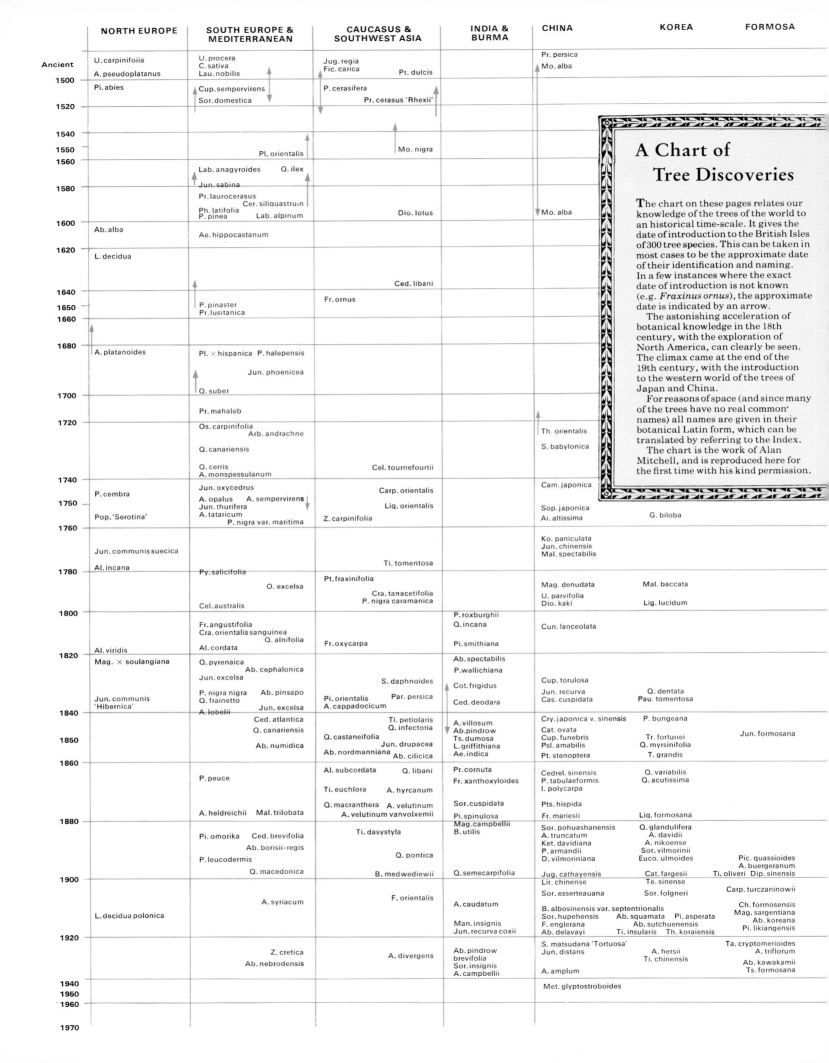

JAPAN & MANCHURIA	NORTH ASIA	AUSTRALASIA	SOUTH AMERICA	EASTERN & CENTRAL NORTH AMERICA	WESTERN NORTH AMERICA & MEXICO

Key to abbreviations

A.	Acer	F.	Fagus	P.	Pinus
Ab.	Abies	Fic.	Ficus	Par.	Parrotia
Ac.	Acacia	Fitz.	Fitzroya	Pau.	Paulownia
Ae.	Aesculus	Fr.	Fraxinus	Ph.	Phillyrea
Ag.	Agathis			Pi.	Picea
Ai.	Ailanthus	G.	Ginkgo	Pic.	Picrasma
Al.	Alnus	Gle.	Gleditsia	Pl.	Platanus
Arau.	Araucaria	Gym.	Gymnocladus	Pod.	Podocarpus
Arb.	Arbutus			Pop.	Populus
Ath.	Athrotaxis	H.	Halesia	Pr.	Prunus
				Psl.	Pseudolarix
B.	Betula	I.	Idesia	Pst.	Pseudotsuga
				Pt.	Pterocarya
C.	Castanea	Jug.	Juglans	Pts.	Pterostyrax
Cam.	Camellia	Jun.	Juniperus	Py.	Pyrus
Car.	Carya				
Carp.	Carpinus	Kal.	Kalopanax	Q.	Quercus
Cas.	Castanopsis	Ket.	Keteleeria		
Cat.	Catalpa	Ko.	Koelreuteria	R.	Robinia
Ced.	Cedrus				
Cedrel.	Cedrela	L.	Larix	S.	Salix
Cel.	Celtis	Lab.	Laburnum	Sass.	Sassafras
Ceph	Cephalotaxus	Lau.	Laurus	Sax.	Saxegothaea
Cer.	Cercis	Laur.	Laurelia	Seq.	Sequoia
Ch.	Chamaecyparis	Lig.	Ligustrum	Seqd.	Sequoiadendron
Cord.	Cordyline	Liq.	Liquidambar	Soph.	Sophora
Cot.	Cotoneaster	Lir.	Liriodendron	Sor.	Sorbus
Cra.	Crataegus			St.	Stewartia
Cry.	Cryptomeria	Mac.	Maclura		
Cun.	Cunninghamia	Mag.	Magnolia	T.	Torreya
Cup.	Cupressus	Mal.	Malus	Ta.	Taiwania
		Man.	Mangletia	Tax.	Taxodium
D.	Davidia	May.	Maytenus	Te.	Tetracentron
Dac.	Dacrydium	Met.	Metasequoia	Th.	Thuja
Dio.	Diospyros	Mo.	Morus	Ti.	Tilia
Dip.	Dipteronia	Myr.	Myrtus	Tr.	Trachycarpus
Dr.	Drimys			Ts.	Tsuga
		N.	Nyssa		
Euc.	Eucalyptus	Not.	Nothofagus	U.	Ulmus
Euco.	Eucommia				
Eucr.	Eucryphia	O.	Olea	Z.	Zelkova
		Os.	Ostrya		

Timeline (dates shown at right)

Eastern & Central North America:
- Th. occidentalis — c. 1535
- P. strobus — c. 1550

c. 1620 (Eastern & Central North America):
- Pr. serotina Car. ovata
- Sass. albidum
- Jug. cinerea Pl. occidentalis
- R. pseudoacacia
- Tax. distichum

c. 1640–1660 (Eastern & Central North America):
- A. rubrum
- Cel. occidentalis
- Lir. tulipifera
- Jun. virginiana

c. 1680–1700 (Eastern & Central North America):
- Liq. styraciflua
- Jug. nigra Pop. tacamahaca
- A. negundo Q. prinus
- Cra. crus-galli Ab. balsamea
- Q. coccinea
- Gle. triacanthos Pi. glauca

Western North America & Mexico:
- Cup. lusitanica — c. 1700

c. 1700 (Eastern & Central North America):
- Pi. mariana
- Ae. pavia

c. 1720–1740 (Eastern & Central North America):
- A. saccharinum Fr. americana Q. phellos
- Cat. bignonioides Q. alba Q. nigra
- Mag. grandiflora Ts. canadensis Q. borealis
- A. saccharum P. palustris Ch. thyoides
- Mag. acuminata P. resinosa B. nigra
- L. laricina P. echinata P. virginiana

c. 1740–1760 (Eastern & Central North America):
- P. taeda R. hispida
- Gym. dioicus
- A. spicatum N. sylvatica B. papyrifera
- Mag. tripetala Ti. americana U. americana
-   H. carolina
- A. pensylvanicum
- B. lenta
- P. rigida Ae. flava
- Car. cordiformis Car. tomentosa
- B. alleghaniensis

Japan & Manchuria:
- T. nucifera — c. 1775

Australasia:
- Soph. tetraptera — c. 1775

c. 1780–1800 (Eastern & Central North America):
- P. banksiana Fr. pensylvanica
- Sor. americana
- Mag. fraseri Q. imbricaria
- Tax. ascendens
- Car. glabra Q. bicolor Q. palustris
- Mag. macrophylla Q. velutina
- Car. laciniosa P. pungens
- Ab. fraseri Ae. glabra Q. macrocarpa

Australasia:
- Euc. obliqua — c. 1790

South America:
- Arau. araucana — c. 1796

Japan & Manchuria:
- Pod. macrophyllus — c. 1800

North Asia:
- L. sibirica
- P. pumila — c. 1800

Australasia: Ac. dealbata | South America: May. boaria | Eastern: Mac. pomifera | Western: A. macrophyllum — c. 1810

c. 1820:
- Japan & Manchuria: A. palmatum
- North Asia: Ab. sibirica L. gmelini
- Australasia: Ag. australis Cord. australis Euc. globulus
- South America: Dr. winteri Not. betuloides Not. antarctica
- Eastern: Q. heterophylla U. rubra
- Western: A. circinatum P. ponderosa Ab. amabilis Pst. menziesii Ab. procera Ab. grandis P. radiata Pi. sitchensis Cup. macrocarpa Ab. religiosa
- Japan & Manchuria: Cep. harringtonia drupacea P. massoniana

c. 1840–1850:
- Japan & Manchuria: Cry. japonica 'Lobbii'
- Japan & Manchuria: Ts. sieboldii Jug. mandshurica P. densiflora P. thunbergii Th. standishii Pi. polita Ch. obtusa
- North Asia: Pi. obovata
- Australasia: Euc. coccifera Euc. gunnii Dac. franklinii
- South America: Myr. apiculata Sax. conspicua Fitz. cupressoides Eucr. cordifolia Pod. salignus
- Eastern: Q. × leana
- Western: Ab. concolor lowiana P. ayacahuite Th. plicata Seq. sempervirens Ch. nootkatensis Ab. magnifica Seqd. giganteum Ab. bracteata Ts. heterophylla

c. 1860–1880:
- Japan & Manchuria: Ab. firma Ts. diversifolia L. kaempferi Mag. obovata Mag. kobus Kal. pictus A. japonicum A. rufinerve albolimbatum A. cissifolium Pi. glehnii Q. acuta Kal. pictus maximowiczii A. argutum
- North Asia: U. pumila Ti. mandshurica Pi. schrenkiana
- Australasia: Ath. spp. Laur. serrata
- South America: Pod. andinus
- Eastern: Cat × erubescens U. thomasii Q. × ludoviciana
- Western: Pi. engelmanii P. aristata Fr. latifolia Q. garryana Ab. concolor Q. wislizenii Q. lobata Q. kelloggii Cup. guadalupensis

c. 1880–1900:
- Japan & Manchuria: Pi. jezoensis A. crataegifolium A. mono A. distylum A. rufinerve A. carpinifolium A. diabolicum B. maximowicziana A. capillipes A. miyabei Mag. salicifolia Pst. japonica B. grossa
- North Asia: B. costata
- South America: Not. fusca Not. cliffortioides Not. moorei
- Eastern: Cat. speciosa Ts. caroliniana Q. × schochiana H. monticola Q. shumardii
- Western: Cup. arizonica L. occidentalis Al. rubra Pi. brewerana Fr. velutina Pop. trichocarpa

c. 1900:
- Japan & Manchuria: S. gracilistyla Pr. yedoensis A. mandshuricum Ab. holophylla St. monodelpha Pi. koyamai Q. aliena Pr. maackii Carp. laxiflora St. serrata
- North Asia: L. gmelini olgensis
- South America: Not. obliqua Not. procera Not. dombeyi
- Eastern: U. serotina Pi. glauca albertiana Cup. glabra Fr. tomentosa
- Western: Jun. deppeana Cup. sargentii Pst. macrocarpa

c. 1920–1940:
- Japan & Manchuria: Ti. kiusiana
- Eastern: Jun. virginiana 'Pseudocupressus'
- Western: Cup. forbesii Jun. ashei Cup. bakeri Cup. abramsiana

c. 1940–1960:
- Eastern: Jun. virginiana 'Skyrocket'
- Western: Ab. vejari P. cooperi

c. 1965:
- South America: Not. pumila

Date scale (right margin): 1500, 1520, 1540, 1550, 1560, 1580, 1600, 1620, 1640, 1650, 1660, 1680, 1700, 1720, 1740, 1750, 1760, 1780, 1800, 1820, 1840, 1850, 1860, 1880, 1900, 1920, 1940, 1950, 1960, 1970

Tree Pests and Diseases

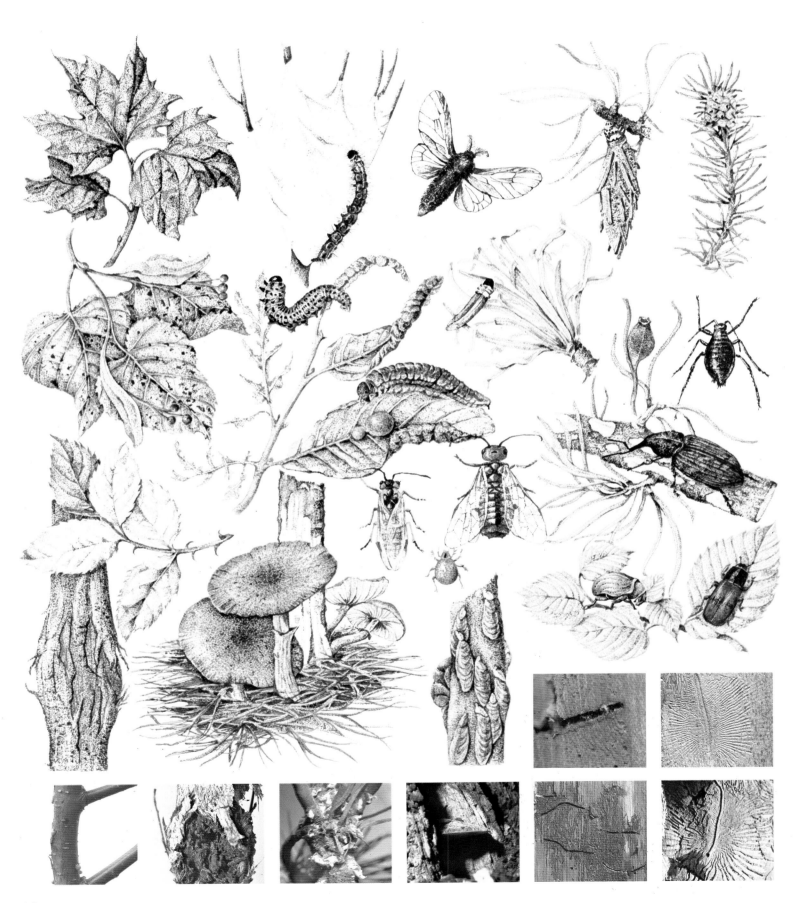

A mighty army of insects, fungi and bacteria relies on trees for food. Most of them are harmless. But a great number can also maim, disfigure and kill when they really take hold.

The list that follows describes some of the commonest pests and diseases, but it is not intended to be an arboricultural medical dictionary. Unless the trouble is obvious it is always worth talking to a qualified tree surgeon before taking action.

Aphids

Aphids are small, generally wingless insects (29). Many secrete honeydew which can act as a germination site for mould. Some can cause galls. Aphids are found mainly on broadleaves; they deform foliage and can deform branches.

Commonest species:

Craphalodes–attacks spruce, causing distortion of the twigs, and pineapple-like galls (27).

Eriosoma lanuginosum–attacks elms, causing irregular, blister-like galls.

Pemphigus bursarius–attacks poplars, causing small oblong galls on the leafstalks and leaves (28).

Tetraneura ulmifoliae–attacks elms, causing club-shaped galls on the leaves.

Control: Tar-oil washes in winter; systemic insecticides; malathion. Birds also help to keep numbers down.

Beetles

Beetles attack both conifers and broadleaves; leaf-eaters are not serious pests; borers can transmit disease and destroy trees by 'ringing'.

Commonest species include:

Copper beech leaf miner (*Rhynchaenus fagi*)–larvae chew winding galleries in leaves of common and copper beech, causing them to turn brown in summer.

Elm bark beetle (*Scolytus scolytus* (16) in Britain, and *Scolytus multistriatus* (15) in America)–see Dutch elm disease.

Large pine weevil (*Hylobius abietis*) (17)–feeds on bark of young conifers (and on broadleaves if no conifers available).

Control: Sprays, burning of infested wood; predatory animals give some control.

Mites

Mites are minature spider-like creatures; their longish, hard mouthparts are specially adapted for penetrating woody substances. They can cause defoliation.

Commonest species:

Red spider mite (*Panonychus ulmi*) (18)–larvae attack mainly apple, pear and cherry tree leaves, leaving a fine web. The leaves eventually die.

Moths

The larvae of various moths, if they occur in large enough numbers, can cause serious defoliation and damage to leader shoots of conifers and broadleaves.

Commonest species:

Bagworm (*Thyridopteryx ephemeraeformis*) – winged male moths (24) are harmless. The wingless females live in a bag made of silk and covered by leaves and leaf-stalks (26). They can cause partial defoliation of young trees.

Buff-tip moth (*Phalera bucephala*)–larvae defoliate a number of small broadleaved species.

Larch case-bearer (*Coleophora laricella*) (25) – larvae hollow out larch needles, causing them to drop off eventually.

Tent caterpillar (*Malocosoma pluvialis*)–larvae live in communal web 'tent' on conifers, especially larch, and cause defoliation.

Control: Caterpillar-eating birds and various bacteria keep down larval populations. Caterpillars can also be picked off and destroyed by hand; use tar-oil washes and pesticides only as a last resort.

Sawflies

The adults (20) are harmless. The caterpillar-like larvae (21) attack both conifers and broadleaves, causing galls and, in large numbers, serious defoliation.

Commonest species:

Larch sawfly (*Lygaenematus erichsoni*)–larvae eat larch needles causing severe defoliation.

Willow sawfly (*Pontania proxima*) (19) and (22)–causes oblong galls on willow leaves.

Control: Various pesticides; smaller insect-eating birds such as tits and warblers.

Scale Insects

Scale insects secrete a waxy protective shield which makes them difficult to eliminate. Only the females are harmful. They mainly attack broadleaves, making leaves curl up and fall off; they also attack and damage fruit.

Commonest species:

Citrus scale (*Aspidiotus perniciosus*)–attacks foliage and fruit of apple and pear trees in Europe, orange and other citrus trees in the United States.

Felted beech scale (*Cryptococcus Fagisuga*)–attacks beech, giving white-washed appearance to tree.

Oystershell scale (*Lepidosaphes ulmi*)–attacks bark of a number of trees and bushes.

Control: Coccinellid beetles will eat the young; otherwise tar-oil and malathion sprays. Some trees are damaged by tar-oil, however, and malathion is ecologically harmful.

Anthracnose

A fungus disease common to broadleaves, particularly willow and plane, which first attacks the foliage in damp seasons, giving it a white spotted appearance (1). It then spreads over the whole tree.

Control: Regular spraying with copper compounds (e.g. Bordeaux mixture). Burn infected leaves. Fertilizer helps.

Bark and Timber Fungi

Fungi can seriously damage wood and kill trees. The fruit of many fungi often appears as a 'bracket fungus' on the bark. Others produce spores which appear on the trunk as small coloured spots (some of which produce canker) (*q.v.*). Beefsteak fungus (*Fistulina hepatica*) 9, which attacks oak, can give a deep brown colour to the wood enhancing its market value. Other fungi attack the roots and show above ground as toadstools. Honey (or bootlace) fungus (*Armillaria mellea*) (6) is the deadliest.

Control: Felling and burning of infected trees and sterilisation of surrounding soil. Soaking the foot of the tree with creosote has destroyed honey fungus.

Canker

A term for several diseases common to conifers and broadleaves. They are caused by bacteria or fungi, whose spores enter open wounds on the tree. The bark usually swells around the wound (7). Balsam poplars are subject to a canker resisted by other poplars.

Control: Infected parts should be cut away cleanly and burned. Badly infected trees must be burned.

Chestnut Blight (*Endothia*)

A fungal disease affecting bark and cambium of chestnuts. The trunk of infected trees is covered with small coloured dots (4). The disease is usually fatal to the top of the tree but new bark often develops beneath the wound.
Control: As for bark and timber fungi.

Dutch Elm Disease

A usually fatal fungal disease affecting elms, spread mainly by elm bark beetles, but also by natural root grafts between healthy and infected trees. The foliage of infected trees turns yellow and wilts.

Adult beetles make breeding galleries in the bark. Those of the American beetle are horizontal (10, 12); those of the European are vertical (11, 13). These galleries and the winding ones made by emerging larvae, are ideal reproduction sites for fungi. Up to 1,000,000 sticky fungal spores are carried to healthy trees by each beetle.

Control: Infected bark should be burnt although the timber is useable. Healthy trees can be sprayed to kill feeding beetles. Recently infected trees can often be saved by injection with fungicide. This is an annual procedure and seldom practicable. Localised injection into the soil of root-killing chemicals, or trenching, will combat the natural spread by root grafts.

Fireblight

A bacterial disease of many members of the Rose family, especially pears, which is spread by pollinating insects. It causes die-back in the flowers and leaves. The twigs of infected trees often exude a bacterial slime (5).

Control: Burning of infected tissue, and complete removal of badly affected trees.

Mildew and Rusts

Fungal diseases which can seriously affect the growth of seedlings and young trees by causing defoliation. In trees affected by mildew the foliage has a whitish powdery coating (3); the foliage of rust-diseased trees is spotted with black, orange-brown or red (2).

White pine blister rust (8) attacks pines (both foliage and, here, shoots) and currant bushes during its life-cycle.

Control: As for Anthracnose.

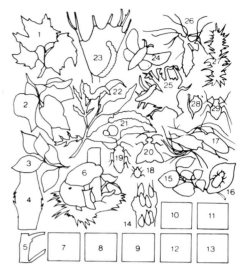

Key
1 *Anthracnose on plane*
2 *Rust fungus on lime*
3 *Mildew*
4 *Chestnut blight*
5 *Fireblight of* Cotoneaster
6 *Honey fungus on pine*
7 *Bacterial canker on poplar*
8 *White pine blister rust on timber pine*
9 *Beefsteak fungus on oak*
10/11 *American elm bark beetle gallery in elm bark/wood*
12/13 *European elm bark beetle galleries on elm wood/bark*
14 *Oystershell scale insects on elm*
15 *American elm bark beetle*
16 *European elm bark beetle*
17 *Pine weevil*
18 *Red spider mite*
19 *Willow sawfly*
20 *Sawfly*
21 *Sawfly larva*
22 *Willow sawfly larva*
23 *Tent caterpillar*
24 *Male bagworm moth*
25 *Larch case-bearer*
26 *Bagworm*
27 *Pineapple gall on spruce (see Craphalodes)*
28 *Aphid purse gall on poplar leaf stalk*
29 *Wingless female aphid*

Rates of Growth

No rate of growth holds good for any species of tree under all circumstances. A tree's performance is governed very much by the area in which it is planted: climate and soil are all-important. Soils vary considerably in depth, moisture content and nutrient supply. These factors in turn depend on temperature and rainfall. Trees, however, have their characteristic patterns of growth. The graphs on the right show how a selection of conifers and of broadleaves reach their maximum growth-rates at different ages: some holding back for the first ten years before putting on three feet a year; others racing away but soon slowing down. The trees illustrated below and on the following pages are chosen for the wide differences in their speed of growth.

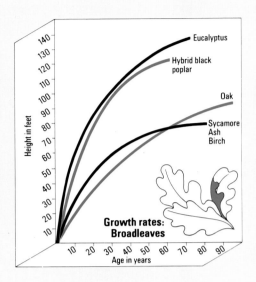

Growth rates: Broadleaves

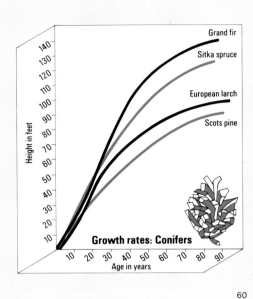

Growth rates: Conifers

The holm oak starts slowly: it barely reaches ten feet in ten years. Then it speeds up to reach 35 feet in 30 years. In the next 70 years it only doubles its height, but spreads hugely.

Wellingtonia (or 'big tree') can be relied on to grow a steady two feet a year for 40 or 50 years, slowing down as it approaches 100 feet.

Cider gum is immensely vigorous from the start, reaching 40 feet in ten years but then slowing down, scarcely doubling its height in the following 20.

White willow makes a really big tree faster than almost any: its height and spread at 30 years make it look twice its age. Thereafter progress is very slow.

Monterey pine is one of the fastest of all conifers: in exceptional conditions it has grown 20 feet in one year: it can be relied on to do three or four.

Silver birch gets away quickly but settles down to a slow advance after 15 or 20 years—making it an excellent garden tree.

English yew is notoriously slow to start with, but grows as wide as it is high—and eventually much wider.

English elm is always vigorous, but most so in middle age: a 100-year-old tree looks 200 or 300 years old.

70 15 years
60
50
40
30
20
10
0

Monterey pine   Common silver birch   English yew   English elm

130 100 years
120
110
100
90
80
70
60
50
40
30
20
10
0

70 15 years
60
50
40
30
20
10
0

Douglas fir   European horse chestnut   Lombardy poplar   English holly

130 100 years
120
110
100
90
80
70
60
50
40
30
20
10
0 Feet

Douglas fir in good damp conditions is a three-feet-a-year tree for the 30 years from five to 35. It then slows down and thickens its stem.

Horse chestnut reaches its full height, like many broadleaf trees, in 50 or 60 years at about two feet a year. Thereafter it just spreads.

Lombardy poplar can grow between two and three feet a year for 25 years before it slows down. Planted at eight feet it should make a 20-foot screen in five years.

English holly starts as slowly as yew. Only after about 15 years does it put on 18-inch shoots in one season.

Rates of Growth

Scots pine grows surprisingly fast after the first three or four years: a three-foot shoot is normal. But it soon loses its upward vigour and spreads out.

Scarlet oak in the acid loam it likes is among the fastest of the oaks. The growth-rates shown here are about average for any oak.

Wingnut is in the championship class for high-speed broadleaves, growing 45 feet in only 15 years, then building a wide symmetrical dome.

Giant Thuja is one of the fastest conifers: a reliable two-feet-a-year tree in gardens, though much more in the Pacific north-west.

Weeping willows usually surprise their owners by their rapid spread: at 15 years 30 feet across as well as high.

15 years

Scots pine   Scarlet oak   Wingnut   Giant thuja   Weeping willow

100 years

15 years

European beech   Serbian spruce   Maidenhair tree   London plane   Big-leafed lime

100 years

0 Feet

Feet 0

European beech is rather slow in its early years but makes up for it in its second and third decades At 100 years it is fully mature: as wide as it is high.

Serbian spruce is the best of the spruces for a confined space, never spreading but mounting at two feet a year in a trim spire.

The gingko or maidenhair tree is never a fast grower. A one-foot shoot is about normal for its formative years.

The London plane is slower than its American parent, but the estimate here is conservative: it should grow two feet a year in its early years.

The big-leafed lime (T. platyphyllos) is not exceptional for speed but keeps a narrow tower-like shape in maturity, unlike most broadleaves.

Spanish chestnut is relatively slow in its earlier years but immensely vigorous in middle age, when it will put out ten-foot shoots in one year if it is cut back hard.

Silver maple is among the fastest of the maples, but has a reputation for making weak wood which is liable to split. Its initial energy fades relatively early in life.

All larches are among the quicker-growing conifers. The speed of the European larch is typical: at 15 years it is growing three feet a year. A hundred years brings it to maturity.

The junipers are a slow-growing race—hence excellent for small gardens. Common European juniper scarcely reaches tree stature—even in 100 years.

15 years

Spanish chestnut

Silver maple

European larch

Common juniper

100 years

15 years

Roblé beech

Swamp cypress

European ash

Cedar of Lebanon

100 years

Feet

The southern beeches (Nothofagus) are among the fastest of all broadleaves: the Roblé beech's 60 feet in 15 years is comparable to the performance of much shorter-lived willows and poplars.

Swamp cypress grows fairly slowly but steadily to a great age. At 100 years it is still not fully grown.

American ash is one of the fastest-growing American hardwoods. European ash (above) is steadier but still vigorous, reaching 100 feet or so in well under 100 years.

Cedar of Lebanon grows and forms its venerable plateaux much faster than you might expect. A hundred years is enough to complete the picture of sublime old age.

A Guide to Choosing Trees

By their shape, colour, performance and preferences

The following lists classify a selection of trees from the Conifers *and* Broadleaves *sections according to their outstanding characteristics.*

SHAPE

Picturesque/romantic/irregular

- **Black mulberry** *Morus nigra*
- **Japanese snowbell** *Styrax japonica*
- **Judas tree** *Cercis siliquastrum*
- **Strawberry tree** *Arbutus unedo*

- **Araucaria** *Araucaria* species
- **Nikko fir** *Abies homolepis*
- **Pines – most with age, especially**
- **Eastern white pine** *Pinus strobus*
- **Japanese black pine** *Pinus thunbergii*
- **Japanese white pine** *Pinus parviflora*
- **Scots pine** *Pinus sylvestris*
- **Umbrella pine** *Pinus pinea*

Broad-domed

- **Algerian oak** *Quercus canariensis*
- **American walnut** *Juglans nigra*
- **Black poplar** *Populus nigra*
- **Blue gum** *Eucalyptus globulus*
- **Broad-leaved lime** *Tilia platyphyllos*
- **California laurel** *Umbellularia californica*
- **Caucasian wingnut** *Pterocarya fraxinifolia*
- **Chestnut-leaved oak** *Quercus castaneifolia*
- **Elm zelkova** *Zelkova carpinifolia*
- **English oak** *Quercus robur*
- **European beech** *Fagus sylvatica*
- **European walnut** *Juglans regia*
- **Hardy rubber tree** *Eucommia ulmoides*
- **Holm oak** *Quercus ilex*
- **Hungarian oak** *Quercus frainetto*
- **Indian bean tree** *Catalpa bignonioides*
- **Italian maple** *Acer opalus*
- **Japanese crab** *Malus floribunda* (and others)
- **Japanese zelkova** *Zelkova serrata*
- **London plane** *Platanus × acerifolia*
- **Lucombe oak** *Quercus × hispanica* 'Lucombeana'
- **Norway maple** *Acer platanoides*
- **Red horse chestnut** *Aesculus × carnea*
- **Red oak** *Quercus rubra*
- **Silk tree** *Albizia julibrissin*
- **Sweet chestnut** *Castanea sativa*
- **Sycamore** *Acer pseudoplatanus*
- **Turkey oak** *Quercus cerris*

- **Cedar of Lebanon** *Cedrus libani*
- **Monterey cypress** *Cupressus macrocarpa*

Tower-like

- **Bat willow** *Salix alba caerulea*
- **Bitternut** *Carya cordiformis*
- **Common lime** *Tilia × vulgaris*
- **Cucumber tree** *Magnolia acuminata*
- **English elm** *Ulmus procera*
- **Mockernut** *Carya tomentosa*
- **Pecan** *Carya illinoensis*
- **Pignut** *Carya glabra*
- **Pin oak** *Quercus palustris*
- **Roblé beech** *Nothofagus obliqua*
- **Shagbark hickory** *Carya ovata*
- **White willow** *Salix alba*

Giant cone

- **Atlantic cedar** *Cedrus lib. atlantica*
- **Big tree** *Sequoiadendron giganteum*
- **European larch** *Larix decidua*
- **Japanese cedar** *Cryptomeria japonica*
- **Japanese larch** *Larix kaempferi*
- **Western hemlock** *Tsuga heterophylla*
- **Western red cedar** *Thuja plicata*

Globular-headed

- **Black locust** *Robinia pseudoacacia* 'Inermis'
- **Cockspur thorn** *Crataegus crus-galli*
- **Norway maple** *Acer platanoides* 'Globosum' and 'Summershade'
- **Sugar maple** *Acer saccharum* 'Globosum'

Horizontally spreading

- **Black mulberry** *Morus nigra*
- **Chinese witch hazel** *Hamamelis mollis*
- **Fig** *Ficus carica*
- **Japanese cherry** *Prunus* 'Kiku-shidare Sakura' and 'Shirofugen'
- **Japanese snowbell** *Styrax japonica*
- **Laburnum** *Laburnum* species
- **Persian parrotia** *Parrotia persica*

- **Silk tree** *Albizia julibrissin*
- **Witch hazel** *Hamamelis virginiana*

- **Golden larch** *Pseudolarix amabilis*

Pyramidal: broad

- **Dove (or handkerchief) tree** *Davidia involucrata* and *D.i.* var. *vilmoriniana*
- **Silver lime** *Tilia tomentosa*
- **Turkish hazel** *Corylus colurna*

- **Golden larch** *Pseudolarix amabilis*

Pyramidal: narrower

- **Alder** *Alnus* species
- **Cornish elm** *Ulmus angustifolia cornubiensis*
- **Jersey elm** *Ulmus × sarniensis*
- **Sweetgum** *Liquidambar styraciflua*
- **Caucasian fir** *Abies nordmanniana*
- **Dawn redwood** *Metasequoia glyptostroboides*
- **Serbian spruce** *Picea omorika*

Upright, columnar or fastigiate

- **Common hawthorn** *Crataegus monogyna* 'Stricta'
- **Crabs** *Malus baccata* 'Columnaris' and *M.* 'Van Eseltine'
- **Dawyck beech** *Fagus sylvatica* 'Dawyck' and *F.s.* 'Dawyck Purple'
- **English oak** *Quercus robur*
- **Honey locust** *Gleditsia triacanthos* 'Columnaris'
- **Japanese cherry** *Prunus* 'Amanogawa'
- **Lombardy poplar** *Populus nigra* 'Italica'
- **Norway maple** *Acer platanoides* 'Columnare' and *A.p.* 'Erectum'
- **Red maple** *Acer rubrum* 'Columnare'
- **Silver birch** *Betula pendula* 'Fastigiata'
- **Small-leaved lime** *Tilia cordata* 'Swedish Upright'
- **Sorbus** *Sorbus × thuringiaca* 'Fastigiata'
- **Sugar maple** *Acer saccharum* 'Temple's Upright'
- **Tulip tree** *Liriodendron tulipifera* 'Fastigiatum'
- **Washington thorn** *Crataegus phaenopyrum* 'Fastigiata'
- **White poplar** *Populus alba* 'Pyramidalis'

- **Arolla pine** *Pinus cembra*
- **Atlantic cedar** *Cedrus libani atlantica* 'Fastigiata'
- **Chinese juniper** *Juniperus chinensis* 'Aurea' and 'Columnaris Glauca'
- **Incense cedar** *Calocedrus decurrens*
- **Irish juniper** *Juniperus communis* 'Hibernica'
- **Irish yew** *Taxus baccata* 'Fastigiata'
- **Italian cypress** *Cupressus sempervirens*
- **Lawson cypress** *Chamaecyparis lawsoniana* 'Columnaris', 'Erecta Viridis' and many others
- **Leyland cypress** *× Cupressocyparis leylandii*
- **Maidenhair tree** *Ginkgo biloba* 'Sentry'
- **Pencil cedar** *Juniperus virginiana* 'Skyrocket'
- **Pond cypress** *Taxodium ascendens*
- **Rocky mountain juniper** *Juniperus scopulorum* 'Skyrocket'
- **Scots pine** *Pinus sylvestris* 'Fastigiata'
- **Syrian juniper** *Juniperus drupacea*
- **Western red cedar** *Thuja plicata* 'Fastigiata'

Pendulous (not weeping)

- **Japanese crab** *Malus floribunda*
- **Silver birch** *Betula pendula*
- **Smooth-leaved elm** *Ulmus carpinifolia*
- **Weeping silver lime** *Tilia petiolaris*
- **White elm** *Ulmus americana*
- **Wych elm** *Ulmus glabra*

- **Brewer's spruce** *Picea breweriana*
- **Deodar** *Cedrus deodara*
- **Drooping juniper** *Juniperus recurva* and *J.r. coxii*
- **European larch** *Larix decidua*
- **Huon pine** *Lagarostrobus franklinii*
- **Kashmir cypress** *Cupressus cashmeriana*
- **Lawson cypress** *Chamaecyparis lawsoniana* 'Intertexta'
- **Nootka cypress** *Chamaecyparis nootkatensis* and *C.n.* 'Pendula'

- **Pencil cedar** *Juniperus virginiana* 'Pendula'
- **Prince Albert's yew** *Saxegothaea conspicua*
- **Westfelton yew** *Taxus baccata* 'Dovastoniana'
- **West Himalayan spruce** *Picea smithiana*

Weeping

- **Camperdown elm** *Ulmus glabra* 'Camperdownii'
- **Perry's silver weeping holly** *Ilex aquifolium* 'Argenteomarginata Pendula'
- **Silver birch** *Betula pendula* 'Tristis'
- **Spring cherry** *Prunus subhirtella* 'Pendula'
- **'Tortuosa' beech** *Fagus sylvatica* 'Tortuosa'
- **Weeping beech** *Fagus sylvatica* 'Pendula'
- **Weeping oak** *Quercus robur* 'Pendula'
- **Weeping purple beech** *Fagus sylvatica* 'Purpurea Pendula'
- **Weeping willow** *Salix babylonica, S. sepulchralis* and var. *chrysocoma*
- **Weeping wych elm** *Ulmus glabra* 'Pendula'
- **Young's weeping birch** *Betula pendula* 'Youngii'

- **Big tree** *Sequoiadendron giganteum* 'Pendulum'
- **Eastern hemlock** *Tsuga canadensis* 'Pendula'
- **Japanese red pine** *Pinus densiflora* 'Umbraculifera'

Weeping–height depending on graft

- **Flowering dogwood** *Cornus florida* 'Pendula'
- **Japanese pagoda tree** *Sophora japonica* 'Pendula'
- **Weeping ash** *Fraxinus excelsior* 'Pendula'
- **Young's weeping birch** *Betula pendula* 'Youngii'

- **Atlantic cedar** *Cedrus atlantica* 'Pendula'

Multistemmed

- **Caucasian wingnut** *Pterocarya fraxinifolia*
- **Hazel** *Corylus avellana*
- **Japanese maple** *Acer japonicum, A. palmatum*
- **Oleaster** *Elaeagnus angustifolia*
- **Olive** *Olea europaea*
- **Rhododendron** *Rhododendron* species
- **Sea buckthorn** *Hippophae rhamnoides*
- **Stewartia** *Stewartia* species
- **Vine maple** *Acer circinatum*

- **Chinese juniper** *Juniperus chinensis* 'Kaizuka'
- **Eastern hemlock** *Tsuga canadensis*
- **Lace-bark pine** *Pinus bungeana*
- **Mountain pine** *Pinus mugo*

Contorted trees

- **Corkscrew hazel** *Corylus avellana* 'Contorta'
- **Corkscrew willow** *Salix matsudana* 'Tortuosa' and *S. × erythroflexuosa*
- **'Tortuosa' beech** *Fagus sylvatica* 'Tortuosa'

LEAVES, FLOWERS, FRUIT AND BARK

Leaves–big

- **American lime** *Tilia americana*
- **American walnut** *Juglans nigra*
- **Bigleaf magnolia** *Magnolia macrophylla*
- **Bigleaf maple** *Acer macrophyllum*
- **Burr oak** *Quercus macrocarpa*
- **Caucasian wingnut** *Pterocarya fraxinifolia*
- **Chinese poplar** *Populus lasiocarpa*
- **Chinese toon** *Toona sinensis*
- **Daimyo oak** *Quercus dentata*
- **'Delavay' magnolia** *Magnolia delavayi*
- **Empress tree** *Paulownia tomentosa*
- **Hercules club** *Aralia spinosa*
- **Himalayan whitebeam** *Sorbus cuspidata* and *S.c.* 'Mitchellii'
- **Idesia** *Idesia polycarpa*
- **Japanese angelica tree** *Aralia elata*
- **Japanese broadleaf holly** *Ilex latifolia*
- **Japanese horse chestnut** *Aesculus turbinata*
- **Kentucky coffee tree** *Gymnocladus dioicus*

- **Mockernut** *Carya tomentosa*
- **Palms** All species
- **Rhododendron** *Rhododendron calophytum, R. falconeri, R. sinogrande*
- **Southern catalpa** *Catalpa bignonioides*
- **Tree of heaven** *Ailanthus altissima*

- **Jelecote pine** *Pinus patula*
- **Montezuma pine** *Pinus montezumae*
- **Pitch pine** *Pinus palustris*

Leaves–very small

- **Antarctic beech** *Nothofagus antarctica*
- **Black beech** *Nothofagus solanderi*
- **Chinese elm** *Ulmus parvifolia*
- **Mountain beech** *Nothofagus cliffortioides*
- **New Zealand sophora** *Sophora tetraptera*
- **Perny holly** *Ilex pernyi*

- **Oriental spruce** *Picea orientalis*

Evergreen trees (not conifers)

- **Acacia** *Acacia* species
- **American holly** *Ilex opaca*
- **Bull bay magnolia** *Magnolia grandiflora*
- **California laurel** *Umbellularia californica*
- **California live oak** *Quercus agrifolia*
- **Camellia** *Camellia* species
- **Carob** *Ceratonia siliqua*
- **Chilean fire-bush** *Embothrium* species
- **Chinese photinia** *Photinia serrulata*
- **Citrus** *Citrus* species
- **Cork oak** *Quercus suber*
- **'Delavay' magnolia** *Magnolia delavayi*
- **English holly** *Ilex aquifolium*
- **Eucalyptus** *Eucalyptus* species
- **Evergreen dogwood** *Cornus capitata*
- **Glossy privet** *Ligustrum lucidum*
- **Golden chestnut** *Chrysolepis chrysophylla*
- **Heath** *Erica* species
- **Highclere holly** *Ilex × altaclerensis*
- **Holm oak** *Quercus ilex*
- **Holly** *Ilex latifolia, I. pedunculosa*
- **Laurel** *Laurus nobilis*
- **Live oak** *Quercus virginiana*
- **New Zealand sophora** *Sophora tetraptera*
- **Oak** *Quercus acuta, Q. glauca*
- **Olive** *Olea europaea*
- **Palms** All species
- **Perny holly** *Ilex pernyi*
- **Portugal laurel** *Prunus lusitanica*
- **Rhododendron** *Rhododendron arboreum, R. barbatum, R. falconeri, R. maximum*
- **Silk oak** *Grevillea robusta*
- **Strawberry tree** *Arbutus* species
- **Tanbark oak** *Lithocarpus* species

Leaves–red/purple

- **Crab** *Malus* 'Lemoinei', *Malus × purpurea*
- **English oak** *Quercus robur* 'Atropurpurea'
- **Japanese maple** *Acer palmatum* 'Atropurpureum'
- **Norway maple** *Acer platanoides* 'Goldsworth Purple' and 'Schwedleri'
- **Purple beech** *Fagus sylvatica* 'Riversii'
- **Purple-leaf filbert** *Corylus maxima* 'Purpurea'
- **Purple-leaved plum** *Prunus cerasifera* 'Pissardii'
- **Smoke tree** *Cotinus coggygria* 'Royal Purple'
- **Sycamore** *Acer pseudoplatanus* 'Purpureum' and 'Spaethii'
- **Japanese cedar** *Cryptomeria japonica* 'Elegans'

Leaves–silver/grey

- **English holly** *Ilex aquifolium* 'Argenteomarginata Pendula', 'Silver Milkboy', 'Silver Queen', 'Silver Sentinel'
- **Olive** *Olea europaea*
- **Russian olive** *Elaeagnus angustifolia*
- **Sea buckthorn** *Hippophae rhamnoides*
- **Silver maple** *Acer saccharinum*
- **Weeping silver lime** *Tilia petiolaris*
- **Whitebeam** *Sorbus aria, S. lanata, S.c.* 'Mitchellii', *S. thibetica*
- **White poplar** *Populus alba*
- **White willow** *Salix alba* 'Sericea'
- **Willow-leaved pear** *Pyrus salicifolia*

- **Arizona cypress** *Cupressus glabra* 'Pyramidalis'
- **Blue spruce** *Picea pungens glauca*
- **Colorado white fir** *Abies concolor* 'Candicans'

Leaves–green and yellow

- **Box elder** *Acer negundo* 'Elegans'
- **Chestnut** *Castanea sativa* 'Aureomarginata'
- **English holly** *Ilex aquifolium* 'Golden Milkboy' and 'Golden Queen'
- **English oak** *Quercus robur* 'Variegata'
- **Highclere holly** *Ilex × altaclerensis* 'Golden King' and 'Lawsoniana'
- **Japanese angelica tree** *Aralia elata* 'Aureovariegata'
- **Sweetgum** *Liquidambar styraciflua* 'Aurea'
- **Tulip tree** *Liriodendron tulipifera* 'Aureomarginatum'

- **Chinese arborvitae** *Thuja orientalis* 'Elegantissima'
- **Golden yew** *Taxus baccata* 'Aurea'
- **Lawson cypress** *Chamaecyparis lawsoniana* 'Lanei', 'Lutea'
- **Oriental spruce** *Picea orientalis* 'Aurea'
- **Western red cedar** *Thuja plicata* 'Zebrina'
- **Yew** *Taxus baccata* 'Standishii'

Leaves–cream/yellow/gold

- **English elm** *Ulmus procera* 'Louis van Houtte'
- **English oak** *Quercus robur* 'Concordia'
- **European alder** *Alnus glutinosa* 'Aurea'
- **European ash** *Fraxinus excelsior* 'Jaspidea'
- **European beech** *Fagus sylvatica* 'Zlatia'
- **False acacia** *Robinia pseudoacacia* 'Frisia'
- **Golden-leaved laburnum** *Laburnum anagyroides* 'Aureum'
- **Golden poplar** *Populus* 'Serotina Aurea'
- **Honey locust** *Gleditsia triacanthos* 'Sunburst'
- **Japanese maple** *Acer japonicum* 'Aureum'
- **Laurel** *Laurus nobilis* 'Aurea'
- **Southern catalpa** *Catalpa bignonioides* 'Aurea'
- **Sycamore** *Acer pseudoplatanus* 'Brilliantissimum' and 'Worleei'
- **White poplar** *Populus alba* 'Richardii'

- **American arborvitae** *Thuja occidentalis* 'Rheingold'
- **Atlantic cedar** *Cedrus atlantica* 'Aurea'
- **Chinese juniper** *Juniperus chinensis* 'Aurea'
- **Hinoki cypress** *Chamaecyparis obtusa* 'Crippsii'
- **Lawson cypress** *Chamaecyparis lawsoniana* 'Winston Churchill'
- **Scots pine** *Pinus sylvestris* 'Aurea'

Leaves–blue-green

- **Eucalypt** *Eucalyptus* species

- **Bhutan pine** *Pinus wallichiana*
- **Blue Cedar** *Cedrus atlantica glauca*
- **Hemlock** *Tsuga mertensiana* 'Glauca'
- **Lawson cypress** *Chamaecyparis lawsoniana* 'Columnaris', 'Pembury Blue', 'Triomf van Boskoop', 'Wisselii', etc
- **Scots pine** *Pinus sylvestris*
- **Weymouth pine** *Pinus strobus*

Leaves–unusual and attractive

- **Camellia** *Camellia* species
- **Cherry laurel** *Prunus laurocerasus* 'Camelliifolia'
- **Chinese persimmon** *Diospyros kaki*
- **European alder** *Alnus glutinosa* 'Imperialis'
- **Fern-leaved beech** *Fagus sylvatica heterophylla*
- **Golden chestnut** *Chrysolepis chrysophylla*
- **Holly** *Ilex* species
- **Hornbeam** *Carpinus betulus* 'Incisa'
- **Hungarian oak** *Quercus frainetto*
- **Japanese maple** *Acer japonicum* 'Aconitifolium' and 'Vitifolium', *A. palmatum* 'Dissectum' and 'Linearilobum'
- **Katsura tree** *Cercidiphyllum japonicum*
- **Oriental plane** *Platanus orientalis*
- **Paper mulberry** *Broussonetia papyrifera*
- **Scarlet oak** *Quercus coccinea*
- **Swedish birch** *Betula pendula* 'Dalecarlica'
- **Sweetgum** *Liquidambar styraciflua*
- **Tulip tree** *Liriodendron tulipifera*

- **Maidenhair tree** *Ginkgo biloba*

Leaves–divided/cut

- **Cut-leaved walnut** *Juglans regia* 'Laciniata'
- **European alder** *Alnus glutinosa* 'Imperialis'
- **Fern-leaved beech** *Fagus sylvatica heterophylla*
- **Hornbeam** *Carpinus betulus* 'Incisa'
- **Japanese maple** *Acer japonicum* 'Aconitifolium', *A. palmatum* 'Dissectum'
- **Mountain ash** *Sorbus aucuparia* 'Asplenifolia'
- **Norway maple** *Acer platanoides* 'Dissectum', 'Laciniatum', 'Lorbergii'
- **Swedish birch** *Betula pendula* 'Dalecarlica'

Leaves–very early

- **Bird cherry** *Prunus padus commutata*
- **Hawthorn** *Crataegus oxyacantha*
- **Horse chestnut** *Aesculus hippocastanum*
- **Japanese flowering crab** *Malus floribunda*
- **Manchurian birch** *Betula platyphylla*
- **Roblé beech** *Nothofagus obliqua*
- **Southern beech** *Nothofagus procera*

- **Dawn redwood** *Metasequoia glyptostroboides*

Leaves–late to drop

- **Algerian oak** *Quercus canariensis*
- **Chinese elm** *Ulmus parvifolia*
- **English elm** *Ulmus procera*
- **Hawthorn** *Crataegus × lavallei*
- **Laurel oak** *Quercus laurifolia*
- **Lucombe oak** *Quercus × hispanica* 'Lucombeana'
- **Water oak** *Quercus nigra*
- **White oak** *Quercus alba*

Autumn colour

- **Amur cork tree** *Phellodendron amurense*
- **Antarctic beech** *Nothofagus antarctica*
- **Aspen** *Populus tremula*
- **Beech** *Fagus* (most species)
- **Birch** *Betula* (most species)
- **Black cottonwood** *Populus trichocarpa*
- **Black tupelo** *Nyssa sylvatica*
- **Buckeye** *Aesculus parviflora*
- **Caucasian wingnut** *Pterocarya fraxinifolia*
- **Cercidiphyllum** *Cercidiphyllum japonicum*
- **Chinese persimmon** *Diospyros kaki*
- **Chinese toon** *Toona sinensis*
- **Chinese witch hazel** *Hamamelis mollis*
- **Crab** *Malus tschonoskii*
- **Disanthus** *Disanthus cercidifolius*
- **English elm** *Ulmus procera*
- **Flowering dogwood** *Cornus florida*
- **Franklinia** *Franklinia* species
- **Giant dogwood** *Cornus controversa*
- **Guelder rose** *Viburnum opulus*
- **Hickory** *Carya* species
- **Japanese cherry** *Prunus sargentii*
- **Japanese dogwood** *Cornus kousa*
- **Japanese maple** *Acer palmatum* 'Ozakazuki'
- **Kentucky coffee tree** *Gymnocladus dioicus*
- **Mountain ash** *Sorbus alnifolia, S. americana, S. aucuparia, S. commixta, S.* 'Embley', *S. sargentiana*
- **Nikko maple** *Acer maximowiczianum*
- **Norway maple** *Acer platanoides*
- **Ohio buckeye** *Aesculus glabra*
- **Pacific dogwood** *Cornus nuttallii*
- **Persian parrotia** *Parrotia persica*
- **Pin oak** *Quercus palustris*
- **Quaking aspen** *Populus tremuloides*
- **Red maple** *Acer rubrum*
- **Red oak** *Quercus rubra*
- **Sassafras** *Sassafras albidum*
- **Scarlet oak** *Quercus coccinea*
- **Smoke tree** *Cotinus* species
- **Snowy mespilus** *Amelanchier* species
- **Sourwood** *Oxydendrum arboreum*
- **Stag's horn sumach** *Rhus typhina*
- **Stewartia** *Stewartia koreana, S. pseudocamellia*
- **Sugar maple** *Acer saccharum*
- **Sweetgum** *Liquidambar styraciflua*
- **Trident maple** *Acer buergerianum*
- **Tulip tree** *Liriodendron tulipifera*
- **White oak** *Quercus alba*
- **White poplar** *Populus alba*
- **Willow oak** *Quercus phellos*

Witch hazel *Hamamelis virginiana*
Yellow wood *Cladrastis* species
Zelkova *Zelkova serrata*

Dawn redwood *Metasequoia glyptostroboides*
Golden larch *Pseudolarix amabilis*
Larch *Larix* species
Maidenhair tree *Ginkgo biloba*
Pond cypress *Taxodium ascendens*
Swamp cypress *Taxodium distichum*

Flowers–early in spring

Alder *Alnus* species
Almond *Prunus dulcis*
Aspen *Populus tremula*
Birch *Betula* species
Camellia *Camellia* species
Cherry plum *Prunus cerasifera*
Elm *Ulmus* species
Goat willow *Salix caprea*
Hazel *Corylus* species
Italian maple *Acer opalus*
Magnolia *Magnolia campbellii*
Norway maple *Acer platanoides*
Silver wattle *Acacia dealbata*
Witch hazel *Hamamelis* species

Flowers–ornamental

Broom *Cytisus battandieri*
Camellia *Camellia* species
Carolina silverball *Halesia tetraptera*
Cherry *Prunus* (most species)
Chilean fire bush *Embothrium coccineum*
Chinese witch hazel *Hamamelis mollis*
Cootamundra wattle *Acacia baileyana*
Crab *Malus* (most species)
Dogwood *Cornus* species
Dove (or handkerchief) tree *Davidia involucrata, D.i.* var. *vilmoriniana*
European pussy willow *Salix caprea*
Golden-rain tree *Koelreuteria paniculata*
Hawthorn *Crataegus* species
Horse chestnut *Aesculus hippocastanum, A.h.* 'Baumannii'
Indian horse chestnut *Aesculus indica*
Japanese witch hazel *Hamamelis japonica* 'Arborea'
Judas tree *Cercis siliquastrum*
Laburnum *Laburnum* species
Magnolia *Magnolia* species
Mountain silverbell *Halesia monticola*
Red buckeye *Aesculus pavia*
Redbud *Cercis canadensis*
Red horse chestnut *Aesculus* × *carnea*
Silk tree *Albizia julibrissin, A.j.* 'Rosea'
Silver wattle *Acacia dealbata, A. decurrens*
Stewartia *Stewartia koreana, S. pseudocamellia*
Sydney golden wattle *Acacia longifolia*
Violet willow *Salix daphnoides*
Willow *Salix gracilistyla*
Wingnut *Pterocarya* species
Witch hazel *Hamamelis virginiana*
Yellow wood *Cladrastis lutea*

Lawson cypress *Chamaecyparis lawsoniana*
Likiang spruce *Picea likiangensis*
Pine *Pinus* (many species)

Fruit–ornamental

American holly *Ilex opaca, I.o.* 'Xanthocarpa'
Black mulberry *Morus nigra*
Blackthorn *Prunus spinosa*
Blueberry elder *Sambucus caerulea*
Campbell's magnolia *Magnolia campbellii mollicomata*
Caucasian wingnut *Pterocarya fraxinifolia*
Chinaberry *Melia azedarach*
Chinese persimmon *Diospyros kaki*
Choke cherry *Prunus virginiana*
Cotoneaster *Cotoneaster* × *watereri*
Crab *Malus* (many species)
Dogwood *Cornus* (many species)
Elder *Sambucus nigra*
English holly *Ilex aquifolium* 'Bacciflava', *I.a.* 'J. C. van Tol'
Hawthorn *Crataegus* (most species)
Highclere holly *Ilex* × *altaclerensis* 'Camelliifolia', 'Golden King'
Italian alder *Alnus cordata*
Japanese broadleaf holly *Ilex latifolia*
Japanese hornbeam *Carpinus japonica*
Japanese whiteleaf magnolia *Magnolia obovata*
Judas tree *Cercis siliquastrum*
Medlar *Mespilus germanica*
Mountain ash *Sorbus* species
Osage orange *Maclura pomifera*
Perny holly *Ilex pernyi*
Persimmon *Diospyros virginiana*
Quince *Cydonia oblonga*
Sea buckthorn *Hippophae rhamnoides*
Strawberry tree *Arbutus unedo*
Tree of heaven *Ailanthus altissima*
Whitebeam *Sorbus* species

Cedar *Cedrus* species
Fir *Abies* species (late summer)
Pine *Pinus* species
Spruce *Picea* species (autumn/winter)
Yew *Taxus* species

Bark–ornamental

Amur cork tree *Phellodendron amurense*
Birch *Betula* (most species)
'Capillipes' maple *Acer capillipes*
Cherry *Prunus serrula*
Cork oak *Quercus suber*
David's maple *Acer davidii*
English walnut *Juglans regia*
Eucalypt *Eucalyptus* (most species)
European beech *Fagus sylvatica*
Japanese maple *Acer palmatum* 'Senkaki'
London plane *Platanus* × *acerifolia* 'Hispanica'
Manchurian cherry *Prunus maackii*
Paperbark maple *Acer griseum*
Persian parrotia *Parrotia persica*
Rhododendron *Rhododendron barbatum*
Shagbark hickory *Carya ovata*
Snakebark maple *Acer davidii* ssp. *grosseri*
Snowgum *Eucalyptus pauciflora* ssp. *niphophila*
Sorbus *Sorbus alnifolia*
Strawberry tree *Arbutus* species
Striped maple *Acer pensylvanicum*
Violet willow *Salix daphnoides*
White willow *Salix alba*
Zelkova *Zelkova carpinifolia*

Coast redwood *Sequoia sempervirens*
Lace-bark pine *Pinus bungeana*
Scots pine *Pinus sylvestris*

SOIL

Soil–able to grow in clay

Alder *Alnus* species
Ash *Fraxinus* species
Birch *Betula* species
Cherry *Prunus* species
Cotoneaster *Cotoneaster* species
Crab *Malus* species
Dogwood *Cornus* species
Eucalypt *Eucalyptus* species
Hawthorn *Crataegus* species
Hazel *Corylus* species
Hornbeam *Carpinus* species
Horse chestnut *Aesculus* species
Laburnum *Laburnum* species
Lime *Tilia* species
Maple *Acer* species
Poplar *Populus* species
Rose *Rosa* species
Smoke tree *Cotinus* species
Sorbus *Sorbus* species
Willow *Salix* species
Witch hazel *Hamamelis* species

Arborvitae *Thuja* species
Fir *Abies* species
Larch *Larix* species
Swamp cypress *Taxodium distichum*

Soil–can be acid

Aspen *Populus tremula*
Birch *Betula* species
Chilean fire bush *Embothrium* species
Cotoneaster *Cotoneaster* species
Disanthus *Disanthus cercidifolius*
English oak *Quercus robur*
Franklinia *Franklinia* species
Grey poplar *Populus* × *canescens*
Heath *Erica* species
Holly *Ilex* species
Rhododendron *Rhododendron* species
Sourwood *Oxydendrum arboreum*
White poplar *Populus alba*

Juniper *Juniperus* species
Pine *Pinus* species
Yew *Taxus* species

Soil–can be alkaline

Ash *Fraxinus* species
Beech *Fagus* species
Birch *Betula* species
Cotoneaster *Cotoneaster* species
Crab *Malus* species
Dogwood *Cornus* species
English holly *Ilex aquifolium*
Hawthorn *Crataegus* species
Hedge maple *Acer campestre*
Highclere holly *Ilex* × *altaclerensis*
Hornbeam *Carpinus* species
Horse chestnut *Aesculus* species
Laurel *Laurus nobilis*
Phillyrea *Phillyrea* species
Whitebeam *Sorbus* species

American arborvitae *Thuja occidentalis*
Austrian pine *Pinus nigra*
English yew *Taxus baccata*
Hiba false arborvitae *Thujopsis dolabrata*
Juniper *Juniperus* species
Western red cedar *Thuja plicata*

Soil–must be lime-free (acid)

Bigleaf magnolia *Magnolia macrophylla*
Black tupelo *Nyssa sylvatica*
Camellia *Camellia* species
Campbell's magnolia *Magnolia campbellii, M.c. mollicomata*
Chilean fire bush *Embothrium* species
Clethra *Clethra* species
Gordonia *Gordonia* species
Japanese whiteleaf magnolia *Magnolia hypoleuca*
Japanese willowleaf magnolia *Magnolia salicifolia*
Lily-flowered magnolia *Magnolia liliiflora, M. l.* 'Nigra'
Pin oak *Quercus palustris*
Red oak *Quercus rubra*
Rhododendron *Rhododendron* species
Scarlet oak *Quercus coccinea*
Shumard oak *Quercus shumardii*
Silverbell *Halesia* species
Snowbell *Styrax* species
Sourwood *Oxydendrum arboreum*
Southern beech *Nothofagus* species
Stewartia *Stewartia* species
Sweetgum *Liquidambar styraciflua*
Veitch magnolia *Magnolia* × *veitchii*
Willow oak *Quercus phellos*
Yulan magnolia *Magnolia denudata*

Soil–very dry, either acid or alkaline

Aspen *Populus tremula*
Chestnut *Castanea* species
Grey poplar *Populus* × *canescens*
Robinia *Robinia* species
Siberian elm *Ulmus pumila*
White poplar *Populus alba*

Cedar *Cedrus* species
Cypress *Cupresses* (some species)
Juniper *Juniperus*
Yew *Taxus* species

Soil–can be badly drained

Alder *Alnus* species
Black tupelo *Nyssa sylvatica*
Caucasian wingnut *Pterocarya fraxinifolia*
Elder *Sambucus* species
European birch *Betula pendula*
Hawthorn *Crataegus oxyacantha*
Medlar *Mespilus germanica*
Mountain ash *Sorbus aucuparia*
Pear *Pyrus communis*
Pin oak *Quercus palustris*
Poplar *Populus* species
Red maple *Acer rubrum*
River birch *Betula nigra*
Swamp bay magnolia *Magnolia virginiana*
Swamp white oak *Quercus bicolor*
Sweetgum *Liquidambar styraciflua*
White birch *Betula pubescens*
Willow *Salix* species

American arborvitae *Thuja occidentalis*
Dawn redwood *Metasequoia glyptostroboides*
Pond cypress *Taxodium ascendens*
Sitka spruce *Picea sitchensis*
Swamp cypress *Taxodium distichum*
Tamarack *Larix laricina*

SPECIAL SITES

Seaside/maritime areas

Aspen *Populus tremula*
Chamaerops *Chamaerops humilis*
English oak *Quercus robur*
Eucalypt *Eucalyptus* species
European ash *Fraxinus excelsior*
Grey poplar *Populus* × *canescens*
Hawthorn *Crataegus* (many species)
Holm oak *Quercus ilex*
Laurel *Laurus nobilis*
Mountain ash *Sorbus aucuparia*
Pittosporum *Pittosporum* species
Sea buckthorn *Hippophae rhamnoides*
Sessile oak *Quercus petraea*
Strawberry tree *Arbutus unedo*
Whitebeam *Sorbus aria*
White poplar *Populus alba*
Willow *Salix* (most species)

Aleppo pine *Pinus halepensis*
Bishop pine *Pinus muricata*
Black pine *Pinus thunbergii*
Juniper *Juniperus* (many species)
Maritime pine *Pinus pinaster*
Monterey cypress *Cupressus macrocarpa*
Monterey pine *Pinus radiata*
Shore pine *Pinus contorta*
Sitka spruce *Picea sitchensis*

Trees which will tolerate industrial or urban atmosphere

Allegheny service-berry *Amelanchier laevis*
Almond *Prunus dulcis*
Ash *Fraxinus* (most species)
Birch *Betula platyphylla*
Bird cherry *Prunus padus*
Black mulberry *Morus nigra*
Box elder *Acer negundo*
Bull bay magnolia *Magnolia grandiflora*
Camellia *Camellia japonica*
Catalpa *Catalpa* species
Caucasian wingnut *Pterocarya fraxinifolia*
Cherry plum *Prunus cerasifera*
Chinaberry *Melia azedarach*
Chinese toon *Cedrela sinensis*
Clethra *Clethra arborea*
Cotoneaster *Cotoneaster* × *watereri*
Crab *Malus* species
Cucumber tree *Magnolia acuminata*
English elm *Ulmus procera*
English holly *Ilex aquifolium*
European birch *Betula pendula*
European hornbeam *Carpinus betulus*
European lime *Tilia* × *vulgaris*
False acacia *Robinia pseudoacacia*
Gean *Prunus avium*
Hackberry *Celtis* species
Hawthorn *Crataegus* species
Hedge maple *Acer campestre*
Highclere holly *Ilex* × *altaclerensis*
Holm oak *Quercus ilex*
Honey locust *Gleditsia triacanthos*
Horse chestnut *Aesculus* species
Japanese cherries *Prunus* species
Japanese pagoda tree *Sophora japonica*
Jersey elm *Ulmus* × *sarniensis*
Laburnum *Laburnum* species
Lime *Tilia* 'Euchlora'
Lucombe oak *Quercus* × *hispanica* 'Lucombeana'
Magnolia *Magnolia kobus, M.* × *soulangiana*
Medlar *Mespilus germanica*
Norway maple *Acer platanoides*
Paper birch *Betula papyrifera*
Poplar *Populus* (most species)
Red-twigged lime *Tilia platyphyllos* 'Rubra'
Snowy mespilus *Amelanchier canadensis, A. lamarckii, A. ovalis*
Strawberry tree *Arbutus unedo*
Sycamore *Acer pseudoplatanus*
Tree of heaven *Ailanthus altissima*
Tulip tree *Liriodendron tulipifera*
White birch *Betula pubescens*
White elm *Ulmus americana*
Wych elm *Ulmus glabra*
Yulan magnolia *Magnolia denudata*

Colorado spruce *Picea pungens*
Maidenhair tree *Ginkgo biloba*
White fir *Abies concolor*

For small gardens

Carolina silverbell *Halesia tetraptera*
Cherry *Prunus* (most species)
Cotoneaster *Cotoneaster* × *watereri*
Crab *Malus* species
Dawyck beech *Fagus sylvatica* 'Dawyck'
Dogwood *Cornus* species
Eastern redbud *Cercis canadensis*
Flowering ash *Fraxinum ornus*
Fragrant snowbell *Styrax obassia*
Franklinia *Franklinia alatamaha*
Genista *Genista* species
Golden-rain tree *Koelreuteria paniculata*
Hawthorn *Crataegus* (most species)
Hazel *Corylus* species
Heath *Erica* species
Holly *Ilex* species
Japanese maple *Acer japonicum, A. palmatum*
Japanese snowbell *Styrax japonica*
Japanese willowleaf magnolia *Magnolia salicifolia*
Judas tree *Cercis siliquastrum*
Katsura tree *Cercidiphyllum japonicum*
Laburnum *Laburnum* species
Medlar *Mespilus germanica*
Ohio buckeye *Aesculus glabra*
Paperbark maple *Acer griseum*
Photinia *Photinia* species
Quince *Cydonia oblonga*
Rhododendron *Rhododendron* species
Russian olive *Elaeagnus angustifolia*
Sea buckthorn *Hippophae rhamnoides*
Silk oak *Grevillea* species
Snowy mespilus *Amelanchier* species
Sorbus *Sorbus* (most species)
Sourwood *Oxydendrum arboreum*
Stewartia *Stewartia* species
Willow *Salix* (some species)
Willow-leaf pear *Pyrus salicifolia* 'Pendula'
Witch hazel *Hamamelis* species

Dwarf conifers
Eastern hemlock *Tsuga canadensis*
Lace-bark pine *Pinus bungeana*

Street trees–big

Buttonwood *Platanus occidentalis*
Castor-aralia *Kalopanax pictus*
False acacia *Robinia pseudoacacia*
Green ash *Fraxinus pensylvanica lanceolata*
Honey locust *Gleditsia triacanthos*
London plane *Platanus* × *acerifolia* 'Hispanica'
Norway maple *Acer platanoides*
Pin oak *Quercus palustris*
Red maple *Acer rubrum*
Red oak *Quercus rubra*
Scarlet oak *Quercus coccinea*
Velvet ash *Fraxinus velutina*
Willow oak *Quercus phellos*

Maidenhair tree *Ginkgo biloba*
Pine *Pinus* (many species)

For narrower streets

Any upright tree (see tables above)
'Capillipes' maple *Acer capillipes*
Cherry *Prunus* (most species)
Chinaberry *Melia azedarach*
Chinese toon *Cedrela sinensis*
Euodia *Tetradium daniellii*
European hornbeam *Carpinus betulus* 'Columnaris'
Flowering ash *Fraxinus ornus*
Flowering dogwood *Cornus florida*
Hawthorn *Crataegus* (most species)
Hedge maple *Acer campestre*
Japanese dogwood *Cornus kousa*
Japanese hornbeam *Carpinus japonica*
Lebanon oak *Quercus libani*
Montpelier maple *Acer monspessulanum*
Paperbark maple *Acer griseum*
Tatarian maple *Acer tataricum*

Screening–(very) fast

Bat willow *Salix alba* var. *caerulea*
Black cottonwood *Populus trichocarpa*
Crack willow *Salix fragilis*
Eucalypt *Eucalyptus* species
Lombardy poplar *Populus nigra* 'Italica'
'Robusta' poplar *Populus* 'Robusta'

Leyland cypress × *Cupressocyparis leylandii*
Monterey cypress *Cupressus macrocarpa*
Monterey pine *Pinus radiata*
Western hemlock *Tsuga heterophylla*

Tolerant of heavy shade

Beech *Fagus* (some species)
Camellia *Camellia japonica*
Cherry laurel *Prunus laurocerasus*
Common elder *Sambucus nigra*
Holly *Ilex* (some species)
Holm oak *Quercus ilex*
Portugal laurel *Prunus lusitanica*
Sycamore *Acer pseudoplatanus*
Cephalotaxus *Cephalotaxus* species
Coast redwood *Sequoia sempervirens*
English yew *Taxus baccata*
Juniper *Juniperus* (most species)
Western hemlock *Tsuga heterophylla*
Western red cedar *Thuja plicata*

Suitable for tubs

Box *Buxus sempervirens*
Camellia *Camellia* species
Citrus *Citrus* (most species)
Holly *Ilex* (some species)
Laurel *Laurus nobilis*

Chinese arborvitae *Platyladus orientalis* 'Elegantissima'
English yew *Taxus baccata* 'Standishii'
False cypress *Chamaecyparis thyoides* 'Andelyensis'
Lawson cypress *Chamaecyparis lawsoniana* 'Ellwoodii'

Resent moving–except when very small

Birch *Betula* species
Black tupelo *Nyssa sylvatica*
Castor-aralia *Kalopanax septemlobus*
Hickory *Carya* species
Holly *Ilex* species
Kentucky coffee tree *Gymnocladus dioicus*
Magnolia *Magnolia* species
Scarlet oak *Quercus coccinea*
Strawberry tree *Arbutus* species
Sweetgum *Liquidambar styraciflua*
Tulip tree *Liriodendron tulipifera*
Walnut *Juglans* species
White oak *Quercus alba*

Cedar *Cedrus* species
Fir *Abies* species
Monterey cypress *Cupressus macrocarpa*
Pine *Pinus* species (except five-needled pines)
Spruce *Picea* species

FEW PESTS OR DISEASES

Alder *Alnus* species
Amur cork tree *Phellodendron amurense*
Castor-aralia *Kalopanax septemlobus*
Dove tree *Davidia* species
English holly *Ilex aquifolium*
Eucalypt *Eucalyptus* species
Glossy privet *Ligustrum lucidum*
Golden-rain tree *Koelreuteria paniculata*
Highclere holly *Ilex* × *altaclerensis*
Honey locust *Gleditsia triacanthos*
Hornbeam *Carpinus* species
Japanese pagoda tree *Sophora japonica*
Katsura tree *Cercidiphyllum* species
Kentucky coffee tree *Gymnocladus dioicus*
Laburnum *Laburnum* species
Magnolia *Magnolia* species
Persian parrotia *Parrotia persica*
Russian olive *Elaeagnus angustifolia*
Snowbell *Styrax* species
Sweetgum *Liquidambar styraciflua*
Tree of heaven *Ailanthus altissima*
White poplar *Populus alba*

Araucaria *Araucaria* species
Coast redwood *Sequoia sempervirens*
Dawn redwood *Metasequoia glyptostroboides*
False cypress *Chamaecyparis* (most species)
Incense cedar *Calocedrus decurrens*
Japanese umbrella pine *Sciadopitys verticillata*
Juniper *Juniperus* species
Maidenhair tree *Ginkgo biloba*
Podocarpus *Podocarpus* species
Swamp cypress *Taxodium* species
Yew *Taxus* species

The Meanings of Botanical Names

Medieval botanical works used descriptive phrases in Latin to identify plants. Carl Linnaeus (1707–1778) did the same, but to each plant (or animal) he also gave a shorter, two-word Latin name: its genus followed by its species. So thorough and indispensable were his books that this convenient two-name system gradually took over completely. Today it is in universal use by all who deal professionally with living organisms.

Every known plant now has a Latin name which identifies it in every country. The advantages of the system are obvious. Most people, however, naturally stick to vernacular names for the few plants they know. For that matter only a minority of plants have vernacular names to stick to. In the United States strenuous efforts are made to give every exotic introduction an English name–but such productions as the Chinese fragrant epaulette tree can hardly be called true vernacular names. And the trouble with the old ones is that they mean different things to different people in different places. Sooner or later one is faced with the need to use, or at least with the value of understanding, the botanical Latin name. The list below demonstrates that for many trees it is a useful description, for others an interesting indication of where it comes from, for others a well-deserved memorial to the explorer who found it. The accent marks the syllable (if any) which is normally stressed. In this list 'ii' is normally pronounced as a long 'i' and 'ae' as a long 'e'.

A

Ábies Old Latin name for fir. From *abire*, to rise, alluding to the great height of some species.
abramsiana In honour of LeRoy Abrams (1874–1956), Professor of Botany at Stamford University, U.S.A.
Acácia Greek name for an African species of *Acacia*; from *akis*, a sharp point.
Ácer Old Latin name for maple; also means sharp; the wood was used for spears.
'Aconitifólium' Has leaves like an aconite.
acumináta Slender-pointed.
acúta Sharply pointed.
acutifólia With sharply pointed leaves or leaflets.
acutíssima Very acutely pointed.
adámii In honour of M. Adam, a nurseryman near Paris, France.
adpréssa Closely pressed together (usually of leaves against shoots).
Áesculus Latin name for a kind of oak, but applied by Linnaeus to the horse chestnut.
aetnénsis From Mt. Etna, Sicily.
agrifólia With rough leaves.
Ailánthus Latinized version of the native Moluccan name *ailanto*, sky tree.
alátamaha From the North American Indian name *Altamaha* for the river where it was first found.
álba White.
albertiána Native of Alberta, Canada.
albicáulis White-stemmed (*albus*=white, *caulis*=stem).
álbidum Whitish.
Albízia In honour of F. del Albizzi, a Florentine nobleman who in 1749 introduced this (the 'silk tree') into cultivation.
albolimbátum Edged with white.
álbosinénsis *Albus*=white, and *sinensis*=China.
aleurítes From the Greek *aleuron*, floury; in some species the young growth has a flour-dusted appearance.
Alexándrae In honour of Queen Alexandra (1844–1925), wife of Edward VII.
alnifólia With leaves like those of alder.
Álnus Old Latin name for the alder.
alpínum From alpine regions.
altaclerénsis Raised at Highclere, a mansion in Hampshire, England.
altíssima Very tall.
amábilis Pleasant, but often used in the sense of lovely.
ambígua Uncertain or doubtful.
Amelánchier From the French Provençal name *amelancier* for *A. ovalis*.
americánus, -a From the Americas.
amurénsis, -e From the region of the Amur River in Manchuria.
amýgdalo-pérsica A combination of *Prunus amygdalus* (*dulcis*), the almond, and *Prunus persica*, the peach.
amygdalóides Resembling almond.
amýgdalus The Greek name for the almond.
anagyróides Resembling *Anagyris*.
'Andelyénsis' From les Andelys, near Paris.
andínus From the Andes of South America.
andráchne Ancient Greek name.
andrachnóides Resembling *Arbutus andrachne* (ancient Greek name for the strawberry tree, used by Linnaeus).
angustifólia Narrow-leaved.
annuláris Ring-shaped.
antárctica Literally from the South Polar region, but used in biology for plants and animals native to south of 45°S.
apiculáta Leaves abruptly tipped with a short point.
aquática Growing in or near water.
aquifólium Latin vernacular name for holly, meaning having leaves with points.
Arália From the Latinization of the French Canadian name *Aralie*.
araucána From the Araucani Indians of central Chile, in whose territory the first discovered species is native.
Araucária *See above.*
arbórea, -éscens, -um Tree-like.
Arbútus Latin name for strawberry tree.
Archonthophoénix From the Greek *archon*, a chieftain, and *phoenix*, the date palm; refers to the stately appearance of these palms.
Arecástrum '-astrum' indicates a resemblance to *Areca*, the Indian betelnut palm.
argéntea, -um Silvery.
'Argénteomarginàta' With silver edges.
ária Old Latin name for whitebeam.
aristáta From the Latin *aristatus*, bearded; so, bearded with awns like ears of barley.
arizónica From the state of Arizona, U.S.A.
armándii The Christian name of l'Abbé Armand David, the French missionary and naturalist who worked in China.
armeniáca From Armenia, on the Black Sea.
articuláta Articulated or jointed.
ascéndens From the Latin *ascendens*, rising upwards.
Asímina The Latinized version of the French form of the Indian vernacular *assimin*.
asperáta From the Latin *asperatus*, roughened.
aspleniifólia With leaves like the spleenwort i.e. fine, feathery, and fernlike.
Athrotáxis From the Greek *athroos*, crowded together, and *taxis*, arrangement; in reference to the crowded nature of the cone scales.
atlántica From the Atlas Mountains of North Africa (also from the shores of the Atlantic).
atropurpúrea, -um Dark purple.
attenuáta Narrowing to a point.
aucupária Old Latin name for rowan tree; from *aucupor*, bird catching, it being used as bait and as an ingredient of bird lime by bird catchers.
aúrea, -um, -us From *aurum*, the Latin for gold; literally, golden.
'Aúrea Nána' Golden-yellow, dwarf.
Aúreomarginátum' With golden edges.
'Aúreospíca' With golden spikes.
'Aúreovariegáta' Gold-variegated.
'Auróra' A fanciful resemblance to the electrical phenomenon of the same name.
austrális Southern, in the sense of southern hemisphere or sometimes of southern Europe.
Aústrocédrus Literally, southern cedar.
autumnális Flowering in the autumn.
avellána From Avella Vecchia in southern Italy.
ávium Of the birds (eaten by).
áyacahuíte The Mexican name for *Pinus ayacahuite*.
azédarach A contracted version of the Persian (Iranian) name *azaddhirakt* for *Melia azedarach*.
azórica From the Azores Islands.

B

babylónica From Babylon.
baccáta From the Latin *baccatus*, berry-like.
'Baccifláva' Yellow-berried.
baileyána In honour of Frederick Manson Bailey (1827–1915), an Australian botanist.
bákeri In honour of John Gilbert Baker (1834–1920), the British botanist who was Keeper of Kew Herbarium from 1890–99.
balsaméa Balsam-like.
balsamifera Balsam-bearing.
banksiána In honour of Sir Joseph Banks (1743–1820), British naturalist who accompanied Captain Cook's round-the-world expedition of 1768–71 in the *Endeavour*.
barbátum Bearded.
battandiéri In honour of Jules Aimé Battandier (1848–1922), a French botanist and an authority on the flora of Algeria.
'Baumannii' In honour of E. N. Baumann of Bolivia.
'Bélgica' From Belgium or the Netherlands.
Bétula The old Latin name for the birch tree.
betulóides Resembling the birch tree, *Betula*.
bétulus Resembling the birch tree, *Betula*.
bícolor Two colours.
bídwillii In honour of J. C. Bidwill (1815–53). Director of the Botanic Garden, Sydney, who collected plants in New Zealand and Australia.
'Biflóra' Two-flowered.
bignonióides Resembling the trumpet creeper, *Bignonia*.
bilóba Two-lobed.
blánda Mild.
boária The Chilean vernacular name meaning loved by cattle (referring to the leaves of *Maytenus boaria*).
boreális Northern.
bracteáta Having conspicuous bracts.
brevifólia With short leaves.
breweriána In honour of William Henry Brewer (1828–1910), American pioneer botanist in California and professor of agriculture at Yale University.
brilliantissimum The most brilliant.
'Briótii' In honour of Pierre Louis Briot (1804–88), a French horticulturist.
Broussonétia In honour of Pierre Marie Auguste Broussonet (1761–1807), professor of botany at Montpellier, France.
brunónii In honour of the botanist Robert Bruon, F.R.S. (1773–1858).
buergeriánum In honour of Heinrich Bürger (1804[6?]–58), German plant collector.
bungeána In honour of Alexander von Bunge (1803–90), a Russian botanist and professor of botany at Dorpat in Estonia.
Búxus The classical Latin name for the box tree.

C

caerúlea Dark blue.
cáesia Lavender blue.
califórnica From California, U.S.A.
calleryána In honour of J. M. Callery (1810–62), a Roman Catholic missionary and botanist in China and Korea.
Callitris From the Greek *kali*, beautiful, and *tris* indicating the arrangement in three of leaves, cone-scabs, etc.
Calocédrus From the Greek *kalos*, beautiful, and the Latin *cedrus*, cedar.
calophýtum From the Greek *kalos*, beautiful, and *phytum*, a plant.
camaldulénsis Named after Camaldule in Australia.
Caméllia In honour of Georg Joseph Kamel (1661–1706), a Jesuit pharmacist and botanist from Moravia who studied the plants of the Philippines and wrote an account of them.
camelliifolia With leaves like a camellia.
campanuláta Bell-shaped.
campbéllii In honour of Dr. Archibald Campbell, Superintendent of Darjeeling and companion of Sir Joseph Hooker on his journey through the Sikkim Himalaya in 1849.
'Camperdównii' Castle in Angus, Scotland, where the elm *Ulmus glabra* 'Camperdownii' arose.
campéstre Of the fields.
cámphora Like camphor.
canadénsis From Canada.
'Canáertii' In honour of the late 19th-century Belgian nurseryman.
canariénsis From the Canary Islands.
cándicans Shining.
canéscens Off-white or ash-grey.
cápillípes With slender feet.
capitáta With a dense knob-like head, meaning flowers, fruits, or whole plant.
cappadócicum From Cappadocia, an ancient province of Asia Minor.
cáprea Favoured by goats.
caramánica From Caramania (Karamania) in southern Asia Minor.
caribáea From the Caribbean area.
caríca From Caria, a district in Asia Minor.
cárnea Flesh or deep pink.
carolína, caroliniána From North or South Carolina, U.S.A.
carpinifólia, -um With leaves like those of *Carpinus* (hornbeam).
Carpínus The classical Latin name for the hornbeam.
Cárya From the Greek *karya*, walnut tree. Its fruit was known as *karyon*, which was also applied to other nuts.
cashmiriána From Kashmir.
cássine The North American Indian name for dahoon holly.
Castánea The Latin name for the sweet chestnut, from Kasanaia, a city in Asia Minor.
castaneifólia With leaves like those of *Castanea* (sweet chestnut).
Castanópsis Related to *Castanea*, the chestnut.
Casuarína The branches have been said to resemble cassowary (*Casuarinus*) feathers.
Catálpa The North American Indian name for *Catalpa bignonioides*, the first species in this genus to be cultivated in Europe.
Cedréla Diminutive of the Latin *cedrus*; from a similarity in the wood and its fragrance.
Cédrus The Latin name for the cedar, though originally the Latin *cedrus* and Greek *kedros* may have applied to species of juniper.
Céltis The Greek name of an unrelated tree, taken up for the hackberry by Linnaeus.
cémbra The Italian name for the Swiss Arolla or stone pine.
cembróides Resembling *Pinus cembra*, the Swiss Arolla pine.
cephalónica From the island of Cephalonia in the Ionian Sea.
Cephalotáxus From the Greek *kephale*, a head, and *taxus*, the yew tree; referring to the relationship to the yew, and resemblance of some species.
cerasífera Cherry-like, referring to the fruits.
cérasus The Latin name for cherry.
Ceratónia The Greek name *keratonia* for the carob.
Cercidiphýllum With leaves like those of the Judas tree, *Cercis*.
Cércis From the Greek name *kerkis* used for the Judas tree.
cerífera Wax-bearing.
cérris A kind of oak, from the old Latin name.
Chámaecýparis From the Greek *chamai*, dwarf, and *kuparissos*, cypress. This now inapt name seems to have been derived from the dwarf juvenile forms formerly known as retinospora.
Chámaerops From the Greek *chamai*, dwarf, and *rhops*, a bush.
'Charles Raffill' In honour of C. P. Raffill (1876–1951), curator of Kew Gardens.
'Chermesína' *Salix alba* 'Chermesina' was named after the Chermes (*Adelges*) insect because of the similar reddish colour of the young shoots.
chilénsis From Chile.
chinénsis From China.
Chionánthus Having snow-white flowers; from the Greek *chión*, snow, and *anthos*, a flower.
chrysocóma With golden hairs.
chrysolépis With golden scales.
chrysophýlla Having golden leaves.
cinérea Ash-coloured.
cinnamómum From the classical Greek name for cinnamon.
circinátum Rolled in a circular fashion.
citriodóra Citrus (lemon) scented.
Cítrus The Latin name for the citron (*Citrus medica*).
Cladrástis From the Greek *klados*, branch, and *thraustos*, fragile; alluding to the brittle twigs.
Cléthra From the Greek *kléthra*, the white alder tree, which has similar leaves.
cliffortioídes Like *Cliffortia*, a South African shrub of the rose family.
coccífera Bearing red berries.
coccínea, -um Scarlet.
Cócos From the Portuguese for monkey (*Cocos*), referring to the nut which suggests a monkey's face.
coeruléa Blue.

coggygria An inaccurate rendering of the Greek *kokkugia*, the vernacular name for the smoke tree (*Cotinus*).
colorata Coloured.
'Cólumnáris', -e In the shape of a column.
colúrna Old Latin name for hazel nut or wood.
'Cómmelin' In honour of the Dutch botanists Johan (1629–92) and Caspar (1667–1731) Commelin.
commíxta Mixed together.
commúnis Growing in company, or common.
commutáta Changed or changing.
compréssa Compressed or flattened.
concolór The same colour throughout.
conférta Crowded.
cónica Cone-shaped.
conradinae In honour of Conradine, wife of the German botanist B. A. E. Koehne (1848–1918).

conspícua From the Latin *conspicuus*, conspicuous, distinctive, remarkable.
contórta From the Latin *contortus*, twisted or irregularly bent.
controvérsa Controversial, doubtful or questionable.
cordáta Heart-shaped.
cordifólia With heart-shaped leaves.
cordifórmis Heart-shaped.
Cordýline From the Greek *kordyle*, a club.
cornúbia Of Cornwall, England.
cornubiénsis Of Cornwall, England.
Córnus The old Latin name for the cornelian cherry, *Cornus mas*.
coronária Used for garlands.
Córylus The Greek name for the hazel bush, *Corylus avellana*.
costáta Ribbed.
Cotínus From the Greek *kotinos*, a name for the wild olive and therefore of obscure meaning, though possibly used as a term for several bushes of no economic value.
Cotoneáster From the Latin *cotoneum*, a quince, and *aster*, superficial or incomplete resemblance to; used to denote a wild or inferior species. Some species of *Cotoneaster* have leaves like those of quince.
cóulteri In honour of Thomas Coulter (1793–1843), an Irish botanist who travelled in the western States.
cóxii In honour of E. H. M. Cox, plant collector and author.
crataegifólium With leaves that resemble those of hawthorn, *Crataegus*.
+ **Crataegoméspilus** The combination of two generic names *Crataegus* and *Mespilus*, the fusion of their tissues forming this graft hybrid.
Crataégus The Greek name for hawthorn.
crenáta Cut in rounded scallops.
'Críppsii' In honour of the nurseryman Cripps of Tunbridge Wells, Kent, England.
crispa Closely curled.
cristáta Crested.
crus-gálli Cock's spur.
Cryptoméria From the Greek *krypto*, to hide, and *meris*, a part; all parts of the flowers (strobili) are concealed.
Cunninghámia In honour of James Cunningham, East India Company surgeon and plant collector.
Cunninghámia In honour of James Cunningham (*see Cunninghamia*).
'Cupréa' Copper-coloured.
cupressínum Resembling *Cupressus* or cypress.
× **Cupréssocypáris** Compounded from *Cupressus* and *Chamaecyparis*, the parents of this bigeneric hybrid.
cúpressoides Resembling *Cupressus* or cypress.
Cupréssus The Latin name for *Cupressus sempervirens*, the Italian cypress tree.
cuspidáta From the Latin *cuspidatus*, bearing a stiff point.
Cyáthea From the Greek *kyatheion*, a little cup; the membrane covering the spore-cases on the underside of the leaves breaks at the top at maturity, forming a cup.
Cydónia The Latin name for this fruit tree, derived from Cydon, a town in Crete.
Cýtisus Broom, from the Greek *kytisos*, a name used for several shrubby members of the pea family (*Leguminosae*).

D

dacrýdióides Resembling *Dacrydium*.
Dacrýdium From the Greek *dakrydion*, a small tear; some of these trees exude small drops of clear resin.
dactylífera Fingerlike.
Dáctylis From the Greek *daktylos*, a finger; the inflorescence appears fingerlike.
'Dalecárlica' From the Swedish province of Dalecarlia or Dalarna.
daniéllii After the surgeon-collector who toured Tientsin in 1860–62.
daphnóides Resembling *Daphne*, from the Greek name for the laurel.
dardárii In honour of M. Dardar of Bronvaux, Metz, in whose garden the graft hybrid *Crataegomespilus dardarii* arose.
Davídia In honour of l'Abbé Armand David (1826–1900), a French missionary and naturalist who worked and collected in China.
davídii In honour of l'Abbé Armand David (*see Davidia*).
'Dáwyck' From the famous Scottish garden on the banks of the River Tweed.
dealbáta Whitened, as with a powder.
'Decaisneána' In honour of Joseph Decaisne (1807–82), a director of the Jardin des Plantes, Paris, and a famous botanist and horticulturist.
decídua Deciduous (leafless in winter).
decóra, -um Decorative.
decúrrens Running down; used when leaf bases are extended down the stem in winglike tapering ridges.
delaváyi In honour of l'Abbé Jean Marie Delavay (1834–95), a missionary who collected plants in western China.
Délonix From the Greek *delos*, evident, and *onux*, a claw; referring to the long clawed (stalked) petals.
deltóides Triangular, like the Greek letter delta.
densiflóra, -us Densely flowered.
dentáta Toothed.
denudáta Bare or naked.
deodára From the native Indian name for the deodar cedar.
deppeaná pachyphláea Thick rinded.
diabólicum Devilish, applied to a plant with horned fruit.
Dicksónia In honour of James Dickson (1738–1822), a British nurseryman and botanist.
dicksónii In honour of James Dickson (*see Dicksonia*).
dioícus Dioecious; the separate-sexed flowers are borne on individual trees.
Diospýros From *dios*, divine, and *pyros*, wheat, a Greek name transferred to the persimmon, *Diospyros kaki*.
Disánthus Paired flowers; from *dis*, twice, and *anthos*, flower.
discólor Of two colours.
disséctum Deeply cut, divided into segments.
distíchum From the Latin *distichus*, in two parallel ranks.
diversifólia From the Latin *diversus*, diverse, and *folium*, leaf, with diverse leaves.
dolabráta Hatchet-shaped.
dombeyi In honour of Joseph Dombey (1742–94), a French botanist.
doméstica Domesticated; much used in gardens.
'Donard Gold' From the Slieve Donard Nursery Co. Ltd., Ireland.
'Dovastónii', -iana *Cephalotaxus x media* 'Dovastonii' was 'found' by Mr. John Dovaston of Westfelton, Shrewsbury, England.
'Drummóndii' In honour of Thomas Drummond (d 1835), nurseryman.
drupácea Bearing a fleshy fruit with a single seed within, like a cherry, an olive or a plum.
dúlcis Sweet.

E

ébenum Ebony-black.
echináta Prickly.
édulis Edible.
Ehrétia In honour of Georg Dionysius Ehret (1708–70), a German botanical artist.
Elaeágnus Said to be derived from the Greek *elaia*, the olive tree, and *agnos*, a name for the chaste-tree (*Vitex*), but more likely from *heleagnos*—*helodes*, marshy, and *hagnos*, pure (or white), in allusion to the white fruits.
eláta Tall.
elegáns Elegant.
elegantíssima Italian word for 'very elegant'.
'Ellwóodii' In honour of Mr. Ellwood, who discovered *Chamaecyparis pisifera* 'Ellwoodii' *c.* 1920 as a chance seedling at Swanmore Park, Bishop's Waltham, England, where he was gardener.
Embóthrium From the Greek *en*, in, and *bothrion*, a little pit; the stamens are borne in recesses or pits in the petals.
engelmánnii In honour of Georg Engelmann (1809–84), a German-born American doctor, greatly interested in plants. He did some collecting, but did more by encouraging others.
erécta, -um Erect or upright.
erecta viridis Erect or upright, and green.
Érica From the Latin *erice*, heath.
ericóides Resembling *Erica*.
ermanii In honour of G. A. Erman (1806–77) of Berlin, who collected in eastern Asia and elsewhere.
erubéscens Reddening.
erythrocládum Red-branched; from the Greek *erythro-*, red, and *klados*, branch.
érythrofléxuosa Red, bent alternately, zigzag.
Eucalýptus From the Greek *eu*, well, and *kalypto*, to cover (as with a lid); alluding to the petals and sepals which are fused together to form a cap, shed when the flower opens.
euchlóra From the Greek *eu*, good, and *chloros*, green.
Eucómmia From the Greek *eu*, good, and *kommi*, gum; the name for the only hardy rubber-producing tree.
Eucrýphia From the Greek *eu*, well, and *kryphios*, covered; referring to the sepals which are joined at the tips to form a protective cap to the bud.
'Eugénei' In honour of the Prince Eugene of Savoy (1663–1736), said to have been a patron of botany.
Euódia From the Greek word meaning a sweet scent; the leaves are fragrant when bruised.
europáea From Europe.
excélsa Tall or high.
excélsior Taller.

F

Fágus The Latin name for the beech tree (*F. sylvatica*).
falcáta The Latin word for sickle-shaped.
falconéri In honour of Hugh Falconer (1808–65), a Scottish doctor, geologist and botanist in India (1830–55).
fargésii In honour of Paul Guillaume Farges (1844–1912), a French missionary and naturalist who worked in central China.
fastigiáta, -um Having erect growth and a columnar habit from the Latin for a gable (which it does not resemble).
férox Ferocious, very thorny.
fémina A female.
ficifólia With leaves like those of a fig (but not the edible fig, *Ficus carica*).
fictolácteum From the Latin *fictus*, false, and *Rhododendron lacteum*, a species with which *Rhododendron fictolacteum* was at one time confused.
Fícus The Latin name for the fig.
filicifólia Fern-leaved.
filicóides Resembling fern, Latin *filix*, a fern.
filifera Thread-bearing.
filifórmis Thread-like.
fílipes With thread-like stalks.
Fitzróya In honour of Vice-Admiral Robert Fitzroy (1805–65), who commanded the five-year surveying expedition in H.M.S. *Beagle*. (Charles Darwin was the naturalist aboard.)
fláva Yellow.
'Flétcheri' Named after Fletcher's Nursery, Kent. Fletcher first distributed the branch mutant *Chamaecyparis lawsoniana* 'Fletcheri', which originally arose in 1913 in the Ottershaw Nursery, Chertsey, Surrey, England.
floribúnda Profusely flowering.
flórida Flowery.
fórdii In honour of Charles Ford (1844–1927), Superintendent of the Hong Kong Botanical Garden.
formosána From the island of Formosa (Taiwan).
forréstii In honour of George Forrest (1873–1932), from Scotland, who collected large numbers of seeds and specimens in western China.
fortúnei In honour of Robert Fortune (1812–80), Scottish horticulturist who collected plants in China and Japan (and introduced tea to India).
Fortunélla The Kumquat, an evergreen shrub, named after Robert Fortune (*see fortunei*).
frágilis Brittle or fragile and easily broken.
frainétto The native name of the Hungarian oak.
Franklínia In honour of Benjamin Franklin (1706–90), American scholar and statesman.
franklínii In honour of Sir John Franklin (1786–1847), naval captain and arctic explorer (discovered the North West Passage), also governor of Tasmania 1836–43.
fráseri In honour of John Fraser (1750–1811).
fraxinifólia With leaves like *Fraxinus* (ash).
Fráxinus The old Latin name for the ash tree (*Fraxinus excelsior*).
frígidus Coming from cold regions.
'Frísia' From Friesland, W. Germany and E. Netherlands.
frúctu-lutéo Yellow-fruited.
fúlvum Tawny-orange.
funébris Funereal, grown in graveyards.
fúsca Dusky brown.

G

garryána In honour of Nicholas Garry, Secretary of the Hudson's Bay Company, who between 1820–30 helped David Douglas in western North America.
generósa Of noble appearance.
Genísta The Latin name for dyer's greenweed, but said to have come from the Celtic *gen*, a bush.
germánica From Germany.
gigánteum From the Latin *giganteus*, gigantic.
Gínkgo A misrendering of the ancient (and now obsolete) Japanese name *gin-kyo* (silver apricot).
gínnala The native vernacular name for this Asiatic maple.
giráldii In honour of Giuseppe Giraldi, an Italian missionary in China, who from 1890–95 collected plants in Shensi Province.
glábra, -áta Smooth, without hairs.
gláuca Blue-grey or blue-white.
Gledítsia In honour of Johann Gottlieb Gleditsch (1714–86), Director of the Berlin Botanic Garden.
globósa, -um Round, or spherical.
glóbulus Rounded or globular.
glutinósa Gluey or sticky (the buds and young leaves).
glyptostrobóides Resembling *Glyptostrobus*.
Glyptostróbus From the Greek *glypto*, to carve, and *strobilos*, a cone; referring to the depressions on the cone scales of *Glyptostrobus*, the deciduous Chinese cypress.
gmelínii In honour of Gottlieb Gmelin (1709–55), a German naturalist who travelled extensively in Siberia and Kamchatka.
'Goldsworth Purple' From the Goldsworth Old Nursery, Surrey.
Gordónia Named in honour of James Gordon (d. 1781), a correspondent of Linnaeus and a nurseryman of Mile End, London.
goveniána In honour of J. R. Gowen, of Highclere, Secretary of the Royal Horticultural Society 1845–50.
gracilistýla With a slender style.
grandidentáta With large teeth.
grandiflóra Large-flowered.
grandifólia Big-leaved.
grándis, -e Big or showy.
Grevíllea In honour of Charles Francis Greville (1749–1809), a founder of the Horticultural Society of London and a Vice-President of the Royal Society.
griffithiána, -um In honour of William Griffith (1810–45), a British doctor and botanist who collected plants in India and Afghanistan.
griffíthii In honour of William Griffith (*see griffithiana*).
grignonénsis Town in France where *Crataegus grignonensis* was first discovered.
griséum Grey.
grósseri *Acer grosseri* was discovered by Giraldi (*see giraldii*) in Shensa, China, and brought to England in 1927. Probably from *grossus*, very big.
gúnnii In honour of R. C. Gunn (1808–81) of Tasmania.
Gymnoclàdus From the Greek *gymnos*, naked, and *klados*, a branch; the tree is leafless in winter.

H

Hákea In honour of Baron Christian von Hake (1745–1818), German patron of botany.
halapénsis From Aleppo (Halep) in Syria.
Halésia In honour of the Rev. Stephen Hales (1677–1761), curate of Teddington, England, and a physiologist, chemist and inventor.
halliána In honour of George Rogers Hall (1820–99), an American doctor who introduced many plants from Japan to the U.S.A.
Hamamélis A Greek name, possibly for the medlar.
harrowiána In honour of George Harrow, manager of Veitch's Coombe Wood Nursery where many of E. H. Wilson's Chinese plants were raised from seeds.
hastáta Spear-shaped.
Hébe Evergreen shrubs from South America and Australasia, named after the Greek goddess of youth.
hénryae In honour of the wife of Augustine Henry (*see henryi*).
hénryi, -ana In honour of Augustine Henry (1857–1930), Irish doctor and plant collector who travelled in China and Formosa (Taiwan), later professor of forestry.
'Heptalóbum' Seven-lobed.
hérsii In honour of Joseph Hers, who, whilst in China, sent back plants to the Arnold Arboretum during the 1920s.
heterophýlla From the Greek *heter* or *hetero*, various or diverse, and *phyllum*, leaf.
'Hibérnica' From Ireland.
highdownénsis After Sir Frederick Stern's garden at Highdown Towers, Sussex.
híllieri After the tree and shrub specialist nurserymen, Hillier & Sons, Winchester, Hampshire.
hippocastánum The Latin name for the horse chestnut; there are horseshoe-shaped leaf scars on the twigs.
Híppophae An old Greek name for a spiny spurge, later transferred to this shrub.
hispánica From Spain.
híspida Bristly.
Hohéria Latinized version of the New Zealand Maori name for these evergreen trees and shrubs, *houhera*.
hollándica From the Netherlands (Holland).
holophylla From the Greek *holo*, entire, and *phyllum*, leaf.
homolépis From the Greek *homo*, same, one kind of, and *lepis*, scale.
horizontális Horizontal.
'Hudsónia' In honour of William Hudson (1730–93), a London apothecary.
húmilis Low-growing, or relatively so.
hupehénsis From Hupeh, China.
hýbrida Of hybrid origin, or appearing so. ▶

The Meanings of Botanical Names

I

Idésia In honour of Eberhard (or Evert) Ides (d. *c.* 1720), a Dutch (or German) explorer of northern Asia.
I'lex From the Latin name for the evergreen holm oak, the more toothed-leaved forms of which it resembles.
illinoénsis From the state of Illinois, U.S.A.
imbricária Overlapping in regular order, like the tiles on a roof.
imperiális Imperial or showy.
incána Hoary or grey.
incísa Deeply cut.
indica From India.
inérmis Unarmed, i.e. having no prickles.
insígnis Remarkable.
intermedia Intermediate.
intertexta Intertwined.
involucráta Surrounded or enclosed by an involucre (leaf, scale or petal-like bracts).
ioénsis From the state of Iowa, U.S.A.
irrorátum From the Latin *irroro*, to wet with dew or to besprinkle.
'Itálica' From Italy.

J

Jacaránda The Latinized form of the Brazilian name for these flowering trees.
jacquemóntii In honour of Victor Jacquemont (1801–32), a French naturalist who visited Asia.
japónica, -um From Japan.
'Jaspidea' Like jasper.
jeffréyi In honour of J. Jeffrey, a Scottish gardener who collected in Oregon, U.S.A., between 1850 and 1853.
jessoénsis, jezoénsis From Jezo, Japan.
'John Downie' In honour of the Scottish nurseryman and florist.
Jubaéa Named for King Juba of Numidia who killed himself when his kingdom was taken over by the Romans in 46 B.C.
Júglans The Latin name, from *jovis*, of Jupiter, and *glans*, acorn.
julibríssin The Persian (Iranian) name for the silk tree.
Juníperus Old Latin name for juniper tree.

K

kaémpferi In honour of Engelbert Kaempfer (1651–1716), a German physician who travelled widely in the East and lived for two years in Japan.
káki An abbreviation of the Japanese name *kaki-no-ki* for this fruit.
Kalópanax From the Greek *kalos*, beautiful, and *Panax*, a related genus.
kellóggii In honour of Albert Kellogg (1813–87), American doctor and botanist.
'Kiftsgate' After the garden at Kiftsgate Court, Gloucestershire.
'Kilmacúrragh' From the Irish garden of this name.
kóbus Latinization of the Japanese name *kobushi*.
Koelreutéria In honour of Joseph Gottlieb Koelreuter (1733–1806), natural history professor and pioneer in plant hybridization.
koraiénsis, koreána From Korea.
koúsa The Japanese name for this *Cornus*.

L

Laburnocýtisus A combination of *Laburnum* and *Cytisus*, parents of this unique graft hybrid.
Labúrnum Old Roman name for laburnum trees.
laciniáta, -um Deeply cut or slashed.
laéta Bright or vivid or pleasing.
laevigáta Smooth.
laévis Smooth or hairless.
lamárckii In honour of Jean Baptiste Antoine Pierre Monet, Chevalier de la Marck (1744–1829), a distinguished French biologist; his work on evolution foreshadowed that of Darwin.
lambertiána In honour of Aylmer Bourke Lambert (1761–1842), English botanist and author of *The Genus Pinus*.
lanáta Woolly.
lanceoláta, -um Lance-shaped.
'Lanei' Named after Lane's Nursery, Berkhamsted, Hertfordshire.
lantána The Latin name for *Viburnum*.
laricína Resembling (common or European) larch.
Lárix The old Latin name for the common larch, *L. decidua*.
lasiánthus With woolly anthers.
lasiocárpa Woolly fruited.
latifólius, -a Broad-leaved; from the Latin *latus*, broad, and *folium*, leaf.
Laurélia From the Spanish name for *Laurus*, the laurel or bay, referring to fragrant leaves.
laurifólia With leaves like those of *Laurus nobilis* (bay laurel).
lauri̇́na Resembling *Laurus*.
laurocerásus A combination of the Latin for laurel and cherry, hence 'cherry laurel'.
Laúrus Latin name for the bay laurel.
lavállei In honour of M. Lavalle, a French nurseryman, *c.* 1870.
lawsoniána In honour of Charles Lawson (1794–1873), nurseryman and author of *Pinetum Britannicum*, whose Edinburgh nursery received the first *Chamaecyparis lawsoniana* seeds from Oregon in 1854.
laxifólia Loose or open; from the Latin *laxus*, loose, and *folium*, leaf.
'Lemóinei' In honour of Victor Lemoine (1823–1911) and his son Emile (1862–1942), French nurserymen and plant breeders who introduced many new garden plants.
'Lénnei' In honour of M. Lanné, Director of Royal Gardens of Prussia.
lénta Tough but flexible.
leucodérmis White-skinned; from the Greek *leukos*, white, and *dermis*, skin.
leucoxyla, -on White-wooded.
leylándii In honour of C. J. Leyland, of Haggerston Hall, Northumberland (see page 101).
libáni From Mount Lebanon.
Líbocédrus From the Greek *libos*, a tear, and *cedrus*, cedar; referring to drops of resin exuded by the incense cedar.
Ligústrum The Latin name for privet.
likiangénsis From the Lichiang range, Yunnan, western China.
liliiflóra Lily-flowered.
'Linearilobum' From the Latin *linear* and *lobum*, lobed.
lineáris Narrow, with nearly parallel sides.
Líquidámbar From the Latin *liquidus*, fluid or liquid, and the Arabic *ambar*, amber, alluding to the fragrant gum which exudes from this tree.
Liriodéndron Derived from the Greek *leirion*, a lily, and *dendron*, a tree.
Lithocárpus From the Greek *lithos*, stone, and *karpos*, fruit; a reference to the hard nuts (acorns).
Litséa Latinization of an old Japanese name.
Livistóna In honour of Baron of Livinstone, founder of Botanic Garden, Edinburgh.
lóbbii In honour of Thomas Lobb (d. 1984) who collected plants for the nursery firm of James Veitch (from 1843 to 1860) in Java, India, Malaya, Borneo and Singapore.
lóebneri After Max Loebner, Prussian nurseryman.
longáeva Of great age.
longifólia With long leaves.
lowiána In honour of Henry Stuart Lowe (1926–90), a nurseryman of Clapton, London.
lúcidum Shining.
'Lucombeána' Originating in the nursery of Lucombe & Pince, Exeter, Devon.
lusitánica From Lusitania—better known as Portugal.
lútea Yellow.
lutéscens Yellowish.
lyállii In honour of Dr. David Lyall (1817–95), botanist on H.M.S. *Terror* and other ships, and who collected plants in New Zealand.
lycopodiióides Resembling *Lycopodium* (ground pine).
lyráta Lyre-shaped.

M

Máackia In honour of Richard Maack (1825–86), a Russian naturalist who explored the Ussuri River region in eastern Asia.
máackii (*as above*).
Maclúra In honour of William Maclure (1763–1840), an American geologist.
macranthéra Having large anthers.
macrocárpa With large fruits.
macrophýllus, -a, -um Large-leaved.
magnífica Splendid, magnificent or great.
Magnólia In honour of Pierre Magnol (1638–1751), professor of botany and director of the Montpellier Botanic Garden, France.
'Majestica' Majestic.
májor Bigger or larger.
Málus The Latin name for the apple.
mandshúrica From Manchuria.
margaríta Pearl-like.
mariána Of Maryland, U.S.A.
mariésii In honour of Charles Maries (d. 1902), a plant collector who worked for the nursery firm of Veitch in China and Japan.
'Marilándica' From Maryland, U.S.A.
marítima From the Latin *maritimus*, maritime, by or near the sea.
más Male or masculine, formerly used to distinguish delicate species from robust ones.
matsudána In honour of Sadahisa Matsúdo (1857–1921), a Japanese botanist who wrote a flora of China.
máxima, -um Largest.
maximowicziána, -ii In honour of Carl Ivanovitch Maximowicz (1827–91), a Russian botanist who specialized in the plants of eastern Asia.
Máytenus From the Chilean name *maitén* for *M. boaria*.
média Intermediate between two types.
medulláris Pithy.
Mélia The Greek name for an ash tree, in allusion to the similarity of the leaves.
menziésii In honour of Archibald Menzies (1754–1842), a Scottish naval doctor who sailed with Vancouver on his 1790–95 expedition to the northwest Pacific.
mertensiána In honour of Franz Carl Mertens (1764–1831), professor of botany at Bremen, Germany.
Méspilus The Latin name for medlar, the fruit.
Metasequoía From the Greek *meta*, meaning 'with', 'after', 'sharing' or 'changed in nature'; alluding to its ancient relationship with *Sequoia*.
'Meyen' In honour of Franz Julius Meyen (1804–40), German physician and plant collector.
meyeri In honour of Frank N. Meyer (d. 1918), a Dutch-American plant collector.
micháuxii In honour of André Michaux (1746–1803), French explorer and plant collector who visited North America, Persia and Madagascar.
microphýlla With small leaves.
mimosifólia With leaves resembling those of *Mimosa*.
miniáta Vermilion-coloured.
minima Smallest.
mitchellii In honour of Dr. John Mitchell (1711–68), American physician.
'Moorheim', -ii Named after a Dutch nursery firm.
mólle As *Rhus molle*, the Peruvian vernacular name for this tree. (*Molle* in Latin means soft, usually in the sense of hairy.)
móllicomáta With soft hairs.
móllis Softly hairy.
mollíssima Very soft, or velvety hairy.
monógyna Having one pistil.
monophýlla One leaved.
monospérma Having one seed.
monspessulánum From Montpellier in France.
montezúmae To honour Montezuma, emperor of Mexico in the 16th century.
montícola Growing on mountains.
Mórus The Latin name for mulberry.
moupinénsis From Mupin, western China (now Pooksing).
múcronátum Mucronate, ending with a spiny tip.
múgo Or *mugho*, the old Tyrolese name for *Pinus mugo*.
muhlenbérgii In honour of Gotthilf Henry Ernest Muhlenberg (1753–1815), Lutheran minister in Pennsylvania, U.S.A., and a noted amateur botanist.
múme From the Japanese name *ume* for the species *Prunus mume*.
muricáta (The cone) roughened with hard points, like the seashell *Murex*.
Mýrtus The Latin name for myrtle (*Myrtus communis*), a plant sacred to Aphrodite and later associated with the Virgin Mary.

N

nána From the Latin *nanus*, dwarf.
nána grácilis Dwarf (*see above*), and *gracilis*, slender; very dwarf and graceful.
negúndo From the Sanskrit and Bengali *nirgundi*, used for a tree with a similar leaf to *Acer negundo*.
nidiformis Nest-shaped.
niedzwetzkyana In honour of the Russian judge Niedzwetzky.
nígra, -um Black.
nikoénse From the mountains near Nikko in Honshu, Japan.
niphophíla Snow-loving, from the Greek *niphas*, snow and *phileo*, to love.
nítida Shining.
nivális Snow-white, or growing near snow.
nóbilis Notable, renowned, famous, stately or noble.
nootkaténsis From the Nootka Sound, Vancouver Island, British Columbia.
nordmanniána In honour of Alexander von Nordmann, professor of zoology at Odessa and Helsinki.
Nothofágus From the Greek *nothos*, false, and *fagus*, beech.
nucífera Nut-bearing.
numídica From Algeria.
núttallii In honour of Thomas Nuttall (1786–1859), an English botanist who collected in North America during 1811–34.
nymansénsis From Nymans, a famous garden in Sussex.
Nýssa Named from Nysa or Nyssa, a water nymph.

O

obássia Said to be from the Japanese name for *Styrax obassia*, but not mentioned in the standard *Flora of Japan*, by Chwi.
oblíqua Oblique or unequal.
oblónga Oblong.
óbovatus, -a An inverted egg-shape.
obtúsa Blunted.
occidentális From the Occident or western world.
odoráta Fragrant.
Oléa The Latin name for the olive.
olerácea Of the vegetable garden.
olivéri In honour of David Oliver (1830–1916), who was Keeper of Kew Herbarium from 1864 to 1890.
omórika The local name of the Serbian spruce.
opáca Dark or dull.
ópalus Probably from *opulus*, an old Latin name for maple, also given to the guelder rose (*Viburnum opulus*) with its maple-like leaves.
ópulus *See* **ópalus.**
orientális From the Orient, or eastern world (eastwards from Europe and Africa).
órnus The old Latin name for the manna ash.
ósteospérma With hard seeds; from the Greek *osteon*, a bone, and *sperma*, a seed.
óstrya From the Greek name *ostrys* for the hop-hornbeam tree.
ovális Oval.
ováta Egg-shaped.
oxyacántha Having sharp thorns.
oxycárpa Bearing pointed fruits.
oxycédrus Ancient Greek name for a juniper.
Oxydéndrum From the Greek *oxys*, sharp (tasting), and *dendron*, a tree; the leaves are bitter.

P

pádus The Greek name for a wild cherry.
palmátum Having hand-like leaves with outspread finger-like lobes.
palmetto The Spanish name for the cabbage palm.
palústris Growing in marshes or liking wet places.
paniculata Having flowers in panicles.
papyrífera Paper-bearing.
paradísi From Paradise.
'Parkmanii' In honour of Francis Parkman, American horticulturist.
Parrótia In honour of F. W. Parrot (1792–1841), a Russian naturalist who climbed Mt. Ararat in 1834.
parviflóra Bearing small flowers.
parvifólia Small-leaved.
pátula Spreading.
Paulównia In honour of the Princess Anna Paulowna (1795–1865), the daughter of Czar Paul I of Russia.
pávia From an old generic name in honour of Peter Paaw (d. 1617).
pedunculósa With well-developed flower stalks (peduncles).
'Pembury Blue' From the estate of this name in Kent, England.
péndula, -um Hanging down.
pensylvánica, -um From Pennsylvania, U.S.A.
pentándra Each flower having five stamens.
perádo The native (Azores) name for *Ilex perado*.
pérnyi In honour of Paul Hubert Perny (1818–1907), a French missionary in China.
pérsica From Persia (now Iran).
petioláris With a leaf stalk.
petraéa Rock-loving, growing in stony places.
peúce The Greek name for *Pinus peuce*.
pfitzeriana In honour of Ernst Hugo Heinrich Pfitzer (1846–1906), a Stuttgart nurseryman.
phaenopýrum Having the appearance of a pear.
Phellodéndron From the Greek *phellos*, cork, and *dendron*, a tree; these trees have a corky bark.
phéllos The Greek name for the cork oak (*Quercus suber*), which Linnaeus used for *Quercus phellos*.
Phillýrea The classical Greek name.
Phoénix The Greek name for the date palm.
Photínia Said to be from the Greek *phos* or *photos*, light, in allusion to the glossy shining leaves of some species.
Pícea From the old Latin name for pitch pine, now used for spruce.
Picrásma From the Greek *picrazein*, bitter.
píctus Painted or coloured.
pináster The old Latin name for a wild pine—as distinct from one (*Pinus pinea*) that was cultivated.
píndrow The native Himalayan name for *Abies pindrow*.
pínea Of the pines or growing on pines (as a parasite).
pinnatífida With leaves pinnately lobed.
pinsápo The Spanish name for *Abies pinsapo*.
Pínus The old Latin name for a pine tree, in particular the stone pine (*Pinus pinea*).
pisífera Pea-bearing.

'Pissardii' In honour of M. Pissard, the Shah of Persia's French gardener 100 years ago.
Pistácia From the Greek *pistake* (in turn probably derived from a Persian name) for the pistachio nut.
Pittospórum From the Greek *pitta*, pitch, and *spora*, seed; the seeds of this genus are embedded in a sticky, resinous substance.
plantierénsis Named after the Plantier nursery near Metz, France.
platanoídes Resembling the plane tree, *Platanus*.
Plátanus The Greek name for the oriental plane tree.
platyphýlla, -os With broad leaves.
'Pléna' Full or double flowered.
plicáta Pleated or folded.
plumósa Feathery.
Podocárpus From the Greek *podos*, a foot, and *karpos*, a fruit; the fruits of these trees (some species, not all) are borne at the summit of a broad, fleshy stalk or receptacle.
pohuashanénsis From Po hua shan, China.
pólita Elegant or neat.
polycárpa Many fruited.
pomífera Bearing pomes or apples.
Poncírus From the French *poncire*, a kind of citrus.
ponderósa Heavy or weighty.
populifólia Having leaves like those of poplar (*Populus*).
Pópulus The Latin name for the poplar tree.
postelense Named after town in Silesia.
potaninii In honour of Grigori Potanin (1835–1920), a Russian who explored and collected in Asia and China.
praécox Developing or flowering earlier than most of its genus.
práttii In honour of Antwerp E. Pratt, an English zoologist who travelled in China in the 1880s.
prínus The Greek name for the common oak (*Quercus robur*), which Linnaeus used for *Quercus prinus*.
prócera Tall or slender.
procúmbens Prostrate.
prunifólia, -um With leaves like those of the cherry (*Prunus*).
Prúnus The Latin name for the cherry tree.
pseudoacácia False acacia.
pseudocamellia False camellia.
Pseudolárix Literally, false larch; the tree resembles true larch (*Larix*).
pseudoplátanus The false plane tree.
Pseudotsúga False *Tsuga* (the hemlock); Douglas fir is not related to tsuga (nor does it look like one).
Ptélea The Greek name for an elm tree; possibly so named because of the somewhat similar flattened, circular, winged fruits.
Pterocárya From the Greek *pteron*, a wing, and *karyon*, a nut.
Pterostýrax From the Greek *pteron*, a wing, and the genus *Styrax*; this genus is distinguished by its winged fruits.
pubéscens Covered with soft, downy hairs.
púmila Dwarf.
punctáta Marked with dots.
púngens From the Latin *pungens*, piercing, so sharp-pointed.
púrpurascens Purplish.
purpuréa, -um Purple.
pygmáea Pygmy.
pyramidalis Pyramidal.
pyráster The wild pear; from the Latin *pyrus*, pear and *aster*, superficial or incomplete resemblance to; used to denote a wild or inferior species.
Pýrus The Latin name for the pear.

Q

quadranguláta With four angles.
Quássia In honour of Graman Quasi, a Negro slave who used this tree bark as a remedy for fever.
quercifólia With leaves like *Quercus* (oak).
Quércus The Latin name for the oak.

R

racemósa The flowers are borne in a raceme.
radiáta Emitting or having rays.
reclináta Bent backward.
recúrva Curved backward.
régia Royal in appearance.
rehderána In honour of Alfred Rehder (1863–1949), a German American dendrologist, Curator of the Herbarium at the Arnold Arboretum, and author of the classic *Manual of Cultivated Trees and Shrubs*.
resinósa Bearing resin.
reticuláta Having a net-like pattern.
retúsus With a rounded or slightly notched tip.
rhamnóides Resembling *Rhamnus*, the buckthorn.
Rhododéndron From the Greek *rhodon*, a rose, and *dendron*, a tree.
rhombifólium Rhomboid-leaved.
Rhus The Greek vernacular name for a species of sumach (probably *Rhus coriaria*) and now used as the scientific generic name.
'Richardii' In honour of L. C. Richard (1754–1821), a French botanist.
rígida Stiff or rigid.
'Rivérsii' Raised at England's oldest nursery firm of Thomas Rivers in Hertfordshire, England.
'Rivers Purple' A beech from the Rivers nursery (*see* 'Riversii').
Robínia In honour of Jean Robin (1550–1629), herbalist to Henri IV and Louis XIII of France, and his son Vespasian Robin, who first grew this tree in Europe.
róbur Latin name for any hard wood, especially oak.
robústa Robust, strong in growth.
romanzoffianum In honour of the Russian, M. P. Romanzoff (1754–1826).
Rósa The Latin name for the rose.
rosácea Rose-like.
rósea, -um Rose-coloured.
'Roseoplena' Rosy in colour and double.
Roystónea In honour of General Roy Stone (1836–1905), American army engineer in Puerto Rico.
rúbens From the Latin *rubens*, red or reddish.
rúbra, -um Red.
rubrifólia Red-leaved.
rufinérve Red veined when leaves first emerge.
rugósa Wrinkled.
rupéstris Liking a rocky habitat.
rústica rúbra From ther Latin *rusticus*, relating to the country, and *ruber*, red.

S

Sábal Possibly derived from the South American name for these palms.
saccharinum Sugary.
sacchárum Sugarcane (from the Greek *sakcharon*, in turn probably derived from the Malay word for the sweet juice of the sugarcane, *singkara*).
salicifólia With leaves like those of *Salix*, the willow.
salígnus Resembling willow (*Salix*).
Sálix The Latin name for the willow.
Sambúcus The old Latin name for these shrubs and small trees, perhaps connected with *sambuca*, the Biblical sackbut.
Sápium The Latin name for a resinous pine; presumably applied here because of the sticky sap which is exuded.
sargentiána, -ii In honour of Charles Sprague Sargent (1841–1927), American botanist and dendrologist, first director of the Arnold Arboretum.
sarniénsis From Guernsey (once Sarnia) in the Channel Islands.
sasánqua From the Japanese name *sasankwa* (more correctly *sazanka*) for the species *Camellia sasanqua*.
Sássafras Probably from a North American Indian name used in Florida.
satíva Cultivated.
Saxegothǽa In honour of Prince Albert of Saxe-Coburg-Gotha (1819–61), Consort of Queen Victoria.
Schínus From the Greek *schinos*, a name for the mastic tree, which this genus resembles in its production of resin and a mastic-like juice.
schrenkiána After the Russian botanist, Schrenk (1816–76).
Sciadopítys From the Greek *skiados*, an umbel, and *pitys*, a fir tree; the whorls of spreading, straight, needle-like leaves resemble the spokes of an umbrella.
Scindápsus Ivy arum; from the Greek for an ivy-like plant.
scopulína Bearing small brushes.
scopulórum Growing on cliffs, crags or rocky outcrops.
seláginoides Resembling club-moss.
semipléna Semi or partly double flowered.
sempervírens Evergreen.
septentrionális Northern.
sepulcrális Growing in burial places.
Sequóia Sequoia or Sequoiah was the Cherokee Indian name (meaning opossum) of the halfcaste George Gist (1770–1843), who had a German American father. He invented the Cherokee alphabet.
Sequoiadéndron From *Sequoia* and the Greek *dendron*, a tree.
sericea Silky.
serotína Late flowering or ripening.
serráta Saw-toothed.
sérrula, -ata With small saw-like teeth.
shasténsis From Shasta in California, U.S.A.
shumárdii In honour of Benjamin Franklin Shumard (1820–69), State Geologist of Texas in 1860.
sibirica From Siberia.
siebóldii In honour of Philipp Franz von Siebold (1796–1866), a German doctor who collected in Japan.
silíqua, -astrum Bearing pods with partitions like the fruits (siliquae) of certain members of the cabbage family (*Cruciferae*).
simónii In honour of Gabriel Eugene Simon (b. 1829), French consul and plant collector.
sinénsis From China.
sinogránde A species allied to *Rhododendron grande* from China.
sitchénsis Of Sitka, Alaska.
smithiána In honour of James Edward Smith (1759–1828), founder and first president of the Linnean Society of London.
smíthii In honour of John Smith (1798–1888), Scottish gardener and fern specialist at the Royal Botanical Gardens, Kew.
solánderi In honour of Daniel Carl Solander (1736–82), a pupil of Linnaeus and botanist with Sir Joseph Banks on Captain Cook's first voyage to the Pacific.
Sóphora From the Arabic name for these shrubs and trees.
Sórbus From the Latin *sorbum*, for the fruit of the service tree (*Sorbus domestica*).
soulangiána In honour of the Chevalier Etienne Soulange-Bodin (1774–1846), a French horticulturist.
'Spaethii' After the Späth Nursery, Berlin.
speciósa Showy.
spectábilis, -e Showy or spectacular.
'Spek' After the Dutch nurseryman.
spinósa Bearing spines.
spiralis Spiral.
spléndens Splendid.
spontanéa Spontaneous, in the sense of not being planted; growing wild.
squamáta Scaly, with small scale-like leaves.
squarrósa Spreading or curved.
standíshii In honour of John Standish (1809–75), a Surrey nurseryman who raised the plants introduced from China and Japan by Robert Fortune.
stelláta Starry.
stenóptera With narrow wings.
Stewártia (*Stuartia* of some botanists) In honour of John Stuart (1713–92), 3rd Earl of Bute (and Prime Minister 1762–63), a keen patron of botany and horticulture.
stricta Upright.
stróbus The old Latin name for an incense-bearing tree.
styraciflúa Flowing with gum.
Stýrax A Greek name derived from the original Semitic name for these plants.
suaveólens Fragrant.
súber Cork.
subhirtélla Somewhat hairy.
'Suécica' Swedish.
sylvática, sylvéstris Forest-loving, growing in woods.

T

taéda The old Latin name for resinous trees, the wood of which was used for torches—*taeda*, a torch.
Taiwánia From Taiwan, formerly Formosa.
tatáricum From Tartary, a region in central Asia.
Taxódium The name for the swamp cypress; from the Latin *Taxus*, the yew, and the Greek *eidios*, resemblance, the leaves of the swamp cypress and yew are somewhat similar in shape.
Táxus The old Latin name for the yew tree.
Tetraclínis From the Greek *tetra*, four and *kline*, bed; referring to the leaves which are in fours.
tetragona aurea From the Greek *tetra*, four, *gonus*, angled, and the Latin *aurum*, gold.
tetraptera From the Greek *tetra*, four, and *terus*, winged. Four wing-like appendages or projections.
thomsonii In honour of Thomas Thompson (1817–78), Scottish physician and Superintendent of Calcutta Botanic Garden.
Thúja From the Greek name *thuia* (*thya* or *thyia*) for a resin-bearing tree, almost certainly a kind of juniper.
Thujópsis Resembling *Thuja*, q.v.
thunbérgii In honour of Carl Peter Thunberg (1743–1828), a student of Linnaeus and later professor of botany at Uppsala, Sweden, who collected in Japan and Batavia.
thuringiáca From Thuringia, central Germany.
thyoídes Resembling *Thuja* (in turn derived from *thya*, *thyia* or *thuia*, Greek names for a resin-bearing tree, probably a juniper).
tíbetica Of Tibet.
Tília The Latin name for the lime or linden tree.
tobira Local name.
tomentósa Covered with short woolly or matted hairs.
toríngoides Like toringo.
torminális Used to alleviate (or capable of giving) a stomach-ache.
Torréya In honour of Dr. John Torrey (1796–1873), one of the most famous of America's botanists who described many thousands of plants brought back by explorers and collectors. Also co-author with Asa Gray of *The Flora of North America*.
torreyana After Dr. John Torrey (see *Torreya*).
tortuósa Twisted as contorted.
tótara The native Maori name (New Zealand).
Trachycárpus From the Greek *trachys*, rough, and *karpos*, a fruit.
trémula Trembling.
trémuloides Like *Populus tremula* (aspen) in general appearance.
triacánthos Three-thorned.
triándra Each flower having three anthers.
trichocárpa With hairy fruits.
tríchotomum Having all divisions in threes.
triflórum *Tri* means three, and *flora*, a flower; the flowers are borne in groups of three.
trifoliáta Having leaves composed of three leaflets.
trilóba Three lobes.
'Triomf van Boskoop' From the nursery area of this name in Holland.
trístis Dull or sad.
tschonoskii In honour of Tschonoski (Chonosuke Sukawa) (1841–1925), who collected for Maximowicz in Japan.
Tsúga The Japanese name for hemlock.
tulipífera Tulip-bearing.
turbináta Shaped like a spinning top.
typhína Resembling reed-mace (*Typha*).

U

'Ukon' From the Japanese for yellow or yellowish.
ulmoídes Like *Ulmus* (elm).
Ulmus The Latin name for the elm.
Umbellulária Bearing umbels; the floral clusters are of this form.
umbraculífera Shade-giving.
undulátum Undulating.
únedo The Latin name for the strawberry tree and its fruit.
ussuriénsis From the vicinity of the Ussuri River in eastern Asia.

V

variábilis Variable.
variegáta, -um Variegated.
végeta Vigorous.
véitchii In honour of the Veitch family, nurserymen of Exeter, Devon, and Chelsea, London. The original nursery was founded in 1808 at Exeter, dividing in 1854, the Chelsea firm finishing on Sir Harry James Veitch's retirement in 1914.
velutína Velvety.
véra True to type.
verniciflua Yielding varnish.
verticilláta Whorled.
vestíta Covered.
Vibúrnum The Latin name of one species of the wayfaring tree.
vilmoriniána, -ii In honour of the French nurseryman Vilmorin-Andrieux.
viminális With long slender shoots like the willow or osier.
violacea Blue-red colour.
virginiána From the states of East or West Virginia, U.S.A.
virgínicus From Virginia, U.S.A.
virídis Green.
viscósa Sticky.
vitellina The colour of an egg-yolk.
'Vitifólium' With leaves like *Vitis* (grapevine).
vomitória Emetic.
vossii In honour of Andreas Voss (1857–1924), German nurseryman.
'Vranja' Named after Vranje in Yugoslavia.

W

wallichiána In honour of Nathaniel Wallich (1786–1854), a Danish doctor and botanist who became Superintendent of the Calcutta Botanic Garden in India from 1814 to 1841.
Washingtónia In honour of George Washington (1732–99), first President of the United States.
wátereri For the nursery firm of John Waterer Sons & Crisp Ltd, Twyford, Berkshire (in the case of *Laburnum anagyroides x watereri*). In honour of the nurseryman Waterer of Surrey (in the case of *Cotoneaster frigidus x watereri*).
wilsónii In honour of Ernest Henry Wilson (1876–1930), the famous plant collector who travelled widely in China and later became curator of the Arnold Arboretum.
'Wissellii' In honour of the Dutch nurseryman Wissel.

X

xanthocárpa Yellow-fruited.

Y

yedoénsis From Tokyo (formerly Yedo), Japan.
'Youngii' In honour of the Young family, nurserymen at Epsom, Surrey, during the first half of the 19th century.
Yucca From the Carib name for cassava, a member of the *Euphorbia* family.
yunnanénsis From Yunnan, western China.

Z

zebrína Zebra-striped.
Zelkóva From the Caucasian native name.

General Index

Index of Tree Species

Descriptions of trees in the Index follow their botanical (Latin) name. To find botanical or horticultural details of (e.g.) western red cedar look up the English name to find the Latin; then look up the Latin (*Thuja plicata*). General notes on the genus *Thuja* are at the head of the entry. Specific notes on the species (*T. plicata*) are listed alphabetically below.

The hardiness zones (e.g. 'Zone 9') referred are those mapped on pages 30-31.

The sign x before a name denotes a natural hybrid, the sign + a graft hybrid.

The words 'big', 'medium', 'small' in relation to leaf-size are based on the following measurements:
'big' – 7 ins upwards: 'medium – 2–6 ins: 'small' – to 2ins.

The height given is that of a mature tree in its native land.

The speed of growth given is that of a known tree in good but not exceptional condition. Statistics are not available for all species.

For space seasons, certain geographical abbreviations have been used including C, – central, E, – eastern etc.

Trees which have been chosen by the Royal Horticultural Society for their Award of Garden Merit, the internationally-recognized commendation of an outstanding garden plant, have the legend 'A.G.M.' with the date of award at the end of their specific entry.

A

ABIES 78-81, 262. 263 Evergreen trees, big, mostly conical. Leaves either spreading around shoot, or directed forward, often notched at tip, smell of turpentine when bruised. Sexes separate on same tree: male 'flowers' in clusters on underside of branches, often brightly coloured: female 'flowers' catkin-like, Cones have spreading scales, cylindrical, upright on branches, breaking up and leaving a central spike on the tree. Some years many, others few or none. Seeds winged. Bark usually resinous. Dislikes shallow chalk. Susceptible to certain insect pests, e.g. woolly aphid and rust fungi in Europe and America.

A. alba 80, 81, 254 Common silver fir, European silver fir. Europe Zone 4. To 150 ft, sometimes with huge branches. Leaves in 2 ranks, upper shorter than lower, dark shiny green. Cones clustered near top of tree, pale green becoming brown-red. Young foliage susceptible to late frosts. 35 ft in 20 years.

A. amabilis 79, 83, 255 Pacific silver fir. Red fir. W. United States Zone 5. To 250 ft. Leaves flattened, crowded on upper surface of twig, brilliant white bands beneath. Cones dark purple-brown. Most soil types, except dry or chalky. Requires deep soil or high rainfall. 30 ft in 20 years.

A. borisii-regis 254 Sturdy, big trees from Balkan Peninsula.

A. bracteata 79, 255 Bristlecone fir. Santa Lucia fir, Fringed spruce. Mts of S. California Zone 7. To 150 ft, broad-conical shape with hanging branchlets. Buds pale, slender, conical. Leaves large, spread horizontally into 2 opposite sets, curved and flattened with sharp tips, icy-white underneath. Grows on deep soil over chalk. 30 ft in 20 years.

A. cephalonica 80, 81, 254 Greek fir. Mts of Greece Zone 5. To 100 ft. broadly conical, becoming more open. Leaves spread round shoots, mostly above; dark shiny green above. 2 narrow white bands beneath, prickly. Male 'flowers' in dense clusters beneath shoots. Cones often at top of crown, green-brown. Early foliage often frost-damaged. Disease-free. Likes chalk. 28 ft in 20 years.

A. cilicica 254 'Cilician fir', from Mt. Lebanon, similar to A. nordmanniana.

A. concolor 79, 255, 263 Colorado white fir. White fir. S.W. United States Zone 4. To 160 ft, narrow. Leaves 2 ins long (longer than most other species), blue-grey, dull green with age. Cones oblong, olive-green becoming purple. 30 ft in 20 years.

'Candicans' 72, 263 Handsome form.

Leaves silver-grey to white.

lowiana 79, 255 Low's silver fir, Pacific white fir. S.W. United States Zone 6. To 250 ft. Leaves horizontal and curving upwards, dark blue-grey or green. Cones green, brown with age, big, smooth barrels. 45 ft in 20 years.

'Violacea' 79 Leaves waxy blue-green.

A. delavayi 254 W. and C. China Zone 7. Medium-size. Densely set leaves, bright shiny green above, gleaming white below. Cones dark bluish-violet. Buds very resinous.

A. fargesii 81 W. and C. China Zone 5. To 100 ft, with massive branches. Leaves long, spreading horizontally in 2 or more ranks, upper rank ½ length of lower. Cones purple to red-brown. 35 ft in 20 years.

A. firma 255 'Japanese fir': big tree, leaves bright green, thick and broad; bark pinkish.

A. forrestii 80, 81 Forrest's fir. W. China Zone 7. To 60 ft. Cones deep blue. 40 ft in 20 years.

A. fraseri 78, 255 Fraser's fir. S.E. United States Zone 4. 50 to 70 ft. open. Leaves short, dark shiny blue-green, 2 broad white bands beneath. Cones purple. Prone to disease.

A. grandis 26–7, 78–9, 255 Grand fir. Giant fir. W. United States Zone 6. To 250 ft, columnar, becoming rounded, sometimes multiple-topped. Leaves double-ranked horizontally, upper shorter than lower, bright green above, 2 narrow bands of silver-white beneath. Cones green-purple summer. Moderately lime-tolerant. Exceedingly vigorous on many soils. 55 ft in 20 years.

A. holophylla 81, 2255 Manchurian fir. Manchuria, Korea Zone 5. 100 to 150 ft, narrow conical or spreading. Leaves medium length, bright green, 2 grey-green bands beneath, sharp pointed. Cones green ripening to light brown.

A. homolepis 80, 81, 262 Nikko fir. Japan Zone 4.80 to 90 ft. Leaves, lower at right angles to shoot, upper directed outwards and upwards, dark green shiny above, two conspicuous white bands on lower leaves. Cones purple, brown when mature. Tough, adaptable, tolerates some pollution. 25 ft in 20 years.

A. kawakamii 254 Small silver fir with white bark from Formosa.

A. koreana 80, 81, 254 Korean fir. Korea Zone 5. To 40 ft, conical, or low, bushy. Leaves nearly covering upper side of shoot, curve upwards to near vertical; black-green above, 2 broad white bands below. Male 'flowers' on side-shoots, ovoid, dark red-brown; female 'flowers' dark-red to purple or pink to bright yellow. Cones freely from early age, dark purple. 10 ft in 20 years.

A. lasiocarpa 26–7. 78, 79 Alpine fir. W. United States Zone 2. Sometimes to 180 ft, beautifully narrow spire (Washington). Leaves irregularly double-ranked, medium length, shorter on higher branches, waxy, blue-green. Cones dark purple. Seeds with a shining purple wing. Does not grow well in lime as Adelges make gouty swellings on shoots.

arizonica 79 Arizona cork fir. Corkbark fir. Arizona Zone 2. 100 or 130 ft, neat, conical, blue tree. Leaves 1 in long, striped blue-grey each side; flat, upward-curving, those in midline covering the stem. Cones dark purple. Seeds with a purple wing. Tolerant of many soils. 15 ft in 20 years.

A. magnifica 79, 255 California red fir. Red fir. W. United States Zone 5. To 200 ft, narrow. Leaves blue to blue-green, later. 4-angled, lower horizontal, upper leaves curve upward. Cones purple-brown. Dislikes chalk. 30 ft in 20 years.

shastensis 79 Shasta red fir. Red fir. Zone 5. To 125 ft. Leaves 4-faceted, curved.

A. mariesii 81 Maries fir. Japan Zone 5. To 80 ft. Leaves 1 in long, shiny, dark green, 2 white bands beneath. Cones violet-blue at first, becoming dark brown, oval.

A. nebrodensis 254 Small silver fir from Sicily.

A. nordmanniana 80, 81, 254, 262 Caucasian fir. W. Caucasus Zone 4. To 200 ft, conical, becoming columnar, pointed or flat-topped. Bright green leaves forward-pointing, 2 sets of lower sides of shoots, upper set shorter. Cones pale green becoming brown, resinous. Generally disease-free. 35 ft in 20 years.

A. numidica 80, 254 Algerian fir. Eastern Algeria Zone 6. 70 or 100 ft, conical. Leaves short, flattened, stiff, broad and thick, dark shining green, broadly branded grey all round shoot, curving upwards. Cones brown. Best Abies near towns.

A. pindrow 81, 254 West Himalayan fir. Afghanistan to Nepal Zone 6. To 200 ft, narrow, pyramidal with short branches becoming open with age. Leaves mainly below shoot, 2 to 3 ins long, dark shiny green. Cones deep purple, becoming brown. Requires high rainfall and cool summers.

A. pinsapo 80, 254 Spanish fir. Mts of S. Spain Zone 6. To 100 ft, narrow cone, becoming more irregular. Leaves all round shoot, very short, blunt, broad, straight or slightly curved, noticeable bands on both sides. Male 'flowers' abundant, round beneath shoot, bright red, opening late spring. Cones tapered, purple-brown. Tolerates lime, chalk, and any dry soils. 25 ft in 20 years.

A. procera 78. 79, 255 Noble fir. W. United States Zone 5. To 250 ft, dome-headed. Leaves slightly 4-angled in section, flatter than A. magnifica; pointed, crowded on upper side of twig, blue-green. Cones olive-green to purple. Dislikes chalk. 30 to 40 ft in 20 years.

A. religiosa 255 'Sacred fir' from Mexico. Hardy in Britain.

A. sibirica 255 Siberian silver fir.

A. spectabilis 81, 254 East Himalayan fir. Himalaya. Sikkim, Bhutan Zone 7. To 150 ft, broad columnar, eventually flat-topped. Leaves on a large scale, dense in 2 ranks, lying slightly forward. Cones pale grey-blue, becoming dull, dark purple by winter. Susceptible to late frosts. 35 ft in 20 years.

A. squamata 254 'Flaky fir', small silver fir with peeling brown bark from W. China.

A. sutchuenensis 254 See A. fargesii

A. veitchii 81 Veitch's silver fir. C. Japan Zone 3. 60 or 70 ft. Leaves as A. nordmanniana but softer to touch. Male 'flowers' orange-red, minute, becoming round, red-brown, female 'flowers' red cylinder. Cone purple-blue to brown. Trunk deeply fluted. Dislikes chalk, thrives in semi-urban conditions. 40 ft in 20 years.

A. vejari 255 Silver fir from Mexico similar to A. religiosa.

ACACIA 208, 209, 211, 262 Mostly evergreen trees and shrubs. Leaves usually doubly pinnate, often replaced by flattened structures developed from leaf-stalks. Flowers bisexual, yellow, winter or spring. Full sun, avid or neutral, dry soils. Tender.

Acacia, False See Robinia pseudoacacia True, See Acacia

A. baileyana 211, 263 Cootamundra wattle. Bailey's mimosa. Australia Zone 8. To 20 ft or more, often weeping. Leaves divided into numerous long, narrow leaflets, obliquely pointed, evergreen, waxy, silvery. Flowers, clusters of small, roundish heads. Fruits in pods 2 to 3 ins long.

A. dealbata 209, 210, 211, 252, 255, 263 Silver wattle. Mimosa. Australia Zone 8. To 50 ft, spreading. Leaves fern-like, downy, silver-green. Flowers, clusters of small, round heads, fragrant. Seed pods flat. 2 to 3 ins long, blue-white. Sun-loving; can be killed by severe or prolonged frost. 50 ft in 20 years.

A. longifolia 211, 263 Sidney golden wattle. Australia Zone 8. To 20 ft, spreading. Leaves long, lance-shaped, simple, evergreen, leathery, dark green. Flowers small, round heads, bright yellow, in spikes 2 to 3 ins long. Seed pods 3 to 4 ins long. Fairly lime-tolerant.

ACER 226–33, 263 Maples. Deciduous, rarely evergreen trees. Opposite, normally lobed leaves often with brilliant autumn colours. Clustered uni- or bi-sexual flowers. Fruits are paired nuts or keys. Usually pest-free. Tolerant of most soil-types.

A. amplum See A. longipes ssp. amplum

A. argutum 255 Small Japanese maple, five-lobed leaves with conspicuous veins.

A. buergerianum 231, 254, 262 Buerger's maple. Trident maple. E. China. Japan Zone 6. 20 ft high, rounded. Leaves 3-lobed, simple, bright green above, paler, waxy beneath, toothed, stalked. Flowers in a flattish cluster.

A. campbellii 254 Medium-sized Himalayan maple; leaves lobed.

A. campestre 233, 263 Hedge or field maple. Europe (incl. British Isles). W. Asia Zone 5–6. To 40 ft, rounded, dense, 5-lobed leaves, 4 ins across, downy beneath, yellowish in autumn. Small green flowers in small clusters, early May. Keys 1 in long, downy. Grows on chalk 30 ft in 20 years.

postelense 233 Zone 5–6. To 25 ft, rounded. Leaves golden yellow in spring, turning clear yellow, sometimes flushed red, in autumn. Ornamental cultivar.

A. capillipes 231, 255, 263 Small Japanese snakebark maple.

A. cappadocicum 233, 254 Caucasian maple. Caucasus and W. Asia to Himalaya Zone 5 or 6. To 65 ft, spreading. Leaves 5- to 7-lobed, 3 to 6 ins across, glossy green, yellow in autumn. Small yellow flowers. Keys in clusters. Shade tolerant. 30 ft in 20 years.

'Rubrum' 233 New shoots blood red.

A. carpinifolium 230, 231, 255 Hornbeam maple. Japan Zone 5. To 35 ft, vase-shaped with a number of stems from the base. Leaves opposite, otherwise hornbeam-like, unlobed, 3 to 4 ins long, golden brown in autumn. Green flowers in spiky clusters. Keys have curved wings. 15 ft in 20 years.

A. caudatum See A. ukurunduense ssp. caudatum

A. circinatum 228–9, 255, 262 Vine maple W. United States Zone 5 Small tree, to 40 ft, wide spreading with several branches from the base. Leaves almost circular, 7 to 9 lobes, orange to red in autumn. Flowers white to purple in drooping clusters, late April. Red keys. Shade-tolerant. 15 ft in 20 years.

A. cissifolium 255 Small Japanese maple with three-piece bronzy leaves.

A. crataegifolium 255 Hawthorn maple. Japan. Zone 5. Small, spreading to 35 ft. Leaves variable, shallow lobes. Yellowish-white flowers on small erect spikes, April. Striped bark. 15 ft in 20 years.

A. davidii 233, 254, 263 David's maple. China Zone 6. To 50 ft, rounded head. Oval, pointed leaves up to 8 ins long, dark, shining green, yellow and purple in autumn. Keys green flushed with red, hanging along branches in autumn. Bark green striped with white. 30 ft in 20 years.

grosseri 231, 263 Grosser's maple. C. China Zone 6. Small, to 20 ft. Leaves sometimes lobed, toothed. Good autumn colour. Keys in long hanging clusters.

A. diabolicum 231, 255 Horned maple. Japan Zone 5. To 40 ft. Big 5-lobed leaves. Yellow flowers, April, in hanging clusters. Bristly reddish fruits.

purpurascens 231 Horned or Red devil maple. Japan Zone 5. To 30 ft, round-topped. Young leaves red, purplish in autumn. Drooping clusters of salmon-pink flowers in spring. Young keys purple, bristly. 15 ft in 20 years.

A. distylum 255 Larger Japanese maple, simple leaves unfolding pink.

A. divergens 254 Similar to A. campestre, leaves three- or five-lobed.

A. ginnala See A. tataricum ssp. ginnala

A. giraldii 231 Yunnan Zone 6. Medium to large with rather gawky habit. Broad-lobed leaves not unlike sycamore, bluish-white and veined beneath. Drooping clusters of big fruits. Bright autumn colours. 25 ft in 20 years.

A. griseum 230–1, 263 Paperbark maple. C. China Zone 5. To 30 ft. Leaves compound. 3 leaflets on a downy stalk, scarlet in autumn. Downy winged fruit. Most striking 3-leafed maple. 15 ft in 20 years. A.G.M. 1936.

A. grosseri See A. davidii ssp. grosseri

A. heldreichii 254 Medium-sized maple with deeply 3-lobed leaves.

A. hyrcanum 254 Small version of A. opalus from eastern Mediterranean.

A. japonicum 230–1. 255. 262. 263 Full-moon maple. Japan Zone 5. Small bushy tree. 30 ft, rounded. Leaves 2 to 5 ins long, roundish. 7 to 11 lobes, bright red in autumn. Purplish-red flowers, April. Keys in clusters. Best in woodland shelter. 10 ft in 20 years.

'Aconitifolium' 230, 262 Japan. Small tree or large bush. Leaves deeply cut and divided, soft green, turning rich crimson in autumn. Flowers red in drooping clusters. Grows well in moist well-drained positions sheltered from cold winds. A.G.M. 1957.

'Aureum' 230, 262 Japan. Soft yellow leaves, liable to scorch in full sun. Slow-growing. A.G.M. 1969.

'Vitifolium' 230, 231, 262 Wide, fan-shaped leaves, 10–12 lobes. Beautiful autumn colour.

A. lobelii 254 An erect form of the Caucasian maple.

A. longipes ssp. amplum 254 Small maple from central China with shiny green stems.

A. macrophyllum 228, 229, 255, 262 Oregon or Big-leaf maple. W. United States Zone 6. To 100 ft, round-headed. Leaves 6 to 12 ins across, dark shining green, orange and scarlet in autumn. Flowers small, yellow in hanging clusters, fragrant, May. Keys in hanging clusters. 35 ft in 20 years.

A. mandshuricum 255 Small Japanese maple like shiny-leaved A. nikoense.

A. maximowiczianum 231, 254, 262 Nikko maple Japan, C. China Zone 5. To 50 ft, round-topped or vase-shaped. Leaves compound on a stout hairy stalk. Brilliant red or purple in autumn. Yellow flowers in threes on a hairy drooping stalk. Keys with hairy nutlets. 20 ft in 20 years.

A. miyabei 255 Smaller Japanese version of the Norway maple.

A. mono 255 Larger Japanese maple, lobed leaves turning yellow in autumn.

A. monspessulanum 233, 254, 263 Montpelier maple. S. Europe, W. Asia Zone 5. To 30 ft, rounded. Leaves 3-lobed, simple, virtually smooth, dark green above, paler beneath. Flowers in drooping, loose clusters, greenish. Fruit red, profuse, winged.

A. negundo 42, 64, 228, 230, 255, 263 Box elder. North America Zone 2. To 65 ft, spreading and rather open. Leaves compound, 3 to 5 leaflets, bright green above, paler beneath. Sexes on separate trees. Male flowers in dense clusters, female flowers in slender drooping clusters. Keys in drooping clusters. 20 ft in 20 years.

'Elegans' (or 'Elegantissimum') 228, 262 Leaves with bright yellow margins. Young shoots with white bloom.

'Variegatum' 228 Leaves white and green.

A. nigrum See A. saccharum ssp. nigrum

A. nikoense See A. maximowiczianum

A. opalus 233, 252, 254, 262, 263 Italian maple. S. Europe Zone 5. To 50 ft, rounded head. Leaves 2½ to 4½ ins wide, 5 shallow lobes, toothed, dark green and hairless above, paler and downy beneath. Clusters of small yellow flowers, March. 20 ft in 20 years.

A. palmatum 230, 255, 262, 263 Japanese maple. Japan, C. China, Korea Zone 5. To 25 ft, low, rounded head. Bright green leaves, 5 to 7 toothed lobes, bronze or purplish in autumn. Small purple flowers on erect stalks. Fairly chalk-tolerant; prefers shelter from cold winds. Moist well-drained loam preferred. 15 ft in 20 years. A.G.M. 1969.

'Atropurpureum' 230, 262 Bloodleaf Japanese maple. Leaves with 5 to 7 lobes, crimson-purple throughout summer. 20 ft in 20 years. A.G.M. 1928.

'Dissectum' 230, 262 To 10 ft, dome-shaped, fernlike. Green leaves with 7, 9 or 11 lobes. Slow-growing. A.G.M. 1956.

'Dissectum Atropurpureum' 230 As above. Leaves deeply cut, purple. A.G.M. 1969.

'Heptalobum Osakazuki' 230, 262 Possibly the most brilliantly-colouring Japanese maple. A.G.M. 1969.

'Linearilobum' 230, 262 Leaves divided into narrow lobes, slightly toothed, reddish when young, green in summer.

'Osakazuki' See Acer palmatum 'Heptalobum Osakazuki'

'Senkaki' 230, 263 Coral bark maple. Shrub or small tree. Young branches coral-red, effective in winter. Leaves yellow in autumn. A.G.M. 1969.

A. pensylvanicum 228, 229, 255, 263 Striped or Snake-bark maple. Moosewood, Eastern N. America Zone 3. To 40 ft open and irregular. Young stems green, becoming striped with pale green and white. Leaves 3-lobed, up to 7 ins long, bright yellow in autumn. Flowers yellow, in hanging clusters, May. Unhappy on chalk. 20 ft in 20 years.

'Erythrocladum' 229 Young winter shoots pink-red, distinctive.

A. platanoides 232, 233, 252, 254, 262, 263 Norway maple. Europe. Caucasus Zone 3. To 100 ft, rounded head. Bright green leaves, 5-lobed, 4 to 7 ins wide, yellow in autumn. Small yellow flowers in clusters, late April. 35 ft in 20 years. A.G.M. 1969.

'Columnare' 262 Erect columnar form becoming conical with age. Leaves smaller with shallower lobes than the type.

'Dissectum' 262 Lobed leaves with crinkled edges and straight points.

'Erectum' 262 Narrow pyramidal form with short ascending branches. Leaves bigger and darker than the type. Slow-growing.

'Faasens's Black' 233 Leaves as A. platanoides 'Goldsworth Purple'.

'Goldsworth Purple' 233, 262 Red-leaved form, becoming purple/black.

'Laciniatum' 262 Eagle's claw maple. Big, upright tree. Leaves wedge-shaped at base; lobes with claw-like points.

'Lorbergii' 262 Medium-size tree. Palmate leaves, pale green.

'Reitenbachii' 233 Medium size. Leaves red at first, green later, red again in autumn.

'Schwedleri' 233, 262 Large leaves and young shoots red-purple, bronzy green later.

A. pseudoplatanus 232–3, 254, 262, 263 Sycamore or Sycamore maple. Europe and W. Asia Zone 5. To 100 ft, wide-spreading. Leaves usually 5-lobed, dark green above, paler below. Yellowish-green flowers in large drooping clusters. Keys in clusters. Succeeds in exposed positions, any soil. 35 ft in 20 years.

'Brilliantissimum' 232–3, 262 Small dense tree, young leaves pink, later yellow-green, finally green. 12 ft in 20 years.

'Purpureum' ('Spaethii') 232, 262 Purple sycamore. Leaves dark purply-red beneath.

'Worleei' 232, 262 Golden sycamore. Medium-size tree. Leaves yellow-green when young, leaf-stalks reddish. 20 ft in 20 years.

A. rubrum 42, 226, 228, 229, 255, 263 Red maple. Swamp maple. Eastern N. America Zone 3. To 120 ft, round head, dense foliage. Leaves medium length, with 3 to 5 toothed lobes, dark shiny green above, waxy bloom underneath. Small red flowers on slender stalks, early spring. Bright red keys in hanging clusters. 35 ft in 20 years.

'Columnare' 228, 262 Columnar red maple. Big, upright, widely columnar.

A. rufinerve 231, 255 Japan Zone 5. To 35 ft. Young stems bluish-grey; older stems and trunk green and white striped. Leaved 3-lobed, similar to A. pensylvanicum; bright red and yellow in autumn.

albolimbatum 231, 255 Leaves mottled or edged with white.

A. saccharinum 43, 228, 255, 261, 262 Silver maple. Eastern N. America Zone 3. To 120 ft, spreading head. Leaves medium length, 5 deep toothed lobes, bright green above, silvery white underneath. Clear yellow in autumn. Small greenish yellow flowers. Keys in hanging clusters. 50 ft in 20 years.

laciniatum 228 Branchlets weeping, leaves deeply lobed.

'Lutescens' 228 Pale yellow leafed form.

A. saccharum 43, 226, 228, 229, 255, 262 Sugar maple. C. and E. America Zone 3. To 120 ft. fluted trunk, rounded head. Leaves medium length, 3 to 5 toothed lobes, bright green, yellow orange or scarlet in autumn. Small greenish-yellow flowers in hanging clusters. Grey furrowed bark. 35 ft in 20 years.

nigrum 228 Black maple. Eastern N. America Zone 3. To 120 ft. Leaves 3-occasionally 5-lobed, simple, furry beneath, dull green above, paler beneath. Flowers in weeping clusters, pale green. Fruit smooth.

'Globosum' 262 Dwarf, rounded form, dense. 10 ft in 20 years.

'Temple's Upright' 228 Columnar., possibly rounded or oval.

A. sempervirens 254 'Cretan maple', similar to A. monspessulanum; keeps shiny leaves very late.

A. syriacum 254 Variable bushy tree from Syria and Cyprus. syn. A. obtusifolium

A. tetaricum 254, 263 'Tatarian maple'. Large shrub or small spreading tree. Leaves dull, pale green, doubly toothed.

ginnala 231 Amur maple. China Zone 2. To 20 ft, upright, rounded, dense branching, vigorous. 3-lobed leaves, toothed margins, bright dark green above, scarlet in autumn. Keys red and conspicuous. Flowers yellowish white, very fragrant, May. 15 ft in 20 years.

A. triflorum 254 Rare small maple like A. maximowiczianum, brilliant in autumn.

A. truncatum 254 Small lobed-leaved maple, leaves truncated at base.

A. ukurunduense caudatum 254 (A. papilio) Maple with five-lobed, toothed leaves; E. Himalayas.

A. velutinum, A. V. vanvolxemii 254 Caucasian maples with enormous leaves.

A. villosum 254 Himalayan maple with very big leaves. syn A. sterculiaceum.

AESCULUS 224–5, 263 Deciduous trees or shrubs, compound leaves usually with 5 to 7 leaflets. Flowers in large conical heads, late spring to summer. 1 or 2 large seeds in a smooth or prickly husk. Hardy. All soils, if not too dry. Prefer open, sunny position. Leaf spot in Europe and America.

A. californica 224 Californian buckeye. California Zone 7. To 35 ft, spreading tree or shrub. Leaves medium length. Flowers white to rose-coloured, 1 in. long, fragrant., April to Aug. Egg-shaped fruit, Aug. and Sept.

A. x carnea 224, 262 Red horse chestnut. Zone 3. Hybrid between A. hippocastanum and A. pavia, to 70 ft, pyramidal when young, becoming round-headed with age. Leaves smaller and darker than common horse chestnut. No autumn colour. Flowers rose-pink in upright clusters 10 ins high, mid-May. 25 ft in 20 years.

'Briotii' 225, 252 Almost identical to the type, but the flowers are a deeper colour and in large clusters.

'Plantierensis' 225, 263 Damask horse chestnut. Zone 3. Backcross between A. carnea and A. hippocastanum, ¾ common horse chestnut and ¼ red buckeye. Flower cluster is like former, but flowers soft pink.

A. flava 224, 255 Sweet buckeye. S.E. United States Zone 3. To 90 ft, round-headed. Leaves opposite, medium length, finely toothed, downy beneath, usually good autumn tints. Flower long, yellow, May to June. Fruit smooth. 20 ft in 20 years.

A. glabra 224, 255, 262, 263 Ohio buckeye. S.E. and C. United States Zone 3. To 30 ft, round-headed. Leaves oval to wedge-shaped, smooth with age. Flowers green-yellow. Fruit ovallish, prickly. 20 ft in 20 years.

A. hippocastanum 224, 252, 254, 259, 262, 263 Common horse chestnut. Greece, Albania Zone 3. To 120 ft, with a rounded spreading head. Leaves medium to long, scattered hairs below, hairless above. Flowers white. May. Fruit spiny. 40 ft in 20 years.

'Baumannii' 224, 225, 263 Baumann's horse chestnut. Zone 3. To 85 ft, rounded at maturity. Flowers double, white mid-May, lasting longer than the type. No fruit.

A. indica 224, 254, 263 Indian horse chestnut. N.W. Himalaya Zone 7. To 100 ft, often with a short, thick trunk. Leaves large, toothed hairless, dark shiny green above. Flowers 1 in long, which flushed with pink, July. Fruit rough. 30 ft in 20 years. A.G.M. 1969.

A. parviflora 224, 262 Shrubby pavia, Dwarf buckeye. S.E. United States Zone 4. To 15 ft, a spreading, suckering shrub with several slender stems. Leaves medium to long, shallow-toothed, beneath. Flowers white with red anthers, July, Aug. Fruit hairless, nearly egg-shaped. Tolerant of shade. 10 ft in 20 years. A.G.M. 1969.

A pavia 224, 255, 263 Red buckeye. S. United States Zone 5. To 20 ft, shrub or small tree. Leaves medium length. Flowers crimson, June. Fruit nearly egg-shaped, August.

A. turbinate 224, 262 Japanese horse chestnut. Japan Zone 5. To 100 ft, with a thick trunk. Leaflets up to 16 ins long, toothed, on a long stalk. Attractive autumn tints. Flowers yellowish-white, June. Fruit pear-shaped, rough. 35 ft in 20 years.

AGATHIS australis 255 Kauri pine. New Zealand Zone 9. Leaves large, evergreen, leathery, stalked, in opposite pairs, 1 in apart, tapering to a blunt point, dull grey-green. Male and female 'flowers' on same tree, but separate. Cones round to oval. Seeds winged. 12 ft in 20 years.

AILANTHUS altissima 242–3, 253–4, 262, 263 Tree of heaven. N. China Zone 4. To 90 ft, usually less. Leaves compound. deciduous, leaflets ovallish, with unpleasant smell, toothed near base. Flowers in small clusters, greenish-yellow, sexes on separate trees, male flowers with unpleasant smell. Fruits dry, winged, reddish-brown, profuse, on female trees only. Tolerant of dryness, shade, acid soil; sun-loving. 45 ft in 20 years.

'Erythrocarpa' 243 Dark green leaves, bright red fruit.

ALBIZIA julibrissin 210, 211, 252, 262, 263 Silk tree. Pink siris. Persia to China Zone 7. To 40 ft. broad, spreading, flat-topped. Leaves doubly pinnate, 9 to 18 ins long. Flowers light pink, brush-like, in rounded heads. June-August. Pods 5 ins long, narrow between seeds, flat, Sept-Nov. 15 ft in 20 years.

'Rosea' 211, 264 Smaller form with pinker flowers, hardy to zone 5.

Alder, Common See Alnus glutinosa

Grey See Alnus incana, A. rugosa

Italian See Alnus cordata

Red See Alnus rubra

Speckled See Alnus incana

Alerce See Tetraclinis articulate

Aleurites fordii 235

Almonds See Prunus dulcis

ALNUS 168–9, 262, 263 Very hardy deciduous trees or shrubs. Toothed leaves. Long make catkins, short female catkins on the same tree form woody cones, ripe in autumn. Seeds are small flat nuts. Flowers produced before the leaves. Mostly moisture-loving, some lime-tolerant. Susceptible to die-back, leaf spot, tent-caterpillar.

A. cordata 168–9, 254, 263 Italian alder. Corsica and S. Italy. Zone 5. To 80 ft. Leaves roundish with abrupt point, medium length, bright green, glossy, finely-toothed. Male catkins 2 to 3 ins long, groups of 3 to 6. Fruit erect, egg-shaped, about 1 in long, in threes. Suited to all types of soil. 50 ft in 20 years.

A. glutinosa 168, 169 Common alder, European alder. Europe (incl. British Isles), W. Asia, N. Africa Zone 3. to 80 ft, with sticky young growth. Broad, pear-shaped leaves, medium length,; dark green and sticky above, pale green below. Male catkins in groups, 2 to 4 ins long. Egg-shaped fruits in clusters. Suited to boggy ground. 40 ft in 20 years.

'Aurea' 169, 262 Leaves golden yellow, particularly in spring and early summer.

'Imperialis' 169, 262 Leaves deeply and finely lobed, the lobes slender and pointed, not toothed. 25 ft in 20 years.

'Laciniata' 169 Sturdy, rather stiff form; leaves not so finely divided as 'Imperialis'.

A. incana 168, 169, 254 Grey alder, American speckled alder. Europe, Caucasus. E. North America Zone 2. Large shrub to medium-sized tree, to 65 ft. Leaves dull green above, grey beneath, downy, oval. Male catkins 2 to 4 ins long in groups. Oval fruits clustered. Good for cold or wet situations. 50 ft in 20 years.

'Aurea; 169 Young shoots and foliage yellow; catkins red-tinted.

'Laciniata' Leaves dissected, grey on lower surface. Very hardy.

A. rubra 168, 255 Red alder. Western N. America Zone 4. Medium-sized tree, to 65 ft, narrow pyramidal head, pendulous branches. Oval leaves medium length. upper surface dark green, lower surface pale or greyish. Male catkins 4 to 6 ins long in groups. Fruits barrel-shaped in clusters. 40 ft in 20 years.

A. rugosa 169 Smooth alder. E. United States Zone 2. Small tree or large shrub. Long

japonica

Monarch See *Betula maximowicziana*

Paper See *Betula papyrifera*

Polar-leaved See *Betula populifolia*

River See *Betula nigra*

Russian rock See *Betula ermanii*

Silver See *Betula pendula*

Southern white Chinese See *Betula albo-sinensis septentrionalis*

Swedish 'Dalecarlica'. 'Tristis' See *Betula pendula*

Yellow See *Betula alleghaniensis*

Young's weeping See *Betula pendula* 'Youngii'

Bitternut See *Carya cordiformis*

Black-gum See *Nyssa sylvatica*

Blackhaw See *Viburnum prunifolium*

Blackthorn See *Prunus spinosa*

Box 65 See also *Buxus*

Broom, Moroccan See *Cytisis battandieri*

Mount Etna See *Genista aetnensis*

BROUSSONETIA papyrifera **142, 143**, 262 Paper mulberry. E. Asia Zone 6. To 45 ft, wide-spreading, broad round head. Leaves variable, oval or lobed, dull green and rough above, woolly beneath. Deciduous. Flowers, sexes on separate plants, male flowers in woolly catkins 1½ to 3 ins; female flowers in small round clusters, May. Round orange-red fruits ¾ in across. Any soil.

Buckeye, California See *Aesculus californica*

Ohio See *Aesculus glabra*

Red See *Aesculus pavia*

Sweet See *Aesculus flava*

Buttonwood See *Platanus occidentalis*

BUXUS sempervirens **223**, 263 Common box S. Europe, N. Africa, W. Asia Zone 5. To 35 ft, evergreen shrub or small tree. Leaves oval, tapering, notched at tip, short, profuse, leathery. Flowers pale green, insignificant, males clustered round female. Fruit, small oval or rounded capsule. Most soils. Sun or shade. Subject to leaf spot, twig dieback. 15 ft in 20 years.

C

CALLITRIS robusta **97** Common cypress pine. Queensland. Tasmania Zone 9. To 15 or 20 ft evergreen, branches spreading or upright. Small leaves in whorls of 3, narrow or scale-like. Male and female 'flowers' separate but on same plant, males cylindrical, females conical. Cones single or clustered. 1 in. long. 10 ft in 20 years.

CALOCEDRUS **104** Evergreen, Leaves flattened, scale-like, overlapping. Male and female 'flowers' on different branches of same tree usually, both solitary; males oblong to oval, females oval to oblong, woody. Cones woody. Seeds winged.

C. decurrens **85, 90, 104**, 262, 263 Incense cedar. S.W. United States Zone 5. Conical in wild, columnar in cultivation, 100 to 150 ft. Shoot covered in scales, becomes red-brown, vertical sprays of foliage, deep green outside, yellow beneath. Male flowers pale yellow. Cones pale yellow-brown, becoming red-brown. Bark dark red-brown, fragrant. Dislikes shallow soils, or very dry, exposed places. 35 ft in 20 years.

CAMELLIA **172–3**, 262, 263. Evergreen trees or shrubs. Leaves alternate, toothed, simple. Flowers bisexual, usually solitary, white to red, showy. Seeds big, oily, in woody capsule; rare in cultivated forms. Neutral, slightly acid soils. Shade-loving. Subject to leaf blotch.

C. japonica **173**, 252, 254, 263 Common camellia. China, Japan Zone 7. To 20 ft. Leaves ovallish, long-pointed, smooth, often black-dotted beneath, leathery, dark green, short-stalked. Flowers single, red, waxy, possibly slightly fragrant, late winter. 15 ft in 20 years. A.G.M. 1930.

'Haku-rakuten' **173** Erect form, vigorous growth. Flowers big, white, semi-double with curved petals.

'Yours Truly' **173** Bushy. Leaves wavy. Flowers semi-double, pink streaked with deeper pink, bordered with white.

C. reticulata **172–3** Yunnan, China Zone 8. To 35 ft, evergreen trees or compact shrub. Rigid leathery leaves, dark dull green. Flowers rose-pink. March. Prefers slightly acid soil.

C. sasanqua **172–3** Japan Zone 7. Shrub or small tree. To 20 ft. Leaves narrowly oval, dark green, leathery. Flowers white, fragrant, early winter. Needs shelter. 12 ft in 20 years.

C. sinensis **172** Tea-tree. Assam to China Zone 7. To 45 ft compact shrub or tree. Leaves variable, broad to lance-shaped. Flowers white, nodding, spring. Slow-growing.

Camphor tree See *Cinnamomum camphora*

Candelabra tree See *Araucaria angustifolia*

Carob tree See *Ceratonia siliqua*

CARPINUS **170–1**, 263 Hardy deciduous trees or shrubs. Leaves toothed in two ranks. Hanging male catkins, spring. Narrow female catkins. Fruit in small ribbed nut, ripe in autumn. Bark smooth or scaly grey. Easily grown. Clay- and chalk-tolerant.

C. betulus **64, 170, 171**, 263 Common hornbeam. European hornbeam. Europe, Asia Minor Zone 5. To 75 ft pyramidal, becoming rounder. Leaves oval, tapering; dark green, downy beneath, turning yellow and smooth by autumn. Unisexual flowers. Male catkins 1½ ins; fruiting catkins 1½ to 3 ins with large, 3-lobed bracts. 35 ft in 20 years.

'Columnaris' **263** Small, compact form, conical becoming columnar. Slower than 'Fastigiata'.

'Fastigiata' **171** Medium-sized tree, erect, columnar, broadening with age. 30 ft in 20 years A.G.M. 1969.

'Incisa' **262** Leaves small, narrow, deeply toothed. Liable to revert.

'Intertexta' **262** Ascending, open. Branchlets drooping. Foliage blue-green, in flat sprays. A.G.M. 1969.

C. caroliniana **170** American hornbeam. Blue beech, or Ironwood. E. United States Zone 2. To 40 ft, branches spreading, arching at tips. Leaves oval, bright green, downy when young, sparsely hairy later; scarlet and orange in autumn. Male catkins 1 to 1½ ins long. Fruiting clusters 3 ins long. 15 ft in 20 years.

C. cordata **170, 171** Japan, N.E. Asia, N. and W. China Zone 5. To 40 or 50 ft. Leaves heart-shaped, pointed, simple, deeply-veined, hairy below, slightly so above. Male catkins with long hairs, female catkins 3 ins long. Fruits small, green, clustered.

C. japonica **170, 171**, 253, 263 Japanese hornbeam. Japan Zone 4. To 50 ft, wide-spreading. Leaves alternate, oval, tapering; medium length, upper surface dark green, lower surface downy on veins, corrugated. Male catkins 1 to 2 ins long with conspicuous scales. Fruit clusters to 2½ ins long, persist on tree. 15 ft in 20 years.

C. laxiflora **255** Japanese hornbeam with ornamental fruit.

C. orientalis **254** Small bushy tree or shrub from S.E. Europe and Asia Minor. Small, sharply toothed leaves.

C. turczaninowii **254** A very graceful thin, spindly hornbeam.

CARYA 132, **144, 145, 146, 147**, 262, 263 Big deciduous trees related to walnuts. Pinnate leaves. Sexes on same tree. Male flowers in branched, slender catkins; female flowers in small clusters. Fruit, nut surrounded by a husk. Deep loamy soil. Subject to canker, leaf blotch and scab in America; pest-free in Europe. Resent transplanting.

C. cordiformis **147**, 255 Bitternut. E. United States Zone 4. To 90 ft broad, rounded. Winter bud scales yellow. Leaves long, 5 to 10 oval, toothed leaflets, yellow in autumn. Male flowers downy. Fruit in twos or threes. 25 ft in 20 years.

C. glabra **147**, 255, 262 Pignut. E. United States Zone 4. To 120 ft. narrow to round. Leaves long, 5 to 7 oval, toothed leaflets, yellow in autumn. Nuts vary in size and shape.

C. illinoensis **146–7**, 262 Pecan. E. United States Zone 5. To 150 ft, rounded head, huge branches 11 to 17 toothed, pointed leaflets, yellow in autumn. Fruits clustered, oblong.

C. laciniosa **255** A shaggy-barked hickory from E. United States.

C. ovata **146, 147**, 255, 262, 263 Shagbark hickory. E. United States Zone 4. To 120 ft, narrow and upright, irregular. Leaves long, 5 to 9 leaflets, hairy beneath. rich yellow to golden brown in autumn. Male catkins hairy, in threes. Fruits roundish. 20 ft in 20 years.

C. tomentosa **147**, 255, 262 Mockernut, Bigbud hickory. S.E. Canada, E. United States Zone 4. To 90 ft, upright with a round head. Leaves long, 5 to 9 toothed, pointed leaflets, dark green above, yellowish, downy below. Male catkins downy, 3 to 5 ins long. Fruit roundish. 20 ft in 20 years.

CASTANEA **162–3**, 263 Leaves toothed, deciduous. Flowers, sexes on separate catkins; males long, hanging, females shorter; both pale yellow. July. Fruit, nuts surrounded by prickly husks. Tolerant of shade. Not suited to shallow, chalky or sandy soils. Subject to chestnut blight in America, canker, die-back, leaf-spot.

A. crenata **163** Japanese chestnut. Japan Zone 5. To 30 ft. Leaves narrow oval, often hairy beneath. Nuts 1 in across, 2 or 3 in each husk.

C. dentata **163** American sweet chestnut. E. United States Zone 4. To 100 ft, upright, broad. Leaves hairless, dull green, narrowly oblong, tapering. Flowers in catkins, bisexual. Fruit 1 to 3 nuts. 15 ft in 20 years.

C. mollissima **163** Chinese chestnut. China, Korea Zone 4. To 65 ft, dense, rounded head. Leaves oval, tapering, sometimes hairy, with short, hairy stalk. Usually 2 or 3 nuts in husk. 10 ft in 20 years. Resists chestnut blight.

C. sativa 64, 132, 148, **162–3**, 253, 259, 261, 262 Spanish chestnut, Sweet chestnut. S. Europe, N. Africa, Asia Minor Zone 5. To 100 ft, spreading. Leaves oblong, tapering hairy beneath at first. Flowers yellowish-green. unpleasant-smelling. Ornamental, especially in flowers. Nuts edible. 35 ft in 20 years.

'Aureomarginata' **262** Leaves bordered yellow.

'Marron de Lyon' **162** Bears fruit at a very early age.

CASTANOPSIS cuspidata **162, 163**, 254 Small evergreen tree between oak and chestnut.

CASUARINA nana **215** Dwarf sheoke. She-oak. Australia Zone 8. Small, bushy evergreen tree or shrub, narrow, with rushlike stems and leaves.

CATALPA 64, **244–5**, 263 Deciduous. Big, opposite leaves, long-stalked, sometimes lobed. Flowers clustered, bisexual. Long, narrow seed capsule. All well-drained soils. Sun-loving. Subject to leaf-spot in America.

C. bignonioides **244**, 253, 255, 262 Indian bean tree. Southern catalpa. E. United States Zone 4. to 65 ft, wide-spreading. Leaves broadly oval, tapering, light green above, pale downy beneath, disagreeable odour when crushed. Flowers upright, white and purple. 20 ft in 20 years. A.G.M. 1960.

'Aurea' **245**, 262 Golden Indian bean tree Zone 4. Leaves rich yellow and velvety.

C. x erubescens **255** To 30 ft. Leaves ovallish, 3-lobed and whole on same tree, purple when unfolding. Flowers similar to *C. bignonioides* but smaller and more numerous, late July.

'J. C. Teas' **245** Double-sized flowers.

'Purpurea' **245** Shoots and leaves black-purple, becoming greener.

C. fargesii **254** Smaller-leaved catalpa with excellent summer flowers.

C. ovata **254** To 40 ft. Leaves usually 3-lobed. Small white flowers with yellow and red markings.

C. speciosa **244**, 253 Western catalpa. C. United States Zone 4. To 100 ft. leaves heart-shaped, tapering, lower side downy. Flowers slightly larger than *C. bignonioides*, less spotted with purple. 20 ft in 20 years.

Cedar, Alaska See *Chamaecyparis nootkatensis*

Atlantic See *Cedrus atlantica*

Chinese See *Toona sinensis*

Deodar See *Cedrus deodara*

Eastern red See *Juniperus virgininiana*

Eastern white See *Thuja occidentalis*

Incense See *Calocedrus decurrens*

Japanese See *Cryptomeria japonica*

of Goa See *Cupressus lusitanica*

of Lebanon See *Cedrus libani*

Port Orford See *Chamaecyparis lawsoniana*

Western red See *Thuja plicata*

White See *Thuja occidentalis*

Yellow See *Chamaecyparis nootkatensis*

Cedars See *Cedrus*

CEDRELA See *Toona*

CEDRUS 69, 70, 83, 85, **90–1**, 94, 97–100, 102–6, 112, 114, 263 Cedars. Hardy evergreen, initially conical, spreading later. Leaves needle-like, in rosettes on old shoots, single on new. Male and female 'flowers' on same or separate trees, males yellow, profuse. Cones barrel-shaped, break up on tree after 2 years. Seeds winged. Few fungal diseases, susceptible to drought.

C. brevifolia See *C. libani* ssp. *brevifolia*

C. deodara **91**, 254, 262 Deodar. W. Himalaya Zone 7. To 200 ft, pendulous. Leaves short, dark green, waxy or silvery, sharply pointed. sexes usually on separate trees. 45 ft in 20 years.

C. libani 41. 43. **90–1**, 254, 261, 262 Cedar of Lebanon, Asia Minor and Syria Zone 5. To 70 or 100 ft, often erect or ascending, flat-topped with age. Leaves short, green or waxy. 30 ft in 20 years.

atlantica **91**, 254, 262 Atlas cedar. Atlas Mts Zone 6. To 120 ft, pyramidical when young. Leaves shorter but similar to *C. libani*, slightly more waxy and numerous. Male 'flowers' erect sugarloaf-shape, pale green summer, purplish Sept; females green, tinged pink in centre of rosette. 40 ft in 20 years.

'Aurea' **263** Leaves shorter than the type, golden yellow.

'Fastigiata' **262** Narrow, pyramidal, ascending branches. Leaves light green above, bluish-green below, on short branchlets.

glauca **91**, 163 Blue cedar. To 120 ft, more pointed, less liable to have multiple stems. Leaves light blue or waxy. Bark pale grey. 40 ft in 20 years.

'Pendula' **262** Small, pendulous branches. Leaves green or greyish green.

brevifolia **91**, 254 Cyprus cedar. Mts of Cyprus Zone 7. Narrowly conical. Leaves rich green to blue- or yellow-green. Cones smooth pale green. 20 ft in 20 years.

CELTIS **140–1**, 263 Medium or large, related to elms. Leaves deciduous, simple. Flowers small, greenish. Separate sexes on same tree, male flowers clustered, female flowers in groups of 1 to 3. Fruit fleshy, single-stoned, sweet, ripe in autumn. Subject to leaf-spot where native, witches' broom in America. Any soil.

C. australis **141**, 254, 263 S. Europe, N. Africa, Asia Minor Zone 6. To 80 ft, round-headed. Leaves toothed, lance-shaped, soft down beneath, harsher above, short-stalked. Sun-loving. 10 ft in 20 years.

C. laevigata **141** Sugar hackberry. Mississippi hackberry. S.E. United States Zone 5. To 100 ft, spreading, sometimes weeping. Leaves oval to lance-shaped, smooth, dark green above, paler with some hairs beneath, few teeth. Male flowers separate from solitary females. Fruits small, oval, orange to black. Sun-loving. Fairly resistant to witches' broom. 12 ft in 20 years.

C. occidentalis **140, 141**, 255 Hackberry. Sugarberry. N. United States Zone 3. Usually to 40 ft, occasionally much more. Leaves oval to oblong, possibly downy, short-toothed near base. Flowers early spring. Fruit ripens purple, small, profuse. Bark warty, corky, rough. 12 ft in 20 years.

C. sinensis **141** Chinese hackberry. E. China, Korea, Japan Zone 6. To 65 ft, spreading. Leaves shiny, dark green, red or yellow, edible. Sun-loving. Resistant to witches' broom disease. 20 ft in 20 years.

C. tournefourtii **254** Small oriental tree, polished leaves and red and yellow fruits.

CEPHALOTAXUS **110–11**, 263 Hardy evergreen shrubs or small trees. Leaves narrow, pointed, dark green above, obvious midrib. Sexes usually on separate trees; male 'flowers' round, females scarce, cup-shaped. Fruit in cup, single seed. Shade-tolerant.

C. fortunei **110** Chinese plum yew. C. and S.W. Chin Zone 6. To 30 ft, slender or bushy. Medium length leaves. Male 'flowers' on short stalks below shoot, females on separate trees. Small fruit, oval, green-white vertically striped green. Lime-tolerant. 12 ft in 20 years.

C. harringtonia drupacea **110**, 255 Cow's tail pine, Japanese plum yew. Japan, Central China Zone 5. To 20 or 40 ft, wide-spreading, bushy crown, rounded. Leaves short, in double ranks, forming narrow V-shaped channel on upper surface of branchlets. Male 'flowers' small, short scaly stalks. Seeds pear-shaped, oily, brown or olive-green. Thrives on chalk soils. 8 ft in 20 years.

Cerasus **200**

CERATONIA siliqua **208, 210**, 262 Carob, St John's bread. Mediterranean Zone 10. To 50 ft, rounded shrub or small tree. Leaves evergreen, pinnate, wavy-edged, glossy, dark green. Flowers, sexes separate, small, red, clustered, spring. Fruits pods 1 ft long, edible, early autumn. Tolerates dry soils.

C. controversa 216, 217, 262 Giant dogwood. Japan, China Zone 5. To 65 ft, horizontal branches in tiers. Leaves alternate, oval, pointed, dark glossy green above, waxy beneath. Flowers white, in flattish heads, profuse. Fruit blue-black, roundish. Chalk-tolerant. 25 ft in 20 years.

'Variegata' 217 Zone 5. Small tree, form similar to type. Leaves with silvery-white to pale yellow border. 12 ft in 20 years.

C. florida 42, 216, 252, 262, 263 Flowering dogwood. E. United States Zone 5. To 40 ft, wide-spreading tree. Leaves oval, dark green with scattered down above, pale beneath. Flowers insignificant, spring, but four white bracts, 2 ins long, expand in May after enclosing bud in winter. Red berries in winter. Sun or semi-shade. Dislikes poor, shallow chalk soils. 10 ft in 20 years.

'Cherokee Chief' 216 Flower bracts deep rose red.

'Pendula' 262 Stiffly pendulous branches.

'Rubra' 216 Variable, flower bracts rosy-pink. Less hardy than the type. A.G.N. 1937.

C. kousa 216. 252–3, 262, 263 Japanese dogwood. Japan. Korea Zone 5. To 25 ft, shrub or small tree. Leaves oval, pointed, crimson-bronze in autumn. Flowers small, inconspicuous, attractive large white bracts. Fruits strawberry-like. Dislikes poor, shallow chalky soils. Moderately sunny location. 12 ft in 20 years. A.G.M. 1969.

chinensis 216 Chinese dogwood. China. Taller, more open than *C. kousa*. Leaves slightly bigger, flower bracts slightly longer. A.G.M. 1969.

C. mas 217, 252 Cornelian cherry C. and S. Europe Zone 4. To 25 ft, shrub or small tree, dense branching. Leaves oval, pointed, dark dull green, reddish-purple in autumn. Flowers small, yellow, late winter, in short-stalked, flat-headed clusters on leafless twigs. Fruit bright red, edible. Resists insect or disease pests in America. Sun-loving; tolerates dryness and exposure. 20 ft in 20 years. A.G.M. 1924.

C. nuttallii 216, 252, 262 Pacific dogwood. W. United States Zone 7. To 80 ft. Leaves oval, downy, good autumn colour. Flowers small, purple and green, surrounded by 4 to 8 large white bracts, flushed with pink; attractive. Dislikes shallow chalk soils, extreme cold. Sun or semi-shade. 25 ft in 20 years.

CORYLUS 171, 263 Deciduous shrubs, rarely trees. Leaves oval, toothed. Flowers, male and female on same tree, male catkins hanging in winter, female flowers in small clusters, opening in spring. Fruit, ovoid nut held in toothed cup, mostly edible, ripen in autumn. Lime-tolerant, suited to chalk soil. Occasional bacterial blight in America, fungal fruit rot, bark fungi in Europe. Nut weevil attacks young nuts.

C. avellana 64, 171, 262 Hazel, Cobnut. Europe, W. Asia, No. Africa Zone 3. To 11 ft, shrub or small tree. Leaves roundish, terminal half open lobed. Nuts in shallow lobed husk. Mainly attractive for male catkins, although leaves turn yellow in autumn. Sun or shade. 15 ft in 20 years.

'Contorta' 171, 262 Corkscrew hazel, Harry Lauder's walking stick. To 10 ft, twigs twisted and curled. Attractive in late winter when in catkin. Slow-growing.

C. californica 171 Californian hazel. California Zone 5. To 10 ft, shrub. Leaves downy beneath. Fruit bristly with a short beak.

C. colurna 171, 262 Turkish hazel, Turkish filbert. S.E. Europe, W. Asia Zone 4. to 80 ft, symmetrical, pyramidal form. Leaves pointed at apex; upper side dark green, lower downy along midrib. Nuts held in husk fringed with lobes, fine down, in groups of 3 or more. Thrives in hot summers and cold winters, as in central Europe. Sun-loving. 35 ft in 20 years.

C. maxima 'Purpurea' 171, 262 Purple-leaf filbert. Leaves and catkins coppery purple.

COTINUS 235, 262, 263 Deciduous shrubs or trees. Simple alternate leaves with slender stalks. Sexes sometimes on separate trees. Small, egg-shaped, fleshy fruit. 12 ft in 20 years.

C. americanus See *C. obovatus*

C. coggygria 235 Smoke tree. Venetian sumach. Central Europe Zone 5. Shrub or small tree, to 15 ft. Smooth rounded green leaves, good autumn colours. Flowers fawn-coloured plumes, turning smoke grey. Preferable to *C. obovatus*. A.G.M. 1969.

'Royal Purple' 262 Leaves deep wine-purple. A.G.M. 1969.

C. obovatus 234–5 American smoke tree. S.E. United States Zone 5. To 40 ft, shrub or small tree. Leaves wedge-shaped ovals, medium length, often reddish purple; brilliant autumn colouring. Flowers in greenish feathery masses; sexes separate. Fruit sparse. Richer soil gives poorer colour. Tolerant of dry soils. Sun-loving.

COTONEASTER 191, 263 Evergreen and deciduous trees and shrubs. Leaves simple, without teeth and lobes, unlike the closely allied *Crataegus*. Flowers all similar, ⅓ to ½ in wide, white or rose-tinted, usually in profuse clusters, attractive to bees. Fruits round to oval; best types brilliant red, thornless. All soils. Sun-loving; some species tolerant of shade. Hardy. Susceptible to fireblight and some rusts.

C. 'Cornubia' 191, 252 Zone 7. To 20 or 30 ft, spreading. Leaves narrow, oval, pointed, semi-evergreen, smooth above, slightly hairy below. Fruit profuse, large. Fast-growing. A.G.M. 1969.

C. frigidus 254 Himalaya Zone 7. To 20 or 40 ft, spreading. Leaves elliptic, deciduous, smooth, woolly below at first, dull green. Flowers, late spring or early summer. Fruit clustered, pea-sized, crimson, autumn to winter. 25 ft in 20 years. A.G.M. 1925.

C. x watereri 191, 263 Zone 7 to 15 ft, spreading, hybrid. Leaves tapered at both ends, semi-evergreen, smooth when fully developed. Fruits small, in clusters. Fast-growing.

Cottonwood See *Populus*

Black See *Populus trichocarpa*

Crab-apples See *MALUS*

Crab, Bechtel's See *Malus ioensis* 'Plena'

'Cherry' See *Malus x robusta*

Cutleaf See *Malus toringoides*

English wild See *Malus sylvestris*

Hupeh See *Malus hupehensis*

Japanese See *Malus floribunda*

Manchurian See *Malus baccata* 'Mandshurica'

Prairie See *Malus ioensis*

Rivers' See *Malus spectabilis* 'Riversii'

Sargent's See *Malus sargentii*

Siberian See *Malus baccata*

Tea See *Malus hupehensis*

Crabs See *MALUS*

+ *CRATAEGPMESPILUS dardarii* 193 Bronvaux medlar. Zone 5. To 15 or 20 ft, spreading, grafted hybrid, consists of core of hawthorn enveloped with medlar. Leaves yellow to orange in autumn, ovallish, simple, deciduous, downy on both sides, possibly finely toothed. short stalk. Flowers white in domed heads, very fluffy. Fruits clustered, like small medlars. Occasionally thorny.

CRATAEGUS 192–3, 263 Deciduous trees or shrubs. Usually thorny. Leaves simple, toothed or lobed. Flowers usually white and clustered, late spring/early summer. Fruit apple-like, small, variously coloured. Susceptible to fireblight, juniper rust, hawthorn blight, lacebugs, mites, leaf miners, various borers and others. Very hardy. All soils.

C. crus-galli 193, 253, 255, 262 Cockspur thorn. E. and C. United States Zone 4. To 40 ft, wide-spreading. leaves wedge-shaped, shiny, smooth, dark green, stalked. Flowers small. Fruits, crimson, winter. Thorns 1½ to 3 ins long, branched.

C. x grignonensis 193 Zone 5. Small hybrid. leaves with 2 to 4 toothed lobes, green until winter. Flowers white, late summer. Fruits bright red.

C, laciniata (*C. orientalis*) 193 S.E. Europe, W. Asis Zone 5. To 20 ft, rounded spreading head. Leaves with 5 to 9 toothed lobes, hairy above, woolly below. Flowers June. Fruit roundish, hairy, orange-red. October.

C. laevigata 192–3, 262, 263 Hawthorn, May. N.W. and C. Europe Zone 4. To 25 ft, spreading. Leaves 3- to 5-lobed, smooth, except at first, glossy, dark green, toothed, stalked. Flowers small, in flat heads. Fruit scarlet, autumn, several-seeded.

'Paul's Scarlet' 193 Double-flowered form. Fruit sparse.

'Plena' 252 White double flowers. A.G.M. 1969.

C. x lavallei 193, 262 Zone 4. To 20 or 25 ft, spreading to upright, hybrid. Leaves long, shiny, dark green, often remain until mid-winter. Flowers small, numerous. fruit orange to brick-red, autumn and winter. Thorns stout, few. 20 ft in 20 years. A.G.M. 1925.

C. mollis 193 Downy hawthorn. C. United States Zone 4. To 35 ft, wide-spreading with stout thorns. Leaves oval with shallow lobes, downy. Flowers profuse, April and May. Fruit pear-shaped, red, Aug.-Sept.

C. monogyna 192–3 Common hawthorn, May. Europe, N. Africa, W. Asia Zone 4. To 35 ft, spreading. Leaves 3- to 7-lobed, dark green, stalked. Flowers in tight clusters, fragrant. Fruits small, red, usually single-seeds, autumn. Many short, rigid thorns.

'Biflora' 193 Glastonbury thorn. Leaves produced earlier than *C. monogyna*. Occasionally flowers in mid-winter (if mild) s well as spring; fewer flowers than species.

'Stricta' 262 Small upright form.

C. nitida 193 Glossy hawthorn. E. United States Zone 4. Top 20 or 35 ft, rounded. Leaves oblong, shiny, roughly lobed, double-toothed. Fruit round, dark red, persists through winter.

C. orientalis See *C. laciniata*

C. orientalis sanguinea 2542 Red fruiting form of *C. orientalis*

C. oxyacantha See *C. laevigata*

C. phaenopyrum 193, 253. 262 Washington hawthorn. S.E. United States Zone 4. To 35 ft, upright, narrow. Leaves triangular, possibly lobed, smooth, glossy, bright green, sharply toothed, stalked. Flowers numerous in flat heads, small. Fruit shiny, scarlet, winter persisting until spring. Slender-thorned. Good autumn colour.

C. pinnatifida major 193 Large Chinese hawthorn. China Zone 5. To 18 ft, spreading. Leaves wedge-shaped to round, downy along the midrib above and below, deep lobe at base, often double-toothed, glossy dark green above, paler below. Flowers small, in flat heads. Fruit shiny, crimson, with tiny dots, winter. Thorns absent or short.

C. tanacetifolia 254 'Tansy-leaved thorn'. Grey-leaved hawthorn with large yellow berries from Asia Minor.

CRYPTOMERIA 9, 98, 116–17 Evergreen tree, sun-loving, fairly hardy.

C. japonica 117–17, 262 Japanese cedar. Japan, C. China Zone 5. To 150 ft, narrowly conical, older trees broader and domed. Leaves spirally arranged, short, blunt points. Sexes separate on same tree; male 'flowers' in terminal clusters, roundish, pale green in summer, pale yellow in winter; female 'flowers' green rosettes. Cones globose, rough, green ripening to dull dark brown. Likes moisture. 40 to 55 ft in 20 years.

'Elegans' 116, 262 Broad, rounded tree to 70 ft. Leaves juvenile, spreading outwards and downwards, grey-glue, soft to touch, short, red-bronze in autumn and winter. Cones rare, smaller and smoother than *C. japonica*. 20 ft in 20 years.

'Lobbii' 252 Zone 5. Narrowly conical. Short branches upturned at ends. Foliage dense. Hardiest form. 35 ft in 20 years.

'Nana' 119 Dwarf, to 3 ft, erect twisted branches with crowded branchlets. Shoot tips curved. Slow-growing.

'Pygmaea' 119 Compact round bush to 6 ft. Leaves short, needle-like, apple-green. Slow growing.

sinensis 254 Commonest form of *Cryptomeria* in cultivation in the West.

Cucumber tree See *Magnolia acuminata*

Yellow See *Magnolia acuminata subcordata*

CUNNINGHAMIA lanceolata 112, 117, 254 Chinese fir. C. and S. China Zone 7. To 150 ft, spreading, weeping branch tips, evergreen. Leaves in spirals, lance-shaped, bright green above, with 2 white bands beneath; bronze in autumn. Male 'flowers' in clusters of about 12, female 'flowers' with leafy scales; both open in spring. Cones single or clustered, oval.

x *CUPRESSOCYPARIS leylandii* 99, 101, 262, 263 Leyland cypress Zone 4. To 90 ft, broadly columnar. tapering. Evergreen. Very adaptable. 50 ft in 20 years.

'Haggerston Grey' 101 Columnar but rather open form with irregular sprays of grey-green foliage.

'Leighton Green' 101 Narrow columnar. Foliage green in flattened fern-like sprays.

CUPRESSUS 94–101, 263 Cypresses. Evergreen, mostly columnar or pyramidal. Leaves minute, scale-like, pressed on branch. 'Flowers' separate on same tree; cylindrical heads on male 'flowers'. Cones round to oval. Tolerant of various soils but often tender.

C. abramsiana 96–7, 255 Santa Cruz cypress. California Zone 7. Conical to columnar. Leaves blunt-pointed, pale green; resin gland inconspicuous or absent. Cones green ripening brown. 50 to 60 ft in 20 years.

C. arizonica glabra 94–5, 96, 97, 255 Smooth Arizona cypress. Central Arizona Zone 6. 20 to 50 ft, conical. Leaves toothed, usually waxy, glandular, resin whitish. 30 ft in 20 years.

C. bakeri 97, 255 Modoc cypress. California Zone 5. To 35 or 50 ft, open, conical. Leaves grey-green, short, pointed, with obvious resin gland. Cones grey-brown, warty. 15 ft in 20 years.

C. forbesii 225 Rare small cypress from California with flaking bark.

C. funebris 254 'Mourning cypress'. C. China Zone 9. To 60 ft. Flat hanging branchlets. Leaves bluish-green. Cones small, dark brown.

'Pyramidalis' 97, 262 Conical or pyramidal. Shoots upturned at tips. Leaves blue-green, heavily white spotted. 25 ft in 20 years. A.G.M. 1969.

C. goveniana 97 Gowen cypress, California cypress. California. 30 or 70 ft, dense, bright green, columnar in Britain; open, wide, conical in California. Leaves pale green or yellow-green, fragrant. Male 'flowers' small, yellow; females small, becoming grey. Cones shiny brown, bunched well back on main shoot. 35 ft in 20 years.

C. guadalupensis 255 'Tecate cypress'. Vigorous, erect, fairly hardy cypress from Mexico. Red bark.

C. himalaica var *darjeelingensis* 97, 262 Kashmir cypress. Zone 8. Conical, spreading, ultimately pendulous. Leaves in opposite pairs, blue-white, sharply acute, hard. Grows fast under glass. 25 ft in 20 years.

C. lusitanica 97, 255 Mexican cypress. Cedar of Goa, Mexico, Guatemala Zone 9. To 100 ft. Branches spreading, slightly pendulous. leaves pointed, grey-green. Cones small, waxy, brown when mature. Unsuited to cold climates. 40 ft in 20 years.

C. macrocarpa 96, 97, 101, 255, 262, 263 Monterey cypress. California Zone 7. 70 or 110 ft, columnar or conical, broadening with age. Leaves bright green, dulling later, triangular, close to stem. Cones purple-brown. May succumb to frost but withstands exposure, especially to sea winds. 45 to 60 ft. in 20 years.

'Donard Gold' 96 Medium height, conical or broadly columnar. Leaves golden yellow. 40 ft in 20 years.

'Goldcrest' 96. 97 Medium height, narrowly columnar. Juvenile leaves rich yellow.

'Lutea' 96 50 to 80 ft, wide, columnar. Leaves yellow, becoming green. cones yellow. Good against sea winds. 40 ft in 20 years.

C. sargentii 255 'Sargent cypress'. Small attractive cypress from California.

C. sempervirens 94, 95, 96, 254, 262 Italian cypress, Mediterranean cypress. Mediterranean Zone 7. To 75 ft, columnar. Leaves dark green, thick and dense on old trees. Male 'flowers' terminal, greenish. Cones shining green, becoming dark brown, each scale with central spike. 35 ft in 20 years.

C. torulosa 254 Bhutan or Himalayan cypress. Tall and cedar-like. Not very hardy.

CYDONIA 194–5 Mostly deciduous trees and shrubs. Leaves simple. Flowers in clusters or solitary. Fruit with many-seeded cells distinguishing group from related *Pyrus*; fragrant, edible when cooked. All soils. Sun-loving. Hardy. Subject to leaf blight, fruit spot, mildew, fire-blight.

C. oblonga 194, 195, 263 Common quince. N. Persia, Turkestan Zone 4. To 25 ft, spreading. Leaves ovallish, deciduous, underside covered with pale grey matted hairs, upper surface dark green, often turning deep yellow before falling. Flowers 2 ins across, solitary, 5-petalled, white or pale pink, late spring. Fruit pear-shaped, golden yellow, acid-tasting when raw.

Cypress, Arizona See *Cupressus arizonica* var. *glabra*

Bald See *Taxodium distichum*

Classic See *Cupressus sempervirens*

Japanese Hinoki See *Chamaecyparis obtusa*

FORTUNELLA margarita 237 Nagami. Kumquat. S.E. China Zone 9. 10 to 15 ft, spreading. Leaves lance-shaped, dark green, paler beneath, partly crinkle-edged, evergreen. Flowers solitary or in small clusters, white, spring. Fruit oval-oblong, pale orange, sweet, slightly acid.

FRANKLINIA alatamaha 172, 173, 262, 263 Georgia, United States Zone 5. To 35 ft, upright. Leaves medium length, narrow, oblong, deciduous, simple, shiny above, dark green becoming red in autumn, minutely toothed. Flowers to 3 ins white, cupped, waxy, single. fragrant, late summer. Fruit woody, round, capsule. Tender in Britain; requires hot summers. Acid or alkaline soil. 10 ft in 20 years.

FRAXINUS 289–9, 263 Deciduous trees, few shrubs. Leaves mostly pinnate. Flowers mainly insignificant, bisexual or unisexual on same tree. Fruits narrowly ovoid, winged, often propellor-like. Hardy.

F. americana 239, 254 White ash, American ash. E. United States Zone 3. To 135 ft, upright. leaves pinnate, leaflets stalked, oval or near, dark green above, whitish-green and downy beneath; end of leaflet may be toothed. Stalk grooved, yellowish white. Flowers petalless. Prefers loamy soil, much moisture. Sun-tolerant. Subject to oyster scale, canker in America. 25 ft in 20 years.

F. angustifolia 239, 254 Narrow-leaved ash. S. Europe Zone 6. To 80 ft. Leaflets slender, lance-shaped, smooth, shiny, dark green above, toothed, stalked. Flowers few, petalless. 30 ft in 20 years.

F. chinensis 241 Chinese ash. China Zone 5. To 45 ft. Leaves with 5 to 9 leaflets, dark dull green above, paler beneath, often purple in autumn. Flowers in big loose clusters, fragrant. May. Fruit narrow. 1½ ins long.

F. excelsior 64, 238, 239, 261, 263 Common ash. Europe (incl. British Isles). Caucasus Zone 3. To 130 ft, spreading. Leaves pinnate, oblong, lance-shaped, smooth above, furry brown by lower midrib, dark green, toothed, leaflets stalkless. Flowers greenish-yellow, clustered, spring. Fruit in bunches. Likes chalk soil. Susceptible to oyster scale. 30 ft in 20 years.

'Diversifolia' 239 One-leaved ash. Leaves simple or 3-part, toothed.

'Jaspidea' 239, 262 Branches yellowish, young shoots golden yellow.

'Pendula' 238, 239, 262 Weeping ash. Height according to graft; spreading. Vigorous. Branches and branchlets stiffly hanging.

F. latifolia 239, 255 Oregon ash. W. United States Zone 6. To 80 ft, narrow, upright to broad. Leaves pinnate, leaflets oval or oblong, pointed, downy, dark green above, furry, pale. Flowers petalless. Fruit to 2 ins long. Susceptible to oyster scale. 20 ft in 20 years.

F. mariesii 239, 254 Flowering ash. Maries' ash. C. China Zone 7. To 30 ft, spreading. Leaves pinnate, leaflets oval, tip tapering, smooth, dull green, toothed or almost toothed, leafstalk purplish. Flowers in terminal clusters, creamy-white, late spring or early summer. Fruits winged, to 1¼ ins long, deep purple, autumn. Sun-loving. Susceptible to oyster scale. 15 ft in 20 years.

F. nigra 239 Black ash. E. United States Zone 2. To 75 ft, 7 to 11 slender pointed leaflets, dark green above, paler beneath. Sexes on separate trees. Fruits 1½ ins long.

F. ornus 238–9, 252, 254, 263 Manna ash. S. Europe, Asia Minor Zone 5. To 50 ft, spreading. Leaves pinnate, broad, oblong leaflets, rusty hairs along midrib beneath, dull green, toothed. Flowers clustered, off-white, spring. Fruit notched at tip. Sun-loving. Susceptible to oyster scale. 15 ft in 20 years.

F. oxycarpa 239, 254 S. Europe to Persia and Turkestan Zone 5. To 30 ft, upright to spreading, but compact. Leaflets narrow, lance-shaped, shiny dark green, downy beneath, sharply toothed. Flowers without petals. Sun-loving. Susceptible to oyster scale. 30 to 50 ft in 20 years.

F. pensylvanica 239, 255 Red ash. E. United States Zone 3. To 60 ft. leaves big. 7 or 9 narrow oval leaflets, dull green, downy beneath. Sexes on separate trees. Fruit to 2 ins long. Fast-growing.

subintegerrima 239, 263 Green ash. E. United States Zone 2 To 60 ft, spreading. Leaflets oblong or narrowly oval, downy beneath, pale green on both sides, obscurely toothed; common stalk grooved and downy. Flowers, sexes on separate trees. Susceptible to oyster scale. 18 ft in 20 years.

F. quadrangulata 239 Blue ash. C. and E. United States Zone 3. To 80 ft with square branchlets. Leaves big, 7 or 11 narrow oval leaflets, yellow-green. Bisexual flowers in short clusters. Fruit oblong. 1 to 2 ins long.

F. tomentosa 255 Ash with big downy leaves. E. United States.

F. velutina 254, 253 Velvet ash. S.W. United States, N. Mexico Zone 5. To 45 ft, round-headed, fairly open. Suitable for dry alkaline soils.

F. xanthoxyloides 254 'Afghan ash'. Small, rounded close-set leaflets on winged stalk.

Fringe-tree, American See *Chionanthus*

Chinese See *Chionanthus*

G

GEAN see *Prunus avium*

GENISTA aetnensis 210, 263 Mount Etna broom. Sardinia, Sicily Zone 3. To 20 ft. Tiny, slender leaves, green, rush-like, sparse, simple, deciduous. Flowers profuse, pea-shaped, golden yellow, summer. Prefers well-drained, light loam, tolerates chalk. Sun-loving. Subject to rust, fungal die-back. A.G.M. 1923.

Ghost tree See *Davidia involucrata*

Ginkgo See *Ginkgo biloba*

GINGKO biloba 68–9, 254, 260, 262, 263 Maidenhair tree. E. China Zone 4. To 80 ft, varies from narrow, upright to broadly spreading. Leaves larger and more deeply cleft at first, green both sides, deciduous. Male 'flowers' rare, thick, yellow; female 'flowers' single or paired, pale yellow becoming orange. Fruits yellow, plum-shaped; offensive smell if crushed. Seeds edible. Tolerates lime. 25 ft in 20 years. A.G.M. 1969.

'Fastigiata' 69, 262 Columnar, upright-branched form.

GLEDITSIA 208–9 Deciduous trees. Leaves pinnate. Flowers small, insignificant, greenish, regularly-petalled, not pea-like as other *Leguminosae*. Most species have large thorns, some thornless. Sun-loving.

G. caspica 209 Caspian locust. M. Persia Zone 6. To 35 ft, very spiny. Leaves pinnate with 12 to 20 oval, toothed leaflets, or doubly pinnate. Pod thin, curved 8 ins long.

G. japonica 209 Japanese locust. Japan Zone 5. To 70 ft, pyramidal, spiny bole. Leaflets roughly lance-shaped, midrib and stalk slightly hairy. Flowers, male and female on separate spikes, yellow-green, bell-shaped, June. Fruit, pods to 10 ins long, curved, eventually twisted. 15 ft in 20 years.

G. triacanthos 208, 209, 255, 263 Honey locust. C. and E. United States Zone 4. To 140 ft, broad, open, spiny trunk and branches. Leaves pinnate, medium to long, glossy dark green. Flowers unisexual on same tree, clustered; male green, females more sparse, June. Pod brown, to 18 ins long. curved, Oct-Dec. Tolerates chalk soils and drought. 25 ft in 20 years.

'Columnaris' 262 Columnar form.

'Moraine' 209 C. and E. United States. Wide-spreading form. Flowers as *G. japonica*. Fruitless; thornless. Many soils.

'Sunburst' 208, 262 Medium-Sized, thornless stems. Young leaves bright yellow.

GLYPTOSTROBUS lineatus 113 Chinese deciduous cypress. S. China Zone 8. Small bush or tree. Leaves either short in 3 ranks. or scale-like, overlapping; both types pale sea-green, rich brown in autumn. Cones pear-shaped, long-stalked. Seeds winged.

GORDONIA 172. 173, 263 Tender evergreen trees or shrubs similar to *Camellia*. Dark glossy green leaves. Conspicuous flowers autumn and winter. Dislikes lime soil.

G. lasianthus 173 Loblolly bay. S.E. United States Zone 8. To 60 ft, narrow. Leaves oblong, pointed, evergreen, simple, shiny, smooth, leathery, dark green, shallow-toothed. Flowers 3 to 6 ins across, white, single, fragrant, mid-summer. Fruits oblong, hard.

Grapefruit See *Citrus paradisi*

GREVILLEA robusta 215, 262, 263 Silk-oak grevillea. Australia Zone 10. To 150 ft in Australia. Leaves feathery, simple, evergreen, white hairs on underside. Flowers bunched, honeysuckle-like, orange to golden yellow. Fruit a boat-shaped capsule. Needs well-drained, lime-free soil. Sun-loving.

Guelder rose See *Viburnum opulus*

Gum, Black See *Nyssa sylvatica*

Blue See *Eucalyptus globulus*

Cider See *Eucalyptus gunnii*

Ghost See *Eucalyptus papuana*

River red See *Eucalyptus camaldulensis*

Snow See *Eucalyptus niphophila*

Spinning See *Eucalyptus perriniana*

Tasmanian cider See *Eucalyptus gunnii*

Tasmanian snow See *Eucalyptus coccifera*

Gwillimia See *MAGNOLIA*

GYMNOCLADUS dioicus 209, 255 Kentucky coffee tree. E. and C. United States Zone 4. To 90 ft, large branches, open. Leaves bi-pinnate (i.e. leafstalk has secondary stalks bearing leaflets), medium to long, green above, grey-green and hairy beneath, yellow in autumn. Small flowers unisexual, clustered, greenish-white, on same or different trees., June. Pods oblong, flat, Oct. through winter. Tolerates chalk. 18 ft in 20 years.

H

Hackberry, American See *Celtis occidentalis*

Chinese See *Celtis sinensis*

Common See *Celtis occidentalis*

Mississippi See *Celtis laevigata*

Southern European See *Celtis australis*

HAKEA laurina 215 Sea-urchin, Pincushion-tree. New Zealand Zone 8. To 30 ft, shrub or small tree. Leaves oblong to lance-shaped, narrow, simple, evergreen. Flowers red-pink, tubular. Fruit a thick woody capsule. Not lime- or chalk-tolerant. Sun-loving.

HALESIA 189, 263 Shrubs or small trees. Leaves simple, deciduous. Flowers hanging, snowdrop-like, clustered. Fruits, pear-shaped winged pods, pale-brown. Tolerates lime if enriched with peat or leaf soil. Sun-loving.

H. monticola 189, 252, 255, 263 Mountain silverbell. Peawood. Mts of S.E. United States Zone 5. To 90 ft, pyramidal. Leaves medium length, ovallish, becoming smooth, scarcely toothed, stalked, yellow in autumn. Flowers white, spring. Resistant to pests and disease. Sun or semi-shade. 25 ft in 20 years.

***H. tetraptera* 189, 255, 263 Snowdrop tree, Silverbell tree. S.E. united States Zone 4. To 35 ft. Leaves ovallish, thick down beneath. Flowers small, white. Bark scaly. 12 ft in 20 years. A.GM. 1946.**

HAMAMELIS 132–3, 263 Deciduous shrubs or small trees. Leaves alternate, with waxy or toothed edge. Flowers bisexual, clustered, thin yellow petals, late autumn to spring. Fruit, capsule holding 2 shiny black seeds.

H. japonica 'Arborea' 132–3, 263 Wide-spreading form sometimes making a small tree. Flowers rich yellow. 10 ft in 20 years.

H. mollis 132–3, 262, 263 Chinese witch-hazel. China Zone 5. To 25 ft, bushy. Leaves roundish, simple, hairy. Flowers fragrant. 8 ft in 20 years. A.G.M. 1922.

H. virginiana 132–3, 262, 263 Virginian witch-hazel. E. United States Zone 4. to 30 ft, often bushy. Leaves oval to triangular, simple, hairy on veins beneath, toothed, hairy stalk. 6 ft in 20 years.

Handkerchief tree See *Davidia involucrata*

Hawthorn, Common See *Crataegus monogyna*

Downy See *Crataegus mollis*

English See *Crataegus laevigata*

Hazel, Californian See *Corylus californica*

European See *Corylus avellana*

Purple'1 See *Corylus maxima purpurea*

Turkish See *Corylus colurna*

Hebe lycopodioides 119 New Zealand Zone 7. To 2 or 3 ft with upright 4-sided yellow-green stems. Leaves minute, triangular, scale-like, evergreen. Flowers small, white, in small clusters. Fruit, small capsule. Thrives in industrial and seaside areas, on all soils.

Hedge=thorn See *Crataegus monogyna*

Hemlock, Carolina See *Tsuga caroliniana*

Eastern See *Tsuga canadensis*

Japanese See *Tsuga diversifolia* and *T. sieboldii*

Mountain See *Tsuga mertensiana*

Western See *Tsuga heterophylla*

Hercules' club See *ARALIA*

Hickories See *CARYA*

Hickory, Shag-bark See *Carya ovata*

HIPPOPHAE rhamnoides 215, 253., 262, 263 Sea buckthorn, Europe, temperate Asia Zone 3. To 30 ft, deciduous shrub or small tree. Leaves short to medium length, narrow, lance-shaped, simple, greyish-green above, silvery-green below. Flowers, sexes on separate trees, small, clustered. Fruit, berry-like, small, orange-yellow, in winter; very acid. Tolerates dry soils, exposure; excellent in coastal areas, sandy soils. Sun-loving. 8 ft in 20 years.

HOHERIA 174, 175 Evergreen or deciduous small trees or shrubs from New Zealand. Leaves alternate, toothed. Flowers white,bisexual, solitary or clustered, summer. Seed-case thin, sometimes winged.

H. glabrata 174 Ribbonwood. Zone 7. To 35 ft. Leaves alternate, toothed, medium length, lance-shaped. Fragrant white flowers in small groups, summer.

Hollies See *ILEX*

Holly, American See *Ilex opaca*

Camellia-leaved See *Ilex x altaclerensis* 'Camelliifolia'

Dahoon See *Ilex cassine*

English See *Ilex aquifolium*

Father Perny's See *Ilex pernyi*

Hedgehog See *Ilex aquifolium* 'Ferox'

Highclere hybrids See *Ilex x altaclerensis*

Japanese broadleaf See *Ilex latifolia*

Weeping silver-variegated See *Ilex aquifolium* 'Argenteomarginata Pendula'

Yellow-berried, English See *Ilex aquifolium* 'Bacciflava'

Honey-locust See *Gleditsia triacanthos*

Hop-hornbeam See *OSTRYA*

Hop-tree See *Ptelea trifoliata*

Hornbeam See *Carpinus betulus*

American See *Carpinus caroliniana*

European See *Carpinus betulus*

Hop See *OSTRYA*

Japanese See *Carpinus cordata, C. japonica*

Horse chestnut, Indian See *Aesculus indica*

Japanese See *Aesculus turbinata*

Red-flowered See *Aesculus x carnea*

I

IDESIA polycarpa 242, 253, 254, 262 Japan, china Zone 6 To 45 ft, horizontal branching. Oval laves, medium to long, red-stalked, deep green above, deciduous. Sexes usually on separate trees; small greenish-yellow, fragrant flowers in hanging clusters to 10 ins long. Red pea-like berries, autumn. Good in neutral or slightly acid, moisture-retentive soil. 30 ft in 20 years.

ILEX 220–3, 262, 263 Deciduous and evergreen trees and shrubs. Leaves simple, stalked. Flowers small, off-white, males and females on separate trees. Fruit small. Most soils. *I. aquifolium* forms hardier than *I. altaclerensis* forms. Sun or semi-shade; injured by cold in N. Europe and America. Mainly pest-free, except holly leaf miner.

I. x altaclerensis 222, 262, 263 Highclere hybrid holly. Zone 7. A group of excellent vigorous hybrids. Small tree or large bush to 50 ft. Leaves evergreen, large, less prickly than *I. aquifolium*. Tolerates seaside and industrial areas. 25 ft in 20 years.

'Camelliifolia' 222, 253 Vigorous, conical. Leaves evergreen, nearly spineless, purplish at first, dark green later. Large fruits. Bark purple. 20 ft in 20 years. A.G.M. 1931.

'Golden King' 222, 262 Golden-variegated female form. Leaves green, edges bright yellow, virtually spineless. 20 ft in 20 years. A.G.M. 1969.

'J. C. van Tol' 222, 253, 263 Dark-green leaved form, nearly spineless. Masses of berries. 20 ft in 20 years. A.G.M. 1969.

'Lawsoniana' 222, 262 Female form of *I. a.* 'Hendersonii' with large, sparsely spined leaves, medium length, yellow edge (broad), marbled centre, deep and pale greens. May revert to plain green. 20 ft in 20 years.

'Purple Shaft' 222 Very vigorous purple-shooting form. Masses of berries. 20 ft in 20 years.

'Silver Sentinel' 222, 262 Female form. leaves dark green, mottled pale green and grey, margins pale yellow or whitish, flat, sparsely spined. 20 ft in 20 years.

I. aquifolium 220–2, 262, 263 English holly. S. Europe, N. Africa, W. Asia to China Zone 6. To 45 or 70 ft, short spreading branches, dense, pyramidal. Leaves oval, spiny, shiny green, evergreen. Flowers small, white, fragrant, May-June. Fruit, red berries, Sept.

'Aureum' 262 Golden-leaved laburnum. Leaves yellow in summer.

L. x vossii See *L. x watereri*
L. x watereri 210 Waterer's laburnum. Zone 5. Hybrid between *L. alpinum* and *L. anagyroides*. To 30 ft, stiffly upright. Leaves glossy green, hairy beneath, elliptic or oval. Flowers pea-like, May-June. Pods usually only partially developed, sometimes sterile. 30 ft in 20 years. A.G.M. 1928.

Lagarostrobus franklinii 111, 255, 262 Huon pine. Tasmania Zone 9. to 100 ft, pyramidal, evergreen with drooping branches. Leaves small, dense, overlapping, bright green. Fruits nutlike. 12 ft in 20 years.

Larch, Dunkeld See *Larix x eurolepis*

Eastern See *Larix laricina*

European See *Larix decidua*

False See *Pseudolarix amabilis*

Himalayan See *Larix griffithiana*

Japanese See *Larix kaempferi*

Water See *Metasequoia glyptostroboides*

Western see *Larix occidentalis*

Larches See *LARIX*

LARIX 42, 70, **92–3**, 112, 262, 263 Larches. Deciduous, conical. Leaves flat, narrow, needle-like, bright green, in rosettes on old shoots, singly on new. Male 'flowers' yellow, females variously coloured. Cone upright, sheds seed in autumn of 1st year, but persists on tree. Successful on many soils except dry, shallow chalk. Sun-loving. Susceptible to 'larch blight' caused by woolly aphid (*Chermes* sp.), also 'larch canker' caused by fungus *Dasyscypha calycina*; leaf-cast and rust in Europe, leaf-cast in U.S.A.

L. decidua 92–3, 254, 261, 262 European Alps and Carpathians Zone 2. To 180 ft, narrowly conical. Leaves darken in summer, turn gold in autumn, soft, thin. Shoots buff-coloured. Male 'flowers' on weak. pendulous shoots. 50 ft in 20 years.

polonica 254 A North European form of common larch.

L. x eurolepis 93 Dunkeld hybrid larch. Scotland Zone 4. To 100 ft Leaves small, dull dark grey-green above, 2 grey bands beneath. Female 'flowers' pink as *L. decidua*. Cones as *L. decidua* but bigger. More resistant to insect and fungal attack than other forms. Vigorous. 55 to 65 ft in 20 years.

L. gmelini 255 'Dahurian larch' from Siberia.

olgensis 255 Siberian larch with red, hairy shoots.

L. griffithiana 93, 254. Sikkim larch. E. Nepal, Sikkim, Tibet Zone 7. To 70 ft, broadly conic with wide-spreading, low branches, hanging shoots. Leaves in whorls, shiny, 2 narrow green-white bands beneath. Cones abundant to 5 ins. Needs mild area. 25 ft in 20 years.

L. kaempferi 93, 255, 262 Japanese larch, Red larch. Japan Zone 7. To 100 ft, broadly conical. Leaves dark grey-green above. 2 broad greenish grey bands beneath, becoming pale yellow, then orange. Male 'flowers' widely spread over crown. 50 ft in 20 years.

L. laricina 93, 255, 263 Tamarack, Eastern larch. E. United States Zone 1. 40 to 80 ft, pyramidal. leaves 3-angled, bright blue-green, yellowing to fall in early winter. Cones very small, ovallish. Tolerates wet, peaty soils. 40 ft in 20 years.

L. occidentalis 92, 93, 255 Western larch. United States Zone 5. 140 to 180 ft, open and rather narrowly conical. Leaves similar to *L. laricina*, but slightly longer. Cones to 1½ ins long. 35 ft in 20 years.
L. sibirica 255 Siberian larch, medium-sized, not hardy in Britain.

Laurel See *Cinnamomum camphora, Laurus nobilis, Prunus laurocerasus, P. lusitanica, Umbellularia californica*

Bay See *Laurus nobilis*
California See *Umbellularia californica*

Camphor See *Cinnamomum camphora*

Cherry See *Prunus laurocerasus*

Common See *Laurus nobilis*

Portugal See *Prunus lusitanica*

True See *Laurus nobilis*

Laurocerasus See *Prunus laurocerasus*

LAURUS 130–1 Evergreen shrubs or small trees. Flowers small, yellowish-green in clusters, Separate trees, April. Fruits on female trees, black, shining. Likes well-drained soil.

L. nobilis 130, 254, 262, 263 Laurel, Sweet bay. Mediterranean Zone 6. To 35 ft, dense, often pyramidal. Narrow or oval aromatic leaves, medium length, dark glossy green, simple. Flowers on spikes. Fruit oval, dark green berry. 15 to 20 ft in 20 years.

angustifolia 130 Willow-leaf bay. leaves long, narrow, leathery, pale green, wavy-edged. Hardier than the type.

'Aurea' 130, 262 Golden-yellow leaves.

L. serrata 253 'Chilean laurel'. Aromatic evergreen laurel from Chile.

Lemon See *Citrus limon*

LIBOCEDRUS decurrens See *Calocedrus decurrens*

LIGUSTRUM lucidum 240–1, 253, 254, 262, 263 China Zone 7. To 30 ft, occasionally to 50 ft, erect shrub or tree, dense branching. Leaves narrow, oval, medium length, glossy dark green above, simple, evergreen. Flowers small, white, bisexual, in clusters to 8 ins long, Aug.-Sept. Fruit oblong, blue-black, Sept.-Oct. Sun-loving; tolerant of shade and dryness; requires shelter. Most soils. Pest-free. 15 ft in 20 years. 'Glossy privet.'

Lily-of-the-valley tree See *Clethra arborea*

Lime, Big-leafed See *Tilia platyphyllos*

Common See *Tilia x vulgaris*

Crimean See *Tilia euchlora*

Silver See *Tilia tomentosa*

Small-leafed See *Tilia cordata*

Weeping silver See *Tilia petiolaris*

Limes See *Citrus aurantifolia*

Lindens See *TILIA*

LIQUIDAMBAR 123–3, 219, 262, 263 Small deciduous group. Leaves maple-like, toothed, good autumn colour. Flowers green-yellow in small round heads, male and female separate, petalless. Round fruiting heads of capsules. Dislikes shallow chalky soil. Young plants liable to frost damage in late spring. No diseases in Britain; sweetgum blight in America.

L. formosana 133, 254 Zone 7. To 120 ft. Leaves medium length, 3-lobed, often hairy beneath. Fruiting heads bristly. Fruits as in *L. styraciflua*. Not lime tolerant. 35 ft in 20 years.

L. orientalis 133, 254 Oriental sweet gum. Asia Minor Zone 6. To 100 ft. Leaves 5-lobed, simple, smooth, lobed or coarsely toothed, stalked. Flowers greenish, spring. Fruit woody.

L. styraciflua 133 Sweet gum. E. United States Zone 5. To 140 ft, narrow, pyramidal, small branches. Leaves alternate, medium length, 5 to 7 lobes, pointed, smooth and glossy above, hairy below, slender stalk. Male flowers on 3-in stalk; female flowers on same tree in larger clusters. 20 ft in 20 years. Usually pest-free. A.G.M. 1969.

'Aurea' 252 Leaves striped and mottled with yellow.

LIRIODENDRON 42, **126, 130** Deciduous, alternate leaves, solitary flowers. Brown cone-like fruit, a cluster of husks each with 1- or 2-seed, winged nuts. Prefer deep soil.

L. chinense 254 Chinese tulip-tree. China Zone 7. To 50 ft, similar to *L. tulipifera*. Leaves with deeper lobes. Flowers smaller, green outside, yellowish inside. 45 ft in 20 years.

L. tulipifera 126–7, 253, 255, 262, 263 Tulip-tree. N. America Zone 4. To 160 ft. Saddle-shape leaves, medium length, rich yellow in autumn. Flowers tulip-shaped, yellow-green, orange markings inside. Flowers May-June, fruit October. 40 ft in 20 years.

'Aureomarginatum' 262 Leaves bordered with yellow.

'Fastigiatum' 262 Broadly columnar, erect.

LITHOCARPUS densiflorus 162, 163, 262 Tanbark oak. California, Oregon Zone 7. To 100 ft, closely related to oak, pyramidal when young, becoming open. Leaves evergreen, substantial, leathery, oval, pointed, toothed; woolly down at first. Flowers unisexual, males on erect spikes. Fruit acorn-like, solitary. Requires sun, sheltered site in moist soil, preferably neutral to acid. Not lime-tolerant. 15 ft in 20 years.

LIVISTONA australis 122–3 Australia Zone 8. To 60 ft, trunk covered with leaf-bases and fibres. Palmate leaves to 4 ft across, on 6 ft stalk; leaflets glossy green with yellow stripe. Unisexual flowers on same tree. Tiny reddish-brown fruit clusters.

Locust See *Ceratonia siliqua*

Black See *Robinia pseudoacacia*

Caspian See *Gleditsia caspica*

Clammy See *Robinia viscosa*

Honey See *Gleditsia triacanthos*

LUMA apiculata 214, 253, 255 Chile Zone 8. To 20 ft, broad. Leaves small, oval, dull green above, paler beneath, evergreen. Flowers small, solitary, white, Aug.-Sept. Fruits small, black, edible. Pretty peeling bark. Tolerant of lime. Best in full sun.

M *MAACKIA* 209 Hardy, deciduous. Leaves pinnate. Flowers white, pea-like, in dense upright clusters. Pods oblong, straight, up to 5 seeds. Slow-growing. Most soils including deep soil over chalk. Full sun.

M. amurensis 209 Manchuria Zone 4. to 20 ft. Leaves dark green above, paler beneath, very pretty at bud-break, shoots silver-hairy. Flowers July-Aug. Pods Sept.-Oct. Prefers light loam. 12 ft in 20 years.

M. sinensis 209 C. China Zone 5. To 70 ft, broad-headed. Leaves with 11 or 13 leaflets, downy beneath. Flowers July-August.

Maclura See *Maclura pomifera*

MACLURA pomifera 142–3, 253, 255, 263 Osage orange. S. and C. United States Zone 5. To 60 ft, rounded top, open and irregular, thorny. Leaves alternate, medium length, oval, pointed, dark green and hairless above, paler and downy beneath, yellow in autumn, deciduous. Flowers, sexes on separate trees. Fruit orange-shaped, yellowish-green, inedible. 20 ft in 20 years.

MAGNOLIA 15, 125, **126–30**, 173, 263 Deciduous or evergreen trees or shrubs. Big simple leaves. Bisexual flowers borne singly. Cone-like fruit, red or pink, a cluster of seed capsules which split open to reveal shiny seeds (usually red). Neutral to acid soil; some species lime-tolerant. Mostly fast. Subject to leaf-spot in Europe and America, canker and die-back in America.

Magnolia, Bigleaf See *Magnolia macrophylla*

Chinese See *Magnolia sinensis*

Japanese 'whiteleaf' See *Magnolia obovata*

Japanese willowleaf See *Magnolia salicifolia*

Lily See *Magnolia liliiflora*

Oyama See *Magnolia sieboldii*

Star See *Magnolia stellata*

Wilson's See *Magnolia wilsonii*

M. acuminata 128, 255, 262, 263 Cucumber tree. E. United States Zone 4. To 100 ft, upright, pyramidal, spreading with age. Leaves oval to oblong, medium to long, pointed, green, downy beneath, deciduous. Flowers inconspicuous, early summer. 35 ft in 20 years. Usually pest-free.

subcordata 127, 128 Yellow cucumber tree. S.E. united States Zone 5. To 35 ft, upright, compact. Leaves medium length, deciduous. Flowers cup-shaped, yellow, summer and early autumn. 25 ft in 20 years.

M. campbellii 128, 129, 252, 254, 263 Pink tulip tree. Sikkim Zone 8–9. to 100 ft, open, few branches. Leaves oval, tapering, long, smooth above, hairy beneath. Flowers cup-shaped, spreading later, shell-pink, to 10 ins across, early spring. Not lime-tolerant. Sheltered position; flowers frosted in cold, exposed areas. 30 ft in 20 years.

mollicomata 128, 263 Slightly hardier than the type; flowers at an earlier age.

M. delavayi 127, 128, 253, 262 **China Zone 7. To 35ft, spreading, flat-topped. Leaves twice size of** *M. grandiflora*, full greyish-green above, finely downy beneath, evergreen. Flowers creamy-white, to 8 ins across, cup-shaped, fragrant, late summer. Buff-white bark. Likes chalk. 20 ft in 20 years.

M. denudata 129, 254, 263 Yulan, Lily tree. China Zone 5. To 50 ft, rounded, many branches. Leaves medium length, oval, downy beneath. Flower buds conspicuous for grey-shaggy hairs in winter. Flowers pure white, early spring. Orange seeds. 20ft in 20 years.

M. fraseri 255 Similar to *M. macrophylla*, bigleaf magnolia, from S.E. united States.

M. grandiflora 43, 126–7, 173, 253, 255, 262, 263 Bull bay, Laurel magnolia, Southern magnolia. S.E. United States Zone 7. To 100 ft, dense, pyramidal. Leaves oval to oblong, long, glossy green above, often reddish-brown beneath, evergreen. Flowers creamy-white, fragrant, 8 ins across, late spring and summer. 20 ft in 20 years.

'Exmouth' 127 Exmouth magnolia. Narrowly pyramidal. Leaves narrow, lance-shaped. furry beneath, hairs rust red. Flowers big, fragrant. A.G.M. 1969.

'Goliath' 127 Leaves broad, dark shiny green. Flowers to 12 ins across. A.G.M. 1969.

M. x highdownensis 128 Small tree, a hybrid between *M. sinensis* and *M. wilsonii*. Flowers big, white petals, purple core, early summer. Succeeds on chalk. 15 ft in 20 years.

M. hypoleuca 128, 252, 255, 263 Whiteleaf Japanese magnolia. Japan Zone 5. To 100 ft, pyramidal and open. Leaves wedge-shaped, to 18 ins long, green and bloomed above, blue-white, slightly downy beneath, deciduous. Flowers fragrant, white petals, stamens purple with yellow anthers, early summer. Orange seeds. Not lime-tolerant. 25 ft in 20 years.

M. kobus 128, 255, 263 Japan Zone 5. To 40 ft, pyramidal, becoming round-headed. Leaves obovate, medium length, leaf-buds downy. Flowers small, white, slightly fragrant, mid-spring, not flowering for 12/15 years. All soils. 20 ft in 20 years. A.G.M. 1936.

M. liliiflora 129, 263 C. China Zone 5. To 12 ft, straggling. Leaves oval, deciduous, shiny, dark green above, furry beneath. Erect flowers 8 ins wide, purple-tinted outside, creamy-white inside, late spring/early summer. Fruit brown, oblong. Dislikes chalk. 10 ft in 20 years.

'Nigra' 129, 263 Japan Zone 5. Form with slightly larger flowers, purple-flushed, spring/summer. A.G.M. 1969.

M. x loebneri 128–9, 252 Zone 4. To 50 ft, variable hybrid, pyramidal, open. Flowers, numerous white petals, fragrant, early spring. All soils. A.G.M. 1969.

M. macrophylla 127–8, 255, 262, 263 Bigleaf magnolia. S.E. United States Zone 5. To 60 ft, open, spreading head. Leaves to 25 ins long, bright shiny green above, bloomed beneath, deciduous. Flowers creamy-white, fragrant, to 12 ins across, summer. orange seeds. Not lime-tolerant. Requires shelter. 25 ft in 20 years.

M. obovata See *M. hypoleuca*

M. salicifolia 129, 255, 263 Anise magnolia. Japan Zone 5. To 30 ft, pyramidal. Leaves lance-shaped, deciduous, smooth, dull green above, waxy, slightly downy beneath. Flowers white, fragrant, early spring. Fruit cucumberlike, early autumn. 25 ft in 20 years. A.G.M. 1941.

M. sargentiana 254 Tree-size magnolia from W. China; very big pink flowers.

M. sieboldii 128 Oyama magnolia, Japan., Korea Zone 5–6. To 30 ft, rounded. Leaves broadly oval, deciduous, hairy and waxy beneath, dark green above. Flowers cup-shaped, white, fragrant, summer. 15 ft in 20 years. A.G.M. 1935.

M. sinensis 128 W. China Zone 7. to 20 ft, wide-spreading. Leaves oval to round, deciduous, shiny, bright green above, furry beneath. Nodding flowers to 5 ins wide, white, saucer-shaped, lemon-smelling, summer. 15 ft in 20 years. A.G.M. 1969.

M. x soulangiana 28–9, **128, 129**, 254, 263 Saucer magnolia. Zone 5. To 25 ft, hybrid between *M. denudata* and *M. liliiflora*, often many-stemmed, low and spreading. Leaves medium length, downy beneath. Flowers tulip-shaped, white, stained rose-purple at base, spring. Other clones have coloured flowers. Tolerates poor soils, pollution; moderately lime-tolerant. Best in full sun. 10 ft in 20 years. Scale pest A.G.M. 1932.

'Lennei' 128 A vigorous clone with purple flowers dark outside and pale within.

M. stellata 128 Star magnolia. Japan Zone 5. To 10 ft, rounded, spreading shrub. Leaves small, dark green. Flowers double, white, fragrant, April. Slow-growing.

M. tripetala 255 Umbrella tree; big spreading magnolia from E. United States. Flowers late spring, very fragrant.

M. x veitchii 129, 252, 263 Veitch magnolia. Zone 7. To 70 ft, vigorous, open. Leaves oblong, long, dark green. Flowers 6 ins across, white flushed purple-pink, spring. Flowers earlier in life than *M. campbellii*. Not lime-tolerant. 35 ft in 20 years.

M. virginiana 42, 127, 263 Swamp bay, Sweet bay. E. United states Zone 5. To 65 ft but more shrub-like in colder areas. Leaves oval or oblong, medium length, glossy green above, blue-white and downy beneath, partially evergreen. Flowers to 3 ins wide, white, very fragrant, early summer.

M. wilsonii 128, 252 Wilson's magnolia. W. China Zone 6. To 24 ft, wide-spreading, often shrubby and open. Small, pointed leaves.

OLEA europaea 240–1, 262 Olive.
Mediterranean Zone 9. 20 to 40 ft, spreading.
Leaves oval or narrowly oval, simple,
evergreen, leathery, shiny or silvery beneath.
Flowers small, whitish, clustered, fragrant, late
summer. Olives green, becoming purple and
wrinkled. Requires shelter; tolerant of
dryness; tender. Slow-growing.

O. excelsa (Notelea excelsa) 254 A hardier
cousin of the olive.

Orangequat 237

OSTRYA 170–1 Hop-hornbeam. Medium to
large deciduous trees. Leaves oval, toothed.
Upright female catkins, drooping male
catkins. Flowers in spring with leaves. Fruit
is a nutlet in a husk, clusters, ripe in
autumn. Any fertile soil. Of easy cultivation.

O. carpinifolia 171, 254 Hop hornbeam. S.
Europe, Asia Minor Zone 5. To 65 ft, round-
headed. Alternate, pointed, medium length,
doubly toothed, dark green above, sparsely
hairy below, clear yellow in autumn. Male
catkins 1½ to 3 ins long. Fruiting clusters to
2ins long. 30 ft in 20 years.

OXYDENDRUM arboreum 185, 253, 262,
263 Sorrel tree. E. United States Zone 5. To
75 ft, slender trunk. Leaves narrow, oblong,
medium to long, tapering, dark green above,
paler beneath, red in autumn. Small cylindrical
white flowers clustered along spike 5 to 10 ins
long, July, August. Fruit greyish, hairy, woody
capsule. Line-free soil. 25 ft in 20 years.
A.G.M. 1947.

P

Padus See *Prunus padus*

Pagoda tree See *Sophora japonica*

Palm. Californian fan See *Washingtonia filifera*

Palms 120–3

Parrotia See *Parrotia persica*

PARROTIA persica 136, 137, 254, 262,
263 Persian parrotia, Ironwood. N. Persia to
Caucasus Zone 5. To 50 ft, widely spreading in
cultivation, with rounded head and usually
several trunks; tall, erect tree in the wild.
Leaves ovate, medium length, coarsely
toothed, almost hairless above, slightly hairy
beneath, deciduous. Flowers, clusters of
crimson stamens, early spring. Fruit, nut-like
seed-vessel. Bark flaking. Thrives on chalk
soils, but does not always colour well. Usually
pest-free. A.G.M. 1969.

PAULOWNIA 244–5 Small genus of Chinese
trees. Leaves large. Flowers foxglove-shaped,
carried in erect panicles, formed in autumn,
open next spring. Sun-loving; needs shelter
from gales. Deep, well-drained soils.
P. fargesii 245 W. China Zone 7. To 65 ft,
spreading. Leaves deciduous, simple. Flowers
absent on young trees, fragrant, dark purple-

speckled, cream at base. Tolerates dryness. 40
ft in 20 years.

P. tomentosa 244, 245, 252, 254,
262 Empress tree, Royal paulownia. China
Zone 5. To 50 ft, spreading, thick, stiff
branches. Leaves simple to 5-lobed, simple,
deciduous, to 3 ft wide, dark green above,
grey beneath, hairy, long-stalked. Flowers
similar to those of *P. fargesii*, violet-scented,
yellow-striped inside, spring. Fruit, oval,
pointed capsule, holding winged seeds. 40 ft
in 20 years. Flowers susceptible to late frost.

PHELLODENDRON amurense 237, 252, 262,
263 Amur cork tree. Japan, Korea, N. China.
Ussuri, Amur, Manchuria Zone 3. To 50 ft
wide-spreading branches. Leaves pinnate,
medium length, deciduous; leaflets ovallish,
bright green, golden in autumn. Flowers small,
off-white in small clusters, smell of turpentine,
late spring. Fruits black, shiny, clustered,
autumn. Bark deeply fissured like black cork.
Likes chalk. Sun-loving 20 ft in 20 years.

PHILLYREA latifolia 240, 254, 263 S.
Europe, W. Asia Zone 7. To 30 ft, spreading
shrub or tree, densely branched. Leaves
variable, ovallish, toothed, dark shiny green
above, paler beneath, evergreen. Flowers
small, greenish white. Fruit small, round, blue-
black. All soils.

PHOENIX canariensis 123 Canary Island
palm. Canary Islands Zone 8. To 60 ft, very
thick trunk covered with old leaf bases. Dense
crown. Pinnate leaves 17 to 20 ft long, short
pointed light green leaflets. Flowerstalk 6 ft
long. Roundish orange fruit 1 in across, hangs
in heavy clusters.

P. dactylifera 123 Date palm. N. Africa Zone
9. to 100 ft, slender, suckering at base. Leaf
bases persist for years, later leaving scars.
Pinnate leaves 20 ft long, grey-green leaflets.
Sexes on separate tree, flowers white,
fragrant, on 4 ft stalk. Oblong fruit, 1 to 2 ins
long, deep orange, edible. Not shade-tolerant;
requires warm, dry climate.

PHOTINIA serrulata 203, 262, 263 Chinese
photinia. China Zone 7. To 40 ft, spreading.
Leaves oblong to oval, simple, evergreen,
leathery, dark, shiny green, roughly-toothed;
young leaves red copper. Flowers small, in
large flat heads, white, spring. Fruits small,
red, fleshy berries, autumn and early winter.
Lime-tolerant. Most soils. Sun-loving. No
diseases in Britain; fungal leaf-spot and fireblight in America.

PICEA 69, 70, 73, 78, 84–7, 93, 98,
263 Spruces. Very hardy evergreen trees,
often conical. Leaves needle-like, short,
4-sided, in 2 ranks. Male and female 'flowers'
on different branches of same tree; male
'flowers' oval, yellow or red, females purple.
Cones hanging, cylindrical to oval. Seeds
winged. Many soils. Subject to aphid attack,
honey fungus, stem canker in Europe; rusts in
Europe and America.

P. abies 86–7, 93, 254 Norway spruce. N.
Europe Zone 5. To 200 ft, usually conical,
except very old trees, which are columnar or
irregular. Leaves forward pointing, lower
leaves spreading, small. Male 'flowers'
infrequent, round, female 'flowers' spread on
crowns of older trees, pink-red. Cones 8 ins
long, 40 ft in 20 years.

'Procumbens' 119 Dwarf, to 3 ft, broad.
Horizontal branches. Foliage in flat, yellow-
green sprays.

P. asperata 86 Chinese spruce. Dragon
spruce. W. China Zone 5. To 100 ft, similar to
P. abies in habit, but more broadly conical.
Male 'flowers' round, shedding pollen in
spring; female 'flowers' scarlet. Branches very
rough. Cones dull brown, 5 ins long. Not for
chalky soils. 30 ft in 20 years.

P. brachytyla 86 Sargent spruce. W. and C.
China Zone 5. To 80 ft, conical, becoming
round-headed. Leaves crowded, firm, yellow
to green, whitish beneath, flattened. Cones to
3½ ins long, green, ripening dull brown.

P. brewerana 83, 85, 87, 98, 255,

262 Brewer's spruce, Weeping Spruce. N.W.
California and S.W. oregon Zone 5. 80 to 100
ft, flat-topped, weeping with curving branches
trailing vertically-hanging branchlets. Leaves all
round shoot, slender, dark green. 15 ft in 20
years.

P. engelmanii 85 Engelmann spruce. W.
United States Zone 2. To 120 ft. Leaves
4-sided, grey-green, small, rank smell. Cones
oblong-cylindrical, to 2 ins long. Dislikes dry or
shallow chalk soil. 20 ft in 20 years.

'Glauca' 85 Foliage more blue-grey.

P. glauca 42, 84–5, 255 White spruce.
Canada, N.E. United States Zone 2. 60 to 70
ft, conical. Leaves small, blue-green,
pungent when crushed. Cones small,
narrow, oblong. 35 ft in 20 years.

albertiana 'Conica' 85, 255 Ovoid-conical
bush. Leaves soft, grassy-green, curved,
pointed, susceptible to frost in bad winters
and to red spider mite. A.G.M. 1969.

P. glehnil 255 'Sakhalin spruce'; small
narrow Japanese spruce, rather like *P. abies*.

P. jezoensis 255 Yezo spruce. N.E. Asia
Japan Zone 4. To 100 or 150 ft, spire-like,
branch ends upturned. Leaves flattened,
shining rich green above, silver white beneath
with 2 white bands, crowded and overlapped
on upper part of shoot, those below curving
upwards. Cones crimson, becoming leathery-
brown, to 3 ins long; scales toothed. Can be
frost-damaged in spring in Europe.

P. koyami 255 Narrow-growing mountain
spruce from Japan.

P. likiangensis 86–7, 254, 263 Likiang
spruce. W. China Zone 5. 50 to 65 ft, conical.
Leaves forward pointing on upper side of
shoot, on lower side in 2 opposite ranks.
Upper leaves blue-grey, lower with 2 broad
white bands. 'Flowers' profuse; male 'flowers'
large, round, crimson; females scarlet, small.
Cones to 5 ins long, slightly tapered. Vigorous
and adaptable. 35 ft in 20 years.

P. mariana 42, 84–5, 255 Black spruce. N.W.
America Zone 2. To 100 ft, dense, pyramidal.
Leaves small, blue-green, blunt-pointed. Cones
small, purplish, becoming brown, persist up to
30 years. 15 ft in 20 years.

'Doumetii' Zone 2. Small, dense, conical,
becoming rounded, irregular. Leaves thin,
sharp-pointed, crowded, pale grey.

P. obovata 255 Siberian spruce, similar to
Norway spruce.

P. omorika 86, 254, 262 Yugoslavia Zone 4.
To 100 ft, narrowly conical. Leaves more or
less horizontally arranged, flattened, small,
glossy greyish green with two white lines
beneath. Cones egg-shaped. Grows on
limestone, very acid peats. Resists frost, town
air. 35 ft in 20 years. A.G.M. 1969.

P. orientalis 69, 86, 87, 254, 262 Oriental
spruce. Caucasian spruce. Asia Minor,
Caucasus Zone 4. To 180 ft, conical. Leaves
shortest amongst spruces, growing all round
shoot, to ⅓ in long, deep shining green. Male
'flowers' deep red. Cones freely borne over
upper crowns of older trees, purple at first,
brown at maturity. 40 ft in 20 years.

'Aurea' 86, 262 Small. leaves pale yellow,
then golden-yellow, finally green. Beautiful for
3 weeks in spring.

P. polita See *P. torano*

P. pungens 85, 263 Colorado spruce. S.W.
United States Zone 2. To 100 ft, stout
horizontal branches. Rigid leaves, small,
pointed, bluish-green. Oblong cones to 4 ins.
Tolerates drought. 25 to 30 ft in 20 years.

'Glauca' 85, 262 Blue spruce. Zone 5. To
75 ft, narrowly conical, columnar at bottom.
leaves waxy, grey-green or green with age. 25
ft in 20 years.

'Koster' 85 Small-medium, conical. Leaves
silver-blue.

'Moerheimii' 85 To 30 ft, conical, dense.
Leaves pale waxy blue. 15 ft in 20 years.

P. rubens 84–5 Red spruce. N.E. United
States Zone 2. 60 to 70 ft, narrowly conical.
Leaves dark yellow-green, wiry, curved.
Cones to 2 ins long, brown at maturity,
falling during first winter or following
spring. Likes moisture, not chalk. 30 ft in 20
years.

P. schrenkiana 255 Schrenk's spruce from
central Asia; similar to *P. smithiana*

'Globosa' 119 Miniature form; broad, low,
cone shape.

P. sitchensis 73, 83, 84, 85, 86, 100, 255,
263 Sitka spruce. W. United States Zone 6.
To 80 or 200 ft, conical. Leaves flattened,
bright blue-green above, blue-white, waxy

beneath, pointed. Cones to 4 ins long, falling
by winter of first year. Pale trunk of big trees
splays out at base. Likes cool, damp
summers; acid or any soils. 55 to 65 ft in 20
years.

P. smithiana 86, 87, 254, 262 West
Himalayan spruce W. Himalaya Zone 6. To 200
ft, pendulous. Leaves slender, curving,
medium length, dark green. Male 'flowers'
small, end of shoots. Cones green becoming
brown, to 7 ins long. 35 ft in 20 years.

P. torano 86, 255 Tiger-tail spruce. Japan
Zone 5. To 100 ft, pyramidal. Leaves dark-shiny
green, rigid-spined, very sharp. Cones ovallish,
shining yellow-brown, to 4 ins long, brown at
maturity. 20 ft in 20 years.

P. spinulosa 254 Eastern Himalayan
weeping spruce, similar to *P. smithiana* but
with sharp prickly needles.

PICRASMA quassioides 254 Small attractive
relation of *Ailanthus*. Good autumn colour.

PINUS 70–7, 263 Evergreen trees, conical,
becoming flat-topped or bushy. Leaves in
groups of 2 to 5 usually, needle-like, long

P. spinosa

Podocarp, Willow-leaf See *Podocarpus salignus*

Podocarps See *PODOCARPUS*

PODOCARPUS 110, 111, 263 Evergreen trees and shrubs. Leaves spirally arranged, vary from scale-like to 12 ins long. Male and female 'flowers' on separate trees. Fruit, a single seed in brightly-coloured cup. Acid or alkaline soils. Some species hardy.

P. andinus **111**, 255 Plum-fruited yew. Andes of S. Chile Zone 7. Pointed, upswept bush, often on many stems, rarely a conical tree. Leaves pointing forwards, short, with acute tips. Male 'flowers' stalked, emerging where branches and leaves join. Fruit yellow-white, plum-shaped. 18 ft in 20 years.

P. dacrydioides **111** New Zealand Zone 9. To 150 ft, branchlets drooping. Leaves on young trees, small, pointed, in a single row, bronze to bronze-green, scale-like; smaller, green or bronze-tinted, spiralled or overlapped on older trees. Seed cup red, waxy.

P. latifolius **111** Real yellow-wood. S. Africa Zone 9. To 100 ft. Leaves oblong to lance-shaped, short. Male 'flowers' small, single. Seed-cups green.

P. macrophyllus **110, 111**, 255 Kusamaki, China, Japan Zone 7. Small tree or upright, narrow bush. Leaves medium length, dark glossy green, often yellowish above, leathery, pliant. Seed cup purple. 8 ft in 20 years.

P. salignus **111**, 255 Willow-leaf podocarp. Chile Zone 7. Usually many-stemmed, bushy tree; occasionally single, irregularly conical, narrow crown and single stem. Leaves medium length, blunt-tipped, shiny deep green above, pale beneath. 20 ft in 20 years.

PONCIRUS trifoliata **237** Japanese bitter orange, Hardy orange. N. China Zone 5. Large shrub or small tree to 15 ft. Attractive spiny green stems with 3-part deciduous leaves. Fragrant blossom, small fruit edible, but bitter. The hardiest 'orange tree'.

P. trifoliata x Citrus sinensis **237** Citrange. Zone 6. Bushy, somewhat erect trees, stiff, angular, often spiny branches, dense foliage. Leaves usually in threes. Fruits very variable, mostly acid and bitter. Flowers fragrant, differ from either parent. Many named cultivars.

x Fortunella **237** Citrangequat. Zone 10. Vigorous evergreen trees, upright; old wood spiny. Leaves singly, paired or in threes, medium length, thick, stiff, dark green. Flowers small, white. Fruit small, yellow or orange-yellow, with thin roughened rind.

Poplar, Balsam See *Populus balsamifera*

Black See *Populus nigra*

Chinese See *Populus simonii*

Golden See *Populus serotina* 'Aurea'

Grey See *Populus x canescens*

Lombardy See *Populus nigra* 'Italica'

Richard's See *Populus alba*

Tacamahac See *Populus balsmifera*

Virginia See *Liriodendron tulipifera*

White See *Populus alba*

Yellow See *Lirodendron tulipifera*

POPULUS 180–3, 263 **Hardy, deciduous trees. Leaves simple, alternate, usually toothed, fairly long-stalked. Flowers usually catkins, sexes on separate trees, before leaves. Seeds, each with long tuft of hairs, in a capsule. Often on wet sites; prefer full sun; many tolerant of exposure. Majority dislike shallow, chalky soils. Fast-growing. Some species susceptible to canker, leaf rusts, leaf blister, leaf blight.**

P. alba **180, 181, 183**, 262, 263 White poplar. C. and S. Europe to W. Siberia and W. Asia Zone 3. to 100 ft, spreading. Leaves variable, oval to 5-lobed, simple, at first hairy, later upper surface smooth, very dark green, underside white. Likes chalk. Tolerates dryness. 40 ft in 20 years.

'Pyramidalis' **180, 183**, 262 Bolle's poplar. To 70 ft, pyramidal form as Lombardy poplar. Leaves, under-surfaces white, flashing in wind.

'Richardii' **183**, 262 Slightly smaller than *P. alba*. Leaves golden yellow, with white wool on underside.

P. balsamifera 42, **180, 183** Balsam poplar. United States Zone 5. To 100 ft, upright. Leaves broad, oval, simple, dark green above, smooth; possibly slightly downy, paler beneath. Smells of balsam. Short-lived on dry, chalky soils. Prone to canker. 50 ft in 20 years.

P. x candicans See ***P. x jackii***

P. x canescens **181, 183**, 263 Grey poplar. W. C. and S. Europe. Zone 4. To 100 ft. Leaves roundish, simple, grey and matted on underside, red and yellow in autumn. Catkins late winter, red. Likes chalk, tolerates exposure and drought. 50 ft in 20 years.

***P. x* 'Eugenei'** **183** Zone 2. To 150 ft, hybrid, columnar. Leaves roughly triangular, short-haired, rough. Male catkins only. Canker-resistant.

***P. x* 'Marilandica'** **183** Wide-spreading. Leaves green. Female catkins only, 2½ ins long. Likes chalk.

***P. x* 'Regenerata'** **183** Hybrid. Leaves long, triangular. Female catkins only, 2½ ins.

***P. x* 'Serotina'** **183**, 254 Black Italian poplar. To 100 ft, spreading. Leaves oval to triangular, simple, edges hairy at first, leaf-stalk flattened. Only male trees of this hybrid known. Very hardy. 65 ft in 20 years.

'Aurea' **183**, 262 Golden poplar. As *P. serotina* but leaves rich yellow, becoming greenish, then rich yellow again.

P. deltoides **180, 183** Cottonwood. Necklace poplar. E. United States Zone 2. To 100 ft, wide-spreading. Leaves heart-shaped, simple, smooth, dark green above, lighter beneath, edges hairy, stalk flattened. Male catkins densely-flowered, females twice as long, 8 ins. 80 ft in 20 year.

P. grandidentata **181** Big-toothed aspen. E. United States Zone 3. To 60 ft Leaves round or oval, grey and furry at first, later dark green above, stalk partly compressed. Catkins to 2½ ins long. 65 ft in 20 years.

***P. x jackii* 'Gileadensis'** **180, 183** Balm of Gilead, Ontario poplar. United States Zone 4. To 100 ft, wide-spreading. Leaves triangular to broadly oval, simple, furry beneath, underside whitish, balsam-scented. Only female trees known 50 ft in 20 years.

'Aurora' **180, 183** Variegated form. Leaves at first creamy-white, pink tinted; older leaves green.

P. lasiocarpa **183**, 262 Chinese poplar. C. China Zone 5. To 65 ft, spreading. Very big leaves, heart-shaped, broad, simple at first hairy, upper surface becoming smooth, veins, midrib and stalk red, otherwise light green. Female catkins to 8 ins long, twice as long as males. 35 ft in 20 years.

P. maximowiczii **182** Japanese poplar. Japan, Korea Zone 4. To 90 ft, wide, open, Leaves roundish, leathery, dull dark green above, whitish beneath, twisted tip. Male catkins to 4 ins, females to 10 ins. Fruit, July.

P. nigra **181, 182, 183**, 262 Black poplar. C. and S. Europe, W. Asia Zone 2. To 130 ft, upright, broad. leaves diamond-shaped to oval, simple, smooth, green. Flowers red catkin. 60 to 70 ft in 20 years.

'Italica' **180, 182, 183**, 259, 262, 263 Lombardy poplar. Zone 2. To 90 ft, narrow, erect. Leaves broad at base, simple. Most specimens are male trees, bearing male catkins only; female trees slightly broader. Mature trees susceptible to canker of upper branches. 40 ft in 20 years.

'Plantierensis' **183** Similar to *P. n.* 'Italica' but broader with more bushy head.

***P.* 'Robusta'** **181, 183**, 263 Big, upright, narrow at first, broadening later. Leaves triangular to oval, simple, copper-coloured at first. Only male trees of this hybrid known. Very fast. 90 ft in 20 years.

P. simonii **180, 183** N. China Zone 2. To 40 ft, narrow. Leaves diamond-shaped or ovallish, smooth, dark green above, paler beneath, short-stalked. Liable to canker. 50 ft in 20 years.

P. tacamahaca 255 Old name for *P. balsamifera*. North American balsam poplar.

P. tremula **181, 182, 183**, 262, 263 Aspen. Europe, Asia, N. Africa Zone 2. To 100 ft, usually less, upright, narrow. Leaves roundish, simple, woolly at fist, later almost smooth, grey-green. Long stalk flattened, so leaves tremble in wind, yellow in autumn. 25ft in 20 years.

P. tremuloides **182, 183**, 262 American aspen. Quaking aspen. From N. Mexico to Alaska Zone 1. To 100 ft, wide-spreading. Leaves roundish, simple, smooth, dark green above,paler beneath, quake in breeze. Short catkins. Larger trees more susceptible to pests.

P. trichocarpa **180, 183**, 262, 263 Black cottonwood. From Alaska to Mexico Zone 4 To 200 ft, pyramidal. Leaves oval, slender-tipped, simple, shiny, dark green above, whitish beneath, balsam-scented. Liable to canker. 65 to 85 ft in 20 years.

Privet, Glossy See *Ligustrum lucidum*

PRUNUS 198–203, 263 Big group of deciduous or evergreen trees. Leaves simple, edges toothed, crushed leaves often fragrant. Flowers 5-petalled, white or pink; in doubled forms number of petals is increased; spring. Fruit has one cell and one seed, fleshy; reduced and inedible in certain ornamental species. Most thrive on lime or chalk. Sun-loving. Usually very hardy. Susceptible to borers, scale and leaf-eating insects and virus diseases.

***P. x amygdalo-persica* 'Pollardii'** **202, 203**, 252 Similar to almond, but flowers richer pink. Fruit intermediate between peach and almond. A.G.M. 1937.

P. armeniaca **202, 203 Apricot. C. Asia, China Zone 5. To 35 ft, spreading. Leaves roundish, pointed, deciduous, smooth, shiny green,stalked. Flowers solitary, small. Fruits 1¼ in wide, larger in cultivation, yellow-orange, red-tinged, early summer, edible.**

P. avium **200**, 263 Gean, Mazzard, Wild cherry. W. Asia Zone 3. To 70 ft, pyramidal, Leaves oval, long-pointed, deciduous, red in autumn, stalked. Flowers clustered, white, small. Fruit small, round, red-black, bitter or sweet. 45 ft in 20 years.

'Plena' **200**, 262 Double Gean. Europe Zone 3. To 60 ft. Flowers profuse, small, double-petalled, drooping masses. Fruits rare. Hardier than oriental cherries. As large as type and longer-lasting. A.G.M. 1924.

P. campanulata **201** Formosan cherry. Bell-flowered cherry, Formosa, S. Japan Zone 7. to 30 ft, bushy. Leaves roughly oval, deciduous, shiny, stalked. Flowers small, rose-pink, bell-shaped at first, opening later.

P. cerasifera **202**, 254 Cherry plum, Myrobalan. W. Asia Zone 3. To 25 ft, sometimes thorny. slender branches. Leaves ovallish, toothed, light green. Flowers solitary, white, March. Fruit round 1 in across, red or yellow, on mature trees.

'Pissardii' **202, 203**, 262, 263 Pissard plum, Purple-leaved plum. Persia Zone 4. To 35 ft, upright, spreading. Leaves ovallish, deciduous, ruby at first, becoming claret then purple. Flowers single, small, profuse. Fruit purple, rarely produced. 25 ft in 20 years. A.G.M. 1928.

P. cerasus **200, 201** Sour cherry, Wild dwarf cherry. S.W. Asia Zone 3. To 35 ft, spreading. Leaves oval, abruptly pointed, deciduous, smooth, shiny, pale green, stalked. Flowers dense-clustered, white. Fruits roundish, red-black, acid-tasting, summer.

'Rhexii' **201**, 254 As *P. cerasus* but flowers doubled, hardier. Last in flower.

P. conradinae See ***P. hirtipes***

P. cornuta **254** Himalayan bird cherry; bigger leaves than *P. padus*.

P. dulcis **200, 202**, 252, 254, 263 Common almond. N. Africa to W. Asia Zone 4. 20 to 30 ft, spreading. Leaves lance-shaped, deciduous, smooth, stalked. Flowers 2 ins across, single or paired, early spring. Fruit to 2½ ins long, velvety. Tolerates dryness. 25 ft in 20 years.

'Roseoplena' **202** Double almond. Flowers pale pink, double, numerous petals.

***P. x hillieri* 'Spire'** **201**, 252 Zone 5. To 25 ft, narrow, pyramidal. Leaves turning red in autumn. Flowers profuse, soft pink.

P. hirtipes **201** C. China Zone 6. To 25 ft, elegant. Leaves ovallish, medium length, toothed. Flowers white or pinkish, profuse, Feb., before leaves. Fruit oval, red.

'Semiplena' **201**, 252 Double Conradine cherry Zone 6. to 35 ft, spreading. Leaves oval, slender-pointed, deciduous, smooth or virtually so above, downy below, short-stalked. Flowers doubled, white or pale pink, profuse, fragrant, long-lasting, late winter or early spring. Fruit small, ovoid, red.

P. laurocerasus **202–3** 254, 263 Cherry laurel, Common laurel, Europe, Asia Minor Zone 6–7. To 40 ft, wide-spreading. Leaves lance-shaped or oblong, tapering, evergreen, leathery, glossy, dark green, short-stalked. Flowers tiny, dull white, upright clusters. Fruit small, conical, red, turning black. Shade-tolerant. 30 ft in 20 years.

'Camelliifolia' **202–3**, 262 Shrub or small tree. Leaves dark green, contorted.

P. lusitanica **203**, 254, 262, 263 Portugal laurel, Spain, Portugal Zone 6–7. To 60 ft, often shrubby. Leaves oblong, medium length, finely toothed, dark shiny green above, paler beneath, evergreen. Flowers tiny, cup-shaped; in slender clusters to 10 ins long. Fruit purple, oval ½ in long. 25 ft in 20 years.

'Angustifolia' **203** To 15 ft, conical, dense. Leaves smaller than *P. lusitanica*, shiny deep green.

azorica **203** Azores. Shrub or small tree. Leaves bigger than the type, bright green.

'Variegata' **203** Leaves variegated white, often with pink flush in winter.

P. maackii **201**, 255, 263 Manchurian cherry, Amur chokecherry. Manchuria, Korea Zone 2. To 50 ft. spreading. Leaves oval, pointed, deciduous, hairy on veins and midrib. Flowers small, white, in downy clusters. Fruit small, black. 30 ft in 20 years.

P. mahaleb **254** 'St Lucie cherry' from southern Europe; fragrant white flowers; small spreading tree.

P. mume **202** Japanese apricot. China, Korea Zone 6. To 20 ft, spreading. Leaves round to oval, long-pointed, deciduous, becoming smooth, short-stalked. Flowers single or paired, early spring, occasionally winter or late spring, almond-scented. Fruit to 1¼ across, round, yellow, hardly edible. Best against a wall in cold, exposed areas.

'Alphandii' **202** Flowers semi-double, pink, March or earlier.

P. padus **201**, 263 Bird cherry. Europe, N. Asia to Japan Zone 3. To 50 ft, spreading. Leaves oval, pointed, rounded at base, deciduous, smooth, dull green above, greyish beneath, short-stalked. Flowers small, in spreading spikes, almond-scented. Fruit small, round, black, harsh, bitter-tasting, summer. Less susceptible to tent caterpillar than other species. 30 ft in 20 years.

'Colorata' **201** Leaves initially purplish-brown, purple coloration retained in veins and on undersides. Shoots dark purple.

commutata **201**, 262 Leaves bright green. Flowers several weeks before other varieties, early spring. One of the first trees into leaf.

'Watereri' **201** Flowers in extra long clusters, up to 8 ins long standing out with great vigour from all over tree. A.G.M. 1930.

P. pensylvanica **201** Wild red cherry. Pin cherry. United States Zone 2. To 40 ft, spreading. Leaves oval, pointed, deciduous, smooth, bright green. Flowers in flat heads, small. Fruit small, red, round, late autumn.

P. persica **202**, 252, 254 Peach. China Zone 4. To 25 ft, spreading. Leaves lance-shaped, deciduous, smooth, short-stalked. Flowers usually single, to 1½ ins across, pink. Fruits to 3 ins wide, slightly furry, round, yellow-orange, red-tinged on sunny side, juicy. Susceptible to trunk borers and peach leaf curl. Dry soils.

'Klara Meyer' **202** Flowers many-petalled, deep, bright pink A.G.M. 1939.

'Laevis' **202** Nectarine. Fruit smooth-skinned, otherwise identical to the type.

P. sargentii **198, 199**, 262 Sargent's cherry. Japan, Sakhalin, Korea Zone 4. To 40 ft, upright, spreading. Leaves oval, slender-pointed, deciduous, smooth, bronze-red, orange and red in autumn, stalked. Flowers deep pink, in small clusters; one of first cherries to flower and to colour in autumn. Fruits tiny. 30 ft in 20 years.

P. serotina **201**, 252, 255 Black cherry, Rum cherry. E. United States, E. and S. Mexico, Guatemala Zone 3. To 100 ft, spreading. Leaves oval to lance-shaped, tapered both ends, deciduous, smooth, glossy above, lighter beneath, pale yellow in autumn, stalked. Flowers in hanging cylindrical clusters, white, small, early summer. Fruit small, shining, black, late summer, sparse. 40 to 50 ft in 20 years.

P. serrula **201**, 263 W. China Zone 5. To 35 ft, wide-spreading. Leaves lance-shaped, deciduous, downy beneath, sometimes becoming smooth. Flowers small, white, in small groups. Fruit oval, red, small. Bark glossy, dark red, peeling. Most soils. 25 ft in 20 years.

P. serrulata **198** Japanese cherry. China Zone 5 to 6. To 80 ft, wide-spreading, flat-topped. Leaves oval to lance-shaped, smooth, waxy beneath, deciduous, short, possibly double-toothed. Flowers to 2½ ins across, single or paired. Fruit small, black.

'Sato Zakura' **198, 199** Japanese cherries of garden origin.

'Amanogawa' **198, 199**, 262 To 30 ft, upright, narrow. Leaves greenish-bronze. Flowers double, fringed, pink, profuse, fragrant. Fruits small, black. Most soils; especially floriferous on chalky soils.

'Hokusai' **198** Vigorous, wide-spreading.

deciduous.

Q. macranthera 156, 254 Caucasus. N. Persia Zone 5. To 65 ft. Leaves long, oval, lobed, green above, pale and downy beneath, deciduous. Acorns 1 in long on short stalk, cup with downy scales. May be grown in deep soils over chalk. 35 ft in 20 years.

Q. macrocarpa 159, 160, 161, 255 Burr oak, Mossy cup oak. N.E. and N.C. United States Zone 2. To 130 ft, spreading. Leaves roughly triangular, medium to long, dark glossy green above, downy beneath, downy stalk, deciduous. Twigs corky, bark like white oak. Acorns to 1½ ins long, usually solitary, fringed cup. Not lime-tolerant. 15 ft in 20 years.

Q. marilandica 160 Blackjack oak. E. United States Zone 6. To 30 ft, spreading. Leaves roughly triangular, deciduous, wide and 3-lobed at tip, medium length, shiny, dark green, yellow-brown beneath. Acorns ¾ in long, solitary or in pair. Good on poor, dry soil.

Q. michauxii 159, 161 Basket oak, Swamp chestnut oak. E. United States Zone 5. To 100 ft, round-headed, compact. Leaves roughly triangular, coarsely toothed, bright green, rich autumn colour, deciduous. Acorns stalked, to 1½ ins long. Not lime-tolerant; prefers moist soil.

Q. muehlenbergii 159, 161 Chinkapin oak, Yellow chestnut oak. S. Canada, E. United States, N.E. Mexico Zone 5. To 80 ft. Leaves oblong, coarsely toothed, yellow-green above, pale and downy beneath with yellow midrib and stalk; rich autumn colour, deciduous. Roundish acorns, ¾ in long. Not lime-tolerant.

Q. myrsinifolia 254 Small evergreen oak with pointed leaves and reddish shoots.

Q. nigra 159, 160, 161, 255, 262 Water oak. S. United States Zone 6. To 80 ft, conical or round-topped, fine-textured foliage. Leaves roughly triangular, sometimes lobed, sometimes entire, medium length, smooth shiny green, short stalk. Acorns, usually single, ½ in long. Not lime-tolerant; likes moist ground.

Q. nuttallii 159, 160 Nuttall oak. Central S. United States Zone 5. To 80 ft. Leaves medium size, deeply lobed with sharp points, deciduous. Roundish acorns.

Q. palustris 159, 160, 161, 255, 262, 263 Pin oak. S.E. Canada, E. United States Zone 4. To 120 ft; dense pyramidal head, branch ends drooping. Leaves medium length, lobed, toothed near tip, glossy green, hairless except where veins join beneath slender stalk, deciduous. Acorn about ½ in long; shallow, saucer-shaped cup. Not lime-tolerant; likes moist soil. 30 ft in 20 years.

Q. petraea 154, 156, 263 Sessile oak, Durmast oak. W., C. and S.E. Europe, Asia Minor Zone 4. To 100 ft. Leaves medium length, stalked, oval, deeply lobed, dark glossy green above, greyish, downy beneath deciduous. Acorns to 1¼ ins long, solitary or clustered, stalkless on twig. 30 ft in 20 years.

Q. phellos 159, 160, 161, 255, 262, 263 Willow oak. E. United States Zone 5. To 100 ft, conical or round-topped head, slender branches. Leaves medium length, narrow, pointed at both ends, entire, pale green, yellow in autumn, deciduous. Acorns tiny. Not lime-tolerant. 30 ft in 20 years.

Q. pontica 254 'Armenian oak'; small deciduous oak with huge yellow-stalked leaves.

Q. prinus 159, 161, 252 Chestnut oak, Basket oak. S.E. Canada, E. United States Zone 5. To 90 ft, open, spreading crown. Leaves medium length, toothed, upper surface dark glossy green and hairless, midrib yellow, lower surface pale grey, downy, rich yellow in autumn, deciduous. Acorns oval, 1¼ ins long, single or paired in thin, stalked cup. Not lime-tolerant; likes dry soils. 15 ft in 20 years.

Q. pyrenaica 254 'Pyrenean oak'; big, often pendulous Mediterranean relation of *Q. robur*

Q. robur 41, 154, 156, 262, 263 Common oak, English oak. Europe, Caucasus, Asia Minor, N. Africa Zone 5. To 100 ft, broad open head, short trunk. Leaves oblong, medium length, lobed, dark green above, greyish, hairless below, deciduous. Acorns to 1¼ ins long, ovoid, one or more on long stalk. 30 to 45 ft in 20 years.

'Atropurpurea' 154, 156, 262 Purple English oak. Small to medium. Leaves and shoots rich purple. Slow-growing.

concordia 154, 262 Golden oak. Small, rounded tree. Leaves golden-yellow, scorched in hot sunshine.

'Fastigiata' 154 Cypress oak. Big, columnar head, upright branches.

'Pendula' 262 Weeping oak. Small to medium-sized, pendular branches.

variegata 154, 262 Leaves with white or yellow markings; leaves of a tree at Kew initially green, variegated later.

Q. x rosacea 'Filicifolia' 154 Leaves divided pinnately into narrow segments. Fruits stalked.

Q. rubra 43, 158, 159, 160, 262, 263 Red oak. E. United States Zone 4. To 80 ft, becoming broad and round-topped. Leaves oval, medium to long, lobed, smooth dark green above, greyish beneath with tufts of hair, stalk yellow, deciduous, red or red-brown in autumn. Acorns to 1¼ ins long. Fast when young. Not lime-tolerant.

Q. x schochiana 255 Hybrid between *Q. palustris* and *Q. phellos.*

Q. shumardii 159, 160, 255, 263 Shumard oak. S. and C. United States Zone 5. To 120 ft, open, round head. Leaves medium length, obovate with sharp-pointed toothed lobes, smooth, dark glossy green above, red or golden-brown in autumn. Acorns 1 in long. Not lime-tolerant.

Q. stellata 161 Post oak. W. and C. United States Zone 5. To 60 ft. Leaves roughly triangular, lobed at tip, medium to long, deciduous, dark green and rough, paler, hairy beneath. Acorns single or paired, downy cup.

Q. suber 155, 156, 254, 262, 263 Cork oak. S. Europe, N. Africa Zone 8. To 65 ft, wide-spreading and rounded, large branches. Leaves oval to oblong, short to medium, toothed, dark glossy green above, downy beneath, evergreen. Acorns ¾ in long, single or paired on short downy stalk. Bark thick, rugged, corky. Needs full sun; dislikes cold, exposure. 12 ft in 20 years.

Q. variabilis 157, 254 Oriental cork oak. Japan, China, Korea Zone 5. To 80 ft, spreading. Leaves oval to oblong, dull green; bristly margin, hairy beneath, deciduous. Bark corky.

Q. velutina 43, 158, 160, 255 Black oak, Yellow-bark oak. E. and C. United States Zone 4. To 100 ft or more, dense rounded head. Leaves oval, medium to long, deeply lobed, glossy green above, downy beneath, rich autumn colours, deciduous. Acorns usually solitary on short stalk, to ¾ in long. Inner bark bright yellow. Not lime-tolerant. 30 ft in 20 years.

'Rubrifolia' Very striking, with leaves up to 16 ins long.

Q. virginiana 160, 161, 262 Live oak. S.E. United States, N.E. Mexico, W. Cuba Zone 7. To 60 ft, very wide-spreading, branches nearly horizontal. Leaves oblong, medium length, leathery, glossy green above, pale downy beneath, evergreen. Acorns oval, 1 in long.

Q. wislizenii 255 Small evergreen oak from California.

Quick See *Crataegus monogyna*

Quince See *Cydonia oblonga*

R

Red-bud, Eastern See *Cercis canadensis*

North American See *Cercis canadensis*

Redwood See *Sequoia sempervirens*

Coast See *Sequoia sempervirens*

Dawn See *Metasequoia glyptostroboides*

Retinospora moss See *Chamaecyparis pisifera* 'Squarrosa'

RHODODENDRON 184, 185, 186, 187, 262, 263 Evergreen or deciduous, some trees, usually shrubs. Simple, entire leaves. Flowers usually in clusters on shoot end, often funnel-like. Fruit, capsule, usually oval or oblong, minute seeds. Not lime-tolerant.

R. arboreum 48, 187, 252, 262 Temperate Himalaya, Kashmir to Bhutan, Khasia Hills, Ceylon Zone 6. 30 to 40 ft in cultivation, evergreen, thick trunk, wide head. Narrow, oblong leaves, medium to long, dark green above, scaly beneath. Dark red, bell-shaped flowers, spring.

R. barbatum 187, 262, 263 Nepal, Sikkim, Bhutan Zone 7. Shrub or small tree, to 40 ft, evergreen, smooth blue-grey branches. Oblong leaves, pointed, medium length, dark dull green above, paler beneath. dark red bell-shaped flowers 4 ins across. Peeling bark.

R. calophytum 262 W. China Zone 7. To 35 ft, often shrubby. Leaves long, narrow. Flowers bell-shaped, white or rose-pink with a maroon blotch.

R. falconeri 187, 262 Sikkim, Nepal, Bhutan Zone 7. To 30 ft. Thick, sparse branches. Oval to oblong evergreen leaves, long, dark green above, rust-coloured felt beneath. Creamy-white flowers shaded with lilac, dark purple blotch at base.

R. giganteum 49 Yunnan Zone 9. 40 to 80 ft. Leaves long, evergreen; green above, reddish-brown felt beneath. Flowers bell-shaped, deep rose-crimson.

R. maximum 187, 262 Great laurel, Rose bay. E. United States Zone 3. To 40 ft. Narrow, oblong leaves, medium to long, dark green above, paler beneath. Rose-purple to pink flowers spotted with olive-green to orange, small, June/July.

R. sinogrande 49, 262 Yunnan, Upper Burma, S.E. Tibet Zone 7. To 45 ft. Evergreen oval or oblong leaves, rounded ends. To 20 ins long; dark green above, silvery grey beneath. Creamy white to yellow bell-shaped flowers, large.

RHUS 235 Deciduous or evergreen shrubs, sometimes trees or climbers. Compound, alternate leaves. Uni- or bi-sexual flowers on same or different trees. Fruits roundish, fleshy, hard stones. Any fertile soil. Subject to coral spot fungus, fungal wilt in America; few diseases in Britain.

Rhus, Chinese See *Rhus verniciflua*

R. typhina 253, 262 Stag's horn sumach. E. United States Zone 5. Small tree or shrub, to 35 ft, wide-spreading; sparse branches thick and pithy, yielding thick white juice when cut. Leaves downy at first, large, turning orange, red, purple in autumn. Male and female flowers clustered on separate trees. Fruits closely packed, hairy, decorative. Good in built-up areas. A.G.M 1969.

R. verniciflua 235 Varnish tree. Japan, China, Himalayas Zone 5. To 65 ft. Large leaves, downy beneath. Flowers inconspicuous, separate trees. Fruits small, yellowish.

Ribbonwood See *HOHERIA*

Rimu, New Zealand See *Dacrydium cupressinum*

ROBINIA 32. 208, 209, 263 Deciduous trees or shrubs. Leaves pinnate. Flowers white to pink or pale purple, pea-like, hanging clusters. summer. Fruits a flattened brown pod, several seeds. Many soils. Hardy. Sun-loving.

R. x ambigua 'Bella-rosae' 208 Shoots sticky. Flowers bigger and deeper t]pink than the type.

R. hispida 255 Rose acacia. S.E. United States Zone 5. Small shrub. Leaves 7 to 13 smooth roundish leaflets. Flowers big, rose-coloured or pale purple, small clusters, May and June. Needs shelter.

R. pseudoacacia 208, 252, 255 Black locust. Common acacia, False acacia. E. United States Zone 3. To 80 ft, upright, open few branches. Leaflets opposite, oval, hairy at first. Flowers white, fragrant, June. Pod to 3½ ins long, upper edge winged. Bark rough, furrowed. Tolerates dryness. Good in industrial areas. Subject to locust borer, locust leaf miner, witches' broom, virus growths. 40 ft in 20 years.

'Frisia' 208. 209, 262 Small-Medium. Leaves golden-yellow. A.G.M. 1969.

'Inermis' 209 Mop-head acacia. Small, compact round head, branches spineless. Flowers rare. A.G.M. 1969.

R. viscosa 208 Clammy locust. S.E. United States Zone 3. To 35 ft, branchlets dark red-brown. Young shoots and leaf stalks sticky. Flowers pink with yellow blotch, May and June. Pod narrow, to 3 ins long.

ROSA 190, 263 Deciduous shrubs, stems thorny. Leaves pinnate. Flowers 5-petalled. Fruit, rose 'hip', a fleshy covering of the true fruit which is bony, seedlike. Succeeds in most except acid soils. Sun-loving. Hardy. Subject to black spot, mildew, leaf-cutting bees, etc.

R. brunonii 190 Himalayan musk rose. Himalaya Zone 7. Climbing form, to 35 ft. Leaves limp, sea green. Flowers white, densely clustered, very fragrant.

R. filipes 'Kiftsgate' 190 Climbing form, to 60 ft. Leaves pale green, brown initially. Flowers white, profuse, large clusters. Fragrant. Fruits small, red, numerous.

Rose, Himalayan musk See *Rosa brunonii*

Rosebay See *Rhododendron maximum*

Rowan See *Sorbus aucuparia*

ROYSTONIA regia 123 Royal palm. Cuba Zone 10. To 70 ft, powdery greyish-white trunk, swollen in middle. Pinnate leaves to 10 ft long, four rows of leaflets. Flowerstalk develops below smooth glossy crownshaft. Purplish fruit, ½ in long.

Rubber plant 141

S

SABAL palmetto 122–3 Caribbean cabbage palm. Caribbean, Central America Zone 9. 20 to 90 ft, very variable. Trunk bare or covered with leaf bases. Palmate leaves 12 ft long, green or blue-green. Unisexual flowers on same tree, flowerstalk to 3 ft long. Roundish shiny black fruit ⅓ in. across.

SALIX 176–9, 263 Mostly deciduous trees and shrubs. Leaves simple, typically alternate, long and narrow, pointed, toothed, but other shapes occur. Flowers, sexes usually on separate trees, without petals, in upright silky or hairy catkins, spring, before or after, leaves. Seeds in small capsules. Tolerant of moisture; prefer full sun. Very hardy. Fast-growing. Subject to watermark disease, rusts, twig blights, cankers, aphids.

S. alba 176, 177, 178, 179, 262, 263 White willow. Europe, N. Asia, N. Africa Zone 2. To 80 ft, rather upright. Leaves lance-shaped, deciduous, white-furred, yellow in autumn, short-stalked. Flowers, spring. Dislikes shallow chalky soils. Susceptible to leaf-eating insects and other pests and diseases. 70 ft in 20 years.

'Britzensis' ('Chermesina') 177, 178, 179 Scarlet willow. Bark striking orange-scarlet colour, most obvious in winter.

'Caerulea' 179,, 262, 263 Cricket-bat willow. British Isles Zone 2. To 100 ft, pyramidal. Leaves lance-shaped, deciduous, downy at first, smooth later, blue-green. Flowers, only female catkins known. 85 ft in 20 years.

'Sericea' 262 Very effective form with silvery-white leaves.

vitellina 177, 178 Golden-stemmed willow. Similar to *S. alba*; only male trees known. Shoots bright yellow. 50 ft in 20 years. A.G.M. 1969.

S. amygdaloides 179 Peach-leafed willow. Canada, E. and W. United States Zone 4. To 60 ft but usually smaller. Ascending branches, branchlets shiny red-brown or orange. Leaves lance-shaped, toothed, pale beneath. Male catkins to 2 ins, female 4 ins.

S. babylonica 1766–7, 178, 179, 180, 254, 260, 262 Weeping willow. China Zone 6. to 40 ft, weeping. Leaves lance-shaped, deciduous, smooth, except at first, dark green above, paler beneath, short-stalked. Flowers early spring. Pests as *S. alba.*

'Annularis' 179 A form with spirally curled leaves.

S. x blanda See *S. x pendulina* var. *blanda*

S. caprea 177, 178, 263 Goat willow, Common sallow. Europe, W. Asia Zone 4. To 30 ft, spreading. Leaves broad, oblong, deciduous, downy at first, woolly beneath, wrinkled above, grey-green, short-stalked. Flowers, sexes on separate trees, spring; male catkins large, yellow; females silver-grey. 35 ft in 20 years.

S. x chrysocoma See *S. sepulcralis*

S. cinerea 177 Grey sallow. Europe, W. Asia Zone 2. To 15 ft, often shrubby. Leaves ovallish, dull green above, grey, woolly beneath. Catkins before the leaves, early spring.

S. daphnoides 178, 252, 254, 263 Violet willow. N. Europe, C. Asia, Himalayas Zone 4. To 30 ft, upright. Leaves oval to lance-shaped, deciduous, smooth, shiny, tough, dark green, short-stalked. Flowers late winter. Pests as *S. alba.* 35 ft in 20 years.

S. discolor 177, 178 E. United States Zone 2. To 35 ft, shrub or small tree. Leaves oval to oblong, grey furry beneath, bright green above, stalked. Catkins in spring, before leaves.

S. elaeagnos 262 Hoary willow. S. and S. Europe, W Asia Zone 4. Dense bushy shrub. Slender reddish-brown stems. Leaves narrow, green above, white beneath, rosemary-like.

S. x erythroflexuosa 179, 262 Zone 4. 20 to 30 ft hybrid. Shoots orange-yellow, weeping, twisted in corkscrew fashion, as are narrow laves.

S. fragilis 177, 179, 263 Crack willow. Europe, N. Asia Zone 4. To 100 ft wide-spreading. Leaves lance-shaped to narrow-oblong, deciduous, smooth, dark green above, blue-green beneath, stalked. Flowers, spring. Fruit stalked. bark roughly channelled, twigs liable to break off. 40 ft in 20 years.

S. gracilistyla 178, 255 Japan, Korea, Manchuria Zone 5. To 10 ft, bushy shrub.

Brewer's See *Picea brewerana*
Colorado See *Picea pungens*
Colorado blue See *Picea pungens*
Dragon See *Picea asperata*
Engelmann See *Picea engelmannii*
Himalayan weeping See *Picea smithiana*
Japanese tiger-tail See *Picea torano*
Likiang See *Picea likiangensis*
Norway See *Picea abies*
Oriental See *Picea orientalis*
Red See *Picea rubens*
Sergent See *Picea brachytyla*
Serbian See *Picea omorika*
Shrenk's See *Picea schrenkiana*
sitka See *Picea sitchensis*
Weeping See *Picea brewerana*
White See *Picea glauca*

Spruces See *PICEA*

STEWARTIA 173, 262, 263 Deciduous shrubs or trees related to camellias. Leaves alternate, finely-toothed, rich autumn colour. Flowers white, cup-shaped, bisexual, often big, July and autumn. Fruit, woody capsule, flattened, usually winged seeds. Warm, lime-free soil; semi-shade.

Stewartia, Japanese See *Stewartia pseudocamellia*
Korean See *Stewartia koreana*

S. koreana 173, 262, 263 Korea Zone 5. To 50 ft. Leaves ovallish, simple, hairy at first, orange-red in autumn, stalked. Flowers 3 ins across, solitary, summer. Fruit, oval, hairy, small. Bark flaking. 10 to 15 ft in 20 years.

S. monadelpha 255 Small Japanese stewartia.

S. pseudocamellia 173, 253, 262, 263 Japanese stewartia. Japan Zone 5. To 65 ft. Leaves ovallish, simple, bright green, red and yellow in autumn. Flowers 2 ins across, single, hairy, summer. Bark reddish, flaking. 25 ft in 20 years.

S. serrata 255 Small Japanese stewartia.

Strawberry tree See *Arbutus unedo*

STYRAX 188–9, 262, 263 Deciduous or evergreen trees and shrubs. Leaves alternate, often downy. Flowers white, clustered in spikes on short side-branches, late spring and summer. Fruit dry or fleshy with 1 or 2 seeds. Needs moist, loamy, lime-free soil. Sun or semi-shade.

S. japonica 189, 252, 262, 263 Japanese snowbell. Japan, Korea Zone 5. To 35 ft, wide-spreading. Leaves oval to oblong, simple, deciduous, almost smooth, shiny, dark green above, minutely toothed, stalked. Flowers small, bell-shaped, waxy. Fruit small ovallish. 20 ft in 20 years. A.G.M. 1969.

S. obassia 189, 263 Fragrant snowbell. Japan Zone 5. To 35 ft, upright, deciduous, upper surface dark green, minutely toothed, downy beneath stalked. Flowers bell-shaped. Fruit small, ovallish. downy. 30 ft in 20 years.

Sumach, Staghorn See *Rhus typhina*

Sweetgum See *LIQUIDAMBAR*

Sycamore See *Acer pseudoplatanus*
Golden See *Acer pseudoplatanus* 'Worleei'
Purple See *Acer pseudoplatanus* 'Purpureum' or 'Spaethii'

Sycamore-maple See *Acer pseudoplatanus*

SYAGURUS *romanzoffianum* 123 Queen palm. Brazil Zone 10. To 30 ft, trunk 6 ft thick, smooth ringed surface. Pinnate leaves 8 to 15 ft long on a 3 ft stalk. Leaflets green. Small cream-coloured unisexual flowers on a 3 ft stalk. Fruit 1 in long, oval, yellow, fleshy.

T

Tamarack See *Larix laricina*

Tangerine See *Citrus reticulata*

Tangor 237

TAXODIUM 112–3, 263 Deciduous trees, usually pyramidal. Leaves narrow, flat or awl-shaped, in 2 ranks, soft, bright green. Male and female 'flowers' separate on same tree; male 'flowers' in drooping clusters. 4 to 5 ins long. Cones round or oval, small. Seeds winged. Dislikes chalk. Sun-loving. Hardy.

T. ascendens 112–3, 262, 263 Pond cypress. S.E. united States Zone 4. 70 to 80 ft, narrowly conical or columnar; base of trunk swollen in wet areas. Leaves lance-shaped, small, deciduous, turn rich brown in autumn. Cones upright, purple-tinted. 18 ft in 20 years.

T. cryptomerioides 254 Cryptomeria-like conifer from Formosa.

T. distichum 42, 112, 113, 261, 262, 263 Bald cypress, Southern cypress, Swamp cypress. S. United States Zone 4. 100 or 120 ft, narrowly pyramidal, flattening later; buttressed roots which, by water, produce woody humps called 'cypress knees'. Leaves deciduous, short, yellow-green. Cones persist after first season. 25 ft in 20 years.

T. mucronatum 113 Mexican cypress. Mexico Zone 8. Leaves semi-evergreen or evergreen occasionally. 'Flowers' open in autumn.

TAXUS 64–5, 108–11, 263 Evergreen shrubs and trees. Leaves needle-like, with 2 yellow bands beneath. Male and female 'flowers' on separate trees, both small, hardly noticeable. Fruit, seed in brightly coloured cup. Good on most soils; chalk tolerant. Very hardy. Subject to shoot dieback in Europe and America.

T. baccata 108, 109, 259, 263 Common yew. Europe, N. Persia, Algeria Zone 6. To 80 ft, young trees broadly conical, open with level, wide-spreading branches; old trees irregular, broadly domed, often many-stemmed. Leaves short, deep shiny green above, pale, yellowish-green beneath. Male 'flowers' beneath new shoots; female 'flowers; on separate trees, dark green. Red, fleshy seed-cup. Survives drought. 20 ft in 20 years. A.G.M. 1969.

'Aurea' 262 Golden yew. Compact shrub. Leaves golden-yellow for one year, turning green.

'Dovastoniana' 108, 262 Westfelton yew. British Isles. Upright with wide-spreading branches, long weeping branchlets. Male and female 'flowers' have appeared on same tree. A.G.M. 1969.

'Fastigiata' 108–9, 262 Irish yew. Ireland. Columnar, compact. Almost all existing trees female, obtained by cuttings or grafts from 2 originals discovered in 1780. A.G.M. 1969.

'Fastigiata Aurea' 109 Sub-variety, initially with golden leaves. Small, good golden form is male.

'Standishii' 262, 263 Female. Dense, columnar. Leaves golden yellow on tightly-packed upright branches.

T. canadensis 108 Canadian yew. Canada, N.E. United States Zone 2. Small, straggling shrub. Leaves short, curved, thin, pointed. 'Flowers', sexes separate on same shrub. Seed-cup bright red. 20 ft in 20 years.

T. cuspidata 108, 109 Japanese yew. Japan Zone 4. To 50 ft, may be bushy. Leaves short, curved or straight, dark green above, golden-green beneath. Red seed-cup. Bark red to grey-brown, slightly fissured. 20 ft in 20 years.

T. x media 109 Hybrid between *T. baccata* and *T. cuspidata* Zone 4. Upright shrub. Leaves short, spines, pale green underneath. fruit abundant, big, shiny, bright scarlet.

Tea-tree See *Camellia sinensis*

TETRACENTRON sinense 254 Rare, small, wide-spreading summer-flowering tree with yellow catkins.

TERTACLINIS articulata 97 Algeria, Morocco, Malta, S.E. Spain Zone 8. 40 to 50 ft, conical, branches ascending, evergreen. Leaves in fours, flattened, scale-like, pointed, lateral ones larger. 'Flowers' separate, but on same tree. Cones small, round, waxy, 4 woody scales.

Thorn, Cockspur See *Srataegus crus-galli*
English See *Crataegus oxyacantha*
Glossy-leaved See *Crataegus nitida*
Washington See *Crataegus phaenopyrum*

THUJA 102–3, 262 Evergreen trees and shrubs, mostly conical. Leaves small, scale-like, pressed closely to branches, sometimes needle-like. Male and female 'flowers' separate on same tree; males round, red; females small, green, purple tinged. Cones small, single. Seeds winged. Succeeds in many soils. Hardy. Susceptible to scale insects, honey-fungus, needle blight.

Thuja, Chinese See *Thuja orientalis*
Japanese See *Thuja standishii*

T. koraiensis 254 Korean arbovitae. Sprays white beneath, bark peeling.

T. occidentalis 102, 103 White cedar. American abor-vitae. Tree of life. E. United States Zone 2. 40 to 50 ft, pyramidal, late more oblong, columnar. Leaves in fan-like sprays, dark green on top, pale underneath. Cones small, persist in winter. Bark thin, furrowed, red to grey-brown. Thrives on limestone outcrops; useful on poorly drained ground and heavy clays. 25 ft in 20 years.

'Lutea' 102, 103 Conical. Young branchlets yellow-green in winter, become greener during second spring. Strongest-growing cultivar of *T. occidentalis.*

'Rheingold' 102, 119, 262, 263 Small, rarely to 12 ft, broadly conical, rounded top. Leaves gold in summer, copper-gold in winter. Male 'flowers' open in spring. Cones rare, green becoming purple, small. Seeds sometimes wingless. Bark thin, scaling. Cones rare. A.G.M. 1969.

'Spiralis' 102 Narrowly columnar small tree, densely branched. Short sprays of dark-green foliage. Very pretty.

'Wintergreen' 102, 103 Small-medium, columnar. Foliage green throughout year.

T. orientalis 102, 103 Chinese thuja. N. and W. China Zone 6. Roughly conical, branches upsweeping. Leaves triangular, blunt-pointed, in vertical plates, mid-green. Cones numerous, often crowded. Prefers limestone; short-lived on very acid soils. Tolerates drought. 15 ft in 20 years.

'Conspicua' 103 Narrow and dense; golden leaves have greenish tinge.

'Elegantissima' 103, 119, 262, 263 Narrow, flame-shaped, gold outer foliage in summer, dull yellow turning green and brown in winter. Broad with age.

T. plicata 102–3, 260, 262, 263 Western red cedar, giant arborvitae. W. United States Zone 5. To 180 ft wide-spreading. Foliage in long, flat, fragrant sprays. Cones green, turning brown, ovallish. Bark red-brown, grey with age, ridged. Tolerates chalk, shade. 45 ft in 20 years.

'Fastigiata' 262 Tall, narrow, columnar form; slender ascending branches.

'Zebrina' 103, 262 To 60 ft, conical. Leaves green, variously barred yellow.

T. standishii 103 Japanese thuja. Central Japan. Zone 5. To 60 ft, broadly cone-shaped. Leaves in dense sprays, dark grey-green or yellow-green, scented when crushed. Bark deep red. 18 ft in 20 years.

THUJOPSIS dolabrata 103, 263 Hiba false arbor-vitae. Japan Zone 6. Form allied to *Thuja* sp. To 45 ft, usually many-stemmed bush, but sometimes single-boled tree with branches sharply down-curved from bole, then upswept. Leaves broad, scaly, shiny green margin, vividly white on underside. 'Flowers', sexes on separate trees; male 'flowers' ovallish, green-black, down-curving on side shoots, females clustered on tips of sprays. Needs cool summer, plenty of moisture. Any soil. 15 ft in 20 years.

TILIA 174–5 Deciduous trees. Leaves alternate, toothed. Flowers small, fragrant, creamy-white, in drooping clusters. Fruit pea-sized, usually one-seeded. Prefer full sun, but tolerates semi-shade. Hardy. Fast-Growing when young. Subject to bark fungi, leaf fungi, leaf-eating insects.

T. americana 175, 262 Basswood, American lime, Linden. E. and C. United States Zone 2. To 135 ft, spreading. Leaves roundish, simple, to 15 ins across, virtually smooth, dark green above, paler beneath, stalked. Flowers early summer. Fruit small, nut-like. 25 ft in 20 years.

T. chinensis 254 Small lime with shiny, toothed leaves.

T. cordata 174, 253 Small-leaved linden, Small-leaved lime. Europe Zone 3. To 100 ft, pyramidal. Leaves small, heart-shaped, simple, smooth above, red-brown hair beneath, dark green, paler beneath, stalked. Flowers very fragrant, summer. Fruit round, thin-shelled, felt-covered. 30 ft in 20 years.

'Swedish Upright' 254 Smallish lime with toothed leaves and red twigs, from Caucasus.

T. 'Euchlora' 175, 262, 263 Crimean linden. Zone 5. To 65 ft, slightly pendulous. Leaves roundish, simple, few hairs beneath. otherwise smooth, glossy, dark green above, paler beneath, stalked. Flowers inconspicuous, narcotic to bees, summer. Fruit oval, pointed, covered with brown wool. Freer from insect pests, such as aphids, than other limes. 20 ft in 20 years. A.G.M. 1969.

T. x europaea See *T. x vulgaris*

T. henryana 175 C. China Zone 6. To 50 ft. A rare tree, distinguished by leaves with a fringe of conspicuous teeth, silver-downy on both sides. 25 ft in 20 years.

T. insularis 254 Large Korean lime with toothed leaves.

T. kiusiana 255 Shrubby lime with small oval leaves. From Japan.

T. mandshurica 255 Small Siberian lime with big leaves like American basswood.

T. oliveri 175 C. China Zone 5. To 40 ft; shoots tend to weep. Leaves oval or round, tapering, smooth above, silver-white felted beneath, rich green above. 25 ft in 20 years.

T. petiolaris 175, 262 Weeping silver lime, Pendant silver linden. Zone 5. To 80 ft; slightly weeping. Leaves roundish, simple, few hairs above, dark green, silver furry beneath, stalked. Flowers extremely fragrant, narcotic to bees, summer. Fruit round, grooved, warty. 35 ft in 20 years. A.G.M. 1969.

T. platyphyllos 174, 175, 260, 262 Big-leafed lime, Big-leaf linden. C. and S. Europe, British Isles Zone 3. To 135 ft, pyramidal. Leaves roundish, largest of slightly downy above, thicker down below, dark green, stalked. Flowers, summer. Fruit pear-shaped, downy, ribbed. 35 ft in 20 years.

T. 'Rubra' 174, 263 Red-twigged lime. Large, vigorous tree, twigs red, conspicuous in winter. Leaves unequally heart-shaped, densely downy beneath. Flowers June, early July.

T. tomentosa 175, 262 Silver linden, silver lime. S.E. and E.C Europe Zone 4. To 100 ft, pyramidal. Leaves ovallish, simple silver-downy beneath. Flowers inconspicuous, narcotic to bees, summer. Fruit oval, pointed, downy, warty. 30 ft in 20 years.

T. x vulgaris 174, 262, 263 Common lime, European linden, Hybrid between *T. cordata* and *T. platyphyllos.* Zone 3. To 130 ft, upright to spreading. Leaves ovallish, simple, smooth except for a few hairs beneath, bright green. Suckers badly, causing unsightly burrs. 30 ft in 20 years.

Tilleuls See *TILIA*

TOONA 242, 243 Deciduous or evergreen trees. Leaves alternate, usually pinnate. Flowers small, whitish or greenish, bisexual, in big clusters. Fruit, a capsule holding many winged seeds.

T. sinensis 242, 243, 254, 262, 263 Chinese toon. N. and W. China Zone 5. To 70 ft, rounded and dense. Leaves pinnate, to 2 ft long, 5 to 12 pairs of leaflets, yellow in autumn, deciduous, taste of onion. Flower clusters 1 ft long, fragrant, June. Any soil.

TORREYA 110 Trees or shrubs with whorled branches. Leaves narrow, spiny tips, pungent. Sexes on same or different trees. Fruit plum-like, thin fleshy coat. Tolerates shade and chalk.

Torreya californica 110 California nutmeg. California Zone 7. 50 to 70 ft. Leaves spirally arranged, persistent; commonly 2-ranked, tapering, dark yellow-green above, two white bands and bright yellow margin below. 'Flowers', sexes separate on same tree, males solitary, females paired. Fruits fleshy, single large seed. Bark red-brown, finely latticed. 18 ft in 20 years.

T. grandis 254 Small Japanese torreya.

T. nucifera 110 Kaya. Japan Zone 5. 20 to 80 ft, slender tree or large bush. Leaves narrow, pointed, stiff, curved, pungent if rubbed, shiny, dark green above. Fruit green, tinted purple, edible. Bark reddish, smooth. Likes chalk. Shade-tolerant.

TRACHYCARPUS fortunei 122 Chinese windmill palm. Asia Zone 7. To 40 ft, trunk covered by mat of fibres. Palmate leaves 3 ft across, dark green above, waxy bloom below. Unisexual flowers on same tree, yellow, fragrant. Fruit small, ripens blue.

Tree of heaven See *Ailanthus altissima*

TSUGA 88–9 Hemlocks, Hemlock spruces, Hemlock firs. Evergreen trees, broadly conical. Leaves needle-like, short, usually in 2 ranks. Male and female 'flowers' separate on same tree. Cones small, pendulous, leathery-scaled. Seeds winged. Shade-tolerant. Virtually disease-free, except for decay.

T. canadensis 89, 262 Eastern hemlock, Canadian hemlock. E. United States Zone 4. 60 to 100 ft, often many-stemmed, broadly conical. Bark brown to black, deeply furrowed when old. Any soil. 30 ft in 20 years.

'Pendula' 89, 262 Irregularly dome-shaped, flat-topped bush with branches drooping to ground. Slow.

T. caroliniana 89 Carolina hemlock. S.E. United States Zone 4. To 75 ft, irregularly conical. Leaves sparse, slightly larger than *T. canadensis*. Bark dark red-brown with large yellow pores, becoming purple-grey, fissured. Dislikes chalk. 20 ft in 20 years.

T. diversifolia 89 Northern Japanese

The publishers wish to extend their thanks to the following artists, photographers and studios:

Photographers
A–Z Botanical Collections Ltd. Abbott/Rapho-Guillumette. Malcolm Aird. Bernard Alfieri. Allen/NHPA. Michael Andrews. Heather Angel. Johannes Apel. The Arnold Arboretum. The Ashmolean Museum. Auvin/Top. Barnaby's Picture Library. Kenneth A. Beckett. Bennett/Colorific. The Bettmann Archive. Christian Bonington. Michael Boys. Stanley Breeden. Pat Brindley. F. Brockman. Brosselin/Jacana. John E. Bryan, Strybing Arboretum. Jock Bryden/Strybing Arboretum Society. René Burri/ Magnum. Burton/Bruce Coleman Ltd. Camera Press Ltd. Coleman/Bruce Coleman Ltd. Robert J. Corbin. Crown Copyright Her Majesty's Stationery Office and the Royal Botanic Gardens, Kew. Dalton/NHPA. W. F. Davidson. Anthony Denney. Douglas Dickins. Patrick Eagar/Report. Edouard/ Explorer. Robert Estall. Mary Evans Picture Library. Fenaux/Jacana. Graham Finlayson. Fletcher/ Natural Science Photos. Foord/NHPA. The Forestry Commission. Fox-Davies/Bruce Coleman Ltd. R. Freeman & Co. Ltd. Hatton Gardner, Georg Gerster/John Hillelson Agency. W. A. T. Gilmour. Burt Glinn/Magnum. Greenhill/Transworld. George Haling. Sonia Halliday. Robert Harding Associates. Erich Hartmann/Magnum. John Hedgecoe. Hedrich-Blessing. Henri/Jacana F. Hepper. J. R. P. van Hoey Smith. The Hunt Botanical Library. David Hurn/Magnum. Anthony Huxley. Hyde/NHPA. Japan Society of London Library. P. Roland Johanson. Hugh Johnson. Kasterine/Daily Telegraph Colour Library. Kinne/Bruce Coleman Ltd. Kraulis/Canada Wide. Gerd Krüssmann. Kuusik/Colorific. Roy Lancaster. Lanceau/Jacana. Harold Langford. Eric Leach. Lecourt/Jacana. Leutscher/Natural Science Photos. The Linnaean Society. William MacQuitty. The Mansell Collection. Fosco Maraini. John Marmaras. André Martin. Matthews/National Science Photos. Pat Matthews. Elsa Megson. Paul Miles. Alan Mitchell/NHPA. Inge Morath/Magnum. N. Morcombe. Jean Mounicq/Fotogram. Margaret Mulligan. Myers/Bruce Coleman Ltd. Nardin/ Jacana. The National Gallery of Scotland. The Natural History Museum. Natural Science Photos. The National Trust. Naturfotograferna. N.Z. Forest Service. Paf. Peters/Transworld. Photo Researchers. Pictor. Picturepoint. Plessey/Explorer. President and Fellows of Trinity College, Oxford. M. C. F. Proctor. Radio Times Hulton Picture Library. Reichel/Top. Simon Relph. Ricard/Top. John Richardson/ John Hillelson Agency. Roger-Viollet. The Royal Horticultural Society. Ruffier-Lanche/ Jacana. Savonius/NHPA. Schmitz/Bruce Coleman Ltd. Schneiders/Bruce Coleman Ltd. Roger Settimo. Simon/Bruce Coleman Ltd. Marcel Sire. Edwin Smith. Harry Smith. Sommer/Explorer. Spectrum Colour Library. Ted Spiegel/John Hillelson Agency. John Massey Stewart. Svenska Porträttarkivet. Teutroy/Jacana. G. S. Thomas. Patrick Thurston. Ann Usborne. U.S. National Park Service. Vala/Jacana. The Victoria & Albert Museum. Christopher Walker. Michael Warren. H. J. Welch. Gerald Wilkinson. David Williamson. Myron Wood/Photo Researchers. Dennis Woodland. Adam Woolfitt.

Page 8: James Merrell

Artists
Arka Graphics. Ken Astrop. S. R. Badmin. Stephen Bishop. Broadway Arts. Jim Bulman. John Collings. Roy Boomces. Terry Dalley. Barry Evans. Sherine Fairclough. Freelance Presentations. Ian Garrard. Gilchrist Studios. Vana Haggerty. Garry Hincks. Allan Hood. Tony Jenkins. Tony Joyce. Patrick Leeson. Linden Artists. Ben Minichip. Brian Morris. Tilley Northage. Richard Orr. Elizabeth Rankin. Charles Raymond. Harry Side. Gwen Simpson. Joyce Tuhill. Eddie Wade. David Watson. John Wilson. Julia Wright.